The Linux A–Z

The Linux A–Z

Phil Cornes
Staffordshire University

Prentice Hall
London   New York   Toronto   Sydney   Tokyo   Singapore
Madrid   Mexico City   Munich

First published 1997 by
Prentice Hall Europe
Campus 400, Maylands Avenue
Hemel Hempstead
Hertfordshire HP2 7EZ
A division of
Simon & Schuster International Group

© Prentice Hall Europe 1997

All rights reserved. No part of this publication may be reproduced, stored in a retrieval system, or transmitted, in any form, or by any means, electronic, mechanical, photocopying, recording or otherwise, without prior permission, in writing, from the publisher.

Printed and bound in Great Britain by
T J Press (Padstow) Ltd

Library of Congress Cataloging-in-Publication Data

Cornes, Phil.
    The Linux A–Z / Phil Cornes.
      p.   cm.
    Includes index.
    ISBN 0–13–234709–1 (pbk. : alk. paper)
    1. Linux.   2. Operating systems (Computers)   I. Title.
QA76.76.O63C675   1997
005.4'469–dc20   96–25462
                                                                                       CIP

British Library Cataloguing in Publication Data

A catalogue record for this book is available from the British Library

ISBN 0–13–234709–1

   3   4   5   01   00   99   98

Contents

List of Figures		**xi**
Preface		**xiii**
I	**BASICS**	**1**
1	**Linux Basics**	**3**
	1.1 Logging In	3
	1.2 The File Hierarchy	5
	1.3 Exploring the File Hierarchy	7
	1.4 The Password File	8
2	**Linux Commands**	**13**
	2.1 Directory Hierarchy	13
	2.2 Filesystems	16
	2.3 Manipulating Files	19
	2.4 On-line Help	21
	2.5 Security	23
	2.6 Processes	26
	2.7 Space	29
3	**Text Editing**	**36**
	3.1 Edit Mode	37
	3.2 Insert Mode	40
	3.3 Command Mode	42

4 Bash   49
   4.1 Pathname Expansion   49
   4.2 I/O Redirection   51
   4.3 Pipes   54
   4.4 Background Jobs   55
   4.5 Job Control   57
   4.6 History   59
   4.7 Command Line Editing   61
   4.8 Command Completion   61
   4.9 Shell Functions   62

5 Tools and Utilities   65
   5.1 Search and Sort   65
   5.2 Modifying Files   75
   5.3 Simple Data Manipulation   82
   5.4 Other Tools   87
   5.5 Dos Files   88

6 Shell Scripts   92
   6.1 Command Files   92
   6.2 Variables   93
   6.3 Shell Script Parameters   96
   6.4 Login Scripts   97
   6.5 More Variable Assignment Methods   98
   6.6 Automatic Status Variables   101
   6.7 Flow Control   102
   6.8 Signals   112

II ADMINISTRATION   119

7 Getting Up and Running   121
   7.1 Hardware   122
   7.2 Distributions   123
   7.3 Installing Linux   126
   7.4 Kernel Build   140

8 Users   146
   8.1 Account Passwords   146
   8.2 Adding User Accounts   147
   8.3 User Groups   149
   8.4 Security   151
   8.5 Batch Jobs   153
   8.6 Archives   156

9	**Peripherals**	**160**
	9.1 Console Terminal	160
	9.2 Modems	165
	9.3 Mice	169
	9.4 Printers	171
10	**X-windows**	**175**
	10.1 Servers and Clients	175
	10.2 X-configuration	176
	10.3 Starting X-windows	181
	10.4 `fvwm`	182
	10.5 `xterm`	184
11	**Communications**	**185**
	11.1 Stand Alone Machines	185
	11.2 TCP/IP	186
	11.3 PPP	192
	11.4 Other Connection Methods	196
12	**Internet**	**201**
	12.1 e-mail	202
	12.2 `telnet`	204
	12.3 `ftp`	205
	12.4 `archie`	208
	12.5 Usenet News	209
	12.6 `gopher`	211
	12.7 world wide web	212
13	**Running DOS**	**215**
	13.1 DOSEMU	215
	13.2 Installation	216
14	**Security**	**219**
	14.1 File Permissions	219
	14.2 Device Access	221
	14.3 Passwords	222
	14.4 Root Accounts	223
III	**SYSTEM PROGRAMMING**	**225**
15	**Files**	**227**
	15.1 Sequential Files	227
	15.2 Random Files	238

15.3 Terminal I/O ... 241
15.4 Inodes ... 248
15.5 Changing File Attributes ... 252
15.6 File Hierarchy ... 255

16 Process Control ... 260
16.1 Process Identity Numbers ... 260
16.2 Creating Processes with `fork` ... 261
16.3 `exec` System Call ... 265
16.4 `wait` and `exit` System Calls ... 268

17 Inter-process Communication (IPC) ... 274
17.1 Pipes ... 275
17.2 I/O Redirection ... 277
17.3 FIFOs ... 281
17.4 System V IPC ... 282
17.5 Sockets ... 286

18 Tiny Socket Library – Case Study ... 297
18.1 Library Functions ... 297
18.2 Example Server ... 305
18.3 Example Client ... 308

19 Signals ... 315
19.1 `signal` System Call ... 316
19.2 `sigaction` System Call ... 318
19.3 `kill` System Call ... 320
19.4 `pause` System Call ... 321
19.5 `alarm` System Call ... 321

20 Tiny Shell – Case Study ... 325
20.1 Data Structures ... 325
20.2 The Code ... 327

21 Miscellaneous System Calls ... 343
21.1 `umask` System Call ... 343
21.2 `mount` System Call ... 344
21.3 `umount` System Call ... 345
21.4 `sync` System Call ... 345
21.5 Telling the Time ... 345
21.6 `select` System Call ... 348

22 Daemons — 352
22.1 Principles — 352
22.2 Practice — 353

23 Tiny Daemon – Case Study — 359
23.1 The Daemon Listing — 359
23.2 Socket Server Additions — 364
23.3 Socket Server Changes — 364

IV DEVICE DRIVERS — 367

24 Device Driver Basics — 369
24.1 Introduction — 369
24.2 Device Driver Routines — 372
24.3 Device Driver Principles — 373

25 Character Device Drivers — 375
25.1 Registering Character Devices — 375
25.2 Working Storage — 376
25.3 Basic Entry Points — 379
25.4 Special Control Functions — 383
25.5 Interrupts — 384
25.6 Device Driver Installation — 385

26 Tiny Device Driver – Case Study — 386
26.1 Header Information — 387
26.2 `init` Function — 390
26.3 `open` Function — 391
26.4 `release` Function — 392
26.5 `write` Function — 392
26.6 `read` Function — 394
26.7 `ioctl` Function — 395

27 Block Device Drivers — 397
27.1 Block Driver Concepts — 397
27.2 Registering Block Devices — 400
27.3 Interrupts — 403
27.4 Timers — 407

V INTERNALS — 409

28 Process Scheduling — 411

28.1 Background 411
28.2 Detail 414

29 Tiny Threads – Case Study **417**
29.1 Library Calls 418
29.2 Calling C Functions 420
29.3 Thread Scheduling 423
29.4 Context Switching 424
29.5 Starting New Threads 427
29.6 Rendezvous 430
29.7 Creating Channels 432
29.8 `send` and `receive` 433
29.9 Unbounded Buffers 436

30 Memory **438**
30.1 Protected Mode Addressing 438
30.2 Paging 440
30.3 Linux Specifics 444

31 Filestore **446**
31.1 VFS 446
31.2 System V 447
31.3 minix 454
31.4 ext2 455

32 System Calls **458**
32.1 Interrupts and Exceptions 458
32.2 System Call Mechanism 459
32.3 Adding New Calls 460

Appendix A Linux Permuted Index **465**

Appendix B GNU General Public Licence (GPL) **518**

Index **525**

Figures

1.1	The main file types form a tree structured hierarchy.	6
1.2	The main Linux directory tree structure.	8
2.1	Three filesystems joined to form one hierarchy.	16
2.2	Single files can have multiple names.	17
3.1	The three main vi operating modes.	37
4.1	The shell waits for a command to finish.	56
4.2	Executing a background job.	57
7.1	Partitioning a 320 Mb hard disk.	127
7.2	Partitioning a 720 Mb hard disk.	128
9.1	A character grid and its encoding, for the letter A.	164
12.1	Passing e-mail from machine to machine.	203
13.1	DOSEMU needs to emulate this PC AT memory map.	216
15.1	The three *base* positions for lseek() *offsets*.	239
15.2	Sessions, process groups and processes.	246
16.1	The parts of programs and processes.	262
16.2	The action of the fork() system call.	263
16.3	Parent and child share open file descriptions.	264
16.4	The life cycle of a child process.	270
17.1	Effect of executing the system call dup(2).	278
20.1	Use of line[], avline[] and cmdlin[] arrays.	327

24.1	User programs access hardware via device drivers.	370
28.1	Simplified state transition diagram for CPU scheduler.	413
29.1	Stack layout in `main()` just before calling `twice()`.	422
29.2	Stack layout in `twice()` just before `return`.	423
29.3	Thread stack layout just before context switch.	426
29.4	Data structures set up in `new_thread`.	429
29.5	Structure links created during rendezvous.	432
30.1	Calculation of a linear address.	439
30.2	How paging translates linear to physical addresses.	441
30.3	Paging allows easy memory segment growth.	442
31.1	System V disk partition layout.	448
31.2	The initial data block free list.	449
31.3	Data block free list after block allocations.	450
31.4	Allocation and release of free inodes.	451
31.5	Data block pointers in an inode.	453
31.6	minix filesystem layout on a disk partition.	455
31.7	ext2 filesystem layout on a disk partition.	456
31.8	Layout of an ext2 block group.	457

Preface

Linux is a POSIX conformant operating system kernel that has been available for several years and operates on any 386, or above, IBM PC or clone. The kernel was initially created entirely by the effort of one man, Linus Torvalds, in Helsinki. Since then many system programming gurus have joined in the effort and now Linux is a fully featured UNIX and POSIX compatible operating system kernel. The Linux source code is licensed under the Free Software Foundation's General Public License. The practical upshot of this is that the Linux kernel with all its source code is freely available for anyone to take, use and pass on at will.

This free availability captured the imagination of the computing enthusiast community around the world and, via Internet, the software's use spread like wildfire. When you add to this the fact that look-alike tools and utilities exist for all the major UNIX functionality and that these are also available under the Free Software Foundation's General Public License, you can see that it has been possible to put together a complete UNIX look and feel product that is freely available to anyone with a network connection.

This was the state of play when Linux was in its infancy. Since then, word of Linux has spread beyond the Internet community into the world of computing at large. The evidence for this is that distributions of Linux, accessible by means other than Internet, are now widely available. These include Bulletin board distributions, sets of floppy disks for sale and many CD-ROM versions.

The Linux A–Z is primarily intended for use in an undergraduate course or course sequence. It can also be used in a graduate-level course (perhaps with the addition of some of the primary sources suggested in the text). It is based on lecture notes and practical case studies developed and used by the author over several years in operating systems courses at Staffordshire University. Its comprehensive coverage makes it useful as a primary reference volume for Linux/operating systems students and professionals wishing to branch out beyond their own subfield.

The only prerequisite is familiarity with basic concepts of computer science at freshman level. In particular, I have assumed that you have a reasonable idea about the PC in general, gained perhaps from the configuration of its hardware and disk partitions, and the installation of system software like DOS and/or windows. For the later parts of the book you will also need a working knowledge of C if you are to derive maximum benefit from the material in those sections.

This book has been written to provide entry points, at several levels, into the Linux operating system and many of its associated tools and utilities. The idea is that you are presented with concepts and then encouraged to experiment with the ideas in order to experience and consolidate the material.

The book itself is split up into five parts which are designed to take you on a tour of Linux from basic user level access, through system installation and administration, to programming with Linux system calls (its API), understanding its interface with the hardware, and an examination of some of its deepest internal secrets.

My personal view is that computing is a practical craft-like skill and that, consequently, there is no substitute for first-hand experience of the material. To this end the book also contains five full practical case studies designed with your own experimentation in mind.

The five parts of the book are made up as follows:

1. BASICS – This is covered by Chapters 1 to 6. The idea here is to take readers with some computing experience, but not in UNIX or Linux, and introduce them to the Linux system as ordinary users. This starts with logging on, a tour around a typical filestore layout and some simple commands, and then progresses on to the use of the vi editor, the standard bash shell, useful tools and utilities and finally a look at writing batch program scripts for the shell to execute.
2. ADMINISTRATION – When a beginner has mastered the basics or, if a more experienced user already has this level of knowledge, then it is possible to move on to learning how to perform administrator functions. Chapters 7 to 14 will deal with these aspects of Linux. The tour starts with a look at how to take a PC which probably has MS-DOS on it and reconfigure it so that Linux can co-reside with the user's existing applications. Once the Linux system has been installed it then needs to be configured to the administrator's specific requirements. This begins by looking at how to configure and rebuild the operating system kernel. After that, user accounts need to be set up and all of the resources need to be configured for use. The list of these includes: printers, modems and mice, X-windows clients and servers, serial, parallel and network communications, the Internet and the DOS emulator.
3. SYSTEM PROGRAMMING – This is the first step on the trek into the Linux internals. It is covered by Chapters 15 to 23. In essence, these chapters cover the important aspects of the Linux system call interface as viewed from an application program. So the topics covered are: file and terminal I/O, process control, various Inter-process Communication mechanisms (IPCs) including intra- and inter-machine varieties, high level software interrupts called signals and stand alone daemon processes. Part 3 also includes three complete case

studies, giving source code and commentary on a simple socket IPC library, a small example shell and a daemon which provides simple file transfer services.
4. DEVICE DRIVERS – Having looked at the Linux interface with its application programs, the next part (Chapters 24 to 27) looks at the other main operating system interface, the one between the kernel and the hardware. This interface is provided by device drivers which come in two varieties (character and block), both of which are covered along with some of the support functions supplied by the Linux kernel for use within the drivers. This part also includes a simple device driver case study to consolidate firmly the ideas presented in the block.
5. INTERNALS – The final part is covered in Chapters 28 to 32 and looks at selected topics in the Linux internals to get a feel for how it all works together. The topics covered are: process scheduling, the operation of Linux memory management, the Virtual Filesystem Switch (VFS) which allows Linux to access many different file system types and, finally, another look at the system call interface but this time from inside the kernel. A very simple user threads library is also presented as a case study in this part.

The source code for the five case studies is freely available under the GNU general public licence for anonymous ftp from the School of Computing ftp server at Staffordshire University:

`ftp.soc.staffs.ac.uk`

under the directory:

`users/phil_cornes/linuxa2z`

Whatever your current level of skill and expertise, in order to benefit from this book your only real requirement is an enthusiasm for the subject and a desire to know more about it.

Part I

BASICS

Chapter 1

Linux Basics

This part of *The Linux A–Z* makes the assumption that you have little or no experience of Linux or any other UNIX-like operating system. It will take you through the basics of Linux, seen through the eyes of a new user who has just visited the system administrator and been given the login name and password to an account on a Linux machine.

This is an ideal situation. However, I realize that there will be many readers who are not only new users but who also have to act as system administrators at the same time. The trick in this case is to interleave the material in Part 1 with the early chapters of Part 2 so that you perform the minimum necessary installation and system administration functions while you learn the basics. In fact, this is not such a daunting task, because many Linux distributions now available have default configurations for most things that make them fully usable, straight out of the box. You will still need to keep your wits about you, however, as some parts of the installation and configuration of a full Linux system remain a little tricky.

1.1 Logging In

To start off with, your Linux system should present you with an invitation to login, in the form of a login prompt:

```
login:
```

Here you type in your user name and press **Enter** or **Return**. If a password has been set on your account, the system will respond with:

```
Password:
```

as a prompt for you to enter your password, again followed by **Enter** or **Return**. The characters you type for your password will not be visible on the screen. If your login name and password are correctly entered, the system will return with a prompt inviting you to enter commands. If you have made any mistakes the system responds with the message:

```
Login incorrect
```

and issues a new login prompt for you to try again. A word of warning here – if you are the system administrator for your machine as well as being a new user, you should avoid using your `root` login account unless you need to perform an administrative task that absolutely requires its use. The reasoning behind this is that `root` is a privileged login with great power for overriding the normal Linux system security and integrity checks. Even for experienced administrators, accidentally making time consuming and/or costly errors is very easy.

Another point to mention here is that Linux (in common with most UNIX-like systems) is case sensitive, so that lower case letters and their upper case equivalents are treated as separate characters. In most cases, Linux expects you to type in lower case words and commands and in these cases the upper case versions just won't work.

For an ordinary user account, when you login successfully, the system will execute a program called the *shell*. Any program, while it is executing within the system, is called a *process*. And it is your shell process that is responsible for giving you a command line prompt. By default, the prompt for a non-privileged user is a dollar ($) symbol, and for a system privileged (`root`) user it is a hash (#) symbol. The shell is also responsible for taking in any commands you type at the keyboard and arranging for them to be executed.

In fact, for historical reasons, there are several different shells available which all offer roughly the same facilities. However, in this book, I shall concentrate on the Free Software Foundation (GNU) shell, called `bash`, which is the default shell used in most Linux distributions anyway.

Once you have a shell prompt, you can enter the names of commands, along with any parameters required by the commands, and the shell will execute them. If a command takes a long time to run or generates a lot of output to the screen, you may want to interrupt it and stop it before it has finished. To most commands, you can send an interrupt signal from the keyboard by pressing `Ctrl-c` (i.e. by pressing the 'c' key while you are already holding the 'Ctrl' key down).

When you have finished your login session, you can logout by entering the command `logout` at the shell prompt. There are other ways to logout, the most common being to send end-of-file (EOF) to the shell at the prompt. This is done from the keyboard by pressing `Ctrl-d`. The problem here is that the shell can be set up to ignore EOF and in some Linux distributions this is done by default. Later on, when we look at the shell in more detail, you will see how to customize some of the ways in which the shell responds.

1.2 The File Hierarchy

Having logged on to the system, the next task is to familiarize yourself with the basic file system layout. The Linux file system consists of files that fall into three basic classes:

Ordinary files. These are just collections of bytes upon which the system imposes no particular structure. They are used for text documents (including program source code), data files for programs to use and even the binary executable program files themselves.

Directory files. A directory is the mechanism that allows sets of files to be grouped together. Conceptually, the directory forms a container into which other files and directories can be placed, though, in fact, the directory itself actually contains only the names of the other files plus some simple information on how to find them on disk. Because a directory can itself contain the names of subdirectories, the file system forms a hierarchy.

Special files. A number of different file types fall into this category and you will see them all as you progress through the book. But, in the main, the special files are associated with communicating between running processes and also allowing processes to communicate with the various hardware devices that are connected to the machine, such as terminals, CD-ROMs, modems, etc.

All these file types are arranged into a large tree structured hierarchy (see Figure 1.1). This tree has a single directory at the top, called the *root* directory (not to be confused with the `root` login name), which is given the symbolic name '/'. Inside the `root` directory are several other standard directories and files which are used for various purposes. The layout of these higher level directories and files is standard only by convention and not by necessity, though it would be most confusing once you knew the conventions to find a directory hierarchy that was not laid out in the standard way.

Figure 1.1 shows a `root` directory (/) that contains the subdirectories `dev`, `bin` and `home`. The directory `home` in turn contains the directories `mike` and `lynne`, and so on. At the lowest levels, the directories contain the ordinary files and special files (like a and b). Given these file relationships, you would say that 'home is the *parent* of mike and that a is a *child* of proj1'.

It is quite possible for two or more files or directories to have the same name as long as they are contained in different parent directories. Obviously, therefore, there has to be some method for referring to a particular file unambiguously. This is done by specifying a *pathname*. A pathname is just a list of names separated by slash (/) characters. If this list of names also begins with a slash character then it is called an *absolute pathname*, which means that it works down from the `root` directory. For example, the absolute pathname for the directory `proj1` is:

```
/home/lynne/proj1
```

and for the special file b it is:

6 Linux Basics

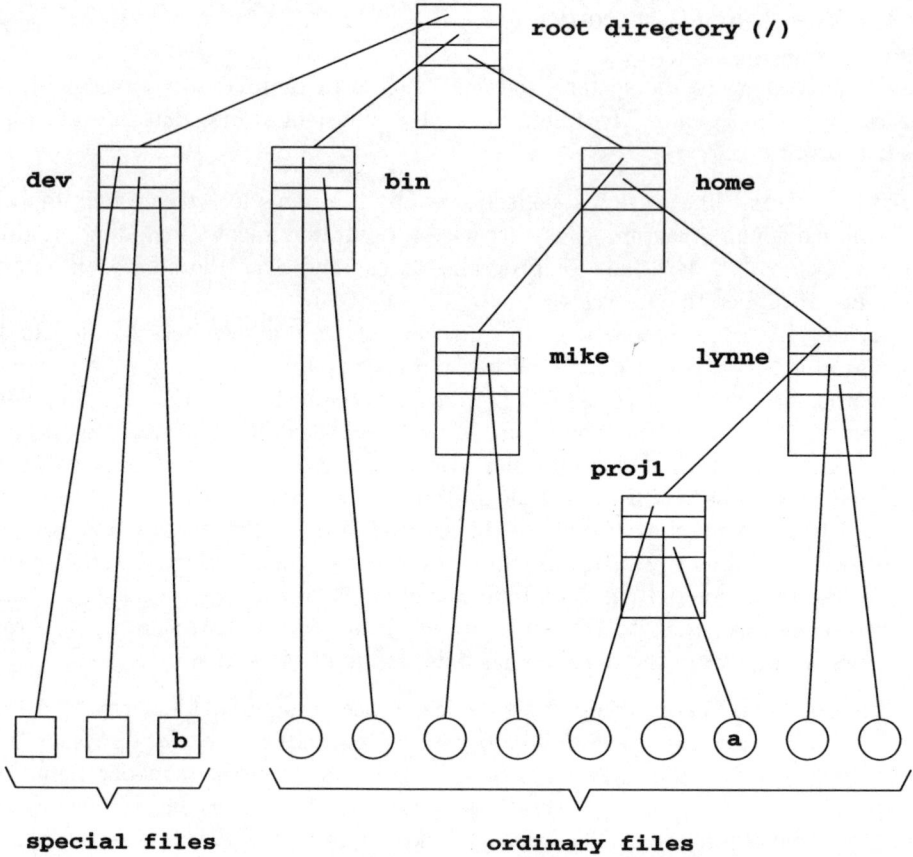

Figure 1.1 The main file types form a tree structured hierarchy.

   /dev/b

As you have seen, absolute pathnames start at the **root** directory and work down from there. It is also possible to specify a pathname starting at some other directory instead. A pathname given in this way is called a *relative pathname*. For example, the relative pathname to the ordinary file a from the directory lynne (or, more properly, /home/lynne) would be:

   proj1/a

showing that the way to get to a from the directory /home/lynne is via the directory proj1 which is contained within it.

When you change directory, the new directory becomes your *current working directory*. This idea of current working directory is quite important. Every time a program is executed in Linux, the resulting process has a current working directory set up as part of its internal state. This is the directory which it uses as the starting point for any files it accesses with a relative pathname. Unless a process makes specific arrangements to set up a particular current working directory for itself (and most don't) the default will be the directory that the user was in when the program was started.

What about trying to specify the relative pathname to the file a from the directory /home/mike? The problem here is that /home/mike and a are in different branches of the directory tree. In order to solve this problem you need to know about two extra names that are automatically included in every Linux directory. They are called . (pronounced dot) and .. (pronounced dot-dot). The name dot is an alias for the current directory and dot-dot is an alias for the parent of the current directory, allowing you to go back up the tree when specifying relative path names. Given the dot-dot notation, the answer to the previous question involves going back up the tree from /home/mike to /home and then back down the right branch to the file a. This would give the relative pathname as:

    ../lynne/proj1/a

Incidentally, even though the root directory does not have a parent directory, it still contains the name dot-dot, which is made to point back to the root directory itself. So, in effect, the root directory is treated specially in that it is its own parent. This also means that it is not an error to specify a relative pathname with too many dot-dots in it.

1.3 Exploring the File Hierarchy

When you login, there is a special directory associated with your login name called your *home directory*. Your home directory is actually your initial current working directory. It is the directory that acts as the starting point (the root if you like) for the part of the overall directory tree that belongs to you. All the files and directories that you create as a part of any work you do on the system will generally be located under your home directory.

The simplest way to find out where in the directory hierarchy your home directory is located is just to use the command pwd straight after you login. The pwd command tells you your *present working directory*. This is the directory you are currently 'in', which will be your home directory when you first login. Using the pwd command from your home directory will give output like this:

    $ pwd
    /home/you

where /home/you will be replaced by the absolute pathname to your home directory.

In order to move your present working directory away from your home directory to somewhere else in the directory hierarchy, you use the cd (*change directory*) command. So, to change directory to the directory hierarchy's root directory you would use the command:

8   *Linux Basics*

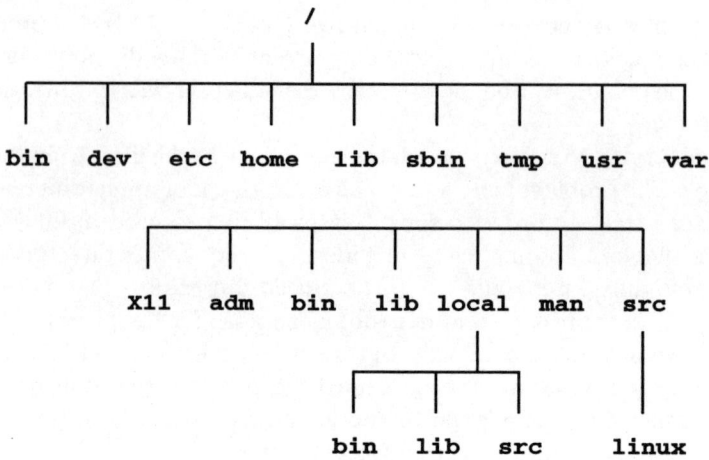

Figure 1.2 The main Linux directory tree structure.

```
$ cd /
```

thus giving the pathname of the required destination directory as a parameter.

In order to obtain a list of the names of the files and directories that are contained in the current directory you use the `ls` command. Using the `ls` command on the `root` directory of a typical Linux system gives an output such as:

```
$ ls
bin       dev       home        mnt       sbin      var
boot      dos       lib         proc      tmp       vmlinuz
cdrom     etc       lost+found  root      usr
```

The most important branches of the Linux directory hierarchy are shown in Figure 1.2. You should use the `pwd`, `cd` and `ls` commands to explore this directory hierarchy on your own machine.

If at any point you want to get back to your home directory you can obviously use the `cd` command and give the appropriate pathname as a command line parameter. But, if you just enter the `cd` command without specifying a destination directory this is a short cut that will also take you straight back to your home directory.

The main branches of the Linux directory hierarchy, as shown in Figure 1.2, contain files which have the general functions given in Table 1.1.

1.4   The Password File

Under Linux, the password file is one of the central data files in the system. It ties together quite a lot of what you have seen so far. The password file contains a list of all the users who have login names; it specifies where the home directories are for

Table 1.1 The main directory list

/bin	Binary executable commands
/dev	Device special files
/etc	System admin. and config. files
/home	Base for user home directories
/lib	Standard programming libraries
/sbin	System admin. commands
/tmp	General store for temporary files
/usr/X11	X windows system files
/usr/adm	System admin. data files
/usr/bin	More executable commands
/usr/lib	Libraries and package config. files
/usr/local/bin	Locally added commands
/usr/local/lib	Locally added libraries
/usr/local/src	Local command source files
/usr/man	System online manual pages
/usr/src/linux	Linux kernel source files
/var	Overflow for some large files

all the users and which shell program they will use when they login. The password file is also responsible for holding user passwords, giving a system identity number to each user and for placing sets of users into groups if they need to co-operate on joint project work.

The password file itself is just an ordinary text file which any user is allowed to read. It is stored in:

    /etc/passwd

The contents of this file can be listed most simply by typing the command line:

    `$ cat /etc/passwd`

The `cat` command is just being used to list the file contents here. Its full use will be covered in the next chapter (Section 2.3).

Each separate line in the password file is a record of information about a single user login name. Each record in the file is divided up into seven fields with colons (:) between them. The records have the format:

    `name:password:uid:gid:comment:home:shell`

From left to right, the seven fields are used as follows:

name This field contains the users login name. It appears exactly as the user must type it to login.

password This is the user's password. Don't be surprised if you don't recognize yours. This is quite correct as the passwords are encrypted. When you enter your password on login it will be encrypted in the same way and compared with this field to allow or deny system access. If this field is empty then no password is required for this user.

uid Once logged in, the system refers to a user by a *user identity number* (`uid`) and not by the login name. This is where the `uid`s are allocated.

gid Sometimes, a team of users will want to be able to work together in a group on a single project. For this, it would be useful to allow them common access to particular directories and files. This is done by allocating all the members of the team the same `gid` (*group identity number*) in this field.

comment This is just a comment field. It is commonly used to hold the user's real name and other personal details.

home This field specifies the absolute pathname to the user's home directory, which the system picks up on login.

shell This is the absolute pathname to a command that will be executed when any successful login is made on this user name. This can be any command, but for an ordinary user account it will be the pathname of a shell. If no pathname is given then this defaults to `/bin/sh`.

Because the password encryption algorithm is deemed to be so secure, the password file (`/etc/passwd`) is made publicly readable. However, if you choose a simple word as a password, such as you might find in a dictionary, then it is a simple matter to encrypt all the words in the dictionary to see if one matches.

There are two ways to overcome this problem. One is to make the encrypted passwords private, and there are packages available for Linux to do just that. In these packages the encrypted passwords are removed and stored in a separate file (typically `/etc/shadow`) to which public read access is denied. Having an extra file available also allows the addition of more fields to a user's record to specify such things as how often the users must change passwords. The other way to overcome the problem is much simpler and equally effective – choose a good password to start with. A good password will be at least six characters long and contain a mix of upper and lower case letters, digits and/or punctuation characters. If that sounds as though it will be hard to remember then make it a simple word, but change some of the characters in it to others that are visually similar (e.g. `shelter` and `5he!tER`). This technique will give a much more secure password, though a more sophisticated password cracking program might still be able to find it.

For maximum security it is also advisable to change your password from time to time. Changing passwords under Linux is easy – you just enter the command:

```
$ passwd
```

and the system will prompt you for your old password, if you have one, and then prompt you twice for your new one. You have to enter the new password twice because the system does not echo the passwords you type so you don't see them on the screen. This allows you to be sure that you have typed your new password correctly because the system will not change your password if the two tries don't match.

Exercises

1. How do you find out the absolute pathname of your home directory, and what is it on your system?
2. How would you find out if any of the users on your system have not got a password set up for them?
3. What commands do you need to give to change your current working directory from /usr/bin to /usr/local/bin first using an absolute pathname and then using a relative pathname?
4. Explore the directory hierarchy on your system and find the absolute pathnames for the ls and pwd commands.

Answers

1. There are several possibilities here. The first could be to look through the password file with the command:

    ```
    $ cat /etc/passwd
    ```

    and then extract your home directory from the sixth field of your password line. Another method would be to use the following command sequence:

    ```
    $ cd
    $ pwd
    ```

    which will change your current working directory back to your home directory from anywhere in the directory hierarchy and then display the present working directory. When I tried this it gave my home directory as:

    ```
    /home/pc
    ```

2. All the passwords are stored in encrypted form in the file /etc/passwd. All you need to do to find user who do not have a password set for them is to examine the contents of this file line by line looking for any entries which have field 2 empty.
3. The command you execute to change your current working directory from /usr/bin to /usr/local/bin using only absolute pathnames it is:

    ```
    $ cd /usr/local/bin
    ```

and to achieve the same result but using only relative pathnames it is:

```
$ cd ../local/bin
```

4. According to Table 1.1 most of the executable user commands are stored in the two directories /bin and /usr/bin. Searching in these two directories with the ls command shows that the two required commands have pathnames:

```
/bin/ls
/bin/pwd
```

There is actually a command, provided on most systems, that will enable you to find the full pathname of any command you can currently execute. It is called which. So, the same result could have been obtained with the command:

```
$ which ls pwd
/bin/ls
/bin/pwd
```

Chapter 2

Linux Commands

Having now logged on and had the chance to explore the layout of the directory hierarchy, it is time to take a look at a small selection of the hundreds of commands that are available. In a volume of this size it is not possible to cover in detail all the commands available. However, as you will soon see, Linux does have a good selection of system documentation on-line for you to explore and more is being added all the time.

In general, you will find that UNIX (and hence Linux) commands are very silent when they execute. That is to say, they don't generate any unnecessary output so that the usual indication you get that a command has executed successfully is the prompt you get for the next command.

2.1 Directory Hierarchy

If you execute the following commands:

```
$ cd /
$ ls
```

you will change your current working directory to `root` (`/`) and then get output from the `ls` command, something like:

bin	dev	home	mnt	sbin	var
boot	dos	lib	proc	tmp	vmlinuz
cdrom	etc	lost+found	root	usr	

However, in the last chapter, I said that every directory also contains the names `dot` and `dot-dot`, so why didn't they appear in the `ls` listing? In fact, as these two names will always be there, there seems little point in listing them. In order to ensure that they don't get listed, `ls` has a built-in rule which says that, by default, names that begin with a period (or full stop '.') should be ignored. This rule not only applies to the names `dot` and `dot-dot` but to *any* names that begin with a period.

This provides a convenient mechanism for having files contained in a directory, but not listed when you look at the directory's contents. Don't get the idea that this provides a mechanism for creating secret files, because it doesn't. It is very easy to get `ls` to list all files, including those that start with a period.

There are many occasions, when entering a command, where you will either want the command to perform some extra action beyond its default function or where you will want to suppress some part of the command's normal operation. In these cases, what you need to do is to pass *command line switches* into the command to switch on (or off) the functionality you require. In order to provide a degree of consistency, the normal way to pass switch values to a command is to use a hyphen (-) before the switch itself, to signify that this *is* a switch and not just a normal command parameter (such as a file name, for example).

In the case of the `ls` command the switch required to get it to list all files is `-a`. Typically this would give:

```
$ cd /
$ ls -a
.            cdrom        etc          mnt          tmp
..           dev          home         proc         usr
bin          dos          lib          root         var
boot         etc          lost+found   sbin         vmlinuz
```

After any command line switches, `ls` can also be given the name of a directory, in which case it will list the contents of the specified directory rather than the contents of the current directory:

```
$ ls -a /tmp
.            .X11-unix    elm.rc.OLD   ls           tagfile
..           NEAT         elv_61.1     modes
.X0-lock     clocks       hosts.OLD    nets.OLD
```

Don't forget that you should expect to obtain different results if you execute this command on your machine because `/tmp` is a publicly available directory for any users to store their own temporary files.

When you start to work on a Linux system, writing programs and running packages, you will start to generate files of your own. In general, you should hang all your files under your home directory. However, if you just put all your files into your home directory then it will soon become difficult to find things (take a look in `/usr/bin`). To overcome this problem you need to impose some sort of order and layout on your file space. You can do this by creating your own mini directory hierarchy under your home directory and imposing some simple self-discipline, to make sure that whenever you store a new file it goes in the right place.

In order to create new directories, you use the `mkdir` command and pass it the names of the new directories as parameters:

```
$ cd
$ mkdir bin text
```

Remember that `cd` on its own takes you back to your home directory. The `mkdir` command then creates two new directories in your home directory, called `bin` and `text`. Any number of directories can be created with a single `mkdir` command. This obviously means that `mkdir` can cope with a variable number of parameter values. In fact, as a general rule, any command where it makes sense (so, not `cd`, for instance) can take a variable list of names as parameters to operate on, and function correctly on the entire set.

Having created the directories, the next task is to copy some files into them. The copy command in Linux is `cp`:

```
$ cp /etc/passwd text/mypass
```

Assuming you are still in your home directory when you type this command, it will take a copy of the system password file (`/etc/passwd`) and store it in your `text` directory under the name `mypass`.

In this form, `cp` just takes the pathnames of two ordinary files as parameters and makes a copy of the first into the second. There is also a second form of the `cp` command, where the last parameter is not an ordinary file name but the name of a directory. In this form, a variable-length list of ordinary file names can be specified instead of the first parameter, and all of the files specified will be copied into the given directory:

```
$ cp /etc/passwd /etc/motd text
$ ls text
motd     mypass   passwd
```

Notice from the above sequence that using the second form of `cp` gives no opportunity to change the names of the files copied.

Incidentally, the file `/etc/motd` contains the system's *message of the day*. By default, the contents of this file are listed to users as they login. This means that if your system administrator needs to get a message to users, entering the message into this file is the easiest way to do it.

Just as files and directories can be created, they can also be removed. In order to remove a directory you use the `rmdir` command:

```
$ rmdir bin
$ rmdir text
rmdir: text: Directory not empty
```

As an added safety feature, the `rmdir` command only works if the directory is empty (except for the `dot` and `dot-dot` entries). So, here, the `bin` directory has been removed but the `text` directory has not. In order to remove the `text` directory you need first to remove the three ordinary files contained in it. Ordinary files can be removed with the `rm` command:

```
$ rm text/mypass
```

16 *Linux Commands*

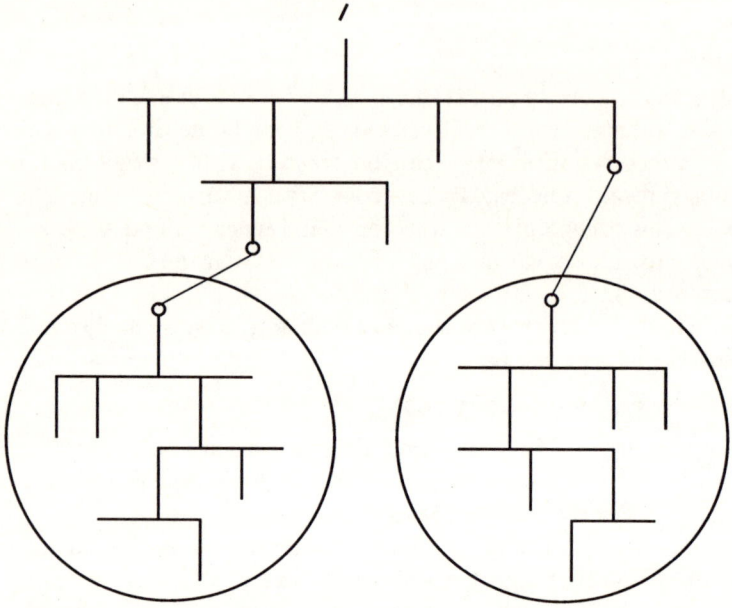

Figure 2.1 Three filesystems joined to form one hierarchy.

2.2 Filesystems

In general, the space on a large hard disk will be split up into convenient-sized pieces, called *disk partitions*. With smaller disks, the whole disk might be treated as a single partition. Either way, once a system is large enough to have several partitions to use for disk storage (on a single disk or on several disks) there is a question to sort out – how should the system treat the various partitions so as to make them all visible to users? One possibility would be to have a separate `root` directory on each partition and then specify file names as pathnames starting from a particular partition `root` directory. But from what you have seen so far there seems to be only a single directory hierarchy and not one for each disk partition.

What happens in Linux is that each partition will have a *filesystem* imprinted on it with its own partition top level directory and its own directory hierarchy underneath. Linux then makes these individual filesystems appear to be one directory hierarchy by mounting the top level directory of one filesystem over a leaf directory of another and making the join appear seamless (see Figure 2.1).

Each file of whatever type, stored in a disk partition, is allocated a number (called its *inode number*) which is actually the index number of an entry in an array stored on the disk. Each element of the array is an inode which stores the administrative information about a single file (such as, when it was created, who owns it and where the data blocks for this file are stored on the disk partition). It is the inode number of a file that is stored in a directory alongside the file's name. So,

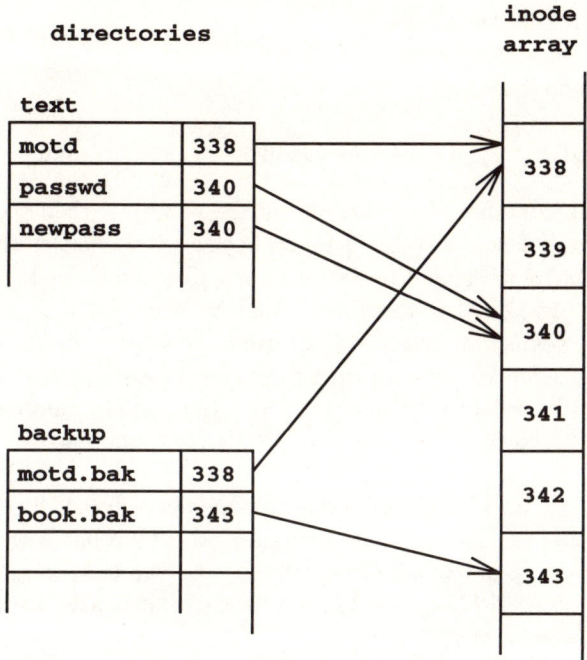

Figure 2.2 Single files can have multiple names.

essentially, directories are just tables that associate file names with inode numbers. Each file name and inode number pair in a directory is called a *link*.

Given that this is so, there is no real reason why the same inode number should not appear in more than one link. What this would mean is that you would have a single file with more than one valid pathname. This is shown diagrammatically in Figure 2.2. There are many instances where this can be useful. One possibility allows you to set up a directory of links to important files in order to provide a kind of 'undelete' facility, against the accidental removal of any of these files. This works because when you issue a remove (rm) command on a file and there is more than one link to the inode, then only your link will be removed. The inode itself and any other links will remain intact. It is not until you rm a file for which only one link exists that the inode itself will be released along with the file data blocks and the directory link.

To create a new link to an existing file you use the ln command and specify as parameters the pathname for the existing file followed by the new link pathname:

```
$ ln text/passwd text/newpass
$ mkdir backup
$ ln text/motd backup/motd.bak
```

In order to see the inode numbers to check that the links are all as expected, you use the -i switch to the ls command, as follows:

```
$ ls -i backup text
backup:
    338 motd.bak
text:
    338 motd          340 newpass      340 passwd
```

If you change the contents of text/motd in the example, then the contents of the file backup/motd.bak will also be changed because it is exactly the same file.

The only problem with all this is that each filesystem (disk partition) has its own array of inodes, so that the inode numbers are only unique within a single filesystem. This means that you could not use ln to set up this kind of link between, say, text/motd under your home directory and another pathname in a different filesystem. This is because, in another filesystem, inode number 338 (the inode number of text/motd in your home directory's filesystem) would be a completely different file.

If you need to set up a link between pathnames in different filesystems it can be done, but not using the shared inode technique above. What you do in this case is to use ln -s to set up a *symbolic link* between the two instead. A symbolic link is one of the Linux special file types and in effect it is just a text file which contains the pathname of the other file to which it provides a link. The other file is the real file which contains all the data. All the commands that read or write the contents of a file, when they are applied to a symbolic link, will follow the link and access the real file instead. Obviously, there is some very small time penalty for having to take this extra step but it is too small to make any real difference.

When you want to create a link between two files and you want to make sure that what you do can be ported to other systems, you should use symbolic links. This is because they can be used both within a single filesystem and between separate filesystems, while inode links can only be used in the first of these situations:

```
$ ln -s text/motd backup/motd2.bak
$ ls -i backup text
backup:
    338 motd.bak     328 motd2.bak
text:
    338 motd         340 newpass      340 passwd
```

Another command that operates by manipulating inode links is mv. This command is used to *move* a directory link from one place to another within the same filesystem. Effectively, it performs the same function as ln to link inodes, but then removes the old link to the file:

```
$ mv text/newpass backup/passwd.bak
$ ls -i backup text
backup:
    338 motd.bak     328 motd2.bak    340 passwd.bak
```

```
text:
    338 motd            340 passwd
```

One side effect of the mv command, which is actually used more than its ability to move files around between directories, is the fact that if the new file is in the same directory as the old file then it performs the same function as a *rename* command. In fact there is no specific rename command in Linux; you just use mv:

```
$ mv backup/motd2.bak backup/motd.sym.link
$ ls -i backup
    338 motd.bak        328 motd.sym.link   340 passwd.bak
```

Just as with the cp command, mv can have its second parameter specified as a directory rather than a file and the first parameter can then be a list of files, all of which will be moved into the specified directory, whilst keeping the same file names as before.

2.3 Manipulating Files

Very often, you will want to examine the contents of a text file. You have already seen one method for doing this – using the cat command. The word cat is an abbreviation of the word *concatenate*, which means *to join together*. The way in which the cat command achieves this joining is by allowing you to specify a list of file names as parameters which it will list one after the other without a break:

```
$ cat /etc/passwd /etc/motd
```

The problem with this is that if the contents of the files you list to the screen are longer than one screenful, then the whole thing just scrolls past too fast to read and you end up only seeing the last screen full at the end of the listing.

What you require is a command which lists files like cat but which will insert pauses at the end of each screen full. The usual command to do this is called more:

```
$ more /etc/passwd /etc/motd
```

When more pauses at the end of a page there are several characters you can type to tell it what to do next:

Space	list next page;
Enter	list next line;
q	quit listing;
:n	list next file.

Another command that works like more but which provides a whole host of facilities in addition to those available with more is (amusingly) called less.

In the situation where you have a file which has new text written to the end of it periodically, you may want to be able to see just the most recent additions to the file without having to page through it from the beginning, especially if it grows to be a large file. The command to do this is called `tail` because it just prints the tail end of a file. By default, `tail` prints the last ten lines of a file, though this can be changed with the -n command line switch:

```
$ tail -n 4 /etc/passwd
user:off:100:50::/home/user:/bin/sh
ftp:*:404:1::/home/ftp:/bin/false
pc:fjKppCZxEvouc:500:500::/usr1/pc:/bin/bash
carey:Yt1a4ffkG2r02:501:500::/usr1/carey:/bin/bash
```

In fact, the '-n 4' can be abbreviated just to '-4' and it will still perform the same function.

Another useful facility is the ability to count the number of lines, words and characters in a file. This can be done with the word count (`wc`) command:

```
$ wc /etc/passwd
      21      42     775 /etc/passwd
```

The three values 21, 42 and 775 are the number of lines, words and characters respectively, in the file `/etc/passwd`. In this case, 21 lines shows that there are 21 account login names set up on this machine. You might have expected there to be somewhat more than 42 individual words in the password file but this is just because of the rather simple definition that `wc` uses for a word. It has nothing to do with looking up words in dictionaries, but is just taken to be any sequence of characters separated by spaces, tabs, newlines etc.

Printing out all three numbers is the default action performed by `wc`. You can obtain just the lines, words or character counts by using one of the command line switches -l, -w or -c:

```
$ wc -l /etc/passwd
      21 /etc/passwd
$ wc -w /etc/passwd
      42 /etc/passwd
$ wc -c /etc/passwd
     775 /etc/passwd
```

It is also possible to use the `wc` command without giving a file name. In this case, the `wc` command will count the lines, words and characters in any text entered directly at the keyboard.

The only problem with entering text from the keyboard comes when you wish to signal to `wc` that you have finished typing and now want to see the counts. The way to do this is to type the end-of-file (`EOF`) character (`Ctrl-d`, remember) at the start of a line on its own. When you press `Ctrl-d`, the `wc` command will get exactly the same end-of-file indication that it would get if it were reading the information from a file and it reached the end.

2.4 On-line Help

In general, there are many more command line switches available for each command than you have seen so far and certainly more than I have space to include here. If you need to find extra detail about the use and format of anything covered in this book, or any other system facility for that matter, then there is a terrific amount of information available in the form of the on-line manual. Linux has a set of manual pages available that are split into sections. The purpose of the pages in each section is as follows:

section 1 This part of the manual details the commands that you type in at the keyboard in response to a shell prompt (such as `cat` and `ls`).
section 2 When you write programs to be compiled under Linux (in C perhaps), you will often want to call on facilities provided for your programs by the kernel of the operating system. These facilities are accessed via a set of *system calls* and it is these calls that are detailed in this manual section.
section 3 In addition to the system calls provided by the operating system, there is also a huge set of programming language function calls collected into libraries and supplied with the compiler. The library function calls are described in manual section 3.
section 4 Under Linux, all input and output is made to look as though is goes to or comes from a file. This means that when you are writing a program to read characters from a keyboard or write characters to a screen or printer, you actually open a file which *is* one of these devices and read or write characters to it. The files which represent the hardware devices of the machine are special files which are stored, by convention, in `/dev`. Any special details about driving the hardware through these files is contained in this manual section.
section 5 This section describes the structure and layout of various system data and administrative configuration files (the password file, for example).
section 6 This is the manual section which describes the games available on the system.
section 7 This is a section for miscellaneous items which don't fit anywhere else.
section 8 This is another section of commands to type in at the keyboard, but they are only intended to be used for system administration, and usually only by the system privileged user (called *root*, not to be confused with the directory of the same name).
section 9 This section is for descriptions of some of the internal workings of the Linux kernel itself.

A command which allows access to all these manual pages is called **man**. It is used as follows:

```
$ man ls
```

This will give a listing of the manual page for the `ls` command. Because most manual pages are longer than a screen in length, the `man` command will use the `more` command (or `less`) to split its output into screens.

Each manual page is split up into several parts. Typically these include:

NAME Under this heading, the name of the manual page entry is given (e.g. `ls`), along with a one-line description of its function (e.g. list the contents of directories).

SYNOPSIS This shows how to use the entry, along with a brief list of all the option switches available and a list of any required or optional parameters (e.g `ls [-adgilCFR] [name...]`). Anything enclosed in square brackets in these listings is optional and anything followed by ellipses (...) may be repeated. So this example says that `ls` can optionally take any or all of the command line switches `adgilCFR` optionally followed by one or more `names`. This matches what you already know about the `ls` command and adds several more command line switches that you have not yet seen. Indeed, the real version of `ls` adds more command line switches even than this.

DESCRIPTION This part gives a much fuller account of the function of the item than the one-liner in the **NAME** part.

OPTIONS The functionality of each of the switches is now described in detail.

RETURN VALUE For the manual sections where some kind of function call is being described, this section details the type of value that will be returned. This might also include the specific values returned if any error occurs.

FILES Here, any associated configuration or data files are listed.

SEE ALSO This part gives a list of other, related, manual page entries that you might want to look at.

BUGS Any known shortcomings or limitations (or even known bugs) are listed here.

Normally, when you ask to see a particular manual entry, the manual is searched sequentially starting with section 1, and it is the first occurrence of the required item which gets displayed. Sometimes, a particular item may occur in more than one manual section. One example of this, which you have already encountered, is the item `passwd`. This occurs not only in manual section 1 as the `passwd` command used to change passwords, but also in section 5, where the format of the `passwd` file in `/etc` is discussed. If you just enter the command:

```
$ man passwd
```

you will always get the section 1 entry if it exists. In order to see the manual entry in a specific manual section you need to give this as an optional parameter to the `man` command. The following example will list the section 5 `passwd` entry:

```
$ man 5 passwd
```

It is also possible to list any relevant entries in all sections of the manual with the -a switch:

```
$ man -a passwd
```

2.5 Security

Linux is a multi-user operating system. This means it can have multiple users simultaneously logged in and working. You have already seen that the system enforces some kind of security arrangement by requiring users to login and supply passwords. This allows the system (via the user's uid) individually to identify what each user does during a login session. In particular, this identification extends to marking as *owned by the user* all the files that the user creates during the login session. When you are the owner of any files, the system gives you permission to exercise control over them, so that you can specify what access other users have to them.

In the case of files and directories, each one has a set of permission flags associated with it, which can be seen by using the -l switch to the ls command:

```
$ cd
$ ls -l text
total 2
-rw-r--r--    2 pc        book            22 Apr 20 20:37 motd
-rw-r--r--    2 pc        book           796 Apr 20 20:37 passwd
```

This switch tells ls to produce a long listing of the files in the given directories, including quite a lot of extra information. The first piece of information in the output gives the total number of disk data blocks (here two, at typically one kilobyte each) occupied by all of the files in the directory. The rest of the output listing is produced with one line per file. The very first character on each line says what kind of file it is. In the example, the hyphen (-) is used to indicate that these are ordinary files. Other characters in this position are possible, the most common being the letter d, which says that this line describes a directory. The rest of the first block of characters on each line are the file's permission flags (I'll come back to these in a moment). After the permission flags is a number which says how many directory links there are to the associated inode. The next field gives the login name of the file's owner. This is followed by the name (or sometimes the gid) of the set of users who share group access to this file. Next comes a number which gives the size of the file in bytes. After that comes the date and time (or, if it was a while ago, the date and year) that the file content was last modified. And, lastly, the name of the file itself.

Incidentally, if you want to find out the extra details for a directory rather than for the files contained within the directory, you can do so with the -d switch to ls as follows:

```
$ ls -ld text
drwxr-x--x   2 pc        book          1024 Apr 20 20:35 text
```

The file access permission arrangements for an ordinary file are based around reading the file's contents, writing new data to the file and being able to execute the file as a command. For a directory, the equivalent permissions are for reading the names of files contained in the directory, writing information to the directory to add or delete inode links and being able to search the directory (i.e. to use the directory in a pathname so as to access a file or subdirectory it contains). For each file (and directory), there are four different classes of user and each class has its own set of access permissions to read, write or execute (search) the file. The four classes of user are:

root This is the class of system privileged users. They all have access to a `root` login account.
owner This is the user who actually owns the file.
group This is the name (or `gid`) of the class of users who will share group access to the file.
world This is the set of all the users who don't fall into any of the other three classes.

In the case of the `root` users, they have complete read, write and search permissions to all files and directories, automatically, so there is no need to specify any permissions for them explicitly. The other three user classes can have the various permissions granted or withdrawn on an individual file and directory basis. For these three classes, therefore, each file and directory in the entire directory hierarchy has associated with its inode a set of nine permission bits giving the read, write and execute (search) permissions for each of the owner, group and world user classes. A few examples should make this clearer:

```
-rw-r--r--   2 pc        book           796 Apr 20 20:37 passwd
```

This line, taken from the previous example, shows that the file *passwd* is owned by the user *pc* and belongs to the user group *book*. The first character on the line (-) shows this to be an ordinary file. The next three characters show the read, write and execute (`rwx`) permissions for the owner. In the example the characters (`rw-`) show that user *pc* has read and write permissions granted but not execute permission. The next three characters are the permissions for the file's group (`r--`). Here the group can read the file but not write to it or execute it. The last three characters in the block (`r--`) are for the world user class (`r--`), who can also read the file but not write or execute it.

```
drwxr-x--x   2 pc        book          1024 Apr 20 20:35 text
```

This second example shows the permission flags for the directory *text*. The first character on the line (`d`) shows that it is a directory. The next three characters (`rwx`) show that the file owner has read, write and search permission. The file's group permissions (r-x) allow read and search access to the group but will not allow group members to add or delete files in the directory. The world permission bits only allow search access to the directory, not read or write access. This stops the world user class from using ls to see what is in the directory (no read permission) but does allow them to access files they already know to be in the directory. The following example shows that a member of the world user class can see the contents of a readable file in a directory, without read permission on the directory itself:

```
$ cd /home/pc
$ ls -l text
ls: text: Permission denied
$ cat text/motd
motd contents in here.
```

One extra privilege granted to the owner of a file, whatever its permission bits show, is the ability to change the permission bits to another value. This is done with the command chmod. The general format of chmod is:

```
chmod mode files...
```

where *mode* specifies the new permission bits and *files* is the list of files whose permissions will be changed. The mode parameter can be specified in either of two different ways – a symbolic representation or a bit pattern given as an octal number. The octal bit pattern is probably the simplest to understand as it just involves writing three octal digits. Each octal digit is just a three-bit bit pattern which specifies the rwx permissions for one of the three user classes: owner, group or world.

Suppose you wanted to change the permissions of the text directory from the values in the previous example to the new values rwxrwxr-x, so that the owner and group classes can read, write and search the directory and the world class can read and search it, but not write to it. The first job is to convert the required permission string (rwxrwxr-x) into a binary bit pattern. This is done by writing a one-bit where a permission is to be granted and a zero-bit otherwise. This gives the nine-bit binary string 111111101 in this example. All that remains now is to split this bit pattern into groups of three bits which can then be converted directly to octal digits. This gives 111 111 101, which in octal becomes 775.

The command required to perform the change would, therefore, be:

```
$ chmod 775 text
$ ls -l
drwxr-x--x   2 pc      book      1024 Apr 20 20:35 backup
drwxrwxr-x   2 pc      book      1024 Apr 20 20:35 text
```

Notice that the permissions of the text directory have been updated as required, while leaving backup unchanged.

2.6 Processes

When you run a program whose executable binary image is stored in a file on disk (perhaps in /bin or /usr/bin), the executable machine code, along with some initialized data, is copied from the file into memory. Here it joins up with an environment provided by Linux to enable it to run. The code and data stored on disk is called a *program*. Once the program is in memory and joined to its run time environment it becomes a *process*. In effect, a program is a static thing stored on disk, whereas a process is dynamic – a program in execution.

Each process in the system is identified by a unique integer value called its *process identity number* (PID).

In Linux, a new process can only be created when an existing process splits into two. The new process is called the *child* of the existing process, and the existing process becomes the *parent*. A single parent process can spawn many child processes, which in turn can then spawn their own child processes. This means that the set of all processes running on a Linux machine forms a tree structured hierarchy, from child to parent to grandparent, and so on. The root of this tree structured hierarchy of processes is a single common ancestor, called the init process, which has a PID value of 1, being the first real process to run when the system boots up.

There are several commands available which will give all sorts of vital statistics about processes. The first one to look at is called ps. Just entering the ps command on its own will tell you what processes you have running specifically for you and will typically generate output like the following:

```
$ ps
  PID TTY STAT  TIME COMMAND
  325 v01 S     0:00 -bash
  359 v01 R     0:00 ps
```

This shows two processes running for the user. The first one, with a PID of 325, is the users login shell (bash). The second, with a PID of 359, is the ps command which produced the output. The hyphen in front of the bash command shows this is a program run as a login shell for a user rather than as a user command at the keyboard. The ps process was created by the shell in response to your command. The other three columns in the output: TTY, STAT and TIME show the process's controlling terminal, its system status and its CPU usage time respectively.

It is possible to obtain a great deal more information out of ps with suitable command line switches. Sadly, much of this will be meaningless to a novice user. There are some worthwhile items however. The -j switch will show the PID of a process's parent under the PPID column:

```
$ ps -j
  PPID  PID PGID  SID TTY TPGID STAT  UID  TIME COMMAND
     1  325  325  325 v01   393 S     500  0:00 -bash
```

```
   325   393   393   325 v01   393 R       500  0:00 ps -j
```

Notice that the parent process of the user's shell is the `init` process as it has a PPID of 1. Also notice that the shell is the parent of the `ps` process and that the PID of the `ps` process is different from that of the previous example, showing that even though the same program is running, it is a different process.

It is possible for the `ps` output to become quite lengthy especially if you get it to output a list of all the process on the system, not just your own. This can be done with two more command line switches: `-x` which will list processes without a terminal to control them and `-a` to obtain a list of processes run by all the other users on the system as well as your own. The following, slightly abbreviated, list gives some typical output:

```
$ ps -ax
  PID TTY STAT  TIME COMMAND
    1 ?   S     0:00 init
    6 ?   S     0:00 bdflush (daemon)
    7 ?   S     0:00 update (bdflush)
   25 ?   S     0:00 /usr/sbin/crond -l10
   41 ?   S     0:00 /usr/sbin/syslogd
   43 ?   S     0:00 /usr/sbin/klogd
   45 ?   S     0:00 /usr/sbin/inetd
   47 ?   S     0:00 /usr/sbin/lpd
   61 v03 S     0:00 /sbin/agetty 38400 tty3
   62 v04 S     0:00 /sbin/agetty 38400 tty4
   63 v05 S     0:00 /sbin/agetty 38400 tty5
   64 v06 S     0:00 /sbin/agetty 38400 tty6
  325 v01 S     0:00 -bash
  460 v02 S     0:00 -bash
  547 v02 R     0:00 ps -ax
```

Linux is a true multi-user multi-tasking operating system, which means that it can handle multiple users logged in simultaneously, all running multiple processes. It is possible to login to a Linux machine in several different ways using one of several entry points. The most common way to login is to use the keyboard and screen built into the machine. Even in this situation it is possible to have multiple users logged in to the system or even a single user logged in multiple times. This can be done because Linux makes provision to support multiple virtual terminals. At any point in time, one of these virtual terminals will be connected to the real keyboard and screen. In effect, the keyboard and screen can be switched between the set of virtual terminals allowing multiple login sessions to be created. The use of these virtual terminals is only possible from the main system keyboard and screen. The selection between the virtual terminals is made by holding the **Alt** key pressed while pressing one of the function keys, usually **F1** to **F6**. This gives easy access to one of six different login sessions. When the system first boots up, the

Alt-F1 terminal is the one used by default. I find virtual terminals most useful when I am developing software – I can be editing code on one terminal, compiling the results on another and looking up information on yet a third.

In the previous ps listing, notice the numbers in the TTY column. They show which processes are associated with each of the virtual terminals (v01 to v06). Notice that the shell with the PID of 325 is the login shell for a user on virtual terminal one. However, the ps command which generated the output listing was executed by a user on virtual terminal two. The other four virtual terminals all have copies of the program

    /sbin/agetty

running against them. This is the program that gives you a login prompt and waits for you to enter your login name. See how all four copies of the program are running as separate processes (i.e. they all have different PIDs).

Normally, when a user logs out, all the processes controlled by the same terminal (in the TTY column) that the user was logged in to will be terminated. However, the processes that have a question mark (or query '?') in the TTY column are all running without an associated terminal, which means that they can continue to run even when there are no users logged in.

If you want to find out quickly what terminal you are logged in to, you can do so by using the tty command:

```
$ tty
/dev/tty1
```

As you can see, the full name for virtual terminal 1 is /dev/tty1. Similarly, virtual terminal 2 would be /dev/tty2, and so on. If you remember, the /dev directory is where the system keeps its special files by convention, and the virtual terminals are one example of what the special files are used for.

Sometimes it can be necessary to force the termination of a process. As long as it is a process over which you have control, usually because you executed it, then it is a simple matter to terminate it using the kill command. All you do is to pass the PID of the process whose execution you wish to terminate as a parameter to the kill command and kill will then send a signal to the process to terminate it. It is possible for a process to ignore the default signal sent to it by kill, in which case a -9 switch to the kill command will send a signal that cannot be ignored. Consider the following command sequence, which demonstrates these points:

```
$ tty
/dev/tty2
$ ps
  PID TTY STAT  TIME COMMAND
  325 v01 S     0:00 -bash
  460 v02 S     0:00 -bash
  557 v02 R     0:00 ps
```

```
$ kill 325
$ ps
  PID TTY STAT  TIME COMMAND
  325 v01 S     0:00 -bash
  460 v02 S     0:00 -bash
  559 v02 R     0:00 ps
$ kill -9 325
$ ps
  PID TTY STAT  TIME COMMAND
  460 v02 S     0:00 -bash
  561 v02 R     0:00 ps
```

First, the `tty` command shows that the user is currently switched to virtual terminal 2. A `ps` command then gives the PID of the shell on virtual terminal 1 as 325. A `kill` command to this PID followed by a second `ps` shows that the shell is able to ignore the default signal to terminate. However, a second `kill` command to the same PID using a -9 switch does terminate the shell, as seen from the final call to `ps`.

2.7 Space

In addition to processes, there are several system resources that it is useful to be able to monitor, the most common being disk space and memory space. In order to see on a per filesystem basis the amount of disk space available and in use, you use the `df` command:

```
$ df
Filesystem       1024-blocks   Used Available Capacity Mounted on
/dev/hda3             199270 182354      6625      96% /
/dev/hda1             610608 209675    369394      36% /usr
/dev/hda4             199271 147953     41027      78% /home/pc
```

The numbers and sizes of partitions on your system will obviously differ from this example, but the principle is the same. The first column in the `df` listing specifies the pathname of the special file that represents the disk partition. The second column gives the number of 1024-byte data blocks contained in the partition, with third and fourth columns being the number of these blocks in use and available respectively. You may be surprised to discover that the values in the fourth column when added to those in the third column do not add up the numbers in the second column. This is because, by default, a small percentage of the space on each partition is reserved for use by the system administrators so that they can login and still have some working space for sorting out problems, even when the filesystems are full as far as ordinary users are concerned.

The *Capacity* column shows the percentage of the ordinary users' space that is in use. This means that when this figure reaches 100% there is still the system administrator's percentage of the partition left to go. Finally, the *Mounted on* column shows where in the directory hierarchy the root directory of each partition is attached to the overall directory tree structure, see Figure 2.1.

The df command is useful when you want to see how much disk space is in use on a particular partition and how much is left. However, it will not help you to find out how much disk space is used up by your home directory and its subdirectories and files. To find out this kind of disk usage information, you use the du command:

```
$ cd /etc
$ du
24      ./rc.d
1       ./fs
4       ./skel/.term
8       ./skel
1       ./lilo
1       ./default
5       ./msgs
389     .
```

By default, the first column in this output listing is the amount of disk space, measured in kilo-bytes, allocated to all of the files in each of the directories listed in the second column.

Notice, that without any command line switches specified, du systematically works its way down the directory hierarchy from the current directory until the sizes of all subdirectories have been reported. This can be rather a lengthy listing, when very often all you want is just a single number giving the total. In this case it is possible to get du to print a summary of what it finds, using the -s command line switch:

```
$ du -s /etc
389     /etc
```

As you can see the name of the directory to use as the start of the disk usage search can be specified as a parameter. In fact, the du command can have a list of directory names specified as command line parameters and it will size each of them separately and generate a list of the results.

Now, we'll move on from disk usage to memory usage. Your machine will have a fixed amount of *random access memory* (RAM) installed in it. This memory is used to hold the running operating system kernel itself, all the processes that are executing on the machine, and all the data on which these processes are operating. In fact, Linux can actually arrange to be dealing with more processes than will fit simultaneously into the memory. It does this by having available a memory overflow area on disk, traditionally called the *swap space*.

In general, all memory starts off as unused (i.e. free). In order to speed up disk access, Linux arranges that once a block of data has been read from a disk file it is stored in memory in a buffer for as long as possible, so that if the contents of the same disk block are required again, the data can be taken from the memory buffer rather than re-reading the disk. Reading disk data from memory like this is orders of magnitude faster than getting the data from disk every time it is required. A similar buffering trick is also done when data is written to the disk.

Another way to use up free memory is to load programs into it for execution as processes. If the number of processes in the system continues to increase, then after a while the quantity of free memory will dwindle down to a small amount that is insufficient to run any new programs. What happens then is that Linux will start to take some of the memory back from the disk buffers in order to run more processes. In this way, as more processes are added to the system, the amount of memory dedicated to disk buffers falls until some minimum required value is reached. When this happens, no more free space or buffer space can be taken up, so Linux now needs to adopt a new strategy. What it does is to look for blocks of memory that are in use but haven't been needed for a while and writes them away to the swap space. This effectively makes those swapped memory blocks free again and available for re-use. At times when the process load on the system lightens, swapped out memory blocks can be brought back into main memory, eventually to re-join the free memory list as the processes terminate.

There is one other technique that Linux uses in order to wring the most use out of the system's main memory – sharing executable code. If two different processes are both executing the same program, or the same program libraries, then there is no reason why they should not both share a single copy of the code in memory rather than loading the same code twice into separate memory areas. And in fact Linux does just this.

This whole thing is a rather dynamic situation with blocks of memory migrating between the free list, the disk buffer cache, process memory and the swap space as the operating system balances out the various requirements for this fixed-size resource. Information about all these areas of memory can be displayed using the `free` command:

```
$ free
             total      used      free    shared   buffers
Mem:         19208     13444      5764      7448      7784
-/+ buffers:            5660     13548
Swap:        32992         0     32992
```

All of the numbers here are given in 1-kilo-byte blocks. Looking at the top row of the output, the *total* figure is the amount of memory that Linux has available and free to start with. If you know how much memory is really installed into your computer then you will find that the total in the `free` output is around 1 mega-byte (Mb) less. This is because the amount of memory used by the kernel has already been removed and is not displayed. The next two numbers in the top row of the output show the amount of memory used so far and the amount left unused in the free memory section. Together these two add up to the total. After that, the next number is the amount of the shared memory used by all the processes. And the final figure is the amount of memory in use for disk buffers at this time.

The second row contains two numbers. These are just the same as the numbers directly above them in the first row, but changed by the size of the buffer memory. This gives an idea of the memory situation just with regard to processes, as buffer memory can be reclaimed for process space anyway.

The final row of the output shows the total, free and used space available on disk for swapping.

It can be quite instructive to watch how the pattern of memory usage changes over time and this can be done with the command **top**. This command is very interesting to see as it provides a large quantity of system statistics in a display which is regularly updated every few seconds. The **top** command itself is actually a cross between the **ps** and **free** commands with a few extras as well. The set of processes that are displayed are listed in the order of how much CPU time they are using, with the heaviest CPU usage at the top. An abbreviated sample output from **top** appears as follows:

```
$ top
1:44pm up 8 days,2:21, 4 users, load average: 0.11, 0.15, 0.14
33 processes: 32 sleeping, 1 running, 0 zombie, 0 stopped
CPU states:  2.1% user,  0.0% nice,  7.4% system, 90.5% idle
Mem: 15040K av, 14340K used,  700K free, 6312K shrd, 6620K buff
Swap: 9208K av, 548K used, 8660K free

  PID USER     PRI  NI  SIZE  RES SHRD STAT %CPU %MEM  TIME COMMAND
  471 pc        20   0   100  308  332 R     9.0  2.0  2:24 top
  273 root       1   0    85  280  352 S     0.5  1.8  0:17 in.tftpd
    1 root       1   0    48  196  280 S     0.0  1.3 26:37 init
  295 cew        1   0   536  656  508 S     0.0  4.3  0:05 -bash
  849 mot        1   0   538  652  504 S     0.0  4.3  0:03 -bash
```

The first line of output shows the current time, the length of time that the machine has been up and running since it was booted, how many users are currently logged in and three numbers on the end showing how heavily loaded the system has been in the recent past. The three system load values are the load averages taken over the past minute, the past five minutes and the past fifteen minutes respectively. The load average effectively tells you how many processors you need in the machine to run all the processes at full speed. This means that the smaller the value of these numbers, the lighter the load on the system. Obviously, when there is only one CPU to share between all the processes, a load average greater than 1 implies that the processes are not getting as much CPU time as they are requesting and, consequently, they will slow down.

The second line in the output says how many processes there are in total on the system and what states they are all in.

The third line of output gives CPU utilization information and shows that currently the CPU is idle for over 90% of the time and used to run user and system code for less than 10% of the time. These figures effectively confirm the load average figures given before.

The next two lines contain just the same information that you would get from running the `free` command. Finally, the rest of the display is `ps` type output, but ordered on %CPU usage.

Exercises

1. Perform some simple experiments to find out if one symbolic link can point to another which then points on to the file. If it can, is there limit to the number of symbolic links you can have in the chain?
2. What is the disadvantage of symbolic links over hard links?
3. Can you find a pair of directory links anywhere, both of which refer to the same file?
4. Execute the following command sequence:

    ```
    $ cd
    $ mkdir temp
    $ cp /etc/passwd temp
    $ chmod 400 temp
    ```

    If you were now to execute the command `ls temp` what would you expect the output to be?
5. Carrying on from the last question, what would you expect to obtain from executing the command `ls -l temp`? Try it. Did you obtain what you expected? If not, why not?

Answers

1. The experiment can easily be performed as follows:

    ```
    $ cp /etc/passwd ./p0
    $ ln -s p0 p1
    $ ln -s p1 p2
    $ cat p2
    root:ltq3uhhA2dnSM:0:0:root:/root:/bin/bash
    ...
    ```

This sequence takes a working copy of the password file into the current directory as p0. The second line creates a symbolic link to your copy of the password file, and calls the link p1. The third line now creates a second symbolic link to p1 and calls the second link p2. Finally, the cat command is used to test if the second link (p2) can be used to access the target file at the end of the chain. And indeed it can.

If you continue to add links to the chain everything seems to work as far as adding the new links is concerned, but when you have more than six links in the chain the commands you use can no longer access the target file:

```
$ ls -l
total 1
-rw-r--r--  1 pc    500       731 Jan 13 16:19 p0
lrwxrwxrwx  1 pc    500         6 Jan 13 18:07 p1 -> p0
lrwxrwxrwx  1 pc    500         2 Jan 13 18:07 p2 -> p1
lrwxrwxrwx  1 pc    500         2 Jan 13 18:08 p3 -> p2
lrwxrwxrwx  1 pc    500         2 Jan 13 18:08 p4 -> p3
lrwxrwxrwx  1 pc    500         2 Jan 13 18:08 p5 -> p4
lrwxrwxrwx  1 pc    500         2 Jan 13 18:08 p6 -> p5
lrwxrwxrwx  1 pc    500         2 Jan 13 18:09 p7 -> p6
$ cat p7
cat: p7: Too many symbolic links encountered
$ cat p6
root:ltq3uhhA2dnSM:0:0:root:/root:/bin/bash
...
```

so while you can chain symbolic links successfully, there is a maximum usable chain length of six links.

2. In order to access the contents of a file you need to obtain its inode number. Bearing this in mind, the only real disadvantage with symbolic links is that each link adds an extra level of indirection to the process of finding the inode number of the target file and thus slows the process down. Hard links don't suffer from this problem as each hard link has its own copy of the number of the inode to which it refers built into it. Another point about symbolic links, which isn't really a disadvantage, but which can come as a surprise, is that a link can exist to a file which does not exist. Try to set this up and see what happens when you attempt to use the link.

3. Probably the most obvious way to tackle this problem is to use the ls command with the -l command line switch to find files with two or more links (these are shown in field 2 of the ls listing. You could then use the -i switch to display the inode numbers of the relevant files to see if you could find a match.

Another possibility is to remember that directories are also files and that every directory has at least two links to its inode, even if it is empty. For example, the directory /bin has a link in the root directory (called bin). But don't forget it also has another link inside the directory /bin itself (called '.' – dot). Using the -d switch to ls, this can be verified as follows:

```
$ cd /
$ ls -id bin
  43478 bin
$ cd /bin
$ ls -id .
  43478 .
```

Obviously, if you try this experiment, the inode number for /bin on your system will most likely be different to mine but the important thing is that the two inode numbers you get out should both be the same.

4. Because you have set the temp directory up with read permission for you as its owner, the ls command which runs on your behalf is able to read the list of file names contained in the directory and list them as expected – no other permissions are required to do this:

```
$ ls temp
passwd
```

5. Now, executing the command with the -l switch will give an output similar to the following:

```
$ ls -l temp
ls: temp/passwd: Permission denied
total 0
```

What this says is that ls discovered the existence of the passwd file in the temp directory (which you know it can, from the previous question) but after that it was denied permission to perform some operation. What actually happens is that with the -l command line switch, ls cannot get all of the information it needs to display just from the directory, so it needs to access the files themselves for the extra information. Now, however, because you do not have search permission on the directory, ls is denied permission to use the directory as a component is a file pathname. Consequently, when ls tries to find the extra information it requires it is denied access to the files, even though it knows they are there, having got the names from the directory itself. To make ls execute as expected you need to change the permission on the temp directory as follows:

```
$ chmod 500 temp
$ ls -l temp
total 1
-rw-r--r--   1 pc        500        731 Jan 13 16:19 passwd
```

Chapter 3

Text Editing

If you are going to do more on your Linux machine than just execute pre-installed software packages, then at some point you will need to learn how to use one of the available text editors. There are a large number of editors to choose from with Linux and if you already know one of them you might as well continue to use it. However, if you don't know one of the editors yet, or if you might wish to migrate to other UNIX like environments in the future, then you should take the opportunity to master the standard UNIX screen editor called `vi`. In fact, the real `vi` editor is a proprietary product not directly available under Linux, although there are several (five or six at least) `vi` clone editors which are freely available for use under many systems, Linux included. If you make sure that you only learn the standard basic set of commands from these `vi` compatible editors, then you will be able to use any of them with equal ease. From now on, I will use the word `vi` in a generic sense to mean any of the editors with `vi` compatibility (including elvis, vim, stevie, nvi, etc.)

The `vi` editor is a screen editor, which basically means that the contents of the screen is a window on the file being edited. In fact, `vi` makes all its changes to a copy of the file being edited, rather than the original. This means that if you make an error in editing you can always abort all the changes and return to the original file. It is only when you decide that things have gone properly, and issue the command to save the changes, that the original file is replaced by the updated version.

In order to get into `vi` you use a command like the following:

```
$ vi filename
```

where *filename* is the pathname to the file you wish to edit. If the file does not already exist it will be created. The `vi` editor has three modes of operation called *edit* mode, *insert* mode and *command* mode (see Figure 3.1). As the diagram shows, when you run `vi` you start in edit mode. For the purposes of experimentation as we go along, it is recommended that you take a copy of one of the system text files

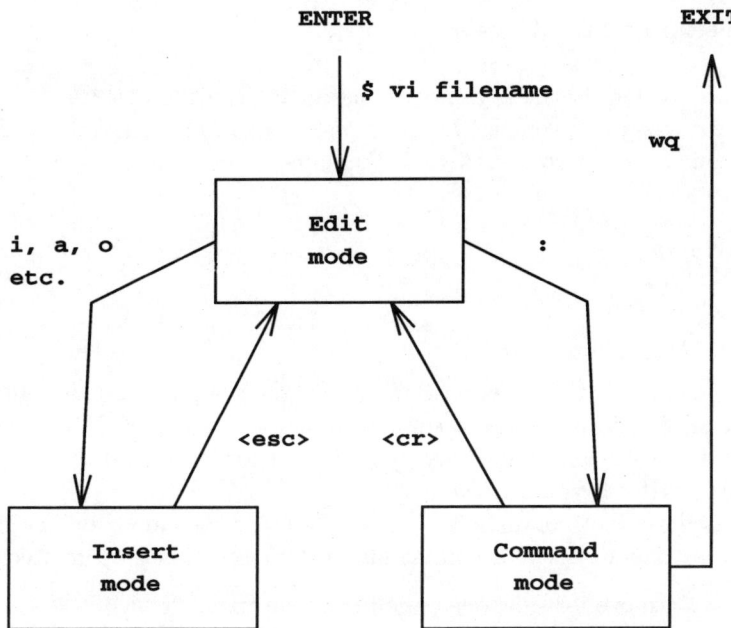

Figure 3.1 The three main vi operating modes.

in the /etc directory (/etc/passwd or /etc/printcap for instance) and use your copy to practice the editor commands as you meet them.

3.1 Edit Mode

The edit mode of vi is used mainly for moving the cursor around the file you are editing to find some position of interest. Once there, you can then cut and paste blocks of text, delete text and insert new text. You may then go back and move the cursor to the next position of interest, and so on.

Because vi doesn't rely on your keyboard having *special* keys (such as cursor control keys), in edit mode, many of the alphabetic keys – and combinations of them – have particular functions. So, for example, when you have finished all your editing, and you want to save your editing changes and quit from the editor back to a shell prompt, you issue the ZZ command, which means just pressing the Z key twice in succession. Note that the editor is case sensitive so you must be sure to use ZZ here and not zz.

3.1.1 Positioning the Cursor

The main cursor movement keys in edit mode are provided by the up, down, left and right arrow keys, if your keyboard supports them. If your keyboard does not properly support the arrow keys then the same effect can be achieved with the following keys:

    `k`   up;
    `j`   down;
    `h`   left;
    `l`   right.

Remember, again, that `vi` was written to run on a system which could support almost any kind of terminal. And some terminal types, especially older ones, just don't have arrow keys or any other special keys for that matter, other than the standard typewriter keyboard layout.

As well as these four commands, which only move the cursor by one line or one character at a time, `vi` also has commands to move the cursor by greater distances:

    `Ctrl-f`   move forward one page in the file (page down);
    `Ctrl-b`   move backward one page in the file (page up).

In fact, these commands move by just under a page to give some degree of continuity as you read through a file.

Once you have the page of interest on the screen you can quickly move the cursor round it with the commands:

    `H`   move the cursor to the home (top) line on the screen;
    `M`   move the cursor to the middle line on the screen;
    `L`   move the cursor to the last line on the screen.

Again, note the case of these letters. In the case of the `H` and `L` commands, they may be preceded by a number, which will move the cursor that many lines into the screen. So, the command `2H` will position the cursor on the second line of the screen, while the command `3L` will move the cursor to the third line from the bottom of the screen.

When you get to the right line in the file, positioning the cursor at the correct point on that line is easy:

    `w`   move right to the start of the next word;
    `e`   move right to the end of the next word;
    `b`   move left to the start of the previous word;
    `0`   (zero) move cursor left to the start of the line;
    `^`   move to the first non-whitespace character on the line;
    `$`   move cursor right to the end of the line.

When the `w`, `e` or `b` commands reach the end (or start) of a line they will wrap around onto the next (or previous) line.

3.1.2 String Searching

If you want to find an occurrence of a particular known word or phrase then you can have vi search for it directly for you rather than moving the cursor around the file and performing the search manually. To do this you type the forward slash (/) character followed by the string of characters to search for, followed by pressing Enter or Return. The editor will search forwards towards the end of the file looking for the specified string. If the string is encountered the editor will stop the search and position the cursor at the start of the string it has found. If this is not the occurrence of the string you were looking for then using the n command will search for the next occurrence of the string. It is also possible to search backwards through the file, towards the start, using the ? character instead of the /. Whichever direction you search in, when you reach the limit of the file, the search will wrap around to the other end of the file and continue on from there. In summary:

/string   search forward for given string;
?string   search backward for given string;
n   search forward or backward for next occurrence of string.

3.1.3 Replace and Delete

With the cursor now located at the required position in the file, there are many options available. The main edit mode options allow you to replace the character the cursor is sitting on with another character or to delete one or more characters from the current cursor position:

rc replace character at current cursor position with c;
x   delete character at current cursor position;
dw   delete the word to the right of the cursor;
db   delete the word before the current cursor;
dd   delete the current cursor line and close the gap.

Putting a number before any of the commands in this block extends their function as follows:

nrc replace n characters from cursor position with c;
nx   delete n characters from cursor position;
$n$dw   delete n words to the right of the cursor;
$n$db   delete the n words before the current cursor;
$n$dd   delete n lines and close the gap.

Other delete commands which can often be of use (but not with preceding numbers) are:

d$ delete characters from current cursor to end of line;
d0   delete characters from current cursor to start of line;
J   delete CR at end of line to join this line to the next.

3.1.4 Cut and Paste

Whenever you delete characters, words or lines from your text, they are not just thrown away, but copied into a memory buffer. This can be very useful because there is a pair of commands which will allow you to paste the contents of this buffer back into your text, either into the same place (if you removed the text in error) or into some new location providing a standard cut and paste facility. The pair of commands is:

    p   (lower case) paste cut buffer after current cursor;
    P   (upper case) paste cut buffer before current cursor.

If the cut buffer contains either characters or words then the paste operations will occur before or after the current cursor position on the same line. If the cut buffer contains whole lines of text then the paste operations take place before or after the line on which the cursor currently sits.

There are several command pairs in vi (like p and P), where a lower and upper case pair provide similar functionality. In these cases, the lower case command is the one which operates after the current position, while the upper case version operates before the current position.

Sometimes you will want to make a copy of a block of text in a new location, rather than moving the block with cut and paste. All you really need for this is to be able to copy a block of text into the cut buffer without also deleting it from the file:

    yy   copy (yank) the current line into the cut buffer;
    $n$yy   copy (yank) n lines into the cut buffer.

3.1.5 Undo and Repeat

The two final edit mode commands to look at here are just for convenience. The first is for use if you make a mistake and you need to undo the ill effects of some command. The second is for the case where you have executed some command and you have now moved the cursor to the next position of interest and wish to repeat the same command again:

    u   undo the effect of the last command;
    .   repeat the last command to change the text.

3.2 Insert Mode

As edit mode uses so many of the ordinary keyboard letters as commands, when you actually want to insert some new text into the file, that you have to switch the editor into a new mode which will treat these characters as ordinary letters to add to the text. Afterwards, when you finish entering text, you need to be able to switch back to edit mode.

This is the purpose of insert mode. As you will see, there are many ways to enter insert mode for different purposes. However, whichever way you use to get into insert mode, there is only one way out – using the Esc key. Some keyboard types do not support an explicit escape key. In these cases the same function can always be achieved by using Ctrl-[.

The usual ways to get into insert mode, once you have positioned the cursor appropriately are:

- i   insert text to the left of the current cursor position;
- a   append text to the right of the current cursor position.

It may seem strange that both of these commands are required, but if either of them were missing it would make inserting in some situations more difficult.

You will often find that you want to add text starting on a new line. In these cases it is possible to move the cursor to the end of the line above the position where the new text will go, and then use the a command followed by pressing Enter or Return to open up a blank line to be filled with the new text. A simpler way to achieve this is to position the cursor anywhere on the line above the required position, then use the o command. This will open a blank line below the current cursor line and enter insert mode at the start of the blank line ready for the entry of text. The O command will do the same thing but will open the gap on the line before the current cursor line:

- o   open a blank line below the current cursor line;
- O   open a blank line above the current cursor line.

Special versions of the insert and append commands can be used to move the cursor to the start of the current line or the end of the current line and enter insert mode there:

- I   insert at the start of the line;
- A   insert after the end of the line.

3.2.1 Text Substitution

In addition to the commands which just enter the insert mode, there are several commands which allow text substitution – effectively deleting a block of text before entering insert mode to accept the replacement text. The main commands for this are:

- s   substitute the current cursor character with new text;
- cw   change the word to the right of the cursor for new text;
- cb   change the word before the current cursor for new text;
- cd   change the current cursor line for new text.

Putting a number before any of the commands in this block extends their function as follows:

    *n*s   substitute next *n* characters with new text;
    *n*cw   change *n* words to the right of the cursor;
    *n*cb   change the *n* words before the current cursor;
    *n*cd   change next *n* lines with new text.

In addition to the previous commands there are also two further change commands which can prove useful:

    c$ change characters to end of line for new text;
    c0   change characters to start of line for new text.

3.3 Command Mode

All the commands covered so far have been fairly simple, at least in terms of the number of keystrokes required to enter them. However, there are a large number of commands with a more complex structure, and also a lot of configuration options which can be set. All of these are entered via command mode. All the command mode features have one thing in common – they all start with a colon (:). As soon as you enter the colon, the cursor will jump to the start of the bottom line of the screen, where a colon will be displayed. Any characters you type now, up to a **Return** or **Enter**, will appear along the bottom line of the display so that you can check and, if necessary, correct your input.

3.3.1 Quit Commands

The only way you have seen to exit from the editor is to use the ZZ command in edit mode. This not only exits but also saves any changes you have made to your text back into the original file, overwriting its previous contents. It may be that you only want to exit from the editor without saving the editor contents. This can be because you have made no changes to the text or because, having changed the text, you now wish to abort the changes and quit the editor anyway. The two commands to do this are:

    :q   quit the editor if no changes have been made;
    :q!   quit the editor aborting any changes made.

It is good practice to get into the habit of using :q where you can as this will reduce the chance of typing :q! by accident, which might result in the loss of some valuable material.

3.3.2 File Manipulation

The next set of colon commands to look at allow you to write and read blocks of text to and from files:

      :w   write editor contents to original file;
      :wq   write file and quit editor (same as ZZ);
      :w *file* write editor contents to named *file*;
      :r *file* read *file* into editor after cursor line;
      :e *file* edit a new *file* replacing old contents;
      :f *file* change the name of the current text to *file*;
      :f   print the name and status of the current text.

The :w command writes the text you are editing back to the file whose name you specified when you first entered vi. This command doesn't exit from the editor but leaves you in edit mode after the file write takes place. This is a command you should use from time to time to save any changes you have made so far. The :wq command just combines the effect of :w followed by :q.

Sometimes you may want to modify the contents of a file, but then write the changed version back to a new file, leaving the original file unchanged. This is done with :w *file*. Another variation on the this command allows you to specify a comma-separated range of line numbers before it. This just writes the appropriately numbered lines to the specified *file*:

      :*a,b*w *file* write lines *a* to *b* inclusive into *file*

The :r command is used to insert the contents of a specified *file* into the current text after the current cursor line. This can be useful for building new files up from previously prepared pieces.

When you finish with the current text, if you want to edit another file without having to exit vi and re-enter it, you use the :e *file* command. At any time during the editing of a file you can change the name that vi will use for the file by default. This is done with the :f *file* command. If you omit the file name after this command then vi will list the current name it is using for the text along with some status information including the number of lines in the text and the line number of the current cursor line.

3.3.3 Line Numbers

All the lines in the text being edited have a line number associated with them. You can move the cursor directly to a particular line with the command:

      :*n* move cursor to line *n*

where *n* is the number of the line to which you wish to move.

It is possible to have vi add line numbers to the text displayed and this is covered later in Section 3.3.8.

Wherever it makes sense, the colon commands can have a range of line numbers specified upon which the command will then operate. There are several different ways in which the line numbers may be given. First, you may specify numeric values, which are treated just as absolute line numbers. A period (or full stop '.') given as a line number refers to the current cursor line, whatever line number it happens to be. And a dollar sign ($) refers to the last line in the file. You can also specify simple numeric expressions for line numbers like .+5, which means five lines on from the current cursor line. Some example commands using these ideas are:

:345	move the cursor to line 345;
:345w *myfile*	writes line 345 out to *myfile*;
:3,8w *myfile*	writes lines 3 to 8 inclusive out to *myfile*;
:1,.w *myfile*	write from line 1 to the current cursor line;
:.,$w *myfile*	write from current cursor line to end of file;
:.,.+4w *myfile*	write five lines from current cursor line;
:1,$w *myfile*	write whole file (same as :w myfile).

3.3.4 String Searching

In addition to specifying lines by number, you can also specify lines by giving a text string to search for, on those lines. The text strings to search for are enclosed between slash (/) characters if you want to search forwards through the text from the current position, or question mark (query '?') characters if you want to search backwards through the text:

:/*str*/	move cursor on to next line containing *str*;
:?*str*?	move cursor back to next line containing *str*;
:/*str*/w *myfile*	write to *myfile* first line containing *str*;
:/*str1*/,/*str2*/w *myfile*	write lines from *str1* to *str2*.

3.3.5 Regular Expressions

When you specify a search string to vi, there are several characters that can be included which have special meanings. Search strings which include these special characters are known as *regular expressions*.

For example, suppose you wanted to search for a line of text which contained the word struct at the start of the line. The command:

:/struct/

would not do, because this would find the first line containing the word **struct** in any position on the line, not just at the beginning. The solution here is to use the ^ (caret) special character at the start of the search string:

   :/^struct/

The ^ character matches the start of the line, so the previous command means: find a line which has the start of the line followed by the string **struct**.

Similarly, you can find words at the end of a line by using the end of line special character ($) at the end of the search string:

   :/struct$/

The following table gives a list of most of the special character sequences and their meanings:

^	at the start of string, matches start of line;
$	at the end of string, matches end of line;
\<	matches the start of a word;
\>	matches the end of a word;
.	matches any single text character;
[*str*]	matches any single character in *str*;
[^*str*]	matches any single character not in *str*;
[*a-b*]	matches any character between *a* and *b*;
*	matches zero or more repeats of the previous character;
\	turns off any special meaning of the character following.

3.3.6 Text Substitution

The :s command is used to substitute one string of characters on a line for another. In fact, there are several variations on this command. These can substitute the first occurrence of a particular string on a line with a new string, or substitute every occurrence of the string on a line, or substitute all occurrences of the string in a block of lines or even the whole file:

:s/*str1*/*str2*/	substitute first *str1* on this line by *str2*;
:s/*str1*/*str2*/g	substitute every *str1* on this line by *str2*;
:.,$s/*str1*/*str2*/g	substitute every *str1* to end of file by *str2*;
:1,$s/*str1*/*str2*/g	substitute every *str1* in whole file by *str2*;
:g/*str1*/s//*str2*/g	another way to substitute every *str1* by *str2*.

In these substitution commands, a g at the end of the command specifies that the command is to be repeated for each occurrence of the search string on the current cursor line. Without the g, the command only operates on the first occurrence of the search string on the line. The g at the start of the command specifies that the command is to be performed for each line in the file which contains the search string.

3.3.7 Deleting Text

Even though deleting text can be performed in edit mode, there is still a colon command to delete lines. This can be very useful for deleting large blocks of text because you can specify a range of lines to be removed in front of the command:

>   :d   delete current cursor line;
>   :3d   delete line three in the text;
>   :.,$d   delete from current cursor line to end of file;
>   :/str1/,/str2/d delete lines from *str1* to *str2*.

3.3.8 Editor Options

In vi there are a large number of internal variables which control the behavior of various editor functions. These variables can have their values changed by the use of the `:set` command:

>   `:set` *option*   set an *option* variable value

where *option* specifies the variable and the value to be set. A few of the more useful options are:

autoindent If this is set, whenever you create a new, blank line the cursor will automatically be moved along the line so as to line up with the first non-blank character on the line above (or the line below for the `O` command). This makes it easy to get the indentation right if, for example, you are entering a computer program as your text. If you do not insert any text on the new line before pressing either `Esc` to quit insert mode, or `Enter` or `Return` to start another new line, then the indentation characters added on that line will be removed so as not to leave indentation characters on otherwise blank lines. Once indentation characters have been added, you may wish to backspace along the line to reduce the indentation for this, and subsequent, lines. This can be done with `Ctrl-d`. This function can be turned off with the `noautoindent` option.

ignorecase When this option is set, then upper and lower case letters in any regular expressions that are used are treated as the same thing. To disable this feature use the `noignorecase` option.

number This causes vi to precede each line it displays on screen with its current line number. The line numbers are only added to the display and not to the file itself. Line numbering is switched off with the `nonumber` option.

ruler Displays the current cursor line number and the cursor character position on the current line as a continuous display on the bottom line of the screen. This allows you to keep track of where you are in the text you are editing. You can turn off this display with the `noruler` option.

tabstop This option allows you to set the number of spaces that will be printed on screen when you press the `Tab` key (i.e. the width of a `Tab` character). The format of the command is `:set tabstop=`n, where n is the required width of a `Tab` in spaces. The default value for this option is 8. There is no special command to turn this option off again, you just set `tabstop` back to the default value.

3.3.9 Shell Escape

While you are in an editing session you will find from time to time that you may wish to run some other Linux command. This would be rather tedious if you had to save your current work, leave the editor, run the required command and then go back to editing the file again. It would be much better if it were possible to run the command whilst remaining in your editing environment. This can easily be done from within `vi`:

> `:!`*command*   execute *command* then return to editor

The `:!` command is called a shell escape, and it allows you run any command that you could run from the standard shell prompt. When the command has finished, control returns to the editor so you can continue your editing session.

Exercises

Identify `vi` colon commands to perform each of the following actions:

1. Find the number of the current cursor line within the file.
2. Delete the current cursor line and the three following lines.
3. Search backwards from the current cursor position for the closest previous occurrence of the string '8.7'.
4. Delete the last ten lines of the file.
5. Search forwards through the file from the current cursor line to find the next number in the file with three or more digits.
6. Delete all the characters on the current line between and including the occurrences of 'aa' and 'zz'.
7. Replace all occurrences of '&' in the whole file with the word 'and'.

Answers

1. `f`
   This command also gives the file name and its current length.

2. `.,.+3d`

   The '`.`' symbol means the current cursor line, so `.,.+3` is a range of lines from the current cursor line to three lines beyond that. The **d** on the end says delete this range.

3. `?8\.7`

   The '`?`' means search backwards from the current position. The '`\`' before the dot ('`.`') is required because otherwise the dot is a wild-card which matches any single character.

4. `$-9,$d`

   The dollar ('`$`') symbol means end of file.

5. `/[0-9][0-9][0-9]`

   Search forward to find three adjacent characters each in the range 0 to 9

6. `s/aa.*zz//`

   The search string here starts with '`aa`' which is followed by any number of single characters ('`.*`') and terminated by '`zz`'. The substitute the search string for nothing – hence delete.

7. `g/&/s//and/g`

   The center part of this line substitutes the '`&`' character for the word '`and`'. The leading '`g`' means for each line in the file, and the trailing '`g`' means for each occurrence on the line.

Chapter 4

Bash

Linux, in common with other UNIX-like systems, makes various shell programs available to users. All these shells have approximately the same objectives – to provide a useful interactive interface between the user and the system, and also to provide a simple programming interface which allows collections of commands to be bolted together and executed as though they were ordinary Linux system commands.

In this chapter we shall examine the interactive interface of one particular shell – **bash** (the Bourne Again SHell).

Bash is distributed by the Free Software Foundation as a Bourne shell compatible program which also incorporates many of the best features of other shells. It is arguably the best shell available for all-round functionality and is supplied with most Linux distributions.

4.1 Pathname Expansion

In all the examples of Linux commands presented in previous chapters, any required pathnames have been specified in full. There are various ways in which the pathnames can be abbreviated and the shell will then expand them before the names are passed to any commands. Pathnames containing these abbreviation characters are called *regular expressions*. For example:

    $ cp text/* backup

Here the asterisk (*) is used to mean any file name (except those that start with a **dot** (.) character which are treated specially by most commands – look back at Section 2.1). This command line therefore says: copy all the visible files in the **text** directory into the **backup** directory, preserving the original names. In actual fact, the **cp** command need know nothing about the * character, because the expansion of this character is performed by the shell before **cp** even gets a look-in. This means that when the cp command is given access to the file names passed to it as command line parameters, what it sees will be a command line like:

```
$ cp text/motd text/passwd backup
```

This is because the shell has looked into the text directory, sorted out the names of all the files in the directory, and explicitly listed them on the command line that it passes to cp. You have already seen that the cp command can cope with copying multiple files into a directory, and consequently it has no problem with executing the shell expanded command line.

Another special character used in file names that the shell will expand is the question mark (query '?'). This character is allowed to stand in for any single character. The following command and its output illustrates the point:

```
$ ls /dev/tty?
/dev/tty0   /dev/tty2   /dev/tty4   /dev/tty6   /dev/tty8
/dev/tty1   /dev/tty3   /dev/tty5   /dev/tty7   /dev/tty9
```

Here, the ten files tty0 through tty9, are listed as the only files in the /dev directory which match the pattern tty? (i.e. tty followed by another single character).

Rather than allowing any single character, it is also possible to give an explicit list of characters, any one of which can be matched. This is done by enclosing the list in square brackets ([ ]):

```
$ ls /dev/tty?[23456]
/dev/ttyS2   /dev/ttyp2   /dev/ttyq2   /dev/ttyr2   /dev/ttys2
/dev/ttyS3   /dev/ttyp3   /dev/ttyq3   /dev/ttyr3   /dev/ttys3
/dev/ttyS4   /dev/ttyp4   /dev/ttyq4   /dev/ttyr4   /dev/ttys4
/dev/ttyS5   /dev/ttyp5   /dev/ttyq5   /dev/ttyr5   /dev/ttys5
/dev/ttyS6   /dev/ttyp6   /dev/ttyq6   /dev/ttyr6   /dev/ttys6
```

Here, all files are listed which match the pattern /dev/tty followed by any single character followed by a digit in the range 2 to 6.

This range could also have been specified as a pair of characters separated by a hyphen (-), as follows:

```
$ ls /dev/tty?[2-6]
```

A final form of expansion for pathnames allows you to specify a list of whole words from which to make a match rather than just single characters. The list of words is separated by commas and enclosed in curly brackets {}, as the following commands show:

```
$ mkdir /usr/tmp/{bin,doc,lib,src}
$ ls /usr/tmp
bin   doc   lib   src
```

Don't forget, that all these pathname expansions are performed by the shell itself and, therefore, the commands invoked by the shell have no need to be able to deal with these special characters. This also has implications if you ever come to write your own commands, perhaps as C programs, because they, too, will be able to take advantage of this service offered by the shell without the need to be able to perform the expansion themselves.

Sometimes, however, you may wish to use a command (or write one of your own) which can have any or all of these special characters passed to it in its parameter list. In this case you need to use a technique called *quoting*, which tells the shell to ignore the special meaning of the quoted characters and just to treat them as though they were ordinary characters instead.

The `bash` shell supports three quoting mechanisms: *escape characters* (\), *single quotes* (´) and *double quotes* (").

A backslash (\) character placed immediately before any of the shell's special characters will tell the shell to ignore its special meaning. If this escape character mechanism is used then a backslash needs to be added before each individual character whose special meaning is to be suppressed:

```
$ cd
$ mv text/motd text/m\*\?
$ ls text
m*?     passwd
```

Any string of characters enclosed in single quotes (´) will suppress the special meaning of all the characters contained in the string:

```
$ cat ´text/m*?´
motd contents in here.
```

Any string of characters enclosed in double quotes (") will suppress the special meaning of all the pathname expansion characters you have seen in this chapter:

```
$ mv "text/m*?" text/motd
$ ls text
motd    passwd
```

You should note, however, that there are some other special characters you have not yet seen that `bash` uses, which retain their special functionality even within double quotes. You will meet these later in Chapter 6, when we look at the non-interactive or programming functionality of the shell.

4.2 I/O Redirection

One of the basic philosophies behind the provision of commands in Linux is to make available many simple functions which perform specific tasks, efficiently. These simple functions can easily be bolted together to build up larger and more complex commands.

Wherever it makes sense, UNIX (and hence Linux) commands are configured so that, by default, they take any input they require from the keyboard and send any ordinary output to the screen. Commands also arrange to send their error output to the screen by default. Sometimes it would be useful if you could take input from or send output to a file instead. In these cases it would be possible to write a command so that you could specify file names as extra or optional command line parameters. Some commands do have this option. However, to provide this functionality for every command on the off chance it might come in handy, would make the executable files rather larger than they would otherwise need to be.

In order to avoid the necessity for this, Linux and the shell together provide facilities that allow a program's standard input and output to be redirected as required. Consider the command:

```
$ ls -l /usr/tmp >dir
```

What this does is to create a long listing of the contents of the directory /usr/tmp. Normally, that listing would be displayed on the screen. But when the command includes a greater than (>) symbol followed by a file name, then the output will be sent to the specified file instead of to the screen. Using this form of output redirection, the specified file will be created if it does not already exist, or its present contents will be overwritten if it does already exist.

That this has actually happened is easy to verify, as follows:

```
$ cat dir
total 4
drwxr-xr-x    2 pc        book         1024 May 22 23:31 bin
drwxr-xr-x    2 pc        book         1024 May 22 23:31 doc
drwxr-xr-x    2 pc        book         1024 May 22 23:31 lib
drwxr-xr-x    2 pc        book         1024 May 22 23:31 src
```

Remember that the ls command does not know about the special function of the > character. In fact, the ls command does not even see the >, as the character and the following file name are removed by the shell before any command line parameters are passed on to the command. When ls runs, it just continues to send its output to the standard output device as usual, except that the shell has redirected the standard output away from the screen and into the specified file before ls was started. The same is true for the other redirection operators, as you will soon see.

Sometimes, when using output redirection, you may have an existing file to which you wish to append the output generated by another command. This can be done by using the append redirection operator >>, which is just made up of two greater than symbols, side by side:

```
$ ls /usr/tmp >>dir
$ cat dir
total 4
drwxr-xr-x   2 pc         book          1024 May 22 23:31 bin
drwxr-xr-x   2 pc         book          1024 May 22 23:31 doc
drwxr-xr-x   2 pc         book          1024 May 22 23:31 lib
drwxr-xr-x   2 pc         book          1024 May 22 23:31 src
bin   doc   lib   src
```

Incidentally, the `cat` command will take its input from the standard input device (keyboard, by default) if no file names are given as command line parameters. Input from the keyboard is terminated by entering the end-of-file character (`Ctrl-d`) at the start of a line on its own. Given this information, and the use of output redirection, the following simple command will allow you to write text directly from the keyboard into a file:

```
$ cat >text.file
any text entered here goes into text.file up to
Ctrl-d
$
```

As well as redirecting a program's standard output, it is also possible to redirect its error output. The standard output and error output from a program are normally treated as two separate things so that you can redirect them individually. So, for example, if you wanted to see the normal output from a program on the screen but wanted to send any output error messages to a file so you could review them later, you could achieve this with:

```
$ ls /usr/tmp 2>err.file
bin   doc   lib   src
```

using the notation 2> (or 2>> to append) to indicate redirection of the error output device.

In order to send both standard output and error output to the same file at the same time, another output redirection operator is used (&>):

```
$ ls /usr/tmp &>output.file
```

Just as a program's output can be written to a file, so its standard input can be read from a file instead of the keyboard. This is done with the less than (<) redirection operator:

```
$ wc </etc/passwd
     21      42     775
```

Notice that the name of the file **/etc/passwd** does not appear in the output from this `wc` command. This is because `wc` does not see the file name – it is dealt with by the shell. The `wc` command operates as though its input was coming from the keyboard, with no file name involved.

Another type of input redirection is known as a *here document*. This type of redirection tells the shell to set up the current command so that its standard input comes from the command line. The redirection operator in this case is << and the text to be redirected into the command is enclosed between a matched pair of delimiter words, as follows:

```
$ wc <<delim
> this text forms the content
> of the here document, which
> continues until the end of
> text delimiter
> delim
      4      17      98
```

When you enter the text for a here document, you do not need to type in the '>' characters at the start of each line – they are supplied by the shell as a prompt. This prompt is used by the shell to tell you that the current command is unfinished and that it still expects more input before it can execute your command.

Any word can be used after the << operator as a start of text delimiter (*delim* in this example). The text of the here document continues until the same delimiter word is encountered again at the start of a line on its own. At that time the text of the here document, excluding the start and end delimiters, is redirected into the command (`wc` in this case) as its standard input text.

It is possible, using redirection, to combine commands to obtain new functionality from the system which no single command provides alone. For instance, to find the number of files in a directory you could use the command sequence:

```
$ ls /usr/bin >/tmp/dir
$ wc -w </tmp/dir
    459
$ rm /tmp/dir
```

This sequence runs the `ls` command on the directory `/usr/bin` and redirects the output to `/tmp/dir`. The second command counts the number of words in the output file from `ls` and displays the result – 459, a lot of files in this particular directory. As in this example, you should always make sure you remove any temporary files you create in `/tmp` as soon as you have finished with them so that they don't just get forgotten and waste disk space.

4.3 Pipes

By writing the standard output from one program into a file and then feeding the contents of this file into the standard input of another command, you are effectively bolting the two commands together via the temporary file so that they work as one. This is such a common thing to want to do that Linux provides a facility, which the shell takes advantage of, to connect the two programs together directly without the need for, or use of, a temporary file. This facility is called a `pipe`.

A pipe uses the | redirection operator. Rewriting the previous example to use a pipe gives:

```
$ ls /usr/bin | wc -w
    459
```

As Linux is a multi-tasking operating system, this command line (or *pipeline* as it is called) will be executed by running the two commands `ls` and `wc` concurrently, so that the output from `ls` can be read by `wc` as it is produced.

A pipeline is not just limited to two commands bolted together. Any number of commands can be joined together, with a pipe operator being used to connect each adjacent pair. With this arrangement, the output from the first command will become the input to the second. The output from the second becomes the input to the third, and so on.

4.4 Background Jobs

In all of the command line examples so far, once you have typed in a command and pressed **Enter** or **Return** the system seems to go away to perform your command. When your command has finished, the shell finally returns a prompt to you as an invitation to enter another command. Figure 4.1 shows why this is so.

As you can see, once the shell has started a new process and set your command running, it then puts itself to sleep to wait for your command to finish. Only when this has happened is a signal sent back to the shell to wake it up so that it can give you a prompt and look for your next command.

Because Linux is multi-tasking, there is no reason why the shell shouldn't be able to run at the same time as your command and hence return a prompt to you immediately, while your command gets on with its task (see Figure 4.2). This is very useful if, for instance, the command you run will take a long time to complete its task, as it allows you to get on with something else.

The decision as to whether the shell will wait for a command to finish, or return to you immediately with a prompt, is made by you when you run the command. All you do is to put an ampersand character (&) at the end of your command line if you do not want the shell to wait but, rather, to return a prompt straight away. This is called putting the command into the *background*:

```
$ ls -lR / >/tmp/ls.lR &
[1] 341
$
```

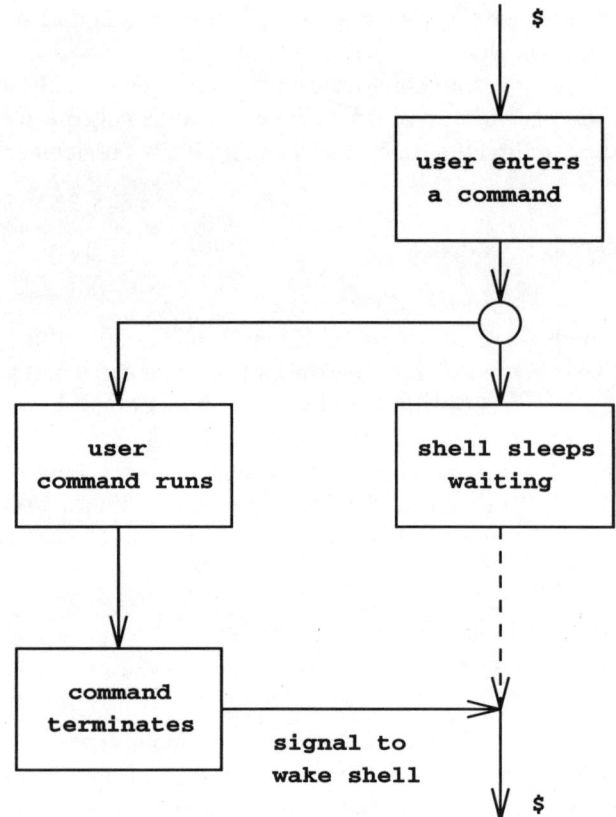

Figure 4.1 The shell waits for a command to finish.

Here the output from an ls command is being written to the file /tmp/ls.1R and, rather than wait while this happens, the command has been run in the background with the & character on the end of the command line. The -R option to ls produces a recursive directory listing that works its way down through all the subdirectories that can be reached from the starting point (/ here). It means that this command produces a sorted long listing of the entire directory hierarchy of the machine – quite a lengthy task. The numbers printed on the line after the command are displayed by the shell. The number in square brackets is the job number for this command line. This is described in Section 4.5. The second number is the PID for the command being executed, or the PID for the last command on the line, if there is a pipeline involved.

In general, commands that you run in the background, must not try to take any input from the keyboard because all the keyboard input will go to the shell, after it gives you a prompt. The default for any background commands that do try to take keyboard input is that their execution is stopped and all their activity is suspended.

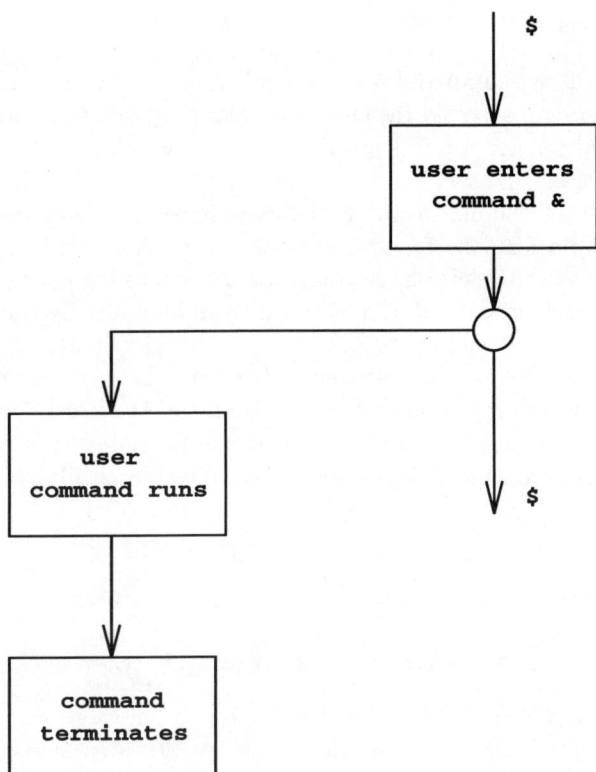

Figure 4.2 Executing a background job.

4.5 Job Control

Every time you execute a command with **bash** a *job number* is allocated to it. For the purposes of this allocation, multiple commands connected together in a pipeline all count as one job which will share a single job number. The shell uses these job numbers as the basis for its job control.

Job control allows you to suspend and subsequently resume the execution of processes at a later time. The shell maintains a list of currently executing jobs which can be displayed with the **jobs** command. In order to suspend the current foreground job you just press the key sequence **Ctrl-z** on the keyboard. When you do this, the job will stop running and a shell prompt will be returned, as in the following example:

```
$ cat >text.file
Ctrl-z
[1]+  Stopped                 cat >text.file
$ jobs
```

```
[1]+  Stopped                 cat >text.file
```

The `Ctrl-z` in the above command sequence indicates that you should press `Ctrl-z` at this point, which will suspend the currently executing `cat` command. The use of the `jobs` command then shows this job in the shell's list along with its job number and its current status.

When you come to resume execution of this process, you have two choices: you can either start it back in the foreground with the `fg` command, in which case it will continue from where it left off, or you can push it into the background with the `bg` command, in which case it will run as though you had initially run the command with an `&` operator on the end of the line.

In this particular case, you should remember that the `cat` command has been started in a mode where it is taking its input from the keyboard. This means that if you resume the command in the background it will immediately perform an illegal read from the keyboard and be suspended again, automatically this time, by the system:

```
$ bg
[1]+ cat >text.file &
$ jobs
[1]+  Stopped (tty input)     cat >text.file
```

The `fg` and `bg` commands operate, by default, on the most recently stopped job. When you use the `jobs` command, this default job will be identified by the `+` symbol immediately following its job number in the shell's output. In general, if you want to refer to any job in the list, not just the default job, you can do this by giving its job number after a percent (%) symbol:

```
$ fg %1
cat >text.file
```

This `fg` command will restart the `cat` job back in the foreground so that any subsequent keyboard input (up to `Ctrl-d`) will be written to the file `text.file`.

Rather than resume a stopped job, you may just wish to terminate the job altogether. This can be done with the `kill` command:

```
$ cat >text.file
Ctrl-z
[1]+  Stopped                 cat >text.file
$ jobs
[1]+  Stopped                 cat >text.file
$ kill %1
[1]+  Terminated              cat >text.file
```

If you try to `logout` of the system while you have any stopped jobs, you will receive a warning error message and the command will fail:

```
$ cat >text.file
Ctrl-z
$ logout
There are stopped jobs.
```

At this point you can either deal with the stopped jobs or, if you `logout` again immediately, the jobs will automatically be terminated and the `logout` will be successful.

4.6 History

As you work under Linux, you will often find that you are repeatedly executing the same small sequence of commands. For example, during program development and debugging you will often iterate around the standard loop: edit the source code, compile the source into an executable file, run the executable file to test its performance and then round again to the start. In order to save you repeatedly having to retype the same commands, `bash` stores your commands as you type them so that you can easily return to them again if you wish. The store that `bash` uses for this purpose is called the *history list* and, by default, this list can store the last 500 command lines you have entered.

A history list this size can quite literally represent all the commands entered during many days of work. In order for it to make sense to use a history list of this size, `bash` automatically arranges to save the current list to a file when you `logout`. The default file name `bash` uses is `.bash_history`, which it stores in your home directory. Notice that the `dot` at the start of the file name means that the file will not be listed by `ls` unless the `-a` command line switch is used. When you login at the start of the next session, the shell will automatically load the contents of the history file into its history list, effectively allowing you to continue on from where you left off at the end of the previous session.

In order to see the stored list of previously entered lines, you use the `history` command. Remember that the list is up to 500 lines long so you may want to pipe the output of the `history` command into `more` or `tail`:

```
$ history | tail -5
  511   cat >text.file
  512   cd ..
  513   ls -al
  514   cd book
  515   history | tail -5
```

The lines in the history list are each called *events* and the numbers along side each line are called *event numbers*. Once you know the event number for the line you want to repeat, it is a simple matter to execute it. Suppose you wanted to repeat the history command (event number 515) in the previous example, you just use the history substitution operator (!) followed by the event number:

```
$ !515
history | tail -5
   512  cd ..
   513  ls -al
   514  cd book
   515  history | tail -5
   516  history | tail -5
```

If the event you wish to repeat happens to be the last command, as in the previous example, you could just use the special notation !!, as in:

```
$ !!
history | tail -5
   513  ls -al
   514  cd book
   515  history | tail -5
   516  history | tail -5
   517  history | tail -5
```

As well as referring to events by number, it is also possible to have the shell search textually through its history list to find a particular command for you. In this case you use the history substitution operator followed by a string of characters. The shell will search backwards through the history list and execute the first event it can find whose command line begins with the specified string:

```
$ !ls
ls -al
-rw-r--r--   1 pc      book      3392 May 29 07:55 .bash_history
-rw-------   1 pc      book        25 Mar 26  1994 .profile
drwxr-xr-x   3 pc      book      1024 May 28 23:30 book
```

Looking at the previous example, it is event 513 which gets executed in this case. If the search string you specify is enclosed in a pair of '?' characters, then the shell will search for the string anywhere along each command line, not just at the start. If there is nothing following the trailing '?' then it may be omitted:

```
$ !?456
ls /dev/tty?[23456]
/dev/ttyS2   /dev/ttyp2   /dev/ttyq2   /dev/ttyr2   /dev/ttys2
/dev/ttyS3   /dev/ttyp3   /dev/ttyq3   /dev/ttyr3   /dev/ttys3
/dev/ttyS4   /dev/ttyp4   /dev/ttyq4   /dev/ttyr4   /dev/ttys4
/dev/ttyS5   /dev/ttyp5   /dev/ttyq5   /dev/ttyr5   /dev/ttys5
/dev/ttyS6   /dev/ttyp6   /dev/ttyq6   /dev/ttyr6   /dev/ttys6
```

In this way you can still repeat an event, even if its command name has been used more recently for another purpose.

Sometimes it will happen that you wish to repeat a previous command, but with some small modification. This can be done by specifying a substitution on the end of the line, of the form :s/old/new/, where the first occurrence of string old on the selected command line will be replaced by the string new, as follows:

```
$ !?456?:s/234/4/
ls /dev/tty?[456]
/dev/ttyS4    /dev/ttyp4    /dev/ttyq4    /dev/ttyr4    /dev/ttys4
/dev/ttyS5    /dev/ttyp5    /dev/ttyq5    /dev/ttyr5    /dev/ttys5
/dev/ttyS6    /dev/ttyp6    /dev/ttyq6    /dev/ttyr6    /dev/ttys6
```

Notice that by the time you reach this level of complexity, it is almost easier just to retype the required command line.

4.7 Command Line Editing

In order to simplify the task of finding, modifying and re-executing events in the history list, bash also allows simple command line editing, if your keyboard supports the cursor movement (arrow) keys. Every time you press the up arrow key, the shell will move back one event in the history list and display the command line it finds there. If you press the down arrow key then you move forwards through the list again. When the required line is displayed, just pressing the Enter or Return key will re-execute the command line and add it to the end of the history list. If you wish to edit the command line before you execute it, you do this by using the left and right arrow keys to move the cursor along the line to the point of interest. You can then use the Backspace key to delete characters before the cursor followed by typing in the replacement characters. When you have completed your changes to the command line, Enter or Return will execute it.

4.8 Command Completion

Another useful feature of bash is its ability to attempt to complete your command lines for you. At any time during the entry of a command you can press the Tab key. When you do this, the shell will attempt to complete whatever part of your command you were typing at the time. For example, suppose you wanted to change your password with the passwd command; you could enter the following (the notation <Tab> means press the Tab key):

```
$ pass<Tab>
```

When you enter this character sequence, bash knows you are entering a command name and it will search for a command that begins with the characters you typed before you pressed the Tab key (pass in this example). The only command that the shell can find starting with these characters is passwd and so it completes the command name for you by adding the extra characters onto the end of what you have already typed.

If the number of characters you type is insufficient for bash to be able uniquely to identify what command it should use, then you will get an audible warning. Pressing the Tab key a second time at this point will cause bash to display a list of all the possible ways the command could be completed:

```
$ pas<Tab><Tab>
passwd   paste
```

You can then add enough characters to your command line to enable the shell to resolve the ambiguity next time you press the Tab key.

In addition to being able to complete command names in this way, the shell can also complete file names for you, when you use them as command parameters:

```
$ tail -2 /etc/p<Tab><Tab>
passwd    printcap   profile
$ tail -2 /etc/pa<Tab>
pc:fjKppCZxEvouc:500:500::/usr1/pc:/bin/bash
carey:Yt1a4ffkG2r02:501:500::/usr1/carey:/bin/bash
```

Here, we are trying to display the last two lines in the password file. The shell was unable to resolve the file name on the first attempt, using the file name /etc/p<Tab>. Pressing <Tab> for a second time displays the three choices passwd, printcap and profile in the directory /etc, because they all start with the letter p. As you can see from this list, adding one extra character (an a in this case) will resolve the ambiguity for the shell, and correctly result in the required command line being executed.

4.9 Shell Functions

Using *shell functions* is a simple way to group and store a set of commands for later execution. The general form of a shell function definition is:

```
name() { list; }
```

where name is the command name you will use to execute the function and list is a list of commands or pipelines, separated by semi-colons, which specify what task the function will perform.

For example, if you enter the following function definition:

```
$ ll() { ls -l; }
```

you will then be able to use ll as a command to perform the same task as ls -l:

```
$ ll
drwxr-xr-x   3 pc      book       1024 May 28 23:30 book
```

You might imagine that if you wanted to execute the command ls -al, given that the definition for ll already exists, you could achieve this with the command ll -a. Sadly, however, it isn't quite that simple. It is possible to do what we want, but in order to do it the definition for the ll function needs to be changed as follows:

```
$ ll() { ls -l $*; }
```

The addition of the $* characters means that any parameters or command line switches entered after the ll command are to be inserted into the ls -l command in place of the $* characters. Using the new definition for ll gives the expected results:

```
$ ll -a
-rw-r--r--   1 pc      book       3392 May 29 07:55 .bash_history
-rw-------   1 pc      book         25 Mar 26  1994 .profile
drwxr-xr-x   3 pc      book       1024 May 28 23:30 book
```

A more complete discussion of $* and related topics is given in Chapter 6, when we look at shell programming.

The body of a shell function (between { and }) can consist of several commands or pipelines, as long as they are separated by semi-colons. Here is an example (coded in a rather inefficient way just for demonstration purposes) to display the number of files contained in a given directory. The function is called lswc as it combines the actions of these two commands:

```
$ lswc() { ls $* >/tmp/dir; wc -w </tmp/dir; rm /tmp/dir; }
```

The use of the $* characters in the definition allows lswc to take a parameter which should be the pathname of the directory upon which the command is to operate:

```
$ lswc /usr/bin
    459
```

Exercises

One of the objectives of this set of exercises is to get you used to looking things up in the system manual pages. Don't worry therefore if you cannot immediately see the solution to a particular exercise, just look in the appropriate manual pages and you should find the extra information you need. Write and test command pipelines to perform each of the following functions:

1. Display the number of different login names currently available on your system.

2. How many processes are there on your system at this time?
   What functions do each of the following pipelines perform:
3. `df -a | wc -l`
4. `who | wc -l`

Answers

1. Several solutions to this problem are possible, all of which count the number of lines in the file `/etc/passwd` as each login name available on the system has its own line in this file:
   - `$ cat /etc/passwd | wc -l` This uses `cat` to list the file and then pipes the result to `wc` to count the lines.
   - `$ wc -l </etc/passwd` This uses `wc` directly, redirecting its input from the password file to achieve the same effect.
   - `$ wc -l /etc/passwd` Lastly, the `wc` command can actually have file names specified to it directly, as extra parameters.
2. The command to list the processes on your system is `ps`. This command lists the processes on the system, one line per process. Counting the number of lines should give a count of the number of processes. One minor problem is that, by default, the `ps` command also displays a header line at the top of its output. This can be suppressed but you need to look at the manual page to find out that the command line switch to do this is `-h`. This gives a solution of:

   `$ ps -axh | wc -l`

3. The `df -a` command lists all the filesystems that are mounted together to generate your overall directory hierarchy. The mounted filesystems are listed one per line so a line count will tell you the number of mounted filesystems. One problem is that the `df` command also generates a header line which, unlike the `ps` command, cannot be suppressed. This means that the number you obtain as output from this pipeline will be one too big. If it is important, it is possible to sort this out, and we'll cover arithmetic expressions in Section 6.7.2
4. This exercise uses a command we have not covered yet, but a quick glance in the manual shows that the `who` command just lists all the users who are logged in, one per line. Counting the number of lines will therefore display the number of user logins currently active.

Chapter 5

Tools and Utilities

There are many more commands available to ordinary users under Linux than you have seen so far. This chapter concentrates on some of the more sophisticated commands available, which singly or in combination make it possible to do many useful things without having to resort to any programming.

Many of the commands described in this chapter are designed to take their input from the standard input device and to send their output to the standard output device. This makes them ideal candidates to use when building up more complex pipelines, where the output from one command is piped into the input of the next. Commands of this type are generally called *filters*. These commands read their standard input, perform some transformation on it and then write the result to the standard output.

5.1 Search and Sort

A very common operation is to want to search through a file for lines containing a particular string, or to search through a list for a particular item. Another common operation is to sort lines into some kind of order. Linux has commands which can perform both of these actions either from the command line or from within a pipeline.

5.1.1 grep

The first command to look at is a filter called **grep**. The name is an acronym for *General Regular Expression Parser*, which translated into English means that **grep** can be used to search for string patterns in its input. The output from **grep** consists of all the lines of input which contained the specified string pattern. For example, to find out whether or not a login for the user *carey* exists on the system, you just need to search for this name string in the password file, as follows:

```
$ grep carey /etc/passwd
carey:Yt1a4ffkG2r02:501:500::/usr1/carey:/bin/bash
```

The fact that the `grep` command produced this line of output shows that, indeed, this user name exists on the system. Note, however, that `grep` was not only looking for the string in the user name field of each password file entry, but anywhere in the file. This means that just because `grep` finds the string you were looking for it doesn't necessarily imply that it was in the context you expected:

```
$ grep public /etc/passwd
uucp:*:10:14:uucp:/var/spool/uucppublic:
```

In this example, there is an output line from `grep`, even though there is no user name *public* registered on the system.

If you wanted to get `grep` to find only the user names in the password file, then you need to make sure that it only looks for the search pattern at the start of each line. The solution to this problem in `grep` is similar to the solution used in `vi` for its search string specifications – regular expressions.

The basic set of special characters used for regular expressions in `grep` is the same as those used in `vi`. There is also an extended set of special characters available which you can use in `grep` if you include the -E switch on the command line. The following table gives a list of most of the special character sequences available in `grep` and their meanings; the B or E in the middle column shows which features are basic and which are extended:

^	B	matches the start of the line;
$	B	matches the end of the line;
\<	B	matches the start of a word;
\>	B	matches the end of a word;
.	B	matches any single text character;
[*str*]	B	matches any single character in *str*;
[^*str*]	B	matches any single character not in *str*;
[*a-b*]	B	matches any character between *a* and *b*;
\	B	turns off any special meaning of the character following;
*	B	matches zero or more repeats of the previous item;
+	E	matches one or more repeats of the previous item;
?	E	matches zero or one repeats of the previous item;
{*j*}	E	matches exactly *j* repeats of the previous item;
{*j*,}	E	matches *j* or more repeats of the previous item;
{,*k*}	E	matches at most *k* repeats of the previous item;
{*j,k*}	E	matches *j* to *k* repeats of the previous item;
s|*t*	E	match one of item *s* or item *t*;
(*exp*)	E	treats *exp* as a single item.

Don't forget that there is one other major difference between using regular expressions in vi and grep. In the editor, any characters you type are only seen and used by the editor itself, whereas, any parameters that grep sees have already passed through the shell first. Since some of the special characters used by grep in regular expressions also have special meaning to the shell, you need to tell the shell to ignore them so that grep gets the chance to see them instead. This is done by quoting the characters you want the shell to ignore. If you need a refresher, the shell's quoting mechanisms were described back in Section 4.1.

Returning to the original problem of searching the password file just for login names, it is now an easy task to construct a grep command line to show that 'public' is not a valid login name:

```
$ grep '^public' /etc/passwd
```

The ^ before the word 'public' forces grep only to look for the word at the start of each line. The whole search pattern is enclosed in single quotes (') so that the shell won't interfere with it, but will pass it (minus the quotes) onto grep. The fact that there is no output from grep shows that none of the lines in the password file starts with the word 'public'.

A slightly more complex example is to display lines from the password file where the login name has no password set on it. This is true if the second field on the line (between the first and second colon characters) is empty:

```
$ grep -E '^[^:]+::' /etc/passwd
sync::3:2::/:/bin/sync
mtos::9876:9876:student login:/mtos/home:/bin/bash
load::9876:9876:mount floppy:/:/mtos/bin/load
unload::9876:9876:umount floppy:/:/mtos/bin/unload
```

You can see from the output that there are four such logins in this example, with login names: sync, mtos, load and unload.

In order to understand it fully, the search pattern ('^[^:]+::') used in the example may need a little explanation. The first and last single-quote characters just tell the shell to ignore the string contents and pass it, unchanged, to grep. The search pattern itself needs to look for three things: the start of a line, followed by a login name, followed by a pair of colons which indicate an empty password field. The start of line is picked up by the initial ^ character. The empty password field is matched by the pair of colons (::) at the end of the string. That just leaves [^:]+ to match any login name. To understand this last part you need to think of a login name as a variable number of characters up to the first colon character, and that is just what [^:]+ means – one or more non-colon characters. The -E command line switch to grep is required in order to be able to use the + repetition operator from the extended feature set.

If you use a grep command without specifying any files to search, then grep takes its input from the standard input device. In this mode grep can have its

68   *Tools and Utilities*

input piped to it from a previous command. Here is an example pipeline to list the names of any subdirectories under the `root` directory that ordinary users have write permission for:

```
$ ls -l / | grep '^d.......w'
drwxrwxrwt  10 root     root         1024 May 30 14:30 tmp
```

As you would have expected, this pipeline shows that ordinary users have write permission in the directory /tmp. It operates by using `ls -l /` to generate a long listing of all the files and directories contained in the `root` directory. The output lines from `ls` are then piped into `grep`, which is set up to search for those lines that begin (^) with a d (directories) and then have a set of permission flags which can have any values (...) for the owner, any values (...) for the group, any value (.) for the world read permission flag and which finally has the world write permission flag set to allow world write access to this directory.

Some useful command line switches for use with `grep` are:

-E	use extended regular expressions for pattern matching;
-i	treat upper and lower case letters as the same;
-n	display line number within file for each output line;
-q	suppress output display, used with other commands;
-s	suppress file read permission error messages;
-num	display the *num* lines before and after each match.

5.1.2   find

The primary action of the `find` command is to traverse the tree structured directory hierarchy from a given starting point right down through all the branches and on to the leaf nodes. For each of the files and subdirectories that `find` discovers on the way, it can be made to perform a set of actions which you program at the command line. The most common use of `find` is just to generate a list of all the files and directories below a given starting point in the directory hierarchy:

```
$ cd
$ find . -print
./backup
./backup/motd.bak
./backup/passwd.bak
./text
./text/passwd
./text/motd
```

This example shows a `cd` command that changes the current working directory to your home directory, followed by the `find` command. The two parameters passed into find are the dot, which tells find to start its search with the current directory, and the -print, which just tells find to display the names of all the files it finds.

Since the file names are written to the standard output device by find, they can also be written to a pipe for use by other commands, as the following example demonstrates:

```
$ find . -print | grep passwd
./backup/passwd.bak
./text/passwd
```

In fact, as you will soon see, this particular application can be performed directly by find without having to use grep at all.

The general format for the find command is:

```
find pathnames -expressions
```

where *pathnames* can be any list of directory names which will each be searched recursively to generate the file names, and *-expressions* is any list of expressions which define conditions and actions to be performed on each of the files found by the search. If no *pathnames* are specified, then the default is the current directory, and if no *-expressions* are given, then the default expression -print is used:

```
$ find
./backup
./backup/motd.bak
./backup/passwd.bak
./text
./text/passwd
./text/motd
```

There are three kinds of expression that can be used with find: options, conditions and actions. Each of these types returns a value which is either *true* or *false* depending on which expression it is and on how its evaluation progressed. Whenever a find command has more than one expression specified, then logical operators are used between successive pairs of expressions to control their execution. Given the expressions *e1* and *e2*:

    e1 -a *e2*   evaluates *e2* only if *e1* is true;
    e1 *e2*   same as *e1* -a *e2*;
    e1 -o *e2*   evaluates *e2* only if *e1* is false;
    e1 , *e2*   evaluates both, in the order *e1* then *e2*.

The values of these compound expressions are the values returned by the last component expression that was actually evaluated. Compound expressions with more than two components are evaluated from left to right unless parentheses () are used to alter the evaluation order, so that:

```
e1 -o e2 -a e3
```

will evaluate as:

```
( e1 -o e2 ) -a e3
```

unless brackets are added explicitly to change this, as in:

```
e1 -o ( e2 -a e3 )
```

A logical not operator is also available, so that:

> ! *e1* is true when *e1* is false, and vice versa

The following table details some of the expressions that are available with `find`, along with the type of each expression and the value it returns:

`-mount`
: An option expression which prevents `find` from searching outside the boundaries of the current filesystem. The return value is always true.

`-group` *grp*
: A condition expression which checks the current file to see if it has a group ID or group name that matches *grp*. Return value is true if file's group ID or group name matches *grp* or false otherwise.

`-name` *pattern*
: A condition expression which looks for a file name that matches *pattern*. The *pattern* can be given as a regular expression which may need quoting from the shell. Returns true if the current file name matches *pattern* or false otherwise.

`-type` *t*
: A condition expression which checks to see if the current file is of type *t*, where *t* can be `d` for a directory, `f` for an ordinary file, `l` for a symbolic link, etc. Returns true if the current file is of type *t* or false otherwise.

`-user` *usr*
: A condition expression which checks the current file to see if it has owner ID or owner name that matches *usr*. Return value is true if file's owner ID or owner name matches *usr* or false otherwise.

`-exec` *cmd* ;
: An action expression which executes the command *cmd*. If you need to pass the current file name to *cmd* this is done with the notation {}. The semicolon (;) is used to mark the end of *cmd* and separate it from any more option expressions that may follow. The return value is true if the *cmd* executes successfully without error or false otherwise.

`-print`
: An action expression which just prints the current file name to the standard output device. Always returns true.

One obvious point to note about `find` is that it will not allow you to bypass the system's file and directory permission arrangements. Consequently, if you start `find` off in a place which has directories below it to which your access is denied, then `find` will generate an error message, sent to the standard error device, for each one. As the default device for standard error messages is the screen, this can make the real output you are looking for (assuming you are using the -print action) rather difficult to see:

```
$ find / -name passwd -print
find: /var/spool/cron: Permission denied
find: /var/spool/atjobs: Permission denied
find: /var/spool/atspool: Permission denied
/usr/bin/passwd
find: /usr/doc/ttysnoop: Permission denied
/etc/passwd
find: /root: Permission denied
```

The simplest thing to do to suppress this unwanted output is to redirect the error output to a file. Ordinarily, this would mean that you would have an unwanted file to delete afterwards; however, there is one file you can use which is specially provided for you to send things to that you really want to throw away. The file's pathname is:

```
/dev/null
```

This file is specially arranged so that any time you write something to it, the characters just get thrown away. It is also arranged so that when you try to read any characters from it you always get an end-of-file indication straight away with no other characters read.

Using this file to suppress the error output from `find`, the previous example becomes:

```
$ find / -name passwd -print 2>/dev/null
/usr/bin/passwd
/etc/passwd
```

Notice that this example is using two `find` expressions, with no operator between them (this arrangement defaults to using the -a operator). For this operator, the first expression is evaluated for each file name generated by `find` and only if the result is true will the second expression be evaluated. The first expression in this example is -name passwd, which looks for the file name passwd at the end of the pathname `find` is currently supplying. If a match is found, the expression returns the value true; otherwise it returns false. This return value determines whether or not to evaluate the second expression. If -name returns the value true then the second expression (-print) will display `find`'s current pathname to the standard output device. The overall effect of this is to print a list of all the pathnames that `find` discovers with the file name `passwd` on the end.

In this way you can `find` a list of pathnames without piping to `grep` as in previous examples. There is a difference, however: the `-name` expression will only look for complete words on the end of a pathname, whereas `grep` can look for substrings:

```
$ cd
$ find . -name motd -print 2>/dev/null
./text/motd
$ find . -print 2>/dev/null | grep motd
./text/motd
./backup/motd.bak
```

As a final, and more complex, example, let us see how we might generate a list of pathnames of all the ordinary files in a directory subtree whose contents include a particular string. One possible solution is to use `find` to generate the pathnames and then to use `grep` to see if the specified string appears in any of the files, printing the pathname of any files for which this is true. The only real problem is that `grep` normally displays any lines that it finds to the standard output as well as sending any error messages to the standard error device. One way round this problem is to redirect both the standard output and error output to `/dev/null`, but, in fact, `grep` provides an easier solution than this because it has command line switches built in to suppress these outputs for you:

```
$ find /etc -type f -exec grep -q -s mycroft {} \; -print
/etc/HOSTNAME
/etc/hosts
/etc/lilo.conf
```

What this command line does is to use `find` to generate a list of all the pathnames under the directory `/etc`. It then evaluates the expression `-type f` which returns the value true if the current pathname is an ordinary file. The second expression (`-exec grep -q -s mycroft {} \;`) is thus evaluated for all the ordinary files, and searches each of them in turn for the string `mycroft`. Don't forget that the notation `{}` is replaced by the current pathname when `grep` is executed. The `-q` and `-s` options stop `grep` from producing its normal display, so that, effectively, this expression is just being used to generate a true or false value which decides whether or not to evaluate the third expression. The `\` before the semi-colon at the end of the second expression is just to quote the semi-colon so the shell will ignore it and pass it to `find` unchanged. If the `-exec grep` expression returns true, then the `-print` expression will be evaluated which, as its action, will display the current pathname, as required.

5.1.3 sort

The **sort** command is a filter which can sort the lines of text in its input into the order you specify on the command line and then send the sorted lines to the standard output device. The **sort** command is very versatile in that it can treat the input lines as a collection of several fields and perform sorting operations using one or more of these fields as the sort key. You can also choose the character that **sort** will use as its field delimiter so that you may sort files of different types.

In the examples that follow we shall make use of the following small (and fictitious) password file, called **pw.test**:

```
root:awmku76tr43d6:0:0::/root/:/bin/sh
pc:bdhd74hs9jh3h:500:50::/usr1/pc:/bin/bash
carey:esJ9ohd8HH89i:501:50::/usr1/carey:/bin/bash
mot:dhjd83kjdJS6D:1500:60::/usr1/mot:/bin/bash
grex:cj8AjoWE8h8fs:1500:60::/usr1/mot:/bin/sh
```

By default, **sort** uses whitespace characters (spaces, tabs, etc.) as its field separators. Therefore, the lines of pw.test, containing no whitespace characters, are each treated as a single field. If **sort** is run on this file, it will treat each line as though it is a single word and sort them into alphabetical order:

```
$ sort pw.test
carey:esJ9ohd8HH89i:501:50::/usr1/carey:/bin/bash
grex:cj8AjoWE8h8fs:1500:60::/usr1/mot:/bin/sh
mot:dhjd83kjdJS6D:1500:60::/usr1/mot:/bin/bash
pc:bdhd74hs9jh3h:500:50::/usr1/pc:/bin/bash
root:awmku76tr43d6:0:0::/root/:/bin/sh
```

The **sort** command will take its input from any files specified on the command line, or from the standard input device if there are none given.

Many command line switches are available with **sort**; the most useful are given in the following table:

-b	ignore leading space characters in sort keys;
-f	treat upper and lower case letters as the same;
-n	treat the sort key as numeric rather that text;
-r	sort from high to low rather than from low to high;
-o *file*	send output to *file* instead of standard output;
-t *s*	use *s* as field separator, instead of whitespace;
-k *s1,s2*	use fields *s1* to (*s2* -1) as the sort key.

Actually, the specification of the sort key is a little more complex than is obvious from the previous table. To start with, it is permitted to give repeated -k switches, so that any combination of fields can be specified. The **sort** command uses the fields in the order given on the command line, which need not be the same as the order of the fields in the file. Each of the field specifiers (*s1* and *s2*) can be given as *f.c*, where *f* is the field number and *c* is the character position within the field. Both of these values start counting at one. Some examples might help to make it clearer:

-k3   The sort key is from the start of the third field to the end of the line.
-k3,6   The sort key here is made up of the third, fourth and fifth fields on the line.
-k4,5 -k1,3   The sort key is field 4 followed by field 1 followed by field 2.
-k3.3,4   The sort key is field 3, but omitting the first two characters in the field.
-k3.2,3.6   The sort key in this case is four characters long, starting at the second character of field 3.

Returning to the `pw.test` file, if you want to do anything sophisticated with this file, the first thing to do is to change the field separator from the whitespace default to a colon, which will allow `sort` to access the individual fields in the file. The following example will sort the file on the UID contained in field 3:

```
$ sort -t: -k3,4 pw.test
root:awmku76tr43d6:0:0::/root/:/bin/sh
grex:cj8AjoWE8h8fs:1500:60::/usr1/mot:/bin/sh
mot:dhjd83kjdJS6D:1500:60::/usr1/mot:/bin/bash
pc:bdhd74hs9jh3h:500:50::/usr1/pc:/bin/bash
carey:esJ9ohd8HH89i:501:50::/usr1/carey:/bin/bash
```

By default, if two lines have the same value for the sort key then they will be ordered as though the whole lines were just single words to be sorted. You can see this in the second and third lines of the output in the last example, which both have the value 1500 in the key field.

Instead of this, you can choose to resolve the problem yourself by specifying a second (or more if needed) key field to use for the sort when the first key field cannot determine the order. If we apply this to the last example and specify that if field 3 cannot determine the order, then field 7 (the shell) field should be used next, we obtain the following result:

```
$ sort -t: -k3,4 -k7 pw.test
root:awmku76tr43d6:0:0::/root/:/bin/sh
mot:dhjd83kjdJS6D:1500:60::/usr1/mot:/bin/bash
grex:cj8AjoWE8h8fs:1500:60::/usr1/mot:/bin/sh
pc:bdhd74hs9jh3h:500:50::/usr1/pc:/bin/bash
carey:esJ9ohd8HH89i:501:50::/usr1/carey:/bin/bash
```

One small problem with both of the previous examples is that the file does not seem to have been sorted properly on the UID field, as the lines have been displayed in key field order 0, 1500, 1500, 500, 501. This is because `sort` is treating the content of the UID field as though it is words and not numbers, in which case `sort` has got it right as 0 comes before 1, which comes before 5. It's not what was required, though. The solution is to use the -n switch so that the field contents will be sorted into numeric order as required:

```
$ sort -t: -n -k3,4 -k7 pw.test
root:awmku76tr43d6:0:0::/root/:/bin/sh
pc:bdhd74hs9jh3h:500:50::/usr1/pc:/bin/bash
carey:esJ9ohd8HH89i:501:50::/usr1/carey:/bin/bash
grex:cj8AjoWE8h8fs:1500:60::/usr1/mot:/bin/sh
mot:dhjd83kjdJS6D:1500:60::/usr1/mot:/bin/bash
```

and this seems to have solved the problem.

One final example of the use of `sort` shows how to use just a small part of a field as the sort key. For this example we shall sort the file on the first two characters of the password field, and also obtain the output displayed in reverse order:

```
$ sort -t: -r -k2.1,2.3 pw.test
carey:esJ9ohd8HH89i:501:50::/usr1/carey:/bin/bash
mot:dhjd83kjdJS6D:1500:60::/usr1/mot:/bin/bash
grex:cj8AjoWE8h8fs:1500:60::/usr1/mot:/bin/sh
pc:bdhd74hs9jh3h:500:50::/usr1/pc:/bin/bash
root:awmku76tr43d6:0:0::/root/:/bin/sh
```

All of the examples of `sort` that you have seen have resulted in a display on the screen. As this is just the standard output device being used, the output could, obviously, have been redirected to a pipe or a file. One word of warning is in order here – don't redirect the output from `sort` back into the file you are reading as the input, or the shell will delete your input file in the process of setting up the redirection. (i.e. don't do this):

```
$ sort somefile >somefile
```

If you need the output to go back into the same file then use the -o switch to `sort` to do it, as in the following example:

```
$ sort somefile -o somefile
```

5.2 Modifying Files

Several Linux commands enable you to modify the contents of some text, either in a file or as it passes by, in a pipe. This section examines some of these commands and demonstrates their power.

5.2.1 sed

If you had a text file which you needed to edit, then you could just do it interactively at the keyboard with vi. If the text you wanted to edit only existed in a pipe between two processes then it would be a different proposition. This is where sed comes in. It is an editor specifically designed to take lines of text from the standard input and send them on to the standard output, performing editing actions on them as they pass through. In order to use sed, you need to specify what editing actions you want it to perform on the command line when you enter the command. Because sed only sees the text once as it passes by, there is a limit to what you can reasonably expect it to do. For instance, trying to compose editing actions that need the editor to move backwards and forwards within the text are out of the question.

The standard action for sed is repeatedly to read a line of input and pass it on to the output unchanged. This sequence continues until the end-of-file is reached. If you introduce any editing actions into this sequence then they are applied, if they are appropriate, to each line after it is read in. The result is then usually passed to the output instead of the original line. The editor also arranges to keep a count of the number of lines passing by, so that your editing actions can refer to particular line numbers or ranges of line numbers in the text.

Usually, sed will take its text from the standard input, but it is also possible to take file input instead if the names of one or more files are specified on the command line. The general form of a sed command is:

```
sed actions files
```

Here, *actions* is a list of one or more editing actions that you want sed to perform. If there is only one action it can just be entered on the command line as it is. If you want to perform more than one action with a particular sed command then there are two choices: either the actions can be introduced on the command line each preceded by a -e switch, or the list of actions can be written to a file and sed directed to consult the file with the -f *file* switch.

Usually, you will need to specify a line or range of lines in the text to which each editing action is appropriate. This is done by giving zero-, one- or two-line addresses before each action. A line address can be given as either a line number or as a regular expression, which then specifies a string pattern to search for on the line. The regular expressions available with sed are just the basic set available with grep. Turn back to Section 5.1.1 if you want a reminder of the format of the basic regular expressions.

Editing actions with no line addresses are applied to every line in the input text. If one line address is given, then the action is just applied to lines which match the address specification. When two line addresses are supplied, the action is applied to a range of lines that starts with the first line that matches the first address and extends to the next line after that which matches the second address. Then, beginning with the next line after the selected range, sed starts looking for another matching range of lines, starting with the first address again.

Let us take a look at some examples of sed in action, using the data file pw.test, which was introduced when we looked at grep. The first example shows the delete action:

```
$ cat pw.test | sed '4,$d'
root:awmku76tr43d6:0:0::/root/:/bin/sh
pc:bdhd74hs9jh3h:500:50::/usr1/pc:/bin/bash
carey:esJ9ohd8HH89i:501:50::/usr1/carey:/bin/bash
```

The cat command is used to list the pw.test file to its standard output. This output from cat is piped into sed, which has a single editing action ('4,$d'). It is necessary to quote this editing action so that it does not get tangled up with the shell. If you are ever in doubt about whether or not something like this needs quoting, just quote it anyway to be on the safe side. The action itself says: delete the range of lines from line 4 to the end of the file (the $ means last line in file).

The same effect could be achieved by getting sed to quit after processing line 3, with the q action, as in the next example:

```
$ sed 3q pw.test
root:awmku76tr43d6:0:0::/root/:/bin/sh
pc:bdhd74hs9jh3h:500:50::/usr1/pc:/bin/bash
carey:esJ9ohd8HH89i:501:50::/usr1/carey:/bin/bash
```

Here, the pw.test file is given as a parameter to sed rather than being piped into it as in the previous example.

Sometimes, you will want to suppress the default action of sending all edited lines to the standard output. This can be done with the -n command line switch. Obviously, if you use the -n switch, you will then need to specify explicitly which lines are to be printed to sed's standard output. This is done with the p editing action. The following example demonstrates these things by just selecting and displaying two lines out of the middle of the file:

```
$ sed -n 2,3p pw.test
pc:bdhd74hs9jh3h:500:50::/usr1/pc:/bin/bash
carey:esJ9ohd8HH89i:501:50::/usr1/carey:/bin/bash
```

The next example is a little more complex, and uses the translate characters action (y). The basic idea behind character translation is that you specify two strings of equal length, then, on any lines that are selected by the line addressing, each of the characters in the first string is translated into the corresponding character in the second string. In the following example, all lines containing the word *bash* are selected and on those lines all the colons are translated to underscore (_) characters and all the zeros are translated to percent (%) symbols:

```
$ sed /bash/y/:0/_%/ pw.test
root:awmku76tr43d6:0:0::/root/:/bin/sh
pc_bdhd74hs9jh3h_5%%_5%__/usr1/pc_/bin/bash
carey_esJ9ohd8HH89i_5%1_5%__/usr1/carey_/bin/bash
mot_dhjd83kjdJS6D_15%%_6%__/usr1/mot_/bin/bash
grex:cj8AjoWE8h8fs:1500:60::/usr1/mot:/bin/sh
```

Inserting an exclamation mark (!) into an editing action after the line addressing, applies the action to all the lines NOT selected by the line addressing rather than applying the action to the lines that ARE selected:

```
$ sed '/bash/!y/:0/_%/' pw.test
root_awmku76tr43d6_%_%__/root/_/bin/sh
pc:bdhd74hs9jh3h:500:50::/usr1/pc:/bin/bash
carey:esJ9ohd8HH89i:501:50::/usr1/carey:/bin/bash
mot:dhjd83kjdJS6D:1500:60::/usr1/mot:/bin/bash
grex_cj8AjoWE8h8fs_15%%_6%__/usr1/mot_/bin/sh
```

The other main editing command (s) gives you the ability to substitute one string, specified as a regular expression, for another. The general format for the substitute action is:

```
s/expr/new/flags
```

where *expr* is the regular expression for which sed is to search, *new* is the text that will replace the regular expression and *flags* can be selected from the following list:

num   Normally, only the first occurrence of *expr* will be substituted, but if *num* is specified (in the range 0 to 9) then that occurrence will be substituted instead.

g   If this flag is specified then every occurrence of *expr* will be replaced with *new*.

p   This flag causes the current line to be printed to the standard output if any substitution has taken place.

w *file*   This flag causes the current line to be appended to the end of the specified *file* if any substitution has taken place. The *file* will be created if it does not exist.

The next example uses the substitution action to modify the example password file so as to prevent all users between pc and mot inclusive from logging in. It does this by removing their encrypted passwords and substituting the string ' off ' instead. A list of all the modified logins is also appended to the file **banned**:

```
$ sed '/^p/,/^m/s/:..............:/:    off   :/w banned' pw.test
root:awmku76tr43d6:0:0::/root/:/bin/sh
pc:    off    :500:50::/usr1/pc:/bin/bash
carey: off    :501:50::/usr1/carey:/bin/bash
mot:   off    :1500:60::/usr1/mot:/bin/bash
grex:cj8AjoWE8h8fs:1500:60::/usr1/mot:/bin/sh
```

Two quick notes here should explain the operation of this example. The ^ character means the start of the line, so the range /^p/,/^m/ means 'from a line starting with a p to a line starting with an m'. The other thing to notice is that all standard encrypted passwords are 13 characters long so the regular expression :..............: matches the first 13 character string enclosed between a pair of colons on the selected lines (i.e the encrypted passwords).

A quick look in the file *banned* shows that it contains the expected lines, listing those users who have had their logins disabled:

```
$ cat banned
pc:    off    :500:50::/usr1/pc:/bin/bash
carey: off    :501:50::/usr1/carey:/bin/bash
mot:   off    :1500:60::/usr1/mot:/bin/bash
```

The next example is interesting in that it introduces several new concepts. To give the example a context, suppose that new versions of both the shell programs run by users of this system (/bin/sh and /bin/bash) have become available. The new versions are stored in the directory /usr/local/bin and you want to modify the shell pathnames in the password file to get the users to try out the new shells:

```
$ sed 's?/bin/.*sh$?/usr/local&?' pw.test
root:awmku76tr43d6:0:0::/root/:/usr/local/bin/sh
pc:bdhd74hs9jh3h:500:50::/usr1/pc:/usr/local/bin/bash
carey:esJ9ohd8HH89i:501:50::/usr1/carey:/usr/local/bin/bash
mot:dhjd83kjdJS6D:1500:60::/usr1/mot:/usr/local/bin/bash
grex:cj8AjoWE8h8fs:1500:60::/usr1/mot:/usr/local/bin/sh
```

The first thing to notice is that the regular expression for which you need to search contains the character (/) normally used as the substitution delimiter. The sed program allows you to overcome this problem by choosing another delimiting character. This can be almost anything you like (? in this example). The next point is that a $ at the end of a regular expression matches the end of the line. Consequently, the expression /bin/.*sh$ will match either /bin/sh or /bin/bash at the end of a line. The final point is that an ampersand (&) appearing in the replacement string will itself be replaced by the text matched by the regular expression. This just puts the correct shell name after the string /usr/local.

The final example shows a sed command containing multiple editing actions and shows that in these cases the editing actions are applied one at a time in a strictly left to right order:

```
$ sed -e s/:/_:/ -e /carey_/s//cew_/ pw.test
root_:awmku76tr43d6:0:0::/root/:/bin/sh
pc_:bdhd74hs9jh3h:500:50::/usr1/pc:/bin/bash
cew_:esJ9ohd8HH89i:501:50::/usr1/carey:/bin/bash
mot_:dhjd83kjdJS6D:1500:60::/usr1/mot:/bin/bash
grex_:cj8AjoWE8h8fs:1500:60::/usr1/mot:/bin/sh
```

The idea here is to append an underscore to the end of each login name and, additionally, change the login name `carey_` to `cew_`. These things are achieved with two editing actions, the first dealing with the underscore for all users, and the second dealing with the name change for `carey`. The only thing to notice here is that the substitution in the second editing action doesn't specify a regular expression. In cases like this, the last regular expression value encountered as part of a line address or previous substitute command will be used instead. This will be `carey_` in this example, from the line address of the second editing action.

5.2.2 Character Translation

The `tr` command performs a character translation function similar to the y editing action of `sed`, with a few extras on top. It is a very quick and simple program to use, with typical applications like translating upper case letters to lower case or deleting punctuation. The `tr` program is a true filter in that it can only read text from the standard input and send the translated version to the standard output. The basic form of the `tr` command is:

```
tr str1 str2
```

where *str1* and *str2* are strings of characters. In general, the characters appearing in *str1* will be translated into the corresponding characters in *str2*. An example of this is:

```
tr ABCDEFGHIJKLMNOPQRSTUVWXYZ abcdefghijklmnopqrstuvwxyz
```

Obviously, this will translate all upper case letters to their lower case equivalents. A rather simpler way to achieve the same thing is to specify a contiguous range of characters by just the first and last characters in the sequence, separated by a hyphen (-), as in:

```
tr A-Z a-z
```

The implication of these examples is that the number of characters specified by the two string parameters needs to be the same. Obviously, there are two ways that this can be different. If *str1* is shorter than *str2* then the second string is truncated to the length of the first. If *str2* is shorter than *str1* then the second string is padded out to the length of first using the rightmost character of *str2*. So that:

    tr ABC abcde

is the same as:

    tr ABC abc

And the other example is that:

    tr ABCDE abc

is the same as:

    tr ABCDE abccc

The first of these two examples is of little practical value, but the second can be put to good use, especially when combined with the action of the -c command line switch. The action of the -c switch is to replace the characters in *str1* with a string containing a list of all the characters not in *str1* (i.e. its complement). This allows you to do things like translate all non-alphabetic and non-numeric characters into space characters:

    tr -c A-Za-z0-9 ´ ´

This particular command line has the side effect that it can leave a lot of contiguous space characters in the output. What is required to solve this problem is some way to squeeze occurrences of multiple spaces down into single space characters. There is a **tr** command line switch which can perform this task – the -s switch. The function of the -s switch is to squeeze multiple occurrences of any characters that appear in *str2* into single occurrences of those characters, as follows:

    tr -cs A-Za-z0-9 ´ ´

Applying this **tr** command to the file pw.test gives output like:

    $ tr -cs A-Za-z0-9 ´ ´ <pw.test
    root awmku76tr43d6 0 0 root bin sh pc bdhd74hs9jh3h 500
    50 usr1 pc bin bash carey esJ9ohd8HH89i 501 50 usr1 car
    ey bin bash mot dhjd83kjdJS6D 1500 60 usr1 mot bin bash
    grex cj8AjoWE8h8fs 1500 60 usr1 mot bin sh

If you just want to use **tr** to squeeze multiple occurrences of some characters into single occurrences, then this is done with a command of the form:

    tr -s str1

where only *str1* is specified and the characters in it are used for the squeeze operation.

Some special characters (such as a newline or escape for instance) can be difficult to enter into the translation strings, so a special notation exists for them, consisting of a backslash character followed by a code to specify which special character is required. The following table is a list of the main codes available:

82   *Tools and Utilities*

\b	backspace character (Ctrl-h);
\n	newline character (Ctrl-j);
\r	carriage return character (Ctrl-m);
\t	tab character (Ctrl-i);
\\	backslash character;
\ooo	any character, given as three octal digits, e.g;
\033	ASCII code for escape character (Ctrl-[).

These are the same special sequences that are used in programming in C when you want to use these characters in a literal string.

One final command line switch available with `tr` is `-d`:

```
tr -d str1
```

The purpose of this switch is to cause `tr` to delete characters. For this option only *str1* is specified, which is used to provide the list of characters to be deleted.

5.3 Simple Data Manipulation

This section details a set of simple commands which allow you to manipulate, in specific and useful ways, the contents of text and data files and the output from other commands.

5.3.1 cut and paste

Commands like `sed` and `tr` are very good at manipulating the rows (or records) in a file. What they don't do so well is to allow the manipulation of columns (specific fields in each record) within a file. The `cut` command provides a simple way to extract particular columns from the lines in its input:

```
$ cut -d: -f1 pw.test
root
pc
carey
mot
grex
```

This command extracts field 1 (`-f1`) using the colon as a field delimiter (`-d:`) from each of the lines in the file `pw.test` (i.e. the login name field from our test password file). Notice that there are a few unfortunate inconsistencies between commands, that will come to light from time to time, in their command line switches. Here in particular `cut` uses `-d` to introduce a field delimiter where the `sort` command we looked at earlier used `-t` for the same job – oops!

The next example shows how to extract the login name and home directory information into two separate files (`/tmp/p1` and `/tmp/p6`) and then use a `paste` command to build up a table of this information from the two files:

```
$ cut -d: -f1 pw.test >/tmp/p1
$ cut -d: -f6 pw.test >/tmp/p6
$ paste /tmp/p1 /tmp/p6
root    /root/
pc      /usr1/pc
carey   /usr1/carey
mot     /usr1/mot
grex    /usr1/mot
$ rm /tmp/p1 /tmp/p6
```

When you use `paste` to connect fields together like this, it automatically inserts a delimiting character between the fields, which, by default, is a `Tab` character (`Ctrl-i`). If you prefer, you can specify your own delimiting character (or even a separate character between each pair of fields) with the `-d` switch.

The previous examples of `cut` have only used fields delimited by particular characters, but it is also possible for the fields to be in fixed-byte positions within a record, and not to use field delimiters at all. In these cases you can specify byte positions with the `-b` command line switch. For both the `-f` and `-b` switches to `cut`, the field or byte positions can be given as either a single number or a set of numbers or ranges of numbers separated by commas. In both cases the numbers count from 1.

A slightly more complex pipeline results as the solution to the next problem. Find a way to extract the minute number from the date and time display output by the `date` command. Just using the `date` command with no parameters will display the date and time in a fixed format output string to the standard output device:

```
$ date
Sun Jun  4 17:27:23 BST 1995
```

This string can be treated as a number of fields separated by space characters. These fields are:

Sun	day name;
Jun	month name;
4	day number in month;
17:27:23	time of day (24 hr clock – hour:minute:second);
BST	time zone (British Summer Time);
1995	year number.

The only problem with using `cut` to extract fields from this string is that the day number within the month (4 in this example) has an extra space in front of it, to pad the field out to the correct width, if the number is less than 10. This will effectively count as an extra field when we tell `cut` that fields are space separated. A simple solution is to use `tr` to squeeze multiple spaces to a single space, as follows:

84   *Tools and Utilities*

```
$ date | tr -s ' '
Sun Jun 4 17:27:23 BST 1995
```

The cut command can now be used with a space field delimiter to extract the time of day field (field four):

```
$ date | tr -s ' ' | cut -d' ' -f4
17:27:23
```

The output from this pipeline is now a string which itself consists of three colon delimited fields of which we want to extract the value in the middle field. Again, cut is the ideal solution, as follows:

```
$ date | tr -s ' ' | cut -d' ' -f4 | cut -d: -f2
27
```

A simpler solution to the same problem will still use cut but relies on noticing that all the fields in the output from date are of fixed size. Even when numeric fields are less than 10, so that they are only one digit instead of two, the sizes of the fields are maintained by padding them out. This allows for a solution which uses the -b switch to cut with a range of byte positions carefully calculated to coincide with the field of interest (bytes 15 to 16 in this example):

```
$ date | cut -b15-16
27
```

5.3.2   Comparing File Contents

There are several commands available for comparing the contents of two files for any differences. The simplest command is effectively used just to tell you whether or not two files are the same. This command is called cmp. All it does is to compare the two files given as parameters byte by byte until it either finds a difference or until it reaches the end of the files. The general form of the command is:

```
cmp file1 file2
```

If either *file1* or *file2* is just a hyphen (-) then the text for this file will be taken from the standard input device, which will be from the keyboard unless input redirection is used. The output from the cmp command is the first byte and the line number where the two files differ.

If the lines in the two files to be compared are sorted into order then it is possible to use the comm command to do the comparison between them. The general form for the comm command is:

```
comm options file1 file2
```

If no options are specified then the output from comm is displayed in three columns. Output lines beginning in column 1 are those lines that appear in *file1* but not in *file2*. Column 2 contains the lines that appear in *file2* but not in *file1* and column 3 lists lines contained in both files.

As an example, let us sort the contents of pw.test into the file pw1.test:

```
$ sort pw.test -o pw1.test
$ cat pw1.test
carey:esJ9ohd8HH89i:501:50::/usr1/carey:/bin/bash
grex:cj8AjoWE8h8fs:1500:60::/usr1/mot:/bin/sh
mot:dhjd83kjdJS6D:1500:60::/usr1/mot:/bin/bash
pc:bdhd74hs9jh3h:500:50::/usr1/pc:/bin/bash
root:awmku76tr43d6:0:0::/root/:/bin/sh
```

Then, modify some of the lines in pw.test with sed and sort the result, sending the sorted output into the file pw2.test:

```
$ sed /pc/,/carey/s/bash/sh/ <pw.test | sort >pw2.test
$ cat pw2.test
carey:esJ9ohd8HH89i:501:50::/usr1/carey:/bin/sh
grex:cj8AjoWE8h8fs:1500:60::/usr1/mot:/bin/sh
mot:dhjd83kjdJS6D:1500:60::/usr1/mot:/bin/bash
pc:bdhd74hs9jh3h:500:50::/usr1/pc:/bin/sh
root:awmku76tr43d6:0:0::/root/:/bin/sh
```

Finally, use comm on the two sorted files to observe the result:

```
$ comm pw1.test pw2.test
carey:esJ9ohd8HH89i:501:50::/usr1/carey:/bin/bash
        carey:esJ9ohd8HH89i:501:50::/usr1/carey:/bin/sh
                grex:cj8AjoWE8h8fs:1500:60::/usr1/mot:/bin/sh
                mot:dhjd83kjdJS6D:1500:60::/usr1/mot:/bin/bash
pc:bdhd74hs9jh3h:500:50::/usr1/pc:/bin/bash
        pc:bdhd74hs9jh3h:500:50::/usr1/pc:/bin/sh
                root:awmku76tr43d6:0:0::/root/:/bin/sh
```

The main *options* you can specify are -1, -2 and -3 which suppress the output of the corresponding columns. For example, to see just the lines in pw1.test which do not occur in pw2.test you need to suppress the column two and column three outputs, as follows:

```
$ comm -2 -3 pw1.test pw2.test
carey:esJ9ohd8HH89i:501:50::/usr1/carey:/bin/bash
pc:bdhd74hs9jh3h:500:50::/usr1/pc:/bin/bash
```

Similarly, to see only the lines which appear in both files, you need to suppress the output from columns 1 and 2:

```
$ comm -1 -2 pw1.test pw2.test
grex:cj8AjoWE8h8fs:1500:60::/usr1/mot:/bin/sh
mot:dhjd83kjdJS6D:1500:60::/usr1/mot:/bin/bash
root:awmku76tr43d6:0:0::/root/:/bin/sh
```

The other main command for comparing file contents is `diff`. This command performs a really sophisticated check compared to `cmp` and `comm`. In fact, this command will systematically work through a pair of files, which need not be sorted in any way, and display all the lines where the two files differ:

```
$ diff pw1.test pw2.test
1c1
< carey:esJ9ohd8HH89i:501:50::/usr1/carey:/bin/bash
---
> carey:esJ9ohd8HH89i:501:50::/usr1/carey:/bin/sh
4c4
< pc:bdhd74hs9jh3h:500:50::/usr1/pc:/bin/bash
---
> pc:bdhd74hs9jh3h:500:50::/usr1/pc:/bin/sh
```

The lines in the output display which are preceded by a less than (<) symbol are the lines in the first input file which do not match the corresponding lines in the second file. Similarly, lines preceded by a greater than (>) symbol are those contained in the second input file, but not in the first.

5.3.3 uniq

Once a file has been manipulated, for example, `cut` and then ordered with `sort`, it is possible for there to be duplicate lines in the output file. These duplicate records can be removed from the file to leave only unique instances of each record with the command `uniq`:

```
$ cat pw.test | cut -d: -f7 | sort | uniq
/bin/bash
/bin/sh
```

This pipeline sends the contents of the file pw.test into the `cut` command, which extracts each user's shell name (i.e. field seven). This is then piped into `sort`, which ensures that any pairs of duplicate lines are next to each other in its output. Finally, this sorted list is piped into `uniq`, which will remove one of any pair of duplicate lines discovered on a pass through its input.

5.4 Other Tools

There are several other tools available under Linux that are worth mentioning at this time. The first of these is the `pr` command. The function of this command is to split a file up into pages of the correct size to send to a printer. By default, the pages have a heading inserted which contains the date and time, the file name and the page number:

```
$ pr pw.test

Jun   1 09:20 1995    pw.test Page 1

root:awmku76tr43d6:0:0::/root/:/bin/sh
pc:bdhd74hs9jh3h:500:50::/usr1/pc:/bin/bash
carey:esJ9ohd8HH89i:501:50::/usr1/carey:/bin/bash
mot:dhjd83kjdJS6D:1500:60::/usr1/mot:/bin/bash
grex:cj8AjoWE8h8fs:1500:60::/usr1/mot:/bin/sh
```

It is also possible to use the -n command line switch to get the `pr` command to add line numbers to the text:

```
$ pr -n pw.test

Jun   1 09:20 1995    pw.test Page 1

      1    root:awmku76tr43d6:0:0::/root/:/bin/sh
      2    pc:bdhd74hs9jh3h:500:50::/usr1/pc:/bin/bash
      3    carey:esJ9ohd8HH89i:501:50::/usr1/carey:/bin/bash
      4    mot:dhjd83kjdJS6D:1500:60::/usr1/mot:/bin/bash
      5    grex:cj8AjoWE8h8fs:1500:60::/usr1/mot:/bin/sh
```

The next command to look at is called `od`. This command allows you to examine the contents of a text or data file as a set of bytes. Each line of output consists of a number which is the current byte offset into the file followed by a set of sixteen byte values. All the data byte and offset values in the output can be displayed in several formats, including ASCII characters, and octal or hexadecimal numbers:

```
$ od /tmp/text/motd
0000000 064514 072556 020170 027061 027062 027061 024040 047520
0000020 044523 024530 005056
0000026
```

The default display from `od` is all in octal, which is where it gets its name from (Octal Dump). This is not usually the most useful display however, and a more informative output can be created with the display set, for instance, to a combination of ASCII characters and hexadecimal values:

88   *Tools and Utilities*

```
$ od -Ax -tcx1 /tmp/text/motd
000000   m   o   t   d       c   o   n   t   e   n   t   s       i   n
        6d  6f  74  64  20  63  6f  6e  74  65  6e  74  73  20  69  6e
000010       h   e   r   e   .  \n
        20  68  65  72  65  2e  0a
000017
```

The `-A` switch allows you to specify what format to use for the offset values. The choices are:

    x   hexadecimal;
    o   octal (default);
    d   decimal;
    n   no offset output.

The `-t` switch lets you specify one or more formats in which to display the byte values in the file. The main choices here are:

    xn hexadecimal;
    on octal (o2 is default);
    dn signed decimal;
    un unsigned decimal;
    c   ASCII character or backslash sequence.

The number given for n specifies how many bytes to use for each value displayed. Other options for this command are explained in the associated manual page.

The final command in this section is called `file`. The purpose of this command is to give you some information about another file to help you to classify its contents. The `file` command runs through a set of tests to try to identify a file's type and stops to print a message as soon as it thinks it has a positive identification. Due to the nature of some of the tests, it is possible for `file` to be fooled, but this is rare and should not present any major problems:

```
$ file *
book.dvi:      TeX DVI file data
book.log:      TeX transcript text
book.ps:       PostScript document
book.tex:      English text
fdr:           ascii text
inc:           directory
```

5.5 Dos Files

A portable set of tools exist, called `mtools`, which allow various operating systems, including Linux, to copy files and directories to and from standard DOS disks. This can be very useful for moving files to or from a DOS environment or for moving files between systems which otherwise do not share a common filesystem format.

The main set of commands available in the `mtools` set are:

`mcd` *dname*	change directory on DOS disk;
`mcopy` *path dname*	copy files to DOS disk;
`mcopy` *dname path*	copy files from DOS disk;
`mdel` *dname*	delete a DOS file;
`mdir` *dname*	display a DOS directory;
`mformat` *drive*	DOS format a low level formatted diskette;
`mlabel` *drive*	change DOS disk volume label;
`mmd` *dname*	make a DOS disk directory;
`mrd` *dname*	remove a DOS disk directory;
`mren` *dname dname*	rename an existing file on DOS disk;
`mtype` *dname*	display contents of DOS text file.

These commands are very similar to their DOS equivalents which have the same name but without the first letter m. In the table, *path* is any standard Linux file pathname, *drive* is a DOS disk drive letter followed by a colon and *dname* is a DOS disk file name. DOS file names are made up of a disk drive letter followed by a colon and then a pathname to a file or directory. The directory separator used in these pathnames can be either the Linux slash (/) character or the DOS backslash (\) character, though, if the backslash is used it will need to be quoted from the shell. To see the contents of the top level directory of a DOS disk:

```
$ mdir a:
 Volume in drive A has no label
 Directory for A:/

BOOK             <DIR>      4-13-95  10:58a
FDR                   70    4-13-95  11:00a
FDW                   83    4-13-95  11:00a
DOT              <DIR>      6-05-95   6:01p
LTI      DOC        5732    5-02-95   9:02a
        8 File(s)     828928 bytes free
```

or the contents of a subdirectory on the same disk:

```
$ mdir a:/dot
 Volume in drive A has no label
 Directory for A:/DOT

.                <DIR>      6-05-95   6:01p
..               <DIR>      6-05-95   6:01p
D10      TGZ       65317    6-05-95   6:02p
        3 File(s)     828928 bytes free
```

90   *Tools and Utilities*

Having discovered a file of interest on the disk it is a simple matter to copy the file from the DOS disk into the current Linux directory, and verify that this has, indeed, taken place:

```
$ mcopy a:/dot/d10.tgz .
Copying D10.TGZ
$ ls -l
-rw-r--r--    1 pc        book        65317 Jun  6 23:13 d10.tgz
```

Exercises

Construct a pipeline or single command to perform each of the following functions:

1. Display a list of all the files called `core` anywhere in the file system, that you have access to as an ordinary user.
2. Display a list of the process IDs of all the processes on the system running on your behalf when you are logged in as an ordinary user.
3. Does the answer to the previous question change if you are logged in as `root`?
4. Display a list of file names, one per line, from the directory `/dev`, which have the format `hda` followed by a number. Display the list in ascending order of the number. (My system has file names `hda1` to `hda12`.)
5. Display a list of byte offsets in hexadecimal for the starting positions of all null terminated strings of printable characters, at least three characters long, in the file `/bin/cat`. The solution to this problem may well involve you in looking carefully at some `man` pages to see which of the commands you have seen so far may help.

Answers

1. One possible solution would be to use the `find` command to generate a list of all the file names on the system starting at the `root` directory and then have it search these for any `core` files and print out their pathnames:

    ```
    $ find / -name core -print 2>/dev/null
    ```

    Don't forget, that as an ordinary user, there are directories to which you have no access and which will normally cause `find` to generate error messages. These messages can be suppressed by redirecting them to `/dev/null`.

2. The `ps` command will provide a list of all your processes which are associated with your terminal. Using the `-x` switch will cause `ps` to display any processes you are running that are not associated with your terminal as well. Suppressing the `ps` header line is done with the `-h` switch. After this, each line output by `ps` has a process ID in the first field, which is made up of

the first five characters on the line. This can be extracted and displayed as follows:

```
$ ps -xh | cut -b1-5
```

3. Logged in as `root`, the command `ps -xh` will list all the processes on the system, not just those owned by `root`. This makes getting a list of just the process IDs of those processes that belong to `root` a little more challenging. However, it can still be done – one way is:

```
$ ps -uxh | grep "^root" | cut -b10-14
```

Here the `-u` switch has been added to `ps` so that it lists the user name to which each process belongs, at the start of the line. This list can then be piped to `grep` to extract just those lines that begin with `root`. Extracting and printing the process ID from those lines is the same as before except that the PID field is in a different place, which can be identified by examining the output from the `ps` command.

4. It is quite straightforward to obtain the correct list of file names generated with an appropriate `ls` command. This can then be piped into the `sort` program using the `-n` switch to give numerical sorting and another parameter to specify where in each line the number may be found:

```
$ ls /dev/hda[0-9]* | sort -n +0.8
```

Notice that `ls` automatically produces its output one file name per line when it is being sent to a pipe, rather than several file names per line, which it gives when its output is being sent to the screen. To demonstrate this try the two command lines:

```
$ ls
$ ls | cat
```

which you might otherwise expect to produce the same output.

5. If you look at the `man` page for the `od` command you will find it has the `-s` switch which does a lot of what is required (i.e. it finds all the strings). The `-Ax` switch will also cause the file offsets to be displayed in hexadecimal, as required. This can then be piped into `cut` just to extract the offset field and leave the strings behind:

```
$ od -s -Ax /bin/cat | cut -b1-6
```

Chapter 6

Shell Scripts

You have seen that `bash` has a very powerful set of interactive facilities available from the keyboard in the form of I/O redirection, pipes, job control, history lists, command line editing, and so on. In this chapter you will see that this is only half of the story. The shell goes on to provide a full programming language interpreter and a mechanism for reading and executing your own shell programs. These shell programs are called *Shell Scripts*.

6.1 Command Files

Any standard Linux command or pipeline, or any sequence of these things, can be entered into a text file with `cat` or with an editor like `vi`, made executable with `chmod` and then executed just by entering its name, like any other system command. The following command sequence shows this idea in action:

```
$ cat >dirsize
ls /usr/bin | wc -w
Ctrl-d
$ chmod 700 dirsize
$ ls -l dirsize
-rwx------    1 pc        book         20 Jun 10 22:04 dirsize
$ dirsize
    459
```

Here, the pipeline `ls /usr/bin | wc -w` is entered into the text file `dirsize`. This file is then flagged as executable, with the command `chmod 700 dirsize`. The following `ls` command now allows you to check that the file's permission flags have been set as required. Finally, using the filename (`dirsize`) as a command name causes the pipeline in the file to be executed by a shell, just as though it had been entered from the command line. The output (`459`) is the count of the number of files in the directory specified in the shell script.

When you write any shell scripts that you will use frequently, they should be placed in a personal directory, which you set aside for the purpose, and executed from there. The best plan is, probably, to create a `bin` directory under your home directory and place the files in there. The question then arises as to how you execute these commands without having to type a long pathname, specifying how the commands can be reached from your current working directory. This question will be answered in the next two sections.

6.2 Variables

In common with most programming languages, the shell provides facilities for declaring and using variables. To the shell, a variable is just a place in memory which has a name, and which can hold a string of characters as its value. As soon as you receive a shell prompt, after a login to the system, the shell will already have quite a few variables defined whose values were set up when the shell began execution.

The name and purpose of some of these variables is:

PS1   This variable holds the shell's command line prompt string. So far, in all the examples, the value of this variable has been '$ '.

PS2   This variable holds the shell's secondary prompt string. It is used when the shell detects that the line you have entered is incomplete and more input is required to finish it. The only example of the use of this prompt that you have seen so far was back in Section 4.2, when we looked at 'here' documents. The value of the variable there was '>'.

PWD   This variable holds the absolute pathname of the current working directory, as set by the `cd` command.

UID   This holds the user identity number of the current user. The value of this variable is stored as a string of characters, even though a user's UID is a numeric quantity.

PATH   When you enter a command at the keyboard, the shell needs to know where to find the executable file. The variable PATH is used to hold a colon (:) separated list of directory pathnames, which will be searched to find your command files. The directories are searched in the order given in PATH and the first executable file found whose name matches the required command will be run.

HOME   When you login to the system this variable holds the full pathname to your home directory.

The simplest way to examine the contents of a shell variable is to use the `echo` command. This command just displays any extra command line parameters you give to it back to the standard output:

```
$ echo three extra parameters
three extra parameters
$ echo UID
UID
```

Obviously, since using `echo` on the name of a shell variable (`UID` in the previous example) just displays the name of the variable and not its contents, there must be some other way to access the contents.

Whenever you wish to extract the value from a shell variable you need to precede its name with a dollar ($) symbol. The dollar is a special symbol whose meaning is interpreted by the shell. This also means that if you need to pass a dollar symbol as a parameter to another command, it will need to be quoted. Note that only the backslash and single-quote mechanisms for quoting will work on a dollar symbol. If you need a reminder about the shell quoting mechanisms, refer back to Section 4.1. The value of the `UID` variable can be displayed as follows:

```
$ echo the value of UID is $UID
the value of UID is 500
```

The `echo` command is very useful in shell scripts, because of its ability to display text messages and the values of shell variables.

A shell variable can have a new value assigned to it with the syntax:

`variable=value`

The following sequence changes the value of `PS1` and, consequently, the shell's primary prompt string will change:

```
$ PS1='hello: '
hello: echo prompt is now $PS1
prompt is now hello:
```

Notice that in the line which actually changes the value of the variable, the variable name does not have a dollar symbol in front of it. The dollar notation is only used when you are extracting a value from a variable, not when a value is being assigned. Also notice that, in the assignment, there are no spaces on either side of the equals (=) sign. If you put spaces into these positions the shell will not recognize the line as a variable assignment and will probably generate an error message.

In addition to the standard set of shell variables you are free to create your own variables and to assign values to them. The shell does not complain if you try to access the value of a variable which has not yet been assigned. The shell just returns an empty string as the value:

```
$ echo $sn flowers are pretty
flowers are pretty
$ sn=sun
$ echo $sn flowers are pretty
sun flowers are pretty
```

If you wanted the previous output to be `sunflowers are pretty` then you would need to eliminate the space between the value of the variable `sn` and the word `flowers`. As you can see in the following example, the obvious solution to this problem doesn't work:

```
$ echo $snflowers are pretty
are pretty
```

Just removing the space on the command line has caused the shell to treat the new word `snflowers` as a variable name, and one which currently has no value. The standard way round this problem is to enclose the required variable name in a pair of curly braces, thus separating the name from the following word, but without having a space between them:

```
$ echo ${sn}flowers are pretty
sunflowers are pretty
```

In general, it is acceptable to change the value of an existing variable just by re-assigning it a new value:

```
$ sn='all kinds of '
$ echo ${sn}flowers are pretty
all kinds of flowers are pretty
```

In this example, the quotes around the string being assigned to the variable `sn` are needed because the string is to contain spaces. Normally, the shell will split a line of input into separate words, using the spaces as the split points. In this example it is required that the string of characters, including its spaces, all be assigned to the shell variable.

Sometimes you will want to declare a variable, set it to a particular value and then want to prevent that value from being changed. This can be done by setting the variable up as `readonly`, once its initial value has been assigned:

```
$ readonly sn
$ sn=sun
bash: sn: read-only variable
$ echo ${sn}flowers are pretty
all kinds of flowers are pretty
```

As another example, there is also a standard shell variable, which you have already seen, that is set up as `readonly` – the `UID` variable. This obviously needs to be `readonly` as its value is set when the user logs in, from the user's UID in the password file, and is not a value which can just be changed at will.

Whenever you create a variable it is just local to the current shell. This means that the values of your local shell variables cannot be seen by other commands or scripts run from your shell. Quite often, it would be useful for these values to be made available to the commands that the shell executes. This can be done with the command `export`. In the previous example, the variable `sn` is a local variable, which can be made available to subsequent commands as follows:

```
$ export sn
```

The `export` operation on a variable can also be performed at the same time as it is assigned a value, as a one line command:

```
$ export sn=sun
```

6.3 Shell Script Parameters

The `dirsize` shell script we wrote earlier has one major problem: it will only give a count of the number of files in the directory `/usr/bin` as this pathname is built into the script. It would be much more useful if it were possible to specify the pathname of the directory to use, so that you could find the number of files in any given directory. Ideally, then, you would want to be able to give a command like the following:

```
$ dirsize /etc
```

and have `dirsize` count the number of files in that directory instead.

In fact, this is quite easy, because the shell automatically splits up any command line you enter into separate words, and then assigns the words to a set of special variables, whose values can be read inside a shell script. The values of these special variables can be accessed with the notation $0, $1, $2, and so on. The value in $0 will be the first word on the line (i.e. the command name), the value in $1 will be the first command line parameter, $2 will be the second command line parameter etc. The values starting with $1, $2, etc., are called *positional parameters*. For example, if a shell script named `test1` was executed as follows:

```
$ test1 param1 param2
```

then inside the shell script, the values of the special variables would be:

```
$0 = test1
$1 = param1
$2 = param2
```

Given this information, it is now a simple matter to modify `dirsize` to perform as required:

```
$ cat >dirsize
ls $1 | wc -w
Ctrl-d
$ chmod 700 dirsize
$ dirsize /etc
```

As you can see, when the shell script is run, the parameter (/etc) is substituted into the ls command in the pipeline, in place of the $1. This substitution is done by the shell and the ls command has no idea that it has taken place.

In order that you can access this new command wherever you are in the directory hierarchy, you need to make sure that the directory which contains the command is listed in your PATH variable. The next example creates a bin directory under your home directory, moves the dirsize command into it and adds this bin directory to the start of your PATH so that the directory will be searched automatically by the shell whenever you enter a command name. The value of the shell variable HOME is used in the example, as it contains the pathname of your home directory:

```
$ echo $PATH
/bin:/usr/bin:.
$ mkdir $HOME/bin
$ mv dirsize $HOME/bin
$ PATH=$HOME/bin:$PATH
$ echo $PATH
/usr1/pc/bin:/bin:/usr/bin:.
```

Remember that the list of directories contained in the PATH variable are separated by colons. The initial contents of PATH show that three directories will be searched for any commands you enter: /bin first, then /usr/bin and, finally, dot, the current directory. The command sequence then modifies the value of PATH by adding /usr1/pc/bin: onto the front of the PATH, so that this directory is searched before the other three, whenever a command is entered.

An alternative notation which you can use when you want to refer to your home directory, in place of $HOME, is to use the *tilde* (~) symbol. Using this notation $HOME/bin is the same as ~/bin. The tilde notation can also be extended by following it with the login name of another user. In this case the notation expands to be the pathname of the home directory of the specified user. For example:

```
$ ls ~carey/bin
```

would list the contents of bin under the home directory of user carey, assuming that I have permission to read the contents of this directory.

6.4 Login Scripts

Performing actions like changing your PS1 shell prompt can be quite fun. And adding personal extras to the contents of PATH can be very useful. However, when you have to perform these actions every time you login before they will take effect, it can soon become quite tedious.

The solution to this problem is to create a personal login script which the shell will automatically read and execute for you when you login. A personal login script is effectively just a shell script that gets executed at login time. If you have a personal login script, it must be stored in your home directory. When you login, `bash` will look in your home directory for one of three specific file names. These are:

```
~/.bash_profile
~/.bash_login
~/.profile
```

`bash` looks for the three file names in this order and just executes the first one of them that it finds.

When you logout, `bash` can also execute a personal logout script. Again, this must be stored in your home directory and under the name:

```
~/.bash_logout
```

In addition to the personal scripts that `bash` can execute, it is also possible for the system administrator to create a global login script called:

```
/etc/profile
```

which `bash` will execute for every user as they login. This allows the system administrator to set up local configurations for the system as a whole. If it exists, the global login script will be executed before your personal script so that your personal script can customize your environment even further. For example, something which often appears in this global file is the line which sets the shell to ignore end-of-file (`Ctrl-d`) for logging out. If the file contains a line with the word `ignoreeof` then removing the line will allow you to log out with `Ctrl-d`.

The next example shows how easy it is to set up a personal login script to customize your shell prompt and add your own `bin` directory to the list in `PATH`:

```
$ cat >~/.profile
PS1='What Now! '
PATH=~/bin:$PATH
Ctrl-d
```

6.5 More Variable Assignment Methods

The previous examples have shown how to assign a simple string to a specified variable. There are two other circumstances under which you might want a value assigned to a variable: first, you may want to have a shell script take a value interactively from the keyboard, which you subsequently wish to store in a variable and, second, you may wish to execute a command and have the standard output from the command redirected into a variable instead of displayed to the screen. As you may have guessed, both of these types of variable assignment are available.

6.5.1 Interactive Input

A shell script can take lines of characters from the standard input and assign them to one or more variables using the **read** command. In its simplest form, the **read** command is just used on its own, with no variables specified. In this case, the string read in from the standard input is assigned to the variable REPLY. If you make an executable shell script called *readtest1* out of the text:

```
echo -n 'Enter some text: '
read
echo The text was: $REPLY
```

and then run it, you will get a result like the following:

```
$ readtest1
Enter some text: THIS IS THE TEXT I ENTERED!!
The text was: THIS IS THE TEXT I ENTERED!!
```

Normally, when **echo** is used, it will automatically add a newline character to the end of the line, so that any further output will begin on the next line. As the example shows, using the -n switch to **echo** causes **echo** to suppress the newline output so that any subsequent characters sent to the display will follow on, on the same line. In this case the text that follows on is the text you enter in response to the **read** command. As you can see, this allows you to give a prompt from within a shell script and take a response immediately after it, on the same line.

If you specify a variable name after a **read** command then the input line will be assigned to that variable instead of the variable REPLY.

A more interesting case is what happens when you specify more than one variable after the **read** command. Consider the shell script *readtest2*:

```
echo -n 'Enter some text: '
read one two restofline
echo The first word was: $one
echo The second word was: $two
echo The rest of the line was: $restofline
```

When executed, this script will **read** a line of input as before. This time, however, the line will be split into separate words. The first word will be assigned to the first variable listed, the second word will be assigned to the second variable, third word to the third variable, and so on, until you run out of either words or variables (or both).

If you run out of words and variables together, then that's fine because each variable will have one word assigned to it:

```
$ readtest2
Enter some text: 1 2 3
```

```
The first word was: 1
The second word was: 2
The rest of the line was: 3
```

If you run out of words first this just means that the later variables will not be assigned a value from the input but will be set to empty (or NULL) instead:

```
$ readtest2
Enter some text: 1 2
The first word was: 1
The second word was: 2
The rest of the line was:
```

If there are more words than variables, then each variable has its expected word assigned to it, but then, rather than throw the extra words away they are appended to the value contained in the last variable in the list:

```
$ readtest2
Enter some text: 1 2 3 4
The first word was: 1
The second word was: 2
The rest of the line was: 3 4
```

The read command has a fairly wide definition for what it counts as a word – any string of characters delimited by a space, a tab or a newline. In fact, this list of delimiters is just the default, and the characters are stored in a shell variable called IFS. Because of this, it is possible to change the set of delimiters to other values, if required.

6.5.2 Command Substitution

Command substitution allows the standard output from a pipeline to be used in place of the pipeline itself. A simple example might help to make this clear:

```
$ date
Wed Jun 14 22:50:52 BST 1995
$ datestore=`date`
$ echo $datestore
Wed Jun 14 22:51:11 BST 1995
```

In this example, the date command is used to show the format of its output. Then, the same command is executed again, this time between a pair of backquotes (`` ` ``), which makes the standard output from date available, here to be assigned to the variable datestore.

An alternative notation which achieves the same effect is to enclose the command or pipeline in parentheses and precede this with a dollar symbol:

```
$ datestore=$(date)
$ echo $datestore
Wed Jun 14 22:53:21 BST 1995
```

Another command which is used quite often in command substitution is called basename. What this command does is to take a full file pathname as a parameter and return the base file name with the path stripped off. For example:

```
$ basefile=`basename /usr/bin/man`
$ echo $basefile
man
```

6.6 Automatic Status Variables

When you execute a Linux command it can either run to completion with no errors, or it can encounter some problem which prevents it from fulfilling its task. If you use a command in a shell script, it can be very useful to know which of these events occurred, so that if there is an error then some kind of remedial action can be taken. All the Linux commands are arranged so that they will return a value when they terminate. This value is called the *exit status*. An exit status of zero means that the command was successful, while any non-zero value means the command was unsuccessful. In the case of a pipeline, the exit status that gets returned is just the exit status of the last (right most) command in the pipeline.

Whenever you run a command or a pipeline, the shell has a special variable called $? which is assigned the value of the returned exit status:

```
$ cd /zz
bash: /zz: No such file or directory
$ echo $?
1
$ echo $?
0
```

In this example, trying to change directory to /zz fails because the directory does not exist. Consequently, displaying the value of $? shows that the exit status from cd was non-zero. Notice that displaying the contents of $? for a second time gives a different result. This is because the variable's value is updated after each command or pipeline is completed, and the second display is actually showing that the first echo command executed successfully.

A shell script can itself return an exit status by using the exit command. You should get into the habit of specifying explicit and appropriate exit status values to be returned by your shell scripts:

```
$ cat >tryexit
```

```
          exit 55
          Ctrl-d
       $ chmod 700 tryexit
       $ tryexit
       $ echo $?
       55
```

The variable $? is just one of several special variables used by bash for various status applications and which are available within a shell script. The main ones are:

- $? This variable holds the exit status returned by the last command to be executed by the shell.
- $$ This variable contains the PID of the current shell. This value is very often used for generating unique temporary file names for use within the script (e.g. /tmp/tmp$$).
- $# This holds the number of command line parameters that were passed to the current script. This value corresponds to the number of the $1, $2, etc., variables currently in use.
- $* This variable contains a list of all command line parameters ($1, $2, etc.) that were passed to the current script.

Each of these special variables may only have its value read. Assignment to them is not allowed, except by the shell, which automatically updates them as given in the previous table.

6.7 Flow Control

In common with other high level programming languages, the shell provides a set of commands which are used to control the flow of execution around the code. These include several selection and looping constructs which allow really sophisticated programs to be constructed.

As you will see, the only slightly unusual thing about these constructs is the way that commands and strings are used to specify conditional values, where in a more conventional language a boolean expression would be used.

6.7.1 if Command

You have seen that when the shell executes a command or pipeline, an exit status is returned. One way to determine what action is to be performed next is to use a construct which can test the value returned by a command and use it to make a selection. The `if` command performs this function. The general format of the `if` command is:

```
if condition_command
then
     true_commands
else
     false_commands
fi
```

What happens is that the `condition_command` is executed and its exit status is then used to determine which of `true_commands` or `false_commands` will be run next. Don't forget that it is the exit status value zero which indicates that a command executed successfully, and hence it is the zero value that is used as the *true* condition. Any non-zero exit status value indicates *false*.

The `else` clause and the `false_commands` are optional and without them the `if` command appears as:

```
if condition_command
then
     true_commands
fi
```

As an example of the use of `if`, consider the following script, which I will call user1, that takes a word as a parameter and checks the password file to see if the parameter is a valid user login name on the system:

```
# usage is: user1 login_name
if grep "^$1:" /etc/passwd >/dev/null 2>/dev/null
then
     echo $1 is a valid login name
else
     echo $1 is not a valid login name
fi
exit 0
```

In this case, the conditional test is performed by a `grep` command whose standard output and error output are discarded, because all that is required is its exit status. This value will be zero (true) if `grep` successfully finds the word it is looking for or non-zero (false) otherwise. A suitable message is then sent to the standard output:

```
$ user1 bash
bash is not a valid login name
$ user1 mot
mot is a valid login name
```

104 *Shell Scripts*

user1 is smart enough in the first run that, even though the word `bash` does appear in the password file, it does not appear at the start of a line followed by a colon (as required by ^$1:). This is not to say that user1 cannot be fooled, as the following example shows:

```
$ user1 carey:esJ9ohd8HH89i
carey:esJ9ohd8HH89i is a valid login name
```

As the code for user1 shows, the use of a hash (#) symbol allows the introduction of comments into a shell script. After the hash, the comment just extends to the end of the current line.

6.7.2   test Command

If there is a standard command which does what you need, then it is now a simple matter to execute it and test its exit status to see if it was successful. If it did not succeed in some way then repeat attempts or remedial action are easy to arrange. This still leaves a large number of conditions for which you might like to test and for which none of the commands you have seen so far will provide a suitable function. There is, however, a command available, called `test`, which doesn't take any input or generate any output, whose sole purpose is to test for a range of conditions and return an appropriate exit status. The `test` command has the general form:

```
test expression
```

If the specified *expression* is true then `test` will return a zero exit status; otherwise, if it is false, an exit status of 1 is returned.

One point worthy of note here is that when you are writing simple shell scripts and programs to test out some idea, it is very easy to give the name `test` to the resulting file. When you come to execute your program then you may actually execute the Linux `test` command instead of your own (depending on the order of directories given in your `PATH` variable). Executing the Linux `test` command with no parameters does nothing and just returns the next shell prompt. This gives the impression that your test program didn't work. The same argument applies to any standard Linux command but `test` is a particularly easy one to get wrong.

There are several types of expression that `test` can test for. The most common expression types check a file for some attribute, perform various string comparisons or perform numeric comparisons.

In the first case, a command line switch is given, followed by a single parameter, which is the name of a file. The `test` command then just checks the file for the attribute specified by the switch and gives an exit status based on the result. The most common of these command line switches are:

-e *f*   returns true if the file *f* exists;
-f *f*   returns true if *f* is an ordinary file;
-d *f*   returns true if *f* is a directory;
-r *f*   true if *f* is readable by you;
-w *f*   true if *f* is writable by you;
-x *f*   true if *f* is executable by you.

Expressions of the string type can have one or two string parameters, which can either be literal strings or the contents of shell variables. The most common string expressions are:

-z *str*   true if length of *str* is zero;
-n *str*   true if length of *str* is non-zero;
str1 = *str2*   true if *str1* and *str2* are equal;
str1 != *str2* true if *str1* and *str2* are not equal.

The numeric expression type gives facilities for treating the contents of a string or variable as a number, and performing standard numeric comparisons. The list of numeric expressions are:

num1 -eq *num2*   true if *num1* equal to *num2*;
num1 -ne *num2*   true if *num1* not equal to *num2*;
num1 -lt *num2*   true if *num1* less than *num2*;
num1 -gt *num2*   true if *num1* greater than *num2*;
num1 -le *num2*   true if *num1* less than or equal to *num2*;
num1 -ge *num2*   true if *num1* greater than or equal to *num2*.

The **test** command can also combine its expressions using the logical AND, OR and NOT operators:

exp1 -a *exp2*   true if both *exp1* and *exp2* are true;
exp1 -o *exp2*   true if either *exp1* or *exp2* is true;
! *exp*   true if *exp* is false and vice versa.

As well as **test** being able to compare strings as though they were numeric values, there is a complementary feature in the shell which allows **bash** to perform simple arithmetic operations and to build arithmetic expressions, with the general form:

    $[expression]

The following example demonstrates this idea in action:

    $ num1=2
    $ num1=$[$num1*3+1]
    $ echo $num1
    7

106 *Shell Scripts*

The following is a simple shell script, called *later*, which makes use of the test command to perform simple comparisons and combines this with the arithmetic expression evaluation features of the shell to work out and display what the time will be a given number of hours from the current time:

```
if test $# -ne 1            # Check for `hours` parameter
then
    echo "usage:   later <hours>"
    exit 1
fi
now=`date`                  # Get and split current time
hour=`echo $now | cut -b 11-12`
minsec=`echo $now | cut -b 13-18`
hour=$[($hour+$1)%24]       # Add `hours` to current hour
if test $hour -ge 12a       # Convert to 12 hour clock
then                        #    and print later time
    echo $[$hour-12]$minsec pm
else
    echo $hour$minsec am
fi
exit 0
```

The script starts off by checking that there is a command line parameter specified. It does this by checking the value of $# and terminating the script with a usage message if the number of parameter values is not equal to 1.

Next, the date command is used to supply the current date and time. The time, which is in 24 hour clock format, is extracted and stored in the variables hour and minsec.

The next line of the script adds the value given on the command line to the current hour and then uses the modulus (%) operator to handle the situation where the new hour value is greater than 24.

Finally, the script does a conversion of the time from 24 hour to 12 hour clock time and displays the 12 hour time, adding am or pm to the end of the string as appropriate.

Executing the later command gives results such as the following:

```
$ later 5
8:32:42 pm
$ later 12
3:32:49 am
```

6.7.3 while Command

The while command allows you to introduce conditional loops into your shell scripts. The general form of the command is:

```
while condition
do
     commands
done
```

The *condition* can be any command or pipeline whose exit status will be used to determine the next action. If the exit status is true (zero) then the commands enclosed between do and done will be executed, followed by a jump back to the top of the loop to re-evaluate the condition. If the exit status is false (non-zero) then the commands are skipped, and execution continues with whatever follows the keyword done.

A simple example will help to make the idea clear. The following shell script, called `filecheck`, will repeatedly test to make sure that a given file still exists. As soon as the file is removed, the loop will terminate and the script will exit:

```
while test -e $1
do
     :
done
exit 0
```

The colon (:) between do and done is just a way of specifying a null command that does nothing. There is no action to perform in the body of this loop, but without the colon bash would generate an error, as it will not allow an empty loop.

Normally, you would run a script like this in the background because, otherwise, you would not get a prompt back from the shell until the specified file had been deleted, and that might be a long wait!

Leaving this command running in the background, it will use up quite a lot of processing power, as it does not pause, but continuously re-tests for the existence of the file. In this particular application it may well be adequate to test for the file once every few seconds, rather than as fast as possible. If this is the case, then the colon command can be replaced by the sleep command, which causes execution of the script to be suspended for a specified number of seconds, during which the script will place no load on the processor so that other processes can make use of the time:

```
while test -e $1
do
     sleep 2
done
echo file $1 does not exist...
exit 0
```

This version of `filecheck` has also had an echo command added to it so that you will receive a message when the specified file no longer exists. The following sequence creates a file, runs `filecheck` in the background to test for this file and then deletes the file to make sure that the *file does not exist* message is displayed:

108 *Shell Scripts*

```
$ cat >lock
Ctrl-d
$ filecheck lock &
[1] 2364
$ rm lock
file lock does not exist...
```

Notice that the `cat` command in this example is just being used to create an empty file. There are other ways that this can be done. One of the simplest is to use the `touch` command. The actual purpose of this command is to update the timestamp on a file (given by `ls -l`) to the current time. However, as a side effect, using `touch` on a file that does not yet exist will create the file first as an empty file, and then update its timestamp:

```
$ ls -l lock
ls: lock: No such file or directory
$ touch lock
$ ls -l lock
-rw-r--r--   1 pc       book            0 Jul  3 21:52 lock
```

6.7.4 until Command

The `until` command is another looping construct. It is very similar to the `while` command, and has the general structure:

```
until condition
do
     commands
done
```

The difference between `while` and `until` is that `while` continues to loop for as long as its condition evaluates to true, whereas `until` does the opposite and continues to loop for as long as its condition evaluates to false.

This would make the `until` command ideal if, for example, you needed a script to wait until a given file existed before it terminated:

```
until test -e $1
do
     sleep 2
done
echo file $1 now exists...
exit 0
```

Sometimes, you need to create a loop that goes round indefinitely. What is required for this is a command that always returns an exit status of zero (to make while loop indefinitely) or non-zero (to make until loop indefinitely). These two commands are called true and false respectively. For example:

```
until false
do
    read firstword restofline
    if test $firstword = end
    then
        exit 0
    else
        echo $firstword $restofline
    fi
done
```

This shell script reads in lines of text and echoes them back to the display. This continues until a line is read that begins with the word *end*.

6.7.5 for Loops

The if, until and while commands all use exit status values to control their actions. There are occasions when you would like to perform looping or selection based on string values rather than exit status values, and bash also makes provision for this need.

Imagine you want to write a shell script that can look to see which, if any, of a given set of login names exist in the password file. In fact, you have already seen a script which can go part of the way towards this, in Section 6.7.1. There, the script called user1 just took one name (in $1) and grepped the password file for it. All you really need is just to apply the user1 script repeatedly for each of a set of names ($1, $2 etc.).

To do this, you use the for command. The general format of this command is:

```
for variable in wordlist
do
    commands
done
```

The idea is that the specified *variable* takes each of the values given in *wordlist* in turn, and then executes *commands* with those values. For example:

```
for i in 1 2 3 4 5
do
    echo value of i is $i
done
```

when executed would give the output:

```
value of i is 1
value of i is 2
value of i is 3
value of i is 4
value of i is 5
```

Now going back to the original problem, all you need to remember is that the special variable $* gives a list of all the positional parameters passed into a shell script, and it then becomes a simple matter to code up a solution to the problem. One possibility (called user2) could be:

```
for i in $*
do
    if grep "^$i:" /etc/passwd >/dev/null 2>/dev/null
    then
        echo $i is a valid login name
    else
        echo $i is not a valid login name
    fi
done
exit 0
```

Running this script gives output such as the following:

```
$ user2 carey jill rnc bill
carey is a valid login name
jill is not a valid login name
rnc is a valid login name
bill is not a valid login name
```

The use of 'for variable in $*' is such a common construction that it can be abbreviated just to 'for variable' and the command will automatically assume the 'in $*' part.

6.7.6 case Selection

Selecting one possibility from a number of choices, based on the contents of a string or variable, is done with the case command. The general form of the command is:

```
case string in
expression_1)
    commands_1
    ;;
expression_2)
    commands_2
```

```
        ;;
     .
     .
     .
*)
        default_commands
        ;;
esac
```

In executing a `case` command, the shell evaluates the *string* and then compares the result with each of *expression_1*, *expression_2*, etc., in turn, until it finds a match. If a match is found, then the associated commands will be executed, up to a double semi-colon (;;).

The `case` expressions may also be given as simple regular expressions, using the same set of special characters that the shell can expand in file names (namely, *, ? and []). This means that using *) as the last expression in a `case` command will match any string and thus act as a default entry if all previous matches fail.

As an example of the use of the `case` command, consider the following script, called **append**, which allows text, either typed at the keyboard or read from an input file, to be added onto the end of a specified output file:

```
case $# in
1)
    cat >>$1
    ;;
2)
    cat >>$1 <$2
    ;;
*)
    echo "usage: append out_file [in_file]"
    ;;
esac
exit 0
```

Remember that the `$#` variable is set to contain the number of positional parameters entered on the command line, excluding the command name itself. For the append script, this value should only be either 1 or 2, depending on the source for the input text.

The square brackets which appear in the usage message are just there to indicate that the enclosed item is optional. This application of square brackets is in fairly common use in Linux command documentation.

6.8 Signals

You already know that you can stop the execution of most running programs by interrupting them from the keyboard, usually with Ctrl-c.

What actually happens is that the part of the Linux kernel software that controls the keyboard, sends a message to the running process. This message is called a *signal*, a concept you saw briefly in Section 2.6 when you first met the kill command. In fact, there are about 30 different signal types that can be sent to a Linux process, each of which is generated by some specific hardware or software condition. In addition to the normal mechanisms for generating and sending signals, the kill command can also be used to send any signal to a process at will.

Each of the signals is given a small integer value which is used as a command line switch to kill, along with the process ID of the process to which the signal should be sent. The general format of the kill command is:

    kill [-sig] pid

where *sig* is the number of the signal to send and *pid* is the process ID to which it should be sent. The square brackets just indicate that the specification of the pid is optional – the brackets themselves should not be typed. If a signal number is not specified to the kill command then the *terminate* signal is used by default.

Some of the more common signals and their numeric values are:

Signal	Value	Notes
hangup	1	used to kill your processes when you logout
interrupt	2	generated from the keyboard (Ctrl-c)
quit	3	generated from the keyboard (Ctrl-\)
kill	9	sure process termination – cannot be ignored
alarm	14	generated at the end of an alarm() system call
terminate	15	default signal sent by kill command

When a process receives a signal, it can normally do one of three different things:

1. ignore the signal;
2. accept the signal's default action;
3. execute some code to deal with the signal.

The default action for most signals is just to terminate the receiving process (this is why Ctrl-c from the keyboard will usually terminate a process). To change from this default action requires a process to perform some positive setup procedure. In the case of the *kill* signal (which is signal number 9) this default action cannot be changed, so that a process which receives a kill signal will be terminated.

From inside a shell script it is possible to trap a signal and then to get a sequence of commands executed when that signal is received. This is done with the trap command. There are three basic forms for the trap command, one for each of the three different signal response types:

```
trap "commands" signal_list
```

In this form, **trap** will execute the *commands* in the quotes when any of the signals corresponding to the numbers in the *signal_list* is received by the script.

To restore signals to their default action, use the **trap** command in the form:

```
trap signal_list
```

without any commands specified.

The third form, which allows signals to be ignored, has the format:

```
trap "" signal_list
```

which just specifies a null commands string.

A typical example of the use of **trap** is to clean up temporary files when abnormal termination of a program occurs which might otherwise leave these files cluttering up your file space. The following code fragment assumes that a unique temporary file, called /tmp/tmp$$, is to be created for use within the script and that if abnormal termination of the script occurs, on receipt of either an interrupt or a quit signal, the temporary file needs to be deleted as a clean up operation before the script terminates:

```
trap "rm -f /tmp/tmp$$; exit 0" 2 3
touch /tmp/tmp$$
#
# Rest of shell script here
#
trap 2 3
```

This script starts by setting itself up to **trap** signals 2 and 3 (Ctrl-c and Ctrl-\ from the keyboard). If either of these two signals occurs, it will usually be because the user is trying to break into the script and abort its operation. After the **trap** has executed, signals 2 and 3 will cause execution of the commands:

```
rm -f /tmp/tmp$$; exit 0
```

The **rm** command will remove the temporary file and the exit command then terminates the script. Notice that multiple commands can be entered on the same line if they are separated by semi-colons.

Once the **trap** command has executed, the rest of the shell script will execute as normal, starting with the creation of the temporary file by the **touch** command. The last line of this script fragment restores the operation of signals 2 and 3 to their default state, presumably after the temporary file is no longer needed and has thus already been deleted.

Exercises

Write shell scripts to perform each of the following actions:

1. Take the names of two directories as parameters. Copy all the files in the first directory into the second directory and translate all of the occurrences of the string SP in any of the files into SU during the copy.
2. Check to see if your PATH variable contains /usr/local/bin as one of the directories to search, and display a suitable message.
3. Read lines of text from the standard input device and copy them to the standard output. Precede each output line with a line number in a similar manner to cat -n (without using the cat command).
4. Accept a number in the range 2 to 15 inclusive as a parameter and draw on the standard output a square of that size using the symbols plus (+), minus (-) and vertical bar (|), so:

    ```
    $ drawsquare 4
    +--+
    |  |
    |  |
    +--+
    ```

    If the number of parameters given to the command is wrong or the parameter is not a number in the correct range, a suitable error message should be displayed and an exit status of one returned.
5. Take two command line parameters, the first of which is the name of a directory, and the second is a file size in bytes. The command should list all the regular files in the directory to which you have read access and that are smaller than the given size. You should check that only two parameters are passed to the command and that the first parameter is in fact a directory.

Answers

1. One possible solution could be to take each source pathname in turn, take the basename from this path, and then use sed to copy the source file to the destination directory using the same base name and performing the required translation as the copy is performed:

    ```
    for i in $1/*
    do
        x=`basename $i`
        sed s/SP/SU/ $i >$2/$x
    done
    exit 0
    ```

2. It is a simple matter to use `grep` to see if `PATH` contains the name of the directory `/usr/local/bin`, and display an appropriate message:

   ```
   if echo $PATH | grep "/usr/local/bin" &>/dev/null
   then
         echo PATH contains /usr/local/bin
   else
         echo PATH does not contain /usr/local/bin
   fi
   exit 0
   ```

   Notice that the output and error output from the `grep` command are both being discarded, as only the exit status from `grep` is significant.

3. The easiest way to sort this out is to use the numeric expression evaluation facilities of the shell to maintain a line count which can be `echo`ed to the standard output at the start of each output line and then incremented ready for the next line:

   ```
   linecount=1
   while read line
   do
         echo $linecount $line
         linecount=$[$linecount+1]
   done
   exit 0
   ```

4. This solution to the problem starts by checking the command line parameter for errors. Then the code works from left to right and top to bottom across the character positions of the output square, working out with some simple logic which of the four characters to display at each position:

   ```
   if test $# -ne "1"
   then
         echo 'usage: drawsquare <n>'
         exit 1
   fi
   if test $1 -lt "2" -o $1 -gt "15"
   then
         echo 'usage: drawsquare <n>'
         echo '       (where 2<=n<=15)'
         exit 1
   fi
   xcount=$1
   ycount=$1
   while test $ycount -gt "0"
   do
   ```

```
            while test $xcount -gt "0"
            do
                if test $xcount -eq "1" -o $xcount -eq $1
                then
                    if test $ycount -eq "1" -o $ycount -eq $1
                    then
                        echo -n "+"
                    else
                        echo -n "|"
                    fi
                else
                    if test $ycount -eq "1" -o $ycount -eq $1
                    then
                        echo -n "-"
                    else
                        echo -n " "
                    fi
                fi
                xcount=$[$xcount-1]
            done
            xcount=$1
            ycount=$[$ycount-1]
            echo
        done
        exit 0
```

5. For each file in the specified directory, tests are made to see if it is readable and a regular file. If this test is true then the file size is checked and the names of files smaller than the second parameter are displayed along with their sizes:

```
        if test $# -ne 2
        then
            echo 'usage: listfiles <dirpath> <size>'
            exit 1
        fi
        if ! test -d $1
        then
            echo 'usage: listfiles <dirpath> <size>'
            exit 1
        fi
        for i in $1/*
        do
            if test -r $i -a -f $i
            then
```

```
            size=`wc -c <$i`
            if test $size -lt $2
            then
                echo `basename $i` has size $size bytes
            fi
      fi
done
```

Part II

ADMINISTRATION

Chapter 7

Getting Up and Running

Ideally, you will come into Linux system administration slowly and after having had plenty of opportunity to explore and use the system as an ordinary user. When you do start the journey into administration you will hopefully have others around you who are already at various stages along the road ahead of you, and who will be able to guide your early steps. Or at least you will be one of a group of computing enthusiasts who want to make this journey together.

While this scenario will apply to many of you, there will still be many more without the necessary experience or assistance. If you really do find that you are initially on your own and that you have only limited experience of Linux, then this will be a slow and error prone business. In this position it is important not to become too frustrated or disheartened when things don't work right first time or when you don't immediately see how to do a particular thing despite having read the manual page a dozen times in order to wring the last drop of sense from it all – just take a deep breath... .

The first thing to remember about Linux, especially if you are running it on a PC and you have a DOS background, is that, despite all appearances, Linux is a big-machine operating system, even though you are running it on a small machine. You *must* cultivate big-machine operating system habits and mental attitudes if you are going to avoid many of the pitfalls which await to trap the unwary. The bottom line is that, even if it is not you, someone will need to be the system administrator for your system – while the amount of administrative effort can be minimal, it cannot be zero.

Even with all these warnings, the worst case scenario is that you manage to do something which trashes your installation. In this case, a very full Linux installation (about 150 Mb) from a very slow distribution medium (about 70 floppy disks) will still take no more than about two hours to complete in order to put you back in business.

7.1 Hardware

In order to run Linux on a PC or clone, the machine must support a minimum hardware configuration. However, the hardware requirements are very modest – the only real restrictions being that the CPU must be at least a 386, and that the size of the main memory should be at least 4 Mb.

In fact, the processor can be any flavor of 386, 486, or above, including SX, DX, SL, DX2, DX4, etc., varieties, produced by any of the leading CPU manufacturers, including AMD, Cyrix and Intel. If the main CPU includes a floating point co-processor, then Linux will use it for any floating point calculations. If there is no co-processor present (386SX and 486SX for example) then the Linux kernel can be configured to include a software floating point co-processor emulator, which will automatically be used instead.

The Linux kernel can drive main motherboards which use any of the standard bus architectures from the list: ISA, EISA, VESA local bus (VLB) or PCI. In addition, the motherboard should be fitted with at least 4 Mb of main memory for a single user machine, or 8 Mb for a single user configuration including X-windows. And 16 Mb, or even more, should be considered as a minimum for a machine which is also network connected and provides multiple user logins or some other network services. In addition to the physical RAM plugged into the motherboard, Linux is also able to treat part of your hard disk as though it is an extension of main memory. This virtual RAM on disk is traditionally known as *swap space*.

Apart from the processor and the memory requirements of a Linux system, the list of supported interface cards for such devices as CD-ROMs, disks, networks, graphics, modems, mice and sound is large and continually growing larger. Any list of supported cards I might give here is bound to be out of date by the time you read this. However, as part of the Linux documentation set, a group of files is provided called the Linux HOWTO documents. These documents give specific information on various aspects of hardware and software configuration for the Linux system, and one of them is particularly relevant at this point – the Hardware HOWTO. The latest version of this document will provide a reasonably up-to-date list of all the hardware supported by Linux and, if necessary, it will tell you how to get hold of any extra driver software you may need to use a particular interface card, though the drivers for most supported cards are supplied with the kernel source code.

Looking in general at the interface cards supported by Linux, the list is quite comprehensive. In terms of disk drives, Linux will support all the common disk controllers, including: MFM, RLL, IDE, most ESDI and many SCSI. The amount of disk space required for any particular installation will depend, to a large extent, upon which Linux distribution and which packages you choose to install. In general, however, a minimal installation will take up about 20 Mb of your hard disk space. Beyond that, you may well want to add some of the larger application programs, a more complete set of software development tools, system documentation and facilities for networking. These will take your installation up to around the 50 Mb to 70 Mb mark. Above that still, you may wish to add X-windows, TeX and LaTeX, more programming languages and tools. Altogether, you would now be looking at a disk space requirement in the 110 to 150 Mb range, and maybe even more. In addition to these sizes you would also need to add the amount of disk space you want to use for virtual RAM (i.e. for swapping) and the amount of space you want to allocate to the users of your machine, for their home directories and working storage.

Most modern PCs have Super VGA video cards and monitors. If you just want to display text on the screen, Linux can support any of these cards, as well as ordinary VGA, EGA, and various CGA and mono cards. However, if you want to be able to use graphics via the super VGA library or X-windows, then the choice is slightly more limited, but still includes the standard SVGA chipsets from Tseng, Western Digital, Trident, ATI, Cirrus Logic and more. Sadly, some SVGA cards are not supported, mainly because their manufacturers will not release details of how to drive them, which means that device drivers for these cards cannot officially be written. For an up-to-date list of the cards supported for graphics applications you should refer to another of the HOWTO documents – XFree86 HOWTO.

Setting up a Linux machine to operate on an Ethernet network is very straightforward – the kernel provides drivers for most inexpensive network cards, including those by 3com, Novell, Western Digital, Hewlett Packard and their clones. Again, for an up-to-date list, there is a HOWTO document available, which should be consulted – the Ethernet HOWTO.

For CD-ROM storage, Linux supports the standard ISO-9660 filesystem. Some CD-ROM drives use either an IDE or a SCSI interface. As long as you have a supported IDE or SCSI interface card, then these should work with no problems. In addition, several CD-ROM drives are supported which have proprietary interface cards, including several Mitsumi, Panasonic, Sony and Philips drives. Look in the CD-ROM HOWTO document for the latest list.

Finally, Linux supports a complete range of parallel printers, serial modems and serial and bus mice.

7.2 Distributions

Distributing Linux is not the responsibility of one person or even of one organization. Linux is freely available software and anyone can collect the necessary component parts and then be free to distribute them (under the Free Software Foundation's GNU General Public License (GPL), a copy of which is reproduced as Appendix B). For a major Linux distribution, the task of maintaining and distributing it is so difficult and time consuming that is is only undertaken by very dedicated and enthusiastic Linux supporters. Even so, there are still quite a number of distributions from which you may choose when you come to install Linux on your own machine.

The smaller distributions may fit on as few as four or five floppy disks, the larger ones may take up to a hundred, and yet others may take anything in between. Obviously, the smaller distributions can only contain a small core of the software available whereas the large distributions contain a very comprehensive set including most of the larger packages available, such as X-windows, emacs, ghostscript, TeX and LaTeX.

Which distribution you choose is purely a matter of personal preference, though to some extent it might also be guided by availability. If you have Internet access, and a growing number of potential Linux users do, then the situation is easy. Linux started as a system available over the Internet and this is still the most convenient way to access distributions and to get your questions answered. The best source of interactive information is via USENET news, which is like a global bulletin board that provides several newsgroups specifically for Linux related topics.

If you do not have Internet access, then there are still other on-line sources of Linux distributions, in the form of many local and national bulletin board systems.

Another, increasingly popular source of Linux distributions is on floppy disks and CD-ROMs available via mail-order, and many weekly or monthly magazines and journals now carry advertisements for these products. And many local computer stores and computer markets now sell floppy disk and CD-ROM distributions of Linux, though many of those I have encountered have no knowledge of the product and would not be able to answer technical questions.

A good source of information about various distributions is provided in another document in the HOWTO series – The Distribution HOWTO.

One of the most popular and complete Linux distributions, and one which seems to pop up all over the place, is called the *Slackware Distribution*. This distribution is supplied as a number of disk sets, each of which contains a number of software packages. The following disk sets are currently available:

- **A**   This is the base disk set which must be installed in a Slackware system, whatever else you choose to do.

- **AP**   Contains various application programs and packages which do not need X-windows to run. This includes lots of manual pages, a spell checker, several extra editors, ghostscript and a player for audio CDs in a CD-ROM drive.

- **D**   Software for program development, including: C/C++ compilers (called `gcc` and `g++`), lexical analyzer and parser generators (BSD `byacc` and GNU `bison` and `flex`), the source code debugger (GNU `gdb`), C libraries including the `SVGAlib` graphics library and the `ncurses` terminal control library, translators for other programming languages including lisp (`clisp`), fortran (`f2c`), pascal (`p2c`) and `perl`, plus the programmer's manual pages.

- **E**   GNU emacs, both with and without X-windows support.

F   A collection of all the HOWTO documents plus the frequently asked questions (FAQ) documents.

K   This set contains the source code for the Linux kernel (this was in the D set in early Slackware distributions).

I   A collection of user and system manuals for many of the GNU software development packages.

IV   Interviews X-windows library, including the sample applications `doc` and `idraw`.

N   Networking packages (TCP/IP, ppp, UUCP), mail packages (`mailx`, `deliver`, `elm`, `pine` and `sendmail`) and network news packages (`cnews`, `tin`, `trn` and `nn`).

OOP   Object oriented programming. Contains the GNU version of `smalltalk` and `STIX`, the smalltalk interface to X-windows.

Q   Lots of extra pre-built kernels for various hardware configurations. Frankly, provided you have the disk space available (up to 20 Mb) it is better to build your own, because then it will be exactly right.

T   TEX and LaTeX. A document formatting system, with professional typesetting rules built in. This book was formatted with LaTeX.

TCL   The `Tcl` scripting language and the `Tk` toolkit for rapid development of X-windows applications.

X   XFree86. The base X-windows system with the `fvwm` window manager.

XAP   Extra applications for X-windows, including: a paint package (`xpaint`), an image processing package (`xv` – Note that `xv` is currently unregistered shareware and not free software!), a spreadsheet `xspread`, several X-windows games, as well as a postscript previewer and print program (`ghostview`) and a modem communications program (`seyon`).

XD   Packages required to develop your own X-servers.

XV   The Xview libraries and the Open Look window managers and an X-windows audio CD player (`workman`).

126 *Getting Up and Running*

Y   Games that do not require X-windows including versions of asteroids, tetris and doom.

From this list you can see that you will end up with a fairly powerful and general system if you choose to install the: A, AP, D, F, K, N, X, XAP and Y disk sets.

In addition to the software packages to install, you will also need to obtain the associated software with which to install them. In the case of the Slackware distribution this is supplied on two extra disks along with the rest of the software. You should always read any README type files available with your distribution as these will often contain the very latest updates or changes to more general documentation.

7.3 Installing Linux

During the installation and configuration of your Linux system it is a good idea to write a log which records everything you did. In particular, you need to record the choices that you made whenever you needed to make a decision. You are bound to make some choices, which, when you appreciate all their implications, will turn out to have been the wrong ones. There are so many choices that you need to make, some of which will be quite arbitrary, that it is not always easy, when you repeat the exercise, to work out what selections you actually made – unless you write them down.

Once you have your distribution, the next step is to plan its installation. This is especially important if you expect Linux to co-exist with another operating system on the same machine – DOS for example. The biggest problem is going to be to decide how much of your disk space to set aside for each system. If you get this wrong then it can only really be solved by taking all the software off the machine, so that you can move the boundary between the two systems, and then re-installing it all again, with the new disk space sizes. Either that, or you will need to add an extra disk drive to cope with the overflow.

7.3.1 Disk Partitions

Assuming that you want DOS and Linux to co-exist on your machine when it is finished, the best starting point is from a machine with empty disks. If the machine is already given over entirely to DOS, then this will mean making a backup (surely you do this already???) of everything you can't replace from master disks, so that you can repartition the hard disk space to make room for the Linux software.

Under DOS, each disk can be split up into partitions. Up to four primary partitions can be created on each drive. For a simple installation on a single hard disk, this will usually be enough. For example, with a single 320 Mb disk, you might partition the space into three pieces, as in Figure 7.1.

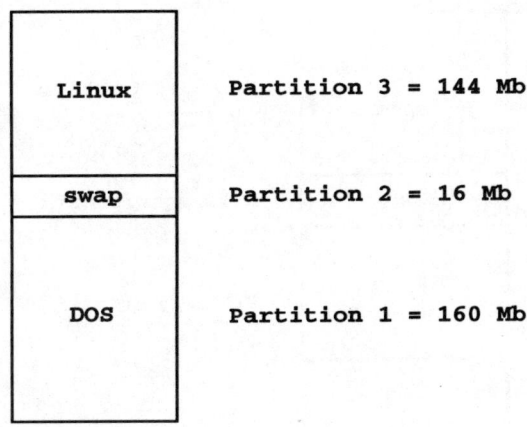

Figure 7.1 Partitioning a 320 Mb hard disk.

Here, the first partition has been set aside for DOS use as the C: drive, the second partition will be used as swap space under Linux and the third partition will be used to hold the Linux root filesystem. Each separate filesystem under Linux will have its own disk partition.

Sometimes you will want to use more than four partitions on a hard drive, especially if it is a rather large drive. In this case, one of the four primary disk partitions can be used as an extended partition. The extended partition is then used like a container to hold a set of logical disk partitions (up to 23 of them under DOS).

In addition to considering extended and logical disk partitions, for really large disk drives, a new problem pops into the frame. Due to a design oversight (the designers couldn't imagine hard drives becoming available that would be big enough to break their design limits...) you cannot generally boot a PC from a disk partition that uses disk cylinder numbers greater than 1023 (unless you have a modern motherboard whose BIOS supports large drives). For Linux, this means that its root filesystem must lie entirely in a partition under the 1024 cylinder boundary. Linux can hold data and programs in partitions above the boundary; you just can't boot Linux from these partitions. For an IDE disk, the 1024 cylinder limit comes at 504 Mb.

Suppose, then, that you have a 720 Mb IDE disk and you want to partition it to give a 150 Mb DOS C: drive, a 200 Mb DOS D: drive (probably to use as a compressed drive), a 16 Mb Linux swap partition and then the rest of the disk (354 Mb) for Linux filesystem space. Figure 7.2 shows one possible disk partitioning arrangement which takes all the constraints into account.

Notice that the Linux space has been split into two parts, so that the partition holding the root filesystem can fit below the 504 Mb boundary. This leaves the problem of where in the Linux directory tree the other Linux filesystem/partition can usefully be mounted. One obvious division, and the one shown here, is to split the Linux space into a system partition and a user partition. All of the Linux in-

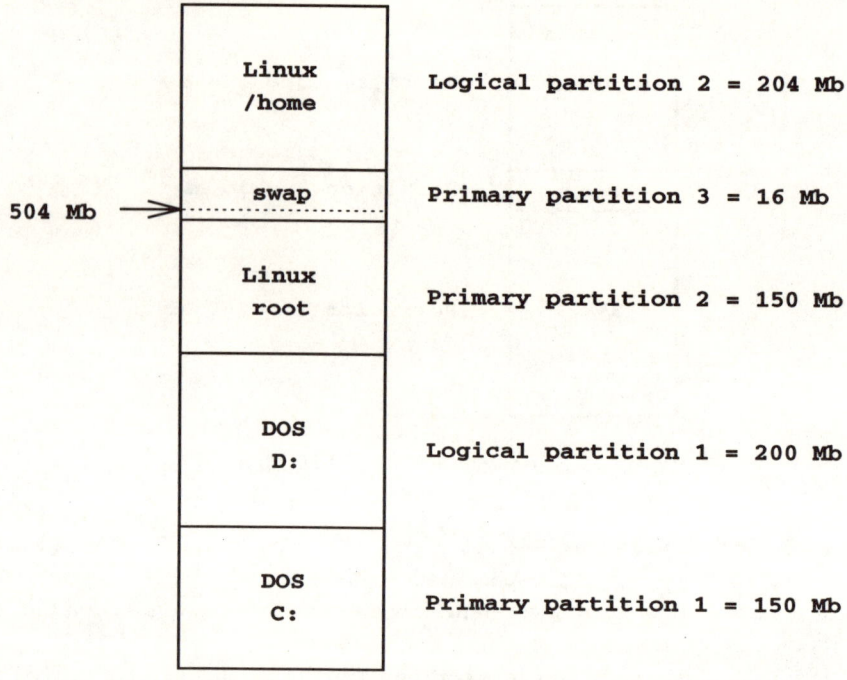

Figure 7.2 Partitioning a 720 Mb hard disk.

stallation will then be made into the `root` partition, which leaves the other partition initially empty and allows it to be used as user home directory and working space, by mounting it as `/home`. Many other arrangements are possible and you may need to experiment until you find the one that suits your own particular circumstances best.

The program used to partition disks is called `fdisk`, both under DOS and under Linux. In general, you should only create the partitions to be used within a particular operating system using that system's own `fdisk` command. So the first task in our example is to install DOS from the master disks, using the DOS `fdisk` command to create just the required DOS partitions, leaving the rest of the disk space unallocated.

Most Linux distributions supply a one- or two-disk set, which you need to use to boot Linux on your machine initially. With the Slackware distribution there are two disks required, called the `boot` and `root` disks. In fact, there are several different versions of each of them, and you will need to select an appropriate one of each. The choice is based on what type of hard disk you will be installing to (SCSI or not) and what medium you will be using as the source of the files to install from (CD-ROM, floppy disk, hard disk or network).

You should consult the release notes supplied with your distribution (probably as a README file or a thin paper leaflet) to help you make the appropriate choice and to tell you how to create the `boot` and `root` disks from the files available.

For the rest of this section I shall assume that you have a 320 Mb IDE hard disk, partitioned as in the example in Figure 7.1, with the DOS partition already created and populated with your DOS software. I shall further assume that you wish to install the A, AP, D, K, N, F, X, XAP and Y software sets from the Slackware distribution and that your installation medium will be floppy disks (though the installation procedure is essentially the same from any other installation medium: CD-ROM, hard disk or network).

Once you have the boot and root disks prepared you should insert the boot disk and reboot the machine. Most distributions, Slackware included, provide a boot disk which will allow you to enter hardware configuration details after a prompt. This should only be necessary in the unlikely event that the boot disk kernel fails to detect, correctly identify or configure a particular hardware device.

Our example configuration should present no problems and so you would just press Enter or Return at the prompt to continue with the boot sequence. After a short time you will be prompted to remove the boot disk, replace it with the root disk and press Enter or Return to complete the initial boot sequence.

At this stage, you will have a minimal Linux system, running entirely in memory, using a ramdisk for its root filesystem and, if all has gone well, you should be looking at a Login: prompt. Now, login as root. There is no password set on the account, so you should be able to log straight in.

By convention (one which I shall follow in the examples in this book) the system administrator or super-user is given a prompt which consists of, or at least ends in, a hash (#) symbol. It is a good idea, when used in a prompt, to keep the hash symbol exclusively for this purpose – it will help to avoid confusion.

In order to set up the Linux partitions you need to run fdisk from the hash prompt, which gives an output as follows:

```
# fdisk
Using /dev/hda as default device!

Command (m for help):
```

The file name /dev/hda is the device special file name corresponding to the whole of the first hard disk drive (/dev/sda for a SCSI disk). This is the drive that fdisk tries to work with by default. If you have a second hard drive, you can get fdisk to work with that instead by specifying the pathname to the device special file for the second drive (/dev/hdb or /dev/sdb) as a parameter to the command:

```
# fdisk /dev/hdb
```

Under Linux, every disk drive and partition is given a name in /dev. These names appear as follows:

```
hda   entire hard drive 1;
sda   entire SCSI hard drive 1;
hdb   entire hard drive 2;
sdb   entire SCSI hard drive 2;
fd0   entire floppy drive 0 (DOS A:);
fd1   entire floppy drive 1 (DOS B:).
```

The partitions on any of the hard drives can be accessed just by adding the appropriate number to the name for the entire drive. The following table shows how to name the partitions on drive hda:

```
hda1   hard drive 1, primary partition 1;
hda2   hard drive 1, primary partition 2;
hda3   hard drive 1, primary partition 3;
hda4   hard drive 1, primary partition 4;
hda5   hard drive 1, logical partition 1;
hda6   hard drive 1, logical partition 2;
hda7   hard drive 1, logical partition 3, etc.
```

The Linux fdisk command looks different to the DOS equivalent, but they both perform similar functions. You can obtain a list of the functions by using the 'm' command once you have fdisk running:

```
# fdisk
Using /dev/hda as default device!

Command (m for help): m
Command action
   a   toggle a bootable flag
   c   toggle the dos compatibility flag
   d   delete a partition
   l   list known partition types
   m   print this menu
   n   add a new partition
   p   print the partition table
   q   quit without saving changes
   t   change a partition's system id
   u   change display/entry units
   v   verify the partition table
   w   write table to disk and exit
   x   extra functionality (experts only)
```

A sensible thing to do at this point is to display the existing partition table, with the 'p' command, to check that the DOS partition has been set up properly:

```
Command (m for help): p

Disk /dev/hda: 16 heads, 40 sectors, 1024 cylinders
Units = cylinders of 640 * 512 bytes

   Device Boot  Begin   Start   End   Blocks   Id   System
/dev/hda1    *      1       1   511   163812+   6   DOS 16-bit >=32M
```

It has, so now you can set up the Linux partitions, starting with the swap space on /dev/hda2. You use the 'n' command to add a new partition, and then fdisk will ask you if you want to create a primary or extended partition. In our example, we want a primary partition, so you would answer 'p' to this prompt. You will then be asked which partition number to use and you would answer '2'. The next question from fdisk asks you to specify at which disk cylinder the new partition should start. In answer to this question, you should give the number of the next free cylinder, after the DOS partition. This will be 512 here. The last question asks you to specify where the new partition ends. This can be given as a cylinder number or you can just specify how big you want the partition in either bytes, kilo-bytes or mega-bytes. To specify a 16 Mb swap partition you would answer '+16M'. The whole sequence appears as:

```
Command (m for help): n
Command action
   e   extended
   p   primary partition (1-4)
p
Partition number (1-4): 2
First cylinder (512-1023): 512
Last cylinder or +size or +sizeM or +sizeK (512-1023): +16M
```

Incidentally, there is nothing to stop you from having multiple swap partitions. If for instance you have more than one hard disk then this arrangement might be the most convenient.

After creating the partition to be used for swap space, a similar sequence can be followed for the Linux root partition on /dev/hda3:

```
Command (m for help): n
Command action
   e   extended
   p   primary partition (1-4)
p
Partition number (1-4): 3
First cylinder (564-1023): 564
Last cylinder or +size or +sizeM or +sizeK (512-1023): 1023
```

132 *Getting Up and Running*

A 'p' command at the end of this sequence will confirm that all has gone according to plan:

```
Command (m for help): p

Disk /dev/hda: 16 heads, 40 sectors, 1024 cylinders
Units = cylinders of 640 * 512 bytes

   Device Boot  Begin   Start     End  Blocks   Id  System
/dev/hda1   *      1       1      511  163812+   6  DOS 16-bit >=32M
/dev/hda2        512     512      563   16640   83  Linux native
/dev/hda3        564     564     1023  147200   83  Linux native
```

This is looking good. However, there is just one more thing to do to finish it off. The system type for partition 2 is still flagged as *Linux native* when it should be *Linux swap*. This can be corrected with the 't' command to toggle the Id from 83 to 82. How do I know what the number should be? You can get `fdisk` to give you a list when you use the 't' command:

```
Command (m for help): t
Partition number (1-4): 2
Hex code (type L to list codes): L

 0  Empty              8  AIX            75  PC/IX         b7  BSDI fs
 1  DOS 12-bit FAT     9  AIX bootable   80  Old MINIX     b8  BSDI swap
 2  XENIX root         a  OS/2 Boot Man  81  Linux/MINIX   c7  Syrinx
 3  XENIX usr         40  Venix 80286    82  Linux swap    db  CP/M
 4  DOS 16-bit <32M   51  Novell?        83  Linux native  e1  DOS access
 5  Extended          52  Microport      93  Amoeba        e3  DOS R/O
 6  DOS 16-bit >=32   63  GNU HURD       94  Amoeba BBT    f2  DOS sec
 7  OS/2 HPFS         64  Novell         a5  BSD/386       ff  BBT
Hex code (type L to list codes): 82
```

And now, at last, the partition table should be set up as required. A final look just to make sure:

```
Command (m for help): p

Disk /dev/hda: 16 heads, 40 sectors, 1024 cylinders
Units = cylinders of 640 * 512 bytes

   Device Boot  Begin   Start     End  Blocks   Id  System
/dev/hda1   *      1       1      511  163812+   6  DOS 16-bit >=32M
/dev/hda2        512     512      563   16640   82  Linux swap
/dev/hda3        564     564     1023  147200   83  Linux native
```

A good tip at this point is to make a note of the numbers of blocks in the Linux partitions for later operations (16640 and 147200 here). Using the 'w' command we will now write this new partition table back to the disk and then quit from `fdisk`. While using `fdisk`, if something should go horribly wrong, you can use the 'q' command to quit from the program without making any changes to the original partition table on disk.

To make sure that the changes to the partition table take effect with all versions of `fdisk` you should now reboot the machine with the `boot` and `root` disks again. Once you have done this and logged back in as `root` again, you are ready to continue.

7.3.2 Creating Filesystems

Having now created the partitions for Linux, the next task is to make the filesystem structures within those partitions. This is just the Linux equivalent of the DOS format operation. Working on the swap partition first, you use two commands: `mkswap` to prepare the partition and `swapon` to tell Linux to bring the partition into use:

```
# mkswap -c /dev/hda2 16640
# swapon /dev/hda2
```

The `-c` switch to `mkswap` forces a check for bad data blocks in the partition. Obviously, if your swap partition is not `hda2`, then you would substitute the name of yours in the command. The number at the end of the line is just the block count of the swap partition, which you noted when you created the partitions. Again, you will substitute your own value in place of the 16640. The `swapon` command just takes a single parameter which is the name of the partition to use (`hda2` here).

Before you can create the filesystems on the Linux native partitions, you have to choose which filesystem type to use. In fact, even though Linux supports several different filesystem structures, the best one all round is called the *Second Extended Filesystem* and it is the one to use. To make a second extended filesystem on a Linux native partition you use the `mke2fs` command:

```
# mke2fs -c /dev/hda3 147200
```

The parameters specify the partition to use and its size in blocks. Again, the `-c` switch forces a bad block check. If you have more than one Linux native partition then you will need to use `mke2fs` on each of them.

7.3.3 Installing Packages

Having prepared the disk partitions, you are now ready to load the Linux software into them. Each different Linux distribution has a different method for performing this operation. But essentially what happens is that your Linux partitions are mounted under the `root` filesystem (which is still in RAM don't forget) and then the various software packages can be unpacked from floppy disk (or other installation medium) and copied into the appropriate places.

Some distributions require you to perform these operations manually, which is not a particularly difficult task, just a bit tedious. Other distributions, Slackware included, provide an installation script to automate the procedure. The installation script in the Slackware distribution is called `setup`:

    # setup

Running this command presents you with a menu which will guide you through the remaining steps of the installation. The various menu options are:

help Displays the `setup` help file.

keymap Allows you to change the keyboard mapping if you have a non-US keyboard. This will be the first option to choose to start the installation proper for non-US keyboard users. When you finish with this option `setup` allows you to move directly to the *addswap* option without coming back to the main menu.

quick Here, you select between quick and verbose installation. As a beginner you should probably use the verbose option, which is the default anyway.

make tags When you gain more expertise with Slackware installation, this option allows you to set up your own tag files to pre-select which software packages to use out of each disk set.

addswap Allows you to specify which of the Linux swap partitions you want your final system to use as swap space. I have already said that it is possible to create and use more than one swap partition, but why you wouldn't want to use all of them automatically I can't imagine. Anyway, this information will be incorporated later into one of the system configuration files.

After making your selections you will be asked if you want to run `mkswap` and `swapon` on these partitions. If you have already used these commands on the partitions before running `setup` (which we did) then you should choose *not* to allow `setup` to do it now.

This menu option will be the first to choose to start the installation proper, if you have a US keyboard. When you finish with this option, `setup` allows you to go on to the next step rather than return to the main menu.

target This is where you specify which of your disk partitions you wish to include in your final directory hierarchy. A list of the available partitions is given and you are asked which to use as the `root` filesystem. In our example there is only one to choose from – `/dev/hda3`. If you haven't already done so (we did) you can now create the filesystem on the `root` partition with `mke2fs`. If applicable, you will then be asked if there are any other partitions you want to use and upon which directories you would like to have their filesystems mounted. This is where you would specify the `/home` partition, for example if we were dealing with the partition layout of Figure 7.2.

source This is where you specify the source medium from which the installation will take place. Generally the choices are: CD-ROM, floppy disk, hard disk or network. If you choose floppy disk here, then a further menu will allow you to specify which floppy drive to use and the size of disks that fit the drive. In fact, whichever option you choose, further questions may be used to determine exactly where the source files will come from.

disk sets This option allows you to choose which disk sets you want to install. You must install the A set. Beyond that, the choice is yours. You will end up with a fairly full and general usage installation if you include the following: A, AP, D, K, N, F, X, XAP and Y.

install This is the menu option which actually unpacks the packages you select for installation and copies their files into your Linux filesystems. Normally, you will arrive at this option directly from the previous option, rather than from the main menu.

You will now be asked how you wish to be prompted and, as a beginner, you should answer by selecting the *normal* option.

Each disk set contains a list of packages. Some of these packages are tagged as REQUIRED and these will be installed automatically, if you choose to install the disk set to which they belong. Other packages within each disk set are tagged as RECOMMENDED or OPTIONAL and in these cases you will be asked whether or not you wish to install them. You should make sure that you read all the on screen information carefully during the installation procedure as, sometimes, you need to make a choice between packages and not just install them all.

configure After the package installation has taken place, this option allows you to set up the mechanism for booting Linux either from floppy disk or hard disk and it also allows you to perform some machine configuration for such things as: mice, modems and networks. Initially, you are probably better skipping some of the configuration options and performing them manually when you have had the chance to look at what is involved. However, you should take the opportunity to create a boot floppy at this time, and perhaps configure lilo (see Section 7.3.6 for information to help you with lilo).

pkgtool This option is only provided for use later, for package maintenance. It will allow individual packages to be added and deleted. The use of this option is quite self-explanatory.

exit Leave setup and return to the shell prompt.

7.3.4 Booting Linux

Whatever Linux distribution you choose to install, it must provide you with some means of booting into Linux when you first switch the machine on. This can be as simple as supplying you with a floppy disk to boot from or you may get to use one of the Linux kernel loaders from your hard disk. The Slackware distribution allows you the opportunity of creating a boot floppy and also of installing the `lilo` boot loader. These things can be done from within the Configure option of the `setup` command.

In order to show how simple it is, we will create a boot floppy manually. This also gives you a spare boot floppy in case anything happens to the one you created at the end of `setup`. In fact, all that you need to do is just to copy the Linux kernel image from your hard disk to a floppy disk and it is automatically bootable.

Different Linux distributions store the kernel image file in different places. The most common places are:

```
/vmlinuz
/zImage
/etc/zImage
```

The Slackware distribution uses `/vmlinuz` by default. Once you have identified the location and name of your kernel image you will need to make sure that it is configured to run from floppy disk properly. To do this you use the `rdev` command. What `rdev` does is to allow you to modify some of the kernel's configuration details directly in the kernel file. What we need to do is to make sure that our kernel file has the name of the `root` partition set correctly and that initially the `root` partition is mounted read-only so that it can be checked. These operations are performed with the following two commands:

```
# rdev /vmlinuz /dev/hda3
# rdev -R /vmlinuz 1
```

Obviously, if your kernel image name or your `root` partition name are different than those used in the example, you will need to substitute your own names into the commands.

All you need now is a blank disk to make the copy (a DOS formatted disk will do). If the disk needs to be formatted this can be done with the `fdformat` command. For example, to format a 1.44 Mb floppy disk in the `A:` drive (`fd0`):

```
# fdformat /dev/fd0H1440
```

Notice the `H1440` after the `fd0` in the device special file name, this forces `fdformat` to treat the disk as high density and 1440 Kb in size (i.e. 1.44 Mb). There are other special files available which force the floppy disks to be treated as other standard sizes, as the following command shows:

```
# ls /dev/fd0*
/dev/fd0         /dev/fd0H1440    /dev/fd0H720     /dev/fd0h360
/dev/fd0D360     /dev/fd0H2880    /dev/fd0d360     /dev/fd0h720
/dev/fd0D720     /dev/fd0H360     /dev/fd0h1200
```

Armed with the blank floppy disk and the name of the kernel image, all that remains is to perform the copy:

```
# cp /vmlinuz /dev/fd0
```

You should now be able to boot the system with your new floppy in just the same way as you will with the floppy created during the **setup** procedure.

7.3.5 The Reboot Procedure

Unless you tried to install `lilo` during **setup** you will have to boot your Linux system from floppy disk for the time being. Having two boot floppy disks available, now is a good time to reboot your system to check that all is well – don't forget you are still running with the `root` filesystem on a RAM disk at the moment!

Reboot time is one of those particular times when you need to remember that Linux is a big-machine operating system. Under *no* normal circumstances should you shut down Linux by just switching the machine off or by pressing the reset switch – Linux needs to be shut down properly. Quite a lot of the work that Linux does is retained in memory for as long as possible rather than writing it to disk. The obvious reason for this is that accessing data in memory is orders of magnitude faster than accessing the same data on disk. One consequence of this, however, is that when you want to shut Linux down you need to give it advanced warning so that it has time to transfer all this memory resident data to disk before you pull the plug.

The safest way to shut Linux down is to use the **shutdown** command. The general form of this command is:

```
shutdown flags time [message]
```

The **shutdown** command can only be executed by a user logged in as `root` and when it is given, *message* is sent to all users. If no message is specified then a default shutdown warning will be given. When shutdown time arrives a SIGTERM signal is sent to all processes to give them the opportunity to terminate cleanly, before the shutdown proper takes place.

The main *flags* are the command line switches: `-h` which means halt the machine after the **shutdown** and `-r` which means reboot the machine instead. The *time* parameter specifies when the shutdown should take place. It can be specified as an absolute time in the format `hh:mm` or it can be given as a number of minutes from the current time, in the format `+mm`. The word *now* can be used to mean +0 minutes.

During its operation, the **shutdown** command ensures that the disk data contents are synchronized with the data stored in memory so that no data will be lost. The following command will shut Linux down immediately and then halt the machine:

```
# shutdown -h now
```

It is also possible to configure the Linux kernel to reboot the machine when you press `Ctrl-Alt-Del`. This action can obviously be performed by anyone, at any time, whether they have a `root` login or not. On Linux machines for home and personal use this may not be a security issue. However, you may want to disable this feature on any machine whose main keyboard and screen are open to unauthorized access. You will see how to do this in Section 7.4 when we look at how to build a custom kernel.

Due to space restrictions on the RAM disk `root` filesystem, many Linux distributions do not supply the `shutdown` program on their setup disks. Therefore, you may need to use `Ctrl-Alt-Del` just for the first shutdown after initial installation.

7.3.6 lilo

Rebooting your Linux system from floppy disk should work fine; however, it is far more convenient if you can boot it directly from the hard disk, especially if you can have the choice of which operating system to boot, where there is more than one from which you might choose.

As I have mentioned briefly before, there is a program called `lilo` which can be used, along with a configuration file, to set the system up so that when the machine boots you can have exactly this choice.

If `lilo` is being used then at the start of the boot sequence the word:

```
LILO
```

will appear on the screen followed by a short pause. If you do nothing during this pause then `lilo` will boot whichever operating system or kernel it has been set up to treat as its default system. If, instead, you press one of the keys: `Shift`, `Ctrl` or `Alt` during the pause, then you will be presented with a:

```
boot:
```

prompt, at which you type in the name of the operating system or kernel you wish to boot. If you press the `Tab` key at the prompt then you will get a list of the names from which you may make your choice.

In order to set up `lilo` to give you these options, you just need to set up a configuration file, called:

```
/etc/lilo.conf
```

with the required information about which operating systems or kernels you want to be able to boot, where they are on your hard disks and what names you want to give them, to use at the `lilo boot:` prompt, and then you just type in the following command to complete the installation:

```
# lilo
```

The easiest way to appreciate what goes into the `/etc/lilo.conf` file is to take a look at one. The following is an example which could be used with our 320 Mb disk to boot DOS by default, but allow the choice of either *dos* or *linux* at the `boot:` prompt:

```
# LILO configuration file
# Global section
boot = /dev/hda
delay = 50

# DOS bootable partition section
other = /dev/hda1
  label = dos
  table = /dev/hda

# Linux bootable partition section
image = /vmlinuz
  root = /dev/hda3
  label = linux
  read-only
```

The configuration file is split up into sections: a global section to start, and then a further section for each operating system or kernel that you want to be able to choose at boot time. The first section after the global section gives the details of the operating system or kernel that lilo will boot by default.

In the example, the global section contains two lines: the first tells lilo from which hard drive it will be booting and, therefore, which disk's boot block it should modify when you install it; the second specifies the length of time (in tenths of a second) that lilo should pause before booting the default system.

Since DOS is to be the default operating system, the DOS section comes next in the configuration file. The three lines in the section specify: which partition holds DOS, the label you will type at the boot: prompt to run DOS and the location of the partition table.

The last section contains four lines of information about booting Linux: the full pathname of the bootable kernel image file, the name of the partition which holds the root filesystem, the label you will type at the boot: prompt to run Linux and a flag which specifies that initially, the root filesystem should be mounted read-only so that it can be checked for integrity by the filesystem check program.

If you want Linux to be the default operating system to boot rather than DOS then all you need to do is to swap over the DOS and Linux information so that the Linux information is given first.

Obviously, when you want to set up a lilo.conf file then you will substitute your own disk, partition, system label and kernel image names into the file in place of my examples.

140   *Getting Up and Running*

You must remember that you need to run the `lilo` command every time you modify the configuration file and every time you change a kernel image file, whether you modify the configuration file or not. Even if you store a new kernel image in the same place as the old one, and with the same name, you must still run the `lilo` command to have the new kernel installed.

7.4 Kernel Build

The Linux kernels supplied with most software distributions are configured to support as wide a range of hardware as possible, so that they will work with as many machines as possible for Linux installation purposes. Once you have an installation running, it is a good idea to build a custom kernel specifically for your machine. In general, this will reduce the size of the kernel and thus increase the amount of memory you have available in which to work. If you only have a limited amount of memory fitted in your machine (4 Mb for example), then this can make a noticeable difference.

Assuming that you have installed the Linux kernel sources and the GNU C/C++ compiler as part of your Linux installation, then building a new kernel is very straightforward.

The first task is to check that your installation of the Linux sources has created two symbolic links in the directory `/usr/include`, as in the following example:

```
# cd /usr/include
# ls -l asm linux
lrwxrwxrwx  1 root    root    26 Jul 4 17:27 asm -> /usr/src/linux
/include/asm
lrwxrwxrwx  1 root    root    28 Jul 4 17:27 linux -> /usr/src/lin
ux/include/linux
```

If the symbolic links already exist then you must not perform the next step. If they do not exist then you will need to set them up manually, probably to replace a pair of directories of the same name. These things can be done as follows:

```
# cd /usr/include
# rm -fr asm linux
# ln -s /usr/src/linux/include/asm asm
# ln -s /usr/src/linux/include/linux linux
```

7.4.1 Configuration

The next step is to choose which facilities and hardware drivers you want to include in your new kernel; you do this with the following commands:

```
# cd /usr/src/linux
# make config
```

You will now be offered a yes/no question and answer session asking which things you wish to include in your new kernel and which you wish to leave out. After each question you will see either [y] or [n]. This is the default answer for the question if you just press Enter. When you have configured your system the answers you have given will be remembered and will become the defaults if you need to run make config again.

Most of the questions have reasonably obvious answers, though one or two deserve a mention here:

```
Kernel math emulation (CONFIG_MATH_EMULATION) [n]
```

If you have a system which does not have a floating point co-processor installed, then you will need to answer *yes* to this question so that a floating point co-processor emulator can be included into the kernel. If you do have a co-processor then you can answer *no* here and reduce your kernel size a little. Answering *yes* to this question with a co-processor fitted will cause no problems as the kernel will detect your co-processor and use it anyway.

```
Networking support (CONFIG_NET) [y]
```

You should probably include network support even if you do not have a network card, because many software packages make use of sockets which comprise the main network interprocess communication mechanism. The kernel can use a local loopback arrangement between processes on a single machine so that they can use sockets to talk to each other as though over a physical network.

```
Limit memory to low 16MB (CONFIG_MAX_16M) [y]
```

Unless you have more than 16 Mb of memory on your machine then you may as well answer *yes* to this question.

```
TCP/IP networking (CONFIG_INET) [y]
IP forwarding/gatewaying (CONFIG_IP_FORWARD) [y]
IP multicasting (CONFIG_IP_MULTICAST) [y]
IP firewalling (CONFIG_IP_FIREWALL) [y]
IP accounting (CONFIG_IP_ACCT) [n]
```

The TCP/IP networking should probably be included, but the IP options that follow are only used if your machine is going to perform some serious network application such as acting as a secure gateway between networks.

```
Standard (minix) fs support (CONFIG_MINIX_FS) [n]
Extended fs support (CONFIG_EXT_FS) [n]
Second extended fs support (CONFIG_EXT2_FS) [y]
xiafs filesystem support (CONFIG_XIA_FS) [n]
msdos fs support (CONFIG_MSDOS_FS) [y]
umsdos: Unix like fs on top of MSDOS fs (CONFIG_UMSDOS_FS) [n]
/proc filesystem support (CONFIG_PROC_FS) [y]
NFS filesystem support (CONFIG_NFS_FS) [y]
ISO9660 cdrom filesystem support (CONFIG_ISO9660_FS) [y]
OS/2 HPFS filesystem support (read only) (CONFIG_HPFS_FS) [n]
System V and Coherent filesystem support (CONFIG_SYSV_FS) [n]
```

Linux is capable of supporting many filesystem types, though there are probably only a few that you will need to include. The second extended filesystem support is essential if you built your Linux native disk partitions using it (as we did in our example installation). Being able to mount DOS hard disk partitions and floppy disks is also very useful. You will almost certainly need the /proc filesystem as versions of many day-to-day Linux commands are configured to use it (like **ps**). The NFS filesystem allows disk partitions on one machine to be mounted over a network into another machine's directory hierarchy. The ISO9660 filesystem is required if you want to operate a CD-ROM drive.

You should edit /usr/src/linux/Makefile after running make config to make sure that the definition for the symbol ROOT_DEV is correct. If the disk partition you want to use as your root filesystem is the same as the one which is currently in use in your running system then the symbol should be set as:

```
ROOT_DEV = CURRENT
```

Otherwise the disk partition name corresponding to the required root filesystem should be assigned to ROOT_DEV instead. For example:

```
ROOT_DEV = /dev/hda3
```

7.4.2 Compilation

Once the configuration is complete, which might initially take two or three attempts to get it how you want it, you can move on to the next stage – preparing and compiling the source tree.

You should start this with the commands:

```
# make dep
# make clean
```

The first of these will configure up all the makefiles for you, to match your particular installation and kernel configuration choices. The second will make sure that there are no old binary files lying about in the source tree to interfere with the compilation of your chosen kernel configuration.

When these have completed successfully, which may take a minute or two, you should go on to start the compilation proper:

```
# make zImage
```

Having entered this command you should now go and take a break because, depending on your processor speed and the amount of memory you have on your system, it could take quite a while to run. A 486DX2/66 with 16 Mb of memory takes about 20 minutes, a 386SX/16 with 4 Mb takes several hours.

Once completed, the system will have generated a ready to install, compressed kernel image in the file:

```
/usr/src/linux/arch/i386/boot/zImage
```

7.4.3 Installation

In order to test the new kernel you should make a bootable floppy disk from it, using the procedure you saw in Section 7.3.4 to configure the `root` filesystem partition name into it first.

If all goes well when you boot the machine from the new floppy disk then you can consider setting up the new kernel to boot from the hard disk, if you wish. Probably the easiest and safest way to do this is to set up an extra kernel in your `lilo.conf` file and re-run `lilo`.

The `lilo.conf` file can be modified as follows:

```
# LILO configuration file
# Global section
boot = /dev/hda
delay = 50

# DOS bootable partition section
other = /dev/hda1
  label = dos
  table = /dev/hda

# New Linux bootable partition section
image = /vmlinuz
  root = /dev/hda3
  label = linux
  read-only

# Old Linux bootable partition section
```

```
    image = /.vmlinuz
      root = /dev/hda3
      label = linux.old
      read-only
```

Notice that there are two bootable Linux kernel sections, one for the new kernel you just created and one for the original kernel so that you can always fall back on the old kernel if any problems show up with the new one.

In order to use the new `lilo.conf` file, you would need to execute the following command sequence:

```
# mv /vmlinuz /.vmlinuz
# cp /usr/src/linux/arch/i386/boot/zImage /vmlinuz
# lilo
```

The first command saves the current kernel image under a new (and invisible) name, the second command places a copy of the new kernel into the place specified in the `lilo.conf` file and the final line performs the `lilo` installation.

Now, when you re-boot your system, you have three choices at the `boot:` prompt. You can type *dos* to boot the DOS operating system, *linux* to boot the new Linux kernel or *linux.old* to boot the original kernel.

7.4.4 `loadlin`

The `lilo` package is only one of the Linux boot loaders available. Another possibility is a package to run under DOS called `loadlin`.

The main difference as far as users are concerned is that `lilo` allows you to make the choice of operating system or kernel at boot time, whereas `loadlin` users need to boot into DOS first, and only when they are there do they then make the choice to stay in DOS or use `loadlin` to boot Linux.

In order to use `loadlin` you must copy it and your Linux kernel file into your DOS partition. The easiest way to do this is to have the DOS partition mounted under Linux and then just use the Linux `cp` command.

Some Linux distributions, including Slackware, offer you the opportunity during the installation procedure of configuring a DOS partition to be mounted into the Linux directory hierarchy automatically during the boot sequence. If your distribution does not offer this opportunity, or if you opted not to take it, then the DOS partition will have to be mounted manually.

The command used to mount the top level directory of one filesystem underneath a leaf level directory in another filesystem is called `mount`. The general format of the `mount` command is:

```
mount -t type device directory
```

where *type* is the filesystem type (e.g. msdos, ext2, iso9660, nfs, etc.), *device* is the name of the device special file which holds the filesystem to be mounted (e.g. /dev/fd0, /dev/hdb1, etc.) and *directory* is the position in the current directory hierarchy where the new filesystem is to go.

When you have finished using it, a filesystem can be unmounted again with the command umount, which has the format:

```
umount directory
```

In the case of a floppy disk filesystem, it is particularly important for you to umount it before you remove the disk from the drive. This is because there may be some filesystem data stored in memory which has not yet been written to the floppy, and the umount command will arrange to flush this data to disk.

The mount and umount commands can only be used by root.

An example mount command to mount our /dev/hda1 DOS partition under the Linux directory /mnt would be:

```
# mount -t msdos /dev/hda1 /mnt
```

You will then need to copy the files loadlin.exe and loadlinx.exe into the DOS partition. In the Slackware distribution these two files are packed into a .zip file in the /root directory. Unpacking them and performing the copy can be done as follows:

```
# cd /root
# unzip lodlin*.zip
# cp /root/LOADLIN/LOADLIN.EXE /mnt/dos
# cp /root/LOADLIN/LOADLINX.EXE /mnt/dos
```

If you don't have the unzip command under Linux, then you could always copy the .zip file to a DOS directory and unpack it with pkunzip.

You can now copy the compressed Linux kernel image to the DOS partition with the command:

```
# cp /usr/src/linux/arch/i386/boot/zImage /mnt/vmlinuz
```

and all should be ready for a reboot.

Once the machine is booted into DOS you should be able to boot Linux just by using the command:

```
c:\> loadlin c:\vmlinuz root=/dev/hda3 ro
```

Chapter 8

Users

Many Linux machines will operate as stand alone boxes, with only a single user (you!) and no connection to the outside world. In a situation like that it seems strange to be thinking about user accounts and system administrator duties – it's just a PC for goodness sake!

However, you should try not to think in this way. Whether you are on a single-user private PC at home or on a 200-user fully Internet connected service machine in a large institution, if you have a `root` account on the machine you should always treat it with respect; you should consider yourself to be in the role of a caretaker rather than a god. When you work on the machine it should be with two separate hats, one labeled *ordinary user* which you should use for all your ordinary day to day work and for as many of the system administrator functions as can be done without a system privileged account, and another hat labeled *caretaker* which you only wear when absolutely necessary and for as short a period of time as is required to perform your task. I cannot emphasize enough that if you have a `root` account on a machine, especially one where other users are involved, then yours is a position of trust and responsibility. A position not to be taken lightly, and certainly not one to be taken with any malicious intent.

8.1 Account Passwords

After you have just installed a Linux distribution there may well be only one usable account – `root`. It usually starts off with no password set, so the first task is to set one. You should choose your `root` password with particular care as it is all that lies between you and anyone else accessing your machine with `root` privilege. You should definitely avoid using any word which might appear in a dictionary, as well as your dog's name or any variation on your birthdate or your partner's name. All these things are easy to guess for anyone who knows you, even slightly. You change the `root` password with the same command as for changing ordinary user passwords:

passwd

Even logged in as root, there is no way that you can find out what someone uses for a password. This means that the best you can do for a user who can't remember his or her password is either to remove the password altogether, which allows the user then to choose a new one the next time they login, or you can set up a new password for the user directly. You tell the new password to the user who can use it to login and then change it for something private. The latter approach is best as it doesn't leave a period of time when the user's account is unprotected. In order to change a user's password directly you use the passwd command with a parameter which is the login name of the user whose password you wish to change:

passwd login_name

An easy way to find out who else is logged into your machine is to use the who command, as follows:

```
# who
pc       tty1     Jul  3 19:25
mot      ttyp0    Jul  3 20:06 (grexiz.soc.staff)
carey    ttyp1    Jul  3 20:08 (gregory.soc.staf)
rvc      ttyp2    Jul  3 20:12 (rachel.soc.staff)
```

The information displayed by the who command is split up into several fields. First comes the user's login name, followed by the name of the terminal that the user is using. This is followed by the date and time at which the user logged in and, finally, if the user logged in to the machine over a network, the name of the machine from which the connection was made.

8.2 Adding User Accounts

Having put a password on your root account, the next task is to create yourself an ordinary user account. Many Linux distributions supply a special command to help you with creating a new user account. This command is called adduser or useradd depending on which distribution you have installed. Either way, the command will ask you a series of questions about the new user account and when you have supplied all the answers (or accepted the defaults, where applicable) the new user account will be created.

I can see that this simplifies the procedure all round but for novice administrators I think it is important to understand what is happening underneath so that you can make more informed choices. Therefore, so you will understand what is going on, we will add your account manually this time and you can look at the special command next time.

In fact, adding a user account manually is quite an easy job, consisting of the following steps:

1. Set up the login entry in /etc/passwd.
2. Create the user's home directory.
3. Set the user as the owner of the home directory.
4. Set up access permissions on the home directory.
5. Set up the user's group entry in /etc/group.

Before you can set up the password file entry, you need to decide on the following account details: the login name, the UID, the GID, the path to the home directory and which shell the user will use.

8.2.1 Password File

Armed with this information you can now edit the password file /etc/passwd and add the following line to the end of the file, substituting your details into the line as appropriate:

```
login_name:OFF:uid:gid:user's_real_name:home_directory:shell
```

Choosing a login name is a matter of personal preference unless your site already has some convention for user names. Remember, however, that the name should be unique and must not be longer than eight characters.

Similarly, the choice of UID and GID are fairly arbitrary, except that the UID should be unique, as it is the UID that the system uses to identify a user. If you intend to make proper use of groups then the GID will just be the group number of the group that the new user is to join. The standard GID for the group users in the Slackware distribution is 100. If you don't need a user to belong to a particular group then you could just set the GID to be the same as the UID so that these users just belong to a group of one.

The user's home directory can be anywhere in the directory hierarchy but you should impose some kind of policy on the location rather than dot them about at random. A good choice is to site ordinary user home directories under /home. If you expect lots of users then it would be reasonable to mount a large disk partition over /home so that the user accounts can have as much space as they need, while also being confined to this space so that they can't use up all the space on your root filesystem.

Finally, arguably the best choice for the shell is bash, though there are others available. A typical line to add to the password file might be:

```
roger:OFF:1234:100:R.N.Foxcroft:/home/roger:/bin/bash
```

8.2.2 Home Directories

The next three steps in the list can be performed with three commands, as follows:

```
# mkdir /home/roger
# chown roger. /home/roger
# chmod 700 /home/roger
```

The first line creates the home directory (/home/roger). The chown command in the second line changes the owner of the home directory to roger. The dot after the user name in this command tells chown to change the group of the home directory to the user's GID at the same time (this could also have been done separately with the chgrp command). The last command gives full read, write and search permission to the directory's owner and no access to anyone else. This last is a bit of a paranoid setting but can be changed by the user (roger) later if required.

The fifth and final step in the list of things to do actually requires no effort at all in this case, because the new user was allocated the GID of a group that already existed in /etc/group. The other case, that of the users who have a GID the same as the UID, would also require no effort for this stage either. If a particular GID does not have a corresponding entry in the group file then the system will just use the GID itself in places where otherwise it would have displayed the group name (ls -l for instance). The only time you want to create or change an entry in the group file is when you add a new group that will actually contain more than one user or when you want to give permission for a user to work in more than one group.

8.3 User Groups

Most installations will make little or no real use of the user group facilities offered by Linux. However, they are available and can offer some elegant solutions to various security problems.

Groups are generally used to allow sets of users to have common access to a collection of files while denying access to the rest of the system's users. It may happen, however, that you want a particular user to be able to join in with more than one group at various times. In these circumstances the group idea is not very helpful unless a user has the ability to change groups. And indeed, under Linux, this is the case.

To understand this better, let us have a look at the format of the group file. It consists of a set of lines with one line per group, and each line has the format:

```
group_name:password:gid:user_list
```

This is loosely analogous to the arrangement in the password file, where each line is split into fields separated by colons. In the case of the group file, each line has four fields which are:

group_name   Name of the group. This name appears in the group column (field four) of an `ls -l` listing.
password   Optional password. If a password is set on a group then it will be requested when changing to that group.
gid   The GID number to be associated with the group_name.
user_list   Optional comma separated user list. This can also be used to permit users to change to this group.

Typical entries in the `/etc/group` file are:

```
root::0:root
bin::1:root,bin,daemon
daemon::2:root,bin,daemon
sys::3:root,bin,adm
adm::4:root,adm,daemon
users::100:
book::500:
```

When a user logs in, the GID in the password file assigns the user to a default group. Taking the user `roger`, whose account we just created, the default GID specified in the password entry is 100. This puts `roger` in the group `users` immediately after logging in. With the contents of the group file shown in the previous example `roger` does not have permission to change to any other group.

Suppose now, you wanted `roger` to be able to change groups to `book` on occasion so as to be able to work with the `book` team. This could be achieved in one of two ways. The best way is to enter `roger` into the `user_list` of the group `book` as follows:

```
book::500:roger
```

All `roger` has to do now to change groups to `book` is to use the `newgrp` command as follows:

```
$ newgrp book
```

and the group change will take place. Using the `newgrp` command without specifying a group parameter will change the user back to their default group.

The other way to allow group changes is to set a password on the group instead of entering the user names. Once the password is in place, `roger` trying to change to group `book` will be asked to supply the group's password before access to the new group is granted.

This may sound a good idea but in reality the second method is not as secure as the first. Admittedly, `roger` has to supply a password now, but any user on the system with the password could also change groups to `book`. So, what if the password falls into unauthorized hands, which must be more likely if it is shared by a large group? Or, how do you go about removing a user with a group password from that group without having to change the password for everyone else?

Just asking these questions should be enough to convince you that listing the names explicitly in the group file is the better approach.

8.4 Security

While we are on the subject of security and passwords another question arises. Given that when you run a program, the process that is created has the same permissions on file accesses that you do, how can you change your password in /etc/passwd when you don't have permission to write to that file as an ordinary user?

In general, the previous statement is true. However, in order for you to be able to write to the password file at all (and when you change passwords, obviously you do), there must be some mechanism for you to run a program but then for the process that gets created to be able to do things as though it was running on behalf of someone else. In the case of the password file the 'someone else' would need to be root as only root has write permission on the file:

```
$ ls -l /etc/passwd
-rw-r--r--  1 root    root    775 Jul 25 15:41 /etc/passwd
```

If we take a look at the file permissions on the executable program for changing passwords (/usr/bin/passwd), we shall get a clue:

```
$ ls -l /usr/bin/passwd
-rws--x--x  1 root    bin    3964 Mar 21 09:37 /usr/bin/passwd
```

As you can see, there is something unusual here. The owner's permission bits are given as rws, but what does the 's' mean in the owner's execute bit position? What it means is that anyone who has execute permission on the file, and in this case that means everyone, will run the program not with their own permissions but with the permissions of the file's owner (root in this case).

It is also possible (though less common) for an 's' to be set in the group execute bit position. Here is an example:

```
$ ls -l /usr/sbin/lpc
-r-xr-s--x  1 root    lp    21508 Feb 14 19:03 /usr/sbin/lpc
```

Any ordinary users on the system who run the lpc command will run it as though they were in the group lp and will therefore obtain lp group permissions on any files accessed by the lpc program. Don't worry for the moment about what lpc does, it is related to the operation of a printer and we will cover its use later.

The way to set these 'extra' permission bits is with the standard chmod command, but using an extra octal digit in front of the normal permission bits. A value of 4 will set the file's setuid bit, the value 2 will set the file's setgid bit and the value 6 will set them both. Obviously, the digit 0 (or no value specified) will turn both bits off. If a lower case 's' is displayed in an ls -l listing it means that the underlying execute bit is set. An upper case 'S' means the underlying execute bit is not set. The following sequence demonstrates some of these ideas:

152   *Users*

```
$ ls -l /tmp/testbits
-rwx--x--x   1 pc      book       0 Jul 26 09:14 /tmp/testbits
$ chmod 4711 /tmp/testbits
$ ls -l /tmp/testbits
-rws--x--x   1 pc      book       0 Jul 26 09:14 /tmp/testbits
$ chmod 2711 /tmp/testbits
$ ls -l /tmp/testbits
-rwx--s--x   1 pc      book       0 Jul 26 09:14 /tmp/testbits
$ chmod 711 /tmp/testbits
$ ls -l /tmp/testbits
-rwx--x--x   1 pc      book       0 Jul 26 09:14 /tmp/testbits
```

8.4.1 umask

As an additional security feature there is a command you can use which will restrict the access permissions that a process running on your behalf can give to a file it creates. The name of this command is umask.

The general form of the umask command is:

umask [permission_mask]

where the *permission_mask* is just a three-digit octal number corresponding to the permission bits you want to have reset by default when a file is created on your behalf.

If you do not specify a permission_mask then the current umask value will be displayed. This will typically be:

```
$ umask
022
```

The following is a simple sequence of commands to demonstrate the use of umask and the effect it has on file permission bits during file creation:

```
$ touch file1
$ umask 027
$ touch file2
$ umask 0
$ touch file3
$ ls -l file?
-rw-r--r--   1 pc      book       0 Aug  3 00:53 file1
-rw-r-----   1 pc      book       0 Aug  3 00:53 file2
-rw-rw-rw-   1 pc      book       0 Aug  3 00:54 file3
```

Here you can see that, left to its own devices (with umask set to zero), the touch command would generate files with permission bits set to rw-rw-rw-. You can also see the effect on permission bits of creating files with umask values of 022 and 027 as well.

8.5 Batch Jobs

Usually, when you enter a command, it is with the intention that it should execute immediately. Sometimes, however, a user will want to have a command executed at some later time as a batch job, perhaps even after the user has logged off.

8.5.1 cron

There is a program called `crond` which most systems arrange to run some time during the boot up sequence. The 'd' on the end of the name indicates that this is the `cron` *daemon*. In common with many daemons, this program continues to run all the time the machine is running and its sole function is periodically to examine the contents of a set of command files and execute the commands in these files at appropriate times.

The command files each consist of a set of command lines. The general format of a command line is:

    minutes hours days months day_names command

The `minutes`, `hours`, `days`, `months` and `day_names` fields allow you to specify when the associated `command` will be executed. For example:

    25 8 27 Jan * birthday

At 08:25 am every 27 January `crond` will execute a user's program called `birthday`. The star (*) in the `day_names` field means 'on whichever day it occurs'.

The star generally means 'match any possible value' and it can be used in the other date and time fields as well:

    25 8 * * * appointments

This says at 08:25 am every day/month/day_name run the user program called `appointments`.

If you only wanted to run `appointments` on working days (i.e. Monday to Friday) then these can be listed in the `day_names` field, separated by commas:

    25 8 * * mon,tue,wed,thu,fri appointments

Lists of consecutive values, like those in the `day_names` field, can also be specified as a simple range, and have the same meaning:

    25 8 * * mon-fri appointments

If you specify `days` and `day_names` in the same command line, then both of them apply:

    0,15,30,45 * 1 * mon oddtimes

This example will execute the user command `oddtimes` every 15 minutes on the first day of every month *and* on every Monday.

Every user login can have its own associated command file to use with `crond`. These command files are stored in the directory:

/usr/spool/cron/crontabs

However, ordinary users do not have direct access to this directory so they must use a special command to create and modify their `crond` command files. This command is called `crontab`. There are several command line switches which can be used to get the `crontab` command to create, modify and delete your personal command files. The main options and command line switches to `crontab` are:

file [-u *user*]	replace current command file with *file*;
- [-u *user*]	replace current command file from standard input;
-l [*user*]	list current command file;
-e [*user*]	edit current command file with `vi`;
-d [*user*]	delete current command file;
-c *dir*	specify a new command file directory.

Only `root` can specify the -c switch to change the directory used to hold the command files, and only `root` can give a *user* name on the end of the command line to apply the given option to the specified user's command file. Don't forget that the square brackets are being used here to enclose optional parameters and should not be entered.

8.5.2 at

The use of `crontab` entries will allow given commands to be executed on a regular basis. However, it may happen that you only have a batch job which you would like to submit to the system to be executed just once, at some specified time.

In order to accommodate this requirement there is another command, called `at` which still relies on `crond` for its operation but which will give the required 'one shot' functionality.

In order for `at` to work there is a special command line in the `crontab` file for `root`. It appears as:

    0,5,10,15,20,25,30,35,40,45,50,55 * * *   /usr/lib/atrun

This line causes /usr/lib/atrun to be executed every five minutes. What `atrun` does when it executes is to look through the pending list of `at` command jobs, to find any that need to be run at the current time, and to run them.

Submitting an `at` job is easy. The general form of the `at` command is:

    at [-f file] time

This will execute all the commands given in *file* at the specified *time*. If the optional file switch is not given, then the commands to execute will be read from the standard input instead (keyboard by default):

```
$ at 10:55
date >/tmp/at.job.test
Ctrl-d
Job c00cd3093.00 will be executed using /bin/sh
```

Remember that pressing `Ctrl-d` on a line on its own is the way to generate an end-of-file from the keyboard. Notice that the `at` command responds at the end of the sequence by allocating a unique job reference number (c00cd3093.00 in this case). The user can check up on the queue of outstanding jobs by using the `atq` command:

```
$ atq
Date                    Owner   Queue   Job#
10:55:00 07/27/95       pc      c       c00cd3093.00
```

Checking on the file `/tmp/at.job.test` after 10:55 am gives:

```
$ cat /tmp/at.job.test
Thu Jul 27 10:55:02 BST 1995
```

It is also possible to remove an `at` job from the queue by using the `atrm` command followed by the job reference number.

The `at` command allows you to specify the job run times in some fairly sophisticated formats including things like:

```
10am Aug 20
6pm tomorrow
7:21 + 4 days
```

The last example means 7:21am in four days' time. In addition, dates can also be given in several formats, including:

```
MM/DD/YY
DD.MM.YY
```

which allows the day and month to be specified either way round.

8.5.3 batch

There is another command, intimately related to `at`, which performs a similar function, called `batch`. Entering a `batch` command is just the same as `at` except that no time needs to be specified. The submitted job will then be run at a time which depends on the load average of the machine – when the machine is sufficiently lightly loaded, the job gets done. The use of the `batch` command depends upon you having installed the `/proc` filesystem from your Linux distribution, because it needs to read the machine's load average from the file:

    /proc/loadavg

Access to the `at` and `batch` facilities can be allowed or denied on an individual user basis by `root`. The rules are as follows:

- The `root` account can always use `at` and `batch`.
- For other users, if the file `/etc/at.allow` exists then only those user login names listed in that file can use the facilities.
- If the file `/etc/at.allow` does not exist but the file `/etc/at.deny` exists then only those user login names *not* listed in the file can use the facilities.
- If neither file exists then no ordinary users can use `at` or `batch`.

The default for the Slackware distribution is that `/etc/at.deny` exists and is empty, thus allowing everyone access to the facilities.

8.6 Archives

Another service that `root` may be required to perform for users on some systems is the production and maintenance of archives and backups.

The most obvious media for storing backups and the one most readily available is floppy disks. If the amount of material to store is only small then it is a simple task to create a Linux second extended filesystem on a floppy disk, `mount` the disk into the `root` filesystem and then just copy the files across. Assuming that you have an unformatted 1.44 Mb floppy disk to start with, the procedure for saving the contents of a given directory (`src_dir` in the example) along with all its subdirectories and files is:

    # fdformat /dev/fd0H1440
    # mke2fs /dev/fd0 1440
    # mount -t ext2 /dev/fd0 /mnt
    # cp -a src_dir /mnt
    # umount /mnt

The five commands in this sequence perform the following functions:

- Low level format the floppy disk. The command line parameter specifies that the floppy disk is in drive `fd0` (`A:`) and that it should be treated as high density with a capacity 1440 Kb (1.44 Mb).
- Make a second extended filesystem on `/dev/fd0`. The second command line parameter gives the size of the device as 1440 blocks.

- Mount the second extended filesystem from the device `/dev/fd0` under the directory `/mnt`. This is an empty directory specifically provided for use by `mount` in this way.
- The `-a` command line switch to `cp` tells it to make an archive copy. This means that all the subdirectories and files under under *src_dir* will be copied into `/mnt` keeping the same file names and directory structures as in the original.
- The final command unmounts the floppy disk from the rest of the directory hierarchy so that you can remove it to a place of safe keeping.

8.6.1 gzip

In situations where there are one or more large files included in the material to archive then you may want to try to compress them to save space on the floppy disk.

The standard command available with Linux distributions for file compression is the GNU `gzip` command. The general form of this command is:

> `gzip [options] file`

The specified *file* will be compressed to generate a new file with the same name as the original, but with the suffix `.gz`. This new file will replace the original.

There are lots of *options* available with `gzip`, the most useful ones are:

> `-1` use fastest compression; output files not as small;
> `-9` use maximum compression; takes longer to run;
> `-l` list some statistics about the files being compressed;
> `-h` display a help screen of information and options.

Typically, a large text file will be compressed by 60% to 70%, which can represent an enormous saving in disk space.

Given a file which was compressed by `gzip`, it can be restored to its original state with the command `gunzip`.

> `gunzip file`

Once again, the output file will replace the input file. It will also have the `.gz` file name extension removed.

A compressed file can also be read while still leaving it compressed at the end, by using the command `zcat`. This command is analogous to the ordinary `cat` command except that it operates on compressed files. The output from `zcat` is sent to the standard output device, which makes the command particularly useful for reading compressed text files, as the following example shows:

> `$ zcat textfile.gz | more`

This command pipes an uncompressed version of the file `textfile.gz` into the `more` command to give a paginated display of the text the file contains.

8.6.2 tar

Once you get up to a certain size, backing files up into a Linux filesystem starts to become unwieldy. What you really need then is to be able to write whole directories with all their subdirectories and files straight out to a tape drive. One of the commands that can perform this operation is called `tar` (i.e. Tape ARchiver).

What this command does effectively, is to pack all the files in the directories it is given into a single huge file, called a `tarfile`, which can then be written to tape.

So far, `tar` would seem to be of limited use as so few systems support a tape drive of any kind. However, `tar` is capable of writing its output file to anywhere including: onto floppy disk, out to the screen or even into an ordinary file. In addition to this, `tar` also has a couple of other tricks it can perform. If the `tarfile` is being written to floppy but it is too large to fit onto a single disk, then `tar` can be instructed to split the file over multiple disks (called a multi-volume archive). It is also possible to instruct `tar` to use the `gzip` algorithm to compress the `tarfile` before writing the result to its output.

The general format of the tar command is:

```
tar [options] files
```

where *files* is the list of files and directories whose contents will be included in or extracted from the archive.

The `tar` command has many *options*, the most useful are:

-c	create a new `tarfile` archive;
-x	extract files from a `tarfile` archive;
-t	display the contents of a `tarfile` archive;
-f *file*	specify `tarfile` name as *file*;
-v	get `tar` to be verbose about what it is doing;
-l	stay in local filesystem, don't cross `mount` points;
-M	create/extract/display a multi-volume archive;
-N *date*	only store files newer than *date*;
-z	use `gzip` to compress/uncompress archive.

By convention, a `tar` archive filename should be given the suffix `.tar` and a compressed archive filename should have the suffix `.tgz` (as all the packages probably had on your Linux distribution disks).

A typical `tar` command to create a compressed archive containing the home directory contents for user `rachel` would be:

```
# tar -cvzf /tmp/rachel.tgz /home/rachel
```

A command to examine the contents of this archive would be:

```
# tar -tzf /tmp/rachel.tgz
```

And a command sequence to restore user rachel's home directory from the archive after some of the original files were accidentally deleted:

```
# cd /
# tar -xvzf /tmp/rachel.tgz
```

The reason for the `cd /` command in this last example is that `tar` has stored all the filenames in the archive as names relative to the `root` directory. So you need to be in the `root` directory to restore the files to their proper place. If you were to unpack this archive from some other directory, then the files would still be unpacked but in places relative to your new position in the directory hierarchy.

Using the `tar -t` option is a simple way to see relative to which directory the archive files were stored.

If it is necessary to allow ordinary users to create archives to floppy disk then there are one or two problems which will need sorting out. To start with, the floppy disk device special files (`/dev/fd*`) usually have read and write permission turned off for ordinary users. As system administrator it is a simple matter to change the permissions appropriately, using the `chmod` command.

A second problem arises if you want ordinary users to be able to mount floppy disks into the directory hierarchy as the `mount` and `umount` commands are `root` only commands. They are set up in this way to prevent ordinary users from rearranging the directory hierarchy, which could lead to all sorts of security problems. Probably the safest solution to this problem is to write a pair of simple programs in C which can only be used to mount and unmount a floppy disk over a specific directory (say `/floppy`). For an implementation of these commands see the exercises at the end of Chapter 21.

Chapter 9

Peripherals

One of the primary functions of any operating system, Linux included, is to provide an interface between the application software and the peripheral hardware of the machine. Common peripheral hardware includes such devices as:

- the console terminal, for video output and keyboard input;
- modems for simple serial communication with other systems;
- mice as alternative input devices;
- printers for output of listings, text and graphics.

This chapter looks at each of these devices in turn to see what facilities exist in Linux to set up and use them.

9.1 Console Terminal

For most Linux systems there will be only one user and the main access to the system will be via the machine's keyboard and screen – the *console terminal*. In fact the console terminal is really two separate peripheral devices: a screen/video output device and keyboard input device. As we shall see, for both of these devices there is quite a bit of setting up which can be performed.

9.1.1 Keyboard Input

The keyboard on a PC seems to be a relatively simple device – it is a box with buttons on it, the buttons are numbered and lettered, you press a button, the appropriate character is displayed on the screen. However, despite the apparent simplicity, there is an awful lot more going on than would seem to be the case at first glance.

To start with, many countries that use PCs need odd extra characters in their character sets in order to be able to cope with the quirks of different spoken languages. This means that many keyboard variations exist, with minor differences in layout and content.

It is much cheaper in a manufacturing sense to be able to produce a single keyboard in terms of its electronics and physical construction and just change the symbols on some of the key-tops, than it is to produce new electronics for each keyboard variation. In order to get this to work, however, it is necessary to have some kind of lookup arrangement so that a single key in a particular physical position on the keyboard can generate different byte values to match the key top on the key.

In Linux, this lookup is done in software inside the kernel in the keyboard driver. Effectively, there is a table in the kernel which gives the byte values to generate for each of the keys on the keyboard and also for the combinations of each key with the various `Ctrl`, `Shift` and `Alt` keys.

Each physical key on the keyboard is given a unique keycode number in the range 1 to 127. A keyboard map file is then used to specify what byte values are to be generated for each keycode or keycode combination you press. By default, the keyboard map files are stored in the directory:

`/usr/lib/kbd/keytables`

Keyboard map files are normally loaded into the kernel at system boot time using the `loadkeys` command. So, for example, to load the map file for a UK keyboard you would use the command:

`$ /usr/bin/loadkeys /usr/lib/kbd/keytables/uk.map`

This command needs to be entered into one of the system startup files. These are normally stored somewhere under the directory `/etc` (though exactly where under `/etc` can vary with different Linux distributions) and have names of the form:

`rc.XXX`

where XXX indicates what the file is used to configure. Under the Slackware distribution the `loadkeys` command appears in the file:

`/etc/rc.d/rc.keymap`

The keyboard map files themselves are just ordinary text files so you can easily view and edit them if you wish to create your own keyboard mappings for special purposes. If you only want to change the mappings of a few keys on top of some otherwise standard layout, then you only need to create a map for the changes, which you can then load after the standard layout has already been set up.

In order to find out what the keycodes are for the keys whose functions you want to change, you need to use the `showkey` command. When this command is running, any key you press or release will cause its keycode to be displayed. In order to terminate the `showkey` program, it is arranged so that it will automatically exit if you don't press any keys for ten seconds:

```
$ showkey
press any key, program terminates after 10s of last keypress
keycode   28 release
keycode   25 press
keycode   25 release
keycode   46 press
keycode   46 release
$
```

Once you know the keycodes that you want to change, it is a simple matter to modify a keyboard map file appropriately and then load it. The format of the map files is quite straightforward and a good description of it is given in the manual page:

```
$ man 5 keytables
```

You may wish to modify the keyboard map table in the kernel incrementally, until you are happy with the way it operates. In these circumstances you can generate a map file for subsequent loading from the current kernel table with the **dumpkeys** command, as follows:

```
$ dumpkeys >newkey.map
```

9.1.2 Video Output

Just as with the keyboard, the screen output also has some lookup tables associated with it, whose values can be altered for special purposes, or just for fun!

Normally, when a byte is sent to the screen, its 8-bit value is used as the code for the character to display. It is possible, however, to insert a translation table into this sequence. This table is just a simple 256-element array of bytes. With this table in use, any time a byte is sent to the screen in order to display the character it represents, what happens is that the byte is used as an index into the table to select one of the 256 elements. It is the 8-bit value in that array element which actually specifies the byte value to display. If, by default, the table is set up so that:

```
table[0]   = 0
table[1]   = 1
table[2]   = 2
     -
     -
table[255] = 255
```

then this has the same effect as when the table isn't there at all. Changing any of the values from the default automatically allows translations to be made from one character to another as they are displayed.

In order to modify the output translation table you use the **mapscrn** command:

```
$ mapscrn filename
```

where `filename` is the name of the file which contains the new character mappings. Once the table has been set up, it can be enabled by sending a special character sequence to the display. This sequence is the `Esc` character followed by '(K'. Use of the translation table can subsequently be disabled by replacing the K in the enable sequence with a B.

The manual page for the `mapscrn` command gives a full description of the formats in which translation entries may be specified in the translation file, but, basically, they all boil down to giving a list of character pairs which specify a character followed by its new translation. A simple example will help to clarify the point.

Suppose for some reason you wanted to translate any of the upper case letters W, X and Y into an asterisk (*). The translation file to specify this could have the contents:

```
'W'  '*'
'X'  '*'
'Y'  '*'
```

This file (called, say, `newtab`) could then be loaded into the console display driver with the command:

```
$ mapscrn newtab
```

The easiest way to send the special escape sequence to the console driver to enable the character translations is with the following `echo` command:

```
$ echo -e '\033(K'
```

After sending this sequence, any attempts to send W, X or Y to the screen will result in the display of an asterisk, as the following command sequence illustrates:

```
$ echo -e '\033(K' VWXYZ
V***Z
$ echo -e '\033(B' V***Z
VWXYZ
```

Obviously, in the second `echo` command, where the three asterisks appear, I actually typed WXY but, because of the translations, they didn't come out that way.

The other table which appears in the display sequence is actually stored on your video card and its contents control the appearance of the displayed characters themselves. Changing the contents of this table allows you to change displayed fonts. Many character fonts are available for Linux and it is also a straightforward (if a little tedious) task to generate your own custom character and graphic shapes.

First, in order to load up one of the standard fonts, you use the `setfont` command and specify the name of a font file:

```
$ setfont sc.fnt
```

164   *Peripherals*

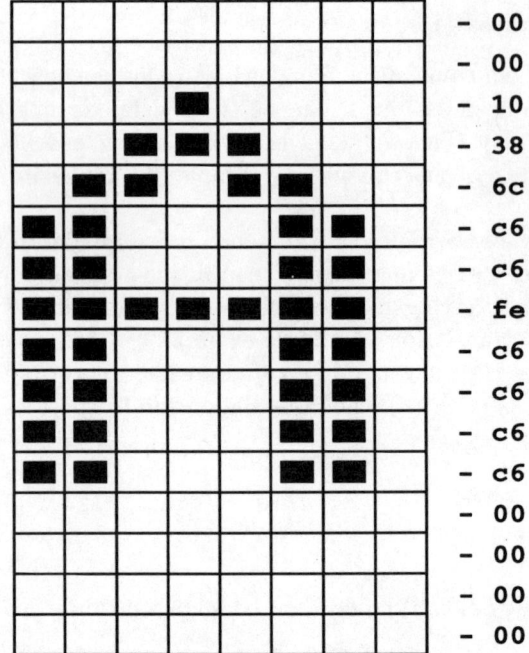

Figure 9.1 A character grid and its encoding, for the letter **A**.

where `sc.fnt` is the name of the font file to load. If you try it, you will find that `sc.fnt` is quite a fun font, though you probably wouldn't want to use it all the time. By default, the font files are stored in the directory:

   `/usr/lib/kbd/consolefonts`

In order to understand the contents and layout of a character font file, we need to take a simplified look at the mechanics of displaying text characters. On a VGA screen when it is displaying 25 lines of text that are 80 characters long, each character occupies a pixel grid on the screen which is eight pixels wide and 16 pixels high.

Next, each displayable character is made up of a set of lit and unlit pixels, also on an 8×16-pixel grid. To display a particular character on the screen in a particular position, all that is required is to copy the pixels from the correct character grid into the appropriate pixel grid position on the screen.

In the character grids, a pixel is represented by a single bit which just specifies whether the corresponding pixel is lit or unlit. This means that an easy way to store the pixel information for a complete 8×16-pixel grid is just as a set of 16 single-byte values – 1 byte for each 8-pixel row in the grid. Figure 9.1 shows a typical pixel grid for the letter **A** and the set of 16 byte values (in hex) that result.

As you can see, the example letter **A** has a grid which is encoded as:

```
00 00 10 38 6c c6 c6 fe c6 c6 c6 c6 00 00 00 00
```

You have already seen that characters sent for display arrive as numbers in the range 0 to 255 (i.e. 256 in total). A complete 8×16-pixel character set, then, is made up of 256 different 8×16-pixel grids. A font file for an 8×16-pixel character set just contains the 256 sets of 16 bytes, one after the other to create a file 4096 bytes long.

Creating your own character set and font file is just a case of working out pixel grids for each of the characters, sorting out the 16 single-byte values for each grid and then writing these values away to a file which you can subsequently load with the `setfont` command and use.

In addition to font files that are 4096 bytes long, you may well find that you have some files of different lengths. In general, these other files contain characters with pixel grids that are 8×8 pixels or 8×14 pixels instead of the 8×16 pixels you have just seen. These other character sets are intended for use in different screen resolution modes or with different graphics adaptors (like EGA). There are still 256 different characters in these other character sets and the pixel rows are still stored as bytes in the same way; there are just less rows to each character. This means that the size of these other font files will be 2048 bytes for 8×8-pixel character sets and 3584 bytes for the 8×14-pixel character sets.

Just to add a final touch of complexity, there is also another font file type which the `setfont` program can use. This other type has exactly the same layout that you have already seen except that there are 4 bytes of header information in the file as well, which makes these files 4 bytes bigger than the files we have considered previously. This makes the full list of file sizes:

```
2048 bytes
2052 bytes
3584 bytes
3588 bytes
4096 bytes
4100 bytes
```

From the file size, `setfont` can work out what the file type is and what the file format is as well.

9.2 Modems

Adding a modem to your system can be quite a tricky operation. In general, a modem is a device which connects your computer to your phone line, so that you can dial the phone number of another computer/modem combination and get your computer to communicate with the remote machine.

When you buy a modem for a PC the first choice is whether it should be internal or external. This is purely a personal choice as there is no operational difference between them. My own preference, for what it is worth, is for external modems, if only because they can be connected to other machines than just PCs.

A modem is a serial device, which means that it requires a serial port (COM1, COM2, etc.) to operate. If you get an internal modem then it will have a serial port built into it which will just need to be configured as detailed in the modem manual. For an external modem, connection is also not a problem as most I/O cards come with two serial ports, one of which most people will use for a mouse, which leaves the other free for your modem. The only extra consideration for an external modem is that if it is a high speed modem (19200 bits per second or higher) then you need an I/O card with buffered UARTs in the serial ports.

The UART is the name of the integrated circuit which performs the serial port functions. In the standard PC design a type of UART is fitted which places a heavy load on the CPU by generating a lot of interrupts (one for each character). At high modem speeds it is possible that the CPU may not be able to keep up with the data and some data may be lost. To overcome this problem I/O cards are available which have UARTs that contain a 16-character buffer. These UARTs only need to interrupt the processor when the buffer is filling up, and during the interrupt the CPU can take all the data in the buffer at the same time. This means many fewer interrupts, so that much higher data transfer rates are possible.

The buffered UARTs (sometimes referred to as FIFO UARTs) have a chip number of 16550A and you need to get a serial card which states that it has these UARTs fitted, if you want to do high speed serial work. In the UK, a multi-function I/O card with primary and secondary EIDE controllers, a floppy disk controller, two 16550A serial ports, one parallel port and one game port can be purchased for around £15 (ummm, that's about $22 US).

The device special files to use for the four serial ports, COM1 to COM4, are given in the following table:

Outgoing device	Incoming device	DOS name
/dev/cua0	/dev/ttyS0	COM1
/dev/cua1	/dev/ttyS1	COM2
/dev/cua2	/dev/ttyS2	COM3
/dev/cua3	/dev/ttyS3	COM4

One reasonable idea that will save you remembering which device your modem is connected to, is to set up a symbolic link to the modem from a device called /dev/modem using a command like:

```
# ln -s /dev/cua0 /dev/modem
```

The next consideration when buying a modem is its speed. The bottom line here is to get the fastest modem you can afford, and in any case at least 14400 bits per second. Most modern modems will talk to your computer at a fixed high speed and then negotiate an operating speed with the remote modem on connection. The modem itself will translate between the two speeds. This makes the setup on your computer rather easier. Many modern modems will also perform data compression where possible, which can increase the effective transmission speed to well beyond the actual speed at which the two modems are talking. For this reason it is a good idea to set the speed at which your computer talks to your modem to the maximum speed the modem can use.

This causes a small problem because the highest standard serial speeds available under Linux, in bits per second are:

   300 600 1200 1800 2400 4800 9600 19200 and 38400

whereas the highest modem speeds are:

   57600 and 115200

In order to solve this problem there is a program available which allows all sorts of low level manipulations on serial ports, called **setserial**. The particular manipulation we are interested in here makes it possible to set up the serial ports so they can reach these higher speeds. This is done with one of the following commands:

```
# setserial /dev/cua0 spd_hi
# setserial /dev/cua0 spd_vhi
```

Using the parameter **spd_hi** sets the maximum speed on /dev/cua0 (COM1) to 57600 bits per second, while the parameter **spd_vhi** sets it to 115200 bits per second. What these commands do is to swap the 38400 standard speed for the new speed you specify, so that when you set the serial port speed to 38400 you actually get the higher speed instead. In all the programs that allow you to change serial port speeds you still have to use the name 38400 as the highest speed but in fact 57600 or 115200 will be used instead.

It is normal to set serial ports up at system boot time, and this is usually done from a startup file called:

   `rc.serial`

which, in the Slackware distribution, is run by a command at the end of the rc.S file (or it is when you uncomment the line).

You will find that the **setserial** program can also handle the setup of serial port addresses and interrupt (IRQ) assignments. Full details of these and other **setserial** functions are in the manual page.

What you have seen so far is all the setup that is required to use your modem for outgoing calls. All you do is to run your favorite terminal emulator program, tell it which device your modem is connected to and the speed to use (38400 don't forget) and then you are ready to dial out and connect to the world.

To use your modem for incoming calls the situation is a little more involved. First you have to set up a program to run on the serial line and give a **login**:

prompt to anyone who calls and, second, you need to set up the modem itself to answer an incoming ring and connect the remote caller to your machine.

The first of these is easy, the program you run to give a `login:` prompt is called `getty`. There are two common versions of this program available to run under Linux, called `agetty` and `getty_ps`. Both perform similar functions in that they set up the serial line characteristics and then give a `login:` prompt. The `getty` program is run by the `init` process as specified in its configuration file:

> /etc/inittab

Typically, using `agetty`, the line in this file needed to set up `/dev/ttyS0` (COM1) to receive incoming login requests at maximum speed would be:

> d1:45:respawn:/sbin/agetty -t60 38400 ttyS0

The configuration lines in `inittab` each contain four colon-separated fields. The fields are:

1. A unique two character identifier (d1 = dialup line 1).
2. A list of the run levels to which this line applies. Here, run levels 4 and 5 are specified which are used when the system is in multi-user mode.
3. This is the action that `init` should take on behalf of this line. The keyword `respawn` indicates that `init` should rerun the command on this line whenever its process terminates.
4. This is the command line for `init` to run. Here, it runs the `agetty` command with speed 38400 on serial line `/dev/ttyS0` and with a 60-second timeout for the user to respond to the `login:` prompt.

For the `getty_ps` program the equivalent `inittab` line would be:

> d1:45:respawn:/sbin/getty -t60 ttyS0 F38400

where F38400 is not directly used as the line speed but is a label on a line in the configuration file:

> /etc/gettydefs

which is used to set up the serial line characteristics.

Having got a `login:` prompt on the line, all that remains now is to set up the modem to monitor the phone line and answer when it rings. The procedure here depends very much on your modem type, though many modems are Hayes compatible in that they accept the Hayes modem command set for their operation.

If your modem is Hayes compatible, then a minimal set of commands to configure it should include:

> ATS0=1
> ATE0
> ATQ1

All the Hayes commands start with AT (a few modems are case sensitive) to grab the modem's attention. This is followed directly by the command you want to execute. The three commands given here operate as follows:

1. Hayes-compatible modems contain a set of internal registers whose values control various aspects of the modem's operation. These registers have the names S0, S1, S2 etc. Register S0 specifies how many bursts of incoming ringing the modem will count before it trips the ring and answers the call. This command sets the count in S0 to 1 so the modem will trip the ring straight away. Setting this register to 0 will disable the modem's auto answer facility.
2. Normally, when you send a command to a Hayes-compatible modem it will echo your command back to you so you can see that you typed it correctly, and so on. However, with a `getty` running on the line waiting for a user to login, any characters echoed by the modem will by treated as the user's login name or password. To prevent this, the echo facility needs to be suppressed. This is done with the command E0. The command E1 turns the echo back on again.
3. Along similar lines to the previous command, your modem will by default send status information and result codes for many of the actions you ask it to perform. And, once again, any of these messages could be mistaken for a login name or password by the `getty` program. The Q1 command sets the modem into quiet mode which suppresses all of these messages. The command Q0 restores normal operation.

Once you have set your modem up you should save the modem settings (if your modem supports this feature – refer to its manual) so that you do not need to set it up again every time you switch the machine and modem on.

9.3 Mice

A mouse is a fairly standard piece of peripheral hardware on a modern PC, and Linux can take full advantage of this device, both in standard text modes and in X windows.

In general, mice come in two flavors: serial and bus (I'm counting the PS/2 mouse as a bus mouse here). This difference just determines what type of interface to your computer they require.

9.3.1 Serial

As its name suggests a serial mouse will plug directly into one of the serial ports on the back of your machine. The device special files to use for a serial mouse are:

```
/dev/ttyS0
/dev/ttyS1
/dev/ttyS2
/dev/ttyS3
```

As in the case of a modem, a common practice is to create a symbolic link to the serial device from /dev/mouse with a command like:

```
# ln -s /dev/ttyS1 /dev/mouse
```

9.3.2 Bus

If you are going out to buy a mouse, then unless you have a good reason to do otherwise, buy a serial mouse. If your computer already has a PS/2 mouse interface, or if you already have a bus mouse, or if you are determined that you want to buy a bus mouse anyway, then that is okay but the installation and configuration of these devices just takes more effort.

In general, a bus mouse will require its own interface card to be fitted inside your computer and the mouse itself will plug into that card. Sometimes a bus mouse interface will be fitted to some other card such as a video adaptor, so that the mouse will not take up an extra slot on your motherboard.

Having fitted the hardware to the machine, you will need to set the interface card up so that it generates an interrupt (IRQ) which does not conflict with any other hardware in your machine and then recompile the kernel to include the appropriate bus mouse support.

By default, most bus mouse interface cards use IRQ 5 as their interrupt number, but lots of other cards also use this as their default, so you will need to take some care over getting the choices right. The IRQ numbers you cannot use are:

```
0 1 2 6 8 13 14 and 15
```

as these are already in use for standard devices and cannot be changed. This leaves you with the choice of:

```
3 4 5 7 9 10 11 and 12
```

Of these, the first four are allocated for use by the standard serial and parallel ports, as follows:

IRQ	Allocation
3	COM2
4	COM1
5	LPT2
7	LPT1

Many machines have two serial ports and one parallel port fitted, which only leaves the LPT2 port's IRQ as spare. The other IRQs (9 to 12), while spare, cannot be accessed by 8-bit ISA cards, which includes most of the stand alone bus mouse interface cards. So you could have some problems.

9.3.3 gpm

One particularly useful application that is available under Linux is **gpm**. This command actually runs as a daemon, and would usually be executed at system boot time from within one of the standard `rc.XXX` files (usually `rc.local`).

What this daemon does is to allow you to use cut and paste facilities on a virtual terminal screen or between virtual terminals. With **gpm** running, moving the mouse will cause a mouse cursor to appear which moves in step with the mouse. Move the mouse cursor to the start of the block of text you wish to cut. Then press the left mouse button, move the mouse to the end of the text block and release the mouse button again. This should have marked the block of text on the screen. Now pressing the center button on a three-button mouse, or the right button on a two-button mouse will paste the marked text in at the current text cursor position. It is also possible to change virtual consoles after marking a block of text so that the block can be pasted into a different application.

When you run the **gpm** command you need to specify the type of mouse you have fitted to your machine with a command like the following:

```
# gpm -t msc &
```

where the list of mouse types supported by **gpm** includes:

- ms   microsoft serial mouse;
- msc   mouse systems serial mouse;
- bm   busmouse protocol bus mouse;
- ps2   PS/2 bus mouse.

9.4 Printers

Most PC printers use a parallel port as a Centronics interface. In a DOS environment the printer ports are called LPT1 and LPT2. The equivalent device special files under Linux are:

`/dev/lp1`
`/dev/lp2`

Most systems will only have one printer installed, usually as `/dev/lp1`.

If you are used to using a printer in a DOS environment then you will be used to having direct and sole access to it. Remember, however, that Linux is a multi-user and multi-tasking operating system so that even though, in your particular case, you may be the only user, provision still needs to be made to operate a printer in an environment where several users may be making simultaneous requests to print.

The standard way to solve this problem is to use a print spooling program. With a print spooler in operation any print requests that are made are not routed directly to the printer but are sent to files in a spool directory instead. Then, a separate program can pick up the print jobs one at a time from the spool directory and send them to the printer.

Under Linux, the situation is slightly more complex than this simple scenario suggests. This is because, as well as printing to a local printer, it is also possible to print on remote printers over a network.

9.4.1 Print Services

The task of scanning the spool directories (there is one directory for each printer) and printing any waiting files is performed by a program called `lpd`. The `lpd` program is actually the line printer daemon which needs to be executed at system boot time, usually from within the startup file `rc.M` or `rc.inet2`.

The four standard commands to submit, remove, monitor and control print jobs are:

lpr This is the command that allows you to submit a print job. Essentially, this means that your document will be copied to the spool directory for the printer, ready for `lpd` to pick up and print.

lpq When it is submitted, each print job is given a unique job number. The `lpq` command will give a list of all the jobs in the spool directory for a particular printer along with the job number for each job on the list.

lprm Once you know the job number for a particular print job (given by `lpq`) you can use the `lprm` command to remove it from the spool directory so it won't be printed. If you specify '-' instead of a job number it will remove all the print jobs belonging to you.

lpc This is the print system control program. It makes several different status and control commands available. However, as an ordinary user you can only use it to display the status of printers, spool queues, and daemons. All the other `lpc` commands which allow you to start and stop printers, spooling and print daemons, require you to be logged in as `root`.

By default, all these commands operate on the printer called `lp`. If you want to specify an alternative printer you can use the `-Pname` command line switch, where `name` is the name of the printer to use. Or, you can set the `PRINTER` shell variable up with the printer name instead.

9.4.2 printcap

All that needs to be done now, is to see how the various print service configuration options are set up. This is all done in the file:

/etc/printcap

This file is just a text file so you can use vi to modify it (if you login as root). The contents of the file are called *printcap enties*. Each printcap entry is just a set of configuration options – one printcap entry for each printer to which you will have access.

Two typical printcap entries are shown next, the first is for output to a local dumb dot matrix printer called lp. The second is for access to an HP 4L laser printer called hp, available over the network on a machine called gregory:

```
lp|starsg10:\
        :lp=/dev/lp1:\
        :sd=/usr/spool/lp:\
        :lf=/usr/spool/lp/err-log:\
        :mx#0:\
        :sh:

hp|hp4l:\
        :lp=:\
        :rm=gregory:\
        :sd=/usr/spool/hp:\
        :lf=/usr/spool/hp/err-log:\
        :if=/usr/local/bin/apsfilter:\
        :mx#0:
```

The first thing to notice is that printcap entries must only occupy a single logical line, with '\' characters used to signify that the the line is not yet complete.

The first field of each printcap entry starts at the beginning of a line and contains a list of names by which the printer may be known. The individual names are separated by '|' characters.

After the first field in each entry there follows a set of options and, where appropriate, their values.

Let us now work through the two printcap entries in turn, lp entry first. After the name field, the second line specifies the device special file to which the printer is attached (/dev/lp1 here). The third line specifies the spool directory for this printer as /usr/spool/lp. The fourth line gives the path to a log file which will be used to record any error messages generated while printing. The mx option specifies the maximum file size (in 1Kb blocks) that can be printed. A value of zero (as here) indicates that the size is unrestricted. The final option in this entry (sh) takes no parameters and just specifies that header page printing should be suppressed.

Now working through the `hp` entry, the second line is to specify the device special file for this printer. Notice, though, that because this printer is attached to a different machine this option specifies an empty parameter. The third line specifies the machine to which print requests for this printer should be sent (`gregory` in this example). The fourth line specifies a spool directory, which is still required even for a network printer to spool the files for printing before they are sent over the network. The fifth line specifies an error log file. The sixth line specifies a filter (`apsfilter` here) through which all documents will be passed on the way to the printer. These filter programs can be written to do anything to the text before it is printed. This particular filter will convert Postscript files into a form which can be printed on the HP 4L which is not a Postscript printer. This conversion is done by using the GNU Ghostscript program. The final line in this entry just specifies that the maximum file size for printing is unrestricted.

If a network printer is to be connected to your machine, then you must specify which remote machines will have permission to use the printer. The simplest way to do this is to enter a list of the machine host names for which permission is to be granted, into the file `/etc/hosts.lpd`.

There are very many more options which can be specified in a `printcap` entry than are shown here, though these examples will allow you to set up simple printer configurations. The `printcap(5)` manual entry contains a full list. Another document well worth reading on printer setup is the Printing-HOWTO document from the Linux Documentation Project.

Chapter 10

X-windows

X-windows is the standard windowing interface for Linux and, indeed, for all UNIX-like operating systems. The X-windows software is supplied in many Linux distributions and can just be installed along with all the other packages. That said, the installation and configuration of X-windows needs to be treated with special care because there are so many options and it is easy to get it wrong the first few times you try.

10.1 Servers and Clients

The X-windows system itself is actually a client–server application which is capable of running clients and servers on the same machine, or over a network.

Within the X-windows system, the server software controls the input and output (such as the keyboard, screen display and mouse), while the X-clients are the application programs that need to make use of the server's I/O. The clients and servers communicate via the X communication protocol.

The server software needs to be run on the machine to which the keyboard, display and mouse devices are connected, and will be specific to the particular hardware configuration of the machine.

When you install the X-windows packages you will have the choice at some point of which one of several different X-servers you should install. The choice will be made on the basis of what graphics display card is installed on your machine. Most graphics cards are supported under X-windows in Linux.

Assuming you have a super VGA card of some variety (though the earlier video standards are also supported) then, unless it is also an accelerated or enhanced card of some type, you will probably need to install the server:

XF86_SVGA

The server will be installed in the directory /usr/X11R6/bin and it should be linked to the command X, also in the same directory. In many cases, this will already have been done by the installation script, but, if not, you can perform the link operation manually, with the command:

```
ln -sf /usr/X11R6/bin/XF86_SVGA /usr/X11R6/bin/X
```

If at any time you need to change the X-server you are using, then this operation will need to be performed again, but with the new server name inserted in the command line as appropriate.

10.2 X-configuration

Once you have selected an X-server, the next task is to configure it. This is done by creating the configuration file:

```
/etc/XF86Config
```

Before you even think about doing this, let me first warn you that it is possible to create a configuration file that can drive your display monitor outside its operating specification. If you do this, there is every chance that you could cause permanent damage to your monitor. For this reason, please exercise the utmost caution when setting up the `XF86Config` file.

The configuration file itself consists of several sections of information about various aspects of your hardware layout. These sections are:

files Specifies the pathnames of the RGB database and the various X-windows character font files.

server flags Used to specify some X-server options.

keyboard Gives keyboard attributes, such as keyboard protocol, auto key repeat characteristics, and num-lock behavior.

pointer Specifies what type of mouse X should look for, what device special file is being used for the mouse, and then such things as baud rate for serial mice and whether or not to emulate the third button on a two-button mouse.

monitor Allows you specify display monitor characteristics such as bandwidth, horizontal sync and vertical refresh frequencies (straight from the monitor manual), as well as giving a list of video modes suitable for use with the monitor.

device This section allows you to specify the technical detail on your video graphics card. If you don't specify all the necessary values in this section, the X-server can often probe the hardware and discover the missing items for itself.

screen This section specifies which video card, monitor and X-server combination will be used.

The manual page for `XF86Config` is particularly useful in creating this file along with the contents of the file:

```
/usr/X11R6/lib/X11/XF86Config.eg
```
as a guide. This file contains an example X-configuration. The simplest way to set up your own X-configuration file is probably to take a copy of this example file and make suitable modifications to it. Do not attempt to use the example configuration file without modifying it for your own setup.

10.2.1 Files Section

In this section you will find definitions for `RgbPath` and `FontPath` similar to the following:

```
Section "Files"
    RgbPath     "/usr/X11R6/lib/X11/rgb"
    FontPath    "/usr/X11R6/lib/X11/fonts/75dpi/"
EndSection
```

For the `RgbPath` definition, the specified pathname should not need to be changed. The `FontPath` definition specifies the pathname to X-windows character font files. As there can be several different sets of fonts, there can be several matching `FontPath` definitions. You just need to make sure that each font directory that appears in `/usr/X11R6/lib/X11/fonts` has a corresponding `FontPath` definition here.

10.2.2 Server Flags Section

This section can specify some global flags for the server. In general, however, the default values are the ones you will want to operate with, so that no server flags need be specified. Even if no flags are specified, the section still needs to be present in the X-configuration file:

```
Section "ServerFlags"
EndSection
```

10.2.3 Keyboard Section

This section specifies some parameters associated with the keyboard. In general, the values in the example configuration file should be just fine:

```
Section "Keyboard"
    Protocol   "Standard"
    AutoRepeat 500 5
EndSection
```

10.2.4 Pointer Section

Several parameters are specified in this section usually relating to the mouse (or track ball, track pad, etc.) First is a specification of what kind of device the pointer is to be, followed by information specifying to which hardware device the mouse is connected. For serial mice, the next item specifies the baud rate (standard is 1200 baud) at which the device operates. Finally, some pointer-related flags can be specified such as `Emulate3Buttons`, which allows the middle button of a three-button mouse to be emulated on a two-button mouse, by pressing both buttons at the same time.

A typical pointer section could be:

```
Section "Pointer"
    Protocol   "Microsoft"
    Device     "/dev/mouse"
    Emulate3Buttons
EndSection
```

10.2.5 Monitor Section

This section specifies the characteristics of your monitor. You should pay particular attention to getting the values in this section right, as the X-server will check to ensure that it does not try to drive your display monitor outside the specifications you give here.

The important values in this section are `Bandwidth`, `HorizSync` and `VertRefresh`, which are taken straight from your monitor manual, and the `ModeLine` entries, which specify each of the resolution modes in which you will operate the monitor:

```
Section "Monitor"
    Identifier   "My monitor"
    Bandwidth    65
    HorizSync    31-49
    VertRefresh  56-87
    ModeLine  "640x480"   25  640  672  768  800   480 491 493 525
    ModeLine  "800x600"   36  800  864  936 1024   600 600 602 625
    ModeLine  "1024x768"  65 1024 1088 1248 1344   768 768 777 806
EndSection
```

Under NO circumstances should you copy the values given here verbatim; they are listed purely for illustrative purposes.

The `Identifier` definition is just to associate a string label, *My monitor* in this example, with this monitor section so that it can be referenced again later in the file.

One of the most difficult parts to sort out in the X-configuration file is the `ModeLine` entries specified in this section. These entries just list sets of closely connected values which are associated with the various screen resolutions available. Again, an examples file is available to give lists of many common `ModeLine` entries:

`/usr/X11R6/lib/X11/doc/modeDB.txt`

If necessary, these values can be calculated, given enough information about all the hardware, but it is beyond the scope of this book to delve so deeply into the workings of X windows, especially when some of the required data about the monitor typically is not available in its specification sheet.

However, if you can't find suitable `ModeLines` in the example file, you should read the documentation in the file:

`/usr/X11R6/lib/X11/doc/VideoModes.doc`

The contents of the quotes (") in each `ModeLine` entry is just a label to allow reference to be made to these lines later in the file. By convention, these labels are given mnemonic significance, though this is not strictly necessary.

10.2.6 Device Section

This is the section which describes your video card and its characteristics to the X-server. Initially, you need not put many values in this section, as, in general, the X-server is capable of probing the hardware to discover most of the values for itself. The only entry you must supply is the `Identifier` definition, which is, again, just a label by which this section can be referenced later.

Once you have used the server to probe the hardware (we'll look at how to do this a little later), then extra details can be filled in to give a device section which could look as follows:

```
Section "Device"
    Identifier   "My video card"
    Chipset      "et4000"
    VideoRam     1024
    Clocks       25.20 28.32 32.50 36.00 40.00 44.90 31.50 37.50
    Clocks       50.30 56.70 64.90 72.00 80.00 89.80 63.00 75.10
EndSection
```

10.2.7 Screen Section

This final section is the place where all the labels from previous sections are drawn together:

180 *X-windows*

```
Section "Screen"
    Driver          "SVGA"
    Device          "My video card"
    Monitor         "My monitor"
    Subsection      "Display"
        Depth       8
        Virtual     1024 1024
        ViewPort    0 0
        Modes       "800x600" "1024x768" " 640x480"
    EndSubsection
EndSection
```

The `Driver` definition specifies which X server you are using – `SVGA` specifies the `XF86_SVGA` server. The `Device` and `Monitor` use previously defined symbolic names to refer back to the appropriate sections.

Then, in the `Display` subsection, more display related details are given. `Depth` specifies the number of bits per pixel. `Virtual` specifies the size of the virtual screen in pixels. The size of the virtual screen must fit into the size of display memory on your video card. `ViewPort` says where on the virtual screen the top left corner of the physical screen will appear. If the current screen resolution is less than the virtual screen size, then it is possible to pan around the virtual screen under the control of the mouse. Finally, `Modes` gives a list of the video modes that you want to be able to use. The first mode in the list will be the default screen resolution when X-windows first executes.

Once X-windows is running, the other video modes can be accessed using the `Ctrl-Alt-Plus` and `Ctrl-Alt-Minus` key combinations. The `Plus` and `Minus` keys in these combinations are the + and - keys on the keyboard's numeric keypad.

10.2.8 Probing the Hardware

When you get to this stage, it is a good idea to start the X-server. However, for the time being, it should be set up only to probe the hardware, so that you can extract the information required to fill in the details in the *device section* that we left out earlier. This is easily done with the `X` command:

```
$ X -probeonly
```

The following listing gives some typical output for the previous command:

```
XF86Config: /etc/XF86Config
(**) stands for supplied, (--) stands for probed/default values
(**) Mouse: type: MouseSystems, device: /dev/mouse, baudrate: 1200
(**) SVGA: Graphics device ID: "ET4000"
(**) SVGA: Monitor ID: "Tatung XGA"
(**) FontPath set to "/usr/X11R6/lib/X11/fonts/misc/,/usr/X11R6/lib/
```

Starting X-windows

```
X11/fonts/Type1/,/usr/X11R6/lib/X11/fonts/Speedo/,/usr/X11R6/lib/X11/
fonts/75dpi/"
(--) SVGA: ET4000: Initial hibit state: high
(--) SVGA: chipset:   et4000
(--) SVGA: videoram: 1024k
(--) SVGA: clocks: 25.14 28.32 32.43 35.93 39.95 44.85 31.44 37.52
(--) SVGA: clocks: 50.28 56.55 64.86 71.96 79.97 89.75 62.94 74.91
(--) SVGA: Maximum allowed dot-clock: 90.000 MHz
(**) SVGA: Mode "800x600": mode clock = 36.000, clock used = 35.930
(**) SVGA: Mode "640x480": mode clock = 25.000, clock used = 25.140
(**) SVGA: Mode "1024x768": mode clock = 65.000, clock used = 64.860
(**) SVGA: Virtual resolution set to 1024x1024
(--) SVGA: Generic SpeedUps selected (Flags=0x30)
(--) SVGA: ET4000: SpeedUps selected (Flags=0xf)
```

As indicated by the second line of the output, lines preceded by (**) are for values that have been specified in the XF86Config file, while lines preceded with (--) contain values which the server discovered by probing the hardware.

This shows where to obtain the values which are subsequently plugged back into the *device section* of the XF86Config file. Once the values have been added to the configuration file, the X-server will not probe the hardware for the values when it is run on subsequent occasions.

10.3 Starting X-windows

Once the XF86Config file is set up, you can start up X-windows properly. On non-Linux systems you may have seen the command xinit to start up X-windows. Under Linux, this is done with the command:

    $ startx

which actually arranges to run xinit anyway. During the X-initialization sequence, xinit will also run any commands found in the file .xinitrc in your home directory (if the file exists). If you don't have a personal .xinitrc file, then xinit will look for the file:

    /usr/X11R6/lib/X11/xinit/xinitrc

and execute the contents of this file instead.

10.3.1 .xinitrc

The .xinitrc file is used to specify the initial configuration of the X-windows display. Typically, it will be used to start X-windows with certain applications already running. It can also be used to determine the initial screen layout, specifying where on the screen the windows for the initial applications should be placed. For example:

```
#!/bin/sh

xterm -geometry 80x43+220+0 -bg gray -fg black &
exec fvwm
```

The first line of this file specifies that the rest of the file should be interpreted using the /bin/sh shell program rather than your current shell. The second line causes the program xterm to be executed. This program is a standard terminal emulator which provides emulation of both the DEC VT102 text terminal and the Tektronics 4014 graphics terminal. The & on the end of the line is needed to push the command into the background so that the rest of the script can be executed without waiting for the xterm to terminate first. The last line in the example starts up a window manager (fvwm here), of which there are many, each offering slightly different look and feel to the X-windows environment.

It is possible to start up several applications between the shell and the window manager. In general, any extra commands should be terminated with an ampersand (&) character, like the xterm line in the example. Note that the line which starts the window manager is not pushed into the background like the rest, but replaces the current process by being run with exec command.

When the window manager terminates, the X-server is shut down, closing your X-windows session. This is normally done with a menu option, as you will see later. The server can also be shut down directly by pressing the keyboard key combination Ctrl-Alt-Backspace.

10.4 fvwm

The fvwm window manager provides a virtual windows system that allows multiple desktops to be accessed via a simple pager window. When fvwm is executed it will search for a configuration file, specified in your home directory, called .fvwmrc.

This file, if it exists, is used to set up a lot of details about the window manager's operation. It covers such things as the colors used for window backgrounds, and active and passive window borders. It specifies which windows will move with you when you switch desktops, and which will be left behind. It allows you to specify which applications are sufficiently important that their windows are not normally overlaid, and thus remain visible however cluttered the desktop gets. It also allows you to set up your own menus and actions to be bound to the mouse buttons (and some of the keys on the keyboard) when various parts of a window's border and background are selected.

Some typical .fvwmrc contents are given in the next example. Full details of all the options can be found in the manual page for the fvwm command:

```
# set up the colors
StdForeColor        Black
StdBackColor        SteelBlue
HiForeColor         Black
HiBackColor         red

#set up the desk top and pager
DeskTopSize 3x2
DeskTopScale 32
Pager 0 0

# list the windows that don't get a decorative border
NoTitle xclock

# list the windows that follow when changing desktop
Sticky xclock

# list windows that "stay on top" of the window stack
StaysOnTop xclock
```

The .fvwmrc file also specifies what happens when you press one of the mouse buttons, either around a window's border or in the desktop's background. The usual options are to allow you to move a window round the desktop, resize a window, alter the stacking order of any windows which overlap, and exit from **fvwm** (and therefore from X-windows as well). A typical specification for an **fvwm** menu might be:

```
Popup "Window Ops"
    Title   "Window Ops"
    Move    "Move Window"
    Resize  "Resize Window"
    Raise   "Raise Window"
    Lower   "Lower Window"
    Iconify "(De)Iconify Window"
    Stick   "(Un)Stick Window"
    Nop     " "
    Destroy "Destroy Window"
    Delete  "Delete Window"
    Nop     " "
    Title   "Exit"
    Quit    "Exit Fvwm"
EndPopup
```

Where the first column specifies the action which should take place when a particular menu option is selected, and the second column gives the text which is to appear on screen, in the menu itself.

The mouse button bindings to the menus are specified later using lines like:

```
# Button      Context Modifiers  Function
Mouse 1          R        N      PopUp "Window Ops"
```

This example says that the *Window Ops* menu should *Popup* when the left mouse button is pressed anywhere in the desktop background (root) window.

10.5 xterm

There are several terminal emulators available to work under X-windows, the most common being **xterm**. In order to provide both VT102 and 4014 emulation, the **xterm** provides two separate windows, either or both of which may be visible at any particular point in time. Even if both of the windows are visible, only one of them can be in use for input and output at a time.

Each of the windows has a set of menus associated with it which can be activated by moving the mouse cursor inside the window boundary and holding down the **Ctrl** key on the keyboard whilst pressing one of the mouse buttons.

Inside the VT102 window there are three menus available, one for each of the three mouse buttons. The left button displays the **main options** menu, the center button gives the **VT options** menu and the right button gives the **VT fonts** menu.

The **VT options** menu provides several control options, the most useful being:

- Enable and disable a scroll bar on the window, allowing you to scroll back through lines of text that have already scrolled off the top of the screen.
- Provide several terminal reset options to get you out of problem situations should the terminal be sent an invalid control character sequence which leaves it in an unusable state.
- Control the display and activation of the Tektronics 4014 window.

From within the 4014 window there are two menus available: the *main options* menu, which is the same as the VT102 equivalent, and the *Tek options* menu, which controls displayed character size and displays and activates the VT102 window.

Chapter 11

Communications

One of the most important modern developments in computing is not related to the size of machines or the speed or type of the processor, but is all about connecting machines together, so that data and other resources can be shared, even over great distances.

Linux is not in any sense being left behind in its ability to connect to other systems – both other Linux and non-Linux systems. Indeed, it makes available all of the popular standard communication mechanisms.

As a system administrator, there are many things you may need to know in order that you can properly establish the communication links between your machine and others. In particular, you may be involved in the installation and setup of serial or parallel line links or ethernet connections, and in the configuration of the machine to operate on these links.

11.1 Stand Alone Machines

Even if your machine is not going to be connected to any others, there is still a lot of software available which has been written to use sockets as an inter-process communication mechanism. The socket mechanism is supported by Linux and it is the standard way by which processes on two separate machines can communicate with each other over a network.

Although socket code assumes that the two communicating processes are on separate machines, there is nothing to prevent the communication from taking place between two processes on the same machine.

In order to do this, it only needs to be configured. First, you need to make sure that the networking packages were loaded onto your machine during system installation. If you installed from the Slackware distribution then the N disk set is the one containing the network software.

Next, when you build a new kernel, you just need to include the basic networking options during the `make config` procedure, though you should not opt to include any of the networking cards themselves, unless you actually have a network card fitted.

Finally, for many distributions, you just need to run the `netconfig` command and answer a few simple questions.

For a stand alone machine, `netconfig` will only ask for three pieces of information, these are:

hostname This is the name you want to give to your machine (strictly, the name is associated with its network interface). The name can be any single word you like. Most people choose something like the dog's name or the name of a fictional character or a role play character – *wendy*, for example.
domain name This is the name of the network to which the machine is connected. If your machine is to be stand alone then the choice here is just academic and it is probably simplest just to provide a single word – something like *mynet* perhaps.
loopback This is where the choice for a stand alone machine is made. A stand alone machine can use only local loopback so you will enter `yes` as the answer to this question.

By this stage, the `netconfig` program has all the information it needs to configure the system just for networking with local loopback only, and no further questions need to be asked. Your machine's full network name is given as the hostname followed by the domain name, and given the previous example values, this would appear as follows:

    wendy.mynet

11.2 TCP/IP

If you do not have a copy of `netconfig` with your Linux distribution so that you have to configure your network software manually, or if you need to configure your machine to run on a network via an ethernet card, then you will need more information than just the hostname and domain name for your system.

hostname As before, the hostname is just a single word to identify your machine connection to the network. If you are adding your machine to an existing network then there could be some local naming convention that you may be required to follow. If you are in this situation then the existing network administrator will be able to advise you.
domain name Here again, if you are connecting to an existing network, there will be an existing domain name which you will be required to use when you add your machine. Again, the local administrator is the person to contact for advice.

IP address Data is moved around a TCP/IP network using the *Internet Protocol* where each machine connection to the network (the network covers the whole world in the case of the Internet) has a unique number which is used to address it, called its *IP address*. These IP addresses are just 32-bit numbers, which are usually given as four separate bytes, and written as four decimal numbers separated by periods (full stops). For example, 199.38.231.66. The first part of the IP address specifies to which network the address refers (network address), and the rest specifies a particular machine connection (host number) on that network.

network mask This is a 4-byte number which specifies how much of an IP address is the network address and how much is the host number on that network. The first part of the network mask (netmask) contains binary 1 bits to indicate the bit positions that specify the network address, and the remainder contains binary 0 bits to indicate the bit positions that specify the host number. By default, it is possible to work out what the netmask value should be, just from the first byte of the IP address, as follows:

IP range	netmask
up to 127	255.0.0.0
128 to 191	255.255.0.0
192 on	255.255.255.0

network address This is a 4-byte number which can be calculated just as the bitwise AND of the IP address and its netmask value. For example, if the IP address is 195.123.48.12 and the netmask, from the previous table, is 255.255.255.0, then the network address is 195.123.48.0.

broadcast address This is also a 4-byte value, calculated as the bitwise OR of the network address and the inverse of the netmask. Continuing with the previous example, the network address is 195.123.48.0 and the inverse of the netmask is 0.0.0.255, which gives a broadcast address of 195.123.48.255.

gateway address This is the IP address of the machine connection on your network through which you can gain access to machines that don't share your network address. These gateway machines will have connections to at least two networks and have the ability to transfer network traffic between the networks, as required. You will need to get this address from your local administrator if you are connecting your machine to an existing network.

name server address A name server is a machine, one of whose functions is to provide the service of translating hostname and domain name pairs into IP addresses. The setup of a small network doesn't need a name server and adding a new machine to an existing network just means getting the name server IP address from the local administrator.

Armed with all these names and numbers you are now ready to do some network setup. Still the easiest option if you have `netconfig` available is to use it, providing the necessary details as it asks for them. But now, if you don't have `netconfig` available, it is a fairly simple task to configure the networking yourself.

11.2.1 Manual Network Configuration

Don't forget, when you add a network card to your machine, you will need to rebuild the Linux kernel and add your particular card type to the kernel configuration, which you supply when you run `make config`.

When your system first boots, one of the things it needs to do, if you want to run networking software, is to start up the networking system.

This involves setting up the machine's network interfaces with the `ifconfig` command, setting up the kernel's routing tables with the `route` command, and then executing the daemons that will provide the various network services.

Unfortunately, when it comes to setting up the files needed to start up networking, there is no single standard to which all Linux distributions adhere to dictate where the files should be stored or even what the files should be called. However, most distributions do store these files in the directory hierarchy, somewhere under `/etc` and the files of interest are given names like `rc.net`, `rc.inet` or `rc.inet1` and `rc.inet2`.

The execution of these and other `rc` files is performed at system boot time. The first process to run when the system boots is process number 1, called `init`. This process periodically consults the file `/etc/inittab` to find out what it should do under various sets of circumstances, and executing appropriate `rc` files is one of its tasks. Sometimes `init` will be configured to execute the network setup files directly, sometimes it will just execute another `rc` file, which will in turn execute the network setup files instead. Either way, when the files execute there are several specific tasks to be performed.

11.2.2 Setting Hostname

The first task is set up your machine's hostname. This is done with the `hostname` command. What you need is for this command to be executed for you each time your machine boots. Normally, the command will be executed by one of the `rc` files run by `init`. The command itself has the format:

```
# hostname grunthos
```

where, in this example, `grunthos` is the hostname to be set up. Instead of setting the hostname directly like this, some Linux distributions use a line like the following:

```
# hostname `cat /etc/HOSTNAME | cut -f1 -d .`
```

and then put the fully qualified host and domain name into the file `/etc/HOSTNAME`, as the following example shows:

```
$ cat /etc/HOSTNAME
grunthos.staffs.ac.uk
```

This is a rather simpler arrangement for an automatic configuration program, which only has to re-write the contents of `/etc/HOSTNAME` when the hostname is set up rather than editing the hostname line in the middle of some other configuration file.

11.2.3 Networking Startup Files

From this point on, the discussion assumes that your system uses the network startup files:

```
/etc/rc.d/rc.inet1
/etc/rc.d/rc.inet2
```

Even if this is not the case, the same tasks need to be performed but just using different files.

The first task (in `rc.inet1`) is to configure the loopback device, with the following command sequence, which involves the `ifconfig` and `route` commands:

```
#!/bin/sh

/sbin/ifconfig lo 127.0.0.1
/sbin/route add -net 127.0.0.0
```

Obviously, if your `ifconfig` and `route` commands are not in the directory `/sbin` then you will need to modify these lines to suit your own directory layout.

The first line here is just to specify which shell should be used to execute the rest of the commands. The `ifconfig` command is used to specify the name of the local loopback interface (`lo`) and its IP address of `127.0.0.1`. The `route` command adds the network to which the local loopback address belongs to the kernel's routing table, so that IP packets sent to the local loopback address will be routed correctly.

After this, if you have an ethernet card fitted then this also needs to be configured by adding lines to the `rc.inet1` file like the following:

```
IPADDR="ip.ip.ip.ip"
NETMASK="nm.nm.nm.nm"
NETWORK="nw.nw.nw.nw"
BROADCAST="bc.bc.bc.bc"
GATEWAY="gw.gw.gw.gw"

/sbin/ifconfig eth0 ${IPADDR} broadcast ${BROADCAST} netmask ${NETMASK}
/sbin/route add -net ${NETWORK} netmask ${NETMASK}

/sbin/route add default gw ${GATEWAY} metric 1
```

Obviously, you need to replace the `ip`, `nm`, `nw`, `bc` and `gw` values above with your own, proper address values.

The `ifconfig` command associates an IP address with the first ethernet interface, called eth0. After that, the `route` command that follows adds an entry to the kernel routing table specifying that network traffic bound for the local network should be sent through this interface. The final line is the routing information for all network traffic outside the local network. It just specifies that this traffic should take the default route through the gateway machine. If you only have a local network so that there is no gateway machine, then this last line should be omitted.

Once the network interfaces and routes are set up the next thing to do is execute the daemons and servers associated with network applications. In our example, these things are arranged by the file `rc.inet2`.

In a simple arrangement, only two servers need to be run from `rc.inet2`. These are `syslogd`, which is used to log system messages and error reports (usually into the file `/var/log/messages`), and `inetd`, which makes a number of services available from your machine, including `telnet`, `ftp`, `finger` and `rlogin`, of which more later.

An `rc.inet2` file to run these daemons could be:

```
# Start the syslogd daemon.
if [ -f /usr/sbin/syslogd ]
then
     /usr/sbin/syslogd
fi

# Start the INET SuperServer
if [ -f /usr/sbin/inetd ]
then
     /usr/sbin/inetd
fi
```

In some Linux distributions the `syslogd` and `inetd` programs may not reside in /usr/bin so you will have to make the appropriate changes to the contents of rc.inet2 to match the arrangement of your system.

All that now remains is to create and/or populate a few simple files to specify some IP names and addresses. Once again, if you have and use the `netconfig` command these files will be set up for you. The four files are called:

```
/etc/networks
/etc/hosts
/etc/host.conf
/etc/resolve.conf
```

Taking each of these files in turn, let us sort out what each is for and also examine their typical contents.

11.2.4 /etc/networks

This file contains a list of network names and their associated network numbers. The file is used by the `route` command in the situation where you want to add a route to a complete network to your kernel's routing table, and you want to specify the network by name rather than by number. In this case, the `route` command will use the file `/etc/networks` to look up the network number from the name. Typical contents for this file could be:

```
loopback        127.0.0.0
phil-net        194.61.21.0
```

Obviously, you would use your own network numbers in your `/etc/networks` file in place of the ones above. If you specify a network number directly to the `route` command rather than a network name, then that entry need not appear in the networks file.

11.2.5 /etc/hosts

This file contains a list of machine IP numbers and their associated IP address names. For large private networks and for the Internet, the names of network hosts are translated into the appropriate IP numbers by requesting the information from a name server. However, for small networks without a name server, or on larger networks, to cover the time at system boot before the name servers are running, you can put a small number of IP numbers and names in `/etc/hosts` and arrange for the system to look in the hosts file for IP name and address translations before it tries to contact a name server. Typical file contents would be:

```
127.0.0.1           localhost
194.61.21.50        grunthos.staffs.ac.uk grunthos
```

This just says that the IP address for the `localhost` is 127.0.0.1 (which is always the case) and that the IP address for the host `grunthos.staffs.ac.uk` is 194.61.21.50. The lines of this file also allow you to specify alias names for the given hostnames. The second line shows the specification of an alias of `grunthos` which can subsequently be used as an abbreviated hostname.

For small, stand alone networks there need not be a name server, and then each machine on the network would just rely on the contents of its own hosts file for hostname to IP address translation.

11.2.6 /etc/host.conf

This file controls how and in what order the system will try to use the various name services. A typical `/etc/host.conf` file would be:

```
order hosts, bind
multi on
```

The first line specifies that when a process requests a hostname to IP number lookup, the request will be ordered as follows: first the file `/etc/hosts` will be consulted and only if the required information is not found there will the `bind` service be used, that is, the local name server will be contacted for the information. The second line in the example specifies that hosts detailed in `/etc/hosts` are allowed to have multiple IP address numbers for the same host.

11.2.7 /etc/resolv.conf

The main uses for the file `resolv.conf` are to specify a list of name servers to try when looking up IP address numbers from hostnames, and to specify a domain name which will be appended to a hostname when `bind` fails to resolve the name with the first lookup. The latter facility allows you to specify hostnames in the local domain as just machine names and still have their IP address numbers correctly resolved, albeit on the second attempt.

A typical `/etc/resolv.conf` file could be:

```
domain staffs.ac.uk
nameserver 194.61.21.1
```

When specifying multiple name servers, each one has its own `nameserver` line in the file `/etc/resolv.conf` and the order of the lines is used to determine the order in which the name servers are contacted.

Whilst this section cannot hope to cover all there is to know about network setup, the previous instructions should cover most simple network configurations. But, if you *are* adding your machine to a more complex network setup then there will, in all probability, be an existing network guru on hand to help you out anyway.

11.3 PPP

In addition to networking using ethernet and local loopback there are also several arrangements for point to point links between pairs of machines using RS232 serial or Centronics parallel ports.

The first one to look at, and probably the best, is PPP which operates over a standard RS232 serial link. PPP stands for point to point protocol and it is a standard internet protocol.

The PPP software comes in two parts. The first part is built into the kernel which means that you will need to build kernels for the machines at each end of the link which have PPP configured into them. This is just a matter of saying yes to the PPP option when running `make config`. The second part is a daemon called pppd which will need to be running on both machines when the PPP link is established.

The most common use of PPP is on modem dial-up connections and that is the setup we will consider here.

Suppose that you have a Linux machine at home and you want to dial up another Linux machine at a remote site which is attached to the Internet. When the PPP link is set up this arrangement will give you full Internet access from your machine at home.

11.3.1 Remote Site Setup

The first thing to consider is the setup at the remote site. The simplest way to get this working is to create a PPP login on that machine specifically for your dial-in purposes. Start by adding a line to the password file such as the following:

```
ppp: off :700:700:PPP account:/home/ppp:/home/ppp/ppplogin
```

You should insert your own ppp account name, uid, gid and home directory in place of my examples. You should then create the account home directory /home/ppp (or whatever yours is called) and change its ownership appropriately:

```
# mkdir /home/ppp
# chown ppp. /home/ppp
```

Notice that the password line you added specifies the login 'shell' as:

```
/home/ppp/ppplogin
```

This isn't actually a shell but a script that will be used to start up the pppd daemon on the remote system. Typical contents for this file would be:

```
#! /bin/sh
exec /usr/sbin/pppd 38400 modem asyncmap 0 proxyarp\
      194.61.21.2:194.61.21.49
```

which probably requires some explanation. The first line specifies that the rest of the script should be executed by /bin/sh. The other line (a \ on the end of a line means that the next line is just a continuation of the current line) runs the exec command which will replace the program in the current process with the specified program (here pppd). The rest of the line is just a set of command line parameters to pppd.

The first parameter (38400) is the speed at which pppd should drive the serial interface to the modem. The modem parameter specifies that pppd should use the modem control lines in the RS232 interface to make sure that the PPP connection is broken cleanly when you hang up the phone line at the local end.

The next parameter is `asyncmap 0`. Depending upon the precise details of your serial connection to the remote machine, it is possible that your connection uses some of the ASCII control codes (codes 0 to 31) for special purposes, so that these codes are not available to be transmitted as part of a data packet. In this case you need to tell `pppd` not to use these control codes but to replace them with special two-character escape sequences. The number after the `asyncmap` keyword is a 32-bit hexadecimal number, where each bit that is set corresponds to an ASCII code which `pppd` must not use. If you have a serial link which is 8-bit clean, then `asyncmap 0` specifies that none of the ASCII control codes needs to be escaped. If no `asyncmap` option is given then the default is to escape all 32 control codes.

The physical ethernet that sits under a TCP/IP network does not know about IP address numbers. It routes its data packets on the basis of hardware ethernet addresses. The protocol that translates IP address numbers to hardware ethernet addresses is called the *Address Resolution Protocol* (`ARP`). A typical machine `ARP` table can be displayed with the `arp` command, as follows:

```
# arp -a
Address            HW type          HW address         Flags Mask
194.61.21.1        10Mbps Ethernet  08:00:2B:F7:E2:44  C     *
194.61.21.6        10Mbps Ethernet  08:00:2B:57:89:CE  C     *
194.61.21.252      10Mbps Ethernet  AA:00:04:40:0A:0C  C     *
194.61.21.50       10Mbps Ethernet  00:40:95:85:0C:B5  CMP   *
194.61.21.49       10Mbps Ethernet  00:40:95:85:0C:B5  CMP   *
```

The `proxyarp` parameter to `pppd` will add an entry to the arp table on the remote machine which contains the IP address number of your local machine listed along side the hardware ethernet address of the remote machine. This makes the remote machine respond with its own hardware ethernet address whenever it sees requests for the hardware ethernet address of your local machine. IP packets addressed to your local machine will then be picked up by the remote machine and routed over the PPP link to your local machine. The last two entries in the example arp table are `proxyarp` entries, both sharing the hardware ethernet address of the remote machine but having the IP address numbers of two machines at the local end of the PPP link.

The last parameter to the `pppd` command specifies the IP address numbers of the remote machine and your local machine respectively, separated by a colon.

There are other options which can be specified, especially if you want to run `pppd` with authentication of machines switched on, for extra security. The details of these options can be found in the `pppd` manual page.

The last thing that needs to be done at the remote site is to set an appropriate password on the `ppp` account.

11.3.2 Local Site Setup

The setup on the local machine is relatively straightforward. It consists of writing a shell script which will run the pppd daemon on your local machine and then dial the remote machine over your modem and log you into its ppp login. The simplest way to do this is to use pppd in conjunction with a dial-up program called chat.

The pppd and chat programs are automatically loaded, along with several other useful programs and scripts, when you install the ppp package from your Linux distribution.

A typical script to connect to the remote machine could be:

```
/usr/sbin/pppd connect '/usr/sbin/chat "" ATDT334566
CONNECT "" ogin: ppp word: PA55word' /dev/modem 38400
modem defaultroute -ip 194.61.21.49:194.61.21.233
```

This script should all be entered as a single long line in a text file and made executable with chmod. This script just runs the pppd command and passes it various parameter values. The first command line parameter to pppd is connect cmd, where cmd is a command or script to run to establish the modem link.

In this example, cmd is everything between the single quotes ('). The contents of the quotes is a call to the chat program with all the parameters it requires to operate. The parameters to the chat program specify a dialogue which is to take place over the serial line to which the modem is attached. This dialogue takes the form of pairs of *expect* and *send* strings. As an expect string, a pair of empty double quotes ("") means expect nothing. The following send string (ATDT334566) is a Hayes-compatible modem command to tell the local modem to dial the number of the remote modem.

The next expect/send string pair is CONNECT "". This says expect to receive the CONNECT string and when that happens send a newline down the line (as a send string, a pair of empty quotes mean send a newline). The word CONNECT is sent by the remote modem when it has answered the local modem's ring and after it has negotiated an operating speed.

In response to the newline, the remote machine should send us a login: prompt and wait for a login name to be sent. Therefore, the next expect/send string pair is ogin: ppp. Using ogin: allows the login prompt to start with either an upper or lower case letter. So, the string pair says: expect to receive a string from the remote system ending in ogin: and when you get it respond with the ppp login name.

Having entered a login name, the remote system should ask for the associated password. Therefore, the last string pair says: expect to receive a string from the remote system ending in word: and respond to it by sending the password to the ppp login (PA55word in this example).

If all goes according to plan then the remote system should now run its ppplogin script which, as you have already seen, will activate the pppd daemon on the remote machine.

The next three parameters to `pppd` in the local startup script specify the device special file associated with the local modem, the baud rate at which to 'talk' to the modem, and an instruction to use modem control lines in the serial link.

The next parameter (`defaultroute`) instructs `pppd` to add a default route to the kernel's routing table which sends network packets for any machines not already specified in the routing table over the PPP link to the remote machine. The `defaultroute` option will only work if the kernel's routing table doesn't already contain a default entry. This means that in order to use this option, your `rc.inet1` file should not contain the last line given in our previous example file, which sets up a default route to your gateway machine. In our PPP scenario the remote machine will be the gateway to the rest of the world and `pppd` will set up the default route to this machine when the link is established.

The final parameters to `pppd` (`-ip 194.61.21.49:194.61.21.233`) tell it not to negotiate IP address numbers with the remote machine but to use the two IP numbers specified, for the local machine and remote machine respectively.

Once the PPP link is established it will operate just as though your local machine was connected directly to the Internet. When you have finished with the link, you just execute the supplied script called `ppp-off` and the link will be terminated and the systems reset ready for the next time the link is required.

Extra information on PPP is available in the `pppd` and `chat` manual pages and in the PPP-HOWTO document supplied as part of the Linux documentation.

11.4 Other Connection Methods

In addition to the networking mechanisms we have already considered, there are also several other possibilities, though in general these are lesser alternatives.

11.4.1 SLIP

SLIP is a serial line IP protocol which is being superseded by PPP. This is largely because PPP is an Internet standard whereas SLIP is not. In concept, SLIP is quite similar to PPP except that SLIP is less robust and rather more error prone.

In order for Linux to support SLIP, it needs to be configured and built into the kernel at kernel build time. As usual, this is just a case of saying *yes* to the appropriate option when you are setting the configuration at the start of the kernel build.

Once SLIP is built into the kernel, a program called `dip` can be run, which acts for SLIP much like the combination of `pppd` and `chat` act for PPP.

The way to use `dip` is to generate a script file which specifies the sequence of actions and operations you need `dip` to perform. See the `dip` manual page for details of generating and modifying script files.

11.4.2 PLIP

PLIP is a parallel line IP protocol. It can be used to connect two machines over standard parallel printer ports. This arrangement might be useful where, for instance, you have a notebook or laptop computer without a standard network interface and would like to be able to connect it, from time to time, to your desktop machine at home or in the office.

Once again, PLIP is an option which needs to be compiled into your kernel before it can be used. However, once it is available in the kernel, setting up the software is quite straightforward. The only difficulty with a PLIP setup is in getting hold of a lead to connect the two machines together. In fact, you can buy the necessary cable as a parallel Laplink cable, or you may opt to build the cable yourself if you are handy with a soldering iron.

If you want to go for the DIY option you will need a pair of 25-way male D-type connectors (to plug into the printer ports of your two machines) and a suitable length of multi-core cable with at least 12 individual wires in it. Once you have assembled the bits, the necessary connections are as follows:

Plug A		Plug B
2	—	15
3	—	13
4	—	12
5	—	10
6	—	11
10	—	5
11	—	6
12	—	4
13	—	3
15	—	2
17	—	17
25	—	25

All the other pins in both plugs should remain unconnected.

In order to get a PLIP link working once the two machines are connected together all you need to do is to add the following lines to the `rc.inet1` configuration files:

```
/sbin/ifconfig plip0 la.la.la.la pointopoint ra.ra.ra.ra up
/sbin/route add -host ra.ra.ra.ra plip0
```

where `la.la.la.la` is the local machine IP address number and `ra.ra.ra.ra` is the remote machine IP address number.

11.4.3 UUCP

Before the advent of the Internet the only real communication between machines was performed over serial links, typically using slow modems. Even in this situation there was still a requirement to send e-mail between users on different machines and a need to upload and download files.

UUCP was designed to fulfill these early requirements by providing a simple dial-up network over ordinary telephone lines with modems. Although UUCP has been around for many years there are still large numbers of machines that use the system.

The setup of UUCP requires the creation and configuration of several files the details of which are beyond the scope of this book. There is, however, a very readable account of the basics of UUCP setup in the Linux Network Administrator's Guide, available as part of the Linux documentation project and also available with the extras in many Linux distributions.

11.4.4 kermit and seyon

Beyond the network interfaces for communication, there are several programs which provide you with the ability to make a connection and login to a remote machine, and which will then act as a dumb terminal emulator for the duration of your login session. As an extra feature, most of the programs of this type also allow you the facility to upload and download files. In general, uploading a file means transferring the contents of a file from your local machine to the machine at the remote end of the link. And downloading a file means transferring it the other way, from the remote machine to your local machine.

Two programs that are easy to obtain for Linux are kermit and seyon. The kermit program will operate directly on a standard terminal screen, while seyon needs to be run within an X-windows environment.

Conceptually, the two programs are very similar, though their user interfaces are very different. In order to give the flavor of the facilities available with these programs we shall look at one of them (kermit) in more detail.

The kermit program can be used in one of several different ways. To start with, kermit can be used in an interactive mode, in which it will repeatedly display a prompt, accept user commands and execute them.

For some options, kermit can also be used in a command line mode, where you run the program and specify the actions you want it to perform as a set of command line parameters. In this mode, the specified actions will be performed and then kermit will terminate and return you to a shell prompt.

When you are transferring files there will be two copies of kermit running, one on each machine. Both copies of kermit are under your control on the local machine. In order to achieve this the kermit running on the remote machine will be placed into a remote server mode, where it takes and executes its commands over the communication link between the two machines.

Whichever way kermit gets run, it can also read a command file called .kermrc in your home directory. This file will normally be used to set up any default parameters you want kermit to use in its operating environment.

A typical sequence of events for transferring a binary data file from a remote machine to your local machine via a dial-up modem connection could be:

- Run the `kermit` program on your local machine with the command:

    kermit

    You may need to add the directory which contains the `kermit` program to your `PATH` environment variable.
- Make the dial-up connection to the remote machine:

    set modem hayes
    set line /dev/modem
    set speed 38400
    dial 334566
    connect

    This sequence is pretty self-explanatory, and after the `connect` command you should be able to get a login prompt from the remote machine. Incidentally, when you enter the `connect` command, make a note of the escape sequence which will get you out of the terminal emulator and back to the `kermit>` prompt (typically it will be something like `Ctrl-\ c`).
- Login to the remote machine, find the file you want to transfer and then run `kermit` on the remote machine. You will now get a `kermit>` prompt from the remote machine.
- In response to the remote prompt you should enter the command:

    server

    This will put the remote `kermit` into server mode ready for file transfer.
- Now you should type your local `kermit`'s escape sequence (which you noted earlier). This will get you back to a `kermit>` prompt but this time it is from your local machine.
- Now you can issue the command to transfer the file:

    set file type binary
    get datafile

    The first command in this sequence tells `kermit` what type of file to expect. As far as `kermit` is concerned there are two types of file: binary data and text. You need to make sure that `kermit` is set to the correct type. If in doubt then use `binary` though the transfer will take longer. Obviously, you should substitute the name `datafile` with the name of the file you want to fetch. In order for this command to work, your local `kermit` will pass commands to the remote `kermit` server, which in turn will send the required file.

- When this file transfer has finished, you can request the transfer of further files just by issuing more `get` commands. After you have got all the files you want you can switch the remote `kermit` out of server mode and back into interactive mode with the command:

    finish

    When the server has shut down, you will get a `kermit>` prompt from the local machine. If at this point you issue a `connect` command then it will switch your local `kermit` back into being a terminal emulator and you will get another `kermit>` prompt, but this time from the remote machine.
- Typing the command:

    quit

    will now terminate the remote `kermit` and return you to a shell prompt from the remote machine.
- When you have finished with your terminal session on the remote machine you should log off. You then type the escape sequence to get back to the `kermit>` prompt from your local machine. Finally, typing the `quit` command to this prompt will terminate the local `kermit` and return you to a shell prompt.

There are many more options to `kermit` than you have seen here, but this should have given you the basic idea. For more information there is a fairly comprehensive help facility built into `kermit` itself, which you can access just by typing `help` to a `kermit>` prompt.

Chapter 12

Internet

The Internet is a world wide collection of separate physical networks, all interconnected, and using the Internet Protocol (IP) to link them all into a single logical network.

But what is it all for? What can you do with it? The simplest way to tackle these questions is to take a look at the main services available to anyone with a full Internet connection. They include:

e-mail Electronic mail (e-mail) is the way that one Internet user can communicate on a one-to-one basis with any other user.

telnet The telnet program allows you to login to any machine on the Internet to which you have a user account and password.

ftp As its name suggests, the file transfer protocol (ftp) program allows files to be transferred between machines.

archie Helps to find information about the kind of files archived at many ftp sites.

usenet news Imagine a world wide bulletin board with many thousands of special interest groups on virtually any topic you want... .

gopher This is another service which allows you to locate and retrieve documents. With its search program (called `veronica`), `gopher` is like a cross between `archie` and `ftp`, only more sophisticated. The `gopher` service is now largely being superseded by the `world wide web`.

world wide web Provides a framework within which hypertext documents can be created and viewed. The documents can contain hypertext links to other documents on any other world wide web (WWW) servers anywhere on the Internet.

In this chapter we'll take a brief look at each of these services to give you a head start when you get an Internet connection sorted out.

12.1 e-mail

Electronic mail (e-mail) is the primary mechanism used to communicate on a one-to-one basis between users on the same machine or, over a network, between users on separate machines.

Sending e-mail is conceptually very similar to sending ordinary postal mail. Anyone who needs to be reached by e-mail has to have an e-mail address, in the same way that in order to receive a letter you have to have a postal address.

Normally, your full postal address will start with your name and then give your house number, street name, town, area, and country. The address provides a hierarchy of information which is used when the mail is delivered, to get it closer and closer to its destination. In the same way, a user's e-mail address has a similar hierarchical structure. For example, my current e-mail address is:

`pc@soc.staffs.ac.uk`

In terms of the hierarchy, the information should be read right to left. This means that the first item is the country code – United Kingdom (`uk`) in my case. All e-mail addresses, except those in the USA, have a country code. The USA is different because it is the default country if no code is given (after all, they did start it all off). Within the `uk`, my e-mail address is in the academic community (`ac`), specifically at Staffordshire University (`staffs`) and, within that, the School of Computing (`soc`).

When someone sends me some e-mail then, in effect, the machine at my local end acts like a post office, in that it receives and stores any incoming mail that is addressed to me until such time as I go to collect it. Similarly, the remote machine from which the mail was sent also acts like a post office for the sender of my message.

As well as passing through the source and destination machines, an e-mail message with any distance to travel will probably pass through several other (post office) machines on the way, though the sender of the message need have no knowledge of these intermediate machines as the mail should be routed automatically. This idea is illustrated in Figure 12.1.

In general, e-mail addresses have the format:

`user@destination`

where the sender need have no knowledge or control of the route taken by the messages. Sometimes, however, you may wish to specify a particular set of machines through which you want the mail to pass. This can be done by specifying the destination address and one or more relay machines as follows:

`user%destination%relay1@relay2`

Using this syntax an e-mail message to `user` on the `destination` machine will be routed via `relay2` and then `relay1`. Notice, that the list of machines is visited in

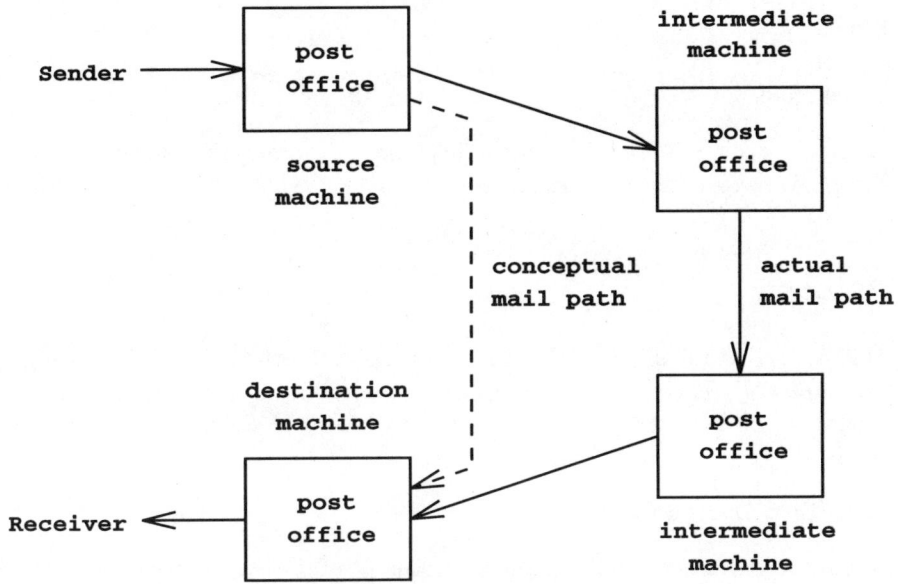

Figure 12.1 Passing e-mail from machine to machine.

right to left order and that the route contains only one @ symbol. The next machine for the mail to get to is the one to the right of the @ symbol. When the mail gets there the @ symbol and the following machine name are stripped from the mail route and then the rightmost % symbol is changed to an @ symbol and the mail is then routed on.

What we have considered so far is just the mail transport part of e-mail delivery – the way e-mail gets from machine to machine. Typically in a Linux installation the e-mail transport will be performed either by a program called smail or one called sendmail. For full Internet connectivity, the configuration of these two programs can be quite involved. Fortunately, several of the more complete Linux distributions come with simple scripts to configure the mail transport program to cover most simple situations.

I strongly recommend that you use one these configuration scripts if you need to set up e-mail for yourself. You should also take a look through the Linux Mail-HOWTO document, which highlights some common problems and solutions for various mail related programs.

In addition to an e-mail transport program, you will also need to provide a means to read and post mail messages, i.e. an e-mail user interface program, or mail reader. There are many mail readers available to run under Linux, several of which are supplied with the main Linux distributions. The list includes:

- elm;
- deliver;

- pine;
- mailx;
- metamail.

My personal favorite is `elm`, but this is just through familiarity, since all the mail readers perform essentially the same task.

12.2 `telnet`

The `telnet` program allows users to communicate between machines using the TELNET protocol. The most common use of `telnet` is to allow users to login to remote machines over the network. The general form of the `telnet` command to do this is:

```
$ telnet host.domain
```

where `host.domain` is the fully qualified hostname of the system to which you wish to connect. If successful, this command will result in a `login:` prompt from the remote machine.

Once you are logged in to a remote machine then `telnet` behaves like a dumb terminal, so that any characters you type are just sent to the remote machine. That is, unless you enter the `telnet` escape sequence. By default, the escape sequence is `Ctrl-]` and if you enter this sequence, your terminal session will be interrupted and you will get the following prompt from your local `telnet` program:

```
telnet>
```

Just pressing `Enter` at this prompt will reconnect you to the remote machine, so that your remote session can continue.

There are many commands that can be entered at the prompt for controlling various aspects of your `telnet` session and they are fully detailed in the `telnet` manual page. For example, the command to change the escape character sequence is:

```
telnet> set escape ^X
escape character is '^X'.
```

After typing `set escape` you just type the character sequence to be used from now on (`Ctrl-X` in this example) and `telnet` responds by confirming your request and resuming your remote session.

All of the Internet services have default port numbers that the servers use and to which the clients must connect when they request a particular service. A list of the default port numbers can be found in the file:

```
/etc/services
```

The default port for `telnet` is port number 23, so that, normally, your `telnet` program will automatically use this port when making a connection to the `telnet` service on a remote machine. However, you can use your local `telnet` program to make a dumb terminal connection to any other port number on a remote machine just by adding the required port number to the initial `telnet` command line:

```
$ telnet host.domain port
```

where `port` will be replaced with the required number.

As an example, the following sequence shows telnet being used to send a mail message by communicating directly with the remote machine's mail transport program on the default e-mail port number, which is port 25:

```
$ telnet grunthos 25
mail from: <pc>
250 <pc>... Sender ok
rcpt to: <saw>
250 <saw>... Recipient ok
data
354 Enter mail, end with "." on a line by itself
Hi
This is just a test message...
.
250 WAA00321 Message accepted for delivery
```

The lines with numbers on the front are confirmation messages and prompts from the remote machine's mail transport program, and the rest of the lines are commands and message text typed into `telnet` on the local machine.

12.3 ftp

The `ftp` command is a user interface to the standard file transfer protocol. The purpose of `ftp` is to allow you to transfer files between a local machine and a remote machine, or vice versa. Running `ftp` is done as follows:

```
$ ftp host.domain
```

where `host.domain` is the fully qualified hostname of the required remote machine. The specification of the hostname on the command line is optional but if it is specified, `ftp` will attempt to make a connection to an `ftp` server on the remote machine. If no hostname is specified then `ftp` will issue a prompt and await user commands:

```
$ ftp
ftp>
```

From the `ftp>` prompt, the `open` command followed by a hostname will attempt to connect to the given host.

Either way, when a successful connection is made with a remote machine, you will be required to login. If you have a user login on the remote machine you can use this account with `ftp` and supply its password. On the remote machine you will then have the read and write permissions of the login name you used. These permissions are used to determine what files you can download from the remote machine and to which directories you can upload files.

If you don't have a specific login account on the remote machine then many `ftp` setups have a special account that you can use instead. The login name for this account is called `anonymous` (hence the phrase `anonymous ftp`). When using this login name, you should enter your full e-mail address as the password.

If the remote system provides an `anonymous ftp` facility then using it will log you in to a special, publicly available, file read and write area. In particular, two directories are provided: `pub`, which contains all the files that the remote site is prepared to make available for public downloads, and `incoming`, into which you may upload files you wish to contribute to the remote site.

Once an `ftp` login to the remote site has been achieved you will receive an `ftp>` prompt from your local `ftp` program. You are then free to use any of the built-in `ftp` commands. You can get a list of the commands supported by using the `help` command. You can also type `help` followed by the name of a specific command, which will give you a little detail about that particular command.

The commands you are most likely to want to use are:

`ls`	list current directory on the remote machine;
`cd`	change working directory on the remote machine;
`lcd`	change working directory on the local machine;
`ascii`	set up subsequent file transfers for ascii text files;
`binary`	set up subsequent file transfers for binary image files;
`hash`	display a # after each 1024 byte data block transferred;
`get`	transfer specified file from remote machine to local machine;
`put`	transfer specified file from local machine to remote machine;
`quit`	break connection to remote machine and exit from `ftp`.

A typical `ftp` session to retrieve a binary data file from a remote machine might appear as follows:

```
$ ftp grunthos
Connected to grunthos
220 grunthos FTP server
Name (grunthos:pc): anonymous
331 Guest login ok, send your complete e-mail address as password.
Password:
230 Guest login ok, access restrictions apply.
Remote system type is UNIX.
```

```
ftp> cd pub
250 CWD command successful.
ftp> ls
200 PORT command successful.
150 Opening ASCII mode data connection for /bin/ls.
total 114
drwxr-xr-x   2 root     wheel        1024 Oct 31 23:45 .
drwxr-xr-x   8 root     wheel        1024 Mar 28  1995 ..
-rw-r--r--   1 root     root        14684 Oct 31 23:45 rog1
-rw-r--r--   1 root     root        96547 Oct 31 23:45 rog2
226 Transfer complete.
ftp> binary
200 Type set to I.
ftp> hash
Hash mark printing on (1024 bytes/hash mark).
ftp> get rog1
200 PORT command successful.
150 Opening BINARY mode data connection for rog1 (14684 bytes).
##############
226 Transfer complete.
14684 bytes received in 0.0473 secs (3e+02 Kbytes/sec)
ftp> quit
221 Goodbye.
$
```

This session starts by running **ftp** and requesting a connection to the hostname **grunthos**. After some messages we receive an invitation to supply a login **Name:**. The contents of the brackets (**grunthos:pc**) form the name that will be used if we just press **Enter** at this point. However, we are going to perform an anonymous **ftp** transfer, so we login as **anonymous**. Next we get a request for a password with a prompt reminding us to supply our e-mail address. The password is not echoed so the characters don't appear, but in the example I typed:

    Password: pc@soc.staffs.ac.uk

Having successfully logged in to the remote system we change to the **pub** directory and then list its contents. Deciding to download the file **rog1** we set **ftp** up for binary file transfer and hash (#) mark displays on receipt of each full 1024-byte data block. We then download the file and quit from **ftp**.

If you want to run an anonymous **ftp** service on your own machine then it needs a little care to make sure your system remains secure. Some Linux distributions are supplied with anonymous **ftp** pre-installed and ready to run 'out of the box'. If you need to install it manually then you will need to create an **ftp** login in your **/etc/passwd** file with a password of '*' and a login shell of **/dev/false**. This is to prevent ordinary logins using the **ftp** account. You will also need to set up an `ftp` home directory and a set of subdirectories, such as `pub` and `incoming`. The full details are a little involved but are well covered in the Linux NET-2-HOWTO document.

12.4 archie

Having `ftp` available gives you a very powerful tool. However, it still leaves the basic problem of sorting out where in the world a particular file can be found. This is where the `archie` program comes in.

Various sites around the world have set up `archie` servers, which essentially contain databases of all the file names on all the `ftp` sites they have encountered. If you make an `archie` query from one of these databases then you will be supplied with a list of all the `ftp` sites and file pathnames on those sites where your required file can be found. You can then use a standard `ftp` session to retrieve the files that you located.

There are many `archie` sites in the world – a list of some of the hostnames and associated countries is as follows:

archie.au	Australia
archie.univie.ac.at	Austria
archie.belnet.be	Belgium
archie.bunyip.com	Canada
archie.cs.mcgill.ca	Canada
archie.funet.fi	Finland
archie.univ-rennes1.fr	France
archie.th-darmstadt.de	Germany
archie.ac.il	Israel
archie.unipi.it	Italy
archie.wide.ad.jp	Japan
archie.hana.nm.kr	Korea
archie.uninett.no	Norway
archie.icm.edu.pl	Poland
archie.rediris.es	Spain
archie.luth.se	Sweden
archie.switch.ch	Switzerland
archie.ncu.edu.tw	Taiwan
archie.doc.ic.ac.uk	UK
archie.hensa.ac.uk	UK
archie.sura.net	USA (MD)
archie.unl.edu	USA (NE)
archie.internic.net	USA (NJ)
archie.rutgers.edu	USA (NJ)
archie.ans.net	USA (NY)

In order to use one of these sites you just `telnet` to one of the hostnames in the list and login as `archie`. Some simple information is then returned by the `archie` server, though for a beginner the most useful thing to find and use is the command:

```
archie> help ?
```

This will give you a list of all the commands available and if you subsequently ask for help on a particular command from the list then it will be explained in more detail. When you have finished with help, pressing `Ctrl-c` or `Ctrl-d` will return you to the `archie>` prompt.

The simple way to use `archie` to locate a specific file is with a command like:

```
archie> find posix.1
```

which, after a short search time, will produce a list of all the sites known to contain the required file and the pathnames at those sites to the file itself. It is then a simple matter to use a conventional anonymous `ftp` to retrieve the file itself.

You must remember that the database stored by each of the `archie` sites is its own snapshot of what files are available in the world and, consequently, a particular file may not be on record at all sites.

12.5 Usenet News

Many people have used bulletin board systems (BBS) as a forum for discussion about whatever specialist topics come under the particular BBS remit. The idea behind Usenet News is that it should provide this bulletin board discussion facility, but on a world wide basis and with a huge number of discussion topics.

Discussion topics are called *news groups* and, using a news reader program, you can post your contributions to news groups and read other users' questions and comments.

In order to participate in network news, you need to know the hostname of a news server machine to which you can connect with your news reader. The news servers are machines connected to the news system which receive, on a regular basis, all the news updates from around the world. All the news articles received by the server are stored by it on local disk storage and from there made available to you via your news reader program.

As there are literally thousands of news groups, it means that network news articles arrive at a rate of many mega-bytes per day – far too much for any individual to keep up with. With news arriving at this rate, it requires a fairly sizeable storage space to keep it in and, even then, most news sites can only afford to keep all the news for a few weeks before removing it from the system to make space for new arrivals. The length of time that the news remains available and the range of news groups offered at a particular site are both controlled by the site administrator.

There are two types of news group called *moderated* and *unmoderated*. As its name implies, a moderated news group has a moderator associated with it, to whom all postings for the news group should be sent. It is the moderator's task to screen all postings to the news group to ensure that they are appropriate, before passing them on to the news group itself. In an unmoderated news group, postings are not screened, so that these news groups contain more open and uncensored discussions.

The news groups are organized into hierarchies under several top level categories, some of which are:

`alt`	alternative/miscellaneous discussions;
`comp`	computing discussions;
`rec`	recreation;
`sci`	science topics.

Underneath each of the main category headings there are several subcategories. For example, two of the subcategories under `comp` are:

`comp.lang`	programming languages;
`comp.os`	operating systems.

Each subcategory can be further subdivided until, eventually, the names of individual news groups are reached, such as:

`comp.lang.c`	C programming language discussions;
`comp.os.linux.announce`	special announcements for Linux users.

A good news reader (my personal favorite) available for Linux is called `tin`. This program has a very similar user interface to the `elm` mail reader we mentioned earlier. In order to use `tin` to connect to a remote news server you should use the following commands:

```
$ export NNTPSERVER=your.news.hostname
$ tin -r
```

where you will obviously substitute `your.news.hostname` with the hostname of the machine which will provide your news service.

When you first use network news via a news reader program, it will create a file in your home directory, typically called `.newsrc`, which contains a list of all the news groups currently available to you and a flag for each group listed to say whether or not you currently subscribe to that group.

It is very easy when you first join a news group to want to get up to speed as fast as possible. This usually tempts you to post all sorts of questions to the news group, many of which are likely to be the same beginners' questions that everyone else asks. In order to avoid annoying others with trivial questions and to reduce the number of postings to the news in general, most news groups have a document which is frequently updated and posted on a regular basis (perhaps once per fortnight or once per month) called the *FAQ*, which stands for *frequently asked questions*. Before you post any question to a news group you should always check to see if the answer is contained in that news group's FAQ or in any of the commonly available documents in the area. Failure to do this may well result in you receiving lots of mail (flames) explaining the error of your ways and probably suggesting that you RTFM (read the fine manual).

12.6 gopher

The **gopher** service is quite sophisticated, in that it allows you easy access to a variety of services on the Internet all rolled into a single package.

Sadly, very few Linux distributions include a **gopher** client so that you will need to get hold of a copy separately before you can use it. This is not as big a problem as it sounds as many of the large Internet Linux mirror sites do carry copies. For example, you can **ftp** to:

    src.doc.ic.ac.uk

and find the Linux specific version of **gopher** in the **sunsite** mirror in the directory:

    /unix/Linux/sunsite.unc-mirror/system/Network/info-systems

The **gopher** service itself is provided by a network of server machines. Each of the servers holds its own list of files and information available on that server plus a set of links to give access to resources on other servers.

When you run the **gopher** client on your local machine, you specify the hostname of the server, which will form your starting point into the **gopher** network. For example:

    $ gopher gopher.doc.ic.ac.uk

Having executed this command, you will be presented with the root menu from your chosen **gopher** server. Typically, this will appear as a numbered list with a highlighting arrow alongside one of the menu items:

```
    Root gopher server: gopher.doc.ic.ac.uk
              1.   Welcome to the src.doc.ic.ac.uk gopher server.
       -->    2.   Gopher Services/
              3.   astronomy/
              4.   biology/
              5.   computing/
              6.   gnu/
              7.   ic.doc/
              8.   info/
              9.   packages/
```

```
        10. rfc/
        11. science/
        12. ukuug/
        13. unix/
        14. usenet/
        15. weather/
```

```
      Press ? for Help, q to Quit, u to go up a menu     Page: 1/1
```

Using the arrow keys to move the pointer up and down the menu, you make a selection by pressing the enter key. This will then take you on to another menu. The following submenu was reached by taking option 2 from the root menu of this gopher server:

```
    Gopher Services

            1.  Hosts and people/
    -->     2.  Other gopher servers/
            3.  Useful college services/
```

```
      Press ? for Help, q to Quit, u to go up a menu     Page: 1/1
```

This process of navigating through menus on your server and following links to menus on other servers continues until you reach documents on your topic of interest. In the menus, items with a slash (/) character after them indicate that selecting this option will get you to another submenu. Other entries are files which will be retrieved if selected.

Even with the menu system for navigating `gopherspace` (as the network of gopher databases is known) there is still the problem of knowing just where to look to find a particular subject area. Just as `ftp` uses `archie` to locate particular files so `gopher` uses its own search program called `veronica`. To use `veronica` you enter a set of keywords as a query and the program searches through a huge database of file and menu titles to locate appropriate items, which you can then retrieve as required.

For all its power and flexibility, `gopher` is rapidly being superseded by the `world wide web` as this provides all the functionality of `gopher` and much more besides.

12.7 world wide web

The `world wide web` (`WWW`), like `gopher`, consists of a network of thousands of server machines, which between them hold documents (called *web pages*) on virtually any conceivable subject.

A web page is a document which can contain text and graphics for display. In addition to this, a web page can also contain hypertext links, which allow one page to refer to other web pages anywhere else on the network.

In order to access the web you will need a *web browser*. In general, Linux distributions are not supplied with a web browser so you will need to download one if you want to use the `world wide web`. Currently, the most common web browser is called `netscape`, versions of which can be found at several of the main Linux archive sites or one of their mirror sites.

Once you have a copy of `netscape` installed you will need to start up X-windows in order to run it. When you have `netscape` running, the front page will be displayed, and one of the boxes on the front page is labeled *Location:*. This box contains the location of the web page you are currently viewing. Web pages are written in a language called `hypertext markup language` (`html`). This uses a simple method for marking sections of the document text as headings or ordinary text, or as links to other web pages or links to other places in the current web page.

Every document available on the web has associated with it a link called its `uniform resource locator` (URL). The URL for a document has the format:

`http://www.server.hostname/pathname/on/server`

The URL consists of three sections, as follows:

1. This is the part up to and including the first colon (`http:` here). This part specifies the communication protocol that will be used to transfer any documents found.
2. This is the part between the double slash (`//`) and the first single slash (`/`) characters (`www.server.hostname` here). It gives the hostname of the machine from which the service is being requested.
3. This part is from the first single slash (`/`) to the end of the line (which, in this example, is `/pathname/on/server`). It gives a pathname on the host machine where the required document is to be found.

The big attraction of the web and its browsers is that many different protocols can be used in addition to `http` such as `email`, `news`, `ftp`, `gopher` and `wais`.

When you are reading `html` documents you will find some words highlighted in the text, by color or by underlining. These highlighted words have hypertext links attached to them and clicking on one of them with the mouse will cause the browser to follow the link and display the contents of the document to which the link points.

Just as with `ftp` and `gopher`, the `world wide web` also has search engines available to help you find the URLs of documents related to particular topics. These include:

yahoo	`http://www.yahoo.com/`
lycos	`http://www.lycos.com/`
excite	`http://www.excite.com/`
altavista	`http://altavista.digital.com/`
webCrawler	`http://webcrawler.com/`
inktomi	`http://inktomi.berkeley.edu/`

These systems are quite sophisticated in their search strategies. In general, they take a list of keywords from you and search through their databases looking for documents containing as many of your keywords as possible. The documents retrieved will then be put into order according to some relevance criteria and their titles listed to you a small number at a time, usually with a short extract from the start of the document. The listed titles are made into hypertext links to the documents themselves so that you can click on any titles in which you are interested to retrieve copies of your chosen documents.

In addition to running a `world wide web` client, if your machine will be attached to the Internet full time, it is also possible to run your own web server under Linux. Once again, most distributions do not include a web server but an `archie` search for `cern-httpd` or `NCSA-httpd` will soon locate a copy of one of these two web servers that you can download with `ftp` and install. Complete installation and running instructions are included in the same `tar` file that you download for the server software.

Chapter 13

Running DOS

Despite the best efforts of everyone who has contributed to the Linux development work, there are still one or two of you out there who feel that for one reason or another you cannot get by without access to DOS. Actually, that is quite understandable because there are one or two application packages available for DOS whose functionality has not yet been matched by the free software brigade (not yet...).

Potentially, there are many problems involved in trying to run DOS software in a Linux environment. The majority of these are centered round the fact that DOS is designed to run on 386, and above, processors only by running the CPU in an 8086 backward compatibility mode (called real-mode). Linux on the other hand, whilst it runs on the same processor, switches the CPU into a completely different mode (called protected-mode) where many of the processor's internal registers have different meanings to those that they have in real-mode.

13.1 DOSEMU

A package which is available to run under Linux and which will allow you to run a great deal of DOS software from within Linux is called DOSEMU. The name suggests that DOSEMU is a DOS emulator – this is not the case. In fact, DOSEMU just emulates the machine environment in which DOS runs. On top of this environment you actually run a real copy of DOS. Since the various versions of DOS with which DOSEMU will run are proprietary products, the DOSEMU package does not include a version of DOS – this means that you will have to buy and use your own copy.

The way that DOSEMU works is to use the virtual 8086 mode of the 80386 processor to provide a hardware environment in which real-mode software will run, while the processor continues operating in protected-mode. Using this arrangement will allow real-mode software to be run at the same time as the Linux operating system.

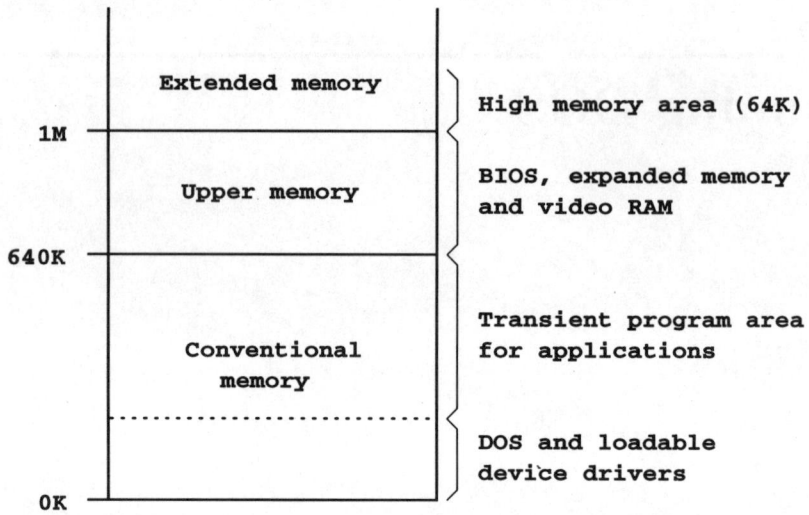

Figure 13.1 DOSEMU needs to emulate this PC AT memory map.

The DOSEMU software then has the task of providing the functionality of the PCs BIOS, with all of its system calls and entry points. In particular, what this means under Linux is that the DOSEMU library uses Linux facilities to emulate the PCs ROM BIOS including:

- int10 video driver;
- int13 disk driver;
- int14 serial driver;
- int15 I/O subsystem extensions;
- int16 keyboard driver;
- int17 parallel printer driver;
- int1a CMOS real time clock.

If the emulation is sufficiently accurate, then any software (DOS, for instance) will run under the emulator and be unaware that it is not running in the real environment. Similarly, with DOS running, other application programs should be able to run, making use of DOS and emulated BIOS calls. Figure 13.1 shows the memory map that DOSEMU needs to emulate to meet the expectations of DOS and its applications.

13.2 Installation

The first thing to remember is that DOSEMU is being modified and upgraded all the time, to add new functionality, take out bugs to improve its reliability and also to keep up with developments and changes in Linux itself. This means that a good idea if you want to install the package is to try to obtain the latest version from the FTP archives.

There are two ways to get hold of the package, one is as a ready-built set of binary, configuration and documentation files, the other is as a set of sources which you need to compile, install and configure yourself. Several Linux distributions arrive with DOSEMU as one of their standard or optional packages, in which case it is usual for the package to be ready-built. This obviously makes the installation of the package a bit easier but may also mean that you won't have the latest version.

Assuming now that you have a set of sources to build and install, the procedure runs something like this:

- To start with, even though DOSEMU is only a user level program (i.e. it doesn't run in the kernel) you may still need to build a new kernel in order to get it to run. This is because it uses the shared memory and semaphore inter-process communication (IPC) mechanisms from the System V IPC package. This means that you must build a new kernel with the IPC software configured into it (unless, of course, your existing kernel already has it in). Also make sure that your kernel version number is high enough for the version of DOSEMU you are trying to install.
- Make sure you are logged in as `root` or you will not be able to complete the installation. Now unpack the software from the archive into a sensible place to build it. This will require about 2Mb of disk space for the sources plus the space that you will use creating all the binaries.
- Building the software, creating the documentation and performing the installation itself couldn't be easier. You just change to the top level directory in which you unpacked the software and type:

    # make doeverything

    and, believe me, it does. Or, at least it does if you have the TEX text processing package installed so that `make` can build the manuals. If you don't have TEX or you don't want to build the manuals, then, instead, you can use the command:

    # make most

    You should finish the installation by copying the file that will become your initial DOS C: drive into the appropriate place, as follows:

    # cp ./hdimage.dist /var/lib/dosemu/hdimage

- Next you need to configure the package by creating the file:.

    /etc/dosemu.conf

    with appropriate contents. The two ways to do this are either to run the `Configure` script and answer lots of questions about your machine's configuration, or copy the example configuration file as:

```
# cp ./examples/config.dist /etc/dosemu.conf
```

and then customize the file, following the instructions in the comments that are contained within it. Also at this time you should create a file called:

```
/etc/dosemu.users
```

into which you should edit a list of login names for those users who have permission to use the DOSEMU package.

- You are now ready to introduce your copy of DOS into the picture. In order to do this you will need a DOS bootable floppy disk onto which you have copied the two DOS files:

```
FDISK.EXE
SYS.COM
```

Insert this floppy disk into your A: drive and then type the command:

```
# dos -A
```

The DOS on your floppy disk should boot up and you should be looking at the familiar `A>` prompt. Try typing `dir c:` to see if you can list the contents of the `hdimage` file. This Linux file is made to appear like your C: drive by the emulator. If you can see the C: drive okay, then you can execute the following commands to install your copy of DOS into the DOSEMU C: drive and make it bootable:

```
A> fdisk /mbr
A> sys c:
A> c:\exitemu
```

The last of these commands will cause DOSEMU to terminate and return you to a Linux shell prompt. You shouldn't need the floppy disk to boot DOS under the emulator any more, you should just type:

```
# dos
```

Having got DOSEMU installed and working you can now spend some time working through its documentation and manuals and then tweak the configuration file to do a more thorough setup.

Chapter 14

Security

In the past, UNIX has had a reputation for being poor with regard to various aspects of system security. One reason for this is that in general the source code is available for study and experimentation, and this inevitably leads to the discovery of security vulnerabilities of various types. Far from being a problem, however, I would argue that this is a positive advantage because it makes the vulnerabilities known so that fixes can be found and distributed quickly and efficiently. I would further suggest that other operating systems must also suffer their share of similar problems, but that these other systems are not so thoroughly explored and, therefore, not so well debugged.

Most of the security problems that are encountered in modern UNIX and Linux installations are due to administrator error, where some available security feature has not been installed or has been configured incorrectly, or where security has been deliberately sacrificed in favor of some degree of user convenience.

14.1 File Permissions

In this section we will look at what permission bits should be set on various files and directories in your Linux directory hierarchy, in order for your system to remain reasonably secure.

In the main, all the standard Linux commands (i.e. the executable commands in the /bin and /usr/bin directories) should be owned by `root` and need have no more permission bits set on them than `rwx--x--x` if they are executable binary files and `rwxr-xr-x` if they are executable shell scripts. Specifically, this set of permission bits will stop users other than `root` from being able to write to the files, so that ordinary users cannot change any of the standard commands. In general, it is good practice to set as few permission bits on a file as are necessary for it to perform its function.

Normally, when a program is executed, it runs with the permissions of the user who executed it. Sometimes, this would not give the process enough privileges to perform its task correctly. In these cases, it is possible to set either the SUID or SGID bits on the program so that users running the program will take on the permissions of the program's owner or group, respectively, rather than their own permissions.

This is the only way to get some programs (such as the `passwd` program) to work properly. It does, however, open up all sorts of possibilities for abuse if the facility should get into the wrong user's hands. For example, if you are logged on as `root` and leave your terminal unattended briefly, it takes only a few moments, while you are away, for a hacker to type:

```
# cp /bin/bash /home/hacker/.innocuous.file
# chmod 4755 /home/hacker/.innocuous.file
# clear
```

and you would probably be none the wiser upon your return. Yet now the hacker has a SUID `root` shell hidden away that can be used anytime without much fear of detection – as long as the hacker doesn't do anything stupidly visible.

It might also be that, on your system, you want to have a group of users who can change the contents of some system data files. In this case it is possible to set up a special user group and have the GID of the relevant files set to be this group. If you then set the permissions on the files to `rw-rw-r--`, it will allow members of the special group to read and write to the files without the need for `root` privileges and will also only allow read access to other system users. Restricting the need for `root` access in this way is an important security consideration.

Don't forget that as an added security feature there is a bit mask value (set by the `umask` command) which will be masked out of the permission bits set on any file when it is created.

As well as setting the correct permission bits on data and executable files, it is also very important (and often overlooked) to get the right permission bits on your directories, too. It is particularly important to make sure that the system directories (with `/tmp` and `/usr/tmp` as obvious exceptions) do not have public write permission associated with them. Remember that write permission on a directory means that you can add new file links to the directory contents and also delete existing links.

Read permission on a directory means that you can read the names of the files contained in the directory – not that you can read the contents of the files themselves. The execute permission bit on a directory is used to allow the directory to be used in a pathname, to access the files below it. Taken together, the read and execute permissions on a directory can be set up so that users are unable to list the contents of a directory to find out what it contains, while at the same time being allowed access to files known to be there. To allow this kind of access, the directory permissions need to be set up as:

```
rwx--x--x
```

These permissions allow the directory owner full access to the directory and its contents, while all other users can only access things in the directory whose names are explicitly known.

14.2 Device Access

When it comes to permissions on device special files, extra vigilance is required because special files give direct access to the hardware of the machine and any mistakes in the setup of these files can lead to serious security problems if one of your users is sufficiently knowledgeable.

The device special files to which you should pay particular attention are those associated with hard disk drives and those associated with memory. Typically these will have names like:

```
/dev/hda    /dev/hda1   /dev/hda2   etc.
/dev/hdb    /dev/hdb1   /dev/hdb2   etc.
/dev/sda    /dev/sda1   etc.
/dev/sdb    etc.
/dev/mem    /dev/kmem
```

All these files should be owned by **root** and have permission settings that are as limited as possible, and in any case without public read or write permission. If a user managed to get read and write access to a disk or a disk partition then that user would be able to circumvent all the standard file and directory permission arrangements on that disk or partition. This is because the user would be able to access the bytes on the drive directly, just as data, without the system imposing any of the usual directory hierarchy on it. Admittedly, the user would then have the task of making sense of the data, splitting it into files and directories manually. But this is not as tough a task as it sounds, especially as it is easy to find out exactly how a file system is laid out on the disk.

A similar problem exists if a user can get read and write access to a memory special file, as these are just mapped directly onto areas of the machine's memory and would thus allow the user to see and modify memory areas in the running system.

Under Linux, another way to access the memory of the machine and the memory associated with each of the running processes is via the contents of the **/proc** directory. In fact, **/proc** and its contents do not literally appear on your hard disk even though you can do an **ls /proc** command and list its contents. The directory and all its contents are just dynamically *fiddled* into place by the kernel.

Obviously, if the memory of a running process can be accessed by a user with sufficient privilege then this will also cause security problems if someone hacks into your **root** account.

Terminal access to most Linux systems will be provided over a network or via the machine's console and its virtual terminals. Some systems, however, will have extra terminals connected to them via serial ports – and this can be the source of another problem. Traditionally, the permissions set on a terminal will allow write access to the terminal special file by anyone. This allows simple messages to be passed around between users using the `write` command. However, this is precisely the source of the problem with some serial terminals.

For many terminals, it is possible to send simple escape and command character sequences to them which can program them to perform simple actions. It is not uncommon for one of these actions to be to send characters from the terminal back to the host machine, just as though the characters had been typed on the terminal's keyboard. Given this scenario it is simple to see that a hacker, using the `write` command, could send a sequence of characters to your terminal which make the terminal send programmed commands back to the computer. These commands will then be executed just as though you had typed them yourself. If you happen to be logged in as `root` at the time... well, you get the picture.

The only way to protect yourself against an attack of this kind is to remove the public write permission from your terminal line. This can be done with the command:

```
$ mesg n
```

Sadly, removing this potential problem also prevents other users from using `write` to send you messages, but you can't have it both ways.

14.3 Passwords

It is a true statement that no system can be any more secure than its passwords. When a user attempts to login to your system, a password will be requested. This password will then be encrypted and compared with the previously encrypted version in the file `/etc/passwd`. If the two encrypted passwords match, the user will be allowed to login to the system. Since the information contained in the password file is generally useful for all sorts of reasons, and since the password itself is securely encrypted, the file has public read access.

So far, so good, but now add the human factor. Most users want a password that is easy to remember – something meaningful to them – their partner's name, their birthdate, or something similar. Passwords like these are just asking for trouble. They are easy to guess by anyone with only a vague knowledge of you and your friends. When you choose a password, it should be something which includes a mixture of upper and lower case characters, digits and punctuation marks and is hence less likely to be discovered by someone trying to guess what it is. In cases where security is particularly strict the important system passwords should be changed quite frequently and should be shared between as few people as is realistically possible. Obviously, for a system with several users on it, the minimum number of privileged users should take into account the fact that you may be away or ill when one of the users needs something done that requires `root` access.

In addition to normal user passwords, it is also possible in Linux to assign passwords to groups of users in the file /etc/group. Putting passwords on groups allows any user with a particular group's password to change to that group using the `newgrp` command. However, it is generally more secure not to put passwords on groups as then only those users actually listed along side each group in the /etc/group file can make these group changes.

14.4 Root Accounts

The first rule for `root` accounts is: if you have one, don't use it unless you absolutely have to. The second rule is: create as few `root` accounts on your machine as are necessary to do the job. Wherever possible, find an alternative way to allow groups of users to do system administration tasks, when necessary, without allocating `root` logins. This can most easily be done with user groups and appropriate permission bits for group access.

As an example of the care you need to take when logged in as `root`, consider the following. When you are logged in as an ordinary user, there is a shell environment variable called PATH which contains a colon-separated list of directories which will be searched, in the order given, to find the executable file associated with any command name you try to run. Typically, the contents of PATH might be:

```
$ echo $PATH
.:/usr/local/bin:/bin:/usr/bin:/usr/X11/bin
```

In the example, five directories are specified in the search path beginning with the current directory (.). Having the current directory first is quite convenient because of the possibility that you might inadvertently create a program file with the same name as some unknown system command. If this happens, then, when you try to run your new command from the current directory, it will be found before the system command with the same name because the current directory is searched first. Without the current directory search, the system command will be executed instead, and cause some degree of confusion.

A favorite version of this occurs for me when I am writing simple little programs to test out new ideas, because I invariably want to call the new program `test` which, of course, is also a standard system command. Unfortunately, if you run the system version of `test` without any parameters, it does absolutely nothing visible and just returns with a shell prompt, convincing me that my trivial `test` program doesn't work... .

Having said that it is useful to start your PATH variable with the current directory, this action is definitely an error in the case of your `root` login. For maximum security, the current directory should not appear at all in `root`'s PATH. To see why this is so consider the following possibility. One of your users calls you over to the terminal to ask you to perform a system administrator function. You go over to the terminal and using the su command change user to root and execute the required system commands, as per your user's request. You then log off as root and carry on with what you were doing previously. What you didn't suspect, however, was that your user was really a hacker and took the opportunity to create a *doctored* version of the command you were going to run as root, which was stored in the user's current directory.

If, as root, your PATH starts with the current directory, then when you perform your task for the user, the user's *doctored* version of your command will be run instead of the real one. Running the user's command as root will give it permission to do anything. A clever hacker will get the *doctored* program to create a root owned SUID shell somewhere safe and then go on to execute the real program so that you will be none the wiser... . Beware!

There are many more security issues than I have space to look at here, but the things you have seen in this chapter should start you thinking in the right direction.

Part III

SYSTEM PROGRAMMING

Chapter 15
Files

The subject of this part of the book is Linux system calls. This, after all, is the main interface between an application program and the services provided for it by the kernel.

One of the basic philosophies behind Linux (in fact, behind all flavors of UNIX) is that the system will try to make its input and output to all kinds of devices, like disks, CD-ROMs, terminals, printers, etc., look as far as possible like input and output to ordinary files.

One of the most obvious reflections of this is that the system calls which are available for use on ordinary files will keep cropping up over and over as we look at driving different device types.

15.1 Sequential Files

An ordinary Linux file is just a set of data bytes stored sequentially one after another in the file. Linux imposes no kind of internal structure on the data so that, as far as Linux is concerned, the data is not split up into records or fields. If for a particular application some kind of internal data structure is required, then it is up to you as the programmer to impose that structure on the data for yourself. This makes the Linux interface to files particularly simple.

15.1.1 File Descriptors

In Linux, files are accessed via a *file descriptor*. Each process can use up to OPEN_MAX file descriptors at the same time. The value OPEN_MAX is accessed through the standard header file <limits.h> and for Linux it has a value of 256.

The definition of OPEN_MAX is actually in <linux/limits.h> but to make your programs portable you should not include this header file in your code directly, because it gets included automatically when you #include <limits.h> anyway.

By convention, file descriptors 0, 1 and 2 are already allocated and available for use when a process starts up. File descriptor 0 is used as the *standard input* device, file descriptor 1 is used as the *standard output* device and file descriptor 2 is used as the *standard error output* device.

Each allocated file descriptor is associated with an *open file description*. The open file descriptions are just structures of information related to the files. This information includes an offset value which specifies where in the file the next access to it will take place, the file's access mode, which specifies whether the associated file can be used for input or output or both, and some other related flags.

The relationship between file descriptors and open file descriptions need not be one-to-one, it can also be many-to-one. This means that it is possible for several file descriptors, even belonging to separate processes, to point at the same open file description. The implication here is that information stored in the open file description data structure will then be shared between all the file descriptors pointing to it.

In fact, as we shall see later, there is also some information stored in the file descriptor structure as well. This means that it is possible for two or more file descriptors to have different values for this information even if they all point to the same open file description.

15.1.2 open System Call

There are several ways of obtaining a file descriptor which will allow you access to a file, the most common is to use the **open()** system call:

```
#include <sys/types.h>
#include <sys/stat.h>
#include <fcntl.h>

int open(const char *path, int flags);
int open(const char *path, int flags, mode_t mode);
```

Notice that there are two different forms for the **open()** system call; the first takes two parameters and the second has three. In fact you will only use the two-parameter version unless there is the possibility that the file you are trying to open does not exist and that in this case you want the file to be created, in which case the three parameter version of **open()** is required.

The *path* parameter is just a pointer to the pathname of the file you wish to open. The *flags* parameter specifies how you want to open the file. This must include one of the three values:

    O_RDONLY   open file for read-only access;
    O_WRONLY   open file for write-only access;
    O_RDWR   open file for read and write access.

In addition any combination of the following flag values may also be included using the bitwise-OR (|) operator:

O_CREAT	open the file and create it if it doesn't exist;
O_EXCL	force open() to fail if O_CREAT is set and file exists;
O_TRUNC	truncate the file to zero length on open();
O_APPEND	force write()s to occur on the end of the file.

There are some other flags which can be specified but they are of no use on ordinary files so we'll cover them later when thay are more relevant. The symbolic names for all these flag values can be accessed via a #include <fcntl.h>.

If you use open() to create a file, then the *mode* parameter is used to specify the access permission bits for the file's owner, the file's group and all other system users. The required combination of the following symbolic constants (defined through <sys/stat.h>) should be created with the bitwise-OR operator:

S_IRUSR	read permission bit for file's owner;
S_IWUSR	write permission bit for file's owner;
S_IXUSR	execute permission bit for file's owner;
S_IRGRP	read permission bit for file's group;
S_IWGRP	write permission bit for file's group;
S_IXGRP	execute permission bit for file's group;
S_IROTH	read permission bit for other file users;
S_IWOTH	write permission bit for other file users;
S_IXOTH	execute permission bit for other file users.

Three useful bitwise-OR combinations are already defined as follows:

S_IRWXU	defined as (S_IRUSR | S_IWUSR | S_IXUSR)
S_IRWXG	defined as (S_IRGRP | S_IWGRP | S_IXGRP)
S_IRWXO	defined as (S_IROTH | S_IWOTH | S_IXOTH)

In addition, it is also possible to specify that the set-uid bit and/or the set-gid bit should be set as well using the constant values:

S_ISUID	set the set-uid bit;
S_ISGID	set the set-gid bit.

Don't forget, when a process creates a file on your behalf, the permission bits are modified by the value of the umask associated with the process. The process effectively uses the formula:

```
mode & (~umask)
```

to determine the permissions with which the file will actually be created. This means that you should not be surprised if the permission bits you get on a file created by one of your programs do not match the *mode* flags you requested in the open() call. We'll look at how to do something about the umask value (in Section 21.1) if this security feature becomes a problem.

Examples of calls to open() using a range of parameter values might be:

```
open("xfile", O_RDONLY);
open("yfile", O_RDWR | O_TRUNC);
open("zfile", O_WRONLY | O_CREAT | O_EXCL, S_IRWXU | S_IXGRP);
```

The first example just opens xfile for read-only access. An error will be returned by open() if xfile does not already exist. The second example opens yfile for reading and writing. The file must already exist and it will be truncated to zero length, thus losing any previous contents. The third example opens zfile for write-only access. The open() call expects to create the file and will return an error if the file already exists. Because zfile is being created, a set of permission bits need to be specified, which in this case are rwx--x---.

Sometimes it can be a bit difficult to read an open() call, especially if the bitwise-OR operator is being used on lots of flags. In this case it is a good idea to #define a suitable symbolic constant at the top of your code. An example which defines the constant MODE755 to give the file permission bits rwxr-xr-x could be:

```
#define MODE755 (S_IRWXU | S_IRGRP | S_IXGRP | S_IROTH | S_IXOTH)
```

When open() detects an error it is indicated by a return value of -1. As there are lots of different conditions which can give rise to an error, an indication of which error occurred is given by the kernel assigning an appropriate value to the external integer variable errno. The main errors from calls to open() are:

ENOENT   You tried to open a file which did not exist without specifying O_CREAT.
EEXIST   You are using O_CREAT | O_EXCL to force the creation of a file which already exists
EACCES   You do not have the requested access permissions to the file, or you do not have search permission on a directory in the file's pathname

These symbols are accessed via <errno.h>.

If no errors occur then the return value from open() is a file descriptor which you will use in all subsequent operations on the file. The file descriptor itself is just a small non-negative integer which is actually the index into an array of pointers to open file descriptions. When a file descriptor is allocated, a search is made through this array to find the first free element. The consequence of this is that Linux will always allocate the lowest numbered free file descriptor when a file is opened – a fact you will see put to good use later when we look at the implementation of I/O redirection to files and pipes.

Sometimes you may wish to check whether or not your process has access to a particular file before you try to open() it. This can be done with the access() system call. The general form of the call is:

```
#include <unistd.h>

int access(char *pathname, int mode);
```

where *pathname* is the name of the file whose access you wish to test and *mode* is one of the following values, which are included via the file <unistd.h>:

    R_OK   check if calling process has read access;
    W_OK   check if calling process has write access;
    X_OK   check if calling process has execute access;
    F_OK   check if specified file exists.

15.1.3   creat System Call

To maintain backward compatibility with earlier UNIX systems, Linux also provides an alternative system call for creating files, named creat().

```
#include <sys/types.h>
#include <sys/stat.h>
#include <fcntl.h>

int creat(const char *path, mode_t mode);
```

In early versions of UNIX the open() system call only existed in the two-parameter flavor, and did not have the capability to open files if they did not already exist. File creation was then performed by the separate system call creat(). In Linux and all modern versions of UNIX the creat system call is redundant. Indeed, the creat call:

```
fd = creat(file, mode);
```

is exactly equivalent to the modern open() call:

```
fd = open(file, O_WRONLY | O_CREAT | O_TRUNC, mode);
```

15.1.4   read System Call

Once you have a file descriptor associated with an open file description then, as long as the file was opened with O_RDONLY or O_RDWR access permission, you can read bytes from the file with the read() system call:

```
#include <sys/types.h>
#include <unistd.h>

int read(int fd, void *buf, size_t nbytes);
```

where *fd* is the file descriptor to the file you want to read, *buf* is a pointer to a block of memory where read() will place the bytes it takes from the file, and *nbytes* is a count of the number of bytes to copy from the file into *buf*.

The function prototype for the `read()` system call is given in `<unistd.h>` and the data type `size_t` is accessed through `<sys/types.h>` and is currently defined to be `unsigned int` which under Linux on a PC are 32-bit values.

The `read()` operation begins at the current file position, which is given by the file offset value contained in the associated open file description, and continues from there until the required number of bytes has been read from the file or until the end-of-file is reached. It is your responsibility to ensure that the data buffer you specify to `read()` is big enough to hold the number of data bytes you request, because the kernel cannot check and will just blindly copy its data regardless.

By the end of the `read()` operation the file offset value will have been incremented beyond the data just copied, to a new position ready for the next `read()`.

The return value from `read()` is -1 if an error occurred, 0 if the file offset value is at the end-of-file, or a count of the number of bytes copied from the file into the specified buffer. The count will normally be the same as the number of bytes you asked for, except when you ask for more bytes than there are left to read. In this case a number less than the number of bytes you asked for will be returned and then, if the file size doesn't change in between, the end-of-file (0) value will be returned on the next `read()`.

Physical disk reads are always done in full disk data blocks, which are then stored in memory buffers. If a file is being read sequentially (i.e. consecutive disk blocks), then in order to improve system performance there are mechanisms in the kernel which can anticipate further data requirements and have the data ready using a read ahead technique.

15.1.5 write System Call

Data is written to a file with the `write()` system call. Superficially, it is easy to think of the `write()` system call as just the opposite of `read()`. It has the format:

```
#include <sys/types.h>
#include <unistd.h>

int write(int fd, void *buf, size_t nbytes);
```

A byte count of *nbytes* is written from the block of memory pointed to by *buf* to the file associated with the file descriptor *fd*.

The data is written to the file starting at the current file offset position and the offset will automatically be incremented by the number of bytes actually written, ready for the next `write()` call. If the file was opened with the `O_APPEND` flag set, then the file offset value will automatically be incremented to the end-of-file position before the `write()` takes place. Using the `O_APPEND` flag helps to prevent you from overwriting data already in the file and is useful when creating log files and audit trails.

Just as with `read()`, memory buffers are used by the kernel to cache the data between the process and the disk. However, there is a subtle difference here which is not immediately apparent. In the case of a `read()` call, if the data is not available in memory then the process must wait while a physical disk read takes place before the `read()` call can return. If any disk errors occur while reading the data then the return value from `read()` and the value of `errno` can reflect this fact.

In the case of `write()` the data is just cached in memory and then the `write()` call returns immediately. In the process, the kernel issues a promise that the data will eventually get onto the disk. Any subsequent reads of the data you just wrote will be taken from the buffer cache rather than from the disk. This means that user programs can't really tell that this trickery is going on, except that data reads and writes to memory are orders of magnitude faster than physical disk reads and writes.

So, where's the problem? The problem is that, despite the promises, the physical disk writes may never take place. If a disk error occurs when the data is written from the buffer cache to disk, then that data will be lost and, worse than that, there is no mechanism for letting the process that wrote the data know about the problem. Errors during physical reads are reported to the reading process by the return value of `read()`. This cannot be done with data writes as the `write()` call returns long before the data is actually transferred to the disk. Indeed, the writing process may even have terminated before the disk write error occurs. Disk hardware failures are not even the only source of problems, anything which prevents a disk write taking place can cause trouble, including such things as: machine power failure, pressing the reset button, removing a mounted floppy disk without using `umount`, accidentally switching the machine off etc.

Generally, modern hardware is so reliable that the performance improvement more than compensates for the slight risk of losing data. However, in situations where even this slight risk is unacceptable, alternative arrangements need to be made.

If you are using the Linux second extended filesystem within a modern Linux kernel then there is an extra flag that can be specified to the `open()` system call – `O_SYNC`:

```
fd = open(file, O_WRONLY | O_SYNC);
```

The effect of this flag is to synchronize `write()` system calls on the appropriate file descriptor (`fd` here) with the corresponding physical disk writes. In effect, the `write()` call doesn't return until the physical disk write has taken place.

A word of warning – if you use this flag then your code may not be portable to other operating systems. In fact, it won't even be portable to files on other filesystem types within Linux. You need to know this because if you do use `O_SYNC` with files on other filesystem types accidentally, you will not get any error indication, the system will just silently fail to perform the expected synchronization.

Outside of the data caching issue, the `write()` call is similar to `read()`, so that it is again your responsibility to ensure you do not try to do things like writing more bytes of data than are contained within your data buffer.

The return value from `write()` is -1 on error with `errno` set appropriately, or a count of the number of bytes actually written to the file. In the case of an ordinary file (though not some other file types) if `write()` fails to return a value which is the same as the number of bytes that were supposed to have been written, then this indicates that something odd happened (you exceeded your maximum file size limit, for example) and you should probably treat it as an error anyway.

15.1.6 `close` System Call

Open file descriptors are released for reuse with the `close` system call:

```
#include <unistd.h>

int close(int fd);
```

Each time a file descriptor is allocated, a reference count in the associated open file description is incremented, so that each open file description knows how many file descriptors are associated with it. Each time `close()` is called on a file descriptor the associated open file description's reference count is decremented. Eventually, a call to `close()` will take the reference count to zero. In this case the `close()` call not only releases the file descriptor but also releases the open file description as well.

The `close()` call returns the value zero on success and -1 on error with `errno` holding the error number. In fact, there is only one error that `close()` can return, and it is:

EBADF   Parameter is not a valid open file descriptor

In fact, no damage is done by calling `close()` with a file descriptor that is not associated with an open file description and, consequently, the return value from `close()` is seldom checked for an error.

It is good programming practice explicitly to `close()` any files that you `open()` although any files that are still open when a process terminates will be closed automatically.

15.1.7 User Buffering

Just because the system call interface is the lowest level access that ordinary application programs have to the operating system's services, you should not get the idea that their use is necessarily the most efficient way to do something – take data buffering as an example.

The following is a very simple function which takes pointers to two file names as parameters and copies the contents of the file named in the first parameter into the file named in the second parameter:

```
#include <fcntl.h>
#include <sys/stat.h>

#define NEWFILE (O_WRONLY | O_CREAT | O_TRUNC)
#define MODE600 (S_IRUSR | S_IWUSR)
#define SIZE 1

void filecopy(char *infile, char *outfile)
{
    char buf[SIZE];
    int infd, outfd, count;

    if ((infd = open(infile, O_RDONLY))==-1)
        fatal("opening infile");

    if ((outfd = open(outfile, NEWFILE, MODE600))==-1)
        fatal("opening outfile");

    while ((count = read(infd, buf, sizeof(buf)))>0)
        if (write(outfd, buf, count)!=count)
            fatal("writing data");

    if (count==-1)
        fatal("reading data");

    close(infd);
    close(outfd);
}
```

The user function `fatal()` is not listed here but all it needs to do is to output an error message containing its parameter string and then terminate execution of the process.

You already know that the system uses large amounts of memory as a buffer cache for disk file reads and writes and that getting bytes to and from memory is a very fast operation. However, in the case of the `filecopy()` function, while it works, in that it performs the required copy, it isn't very efficient. There is quite a time overhead for running a system call and this function makes two system calls (one `read()` and one `write()`) for every byte copied.

Using the `filecopy()` function exactly as listed, I ran a few simple timing tests (using the `time` command) and discovered that on my system I could copy files at about 6.4 kilo-bytes per second.

Now it is quite a simple matter to reduce the number of system calls involved in the copy operation – you just increase the value of the SIZE constant. The effect of this is to copy the file in a smaller number of larger-sized chunks. A natural SIZE to choose would be something related to the size of a disk data block.

Repeating the experiments after changing the value of SIZE to 1024 (but making no other changes) increased the file copy rate to a staggering (well I was impressed anyway) 1.3 mega-bytes per second – a speed improvement of over 200 times!

Even taking the speed increase into account, it is sometimes just not convenient to read the data in such large blocks. In this case you can achieve the best of both worlds by doing the data buffering yourself, in user memory space, and taking your small chunks of data from there.

The following code example shows a small amendment to the `filecopy()` function so that it calls the functions `my_read()` and `my_write()` which perform exactly the same as the `read()` and `write()` system calls except that they use internal 1024 byte buffers to cut down on the number of times the system calls get used. Using `write_close()` to close the output file rather than the `close()` system call is necessary in order to flush any partial `write_buf[]` contents before closing the file:

```
#include <fcntl.h>
#include <sys/stat.h>

#define NEWFILE (O_WRONLY | O_CREAT | O_TRUNC)
#define MODE600 (S_IRUSR | S_IWUSR)
#define SIZE 1
#define BUF_SIZE 1024

void filecopy(char *infile, char *outfile)
{
    char buf[SIZE];
    int infd, outfd, count;

    if ((infd = open(infile, O_RDONLY))==-1)
        fatal("opening infile");

    if ((outfd = open(outfile, NEWFILE, MODE600))==-1)
        fatal("opening outfile");

    while ((count = my_read(infd, buf, sizeof(buf)))>0)
        if (my_write(outfd, buf, count)!=count)
            fatal("writing data");

    if (count==-1)
        fatal("reading data");

    close(infd);
    write_close(outfd);
}
```

Sequential Files 237

```c
int my_read(int fd, char *buf, size_t count)
{
    static char read_buf[BUF_SIZE];
    static int read_offset = BUF_SIZE;
    static int read_max = BUF_SIZE;
    int i;

    for (i = 0; i<count; ++i)
    {
        if (read_offset==read_max)
        {
            read_offset = 0;
            read_max = read(fd, read_buf, sizeof(read_buf));

            if (read_max==-1)
                return -1;

            if (read_max==0)
                return i;
        }

        *buf++ = read_buf[read_offset++];
    }

    return i;
}


static char write_buf[BUF_SIZE];
static int write_offset = 0;

int my_write(int fd, char *buf, size_t count)
{
    int i, n;

    for (i = 0; i<count; ++i)
    {
        write_buf[write_offset++] = *buf++;

        if (write_offset==BUF_SIZE)
        {
            write_offset = 0;
```

```
                n = write(fd, write_buf, sizeof(write_buf));

            if (n!=BUF_SIZE)
                return -1;
        }
    }

    return i;
}


int write_close(int fd)
{
    if (write_offset>0)
        write(fd, write_buf, write_offset);

    write_offset = 0;
    return close(fd);
}
```

This code is only intended to give you the flavor of user buffering because normally you wouldn't write your own – there is a perfectly good user buffering file I/O package in the C standard library (`fopen()`, `fclose()` etc.)

Notice that in performing user buffering for writing to files, you encounter the same kind of problems over what to do about reporting errors that we encountered looking at the `write()` system call itself.

Testing the data transfer rate of the `filecopy()` function using one byte reads and writes and the user buffering functions gives 330 kilo-bytes per second. As you would expect, this is not as fast as direct large buffer calls to `read()` and `write()` because of the overhead of calling the extra functions, but it still shows more than a 50 times' speed improvement over the direct one byte read and write case.

15.2 Random Files

All the file access to date has been sequential access by default. This is because all the reads and writes take place starting from the current file offset position. The file offset value is then automatically incremented to just beyond the position where the read or write finishes, which makes it ready for the next access to take place.

Given this scenario, random access under Linux couldn't be simpler. All you need to do is to alter the current file offset value to the position of interest which will automatically force the next `read()` or `write()` to take place at this position (unless the file was opened `O_APPEND` of course, in which case any `write()` calls will still take place at the end-of-file position).

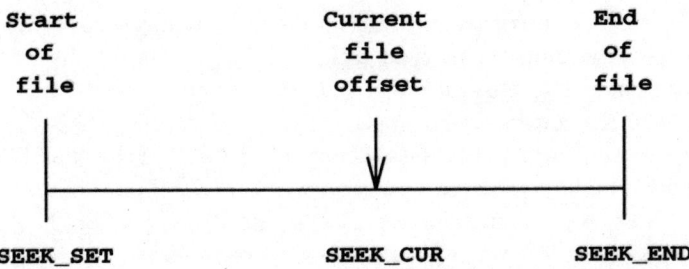

Figure 15.1 The three *base* positions for lseek() *offsets*.

The system call required to perform this task is lseek():

```
#include <sys/types.h>
#include <unistd.h>

off_t lseek(int fd, off_t offset, int base);
```

The *fd* parameter is the file descriptor whose associated open file description will be modified by the call.

When specifying a new position for the file offset value, you may just want to give a number which should be taken as the new value. This is effectively providing a position relative to the start of the file. Two other possibilities are that you may want to give a number relative to the current file offset value, or that you wish to give a number relative to the end of the file. Each of these three possibilities is shown in Figure 15.1, along with the symbolic constants used to select them.

The *offset* parameter is a relative value which is added to the selected *base* position to give the new file offset value. The *base* parameter can have one of three values, defined in <unistd.h>:

   SEEK_SET   count *offset* from start of file;
   SEEK_CUR   count *offset* from current file offset value;
   SEEK_END   count *offset* from end-of-file.

The data type of the *offset* parameter and the return value of lseek() itself are given as off_t. This doesn't really give any indication of what sort of values would be valid here, though the typedef for off_t in <sys/types.h> gives it as:

```
typedef long off_t;
```

A few simple examples should help to clarify the use of lseek():

```
lseek(fd, (off_t) 0, SEEK_SET);
lseek(fd, (off_t) -50, SEEK_CUR);
lseek(fd, (off_t) 5000, SEEK_END);
```

The first thing to notice is that in order to be pedantically correct, it is necessary to cast the *offset* parameters to type `off_t`. This allows for the possibility that the *offset* parameter may have different underlying data types on different ports of Linux, now or in the future.

The first example `lseek()` call sets the file offset value in the open file description associated with file descriptor `fd` to the sum of the *offset* parameter value (0) and the file offset value of the start of the file, as specified by `SEEK_SET` (also 0). So this call sets the file offset value to 0 – the start of the file.

The second example moves the file offset value backwards through the file by 50 bytes from its current position (`SEEK_CUR`). Don't forget that writing to the file will automatically advance the file offset value ready for the next read or write operation. Therefore, if you want to work backwards through a file one byte at a time, writing new byte values as you go, you will need an `lseek()` *offset* value of -2 and not -1, as you might at first expect.

The third example moves the file offset value forwards by 5000 bytes from the end-of-file position (`SEEK_END`). To move the file offset value beyond the end-of-file like this may seem very strange at first, but this is precisely what is happening here. If you were now to write data at this new position then the file size would become the file offset value of the new end-of-file. What happens to the bytes in the gap between the old end-of-file position and the new one? I'm glad you asked that! In fact, nothing happens to them – they are not even allocated any data blocks on the disk (not even when the data really gets written to the disk, eventually). What you then end up with is a file with gaps in it, whose logical size (reported by `ls -l`) is the file offset value of the file's end-of-file position, while the physical size (the number of data blocks it occupies on disk) may be significantly less.

It is easy to convince yourself that this is possible; you just write a program to create a new file and then use `lseek()` to move the file offset value a long way into the file. To be really convincing try a value which is bigger than the size of the filesystem in which the file will be stored. Then `write()` a byte and `close()` the file. Now use the `ls -l` command to see that the size of the file you have just created is larger than could possibly have been written in the filesystem where it appears.

If at some later time you open the file again and seek and write to a position somewhere in the gap, then data blocks will be allocated to the file as required to hold the new data. This will increase the physical size of the file but not its logical size. If at any time you attempt to read data from a gap in the file then Linux will not allocate data blocks for the positions read but will just return zero-byte values for those byte positions instead.

The only restriction placed on `lseek()` when it moves the file offset value, is that it cannot be moved to before the beginning of the file (i.e. the final file offset value cannot be negative).

The return value from `lseek()` is -1 on error with an error number in `errno`, or the new value of the file offset position (given in bytes from the start of the file). For example:

```
pos = lseek(fd, (off_t) 0, SEEK_CUR);
```

would set `pos` to the current file offset value, and:

```
pos = lseek(fd, (off_t) 0, SEEK_END);
```

would set `pos` to the length of the file (though there are other ways to do this which don't change the current file offset value).

15.3 Terminal I/O

As far as possible all input and output in Linux is made to look like input and output to an ordinary file. However, terminal I/O is one of the more difficult cases. As long as you just want to treat your terminal like a sequential access file for input and output, then you can use the `open()`, `close()`, `read()` and `write()` system calls you have already seen. Even so, there are some differences.

Normally, a process will automatically be attached to a terminal, via file descriptors 0, 1 and 2, which it will inherit from its parent process. If this is the case, then the `open()` calls have already been done on behalf of the process and the attached terminal will be the control terminal for the process (we'll see the implications of control terminals later).

If you need to open a terminal for yourself then you will need a file name to pass as a parameter to `open()`. There are basically two possibilities: either you can use the special file name `/dev/tty` which refers to your control terminal, if you have one, or you need know the name of a specific terminal device special file, such as `/dev/tty1`, `/dev/tty2` etc. for the file names of the virtual console terminals.

A moment's thought will convince you that the O_CREAT, O_EXCL, O_TRUNC and O_APPEND flags don't make any sense when applied to terminal files. There are, however, two new flags that do:

    O_NOCTTY   stop this terminal being the control terminal;
    O_NONBLOCK stop `open()`, `read()` and `write()` from blocking.

For superficial compatibility with some other UNIX systems an O_NDELAY flag is also provided. Under Linux, O_NDELAY is exactly the same as O_NONBLOCK, though its semantics should really be slightly different.

Once again, we'll look at control terminals a little later, but what is this idea about blocking? Suppose you do a `read()` on a terminal keyboard and the user hasn't pressed any keys, what should happen?

In fact what does happen is that when you are reading from a terminal and no keys have been pressed the `read()` call doesn't return. Effectively, the process is blocked or suspended until the `read()` request can be satisfied in some way.

Inside the Linux kernel there are data buffers associated with each terminal file. These are used by default to buffer characters as they are sent to and received from the terminal device files. The default action of these buffers is to store up characters until a newline (\n) is encountered. In the case of the keyboard buffer, only when the newline has been received will a blocked `read()` call be released and the characters be made available to the reading process. It doesn't matter how many bytes were requested, the `read()` call cannot return more characters than are in the buffer up to the first newline character. If less than this number of characters is requested then `read()` will just return the number of characters asked for. Either way, the return value from `read()` will be the number of characters actually read.

If the O_NONBLOCK flag is set on `open()` then the blocking behavior of `read()` is suppressed. Now if there is no data ready when the terminal is read then the `read()` call returns the value -1 and `errno` is set to the value EAGAIN, to indicate that the `read()` attempt should be retried. For compatibility with other UNIX flavors the `errno` error value EWOULDBLOCK is also defined and has exactly the same value as EAGAIN.

In the case of a `write()` call to a terminal device, blocking is not an issue and the characters written are just buffered until a newline is sent, when the buffer contents will be displayed.

The `close()` call works on a terminal device just like an ordinary file and releases the file descriptor for further use.

15.3.1 Terminal Control Functions

As long as all you want to do with a terminal device is to use `open()`, `close()`, `read()` and `write()` then the *feel* of terminal access is very similar to ordinary file access. However, there are many things you may wish to do to set up a terminal interface that do not fit into this model. For example, it is not clear how you would use `read()` and `write()` calls to set the baud rate on a terminal line.

For tasks like this there is a general purpose I/O control system call called `ioctl()`:

```
#include <sys/ioctl.h>

int ioctl(int fd, int cmd, int arg)
```

where *fd* is the appropriate file descriptor, *cmd* is the command function you want `ioctl()` to perform, and *arg* is an optional parameter to be used by the *cmd*. In fact, the *arg* parameter can be any 4-byte-sized thing, typically an `int` or a pointer to a block of memory (usually a `struct`) which contains any parameter data required by the specified *cmd*.

The `ioctl()` call is available for use on many I/O devices, not just terminals. As a consequence, each kind of I/O device that uses `ioctl()` has its own set of *cmd* and *arg* parameter values to pass into the call. Because the POSIX committee felt it to have become overworked, the `ioctl()` call has been replaced for terminal I/O in the POSIX.1 standard by a collection of separate functions.

In general, Linux tries to be compatible with as many different flavors of UNIX as possible. There is always the overriding consideration that in the case of a direct conflict between systems, POSIX compatibility comes first and, after that, whichever option seems most popular by common usage.

In the case of terminal I/O it has proved possible to offer the POSIX.1 facilities as well as the ioctl() system call because the underlying data structures that hold the basic information about terminal characteristics are essentially the same for the two systems.

In Linux there is a data structure called struct termios which is accessed via <termios.h> (for compatibility struct termio is also available accessed via <termio.h>). These structures have the following basic layout:

```
#define NCCS 19

struct termios
{
    tcflag_t c_iflag;          /* input mode flags */
    tcflag_t c_oflag;          /* output mode flags */
    tcflag_t c_cflag;          /* control mode flags */
    tcflag_t c_lflag;          /* local mode flags */
    cc_t c_line;               /* line discipline */
    cc_t c_cc[NCCS];           /* control characters */
};
```

One of these structures is associated with each terminal device, and the sets of flags contained in the structure control the various characteristics of the terminal interface.

The main functions performed by each of the sets of flags in the termios structure are:

c_iflag The flags in this set basically allow character mapping to take place on input, for things like translating UPPER case characters to lower case, \r to \n, and 8-bit input to 7-bit. These flags also allow input parity to be controlled and checked as well as I/O flow control (x-on, x-off).

c_oflag These flags allow character mapping on output. For example \n to \r\n, or tab characters to spaces. It is also possible to add transmission delays to characters like form feed, \n. horizontal and vertical tab, etc. This is a throwback to the days when slow printing terminals were common and these devices needed time to perform some of these control functions.

c_cflag These flags control changes to the terminal line's baud rate, the character size (5, 6, 7 or 8 bits per character) and allow control of the generation and checking of data parity bits.

c_lflag This particular set of flags has some very powerful functions, the most important of which are:

- Enable/disable keyboard generated signals – causes input characters to be searched for Ctrl-c and Ctrl-\.

- Enable/disable the character echo function – echo automatically sends typed input characters back to the output for display. With echo switched off the user can secretly enter passwords, etc.

- Enable/disable canonical input – when enabled, input characters are automatically buffered into \n terminated lines and the backspace and line kill characters operate on the buffer. When disabled the read() call can return characters as they are typed rather than waiting for the newline to be typed.

c_cc This is an array of values whose function changes depending upon whether cannonical input is enabled or not. If it is enabled (i.e. input is line buffered) then the array contains the characters that will be used for such things as end-of-file, interrupt, quit and stop (by default these are Ctrl-d, Ctrl-c, Ctrl-\ and Ctrl-z respectively). If canonical input is disabled then two of the values change meaning and become a timeout and minimum character count, one of which must be satisfied before a read() will return. The usual thing is to set both of these values to zero, which allows immediate return of characters as they are typed.

The symbolic constants for all the individual flags in a struct termios are accessed via <termios.h>. This file includes <linux/termios.h>, which is where the constants are actually defined.

The main POSIX functions for accessing and modifying the contents of a termios structure are:

```
#include <termios.h>

int tcgetattr(int fd, struct termios *tptr)
int tcsetattr(int fd, int action, struct termios *tptr)
```

where *fd* is the appropriate file descriptor and *tptr* is a pointer to a termios structure which is filled from the terminal structure by tcgetattr(), and which is used to fill the terminal structure by tcsetattr(). The possible values of the *action* parameter to the tcsetattr() function and their meanings are:

TCSANOW	fill the terminal stucture immediately;
TCSADRAIN	fill the terminal structure after the current output buffer contents have been sent to the terminal;
TCSAFLUSH	same as TCSADRAIN but also discard any unread input buffer contents.

The same functionality can be obtained by using the TCGETA and TCSETA *cmd* values to the ioctl() call, using a pointer to a struct termio as its third parameter.

The following code example is a pair of simple functions to enable you to switch the standard input and output (if it is a terminal) into 'scan' mode and back (i.e. with echo off, signals off, canonical mode disabled and set to give immediate character returns from read()):

```
#include <termios.h>

struct termios tsave;

void scan_mode(void)
{
    struct termios tbuf;

    if (!isatty(0))
        fatal("standard input is not a terminal");

    if (tcgetattr(0, &tbuf)==-1)
        fatal("getting terminal attributes");

    tsave = tbuf;
    tbuf.c_lflag &= ~(ECHO | ICANON | ISIG);
    tbuf.c_cc[VMIN] = tbuf.c_cc[VTIME] = 0;

    if (tcsetattr(0, TCSANOW, &tbuf)==-1)
        fatal("setting terminal attributes");
}


void restore_mode(void)
{
    if (tcsetattr(0, TCSANOW, &tsave)==-1)
        fatal("restoring terminal attributes");
}
```

Notice the use of the isatty() function within scan_mode(). The isatty() function has the prototype:

```
#include <unistd.h>

int isatty(int fd);
```

where *fd* is a file descriptor. If *fd* is associated with an open terminal then isatty() returns 1, otherwise it returns 0.

There is a standard command available which will allow you full control over all the flags in the termios structure; it is called stty and its manual page gives a

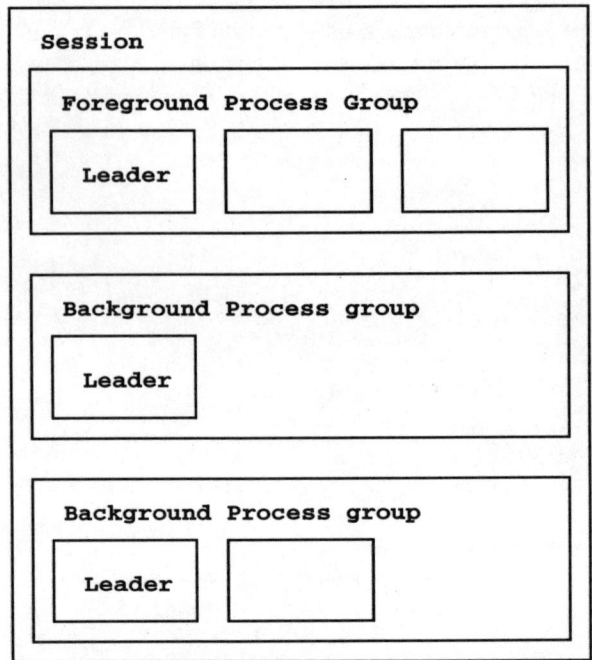

Figure 15.2 Sessions, process groups and processes.

full list of the flags and their use. For example, the scan_mode() settings in the previous code could be set up with an stty command as follows:

```
$ stty -echo -icanon -isig min 0 time 0
```

15.3.2 Control Terminals

Every process is a member of a process group and every process group is a member of a session. In every process group there is one process whose process ID (PID) is the same as its process group ID (PGID). This process is the leader of the process group to which it belongs. Similarly, each session has a single process which acts as the session leader (see Figure 15.2).

The processes in a session, via the session leader, can be associated with a terminal which will act as the session's controlling terminal. A session can only have one controlling terminal and any terminal can only control at most one session. If a session has a controlling terminal then this is the terminal from which keyboard generated signals (like Ctrl-c, Ctrl-\, etc.) can be sent to processes in the session.

Within a session, one of the process groups will be the foreground process group and any other process groups within the session will be background process groups. Only the processes within the foreground process group are allowed to take input from the session's controlling terminal. Controlling terminal output can also be restricted to this process group.

This all sounds very complicated but these things are all set up automatically for you when you login and, generally, there is no reason why you would want to change them.

If you really need to set up your own sessions and process groups, then there are two functions available for this purpose. The first one, called `setsid()`, allows you to set up your own sessions:

```
#include <unistd.h>
#include <sys/types.h>

pid_t setsid(void);
```

A successful call to `setsid()` creates a new session, which contains a new process group, which in turn contains the current process as both the new session and process group leader. However, `setsid()` cannot be called successfully by a process which is already a process group leader. We'll look at the solution to this problem in Section 22.2.3.

As a terminal cannot be a controlling terminal for more than one session, then a side effect of `setsid()` is that the new session will not have a controlling terminal because, even if it had one before, it would have been left behind with the old session.

If you want the new session to have a controlling terminal then all you do is get the session leader to `open()` a terminal which isn't already the controlling terminal for another session and your new session will automatically acquire the terminal as its controlling terminal.

If the new session needs to `open()` a terminal, but you don't want the session to acquire the terminal as its controlling terminal, then you should use the `O_NOCTTY` flag in the `open()` call.

The second function, which allows you to manipulate process groups, is called `setpgid()`. In general, a process can only change its own PGID or the PGID of one of its child processes. The prototype for `setpgid()` is:

```
#include <unistd.h>
#include <sys/types.h>

pid_t setpgid(pid_t pid, pid_t pgid);
```

The parameters *pid* and *pgid* are obviously a process ID and a process group ID respectively. There are three cases to consider for the values of these parameters:

- *pid* and *pgid* are both non-zero – The process *pid* is moved into the process group *pgid*. The value of *pgid* must either refer to a process group in the current session, or it must be the same as *pid*, in which case a new process group is created in the current session with process *pid* as its leader.

- *pid* is zero – This is the same as the previous case except that the PID of the calling process is used instead of *pid*.
- *pgid* is zero – This is also the same as the first case except that the PID of the calling process is used instead of *pgid*.

For compatibility with other flavors of UNIX, another call is also provided which can change the process group of the calling process:

```
#include <unistd.h>

int setpgrp(void);
```

Under Linux the `setpgrp()` call is exactly equivalent to the `setpgid()` call:

```
setpgid(0, 0);
```

15.4 Inodes

You have already seen that all the files and devices in a Linux system have an `inode` associated with them, through which they are accessed. The inode itself contains quite a lot of information related to the file, including:

- file's device and inode numbers giving unique file identity;
- file's type (ordinary file, directory, special file etc.);
- file's access permission bits;
- link count (number of directory entries linked to this file);
- file's UID and GID;
- major and minor device numbers for device special files;
- file's size in bytes (where it makes sense);
- times for last file access/modification/status change;
- other information leading to disk blocks containing the file's data (if appropriate).

With the exception of the last item, the values of all these attributes are readily available to a process if it knows the pathname to the file or if it has a file descriptor to an open file description associated with it.

In order to access them, the status attributes that are available to a process are copied into a `struct stat`, which is defined via `<sys/stat.h>`. The main fields in this structure are:

```
        dev_t     st_dev;                    /* device number */
        ino_t     st_ino;                    /* inode number */
        umode_t   st_mode;           /* file type and permissions */
        nlink_t   st_nlink;                    /* link count */
        uid_t     st_uid;                  /* owner ID of file */
```

```
    gid_t      st_gid;                 /* group ID of file */
    dev_t      st_rdev;       /* device numbers for device file */
    off_t      st_size;                /* file size, in bytes */
    time_t     st_atime;               /* time of last access */
    time_t     st_mtime;            /* time of last modification */
    time_t     st_ctime;           /* time of last status change */
```

Symbolic constants giving values for the st_mode field in this structure are defined via <sys/stat.h>.

The information in this structure can be recovered using one of the three system calls fstat(), stat() or lstat():

```
#include <sys/stat.h>
#include <unistd.h>

int fstat(int fd, struct stat *sbuf);
int stat(char *pathname, struct stat *sbuf);
int lstat(char *pathname, struct stat *sbuf);
```

For fstat(), the *fd* parameter is a file descriptor to an open file description and *sbuf* is a pointer to a struct stat which will be filled with the appropriate status details by the call.

The stat() call is the same as fstat() except that the first parameter is the *pathname* to the file and not a file descriptor.

The lstat() call is the same as stat() except that if the file is a symbolic link lstat() will give the status details about the link file itself, whereas stat() will follow the link and give details about the file to which the link points.

All three system calls return 0 on successful completion, or -1 on error, with errno set to an appropriate value.

The following code is a simple program which will display human readable versions of the information in the struct stat associated with any given file pathnames:

```
#include <stdio.h>
#include <sys/stat.h>

#define MAJOR(a) (int)((unsigned short)(a) >> 8)
#define MINOR(a) (int)((unsigned short)(a) & 0xFF)

main(int argc, char **argv)
{
    struct stat sbuf;
    int dev_flag;

    for (; argc>1; --argc)
```

```
        {
            printf("\nFile name: %s\n", argv[argc-1]);

            if (stat(argv[argc-1], &sbuf)==-1)
                fatal("obtaining status details");

            dev_flag = file_type(&sbuf);
            printf("Permission bits: %o\n", sbuf.st_mode & 07777);
            printf("File numbers: ");
            printf("major %d, ", MAJOR(sbuf.st_dev));
            printf("minor %d, ", MINOR(sbuf.st_dev));
            printf("inode %d\n", sbuf.st_ino);
            printf("Link count: %d\n", sbuf.st_nlink);

            if (dev_flag)
            {
                printf("Device numbers: ");
                printf("major %d, ", MAJOR(sbuf.st_rdev));
                printf("minor %d\n", MINOR(sbuf.st_rdev));
            }
            else
                printf("File size: %ld\n", sbuf.st_size);

            printf("File owner ID: %d\n", sbuf.st_uid);
            printf("File group ID: %d\n", sbuf.st_gid);
        }
    }


    file_type(struct stat *sbufp)
    {
        printf("File type: ");

        switch (sbufp->st_mode & S_IFMT)
        {
        case S_IFREG:
            printf("Ordinary file\n");
            return 0;

        case S_IFDIR:
            printf("Directory\n");
            return 0;

        case S_IFIFO:
```

```
            printf("Named pipe (FIFO)\n");
            return 0;

        case S_IFBLK:
            printf("Block device special file\n");
            return 1;

        case S_IFCHR:
            printf("Character device special file\n");
            return 1;

        default:
            printf("Unknown...\n");
            exit(1);
        }
    }


    fatal(char *mess)
    {
        fprintf(stderr, "Error: %s\n", mess);
        exit(1);
    }
```

Notice that the program is capable of dealing with multiple file names on the command line. Typical output from the program appears as follows:

```
$ file_status /etc ./book.ps /dev/modem

File name: /dev/modem
File type: Character device special file
Permission bits: 660
File numbers: major 3, minor 65, inode 47638
Link count: 1
Device numbers: major 5, minor 64
File owner ID: 0
File group ID: 14

File name: ./book.ps
File type: Ordinary file
Permission bits: 644
File numbers: major 3, minor 66, inode 34876
Link count: 1
File size: 1049173
File owner ID: 500
```

```
File group ID: 500

File name: /etc
File type: Directory
Permission bits: 755
File numbers: major 3, minor 65, inode 45701
Link count: 8
File size: 2048
File owner ID: 0
File group ID: 0
```

15.5 Changing File Attributes

Out of all of the information you can collect about a file there is only a relatively small amount of it that you can change. This section looks at most of the things over which you have this control.

15.5.1 chmod and fchmod System Calls

The first thing to look at is the file permission bits. The system calls used to change them are called chmod() and fchmod(). The bits that can be changed by these system calls are exactly the same as those which can be changed by the chmod command. This includes the read, write and execute bits for the owner, group and world user classes. It also includes the setuid bit and the setgid bit. The prototypes for chmod() and fchmod() are:

```
#include <sys/types.h>
#include <sys/stat.h>

int chmod(char *pathname, mode_t mode);
int fchmod(int fd, mode_t mode);
```

The chmod() call changes the *mode* bits of the file at the given *pathname*, while fchmod() changes the *mode* bits of the file associated with the file descriptor *fd*.

Notice that the *mode* parameter has the POSIX data type mode_t and so to be properly portable you should use the symbolic bit mask names for the mode bits from <sys/stat.h> and not the octal number versions. Linux, however, will accept either so that the following two fchmod() system calls perform exactly the same function:

```
fchmod(fd, S_ISUID | S_IRWXU | S_IXGRP | S_IXOTH);

fchmod(fd, 04711);
```

Both of these system calls return the value 0 if they complete successfully, or -1 on error, with an appropriate error value in `errno`.

15.5.2 `umask` System Call

Don't forget when you change the mode bits on a file, that the bits you specify will automatically be modified by the current `umask` value according to the formula:

    mode & (~umask)

The functionality of the `umask` command which you have seen previously, is provided at the system programming level by a `umask()` system call:

    #include <unistd.h>

    mode_t umask(mode_t mask);

The *mask* parameter is specified using the same set of symbolic bit mask names as `chmod()`.

The return value from `umask()` is the current value of the `umask` that your new *mask* parameter replaces. This allows you to discover the current `umask` value as follows:

    oldmask = umask(0);
    (void)umask(oldmask);

The second call to `umask()` is required to restore the `umask` value that was discovered.

15.5.3 `chown` and `fchown` System Calls

The `chown()` and `fchown()` system calls are used to change a file's owner ID or its group ID. The prototype for these calls is:

    #include <sys/types.h>
    #include <unistd.h>

    int chown(char *pathname, uid_t owner, gid_t group);
    int fchown(int fd, uid_t owner, gid_t group);

The `chown()` and `fchown()` system calls assign the new *owner* and *group* IDs to a file specified by *pathname* or file descriptor *fd* respectively.

Under Linux, only `root` can make sensible use of the `chown()` and `fchown()` system calls.

15.5.4 fcntl System Call

Another thing which can be examined and changed are the flags which were set up for the file by the second parameter to the open() call. The system call to do this is called fcntl(). Obviously, since it is working with the flags set up when the file was opened, fcntl() only has a version that works on a file descriptor, and not one that works from a pathname. The prototype for fcntl() is:

```
#include <unistd.h>
#include <fcntl.h>

int fcntl(int fd, int cmd);
int fcntl(int fd, int cmd, long setval);
```

There is a whole collection of miscellaneous file control facilities which can be provided by the fcntl() call on a file, via the file descriptor *fd*. Here we shall look at only two of them (we will come back to look at others in later chapters).

The fcntl() call takes two or three parameters depending on the value of the command (*cmd*) parameter. In general, commands which get the value of some attribute or flag use the two-parameter version of fcntl() and supply the required value as its return value. Similarly, commands that set the value of some attribute or flag typically use the three-parameter version of fcntl() and set the attribute or flag from the *setval* parameter.

The two commands required for getting and setting some of the open() flags are:

F_GETFL   return flags and access mode associated with *fd*;
F_SETFL   set flags associated with *fd*.

The F_GETFL command can return any of the flags and access mode values set by open() (such as O_RDONLY, O_WRONLY, O_APPEND, etc.), but the F_SETFL command can only set or reset the O_APPEND and O_NONBLOCK flags.

As the access mode values returned by the O_GETFL command are not single-bit flags, the safest way to test if a particular mode value is set is to use a test of the following form (testing for O_RDONLY in this example):

```
if ((fcntl(fd, F_GETFL) & O_ACCMODE) == O_RDONLY)
    /* code if fd is open read only */
```

where O_ACCMODE is specifically designed to mask out the access mode bits from the fcntl() return value.

15.5.5 truncate and ftruncate System Calls

The final system calls in this section can be used to truncate a file to a specified length given either a pathname to the file or a file descriptor associated with the file:

```
#include <unistd.h>

int truncate(char *pathname, size_t len);
int ftruncate(int fd, size_t len);
```

If the file referred to in these calls is longer than *len* bytes in length, then it will be truncated to the specified size and the extra bytes will be lost.

In order for `ftruncate()` to operate successfully *fd* must be associated with an open file description that is open for writing (i.e either `O_WRONLY` or `O_RDWR`).

15.6 File Hierarchy

In order to create, modify and maintain the Linux file and directory hierarchy it is necessary to be able to create and remove directories, and create and remove links in directories to files. All of these things are easy to achieve, especially since they all have their own system calls.

15.6.1 mkdir and rmdir System Calls

A Linux process can create a directory with the `mkdir()` system call. The prototype for the call is:

```
#include <sys/types.h>
#include <fcntl.h>
#include <unistd.h>

int mkdir(char *pathname, mode_t mode);
```

assuming your process has appropriate permissions, a call to `mkdir()` will create a new directory named *pathname* with its permission bits set to *mode*. The value of the *mode* parameter is modified by the current umask value in the usual way. The new directory will be owned by the effective user ID of the calling process and it will automatically be initialized to contain the `dot` and `dot-dot` entries.

If a directory is empty (apart from the `dot` and `dot-dot` entries) then it can be removed from the directory hierarchy with the `rmdir()` system call:

```
#include <unistd.h>

int rmdir(char *pathname);
```

15.6.2 Directory Access

Because of the special importance of directories in the file system hierarchy, special system calls are required to access their contents. To open a directory you need to use the `opendir()` system call which has the prototype:

```
#include <dirent.h>

DIR *opendir(char *pathname);
```

This call opens the specified directory and returns a directory pointer if successful or zero on error. The directory pointer is passed into the related system calls, the main ones being `readdir()` and `closedir()`.

The `readdir()` system call has the prototype:

```
#include <dirent.h>

struct dirent *readdir(DIR *dirptr);
```

This call returns a pointer to a `struct dirent` which contains the details of the next link in the specified directory. The name of the file in the link is stored in the d_name element of the structure, which is a `char` array. Calling `readdir()` repeatedly will result in a sequential walk throught the links in the directory. A zero value is returned when there are no more links left to read.

Once you have finished with a directory, it can be closed with the `closedir()` system call. This call has the prototype:

```
#include <dirent.h>

int closedir(DIR *dirptr);
```

15.6.3 link and unlink System Calls

A directory entry for a file is called a *link*. A link to a file is automatically generated from its given pathname when the file is first created. Thereafter, extra links to the file can be generated by th `link()` system call:

```
#include <unistd.h>

int link(char *pathname1, char *pathname2);
```

A new directory link, called *pathname2*, is created to point to the existing file *pathname1*. In order for the `link()` call to work, both *pathname1* and *pathname2* must be on the same filesystem and the calling process must have appropriate permission to write to the target directory.

Ordinary file links can be removed with the `unlink()` system call.

```
#include <unistd.h>

int unlink(char *pathname)
```

This call removes the specified directory link and decrements the link count to the file in its inode. After this, if the link count has gone to zero then the inode and the file's data blocks are all freed back to the system. If some process should happen to have the file open when it is scheduled for removal then the recovery of the inode and data blocks will be delayed until the process terminates, though the directory link will still be removed so that no other process can `open()` the file and further prolong its life.

Exercises

1. Write a simplified version of the `ls` command which just takes the name of a single directory as its only command line parameter and lists the names of all the files in the directory, one name per line. It will be simpler if you do not try to sort the list of names.
2. Write a program which gets a copy of the `struct termios` associated with your terminal and displays in a sensible human readable form the values of the settings it finds.
3. Write a C program which prompts a user for a name and password and takes string values from the user in response to the prompts. Make sure that you suppress character echo while the password is being entered, and restore the echo afterwards, before your program prints the values it obtains and then terminates.
4. Write a simple `rename` command which will allow you to rename any file owned by you in the current directory. The format of the command should be:

   ```
   $ rename <oldname> <newname>
   ```

Answers

1. The code which follows is very simple, partly because it does none of the checks that would normally be required to verify the correct number and types of command line parameters and also to verify the correct operation of the system calls made. However, it does make the code very easy to read:

   ```
   #include <stdio.h>
   #include <dirent.h>
   ```

```
main(int argc, char **argv)
{
    DIR *dp;
    struct dirent *link;

    dp = opendir(argv[1]);

    while ((link = readdir(dp))!=0)
        printf("%s\n", link->d_name);

    closedir(dp);
}
```

2. The way to tackle this problem is to use either `ioctl()` or `tcgetattr()` to pick up the contents of the structure associated with the terminal. The information you need about the meanings and values for each of the flags and bytes in the structure is contained in the header file `/usr/include/linux/termios.h`, with some extra information in the manual page for the `stty` command. From this information it is quite easy to work out what flags are set and reset and what their effects will be. This can then be displayed in any appropriate form.

3. The following shell script performs the required task and will work nicely as a pseudo code program for you to follow for your solution to the problem in C:

```
echo -n "enter name: "
read name
stty -echo
echo -n "enter password: "
read password
stty echo
echo
echo name: $name
echo password: $password
```

4. A pseudo code solution to this problem would look something like:

```
main(argc, argv)
    if argc!=3
        give error and usage message and exit
    if argv[1] or argv[2] outside current directory
        i.e. if they contain a '/', give error and exit
    if argv[1] not in current directory
        give error and exit
    link(argv[1], argv[2])
    unlink(argv[1])
```

Your C solution should follow this basic pattern. Try to make it as bullet proof as possible by trying to deal with as many error conditions as you can find, including checking error returns from system calls.

Chapter 16

Process Control

Linux is a true multi-tasking operating system. If you have an application that requires several processes to cooperate concurrently then Linux can arrange to have them run concurrently and take care of all the scheduling and administration of the processes on your behalf. In fact, you have already seen that this is so. Every time you use the shell to run a pipeline such as:

```
$ ls | wc -w
```

it involves multiple commands (`ls` and `wc` in this example) running concurrently and with a communication channel between them so that they can co-operate to perform a single task. When the shell arranges to run concurrent processes on your behalf it only uses ordinary user facilities which you are also free to use in your own programs. It is these facilities which form the subject of this chapter.

16.1 Process Identity Numbers

Every process that runs under Linux has a unique process ID number (PID) by which it is known to the system. Each process from process 1 (`init`) onwards has a parent process whose process ID it can also access.

Every process also belongs to a process group, with a process group ID which is just the process ID of the process group leader.

When it comes to sorting out what permissions a process has to access various files, the process uses another set of four IDs. These are known as the *real* user and group IDs and the **effective** user and group IDs. The real IDs of a process are just the UID and GID of the user for whom the process runs. The effective IDs are nomally the same as the real IDs except for the case when a program has its setuid or setgid bits set. If one or both of these bits is set, then the corresponding effective user or group ID will be set to the file owner ID or the file group ID associated with the program file from which the process is running.

That sounds complicated, so an example is in order. Suppose a user with a UID of 200 and a GID of 20 were to run the program /usr/bin/passwd. This program has a file owner ID of 0 (root), a file group ID of 1 (bin) and it also has its setuid bit set.

When the passwd program is run, the associated process will have a real user ID of 200, a real group ID of 20, an effective user ID of 0 because the setuid bit is set, and an effective group ID of 20.

The real IDs are used to sort out the identity of the user for whom the process is running. The effective IDs are used to sort out the privileges and permissions that processes have when accessing a file, according to the following algorithm (which starts at rule 1):

Rule 1 If the effective user ID of the process is 0 (root) then permission is granted automatically for most things. If not, goto rule 2

Rule 2 If the effective user ID of the process is the same as the user ID of the file, then access is granted to the file according to the owner permission bits on the file. If not, goto rule 3.

Rule 3 If the effective group ID of the process is the same as the group ID of the file, then access is granted to the file according to the group permission bits on the file. If not, goto rule 4.

Rule 4 Access is granted to the file according to the world permission bits on the file.

All of the various IDs associated with a process can be accessed via a set of 'get ID' system calls:

```
uid_t getuid(void)        /* get real user ID */
uid_t getgid(void)        /* get real group ID */
uid_t geteuid(void)       /* get effective user ID */
uid_t getegid(void)       /* get effective group ID */
pid_t getpid(void)        /* get process ID */
pid_t getppid(void)       /* get parent process ID */
pid_t getpgrp(void)       /* get process group ID */
```

16.2 Creating Processes with fork

For the purposes of this discussion we will consider that a process consists of three separate parts, illustrated in Figure 16.1.

The *text* segment holds the machine code instructions that are to be executed. The segment is read-only (so you can't write self-modifying code here), which allows the possibility of sharing the segment between two or more process on the system that are running the same program. For instance, if several users are all running bash as their shell, there need only be one copy of the program instructions in memory, which they can all share.

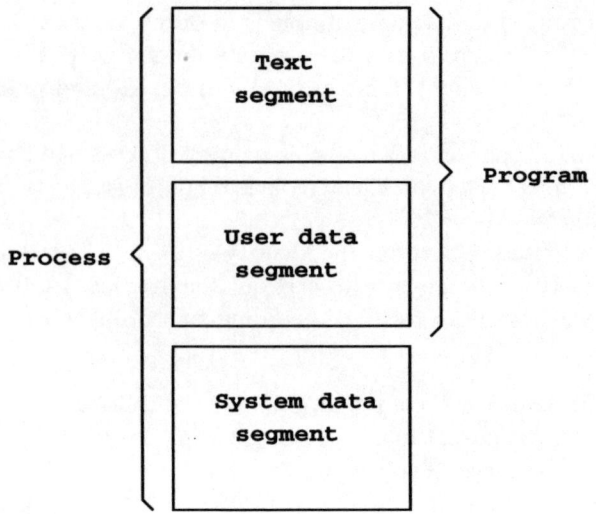

Figure 16.1 The parts of programs and processes.

The *user data* segment holds all the data upon which the process will operate directly as it executes, including all the variables that the process will use. Obviously, as the information contained here can be changed, each process needs its own private user data segment, even processes which are sharing a text segment.

The *system data* segment effectively holds the environment in which the program will run. Indeed, this is the distinction between programs and processes. A program is a static thing on disk consisting of a set of instructions and data which are used to initialize the text and user data segments of a process. The process is a dynamic thing, an execution environment requiring the interaction of the text, user data and system data segment information all running together.

Under Linux, there is only one way that an existing process can start up a new process for you and that is to use the `fork()` system call:

```
#include <unistd.h>

pid_t fork(void);
```

Conceptually, what happens with `fork()` is that the process which makes the `fork()` call becomes the parent of a new process which is created. The two processes are identical in terms of the contents of their text and user data segments, and almost identical in terms of their system data segments as well. The only difference between the processes is in a small number of attributes which have to be different (such as the `PID`, for instance, which has to be unique for each process). Once the child process has been created, then both the parent and child continue execution from inside the `fork()` call. This means that the next action for both processes is to return from `fork()` with its return value.

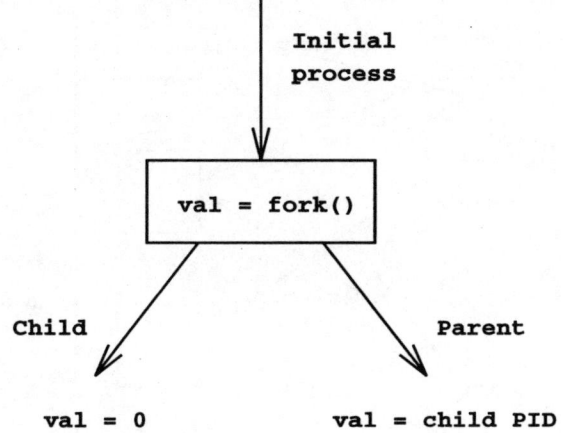

Figure 16.2 The action of the fork() system call.

There doesn't seem much point in having two virtually identical processes running, unless there is some way to get them subsequently to perform different actions. This is made relatively simple by the fact that fork() returns a different value to the two processes. To the parent process it returns the PID of the newly created child, while to the child process it returns the value 0. As normal process IDs only start numbering from 1 with the init process, the fork() system call cannot return the value 0 to the parent as the PID of the new child. Therefore, if fork() does return a 0 then it must be to a new child process. If it returns a non-zero value then it must be the PID of a child process being returned to the parent (or -1 on error). This idea is illustrated in Figure 16.2.

The following code is a simple program to demonstrate the fork() call in action:

```
#include <sys/types.h>
#include <unistd.h>

main()
{
    pid_t val;

    printf("PID before fork(): %d\n", (int) getpid());

    if (val = fork())
        printf("Parent PID: %d\n", (int) getpid());
    else
        printf("Child PID: %d\n", (int) getpid());
}
```

When this program is run it should generate three lines of output. The first will display the PID of the process before the fork() call is executed, and the other

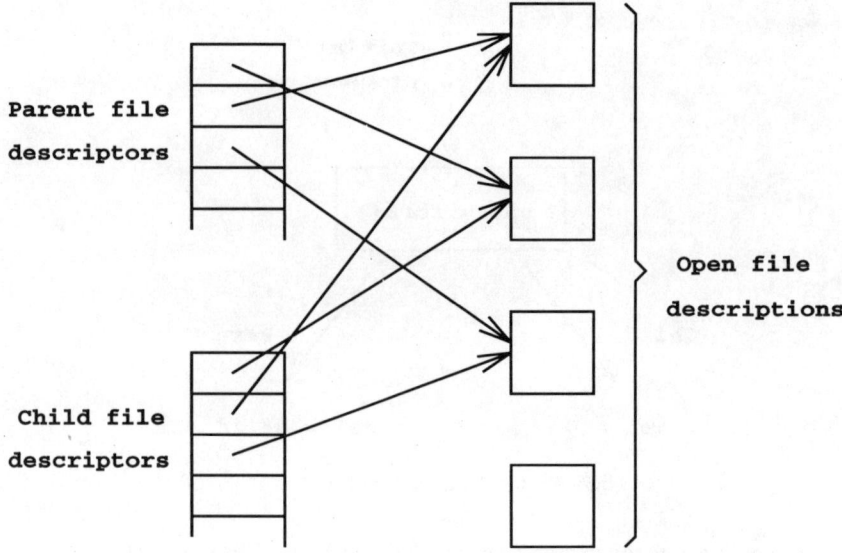

Figure 16.3 Parent and child share open file descriptions.

two lines of output will be generated by the parent and child processes after the fork(), giving the PID of each process. A typical output from the program could be:

```
$ forktest
PID before fork(): 490
Parent PID: 490
Child PID: 491
```

After the execution of a fork() call most of the attributes of the parent process are available unchanged in the child. The main unchanged attributes are:

- session and process group membership;
- controlling terminal (if any);
- real and effective UIDs and GIDs;
- current working directory;
- file mode creation mask (umask).

In addition to this, all of the file descriptors which are associated with open file descriptions in the parent process will be duplicated in the child. This means that the child's file descriptors and the parent's file descriptors will both point to the same open file descriptions, as shown in Figure 16.3

This is a very important concept, as we shall see later, because it allows a process to open files in advance, knowing that they will be pre-opened and immediately available to its child processes after a fork() call.

16.3 exec System Call

When you use the shell to run a command (ls, say) then at some point the shell will execute a `fork()` call to get a new process running. Having done that, how does the shell then get ls to run in the child process instead of the duplicate copy of the shell, which is what will be running immediately after the `fork()` call?

The solution in this case is to use an `exec()` system call. In fact, there are several different flavors of the `exec()` call, but they all perform essentially the same task. Use of the `exec()` system call is the only way to get a program executed under Linux. The way that it does this is to replace the text and user data segments of the process that executes the `exec()` call with the text and user data contained in the program file whose name is passed as a parameter to `exec()`. This is probably best illustrated with a simple example.

Before we do that, however, I need to digress slightly to explain a little more about `exec()`. When you execute a program from the shell, you have seen that it is possible to specify parameters and switches to the program on the command line. From your knowledge of C you also know that these command line values are made available to a program via the `argc` and `argv` parameters to `main()`. Somehow the shell needs to be able to take your command line values and pass them on to the programs it runs on your behalf as their `argc` and `argv`. This is done by passing your command line values in a suitable form to `exec()` which will arrange for them to appear as `argc` and `argv` to the new program about to be run.

The simplest version of `exec()` with which to demonstrate these things is called `execl()`. The prototype for this is:

```
#include <unistd.h>

int execl(char *pathname, char *arg0, ...);
```

The *pathname* is the full path to the command to execute. This is followed by a variable length list of pointers to character strings. These will become the contents of the array pointed to by `argv` in the new program. The list of pointers in `execl()` should be terminated by a NULL pointer. The following example program uses `execl()` to execute the simple command – ls -l:

```
#include <stdio.h>

main()
{
    execl("/bin/ls", "ls", "-l", 0);
    printf("Can only get here on error\n");
}
```

The first parameter to `execl()` in this example is the full pathname to the ls command. This is the file whose contents will be run, provided the process has execute permission on the file. The rest of the `execl()` parameters provide the strings to which the `argv` array elements in the new program will point. In this example, it means that the `ls` program will see the string *ls* pointed to by its `argv[0]`, and the string *-l* pointed to by its `argv[1]`.

Normally the `exec()` calls don't return. In general, they can't because their function is to replace the text and user data segments in the process that calls them for some other program – so there will be nothing to return to!

However, if the `exec()` calls fail for any reason (usually because the file you are trying to execute doesn't exist or because you don't have execute permission for it) then they will return so that you can have the opportunity to do something about the error.

In addition to making all these parameters available to the new program, the `exec()` calls also pass a value for the variable:

```
extern char **environ;
```

This variable has the same format as the `argv` variable except that the items passed via `environ` are the values in the environment of the process (like any exported shell variables), rather than the command line parameters. In the case of `execl()`, the value of the `environ` variable in the new program will be a copy of the value of this variable in the calling process.

The `execl()` version of `exec()` is fine in the circumstances where you can explicitly list all of the parameters, as in the previous example. Now suppose you want to write a program that doesn't just run `ls`, but will run any program you wish, and pass it any number of appropriate command line parameters. Obviously, `execl()` won't do the job.

The example program below, which implements this requirement, shows, however, that the system call `execv()` will perform as required:

```
#include <stdio.h>

main(int argc, char **argv)
{
    if (argc==1)
    {
        printf("Usage: run <command> [<parameters>]\n");
        exit(1);
    }

    execv(argv[1], &argv[1]);
    printf("Sorry... couldn't run that!\n");
}
```

The prototype for `execv()` shows that it only takes two parameters, the first is the full pathname to the command to execute and the second is the `argv` value you want to pass into the new program. In the previous example this value was derived from the `argv` value passed into the run command, so that the run command can take the command line parameter values you pass it and just pass them on.

The following is a typical command sequence using the run command:

```
$ run ls -l mtos
Sorry... couldn't run that!
$ run /bin/ls -l mtos
total 2
drwxr-xr-x   2 pc      book          1024 Apr  2 20:11 tdd
drwxr-xr-x   2 pc      book          1024 Apr  2 20:11 tsh
```

Notice the failure on the first attempt, this is because you need to specify the full pathname to the command you want to run when you are using `execv()` (or `execl()`), as can be seen from the result of the second attempt.

The problem here is that the two versions of `exec()` covered so far do not use the values in your PATH environment variable when looking for the command you specify. As you may have guessed, however, there are versions of `exec()` that do. These are called `execlp()` and `execvp()`, which are exactly the same as the first pair but they also use the value of PATH to find the required command.

The final two versions of `exec()` are the same as the first two (i.e. they don't use PATH) but they do allow you manually to specify the value to appear in `environ` in the new program rather than accepting the automatic default. They are called `execle()` and `execve()`. The following is a list of all six `exec()` variants and the parameter numbers and types they take:

```
int execl(pathname, arg0, ..., argn, 0);
int execv(pathname, argv);
int execlp(cmdname, arg0, ..., argn, 0);
int execvp(cmdname, argv);
int execle(pathname, arg0, ..., argn, 0, envp);
int execve(pathname, argv, envp);

char *pathname, *cmdname;
char *arg0, ..., *argn;
char **argv, **envp;
```

Just as with `fork()`, most process attributes are preserved across an `exec()` call. This is because the system data segment remains intact during an `exec()`, which only changes the text and user data segments. Most important is the fact that the file descriptors which were associated with open file descriptions before the call are normally still available after it. The exception to this is that a flag exists within each file descriptor (not the open file description) called the *close on exec* flag (guess what that does).

Setting the close on exec flag is another one of the miscellaneous facilities provided by a call to `fcntl()`. The form of the call for setting the close on exec flag on a particular file descriptor (fd) is:

```
fcntl(fd, F_SETFD, FD_CLOEXEC);
```

Just to recap for a moment, when you want a running process to organize the execution of another program as part of its operation, the sequence of steps is as follows:

- The running process gets or generates the command that is to be executed.
- The process does a `fork()` system call. This starts up a new process which is a copy of, and runs concurrently with, the original process. The original process is called the parent and the new one is called the child.
- The child process now executes an `exec()` call which scraps the text and user data segments of the child process and replaces them with the text and user data in the command file that is to be run.

Two obvious questions arise on looking at this scenario. First, wasn't it rather a waste of effort creating the child process as an exact duplicate of the parent only to scrap that immediately and replace it with a new program? And, second, what does the parent process do while the child process is executing?

Taking the questions in that order – Linux implements its `fork()` system call in a very efficient way. In effect, Linux cheats. It doesn't really make a full copy of the process at all, it just has two sets of pointers, one for each process, that both point to the same real text and data segments. In the case of the text segment, this doesn't matter because the segment is read-only anyway. In the case of the data segments, however, it decidedly does matter because these are supposed to be a pair of independent processes. But, thinking about it for a moment, as long as the two processes only read data from the data segments and don't do any writing of new values, then neither process will know that the cheat is taking place. In order for this scheme to work completely, all Linux has to do is to spot when one of the two processes tries to write something to one of the data segments and create a copy of just that little bit when it is needed. This technique is called *copy on write*.

In essence, any area that gets written to by either process gets copied so that both processes then have their own copies of those areas. If the child process immediately performs an `exec()` call, then very little of the shared data segment space will have been copied before the `exec()` takes place – a huge saving in time and resources.

16.4 wait and exit System Calls

The answer to the question of what the parent process does while the child process runs is quite simple – either it waits for the child process to terminate or it just gets on with whatever else it needs to do.

In the case of the shell, for instance, the choice is given to the user. Normally, if you just enter a command to the shell, it will wait until the command has finished before it gives you another prompt. If you put an ampersand (&) on the end of the line then the shell will not wait but will return a new prompt immediately.

In order to wait for a child process to terminate, a parent process will just execute a `wait()` system call. This call will suspend the parent process until any of its child processes terminates, at which time the `wait()` call returns and the parent process can continue.

The prototype for the `wait()` call is:

```
#include <sys/types.h>
#include <sys/wait.h>

pid_t wait(int *status);
```

The return value from wait is the PID of the child process which terminated. The parameter to `wait()` is a pointer to a location which will receive the child's exit status value when it terminates.

When a process terminates it executes an `exit()` system call, either directly in its own code, or indirectly via library code. The prototype for the `exit()` call is:

```
#include <stdlib.h>

void exit(int status);
```

The `exit()` call has no return value as the process that calls it terminates and so couldn't receive a value anyway. Notice, however, that `exit()` does take a parameter value – *status*. As well as causing a waiting parent process to resume execution, `exit()` also returns the *status* parameter value to the parent process via the location pointed to by the `wait()` parameter.

In fact, `wait()` can return several different pieces of information via the value to which the status parameter points. Consequently, a macro is provided called WEXITSTATUS() (accessed via <sys/wait.h>) which can extract and return the child's exit status. The following code fragment shows its use:

```
#include <sys/wait.h>

int statval, exstat;
pid_t pid;

pid = wait(&statval);
exstat = WEXITSTATUS(statval);
```

It is now possible to draw up a picture of the life of a child process from creation by `fork()`, through execution via `exec()`, then termination with `exit()`,

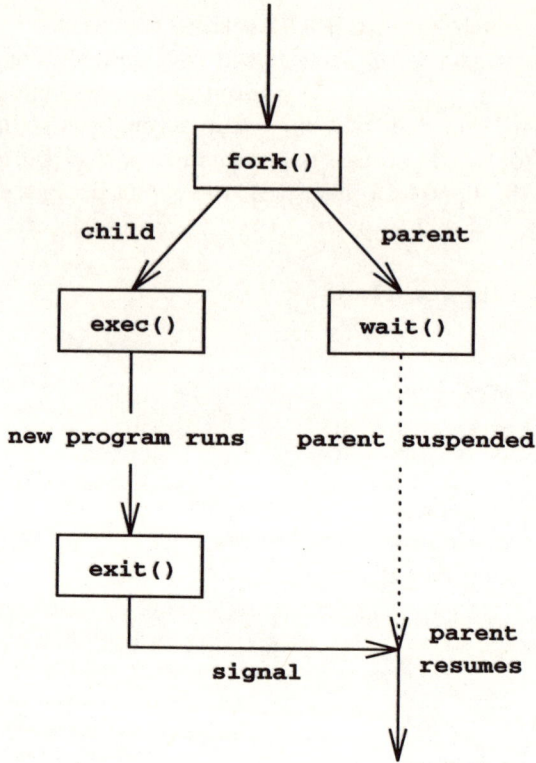

Figure 16.4 The life cycle of a child process.

while the parent process is suspended with `wait()`. This sequence is illustrated in Figure 16.4.

In fact, the version of `wait()` that we have just seen is only the simplest version available under Linux. The new POSIX version is called `waitpid`. The prototype for `waitpid()` is:

```
#include <sys/types.h>
#include <sys/wait.h>

pid_t waitpid(pid_t pid, int *status, int options);
```

where *pid* specifies what to wait for, *status* is the same as the simple `wait()` parameter and *options* allows you to specify that a call to `waitpid()` should not suspend the parent process if no child process is ready to report its exit status.

The various possibilities for the *pid* parameter are:

pid	meaning
< -1	wait for a child whose PGID is -pid
-1	same behavior as standard `wait()`
0	wait for child whose PGID = PGID of calling process
> 0	wait for a child whose PID = pid

The standard `wait()` call is now redundant as the following `waitpid()` call is exactly equivalent:

```
#include <sys/wait.h>

int statval;
pid_t pid;

pid = waitpid(-1, &statval, 0);
```

It is possible for a child process which only executes for a very short time to terminate before its parent process has had the chance to `wait()` for it. In these circumstances the child process will enter a state, known as a *zombie* state, in which all its resources have been released back to the system except for its process data structure, which holds its exit status. When the parent eventually `wait()`s for the child, the exit status is delivered immediately and then the process data structure can also be released back to the system.

Exercises

1. Write a C program which can determine whether or not it is a process group leader and print a suitable message.
2. Write a C program which can determine whether or not it is running set UID and print a suitable message.
3. Write a simple test program with `fork()` that prints messages from the parent and child processes. The messages should include the words `parent` and `child` as appropriate and should also include the PID of the process doing the printing. Execute the program several times. Are the two messages always printed in the same order?
4. Add `wait()` and `exit()` system calls to the program you wrote for the previous exercise, so that an exit status is returned by the child to the parent, and included in the message the parent prints. Execute this program several times. Is the message order different from the previous exercise? Are the messages always printed in the same order?
5. Write a C program which will execute the following series of Linux commands:

   ```
   cp /etc/fstab .
   sort fstab -o myfstab
   cat myfstab
   ```

Answers

1. Your solution will use `getpid()` and `getpgrp()` to get the process ID and process group ID. If these are the same then the process is a process group leader, and not otherwise.
2. Your solution will use `getuid()` and `geteuid()` to get the process real user ID and effective user ID. If these are not the same then the process is running set UID, and not otherwise.
3. The code for this question is very straightforward, as follows:

   ```
   main()
   {
       if (fork())
           printf("parent PID = %d\n", getpid());
       else
           printf("child PID = %d\n", getpid());
   }
   ```

   In general, some flavors of UNIX will run the parent process first, others will run the child first, and yet others have no fixed order. In Linux, the current source code for `fork()` shows that the parent process should always run first, and your experiments should bear this out.
4. The whole idea behind adding `exit()` and `wait()` to a program is to force the parent to wait for execution of the child to terminate before it proceeds. The new code appears as:

   ```
   #include <sys/wait.h>

   main()
   {
       int status;

       if (fork())
       {
           wait(&status);
           printf("parent PID = %d, child ", getpid());
           printf("exit status = %d\n", WEXITSTATUS(statval));
       }
       else
       {
           printf("child PID = %d\n", getpid());
           exit(55);
       }
   }
   ```

When this is run, the use of exit() and wait() ensure that the child message will always be displayed first, and this applies not only to Linux, but to any version of UNIX as well.

5. The best way to guarantee a particular order of execution for the three commands is to fork() child processes to execute each of the commands in turn, making the parent wait() for the termination of one child process before executing the next:

```
main()
{
    if (!fork())
    {
        execlp("cp", "cp", "/etc/fstab", ".", 0);
        printf("error executing cp\n");
        exit(1);
    }

    wait(0);

    if (!fork())
    {
        execlp("sort", "sort", "fstab", "-o", "myfstab", 0);
        printf("error executing sort\n");
        exit(1);
    }

    wait(0);
    execlp("cat", "cat", "myfstab", 0);
    printf("error executing cat\n");
    exit(1);
}
```

In order to simplify the code slightly the return value from fork() is not checked here for an error value. It would also be a good idea to check the exit status returned to wait() for and error value and deal with it appropriately. I leave these things for you to do... .

Chapter 17

Inter-process Communication (IPC)

In order for processes to co-operate on some task they must be able to communicate with each other. Linux supports many different forms of inter-process communication (IPC) mechanism, each of which has advantages and disadvantages in particular circumstances. The purpose of this chapter is to review the most useful IPC mechanisms so that you can make sensible choices when you come to write co-operating concurrent processes.

The simplest way to communicate values between processes is via a file. One process writes to the file and another process reads from it. This is a surprisingly simple mechanism which has several advantages:

- It will allow any pair of processes with access permission to the file to use it for communication.
- It can allow the transfer of very large amounts of data between processes.

Despite these advantages, the use of files as a major IPC mechanism has two big drawbacks:

- In order to make sure that the reader has the opportunity to see all the data sent to it, the writer must only add new data to the end of the file. This means the file can grow very large for long lived processes.
- If the reader performs its task faster than the writer then it will frequently catch up with the writer and have nothing to read. This means that the reader will constantly be reading end-of-file and not be able to tell whether this is because the writer has finished and closed the file, or the writer is still computing values to pass to the reader and there will be more to follow.

The simplest IPC mechanism which overcomes the problems inherent in the use of files is the *pipe*.

17.1 Pipes

You will certainly have encountered pipes before, even if you have not yet written any programs that use one – the shell uses them all the time, whenever you get it to execute a pipeline where the output of one process is sent to the input of another:

```
$ ls | wc -w
```

The pipe overcomes both the problems of using files. First, a pipe is a fixed-size buffer (4096 bytes in Linux) so that its size can't grow unchecked like a file.

The consequence of using a single fixed-sized buffer is that, on writing, the pipe can become full. When this happens subsequent `write()` calls to the pipe will block by default, waiting for some data to be read to make enough room for the `write()` to take place. Notice that reading data from a pipe is a one-off operation and that the data, once read, is discarded from the pipe to free up the space for more data to be written.

Second, it is also possible, if the reader is working faster than the writer, for the pipe to become empty when all the current data has been read. When this happens a subsequent `read()` call will block by default, waiting for more data to be written. This solves the `read()` returning end-of-file problem.

A pipe is created using the `pipe()` system call rather than `open()` because different parameters are required and `open()` could not easily have been pressed into service in this case. The prototype for the `pipe()` call is:

```
#include <unistd.h>

int pipe(int fd[2]);
```

There are two file descriptors associated with a pipe, one for the `read()` end and one for the `write()` end. Because a function call cannot return two values, the parameter to `pipe()` is a pointer to a two-element `int` array which will be filled by the `pipe()` call with the two required file descriptors. The `fd[0]` element will contain the file descriptor for the `read()` end of the pipe, while `fd[1]` contains the file descriptor for the `write()` end.

Notice that there is no pathname given as a parameter to `pipe()`. This means that when a pipe is created it does not have a directory link created for it. As a consequence, other existing processes have no means of obtaining a file descriptor for the pipe and thus cannot access it. How, then, do two processes manage to use a pipe to communicate?

Remember that the `fork()` and `exec()` system calls can ensure that copies of the file descriptors available to a parent process are also available to its children. This information gives the required mechanism. What happens is that a process will create the pipe with a `pipe()` system call and then `fork()` one or more child processes, all of which will have file descriptors to the pipe available to them.

Inter-process Communication (IPC)

The implication here is that an ordinary pipe can only be used between two processes that share a common ancestor, and that this ancestor must have created the pipe for them both to use.

The data in a pipe is always read in the same order that it was written. This means that the lseek() system call has no effect with pipes.

A simple program to set up and use a pipe between two proceses follows:

```
#include <unistd.h>
#include <stdio.h>

main()
{
    int fda[2];
    char buf[1];

    if (pipe(fda)==-1)                          /* Create the pipe */
        fatal("creating pipe");

    switch (fork())
    {
    case -1:
        fatal("forking child");
        break;

    case 0:                     /* Child process is pipe reader */
        close(fda[1]);          /* Close write end of pipe */
        read(fda[0], buf, 1);
        printf("%c\n", buf[0]);
        break;

    default:                    /* Parent process is pipe writer */
        close(fda[0]);          /* Close read end of pipe */
        write(fda[1], "a", 1);
        break;
    }
}

fatal(char *mess)
{
    fprintf(stderr, "Error: %s\n", mess);
    exit(1);
}
```

Notice in this example that each of the two processes closes the end of the pipe that it does not need. This is important so that the end-of-file condition is transmitted properly to reading processes when the writing processes all close the pipe.

Blocking reads and writes form the default action for a pipe which is empty or full respectively. These defaults can be overridden by setting the O_NONBLOCK flag on the pipe file descriptors with the fcntl() system call:

```
#include <fcntl.h>

fcntl(fd, F_SETFL, O_NONBLOCK);
```

17.2 I/O Redirection

With the aid of one additional system call, all the I/O redirection functionality available through the shell can be programmed in your own code. The additional system call is called dup(). The prototype for dup() is:

```
#include <unistd.h>

int dup(int fd);
```

What the dup() call does is to take a file descriptor as its parameter and return another file descriptor that is a duplicate copy of the first. This means that both file descriptors are associated with the same open file description. The dup() call searches through the file descriptor array from the beginning and makes its copy into the first free file descriptor it encounters. This is illustrated in Figure 17.1, which shows the effect of using the dup() system call on file descriptor 2. The file descriptor is duplicated into the first free slot in the file descriptor array. In this example, file descriptor 0 is free to be used and, consequently, the value 0 will be returned from the dup() call.

I/O redirection and pipes between processes, such as are used by the shell, are now easy to set up. Looking at pipes first, the scenario is that you enter a pipeline as a command to the shell such as:

```
$ ls | wc -w
```

Remember that the ls and wc commands do not need to be aware that the redirection is taking place; they just continue to use their standard input and standard output files for all their input and output requirements.

This means that the shell has to create a pipe and then fork() the two child processes, manipulating their file descriptors to make the pipe correspond to the output of the first process in the pipeline and to the input of the second.

The following listing is a simple program which executes the pipeline ls | wc -w from the previous example:

278 *Inter-process Communication (IPC)*

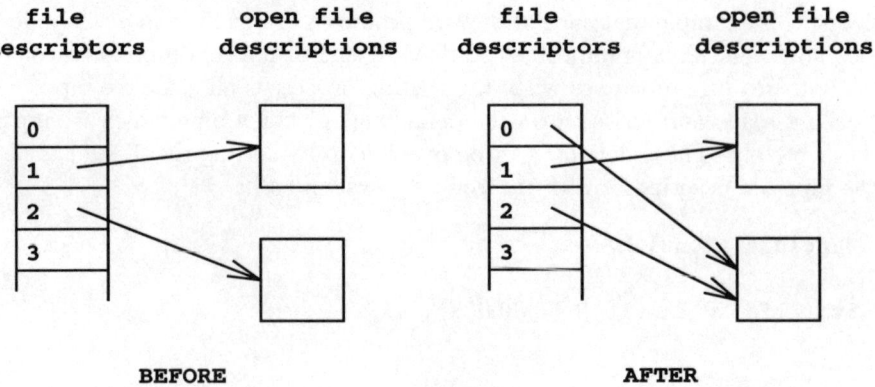

Figure 17.1 Effect of executing the system call dup(2).

```
#include <unistd.h>
#include <stdio.h>

main()
{
    int fda[2];

    if (pipe(fda)==-1)                           /* Create pipe */
        fatal("creating pipe");

    switch (fork())                              /* Create child */
    {
    case -1:
        fatal("forking child");
        break;

    case 0:                                      /* Run ls in child */
        close(1);                                /* Close standard output */
        dup(fda[1]);                             /* Duplicate pipe write end */
        close(fda[1]);                           /* Close pipe write end */
        close(fda[0]);                           /* Close pipe read end */
        execlp("ls", "ls", 0);                   /* Execute ls command */
        fatal("trying to exec ls");
        break;

    default:                                     /* Run wc in parent */
        close(0);                                /* Close standard input */
        dup(fda[0]);                             /* Duplicate pipe read end */
        close(fda[0]);                           /* Close pipe read end */
```

```
            close(fda[1]);                 /* Close pipe write end */
            execlp("wc", "wc", "-w", 0);   /* Execute wc command */
            fatal("trying to exec wc");
            break;
    }
}

fatal(char *mess)
{
    fprintf(stderr, "Error: %s\n", mess);
    exit(1);
}
```

Notice how the redirection into and out of the pipe is accomplished before the exec() calls are made to execute the ls and wc commands.

The child process will be used to execute the ls command. In this case, it is necessary to set things up so that when ls writes to the standard output device it will actually be writing to the pipe. To do this, the first step is to close() the current standard output device and then use dup() to duplicate the write end of the pipe. Remember, dup() will make its copy in the lowest numbered free file descriptor, which in this case will be the standard output file descriptor that we just closed. As standard output is now associated with the write end of the pipe, any write() calls to this file descriptor will automatically send the data to the pipe.

After this, both of the original file descriptors to the pipe can be closed and it is this arrangement of file descriptors that will then be passed on to the ls command by the execlp() call.

Similarly, the parent process will be used to execute the wc command, meaning that it must be re-arranged to take its input from the pipe. This is achieved using the same method as in the previous case. The current standard input file descriptor is closed so that, using dup(), it can be reallocated as the read end of the pipe. Then both the original pipe file descriptors can be closed before the execlp() call executes the wc command with this arrangement of file descriptors set up.

The ls and wc commands will then both execute as normal, reading and writing their standard input and output file descriptors, unaware that they are in communication.

Standard input and output redirection to files is achieved in similar ways, as the following example code shows. The code is designed to execute the command:

```
$ cat <file1 >file2
```

In this case the program will close each of its standard input and output file descriptors in turn and use open() to open the required files and have them associated with the standard input and output file descriptors:

```
#include <unistd.h>
#include <stdio.h>
#include <sys/stat.h>
#include <fcntl.h>

#define WRFLAGS (O_WRONLY | O_CREAT | O_TRUNC)
#define MODE600 (S_IRUSR | S_IWUSR)

main()
{
    close(0);                       /* Close standard input */

    if (open("file1", O_RDONLY)==-1)
        fatal("opening input file");

    close(1);                       /* Close standard output */

    if (open("file2", WRFLAGS, MODE600)==-1)
        fatal("opening output file");

    execlp("cat", "cat", 0);    /* Execute cat command */
    fatal("trying to exec cat");
}


fatal(char *mess)
{
    fprintf(stderr, "Error: %s\n", mess);
    exit(1);
}
```

There are two other system calls which can duplicate file descriptors. the first is dup2(), with the prototype:

```
#include <unistd.h>

int dup2(int oldfd, int newfd);
```

This call makes *newfd* a copy of *oldfd*. It will also close *newfd* before the duplication operation if it is already open.

The other way to duplicate file descriptors is to use another of the miscellaneous facilities of the fcntl() system call:

```
#include <fcntl.h>

newfd = fcntl(oldfd, F_DUPFD, minfd);
```

This provides a facility which is a cross between dup() and dup2(). The fcntl() call looks for a free file descriptor starting with *minfd*. When it finds one it uses it to duplicate *oldfd*. The duplicate file descriptor is then returned by fcntl() as *newfd*.

17.3 FIFOs

Anonymous pipes overcome the main problems with using files for inter-process communication. However, pipes have one drawback not shared by files – they can only be used by processes that have a common ancestor which created the pipe for them and passed on its file descriptors to them.

FIFO files (also known as *named pipes*) solve even this problem, while still maintaining all the advantages of anonymous pipes. The way FIFO files solve the problem is that they have file names (i.e. directory links) and so can be open()ed and used by any processes, whether they are related or not, as long as they have appropriate access permissions to the file.

In order to create a FIFO file you can either use the command mknod from the shell prompt or you can use the mknod() system call from within one of your programs. Both the mknod command and the system call can be used to create more than just FIFO files. We'll see other uses of mknod when we look at writing device drivers.

Using the mknod command to create a FIFO file from the shell prompt is easy – the command has the format:

```
$ mknod filename p
```

This command will create a FIFO file called *filename* with access permissions 666 minus the current value of umask.

The mknod() system call has the prototype:

```
#include <sys/types.h>
#include <sys/stat.h>
#include <fcntl.h>
#include <unistd.h>

int mknod(char *pathname, mode_t mode, dev_t dev);
```

Where *pathname* is the name of the file to be created, *mode* is a combination of the permission bits to be set on the file and a specification of the type of file to be created (S_IFIFO in this case), and *dev* is a value which is used when creating device special files and so, for a FIFO, this has the value zero. For example:

```
#define MYMODE (S_IFIFO | S_IRUSR | S_IWUSR)

mknod{"myfifo", MYMODE, 0);
```

Once a FIFO file has been created it can be accessed using just the standard `open()` system call by any process with appropriate permissions. When `open()`, a FIFO file has the same basic functionality as an anonymous pipe, i.e. `read()`s block when the pipe is empty, `write()`s block when the pipe is full and setting the `O_NONBLOCK` flag with `fcntl()` will cause `read()` and `write()` to return immediately with an `EAGAIN` error in situations where they would otherwise have blocked.

Because they can be accessed simultaneously by many unrelated processes, FIFOs are useful in applications where there are multiple readers and/or multiple writers. In this situation there needs to be a rule to determine what happens if two writers try to write to the FIFO at the same time. The rule is that a `write()` of any number of bytes up to the size of the pipe (4096 bytes in Linux) is guaranteed to be atomic. This means that the data from multiple `write()` operations will not intermingle in the FIFO but will be maintained as separate messages. Exactly the same rule applies to anonymous pipes, but here it is less useful because they are less often used in these types of application.

17.4 System V IPC

In order to provide compatibility with other systems, Linux also provides an option to support the three System V IPC mechanisms: shared memory, messages and semaphores. Each of these has approximately the same kind of interface so we'll just briefly look at one of them – shared memory.

The use of pipes and FIFOs still suffers from one disadvantage and that is the amount of data copying and processor context switching that goes on to transfer the data.

Shared memory overcomes this problem by making the same block of memory simultaneously visible in the address spaces of two or more processes. This means that as soon as one process has written some information into the memory, it is immediately available to the other processes which share this memory block without any further copying operations taking place.

Before any process can attach to a shared memory segment it first needs to be created. This is done with the `shmget()` call, which has the prototype:

```
#include <sys/ipc.h>
#include <sys/shm.h>

int shmget(key_t key, int size, int flags);
```

where *size* is the number of bytes required (rounded up to the smallest whole number of memory pages), *key* is a numeric value (which for a shared memory segment has a similar role to a file's name), and *flags* is a set of bit masks ORed together to specify access permissions and creation flags when a sheared memory segment is created (rather like a combination of the second and third parameters to an `open()` system call).

A value of IPC_CREAT as part of the *flags* parameter will cause a shared memory segment associated with the given *key* to be created if it does not already exist. Including the IPC_EXCL flag will cause a shmget() call to fail if a shared memory segment with the specified *key* already exists.

Using a value of IPC_PRIVATE in the *key* field is a way of creating a shared memory segment without worrying about whether or not the segment already exists.

The return value from shmget() is a shared memory segment ID which is similar in concept to a file descriptor returned by open(), in that the value needs to be passed into the other calls related to the segment. The big difference, however, is that any process which has the value of a shared memory segment ID can access the segment, not just descendant processes as in the file descriptor case.

A simple example program to create a shared memory segment could be:

```
#include <stdio.h>
#include <sys/ipc.h>
#include <sys/shm.h>

#define SHM_SIZE 4096
#define SHM_FLAGS IPC_CREAT | 0644

main()
{
    int shmid;

    shmid = shmget(IPC_PRIVATE, SHM_SIZE, SHM_FLAGS);

    if (shmid==-1)
        fatal("creating shared memory segment");

    printf("shared memory segment ID = %d\n", shm_id);
}


fatal(char *mess)
{
    fprintf(stderr, "Error: %s\n", mess);
    exit(1);
}
```

The status of any System V IPC resources can be examined, once created, with the ipcs command. A -m switch to the command gives information about shared memory segments, a -s switch lists semaphore arrays and -q is for message queues. If no switch is specified then all three resource lists will be displayed.

If the program in the previous listing is called make_shm then it can be used and its results examined with the following command sequence:

```
$ make_shm
shared memory segment ID = 1408
$ ipcs

------ Shared Memory Segments --------
shmid      owner      perms      bytes      nattch     status
1408       pc         644        4096       0

------ Semaphore Arrays --------
semid      owner      perms      nsems      status

------ Message Queues --------
msqid      owner      perms      used-bytes messages
```

Once the shared memory segment exists it can be attached to the memory of a running process with the `shmat()` call, the prototype for which is:

```
# include <sys/types.h>
# include <sys/ipc.h>
# include <sys/shm.h>

char *shmat(int shmid, char *shmaddr, int flags);
```

where *shmid* is the shared memory segment ID returned by the `shmget()` call, *shmaddr* is the address where you want the shared memory segment to be attached and *flags* allows you to specify that you want to attach the segment read-only (using the SHM_RDONLY flag) instead of read-write. Normally, you will not want to specify your own *shmaddr* and you can get the system to pick an address for you by passing the parameter value zero.

The return value from `shmat()` is a pointer (C type pointer) to the shared memory segment, which you can then use just like a pointer to any other block of memory.

When you have finished with a shared memory segment, you can detach it from your process with a `shmdt()` call:

```
# include <sys/types.h>
# include <sys/ipc.h>
# include <sys/shm.h>

int shmdt (char *shmaddr);
```

passing the memory address returned by the corresponding `shmat()` call as the *shmaddr* parameter.

The `shmdt()` call does not destroy the shared memory segment, even if no other process is attached to it. Indeed, anything written into the segment will remain intact so that subsequent shmat() calls will give access to the memory segment and to the data it contains.

If you actually want to destroy a shared memory segment (which you should do when you have really finished with it) this can be done with a control function call named shmctl():

```
#include <sys/ipc.h>
#include <sys/shm.h>

int shmctl(int shmid, int cmd, struct shmid_ds *buf);
```

This function is similar in concept to ioctl() and fcntl() in that it allows both read and write access to a structure of information related to a shared memory segment specified by *shmid*. The *cmd* parameter specifies the actual operation to perform and *buf* is a pointer to a shared memory structure which is used for passing data about as required. The following *cmd* values are available:

    IPC_STAT   copy shared memory structure into *buf*;
    IPC_SET   set shared memory structure from *buf*;
    IPC_RMID   destroy shared memory segment given by *shmid*.

An alternative way to destroy a shared memory segment is to use the command ipcrm:

    $ ipcrm shm shmid

where *shmid* is the shared memory segment ID given in the ipcs display. For example:

    $ ipcrm shm 1408

The following is a short program to demonstrate attaching the memory segment with ID = 1408 to the process, writing some data to the segment and then detaching it to await reading by some other process:

```
#include <stdio.h>
#include <sys/ipc.h>
#include <sys/shm.h>

#define SHM_ID 1408

main()
{
    char *shmaddr;

    if ((shmaddr = shmat(SHM_ID, 0, 0))==(char *)-1)
        fatal("attaching shared memory segment");
```

```
        strcpy(shmaddr, "Some test message");

        if (shmdt(shmaddr)==-1)
            fatal("detaching shared memory segment");
}


    fatal(char *mess)
    {
        fprintf(stderr, "Error: %s\n", mess);
        exit(1);
    }
```

Notice that, in common with the system calls, the shm functions all return -1 on error. Since shmat() actually returns a pointer to a block of memory it is necessary to cast the -1 value to char * in order to perform the comparison.

Though they operate on different data structures, the other System V IPC mechanisms (semaphores and messages) are very similar in concept and usage to shared memory, in that they each have a call to create the resource in the first place; they also have calls for access and control operations:

	shared memory	*semaphores*	*messages*
creation	shmget()	semget()	msgget()
access	shmat()	semop()	msgsnd()
	shmdt()		msgrcv()
control	shmctl()	semctl()	msgctl()

17.5 Sockets

All the IPC mechanisms discussed so far have only been useful for communication between processes on the same machine. With the modern trend towards networks, it is important for Linux to support an IPC mechanism which allows it to be fully network compatible. Sockets is that mechanism.

Sockets made a first appearance in early versions of BSD UNIX. Here the designers tried to build a very general mechanism that would be able to accommodate many network protocols. To a large extent the designers were successful, but, in order to allow all the necessary flexibility, programming with sockets requires the specification of values for a number of variable parameters. In order to make more sense of some of the parameters, it is necessary to look first at some of the underlying network principles.

The Internet Protocol (IP) sits on top of lower level software protocols and the network hardware, and hides these network structures from the application software.

This means that applications do not need to know what kind of network hardware they are using (Ethernet, serial lines, parallel lines).

IP is what is known as a connectionless service, which means that the network doesn't have any fixed data connections between particular machines, just lots of machines all conceptually connected on a common highway. In order to make message routing possible, each interface on each host machine on the network is given a unique IP address. Each address is just a 32-bit number, usually given as four 8-bit values, printed in decimal and with periods (full stops) between (for example 194.61.21.6). If you are only using a stand alone machine, or your own local network, then you are free to choose your own IP addresses. If, however, you will be connecting your machine to a network that has global Internet access, you will need to have a globally registered Internet address allocated to you by your network administrator. Each IP data packet (called a datagram) transmitted on the network carries its source and destination IP address information with it, and may get routed through a number of machines to reach its destination. Because each IP datagram is carried separately, maybe even over different routes, the connectionless service does not guarantee that the packets will arrive in the same order as they were sent, or even that they will arrive at all.

17.5.1 The User Datagram Protocol

At the IP level, the addresses in the datagrams only specify machine interface IP numbers; they do not specify any particular processes or applications on those machines. To overcome this problem, the User Datagram Protocol (UDP) sits on top of the basic IP layer and provides a set of communication end points called ports, each identified by a small integer value. The UDP message packets contain both source and destination port numbers which are used to allow the UDP software at the destination to deliver an incoming message to the correct process, and for that process to be able to return a reply to the original sender.

Using UDP, each message packet is a self-contained entity. This means that each packet of data also carries with it all the information required to deliver it, so that a sequence of packets, transmitted from a particular process via a given UDP port, need not all have the same destination.

UDP simply uses the underlying Internet Protocol to send its messages, and so it, too, provides the same, unreliable, connectionless message passing as IP. Unreliable, here, is not intended to mean that messages are unlikely to get through, just that it is not guaranteed.

17.5.2 The Transmission Control Protocol

At the application program level, there is often a need to transfer large quantities of data between two fixed processes. In this kind of scenario, using an unreliable connectionless protocol means that application programs would have to have sophisticated error detection and correction mechanisms built into them. In order to avoid this unnecessary overhead on the design and construction of application programs, what is required is a reliable protocol which guarantees the delivery of data between two fixed processes and also guarantees that the data will be received in the same order that it was sent. The Transmission Control Protocol (TCP) is the standard solution.

Like UDP, TCP also sits on top of the basic IP layer and provides protocol ports to allow multiple-destination processes on a single machine. Unlike UDP, however, TCP is a connection based protocol. This means that both ends of the communication link must agree to participate before any data can be exchanged, and that sequences of packets transmitted at one end are all intended for the same destination. As all the data packets sent over a particular TCP connection are intended for the same destination, and their order of arrival is guaranteed to be the same as their order of transmission, there is no need for any kind of message boundaries to be observed by the protocol itself. So, for example, using the `read()` and `write()` system calls, a message of 100 bytes transmitted by the sender may legitimately be received at the destination as four separate 25-byte messages. This means that it is up to the processes at each end of the connection to impose any required structure on the data transmitted, as it is not necessarily preserved by TCP.

A socket is a communication end point and as such can be mapped quite nicely onto a UDP or TCP port. Although these are not the only possible mappings they are by far the most common and are the ones considered in most detail here.

17.5.3 Clients and Servers

A server is a process that offers some kind of service to other processes, and clients are the server's customer processes. In the case where the client and server are to communicate using TCP, the server will usually open its end of the link and passively wait for connections to arrive. The client, on the other hand, will take the active role in opening the connection to the server.

Once a TCP-socket connection between two processes has been established, the end points of the connection are made to perform like ordinary Linux files, so that standard system calls, like `read()` and `write()`, can be used to transfer the data. To make this possible, sockets have descriptors associated with them analogous to the file descriptors associated with ordinary files. The main difference between socket descriptors and file descriptors is that the socket descriptors do not automatically have specific destination addresses bound to them when the socket is created, whereas file descriptors are bound to specific file names by the `open()` system call. To enable the `read()` and `write()` system calls to be used in both cases like this, it is necessary for Linux to ensure that socket and file descriptors are in the same numeric range and that there is no duplication of numeric values in a given application. This is done by allocating them both from the same per process table.

17.5.4 Creating a Socket

Sockets are created using the `socket()` system call. The `socket()` call takes three parameters: *family*, *type* and *protocol*, and returns an integer socket descriptor as its return value. The general form of the call is:

    sd = socket(family, type, protocol)

The *family* parameter names the address family to use with the socket. The address family specifies the format for addresses when they are given. The two main families are `AF_INET` where addresses are given as 32-bit IP addresses (standard Internet format) and `AF_UNIX`, where the addresses are path names in the Linux file system.

The *type* parameter specifies the type of communication required. The main choice is between a connectionless datagram (UDP type) service, called `SOCK_DGRAM` and a reliable, connection based (TCP type) service, called `SOCK_STREAM`. If only from the point of view of simplicity and reliability, most home-grown application will be written using `SOCK_STREAM`.

In the majority of cases, specifying the address family and socket type is sufficient to determine the communication protocol to use over the new socket. In these cases, the *protocol* parameter is given the value zero so that a default protocol will automatically be selected. Protocol values other than zero are normally only used when making direct, low level, access to hardware interfaces.

If the `socket()` call is successful, the return value is a socket descriptor of type `int`. A -1 is returned on error. The socket descriptor is used as a parameter to other calls in setting up socket connections.

The standard `close()` system call should be used on a socket descriptor to shut it down at the end of a session.

17.5.5 Binding a Local Address

When a socket is first created, it has no specific address associated with it and so remote processes have no way to refer to it. The format of an address for a particular socket will depend upon the address family that was specified when the socket was created. For example, in the Internet address family (`AF_INET`), a socket address would be a machine interface IP address and a port number on that machine.

Very often a client process will not care what port number is assigned to its socket and will allow the system to pick one. Server processes, on the other hand, need to be able to specify their addresses to the system because they will usually be operating at a fixed port number which is known to their clients and which the clients will need to use to establish a connection.

To bind a specific address to a socket, a server process uses the `bind()` system call, as follows:

```
bind(sd, address, addrlen)
```

The *sd* parameter is just the socket descriptor that was returned by the `socket()` call. The *address* parameter is a pointer to a structure that contains an address of an appropriate type for the socket type being bound, and the *addrlen* parameter specifies the length of the address, in bytes. This arrangement is necessary in order to permit the wide variety of address formats that may be encountered between different address families.

17.5.6 Clients Connecting to a Server

In connection based (TCP type) communication links, a client process needs to initiate the connection to the server. In order to do this, the client needs to know the address and port number that the server will use to provide its service. With this information, the client uses the `connect()` system call:

```
connect(sd, address, addrlen)
```

The *sd* parameter is the socket descriptor of the client's local socket. The *address* parameter specifies the address that the server is using on the destination machine, *addrlen* being the length of the specified address, in bytes.

If the client's socket has not been bound to a specified local address when the `connect()` call is made, then the system will automatically pick a local address and an appropriate local port number and bind them to the client's socket.

The `connect()` call returns the value 0 if a connection is successfully established or the value -1 on error. Once a client has successfully established a connection, the socket can then be used to send and receive data. There are several possibilities here, the most common being the use of the `read()` and `write()` system calls. These are exactly the same calls as are used on files but are given the local socket descriptor as their first parameter.

17.5.7 Setting up a Server

Once a server process has used the `socket()` and `bind()` system calls to create itself a socket and bind a local address and port to the socket, it then needs to prepare the socket to take incoming connection requests. The `listen()` system call is used to perform this function. At the same time, this system call is also used to set the size of a queue that Linux will use to allow queuing of simultaneous connection requests from multiple clients. The general form of the `listen()` system call is:

    listen(sd, qlen)

where the *sd* parameter is the socket descriptor returned by a `socket()` call and *qlen* is the permitted size of the queue given as the maximum number of pending client connection requests.

Once a socket has been set up in this manner, the server now only needs to wait for a connection. To do this it uses the `accept()` system call as follows:

    newsd = accept(sd, address, addrlen)

Once again, the *sd* parameter is the socket descriptor associated with the server's socket. The *address* parameter is a pointer to a socket address structure which will be filled in by the `accept()` call with the address and port number bound to the client's socket when a connection is established. The *addrlen* parameter is a pointer to an integer which is also filled in by the `accept()` call to give the size, in bytes, of the client's address.

The return value from `accept()` is a new socket descriptor which has as its destination the established client, and which will be used in all further communication with that client. The original socket descriptor that was passed as a parameter to `accept()` is still open at this point and may be used again in another call to `accept()` to establish a connection with another client process.

Once a socket descriptor has been returned by `accept()`, the server can communicate with the new client using the normal `read()` and `write()` system calls.

17.5.8 Blocking and Non-blocking Sockets

By default, a call to `accept()` will block if no client process is waiting to establish a connection. This means that the `accept()` call does not return until there is a client ready to communicate. Consequently, the server process cannot proceed with any other tasks until a connection is made.

Sometimes it is required that a server just look to see if a client is waiting to connect, accepting the connection if it is, but getting on with something else if there is no pending connection. This is done by making the socket non-blocking so that the `accept()` call returns immediately, even if no client is waiting. The `fcntl()` system call is used to set or reset the O_NDELAY flag on the associated socket descriptor to achieve this result. First get the flags associated with the socket descriptor:

    flags = fcntl(sd, F_GETFL);

And then set O_NDELAY as follows:

    fcntl(sd, F_SETFL, flags|O_NDELAY);

Or to reset O_NDELAY:

```
fcntl(sd, F_SETFL, flags&~O_NDELAY);
```

17.5.9 Connectionless Communication

In addition to connection based communication, there is also support for connectionless arrangements based on UDP datagram sockets. These sockets are created in the same way as stream based sockets except that the *type* parameter in the socket() call is SOCK_DGRAM instead of SOCK_STREAM. Once the datagram socket is created, if a particular local address needs to be used it can be bound to the socket with the bind() system call. If the use of bind() is required then this must precede the first use of the socket for data transmission. If bind() is not used then the system will automatically allocate a local address and port number the first time data is sent.

A process should use the system calls sendto() and recvfrom() for sending and receiving data, because they include a parameter to hold the address and port number of the communication partner in their parameter lists. The general form of the sendto() call is:

```
sendto(sd, buf, len, flags, addr, addrlen)
```

where *sd*, *buf* and *len* have the same types and actions as the parameters in the write() system call. The *flags* parameter, whose values are defined in the header file <linux/socket.h> is used for several special message options. The *addr* parameter is a pointer to a structure containing the destination address and port, and *addrlen* is the size, in bytes, of the address structure.

The recvfrom() system call has the general form:

```
recvfrom(sd, buf, len, flags, addr, lenptr)
```

Its parameter list is similar to the list for sendto(), with *sd*, *buf* and *len* acting like the read() system call. The *addr* and *lenptr* parameters are pointers to an address structure and an integer respectively and are filled in by the recvfrom() call with the appropriate information about the communication partner.

Datagram sockets can also use the connect() system call. In this case there is no attempt to establish a connection with another process; the connect() call is just used to specify an association between a datagram socket and a particular destination address and port. Once connect() has been used, any data sent on the socket is automatically routed to the associated destination. This allows the use of the send() and recv() system calls for passing data. The general form of these calls is:

```
send(sd, buf, len, flags)
recv(sd, buf, len, flags)
```

These two calls are exactly the same as `sendto()` and `recvfrom()`, but without the last two parameters, as this information has already been set up by `connect()`.

The `send()` and `recv()` calls can also be used for communication on connection based sockets, as here a process's communication partner has already been permanently established.

17.5.10 Socket Support Calls

In addition to the main set of system calls associated with socket use, which you have now seen, there are a number of support functions which also need a mention. These are related to hostnames, port numbers, standard network services and network byte ordering.

The `gethostname()` system call allows processes to have access to the local hostname. The form of the call is:

    gethostname(name, len)

Where *name* is a pointer to a char array that will hold the host's domain name, and *len* is the maximum name length that the array can hold. For privileged (EUID=0) processes, `sethostname()` can be used to set the local hostname to a specified string.

Once you have a host's domain name available you need to be able to get its IP address or vice versa. The library functions `gethostbyname()` and `gethostbyaddr()` perform these tasks. The general form of these calls is:

    hostent = gethostbyname(name)
    hostent = gethostbyaddr(addr, len, type)

The *name* parameter is a pointer to a char array containing the host's domain name. The *addr* parameter is a pointer to a host address of length *len* and address type *type*. Both calls return a pointer to a `struct hostent`, defined in `<netdb.h>`, which contains name, address and address type information for the required host.

There are a set of *well-known* ports for all the standard network services, and to find the port associated with a particular service name and protocol there is a standard library function called `getservbyname()`. This has the general form:

    servent = getservbyname(name, protocol)

The *name* parameter is a pointer to a string containing the name of the required service and the *prototype* parameter is a pointer to a string containing the appropriate communication protocol (udp or tcp). This function looks up the required information in the file `/etc/services` and returns a pointer to a structure of type `struct servent` filled in appropriately. The servent structure is declared in `<netdb.h>`.

Different machines with different processor architectures store integer values in several different ways. The most important difference as far as networking is concerned is the order in which the bytes are stored in an integer. Some processors, including the 80×86 family, store the bytes in an integer with the low byte first. This means that, on these machines, a pointer to an integer is actually pointing at the least significant byte in the multi-byte value. Other processors store the bytes that make up an integer, high byte first so that an `int *` in this case points to the high byte of the multi-byte value.

If steps were not taken to avoid the problem, then machines of opposite types would have trouble communicating integer values to each other over a network link. The solution to this problem is to agree that all machines will send multi-byte values to each other one way or the other. In fact, the agreed standard is to send high byte first. This means that the low byte first machines (80x86 and Linux included) need to reverse their byte order whenever integers are input from or output to the network. To do this conversion, four functions are provided, two to input and output 16-bit values (short) and two more for the input and output of 32-bit values (long). The functions are:

```
netval = htonl(hostval) - host to network long;
netval = htons(hostval) - host to network short;
hostval = ntohl(netval) - network to host long;
hostval = ntohs(netval) - network to host short.
```

All machines supply these functions. On machines that already use the correct byte ordering they are just dummy functions, or macros that do nothing. They are still supplied, however, so that code written on one machine can be portable, even to machines with the opposite processor architectures.

Obviously, if you only want to transmit streams of bytes (such as strings) then no use of these functions is required.

More information on these and related calls are available in sections 2 and 3 of the manual pages.

Exercises

1. Write a function called `mydup2()` which provides the functionality of the `dup2()` system call but written using only `dup()`.
2. Devise and run an experiment to discover the size of a pipe in Linux.
3. Write a simple program which creates a pipe and then executes a `fork()` call so that two independent processes are running. The two processes should then use the pipe to pass the contents of a large file from one process to the other.
4. Rewrite the program from the previous question to use shared memory to pass the contents of the file between the two processes. What are the extra problems you encounter in doing it this way? Which of your programs would you expect to run faster, and which one does?

Answers

1. In order to solve this problem you will need to keep a track of those file descriptors you take into service before you reach the file descriptor you want, so that you can release them again afterwards. The basic function appears as:

    ```
    #include <linux/limits.h>

    int mydup2(int oldfd, int newfd)
    {
        int i, fd, fdtable[OPEN_MAX];

        if (newfd<0 || newfd>OPEN_MAX)
            return -1;

        if (oldfd<0 || oldfd>OPEN_MAX)
            return -1;

        if (newfd==oldfd)
            return newfd;

        for (i = 0; i<OPEN_MAX; ++i)
            fdtable[i] = 0;

        close(newfd);

        while ((fd = dup(oldfd))!=newfd && fd!=-1)
            fdtable[fd] = 1;

        for (i = 0; i<OPEN_MAX; ++i)
            if (fdtable[i])
                close(i);

        return fd;
    }
    ```

2. This is just a case of creating a pipe, setting it O_NONBLOCK and then counting and writing bytes into it until the write() call indicates, by its return value, that bytes are no longer being stored in the pipe. Looking at the source code a pipe should be 4 K.

3. A pseudo code program to perform this task could be:

    ```
    create pipe
    if (fork()
    ```

```
              In parent, open() file
              while not end of file
                     read a character and write it to the pipe
       else
              In child
              while not end of pipe data
                     read a character from pipe and discard
```

You should run this program a couple of times to make sure that the file you are copying is all stored in the buffer cache – it is much faster to read from memory than from disk.

4. This program will be similar to the previous one except that you will create a shared memory segment instead of a pipe and then shmat() to the segment from within the parent and child processes after the fork() call. The extra problem with a shared memory solution is that you will need some form of synchronization between the two processes, so that the writer will not overwrite the character being transferred before the reader has read it, and vice-versa. An obvious way to do this is to use a semaphore which you can either implement yourself in shared memory or you could use the semaphore IPC mechanism provided. I leave you to do the experiment to work out which solution to the problem will be faster, pipes or shared memory.

Chapter 18
Tiny Socket Library – Case Study

As we have now covered quite a bit of the theory behind setting up network communication with sockets, it is time to put some of it into practice. Most socket code will be written to use a reliable, stream based, client/server protocol. This means that whenever a programmer comes to write a socket application for the first time, this will involve searching through the manual pages to find out about all the system calls involved, and then trying to make sense of all the options available with each call, only to come up with essentially the same solution as everyone else. This may be a bit of an overgeneralization, but it is surprising how many programmers effectively re-invent the same solution to the socket communication problem.

18.1 Library Functions

What is required is some sort of simple library of functions which will provide the standard, reliable, stream based, client/server communication facilities by default. Only if you require something out of the ordinary will you then need to delve deeper into the manual to sort out the options. This is a bit like the idea behind the standard I/O library functions for files (`fopen()`, `fclose()` etc.).

The simplest arrangement is just to have a function to call if you want to set up a server and another function to call to set up a client. Two further calls will create and destroy the sockets over which the server and client communicate. In addition to this, you also want to make sure that as few parameters as possible need to be specified so that, where ever possible, sensible defaults are chosen instead.

The following code presents a tiny socket library, which you can include in your own code, and which provides exactly this functionality. After that, a simple application is also presented to demonstrate the use of the library.

The library itself consists of two files: the source code, which you compile and link into your applications, and a header file, to `#include` into your code, which declares some symbolic constants, a data structure and the prototypes for the library functions themselves.

298 *Tiny Socket Library – Case Study*

The functions in the library are sopen(), sclose(), sserver() and sclient(). In essence, a server process will call the sopen() function, which creates a socket and stores the socket descriptor, along with some administrative information, in a structure. The function then returns a pointer to this structure as its return value. You then pass the socket structure pointer, along with the port number that the server will use to offer connections to clients, as parameters to the sserver() call. When a client connects with the server the sserver() call returns with a socket descriptor which can then be used to communicate with the client using, for example, read() and write(). Connections with other clients can be made by further calls to sserver(), using the same socket structure pointer and port number as before. Socket descriptors returned by sserver() should be released with close() when the client communication is over, and the socket pointer returned by sopen() should be released with sclose() when the server shuts down.

At the client end, a call to sopen() will create a socket and return a socket pointer as before. This pointer can then be passed, along with the server's address and port number, into sclient(). When the connection is established, sclient() returns a socket descriptor to communicate with the server. As in the server case, close() and sclose() should be used when the client finishes its task.

18.1.1 The sopen() Function

```
/* 1 */
SOCKET *sopen(void)
{
    /* 2 */
    SOCKET *sp;

    /* 3 */
    if ((sp = (SOCKET *)malloc(sizeof(SOCKET)))==0)
        return 0;

    /* 4 */
    if ((sp->sd = socket(AF_INET, SOCK_STREAM, 0))==-1)
    {
        free(sp);
        return 0;
    }

    /* 5 */
    sp->sinlen = sizeof(sp->sin);
    sp->bindflag = S_RESET;
    /* 6 */
    return sp;
}
```

Working down the numbered comments in turn:

1. The `sopen()` function is called to create a socket. The socket descriptor, along with some internal administrative information, is stored in a `SOCKET` structure (defined in `socklib.h`). A pointer to the `SOCKET` structure is returned by `sopen()` if the call is successful (a zero is returned on error). The pointer should be saved, to pass into other socket library functions. The `SOCKET` structure is a defined type, as follows:

   ```
   typedef struct
   {
       struct sockaddr_in sin;
       int sinlen;
       int bindflag;
       int sd;
   } SOCKET;
   ```

   Where *sd* is the socket descriptor returned when the socket is created, *sin* and *sinlen* are the address and length information of the server socket, and *bindflag* is used in the server to ensure that the `bind()` system call is only used once on the server's socket.

2. A pointer to a `SOCKET` is declared, whose value will eventually be the return value from `sopen()`.
3. A call to `malloc()` is made to obtain a block of memory big enough to store a `SOCKET` struct. If `malloc()` fails then `sopen()` returns the value 0 here.
4. This code section creates a TCP socket (`SOCK_STREAM`) in the IP address family (`AF_INET`). If there are no errors, the socket descriptor returned by the `socket()` call is stored in the *sd* field of the previously `malloc()`ed structure. Otherwise, the allocated memory is released with `free()` and an error value of zero is returned.
5. Once a socket has been successfully created, the *sinlen* and *bindflag* fields of the allocated structure are initialized.
6. Finally a pointer to the initialized `SOCKET` structure is returned by `sopen()` to be passed on to other socket library calls.

18.1.2 The `sclose()` Function

```
/* 1 */
sclose(SOCKET *sp)
{
    int sd;

    /* 2 */
    sd = sp->sd;
    free(sp);
```

```
            /* 3 */
            return close(sd);
}
```

1. The function `sclose()` closes the socket associated with a given SOCKET pointer. The pointer is passed to the function as a parameter. A value of 0 is returned if the call is successful, otherwise, a -1 is returned on error.
2. The socket descriptor in the *sd* field of the socket pointer structure is saved in a local variable so that the memory block pointed to by *sp* can safely be released with `free()`.
3. The saved socket descriptor can now be closed with the `close()` system call. This system call returns 0 if successful or -1 on error, which is exactly what `sclose()` should return, so this can all be done in one line.

18.1.3 The sserver() Function

```
/* 1 */
sserver(SOCKET *sp, int port, int sync)
SOCKET *sp;
int port, sync;
{
    int flags;
    struct hostent *hostent;
    char localhost[S_NAMLEN+1];

    /* 2 */
    if (sp->bindflag==S_RESET)
    {
        /* 3 */
        if (gethostname(localhost, S_NAMLEN)==-1
        || (hostent = gethostbyname(localhost))==0)
            return -1;

        /* 4 */
        sp->sin.sin_family = (short)hostent->h_addrtype;
        sp->sin.sin_port = htons((unsigned short)port);
        sp->sin.sin_addr.s_addr = *(unsigned long *)hostent->h_addr;

        /* 5 */
        if (bind(sp->sd, (struct sockaddr *)&sp->sin, sp->sinlen)==-1
        || listen(sp->sd, 5)==-1)
            return -1;

        /* 6 */
```

```
            sp->bindflag = S_SET;
    }

    /* 7 */
    switch (sync)
    {
    case S_DELAY:
        if ((flags = fcntl(sp->sd, F_GETFL))==-1
        || fcntl(sp->sd, F_SETFL, flags&~O_NDELAY)==-1)
            return -1;

        break;

    case S_NDELAY:
        if ((flags = fcntl(sp->sd, F_GETFL))==-1
        || fcntl(sp->sd, F_SETFL, flags|O_NDELAY)==-1)
            return -1;

        break;

    default:
        return -1;
    }

    /* 8 */
    return accept(sp->sd, (struct sockaddr *)&sp->sin, &sp->sinlen);
}
```

1. The sserver() function sets up the calling process as a network server, and establishes client connections. The *sp* parameter is a SOCKET pointer previously returned by sopen(). The *port* parameter is the port number which should be bound with the local host IP address to the open socket, and the *sync* parameter specifies whether or not calls to sserver() will block if no client is waiting to establish a connection. The two possible values for *sync* are S_DELAY and S_NDELAY, which are defined in socklib.h. A call to sserver() will return -1 if an error occurs or if S_NDELAY is specified and no client connections are waiting to be accepted. In the latter case the externally declared integer errno will be set to the value EWOULDBLOCK. If a connection with a client is established then the return value from sserver() will be a socket descriptor which can be used with read(), write(), etc., to communicate with the new client.
2. The next task is to bind an address to the socket and then set up a queue to listen for connection requests. However, this should only be done the first time sserver() is called. In order to make sure that this is so, a flag called bindflag contained in the SOCKET structure associated with socket pointer *sp*,

is tested, and only if it is reset will the body of the `if` construct be executed to call `bind()` and `listen()`.
3. Using the `gethostname()` function, the hostname for the local machine is copied into the `localhost[]` array. This is then passed into `gethostbyname()`, which returns a pointer to a `hostent` structure, filled with the appropriate information. If an error occurs in either of these function calls then a -1 is returned.
4. The address family, port number and IP address are now copied from the `hostent` structure and the *port* parameter, into the socket address structure, which is stored in the `SOCKET` that is pointed to by the *sp* parameter.
5. When everything is properly set up, the calls to `bind()` and `listen()` take place. If either of these calls generates an error then -1 is returned.
6. To ensure that the preceding block of code can only execute once per socket, the `bindflag` is now set.
7. The next job is to sort out the *sync* parameter. If *sync* has the value `S_DELAY` then `fcntl()` is used to reset the `O_NDELAY` flag in the associated socket descriptor. A *sync* value of `S_NDELAY` is used to set the associated `O_NDELAY` flag. Any other value of *sync* causes the `default` case to execute and return -1 as an error value.
8. Finally, `accept()` is called to establish a connection with any waiting client. On success, the return value from `accept()` is a socket descriptor connected to the client and ready to go. This value is also returned by `sserver()`. If there is no client waiting, and the socket is set up to block, the `accept()` call will not return until a client makes a connection request, If there is no client and the socket is non-blocking, then `accept` will return -1 and set `errno` to the value `EWOULDBLOCK`. This value is also returned by `sserver()`.

18.1.4 The sclient() Function

```
/* 1 */
sclient(SOCKET *sp, char *name, int port)
{
    struct hostent *hostent;

    /* 2 */
    if ((hostent = gethostbyname(name))==0)
        return -1;

    /* 3 */
    sp->sin.sin_family = (short)hostent->h_addrtype;
    sp->sin.sin_port = htons((unsigned short)port);
    sp->sin.sin_addr.s_addr = *(unsigned long *)hostent->h_addr;
```

```
    /* 4 */
    if (connect(sp->sd, (struct sockaddr *)&sp->sin, sp->sinlen)==-1)
        return -1;

    /* 5 */
    return sp->sd;
}
```

1. The `sclient()` function tries to connect to a specified server on a given machine. Its three parameters are *sp*, which is a socket pointer returned from `sopen()`, *name*, which is the machine name of the server, and *port*, which is the server's port number on the machine. The function waits until a connection with the server is established and then returns a socket descriptor connected to the server, or -1 on error.
2. The `gethostbyname()` function is used to fill a `hostent` structure given the server's hostname.
3. The socket address structure associated with this `SOCKET` is filled in from the `hostent` structure and the *port* parameter.
4. The `connect()` system call is now used to bind a local address to the local socket and attempts to make contact with the chosen server. If the server has got as far as doing a `listen()` call then the client's `connect()` request will be queued at the server, waiting for it to call `accept()`.
5. Once the `connect()` call returns without error, and the connection is established, the `sclient()` function returns the socket descriptor associated with the client's socket.

18.1.5 Library Preamble

```
#include <stdio.h>
#include <fcntl.h>
#include <sys/types.h>
#include <sys/socket.h>
#include <netdb.h>
#include <netinet/in.h>

#define S_LIBRARY
#include "socklib.h"
```

This is the set of standard #include files for socket library applications and also the definition of a symbol which will signify to the socket library header file that it is being included in the socket library code. This will cause the definition of some extra symbols in the header file that are only defined and used within the library routines themselves.

18.1.6 The socklib.h Header File

```c
#include <netinet/in.h>


/* 1 */
#define S_DELAY 0
#define S_NDELAY 1


/* 2 */
#ifdef S_LIBRARY
#    define S_RESET 0
#    define S_SET 1
#    define S_NAMLEN 64
#endif


/* 3 */
typedef struct
{
    struct sockaddr_in sin;
    int sinlen;
    int bindflag;
    int sd;
} SOCKET;


/* 4 */
SOCKET *sopen(void);
int sclose(SOCKET *);
int sserver(SOCKET *, int, int);
int sclient(SOCKET *, char *, int);
```

1. These are the definitions of the S_DELAY and S_NDELAY symbolic constants used to select blocking or non-blocking server operation.
2. Extra symbols only defined within the library itself.
3. Definition of the SOCKET structure. This is the socket library equivalent of the FILE structure in the standard I/O library. The #include <netinet/in.h> line at the top of the file is for the definition of struct sockaddr_in used within the SOCKET structure.
4. ANSI function protocols for the functions in the socket library so the compiler can check the correct usage of parameter numbers and types in application code.

18.2 Example Server

There are many ways to transfer files between two machines; each has its own advantages and disadvantages. The majority require a user wishing to transfer files from a particular machine to have some kind of login to that machine before the transfers can take place. The following piece of C code illustrates the use of sockets and the tiny socket library to implement a simple server which allows clients to make requests to download files with a simpler protocol.

On the server machine, all the files that remote users can access are placed into a single directory. The server is then executed from that directory. Subsequent client requests for any files in that directory will be supplied by the server, without any kind of login procedure or security checks being made. In other words, the server provides access to a set of files that are offered freely to anyone with a copy of the client software and a connection to the network used by the server machine.

Because downloading a large file can take an appreciable amount of time, some mechanism is required to deal with subsequent client requests while the current request is still in progress. The example server given below, deals with this situation by calling `sserver()` in an infinite loop. As soon as a client connection is established and `sserver()` returns with a socket descriptor, the server uses the `fork()` system call to create a child process which, because it has access to all of the parent's open files and sockets, can deal with the file transfer request while the parent process loops back to await further client connections. A large number of clients can transfer files simultaneously by this method, as each has its own child process created specifically to deal with its requirements.

The simple request/response protocol used by the example client and server is that the client specifies a file name to the server and the server then sends the contents of that file back to the client. The required file name is given to the server in two parts: first a byte is sent which specifies to the server the length of the file name, and then the bytes of the file name itself are sent. The server makes some simple checks regarding the validity and availability of the file name and, if these are passed, the server then sends the bytes of the file to the client. At the end of the transfer, the server (child) process terminates breaking the connection with this client.

```
/************************************************************************
EXAMPLE SOCKET SERVER
************************************************************************/

#include <stdio.h>
#include <string.h>
#include <signal.h>
#include <fcntl.h>
#include "socklib.h"

/* Server's communication port number */
```

```c
#define PORT 2121


/*************************************************************************
MAIN - A very simple file tranfer program, which sets up a concurrent
    socket server on the host machine on port number PORT to transfer
    any files from the current directory on request.
*************************************************************************/
main(void)
{
    SOCKET *sp;
    int sd;

    /* Set SIGCHLD for no zombies */
    signal(SIGCHLD, SIG_IGN);

    /* Create server's socket */
    if ((sp = sopen())==0)
        /* Exit server if this fails */
        fatal("sopen()");

    /* Repeatedly accept and service client requests */
    for (;;)
    {
        /* Connect to client */
        if ((sd = sserver(sp, PORT, S_DELAY))==-1)
            fatal("sserver()");

        /* Fork() a child process */
        switch (fork())
        {
        /* Deal with client request in child */
        case 0:
            do_service(sd);

        /* Deal with fork() failure */
        case -1:
            fatal("fork()");
        }

        /* In parent, close client and loop for next connection */
        close(sd);
    }
}
```

/***
FATAL - This routine is called when an error condition is returned
    to the daemon, usually from one of the system calls it makes.
    The function first prints the message pointed to by <text> and
    then terminates the process.
***/
```
fatal(char *text)
{
    fprintf(stderr, "Error in %s\n", text);
    exit(1);
}
```


/***
DO_SERVICE - This function is called in the child process that is
    created when a client makes a successful connection. Its task is
    to service the client's request and supervise the required file
    transfer. The parameter <sd> is the socket descriptor to use for
    the communication.
***/
```
do_service(int sd)
{
    int i, fd;
    char *name;
    char c, namlen;

    /* Get length of file name */
    if (read(sd, &namlen, 1)!=1)
        fatal("namlen read()");

    /* Space for name + " open()" */
    if ((name = (char *)malloc(namlen+8))==0)
        fatal("malloc()");

    /* Get required file name into name[] */
    for (i = 0; i<namlen; ++i)
        if (read(sd, &name[i], 1)!=1)
            fatal("file name read()");

    /* Make name[] a string */
    name[i] = '\0';

    /* Check name[] is in current directory */
    if (strchr(name, '/'))
        fatal("illegal file name");
```

```
    /* Open specified file */
    if ((fd = open(name, O_RDONLY))==-1)
        fatal(strcat(name, " open()"));

    /* Transfer contents to client */
    while ((i = read(fd, &c, 1))!=0)
        if (i==-1)
            fatal("file read()");
        else if (write(sd, &c, 1)!=1)
            fatal("write()");

    /* Terminate child and with it the connection to this client */
    exit(0);
}
```

Even though it works, the way the server is coded at the moment is not sufficiently robust to allow it to be used in anger. We shall, however, return to this code again after we have looked at daemon processes.

18.3 Example Client

The C code given below is the matching client for the server just presented. Assuming that the client is called `getfile`, then it should be invoked as:

   getfile host remote_file local_file

where *host* is the hostname of the machine running the server, *remote_file* is the name of the file to get from the server, and *local_file* is the name the client should use for its copy of the transferred file.

```
/************************************************************************
EXAMPLE SOCKET CLIENT
************************************************************************/

#include <stdio.h>
#include <string.h>
#include "socklib.h"

/* Server's communication port number */
#define PORT 2121


/************************************************************************
MAIN - This program implements the client end of a simple file transfer
```

```
    system using the tiny socket library. It should be invoked with:
    getfile <machine_name> <remote_file_name> <local_file_name>
*******************************************************************/
main(int argc, char **argv)
{
    SOCKET *sp;
    FILE *fp;
    int sd, i;
    char namlen, c;

    /* Check correct usage */
    if (argc!=4)
        fatal("command line parameters");

    /* Open local file */
    if ((fp = fopen(argv[3], "w"))==0)
        fatal("opening local file");

    /* Create client's socket */
    if ((sp = sopen())==0)
        fatal("sopen()");

    /* Make contact with server */
    if ((sd = sclient(sp, argv[1], PORT))==-1)
        fatal("sclient()");

    /* Get length of remote file name */
    namlen = strlen(argv[2]);

    /* Send name length to server */
    if (write(sd, &namlen, 1)!=1)
        fatal("sending namlen");

    /* Send name to server */
    for (i = 0; i<namlen; ++i)
        if (write(sd, &argv[2][i], 1)!=1)
            fatal("sending file name");

    /* Read file bytes from server */
    while ((i = read(sd, &c, 1))!=0)
        if (i==-1)
            fatal("reading remote file");
        /* Write bytes to local file */
        else if (putc(c, fp)==EOF)
            fatal("writing local file");
```

```
    /* Tidy up open files and sockets */
    close(sd);
    fclose(fp);
    sclose(sp);
}



/***********************************************************************
FATAL - Function to print a fatal error message to the standard error
    device and then terminate the client process.
***********************************************************************/
fatal(char *text)
{
    fprintf(stderr, "Error in %s\n", text);
    exit(1);
}
```

Exercises

1. Write a simple program to determine how many sockets you can have open at the same time from within a single process.
2. Write simple client and server programs using the tiny socket library to provide clients with some information about the system on which the server is running (such as the number of users currently logged in, or the number of non-root user IDs in the password file, etc.)
3. Write a simple chat server using the tiny socket library which will allow multiple clients to connect and sent text messages to the server. The server, when it receives a message from a client, will broadcast the message to all the currently connected clients. Users should use `telnet` as the client program.

Answers

1. Assuming that the number is not greater than 1000, then the following piece of code will show a list of numbers, the last of which is the number you require:

```
#include <stdio.h>
#include "socklib.h"

#define MAX 1000

main()
{
```

```
        SOCKET *sp[MAX];
        int i, j;

        for (i = 0; (sp[i] = sopen())!=0 && i<MAX; ++i)
            printf("%d\n", i);

        for (j = 0; j<i; ++j)
            sclose(sp[j]);
    }
```

2. This is a straightforward exercise whose solution can be based almost directly on the example client and server programs given in the chapter.
3. In order to make this program work within a single process, it is necessary to use O_NDELAY on the sockets so that reads from the clients won't block when there is no text available. This allows the server to go on to other clients to see if they have any text ready. The following code is a complete, if skeletal, solution to the problem. Three #defines at the start of the code specify the port to use on the server, the maximum line length accepted by the server and the maximum number of simultaneous client connections that the server will accept:

```
#include <stdio.h>
#include <string.h>
#include <fcntl.h>
#include <errno.h>
#include "socklib.h"

#define PORT 2121
#define MAX_LEN 80
#define MAX_USERS 10

#define LINE_READY 1
#define LOGGED_OUT 2

struct client
{
    int sd;
    char in_use;
    char next;
    char text[MAX_LEN+1];
} user[MAX_USERS];

main()
{
    SOCKET *sp;
```

```c
    int i, sd, flags;

    if ((sp = sopen())==0)
        fatal("sopen()");

loop:
    if ((sd = sserver(sp, PORT, S_NDELAY))!=-1)
        grab_user_slot(sd);
    else if (errno!=EWOULDBLOCK)
        fatal("sserver()");

    for (i = 0; i<MAX_USERS; ++i)
        if (user[i].in_use)
            switch(user_state(i))
            {
            case LINE_READY:
                broadcast_line(i);
                break;

            case LOGGED_OUT:
                free_user_slot(i);
                break;
            }

    goto loop;
}

user_state(int slot)
{
    char *ptr;
    int n;

    ptr = &user[slot].text[user[slot].next];

    while ((n = read(user[slot].sd, ptr, 1))==1)
    {
        if (*ptr=='\n')
        {
            *(ptr+1) = '\0';
            user[slot].next = 0;
            return LINE_READY;
        }

        if (++user[slot].next==MAX_LEN)
```

```
                --user[slot].next;
            else
                ++ptr;
    }

    if (n==0)
        return LOGGED_OUT;

    return 0;
}

broadcast_line(int slot)
{
    int i, n;

    for (i = 0; i<MAX_USERS; ++i)
        if (user[i].in_use && i!=slot)
        {
            n = strlen(user[slot].text);
            write(user[i].sd, user[slot].text, n);
        }
}

grab_user_slot(int sd)
{
    int i, flags;

    for (i = 0; i<MAX_USERS; ++i)
    {
        if (!user[i].in_use)
        {
            user[i].in_use = 1;
            user[i].sd = sd;
            user[i].next = 0;

            if ((flags = fcntl(sd, F_GETFL))==-1
             || fcntl(sd, F_SETFL, flags|O_NDELAY)==-1)
                fatal("fcntl()");

            break;
        }
    }

    if (i==MAX_USERS)
```

```
        {
            write(sd, "Too many users - sorry...\n", 26);
            close(sd);
        }
    }

    free_user_slot(int slot)
    {
        user[slot].in_use = 0;
        close(user[slot].sd);
    }

    fatal(char *mess)
    {
        printf("Error: %s\n", mess);
        exit(1);
    }
```

Chapter 19

Signals

Signals is the mechanism by which processes are made aware of events occurring in the system. An important feature of signals is that they are asynchronous, which means that a process may receive a signal at any time during its execution, and must be prepared to respond to the signal at that time. It is even possible for a process to receive a signal while it is executing a system call. Generally, if a system call is interrupted by a signal, then it will return its error value and set `errno` to the value `EINTR`. It is then the responsibility of the signaled process to re-try the interrupted call.

Each of the signal types, of which there are currently thirty odd, is given a symbolic name accessed via the `<signal.h>` header file. The most common signal values and their symbolic names are:

value	symbol	purpose
1	SIGHUP	hangup on control terminal
2	SIGINT	interrupt from keyboard (`Ctrl-c`)
3	SIGQUIT	quit from keyboard (`Ctrl-\`)
8	SIGFPE	floating point exception (e.g. divide by 0)
9	SIGKILL	terminate receiving process
14	SIGALRM	end of `alarm()` system call timeout
15	SIGTERM	default `kill` command signal
17	SIGCHLD	child process stopped or terminated
19	SIGSTOP	stop execution from keyboard `Ctrl-z`

Each signal type has associated with it an action which the kernel will perform on behalf of a process when the process is sent that signal. For most of the signals, the default action is to terminate the receiving process, though, usually, a process can request some alternative action of the system. The various alternatives are:

- Ignore the signal. With this option set, the process will be unaware that a signal has occurred. Two of the signals cannot be ignored: `SIGKILL`, which will terminate the process, and `SIGSTOP`, which will suspend its execution as part of the job control mechanism.

316 *Signals*

- Restore the signal's default action.
- Execute a pre-arranged signal handling function. A process can register a special signal handling function which will be called like an interrupt service routine when the signal is received by the process. When the handler returns, control is passed back to the main code and normal process execution continues.

19.1 signal System Call

Several system calls exist in Linux to allow the various actions to be set up on an individual signal basis. For compatibility with other UNIX flavors, Linux supports the `signal()` system call, in addition to the POSIX specified calls that we shall see later. The prototype for the `signal()` call is:

```
#include <signal.h>
#include <unistd.h>

void (*signal(int signum, void (*handler)(int)))(int);
```

This prototype looks horribly complicated, but all it says is that `signal()` is a call that takes two parameters: the first (*signum*) is the signal number from the previous list for which an action is being set, and the second (*handler*) is a pointer to a function which takes a single integer parameter and returns nothing (`void`). The return value from `signal()` is itself a pointer to a function which takes a single integer parameter and returns nothing (`void`). A simple code fragment should help to illustrate the point:

```
#include <stdio.h>
#include <signal.h>
#include <unistd.h>

int ctrl_c_count = 0;
void (* old_handler)(int);
void ctrl_c(int);

main()
{
    int c;

    old_handler = signal(SIGINT, ctrl_c);

    while ((c = getchar())!='\n');

    printf("ctrl-c count = %d\n", ctrl_c_count);
```

```
        (void) signal(SIGINT, old_handler);

        for (;;);
}


void ctrl_c(int signum)
{
        (void) signal(SIGINT, ctrl_c);
        ++ctrl_c_count;
}
```

This program effectively performs the trivial operation of getting characters until a newline character is typed and then going into an infinite loop. Breaking out of such a program could normally be achieved with a keyboard generated interrupt signal (such as Ctrl-c). However, in this case the program arranges to catch the Ctrl-c signal (SIGINT) and use it to execute a signal handler function called ctrl_c(). Only after a newline is entered at the keyboard is the previous (probably default) action of SIGINT restored.

Setting up the signal handler is done by the first statement in the main() function:

```
        old_handler = signal(SIGINT, ctrl_c);
```

The two parameters to signal() are the signal number whose action is to be set (here SIGINT, the keyboard interrupt signal), and a pointer to the function that will be called when this interrupt signal occurs. The signal() call returns the old signal handler address, which in this case is being assigned to the variable old_handler so that the original signal handler can be restored later.

Once the signal handler is in place, any interrupt (SIGINT) signals that the process receives will cause the execution of the handler function. This function just increments the value of the ctrl_c_count variable to keep a count of the number of SIGINT events that occur. Notice that the handler function also executes another signal() call which re-establishes the connection between the SIGINT signal and the ctrl_c() function. This is necessary because signal handlers set up with the signal() call are automatically reset when the signal occurs so that a subsequent signal of that type would otherwise just perform the signal's default action.

This is the main problem with the early UNIX signal() call (and the reason why POSIX signals are different). The problem is that there is a small (but real) time interval between a signal's action being reset to the default when the signal occurs, and the handler being executed so that the signal's action of calling the handler can be re-established. In this interval if another signal of the same type were to be received then the default action would take place, which would usually terminate the process.

19.2 sigaction System Call

The POSIX committee's version of signal handling is a little more complex than the earlier `signal()` call (isn't that what committees are for?) but it does specify signal semantics which overcome the earlier problems.

Under POSIX, each process has a *signal mask* which is a set of signals that are currently blocked from delivery. If a blocked signal is sent to a process anyway, it will be added to a set of pending signals for the process which will be delivered when the block is removed.

When a signal is sent it is automatically added to the signal mask of the receiving process so that further instances of that signal are blocked while the current instance is being serviced. When the signal handler returns normally, the signal mask is then restored to its previous value.

The main system call for setting up signal handlers is called `sigaction()` and its prototype is:

```
#include <signal.h>
#include <unistd.h>

int sigaction(int signum, struct sigaction *new,
                          struct sigaction *old);
```

Instead of just specifying a handler function for a signal, the `sigaction()` call takes a pointer to a `struct sigaction` (*new*) as a parameter. The layout of a `struct sigaction` is:

```
struct sigaction
{
    void (*sa_handler)(int);
    sigset_t sa_mask;
    unsigned long sa_flags;
    void (*sa_restorer)(void);
};
```

As you can see, the pointer to the handler function has been moved into this structure in the `sa_handler` field. The `sa_mask` field in the structure is an extra signal mask which is ORed into the signal mask of the process when this signal occurs. This extra mask stays in force while the signal handler executes. The `sa_flags` field is an ORed combination of several bit flags, the two main ones being:

SA_ONESHOT   set signal action to default when signal occurs;
SA_NOMASK   ignore `struct sigaction sa_mask` field.

Both flags are set by default if you use the `signal()` call rather than `sigaction()`.

The return value from `sigaction()` does not include a pointer to the old signal handler as it does with the `signal()` call. Instead, an extra parameter (*old*) is passed into `sigaction()`. This is just a pointer to another `struct sigaction` which will be filled by the `sigaction()` call with the details from the old sigaction structure. This allows the old values to be restored later if required.

19.2.1 Special `SIGCHLD` Behavior

Sometimes you will want to run a process which generates lots of child processes but which does not wish to `wait()` for them. By default, child processes in this position will become zombies until some process (probably `init`) waits for them in the future. If the parent is a very long lived process then the zombies will be hanging around in the system for a long time. The creation of zombies under these circumstances just wastes system resources. There are several ways round the problem under Linux, the simplest being to set the action of the `SIGCHLD` signal to `SIG_IGN`, as follows:

```
signal(SIGCHLD, SIG_IGN);
```

As the default action of `SIGCHLD` is to be ignored anyway, setting this signal to `SIG_IGN` serves no other useful purpose. This is therefore used as a special feature in Linux to tell the kernel not to generate zombies from the children of the calling process.

19.2.2 Signal Masks

Setting and modifying signal masks is performed by a special set of functions, whose prototypes are:

```
#include <signal.h>

int sigemptyset(sigset_t *mask);
int sigfillset(sigset_t *mask);
int sigaddset(sigset_t *mask, int signum);
int sigdelset(sigset_t *mask, int signum);
int sigismember(sigset_t *mask, int signum);
```

The `sigemptyset()` function takes a pointer (*mask*) to a signal mask (of type sigset_t) and clears it to ensure that no signals are flagged as blocked. The function `sigfillset()` fills a signal mask to ensure that all signals are flagged as blocked. The `sigaddset()` and `sigdelset()` functions allow signal blocks for individual signals (*signum*) to be added and deleted respectively. The final function (`sigismember()`) allows you to determine if a particular *signum* is flagged as blocked in *mask.

A process can also change and examine the value of its own signal mask using the `sigprocmask()` system call:

320 Signals

```
#include <signals.h>

int sigprocmask(int fcn, sigset_t *mask, sigset_t *old);
```

The *mask* parameter points to a signal mask value which will be applied to the signal mask of the process according to the specification of *fcn*. The various values for *fcn* and their meanings are:

    SIG_BLOCK   *mask* specifies the extra signals to block;
    SIG_UNBLOCK   *mask* gives a set of signals to unblock;
    SIG_SETMASK   *mask* becomes the new process signal mask.

The SIGKILL and SIGSTOP signals cannot be blocked and any attempt to do so will just be silently ignored.

The *old* parameter is a pointer to a signal mask which will contain the previous signal mask value after the call, so that this can be restored later if required.

A process can see if it has any blocked signals pending by calling the sigpending() system call:

```
#include <signals.h>

int sigpending(sigset_t *mask);
```

The signal mask pointed to by *mask* is set to indicate any pending signals.

19.3 kill System Call

Most of the signals considered so far have been generated either automatically by a process changing state, by a hardware error like a floating point exception, or they have been generated by user intervention at the keyboard with interrupt and quit signals. In addition to this, it is also possible for a process to send any signal to another process deliberately if it has appropriate permissions. This is done by using the kill() system call:

```
#include <signal.h>
#include <sys/types.h>

int kill(pid_t pid, int sig);
```

The *sig* parameter specifies which signal to send and the *pid* parameter specifies where to send it. The various values of *pid* have the following meanings:

pid > 0 This will send signal *sig* to the process whose process ID is *pid*.
pid = 0 Sends signal *sig* to all processes with the same process group ID as the calling process.

pid = -1 Sends signal *sig* to all processes in the system except the `init` process and the calling process. (This is Linux specific.)

pid < -1 Sends signal *sig* to all the processes in the process group whose process group ID matches the absolute value of *pid* (i.e. to process group *-pid*).

In order for `kill()` to send a signal, the effective user ID of the calling process must be `root`, or it must match either the real or effective user ID of the receiving process.

19.4   pause System Call

Sometimes you may wish to write a program which needs to co-operate with another program to perform its function. Suppose, for example, that two processes are to communicate via a FIFO file. One of these two processes will create the FIFO and then both of them will use it to communicate.

Obviously, the process which does not create the FIFO file needs to wait for the other process to create the file before it may proceed. One way to achieve this process synchronization is to use the `pause()` system call:

    #include <unistd.h>

    int pause(void);

This system call does nothing except suspend the execution of the process from which it is called. If the process subsequently receives a signal for which it has a signal handler in place, then, when the handler has executed, the `pause()` call will return with an error value and `errno` set to `EINTR`. This return value and error condition can be ignored because this is the only way for `pause()` to return.

The upshot of this is that one process will execute a `pause()` call when it needs to wait for another process to perform some action. When the action has been performed the other process can send a pre-arranged signal to the paused process which will force `pause()` to return and allow execution of the signaled process to resume, knowing that the event for which it was waiting has now occurred.

19.5   alarm System Call

A final system call related to signals is called `alarm()`. The prototype for this call is:

    #include <unistd.h>

    long alarm(long secs);

Each process has an alarm clock timer associated with it which it can use to send itself SIGALRM signals after preset amounts of time have elapsed. The alarm() call takes a single parameter (*secs*), which is the number of seconds to elapse before the alarm goes off. If a value of zero is passed to alarm() then this will switch off any currently running alarm timer.

The return value from alarm() is the previous alarm timer value. This will be zero if no timer is currently set, or the time which remained in the clock when the call was made.

Exercises

1. Write a C program which traps all the signals (that can be trapped) and displays a suitable message when any signal is received by the process.
2. Write a program which reads and displays characters typed at the keyboard. Set up an alarm() which will print a message if no characters are typed within a short space of time.
3. Write a program to send SIGKILL signals to all of your running processes except your current shell (and the current process) based on the following shell script:

```
pidlist=`ps -aux | grep "^$LOGNAME" | grep -v $$ | \
    tr -s " " | cut -f 2 -d " "`
for pid in pidlist
do
    kill -9 $pid >/dev/null 2>/dev/null
done
```

Answers

1. This can all be done with a single signal handler, as the received signal number is passed to the handler as a parameter:

```
void trapper(int);

main()
{
    int i;

    for (i = 0; i<32; ++i)
        signal(i, trapper);

    for (;;);
```

```
    }

    void trapper(int sig)
    {
        signal(sig, trapper);
        printf("Just received signal number: %d\n", sig);
    }
```

2. In the following code, the **while** loop is used to read characters from the keyboard and display them on the screen. When no characters are being typed, the loop is blocked in the **read()** call. A 20-second alarm is started just before the loop commences. Each time a character is written the alarm is reset back to 20 seconds. When no characters have been written for 20 seconds, the alarm goes off, interrupting the **read()** and calling the **trapper()** function:

```
    #include <signal.h>
    #include <unistd.h>

    void trapper(int);

    main()
    {
        char c;

        signal(SIGALRM, trapper);
        alarm(20L);

        while (read(0, &c, 1)==1)
        {
            write(1, &c, 1);
            alarm(20L);
        }

        printf("read() interrupted...\n");
    }

    void trapper(int sig)
    {
        printf("You stopped typing...\n");
    }
```

3. This problem can easily be solved by translating the shell script into C code using the **pipe()**, **dup()**, **fork()** and **exec()** system calls. Where the shell script does the **grep -v** for the shell's PID, when you translate this to C code

you will also need to grep -v for your own PID as well so that you don't kill your own process while it is running. You can create all the pipes at the start of the program so that they are all available when required. Don't forget, after doing the I/O redirection, and before calling `exec()` for each command, you should close all the file descriptors that the process doesn't need (all except 0, 1 and 2), otherwise you will not get end-of-file propagated along the pipeline.

Chapter 20

Tiny Shell – Case Study

You have now seen enough system calls to understand what needs to happen when the shell executes a simple command pipeline. Rather than examine the code for a real shell, which is just too complex to cover in any sensible way here, we will look at the code for a tiny shell which just has the bare essentials in place – just enough to demonstrate some principles.

The tiny shell will present you with a prompt, in response to which you can type in any simple command followed by the parameters that the command requires. The tiny shell will execute your command and then return to you with another prompt. You should note that the tiny shell can cope with none of the regular expressions accepted by the real shell.

In addition to this simple scenario the tiny shell also allows you to use pipes and I/O redirection using the familiar |, <, > and >> operators, as well as allowing a pipeline to be executed in the background with the & operator.

20.1 Data Structures

In order to understand the operation of the tiny shell, the first things to look at are the data structures involved. To simplify the internals of the tiny shell, its data structures are all statically allocated at compile time. This means, for example, using arrays to store things rather than dynamically allocated linked lists. The consequence of this is that the tiny shell imposes fixed limits on the sizes of certain things, where a real shell need impose no such limits. In particular, the following things are fixed, in that you need to re-compile the tiny shell to change them: the maximum length of line entered at the shell prompt, the maximum length of a file name used for I/O redirection, the maximum number of command line parameters for each simple command and the maximum number of simple commands in a pipeline.

All these definitions and the declarations of the global variables and data structures appear in the file def.h, as follows:

```
#include <stdio.h>
#include <limits.h>
#include <signal.h>
#include <fcntl.h>

#define TRUE 1
#define FALSE 0
#define OKAY 1
#define ERROR 0
#define MAXLINE 200             /* Maximum length of input line */
#define MAXARG 20       /* Max number of args for each simple command */
#define PIPELINE 5      /* Max number of simple commands in a pipeline */
#define MAXNAME 100     /* Maximum length of i/o redirection filename */

char line[MAXLINE+1];                   /* User typed input line */
char *lineptr;          /* Pointer to current position in line[] */
char avline[MAXLINE+1];         /* Argv strings taken from line[] */
char *avptr;            /* Pointer to current position in avline[] */
char infile[MAXNAME+1];         /* Input redirection filename */
char outfile[MAXNAME+1];        /* Ouput redirection filename */

int backgnd;            /* TRUE if & ends pipeline else FALSE */
int lastpid;            /* PID of last simple command in pipeline */
int append;         /* TRUE for append redirection (>>) else FALSE */

struct cmd
{
    char *av[MAXARG];
    int infd;
    int outfd;
} cmdlin[PIPELINE];         /* Argvs and fds, one per simple command */
```

When you type a command line to the tiny shell in response to its prompt, the characters you enter are stored directly into the line[] array. Suppose you enter the command:

    tsh: echo hello world

you already know that in order to execute this command the tiny shell needs to fork() a child process and then exec() the echo command in the child. As the echo command takes parameters it is necessary to extract them from the command line (in the line[] array) and parcel them up into an argv type data structure to pass into exec() (the execvp() system call in this case).

In the tiny shell, the separate words on the command line are extracted and stored as a set of separate strings in the avline[] array. Then for each simple command in

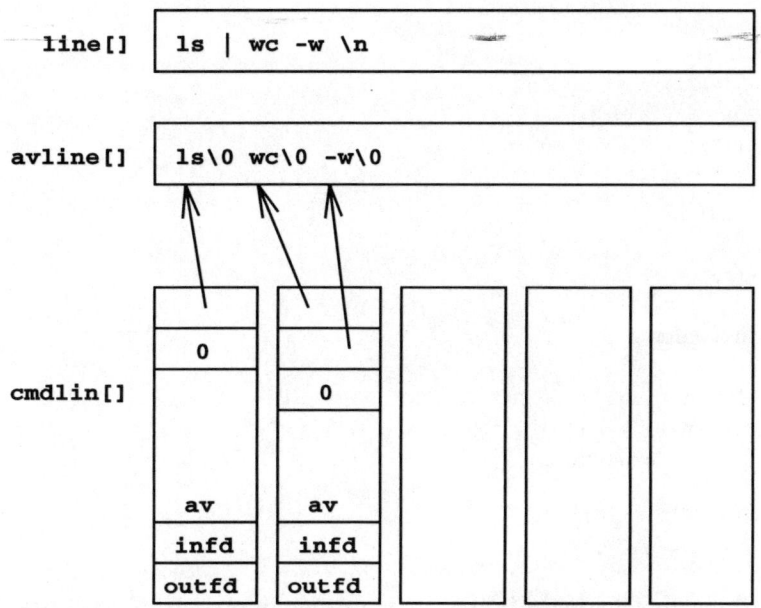

Figure 20.1 Use of line[], avline[] and cmdlin[] arrays.

the command line an array of pointers is set up to point to the appropriate individual command line words for that command. The array of pointers is contained in the struct cmd structure, one of which is available for each simple command in the pipeline. This set of structures is itself stored as an array called cmdlin[].

Figure 20.1 is intended to illustrate this idea by showing the contents of the line[], avline[] and cmdlin[] arrays when the entered command pipeline is:

```
tsh: ls | wc -w
```

20.2 The Code

Having seen the basic data structures and their use let us now take a look through the code. The tiny shell has been designed in a basically top-down fashion and that is the order in which we'll work through it.

20.2.1 main Function

The top level design of any interpreter is basically a loop which just gets something to do and then goes away to do it. The tiny shell is no exception so that the main() function is particularly simple:

328   Tiny Shell – Case Study

```
#include "def.h"

main(void)
{
    int i;

    initcold();

    for (;;)
    {
        initwarm();

        if (getline())
            if (i = parse())
                execute(i);
    }
}
```

The first thing that happens is that `main()` calls a one-off initialization function called `initcold()`. This is followed by an endless loop which repeatedly prints a prompt, gets lines of input, parses them to extract the simple commands and their parameters, and then executes each of the simple commands, dealing with I/O redirection and pipes as appropriate.

In detail, the body of the loop first calls `initwarm()` to initialize things for each input command line and display the `tsh:` prompt. This is followed by a call to `getline()`, which copies the user's command line into the `line[]` array and returns a non-zero value if the length of the entered line was less than `MAXLINE`.

If a non-zero value is returned by `getline()`, then the `parse()` function is called next. This function has the task of parsing the contents of the `line[]` array and extracting the relevant information from it. This includes the simple command names and their associated parameters, the input and output file names for any I/O redirection, and the pipeline background (`&`) operator, if specified.

Assuming there are no errors, the `parse()` function returns a positive value which is the number of simple commands in the input command pipeline. On error, `parse()` returns the value zero. If there have been no errors so far, then, finally, the `execute()` function is called with the count returned by `parse()` passed in as a parameter. The `execute()` function uses `fork()` and `exec()` to execute each of the simple commands in turn, creating pipes and opening I/O redirection files as required.

20.2.2 Initialization Functions

The contents of the `initcold()` initialization function are currently commented out so that the function actually does nothing. This is because the tiny shell has no built-in commands like the real shell. What this means is that shell commands like `exit`, which will terminate the real shell, cannot be used with the tiny shell in the same way. The easiest way to terminate the tiny shell is therefore to send it an interrupt (`Ctrl-c`) or quit (`Ctrl-\`) signal from the keyboard. Obviously, if the contents of `initcold()` were uncommented, then this would not be possible and the tiny shell would then be more difficult to terminate.

```
initcold(void)
{
/*
    signal(SIGINT, SIG_IGN);
    signal(SIGQUIT, SIG_IGN);
*/
}


initwarm(void)
{
    int i;

    backgnd = FALSE;
    lineptr = line;
    avptr = avline;
    infile[0] = '\0';
    outfile[0] = '\0';
    append = FALSE;

    for (i = 0; i<PIPELINE; ++i)
    {
        cmdlin[i].infd = 0;
        cmdlin[i].outfd = 1;
    }

    for (i = 3; i<OPEN_MAX; ++i)
        close(i);

    printf("tsh: ");
    fflush(stdout);
}
```

The `initwarm()` function is executed at the start of each iteration of the 'get a command, execute a command' loop. Essentially, it just initializes the global

330 Tiny Shell – Case Study

variables, sets the `infd` and `outfd` file descriptors for each of the simple command structures in the `cmdlin[]` array to their default values, `close()`s all file descriptors other than the standard input, output and error output devices, and finally displays the `tsh:` prompt.

20.2.3 getline Function

```
getline(void)
{
    int i;

    for (i = 0; (line[i] = getchar())!='\n' && i<MAXLINE; ++i);

    if (i==MAXLINE)
    {
        fprintf(stderr, "Command line too long\n");
        return(ERROR);
    }

    line[i+1] = '\0';
    return(OKAY);
}
```

This function just takes characters from the standard input device and copies them into the `line[]` array, until either a newline (\n) character is encountered or `MAXLINE` number of characters have been entered, in which case the `line[]` array is full.

If `MAXLINE` characters have been entered then the function returns `ERROR`; otherwise a string terminator (\0) is added after the last character entered, and the `OKAY` value is returned instead.

20.2.4 parse Function

The syntax of a command pipeline looks as follows:

```
cmd [ < filename ] [ | cmd ]... [ or filename ] [ & ]
```

Here *cmd* means any simple command including its parameters, and *or* is either of the output redirection operators (> or >>). Square brackets are used to enclose optional items and the ellipses (...) mean that the preceding bracket contents may be repeated zero or more times.

Piecing it all together, what this says is that a tiny shell command pipeline starts with a simple command. This is then optionally followed by an input redirection operator and its associated *filename*. This in turn can optionally and repeatedly be followed by a pipe operator and then another simple command. After the last simple command, which may also be the first if no pipes are used, an optional output redirection operator and its associated *filename* may be specified. Finally, the whole pipeline may optionally be set to run in the background by specifying the & operator.

The `parse()` function needs to make sure that the syntax of its input conforms to this specification, whilst at the same time extracting the tokens belonging to each simple command and the file names for any input or output redirection that might be specified.

```
parse(void)
{
    int i;

    /* 1 */
    command(0);

    /* 2 */
    if (check("<"))
        getname(infile);

    /* 3 */
    for (i = 1; i<PIPELINE; ++i)
        if (check("|"))
            command(i);
        else
            break;

    /* 4 */
    if (check(">"))
    {
        if (check(">"))
            append = TRUE;

        getname(outfile);
    }

    /* 5 */
    if (check("&"))
        backgnd = TRUE;

    /* 6 */
    if (check("\n"))
        return(i);
    else
    {
```

```
        fprintf(stderr, "Command line syntax error\n");
        return(ERROR);
    }
}
```

The numbered comments in this listing are described as follows:

1. The first thing that happens is that a call is made to the `command()` function, which, as we shall see later, knows how to extract the words from the command line associated with a single simple command. These words will be copied into the `avline[]` array as separate strings and the `av[]` pointers in the appropriate `struct cmd` will be set up to point to these strings. The parameter passed into the `command()` function is used to tell it which `struct cmd` in the `cmdlin[]` array to use.

2. After the first command has been parsed, the next section looks for the optional input redirection operator using the `check()` function. If `check()` finds a match for its parameter string at the current position in the `line[]` array it will return a true value and the `getname()` function will then be called to extract the following file name into the `infile[]` array.

3. Simple command zero has already been parsed so the next code section looks for the optional pipe operators followed by simple commands one, two, and so on. Inside the `for` loop, if a pipe operator is found then the `command()` function is called again to parse the next simple command. The parameter to `command()` is supplied this time by the `for` loop control variable (`i`). The `for` loop repeats until no more pipe operators are found or until the 'maximum number of simple commands in a pipeline' limit has been reached.

4. This section checks for the output redirection operator, and then checks whether or not this is append output redirection by looking for the second `>` symbol. If it is append output redirection then the `append` flag is set to TRUE (from its FALSE default set up in `initwarm()`). If either output redirection operator is present, then the `getname()` function is used to copy the associated file name into the `outfile[]` array.

5. The specification now allows for an optional `&` operator, and this is checked next. If the operator is present then the `backgnd` flag will be set to TRUE (the FALSE value was set in `initwarm()`).

6. Whatever path was taken through the preceding code, the input line should now have been parsed to completion and all that should remain is the newline (`\n`) character on the end. If this is so, then parse returns the value of the variable `i` which gives the number of simple commands found in this command line. If a newline is not the next character, then an error message is displayed and the value ERROR is returned from `parse()` instead.

20.2.5 command Function

Basically, this function copies the names of commands and their parameters one word at a time from the `line[]` array to the `avline[]` array. Each time a word is copied, a pointer is set up to point to the start of the word in one of the `av[]` arrays in the `cmdlin[]` array of structures:

```
command(int i)
{
    int j, flag, inword;

    for (j = 0; j<MAXARG-1; ++j)
    {
        while (*lineptr==' ' || *lineptr=='\t')
            ++lineptr;

        cmdlin[i].av[j] = avptr;
        cmdlin[i].av[j+1] = NULL;

        for (flag = 0; flag==0;)
        {
            switch (*lineptr)
            {
            case '>':
            case '<':
            case '|':
            case '&':
            case '\n':
                if (inword==FALSE)
                    cmdlin[i].av[j] = NULL;

                *avptr++ = '\0';
                return;
            case ' ':
            case '\t':
                inword = FALSE;
                *avptr++ = '\0';
                flag = 1;
                break;
            default:
                inword = TRUE;
                *avptr++ = *lineptr++;
                break;
            }
        }
    }
}
```

Within the tiny shell in general, and this function in particular, the variable `lineptr` points to the current place of interest within the `line[]` array and the variable `avptr` points to the next character position to use in the `avline[]` array.

The `command()` function consists of a pair of nested `for` loops. The inner loop copies the characters of a word from the `line[]` array to the `avline[]` array and terminates the word in the `avline[]` array with a `\0` byte. The outer loop is responsible for setting up pointers to the words in the appropriate `av[]` array elements.

20.2.6 execute Function

In each complete pipeline there can only be one input redirection file specified, attached to the first simple command, and only one output redirection file can be specified, attached to the last simple command. Obviously, if there is only one simple command in the pipeline then it qualifies as both the first and the last command on the line and, consequently, it can have both its input and output redirected to files.

If there is more than one simple command in a pipeline, say j of them, then j-1 pipes will need to be created to connect the simple commands together. Bearing these points in mind we can now look at the code for the `execute()` function:

```
execute(int j)
{
    int i, fd, fds[2];

    /* 1 */
    if (infile[0]!='\0')
        cmdlin[0].infd = open(infile, O_RDONLY);

    /* 2 */
    if (outfile[0]!='\0')
        if (append==FALSE)
            cmdlin[j-1].outfd = open(outfile, O_WRONLY | O_CREAT
                | O_TRUNC, 0666);
        else
            cmdlin[j-1].outfd = open(outfile, O_WRONLY | O_CREAT
                | O_APPEND, 0666);

    /* 3 */
    if (backgnd==TRUE)
        signal(SIGCHLD, SIG_IGN);
    else
        signal(SIGCHLD, SIG_DFL);

    /* 4 */
```

```c
    for (i = 0; i<j; ++i)
    {
        /* 5 */
        if (i<j-1)
        {
            pipe(fds);
            cmdlin[i].outfd = fds[1];
            cmdlin[i+1].infd = fds[0];
        }

        /* 6 */
        forkexec(&cmdlin[i]);

        /* 7 */
        if ((fd = cmdlin[i].infd)!=0)
            close(fd);

        if ((fd = cmdlin[i].outfd)!=1)
            close(fd);
    }

    /* 8 */
    if (backgnd==FALSE)
        while (wait(NULL)!=lastpid);
}
```

Remember that the **execute()** function takes a single integer parameter, which is the number of simple commands in the command pipeline. This value is assigned to the variable j. The numbered comments in the listing are explained as follows:

1. If an input redirection file has been specified then **open()** the file and assign the resulting file descriptor to the **infd** field in the **struct cmd** associated with simple command zero (i.e. the first simple command on the command line). Notice that the tiny shell code commits one of the biggest deadly sins of Linux programming – it doesn't check the return values of most of the system calls it makes, to look for error returns. Adding the check code is a very easy task (left as an exercise for the reader) which has been omitted simply to make the code easier to read.
2. Similarly, if an output redirection file has been specified then it will be **open()**ed and the resulting file descriptor assigned to the **outfd** structure member associated with the last (j-1 th) simple command on the command line. One extra twist here is that there are two sorts of output redirection (overwrite and append) which need the file to be opened in two different ways. The selection is made in this case just by testing the value of the **append** flag.
3. The next section is involved with zombie child processes. If the command line

is to be run in the background (`backgnd==TRUE`) then `SIGCHLD` is set so that zombie child processes will not be created when the child processes terminate. This is the correct action here because the shell won't be `wait()`ing for them. If the command line will be run in the foreground then `SIGCHLD` is set to its default action, which also causes the system to generate zombies from child processes when they die, until the shell `wait()`s for them.

4. The next section is a loop, the body of which will be executed once for each simple command in the command line, with the variable `i` specifying which simple command to work on next.
5. The value `j-1` gives the command number of the last simple command in the command line. Where this value is greater than zero, it means that there is more than one simple command in the pipeline. For each simple command whose number is less than `j-1` a pipe needs to be created to pipe the output (`outfd`) of command number `i` to the input (`infd`) of command number `i+1`.
6. All the file descriptors and command line parameters needed by command number `i` are now available and ready so that simple command `i` can now be executed. The `forkexec()` function does just what its name implies – it creates a child process to run a simple command. Therefore, only in the parent process does the `forkexec()` function return.
7. If any I/O redirection or pipes were involved in the simple command that has just been started then the parent's copies of the file descriptors are closed here.
8. Finally, when all the simple commands have been started, if this command line is running in the foreground then the parent (tiny shell) process enters a loop to `wait()` for the termination of the last process in the pipeline, whose process ID will have been set in `lastpid` by the `forkexec()` function.

20.2.7 `forkexec` Function

The `forkexec()` function has the task of creating a child process with the `fork()` system call Then within the child process it performs any required I/O redirection before using `execvp()` to execute the required command.

```
forkexec(struct cmd *ptr)
{
    int i,pid;

    /* 1 */
    if (pid = fork())
    {
        /* 2 */
        if (backgnd==TRUE)
            printf("%d\n", pid);
```

```
            lastpid = pid;
    }
    else
    {
        /* 3 */
        if (ptr->infd==0 && backgnd==TRUE)
            ptr->infd = open("/dev/null", O_RDONLY);

        /* 4 */
        if (ptr->infd!=0)
        {
            close(0);
            dup(ptr->infd);
        }

        if (ptr->outfd!=1)
        {
            close(1);
            dup(ptr->outfd);
        }

        /* 5 */
        if (backgnd==FALSE)
        {
            signal(SIGINT, SIG_DFL);
            signal(SIGQUIT, SIG_DFL);
        }

        /* 6 */
        for (i = 3; i<OPEN_MAX; ++i)
            close(i);

        /* 7 */
        execvp(ptr->av[0], ptr->av);
        exit(1);
    }
}
```

The `forkexec()` function takes as its parameter a pointer to the `struct cmd` associated with the simple command it is about to execute. Remember that this structure contains the file descriptors that the command is to use for its standard input and standard output (though the redirection has not taken place yet) and it also contains an array of pointers to command line parameters (including the command name itself) that will become the command's `argv` parameter.

The numbered comments in this function are described as follows:

1. The first task is to `fork()` a child process and store the process ID that is returned.
2. In the parent process, if this command line is to be run in the background then the process ID of each child process will be displayed as it is created. The process ID of each child is also stored in the variable `lastpid`. As the simple commands in the command line are executed from left to right, the final value of `lastpid` will be the process ID of the last simple command to be created (i.e. the right-most simple command). This is the process ID that `wait()` will be looking for if this is a command line to execute in the foreground.
3. In the child process the first thing to happen is a rather subtle test. If this is to be a background command line then it must be prevented from taking input from the keyboard. In fact, only the first simple command in a pipeline can take its input from the keyboard as all the rest of the commands will take their standard input from pipes, by redirection. So, if this is to be a background command line, and the file descriptor which is to be the standard input for the current simple command (`infd`) is still set up as the keyboard (`infd==0`), then this must be the first simple command in the pipeline and it needs to have its standard input diverted away from the keyboard so there is no chance that it will try to read from it. The simplest and safest way to do this is just to set up an automatic input redirection in this case. The obvious file to use for this redirection is just the standard file `/dev/null`, which will immediately return EOF if the process tries to `read()` from it. Using this simple mechanism saves the tiny shell from being involved in any kind of job control functions.
4. The next stage is actually to perform the input and output redirection by manipulation of the file descriptors if they have changed from their default values.
5. If this is a foreground pipeline then the current simple command is set up so that it can be terminated by an interrupt or quit signal from the keyboard, unless it makes a subsequent and specific provision to the contrary.
6. The next step is that all the file descriptors except the standard input, output and error output are `close()`d so that this process cannot interfere with any of the pipes or I/O redirection files that the shell has set up, except those it is supposed to see via the standard file descriptors 0, 1 and 2.
7. Finally, the simple command is executed by the `execvp()` system call, using the values in its `av[]` array for the command name and the `argv` pointer.

20.2.8 check Function

```
check(char *ptr)
{
    char *tptr;
```

```
        while (*lineptr==' ')
            lineptr++;

        tptr = lineptr;

        while (*ptr!='\0' && *ptr==*tptr)
        {
            ptr++;
            tptr++;
        }

        if (*ptr!='\0')
            return(FALSE);
        else
        {
            lineptr = tptr;
            return(TRUE);
        }
}
```

The check() function compares the string passed to it as a parameter with the characters in the line[] array starting at the position of lineptr. If a match is found then lineptr is moved on beyond the characters matched and the value TRUE is returned. If check() doesn't find a match then a value of FALSE is returned and lineptr is left unchanged so that checks can be performed for other strings starting in the same place in the line[] array.

20.2.9 getname Function

```
getname(char *name)
{
    int i;

    for (i = 0; i<MAXNAME; ++i)
    {
        switch (*lineptr)
        {
        case '>':
        case '<':
        case '|':
        case '&':
        case ' ':
        case '\n':
```

```
        case '\t':
            *name = '\0';
            return;

        default:
            *name++ = *lineptr++;
            break;
        }
    }
    *name = '\0';
}
```

This function just copies a file name up to MAXNAME characters long into the char array pointed to by its name parameter.

Exercises

1. Using bash and tsh type in the following command lines, each of which contains errors, to see what the shell does. Is what you observe what you expected? what you would have wanted? Try other commands and other shells (if you have them), what do you think now?

    ```
    $ cat /etc/passwd >output1 >output2
    $ cat </etc/passwd </etc/motd
    $ cat /etc/passwd | | grep root
    $ cat /etc/passwd >output3 | grep root
    ```

2. Add a simple mechanism to the tiny shell to allow it to execute built-in commands.
3. Add the cd and history built-in commands to the tiny shell and allow it to repeat previous commands in the history list with the ! operator.

Answers

1. Ooops... . Assuming you think that error messages are the order of the day, the standard shells don't do too well, do they?
2. The simple way to add built-in commands is to add the following code at the top of the parse() function:

    ```
    parse()
    {
    ```

```
    int i;

    if (builtin())
        return 0;

    /* 1 */
    command(0);
/* etc...*/
```

and then to write a `builtin()` function which checks for built-in command keywords and performs any required actions when it finds them. If the `builtin()` function returns a true (non-zero) value to say that a built-in command was found, then `parse()` will return at that point and not try to execute the command line further:

```
builtin()
{
    if (check("exit"))
        exit(0);
    else
        return 0;
}
```

3. To add these three extra built-in commands, the `builtin()` function can be modified as follows:

```
builtin()
{
    if (check("exit"))
        exit(0);
    else if (check("cd"))
        return do_cd();
    else if (check("history"))
        return do_history();
    else if (check("!"))
        return do_repeat_command();
    else
        return 0;
}
```

The `do_cd()` function can then extract a directory name from the `line[]` array and use the `chdir()` system call to make the change. For the `!` and `history` commands, you need to modify the `getline()` function so that lines entered at the keyboard are stored as they are entered. The `history` command can then list all the commands in the store and the `!` command can copy the appropriate stored command back into the `line[]`

array. `do_repeat_command()` can then return a zero from `builtin()` so that `line[]` will be parsed as normal.

Chapter 21

Miscellaneous System Calls

There are far more system calls (one hundred and forty something at the present time) than I have space to describe in detail here. However, there are still a few more that we should look at before we finish.

All the commands that can be executed from a shell command prompt can only perform their operations by calling on some underlying system calls to get the required system services from the operating system. In several cases this means a new system call specifically to provide a particular service.

The next set of system calls is of this type.

21.1   umask System Call

You will remember that the **umask** command is used to set up the file creation mask. The **umask** value is used every time a file is created as a security measure to make sure that the processes you run cannot create new files with any more access permission than you want to give. This is done by having the permission bits in the **umask** value reset in the mode bits of any file that gets created on your behalf.

The **umask** command is implemented internally by a call to an underlying system call of the same name:

```
#include <sys/types.h>
#include <sys/stat.h>

mode_t umask(mode_t mask);
```

A call to the **umask()** system call sets the file creation mask to the specified *mask* value. Only the permission bits in *mask* are saved, the values of the other bits are ignored.

The return value from **umask()** is just the previous value of the file creation mask, so that this system call can be used both to get and set the required values.

Sadly, however, there is no way to get the old umask value without setting a new value at the same time.

This means that in order just to see the current value, it is necessary to execute a piece of code like the following function:

```
#include <sys/types.h>
#include <sys/stat.h>

mode_t get_umask()
{
    mode_t old;

    old = umask((mode_t)0);
    (void) umask(old);
    return old;
}
```

The first line of this function sets the umask value to zero, and as a side effect returns the value of interest, which then gets assigned to the variable old. The second line then restores the umask to its original value. And the final line returns the required umask value to the caller.

21.2 mount System Call

Remember that physical disks are very often split into separate partitions and that each partition has a filesystem recorded on it. Each of these filesystems may be mounted into the directory hierarchy, and thus become a part of it. This filesystem mount operation is performed by use of the mount command, which itself uses an underlying mount() system call:

```
#include <sys/mount.h>

int mount(char *fspath, char *dir, char *fstype,
                   unsigned long flags, void *data);
```

It is unusual to want to call the mount() system call directly, especially as it can only be used by the root user.

The *fspath* parameter is the pathname to the disk partition whose filesystem you wish to mount (e.g. /dev/hdb2), *dir* gives the directory over which the filesystem is to be mounted. The *fstype* parameter specifies what filesystem type is on the disk partition (e.g. second extended, minix or DOS), *flags* specifies how the filesystem is to be mounted (e.g. read-only or read-write) and *data* is a pointer to an arbitrary structure of information whose contents (or even existence) depend on the particular filesystem type to be mounted.

21.3 umount System Call

A filesystem, once mounted, can be removed from the directory hierarchy again with the umount command. This uses the underlying umount() system call:

```
#include <sys/mount.h>

int umount(char *path);
```

The *path* parameter is either the pathname to the mounted disk partition or the pathname to the directory over which the filesystem is mounted.

Once again, this system call can only be used by root.

21.4 sync System Call

You already know that when data is written to a file, the kernel arranges to write the data into a memory buffer and not straight out to disk. You have also seen that data writes can be forced by the use of the sync command. This command uses the underlying sync() system call:

```
#include <unistd.h>

int sync(void);
```

You should appreciate, if you intend to use this system call, that it only schedules the disk data to be written out to disk; it doesn't wait for the physical writes to take place. This means that you must not assume that the disk writes have actually taken place when the sync() call returns to your program, only that they have been scheduled to take place as soon as possible.

In fact, it is very rare that you will need to call sync() yourself as there is a pair of programs called update and bdflush which most Linux distributions arrange to execute automatically at system boot time. These commands remain active the whole time the system is running, and they flush the disk buffer cache out to disk on a regular basis, every 30 seconds (more often for really important data). In this way even a bad machine crash should lose no more than 30 seconds worth of work.

Unlike mount() and umount(), the sync() system call can be used at any time by any user.

21.5 Telling the Time

Many programs have a need to measure time. This can be in terms of what the wall clock time is now, or in terms of how much CPU time a process is using. Measurements of time in both these senses are available via system calls in Linux.

21.5.1 `time` System Call

The hardware of a PC contains a system clock. Linux reads the clock during system boot and then maintains its own clock counter which it uses to time stamp events within the system, like the creation of a file or the time a user logs in. The value of this (wall) clock is also available to your own programs by using the `time()` system call:

```
#include <sys/types.h>
#include <time.h>

time_t time(time_t *loc);
```

This system call returns a `time_t` value and, if the parameter *loc* is a pointer to a variable of this type, then the return value is also copied into the variable to which this pointer points.

The data type `time_t` is actually defined by a `typedef`, which is accessed via `<time.h>` and has an underlying data type of `long`. Therefore, the `time()` system call returns the current wall clock time in a `long`, but in a strange format – the number of seconds that have elapsed since midnight on 1 January 1970 GMT. (I suppose the clock had to start somewhere... .)

A side issue at this point is just how much time can be counted by a `long` before it runs out? If you restrict yourself to the positive range of values that can be held in a 32-bit `long` (I'm not sure what a negative time means anyway!), then it comes to just over 68 years, or up to the start of the year 2038 (plenty of time to dream up a replacement).

This format for times is actually quite useful if you want to work out how much time passed between two events (e.g the time you login and the time you logout), as you just subtract the later time from the earlier time to obtain the number of seconds between the events.

The format is less useful, however, where you want to display the day, the month, the year or the time of day. To simplify these applications the standard library contains some useful functions to do the conversions for you. Two such functions are:

```
#include <time.h>

struct tm *gmtime(time_t *loc);
struct tm *localtime(time_t *loc);
```

Both functions take a parameter which is a pointer to a variable containing a value of the 'seconds since 1970' variety. And both functions return a pointer to a structure whose fields contain all the required information:

```
struct tm {
    int tm_sec;
```

```
        int tm_min;
        int tm_hour;
        int tm_mday;
        int tm_mon;
        int tm_year;
        int tm_wday;
        int tm_yday;
        int tm_isdst;
    };
```

The fields `tm_hour`, `tm_min` and `tm_sec` give the wall clock time in 24-hour clock format, `tm_mday` is the day of the month in the range 1 to 31, `tm_mon` is the month number in the range 0 to 11, with January as 0, `tm_year` is the number of years since 1900, `tm_wday` is the day of the week in the range 0 to 6, with Sunday as 0, `tm_yday` is the day of the year in the range 0 to 365, with 1 January as 0, and `tm_isdst` is a flag to specify whether or not daylight saving time is in effect (if the information is available).

The main difference between the two functions is that `gmtime()` gives its information relative to Greenwich Mean Time (GMT), whereas `localtime()` gives its information relative to your local timezone (which was set up during system installation and configuration).

21.5.2   times System Call

The other times that may be of interest are those related to processes and their CPU usage. This information may be obtained by the use of the `times()` system call:

```
    #include <sys/times.h>

    clock_t times(struct tms *buf);
```

Here the parameter to `times()` is a pointer to a `struct tms` which will be filled in by the call. The definition of this structure is:

```
    struct tms {
        clock_t tms_utime;
        clock_t tms_stime;
        clock_t tms_cutime;
        clock_t tms_cstime;
    };
```

The CPU time for a process is split into two parts: the time it spends executing instructions in its own text segment (user time) and the time it spends executing instructions in the kernel, usually via a system call (system time).

The `tms_utime` field is the total user time used by the calling process and the `tms_stime` is its total system time. The other two fields (`tms_cutime` and `tms_cstime`) are the same thing but totalled over all the child processes of the calling process, for which a successful `wait()` has been performed.

The return value from the `times()` system call is the amount of time that has elapsed since the system was last booted up.

All of the times associated with the `times()` system call are measured (for Linux) in hundredths of a second.

21.6 `select` System Call

The final system call in this chapter has the power to decrease the CPU usage of your programs very significantly in the situations where it is applicable.

Consider the following scenario. Suppose you wish to write a program which may take input from a terminal keyboard and which also may take input from the read end of a named pipe. If it can be guaranteed that the input from these two sources will arrive in a strictly alternating fashion so that first one then the other may be read, then producing code to achieve this is a simple matter. However, if (as is more likely) the input from the two sources is free to arrive in any order, then there is a problem because both of these input devices will block on `read()` if no data is ready when the call takes place.

This means that a `read()` from the keyboard could suspend the process if no input is ready. Even though there may be plenty of input arriving from the pipe, the process will be unable to do anything about it.

The obvious solution to this problem is to use `O_NONBLOCK` on the two input devices, so that they both return immediately on `read()`, even if no input characters are ready. You can then write your code repeatedly to poll the two devices in turn, dealing with inputs from each as they occur.

This solution will work. However, repeated polling in this fashion does place a continuous load on the CPU, with no effective work being done except when input characters arrive.

The `select()` system call provides the perfect solution to the problem because it allows you to specify that you want your process to suspend itself while at the same time getting the kernel to monitor any desired collection of file descriptors looking for any activity. As soon as activity is spotted on any of the file descriptors being monitored, the `select()` call will return saying which file descriptor is ready to use.

This allows multiple randomly ordered inputs to a process to be sorted out without the heavy CPU overhead of polling for the inputs yourself. The prototype for the `select()` call is:

```
#include <sys/time.h>
#include <sys/types.h>
```

```
#include <unistd.h>

int select(int nfds, fd_set *rdfds, fd_set *wrfds,
                  fd_set *exfds, struct timeval *timeout);
```

where *rdfds*, *wrfds* and *exfds* are the set of read, write and exception handling file descriptors, respectively, that are to be monitored by `select()`, *nfds* is the highest numbered file descriptor that needs to be checked and the *timeout* parameter can cause `select()` to return early even if no file descriptors are ready.

The fd_sets pointed to by *rdfds*, *wrfds* and *exfds* are modified by the call to show which file descriptors are ready and the `select()` call returns a total of the number of ready file descriptors.

In order to simplify the setting, resetting and testing of appropriate file descriptor bits within an fd_set a set of macros is defined as follows:

FD_SET(fd, setptr)	set *fd* bit pointed to by *setptr*;
FD_CLR(fd, setptr)	clear *fd* bit pointed to by *setptr*;
FD_ZERO(setptr)	clear all bits pointed to by *setptr*;
FD_ISSET(fd, setptr)	test *fd* bit pointed to by *setptr*.

These macro definitions are made available by including the header file `<types.h>` in your code.

Exercises

1. Modify the chat program you wrote in the exercises at the end of the socket library case study to use the `select()` system call to work out when there is something for it to do, rather than repeatedly polling around all of the open socket descriptors to find out if any of them is ready to be `read()`.
2. Implement your own version of the standard `date` command which displays the current wall clock date and time in a suitable format.
3. Implement your own version of the standard `time` command which takes another command and parameters as its own command line arguments, executes the given command, and then displays the kernel and user times used by the controlled command during its execution.
4. Write a pair of simple commands which can be set up as setuid root and which will allow ordinary users to mount and unmount a floppy disk at a fixed point in the directory hierachy (say `/floppy`).

Answers

1. In order to do this, you will need to use the `select()` system call at the top of the infinite loop in `main()`. In order to be fully effective the socket

descriptor inside the SOCKET structure pointed to by sp will also need to be included. As new clients join the chat and existing clients leave, the bits in the read file descriptor set (rdfs) need to be set and reset as appropriate so that select() continually monitors only those file/socket descriptors currently in use.

2. This just involves using the time() system call to obtain the current time in seconds since 1 January 1970 and then using one of the conversion functions on this value to get a struct tm filled appropriately. The required values can then be extracted from this structure and displayed in the correct date format.

3. The easiest way to implement this command is just to fork() a child process which will use execvp() to execute the specified command, and then use the times() call in the parent process after wait()ing for the child to finish, to obtain access to the child's system and user time information:

```
#include <sys/times.h>

main(int argc, char **argv)
{
    struct tms tm;

    if (fork())
    {
        wait(0);
        times(&tm);
        printf("User CPU time = %d.%d secs\n"
            , tm.tms_cutime/100, tm.tms_cutime%100);
        printf("System CPU time = %d.%d secs\n"
            , tm.tms_cstime/100, tm.tms_cstime%100);
    }
    else
    {
        execvp(argv[1], &argv[1]);
        exit(1);
    }
}
```

4. One possible solution is to call the mount and umount system calls with appropriate fixed parameters as follows:

```
/* mountfd0 command - must be setuid root to work */
main()
{
    setuid(0);
```

```
        if (mount("/dev/fd0", "/floppy", "ext2", 0, 0))
            puts("mountfd0 failed!!!\n");
}

/* umountfd0 command - must be setuid root to work */
main()
{
    setuid(0);

    if (umount("/dev/fd0"))
        puts(umountfd0 failed!!!\n);
}
```

The call to `setuid(0)` is needed to set the real uid of the process to 0, as the `mount` system call tests the real uid rather than the effective uid when it looks to make sure it is being run by `root`.

Chapter 22

Daemons

A daemon (pronounced dee-mon, not day-mon) is a process that runs in the background without an associated terminal or login shell. There are many standard daemons, some of which run periodically to perform particular tasks (like `atrun`, typically executed every five minutes by `cron`), while others run continuously, waiting to deal with some specific event (like `inetd` and `lpd`).

22.1 Principles

There are several ways to start up a daemon. The most common are:

- When the system is booted. Daemons run at this time are usually started during the execution of the system startup scripts, which are typically stored in the directory `/etc/rc.d`.
- Manually, from a shell prompt. It should be possible for any user with suitable execute permission to start any daemon in this way.
- By the `crond` daemon. This program consults a set of files typically in the directory `/var/spool/cron/crontabs`, which specify periodic tasks to perform.
- By executing an `at` command. This will cause a program to be executed once at a specified date and time.

In order to be completely sound, a daemon should be capable of being executed correctly in all of these ways. The only problem is that some of these startup methods leave the daemon in a vulnerable state, where it can be influenced by the environment that was set up on its behalf before it was run. Much of the code that you will write to convert an ordinary program (such as the example socket server in Section 18.2) into a daemon will be concerned with isolating your program from these influences. In addition to this, program code intended for daemon use will usually have to be more robust than ordinary user code. This is because you will often want to program a daemon so that even if system errors of various types occur while the daemon is running they do not cause the program to crash.

22.2 Practice

There are more steps involved in starting a daemon than you would probably imagine, though they can all be accomplished with a surprisingly small amount of code. The rest of this section presents a step-by-step guide to the more important aspects of the process.

22.2.1 Close File Descriptors

The first task is to close all unnecessary file descriptors. If your daemon were to leave an ordinary file open, this would prevent the file from being deleted from the filesystem by any other process. It would also prevent a mounted file system containing the open file from being unmounted. In the case of terminal files (usually stdin, stdout and stderr), closing unnecessary connections is even more important, because here the daemon's access rights to the terminal will be revoked by the execution of the vhangup() system call after the user at the terminal logs out. This means that the daemon will have file descriptors which it thinks are in an open state, when in reality there is no longer any access to the terminal via these descriptors.

The simplest thing to do is just to close all file descriptors, which will isolate the daemon from these problems. There is no problem with using the close() system call on a file descriptor which is not open, and so the following code fragment can be used:

```
#include <sys/param.h>

for (i = 0; i<NOFILE; ++i)
    close(i);
```

The symbolic constant NOFILE gives the maximum number of files that a process can have open at once.

22.2.2 Lose Controlling Terminal

If a process is started from within a login session then it will have a controlling terminal associated with it, inherited from the session. For a daemon, the consequence of this is that it can receive signals generated by the controlling terminal (such as SIGINT and SIGQUIT) which, if they are not caught, will terminate the process. This problem could be overcome by having the daemon ignore all the signals it can, but this would prevent the daemon from using signals for simple IPC purposes. A better solution is to have the daemon disassociate itself from the controlling terminal so that these signals are not propagated to the daemon in the first place.

One way to do this under Linux is to open the file /dev/tty and use ioctl() on the file with the command TIOCNOTTY. It is arranged so that every process which has a controlling terminal has access to that terminal via the file /dev/tty.

A short piece of code to do this could be:

```
if ((fd = open("/dev/tty", O_RDWR))>=0)
{
    ioctl(fd, TIOCNOTTY, 0);
    close(fd);
}
```

Under Linux, this is not the only way for a process to disassociate itself from its controlling terminal. Indeed, there is a simpler way to do this that we look at now, in the next section.

22.2.3 Lose Session and Process Group

A process gets its session and process group IDs from its parent process. Because it belongs to a session and a process group, a process will receive any signals that are sent to the session or process group as a whole. This is a similar problem to receiving signals from the controlling terminal, and the solution is essentially the same, i.e. to disassociate the process from this environmental influence.

In POSIX (and, therefore, in Linux) there is a single system call which will disassociate a process from its current session and process group, and set it up as a new session leader. The system call is set session ID:

```
setsid()
```

Because a controlling terminal can only be associated with a single session, the setsid() call has the side effect that it also disassociates a process from its controlling terminal (if it has one).

The only problem with setsid() is that it only works if the process which executes it is not already a session leader. In our case it is easy to suppose that the daemon won't be a session leader, but this cannot be guaranteed unless specific steps are taken to make it so. One thing you can say for sure is that if a particular process which is a session leader executes the fork() system call, then, by default, the child process won't be a session leader. This, then, provides the mechanism for making sure that the daemon process is not a session leader when it executes setsid(). All that the daemon needs to do is to execute a fork() call, then exit() in the parent process and execute setsid() in the child process, as follows:

```
/* After this, child process is not a session leader */
if (fork())
    /* Terminate parent process whatever its status */
    exit(0);

/* Disassociate child from session, process group and tty */
setsid();
```

Even these measures do not solve all the problems surrounding disassociating a daemon from its controlling terminal. This is due to the fact that when a session leader without a controlling terminal (such as ours is now) opens a terminal device which itself is not already the control terminal for another session, the terminal automatically becomes the controlling terminal for the new session.

Notice, however, that acquiring a controlling terminal in this way can only be done by a session leader. The solution, therefore, is obviously to make sure that our process is not a session leader. This can be done by executing fork() for a second time and once again terminating the parent process. This leaves a child process which does not belong to its initial session or process group, does not have a controlling terminal and, now, cannot reacquire one. The required code fragment now appears as follows:

```
/* Start up new session, to lose old session and process group */
if (fork())
    exit(0);

/* Disassociate process group and controlling terminal */
setsid();

/* Become a NON-session leader so that a */
/* control terminal can't be reacquired */
if (fork())
    exit(0);
```

22.2.4 Change Working Directory

The kernel holds open the current working directory of any process on the system for the life of the process. This does not normally present a problem, but if the process has a current directory in a mounted filesystem then that filesystem is flagged as 'in use' and, as such, it cannot be unmounted. To allow a system super-user to umount a filesystem, the daemon could execute:

```
chdir("/");
```

It is also possible that in order to operate properly a daemon has to chdir() to a particular directory. The example socket server is a case in point, where the files in the daemon's current working directory are the only files the server can supply. In cases like this you just have to accept the limitation, or arrange with a system administrator to provide for a place in the root filesystem from which the daemon can run. One possible problem can occur with changing the current working directory to the root. If there is any chance of the daemon terminating and dumping a core file, the kernel will try to open the file in the current directory and if this is the root directory then the operation will fail unless the daemon is running with super-user privileges. To overcome this problem, the following:

```
chdir("/tmp");
```

will make /tmp the current working directory, which is usually just a subdirectory of the root filesystem and also gives all processes write permission.

22.2.5 Reset the File Creation Mask

When a process is started off, its file creation mask is inherited from its parent. Typically, this will have a value of 022, meaning that any files created by the daemon will not give write permission to group or world users, whatever permission bits are specified by the daemon itself. Depending upon the nature of the daemon, this action may or may not present a problem. However, it is a simple matter to include the following line into your code to undo the effect of the file creation mask value set by the parent process, whatever it was:

```
umask(0);
```

Even now, there are still features in the environment, inherited from the parent process, which can cause a daemon some problems. For example, the nice() process priority setting, or the time remaining on an alarm clock signal, set up with alarm(). However, even though these things are possible, it would be a pretty malicious parent process that would set any of them up to trap an unwary daemon process.

22.2.6 Handle SIGCHLD Signals

Sometimes daemons are written that create child processes. Making the example socket server into a daemon will demonstrate this type of code. In this case, the parent process keeps looping back to accept more client connections, whilst the child processes service the client requests. Notice that the parent process does not execute a wait() system call to wait for the termination of its child processes. By default, child processes in this position become zombies until some process (probably init) waits for them in the future. The creation of zombies under these circumstances just wastes system resources. There are several ways round the problem under Linux, the simplest being to set the action of the SIGCHLD signal to SIG_IGN, as follows:

```
signal(SIGCHLD, SIG_IGN);
```

This is a special feature of `SIGCHLD` which tells the kernel not to generate zombies from the children of the calling process.

Exercises

1. Create a pseudo code program skeleton for a server daemon which will allow multiple network client requests over a socket to be served concurrently.
2. Write the code for a new command which can be used to launch another program as a daemon process. For example:

    ```
    $ launch myprog param1 param2
    ```

    will execute the command `myprog param1 param2` after setting up its environment so that it runs as a daemon. This will allow you to write commands in such a way that you can run them as ordinary commands while you are logged on, or run them as daemons so that they will continue to execute even after you logout.

Answers

1. This is actually the arrangement suggested in Section 22.2.6, which gives clues as to the required answer. What you do is to make the process into a daemon, set up the socket and then go into a loop accepting client connections. Each time you get a client connection you fork a child process to deal with it while the parent loops back to accept another connection. The pseudo code could be:

    ```
    Setup current process as a daemon (fork, setsid, fork etc.)
    Create a socket on a well known port
    while (true)
        Get a client connection
        if (fork()==0)
            Close parent's copy of client connection
        else
            In child, deal with client request
            exit child process
        endif
    endwhile
    ```

    You will see essentially this solution used in the Tiny Daemon case study in the next chapter.

2. The solution to this problem just requires you to set up your *launch* command as a daemon to make the process run as a daemon and then use `exec()` to change the program in the daemon process to the one given on the command line. This can be done as follows:

```
main(int argc, char **argv)
{
    Setup process as a daemon (fork, setsid, fork etc.)

    execvp(argv[1], &argv[1]);
}
```

Chapter 23

Tiny Daemon – Case Study

Having looked at the principles involved in setting up a daemon process we will now go back to the example socket server program we looked at in Section 18.2 and see how to make it into a proper daemon process which will continue to run and provide its service even after you log off the machine.

23.1 The Daemon Listing

The following program shows the complete listing of the example socket server from Section 18.2, modified to operate as a robust daemon process. You will notice that some changes have been made to the original server code itself, as well as the addition of the `setup_daemon()` function. All of these will be explained in detail after the listing:

```
/*********************************************************************
THE SOCKET SERVER DAEMON
*********************************************************************/

#include <stdio.h>
#include <string.h>
#include <signal.h>
#include <fcntl.h>
#include <setjmp.h>
#include <sys/param.h>
#include "socklib.h"

/* Server's communication port number */
#define PORT 2121

/* Values for the next_action parameter to fatal() */
#define NA_EXIT 0
```

360 Tiny Daemon – Case Study

```c
#define NA_RESTART 1

/* Global environment store for setjmp/longjmp */
jmp_buf env;


/***********************************************************************
MAIN - A very simple file tranfer daemon, which sets up a concurrent
    socket server on the host machine on port number PORT to transfer
    any files from the current directory on request.
***********************************************************************/
main(void)
{
    SOCKET *sp;
    int sd;

    /* Rearrange operating environment for daemon working */
    setup_daemon();
    /* Set SIGCHLD for no zombies */
    signal(SIGCHLD, SIG_IGN);

    /* Create server's socket */
    if ((sp = sopen())==0)
        /* Exit server if this fails */
        fatal("sopen()", NA_EXIT);

    /* Setup the NA_RESTART (post error) entry point */
    setjmp(env);

    /* Repeatedly accept and service client requests */
    for (;;)
    {
        /* Connect to client or restart on failure */
        if ((sd = sserver(sp, PORT, S_DELAY))==-1)
            fatal("sserver()", NA_RESTART);

        /* Fork() a child process */
        switch (fork())
        {
        /* Deal with client request in child */
        case 0:
            do_service(sd);

        /* Deal with fork() failure */
        case -1:
            close(sd);
```

```c
            /* Restart for next client */
            fatal("fork()", NA_RESTART);
        }

        /* In parent, close client and loop for next connection */
        close(sd);
    }
}


/************************************************************************
SETUP_DAEMON - This function is responsible for modifying the current
    working environment of the process to that required by a daemon.
    I.e.  it closes unnecessary file descriptors, disassociates itself
    from the current controlling terminal, session and process group
    and modifies the current file creation mask.
************************************************************************/
setup_daemon(void)
{
    int i;

    /* Close all open file descriptors */
    for (i = 0; i<NOFILE; ++i)
        close(i);

    /* 1st fork() call */
    switch (fork())
    {
    /* Error in 1st fork() */
    case -1:
        fatal("setup_daemon(), 1st fork()", NA_EXIT);

    /* Exit 1st parent */
    default:
        exit(0);

    /* Continue in 1st child (2nd parent) */
    case 0:
        /* Start new session exit() on error */
        if (setsid()==-1)
            fatal("setup_daemon(), setsid()", NA_EXIT);

        /* 2nd fork() call */
        switch (fork())
        {
        /* Error in 2nd fork() */
```

```
            case -1:
                fatal("setup_daemon(), 2nd fork()", NA_EXIT);

            /* Exit 2nd parent */
            default:
                exit(0);

            /* Continue in 2nd child */
            case 0:
                /* Reset file creation mask for ERROR.LOG */
                umask(0);
                /* and return with daemon set up */
                return;
        }
    }
}


/************************************************************************
FATAL - This routine is called when an error condition is returned to
    the daemon, usually from one of the system calls it makes. The
    function first prints the message pointed to by <text> and then
    either terminates the process or restarts it with longjmp(),
    depending on the value of the <next_action> parameter.
************************************************************************/
fatal(char *text, int next_action)
{
    FILE *fp;

    /* Open the error log file */
    if ((fp = fopen("ERROR.LOG", "a"))==0)
        /* exit() on failure here, with error unreported... */
        exit(1);

    /* Write the error message */
    fprintf(fp, "Error in %s\n", text);
    fclose(fp);

    if (next_action==NA_RESTART)
        /* Restart calling process */
        longjmp(env, 1);
    else
        /* Terminate calling process */
        exit(1);
```

```
/************************************************************************
DO_SERVICE - This function is called in the child process that is
    created when a client makes a successful connection. Its task is
    to service the client's request and supervise the required file
    transfer. The parameter <sd> is the socket descriptor to use for
    the communication.
************************************************************************/
do_service(int sd)
{
    int i, fd;
    char *name;
    char c, namlen;

    /* Get length of file name */
    if (read(sd, &namlen, 1)!=1)
        fatal("namlen read()", NA_EXIT);

    /* Space for name + " open()" */
    if ((name = (char *)malloc(namlen+8))==0)
        fatal("malloc()", NA_EXIT);

    /* Get required file name into name[] */
    for (i = 0; i<namlen; ++i)
        if (read(sd, &name[i], 1)!=1)
            fatal("file name read()", NA_EXIT);

    /* Make name[] a string */
    name[i] = '\0';

    /* Check name[] is in current directory */
    if (strchr(name, '/'))
        fatal("illegal file name", NA_EXIT);

    /* Open specified file */
    if ((fd = open(name, O_RDONLY))==-1)
        fatal(strcat(name, " open()"), NA_EXIT);

    /* Transfer contents to client */
    while ((i = read(fd, &c, 1))!=0)
        if (i==-1)
            fatal("file read()", NA_EXIT);
        else if (write(sd, &c, 1)!=1)
            fatal("write()", NA_EXIT);

    /* Terminate child and with it the connection to this client */
```

```
        exit(0);
}
```

23.2 Socket Server Additions

The most obvious change to the program is the addition of the `setup_daemon()` function which is called as the first statement of `main()`. There are no surprises about what the function does but the way it is coded is different from the conceptual method we looked at earlier.

The first task is to close all the file descriptors. This is done regardless of whether or not they are open. Then, there follows a section which disassociates the daemon from its controlling terminal, session and process group, and stops it from reacquiring another terminal in the future. This is done with the usual `fork()`, `setsid()`, `fork()` sequence but embedded in a pair of `switch()` constructs to make it easier to deal with any possible errors from the `fork()` calls. Remember that `fork()` returns three different values: -1 on error, 0 to the child process and a non-zero value, dealt with by the `default:` case, to the parent process. Finally, in the second child process, a call is made to `umask()` to set the file creation mask to 0. This is because the daemon may need to create the file `ERROR.LOG` if any serious errors occur, and without this call the current `umask()` value may be unsuitable.

23.3 Socket Server Changes

All the other changes to the original example socket server are directly related to enabling the daemon to deal with errors returned from system and library calls. This is done by restarting the daemon's main loop where appropriate, rather than just terminating the daemon when any error occurs. The implementation of this idea has been achieved by adding an extra parameter to the `fatal()` function to specify what its `next_action` should be, after printing out its error message. The options are: `NA_EXIT`, in which case the the calling process terminates, or `NA_RESTART`, where use is made of the `setjmp()` and `longjmp()` library routines to cause a non-local jump back to the start of the main server loop. In fact, this restart facility is only used for errors detected within the main loop of the parent process. If any errors are detected within a client serving child process, then this process is allowed to terminate as before.

Exercises

1. Modify the chat program you wrote in the exercises at the end of the socket library case study to make your server into a daemon.
2. Add a built-in command to the tiny shell which allows shell users to store simple messages for the system administrator. This new command should operate by taking the message, adding the user's login name to the start of it and sending the completed string to a named pipe called /tmp/messfifo which has previously been created. Then write a daemon process which continuously monitors the read end of the named pipe and transfers any messages it receives to the message file (/tmp/sysmess), along with a time stamp to say when the message was written. If you have sufficient privilege on the machine, you should set the system up so that user shells cannot write directly to the message file.

Answers

1. This is just a case of adding the daemon startup code to the beginning of the previous exercise. You might also take the opportunity to make your chat program more robust in its error checking and more fully featured in its facilities. For example, you might like to get users to follow some login protocol so that their login names can be added to all their messages to identify message sources to other chat users.
2. Adding a message command to the tiny shell just involves adding a call to a do_message() function into builtin(). The do_message() function will extract the user's login name from the system (look at getenv("LOGNAME") or getpwuid()) and the message from the line[] array and write() these to the named pipe. The daemon will open the named pipe for read() access, take message lines from the pipe as they arrive, read the wall clock time with the time() call and write the message and time information to the message file. With root access you can make the daemon program, the pipe and the message file owned by root. Then give the daemon program read access to the pipe and write access to the message file. Other users should get write access to the pipe and no access to the message file.

Part IV
DEVICE DRIVERS

Chapter 24

Device Driver Basics

The system calls studied in Part III presented the interface between the operating system kernel and application programs. Device drivers present the interface at the other end of the operating system, between the kernel and the hardware of the machine.

Remember, that great care was taken when receiving input from and sending output to files and devices to make them all look, as far as possible, just like files, all using the open(), close(), read() and write() interface. As we shall see, it is in the device drivers themselves that this file appearance is created.

24.1 Introduction

There are two main classes of device which the kernel needs to be able to access: those with a simple character based interface, like keyboards and printers, and those with a data block based interface like hard disks, floppy disks and CD-ROMs. As the names imply, character based devices send and receive data in single character chunks, whereas block based devices, in order to improve speed and efficiency, do their data transfers a whole data buffer full at a time.

From this, it should come as no surprise that there are also basically two kinds of device driver called *character device drivers* and *block device drivers*. The major difference between the two is that system calls involving character devices are almost directly associated with functions inside the device driver, whereas reads and writes to block devices interact primarily with the buffer cache mechanism, only calling block device driver routines when it is necessary to perform physical input and output. Figure 24.1 shows how these pieces fit together.

Generally, a different device driver is required for each type of device that needs to be controlled. So, for example, there is a device driver to control floppy disks and it knows how to interface with all the standard floppy disk types and sizes. Indeed, if you had a system with more than one floppy disk drive installed then the

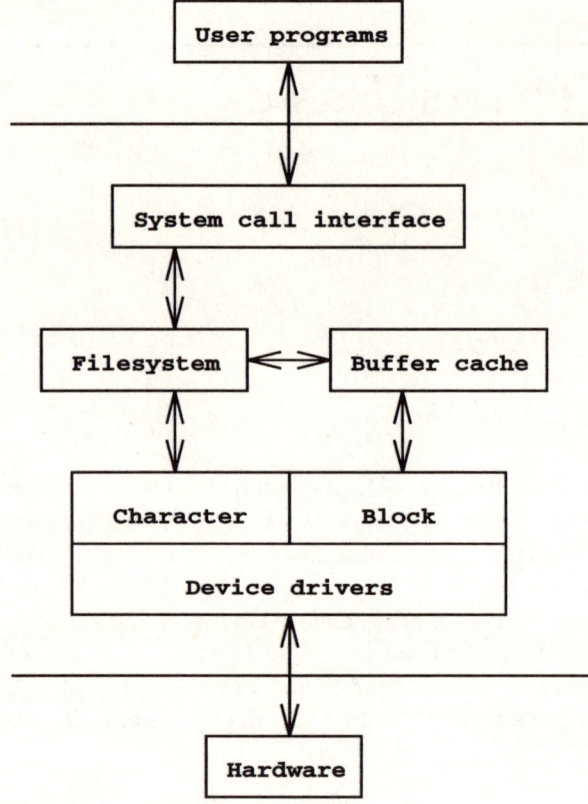

Figure 24.1 User programs access hardware via device drivers.

same device driver would be used for them all.

The main functions of a Linux device driver are:

- setting up hardware on initialization;
- bringing the associated devices into and out of service;
- receiving data from the hardware and passing it back to the kernel;
- sending data from the kernel to the device;
- detecting and handling device errors.

In order to access a device you need to be able to treat it like a file. This means that there must be a file name for all devices in the directory hierarchy somewhere, so that you can use the open(), close(), etc., system calls on them.

These files are called *character device special files* and *block device special files* and, by convention, they are stored in the directory /dev. Some of the files in that directory might be:

```
brw-rw----  1 root    floppy  2,  0 Jul 18  1994 fd0
brw-rw----  1 root    floppy  2,  1 Jul 18  1994 fd1
brw-rw----  1 root    disk    3,  0 Jul 18  1994 hda
brw-rw----  1 root    disk    3,  1 Jul 18  1994 hda1
brw-rw----  1 root    disk    3,  2 Jul 18  1994 hda2
brw-rw----  1 root    disk    3,  3 Jul 18  1994 hda3
brw-rw----  1 root    disk    3,  4 Jul 18  1994 hda4
crw-rw----  1 root    daemon  6,  0 Jul 18  1994 lp0
crw-rw-rw-  1 root    sys     1,  3 Jul 18  1994 null
crw-rw-rw-  1 root    tty     5,  0 Jul 18  1994 tty
crw--w--w-  1 pc      book    4,  0 Jul 18  1994 tty0
crw--w--w-  1 pc      book    4,  1 Aug 30 15:16 tty1
```

Notice that these files have a type, given by the first character on each line, of either c or b, meaning character or block special file respectively. Also notice that the special files have a pair of comma-separated numbers just before the date, where ordinary files would display their file size. The first of these two numbers is called the *major device number* of the device and the second number is called the *minor device number* of the device.

The major device numbers for block and character devices are used to identify the particular device driver whose internal functions will be called to deal with I/O requests for this device. The minor device number will be made available to the device driver routines and will be used by them to identify to which particular device the current I/O request relates. For example, the previous listing shows both floppy disk 0 and floppy disk 1 (fd0 and fd1) to have block major device number 2. This identifies the device driver to call when I/O requests are taken for /dev/fd0 and /dev/fd1. Inside the device driver the minor device numbers (0 for fd0 and 1 for fd1) will be used to tell the two drives apart.

24.1.1 The mknod Command

The device special files are created with the mknod command (or the mknod() system call). Only root can create these files. The general form of the mknod command is:

    mknod filename type major minor

Where *filename* is the path to the special file to be created, *type* is either c or b for character or block files respectively, and *major* and *minor* are the major and minor device numbers to associate with the file. For example:

    # mknod /dev/mytty1 c 4 1

will create the character special file /dev/mytty1 with major device number four and minor device number zero. As this major/minor combination already exists (/dev/tty1) all that this command has done is to create an alternative special file which may be used to access the same device.

24.2 Device Driver Routines

When you try to open() a device special file it will cause an open() function in the associated device driver to be called. The way that this works is that each device driver is just a collection of functions that you write to perform a set of specific tasks. Associated with each device driver is a data structure called struct file_operations, which contains a set of pointers to most of the main functions in your device driver.

When the system boots, an initialization function in each device driver is called by the kernel. One of the tasks performed by this function is to tell the kernel which major device number this device driver will use. At the same time, the initialization function will pass to the kernel a pointer to the structure of function addresses contained within the driver.

The file_operations structure contains many elements, only some of which will be required for most drivers. The full structure appears as follows, showing a collection of pointers to functions:

```
struct file_operations {
    int (*lseek)();
    int (*read)();
    int (*write)();
    int (*readdir)();
    int (*select)();
    int (*ioctl)();
    int (*mmap)();
    int (*open)();
    void (*release)();
    int (*fsync)();
    int (*fasync)();
    int (*check_media_change)();
    int (*revalidate)();
};
```

Here, there are obvious entry points for open(), read() and write(), though some others are less obvious. I'll describe the entry points in more detail when we need them.

Inside the kernel there are two tables, one for character device drivers and one for block device drivers. The tables are used to hold pointers to file_operations structures with the device driver function addresses stored in them. The major device numbers are used as an index to the appropriate table to access the file_operations structure associated with that major device number, and thus allow the kernel access to the addresses of the routines within the driver.

24.3 Device Driver Principles

So far, you have seen how the kernel can identify which set of device driver functions are the appropriate ones to call for operations on a particular device special file. Now we'll look at some of the more general aspects of device drivers, including their relationship to the user processes that call them.

When a process is actually running on the CPU, Linux treats it as the *current* process. When the current process executes a system call that results in the execution of a device driver internal function, the context of the current process is still available even within the device driver routines. This makes it a relatively simple task to copy data to buffers in the process from buffers in the device driver, and vice-versa.

Sometimes, calls to device driver functions will require input or output to a piece of hardware, like a disk drive. In these circumstances, the hardware operates orders of magnitude slower than the CPU. If steps weren't taken to do something about it, these I/O bursts would dramatically slow the system down as the CPU waited for the I/O to complete. In reality, the CPU is not expected to wait for the hardware I/O to finish. What happens is that the I/O is scheduled to take place and then the current process suspends its execution, thus allowing other processes to get on with some useful work while the first process waits for its I/O to happen.

Obviously, some mechanism needs to be provided to resume the suspended process once its I/O has taken place. This mechanism is called `interrupts`. Interrupts are to the kernel what signals are to user processes except that interrupts are generated by hardware events. Just like signals, interrupts can be caught and can be made to cause special service routines to execute to deal with the condition that caused the interrupt.

When some I/O takes place for which a process is waiting, an interrupt can be generated which executes the associated interrupt service routine. It is part of the task of the interrupt service routine to resume any processes that were suspended waiting for the completion of this I/O event to take place.

Care must be taken inside the interrupt service routine, however, as the CPU has moved on to execute other processes so that when the interrupt (a strictly asynchronous event) takes place and the service routine executes, the kernel will not be executing in the context of the suspended process. This means that the interrupt service routine must not try to perform any operation which requires access to the context of the suspended process as this is not immediately available.

Another point to bear in mind when you write a device driver is that the driver will run as an integral part of the operating system kernel and that the kernel cannot be preempted. What this means is that, unlike ordinary user processes, there is no mechanism in the kernel to force a kernel routine to relinquish control of the CPU in favor of some other routine. The only way that kernel routines terminate is if they return at the end of the function or if they voluntarily give up the CPU in favor of some other process by suspending the current process on whose behalf they are running.

Whenever you add code to the Linux kernel you must always be aware that Linux will trust your new code completely. This means that if your code goes into an infinite loop then the kernel will effectively just 'hang' as far as all the other processes on the system are concerned. Even if your kernel code is logically correct, if it is inefficient in its use of the CPU, memory or hardware it can still cause major system performance penalties.

These are the main things to keep in mind as we go on to look at character device drivers.

Chapter 25

Character Device Drivers

In this chapter we will look at the basics of character device drivers. We are going to look at character device drivers first because it is much easier to write a simple character device driver than it is to write a simple block device driver, although, by the time you get on to writing a serious device driver for a new piece of hardware it doesn't matter which type you are working on, they are equally complex. As the operation of a serious device driver is very hardware specific it would not make a particularly good example to work through. To start with we shall be more concerned with the principles involved rather than hardware specifics.

A device driver is just a collection of routines with various specific tasks to perform. Each device driver has essentially the same set of routines and so some mechanism is required to prevent name clashes between drivers. A simple mechanism is to make all the names unique. This is done by choosing a simple unique prefix for each device driver which will be added to the start of all the function names in the driver. This means that even though most device drivers will provide an open() routine, for instance, the prefix for each driver will make all the open() routine names unique within the kernel.

25.1 Registering Character Devices

Each device driver gets the opportunity to initialize itself and its hardware at system boot time. For character device drivers, this is achieved by having an initialization function (init()) in the driver and then placing a call to this function into the kernel chr_dev_init() function. The chr_dev_init() function is contained in the file:

    /usr/src/linux/drivers/char/mem.c

assuming that your kernel sources are in the default location /usr/src/linux.

Suppose your device driver has the name prefix `tdd_`, then the `init()` routine would be called `tdd_init()`. For kernels up to 1.1.32 you would need to add the line:

```
mem_start = tdd_init(mem_start);
```

to the end of the `chr_dev_init()` function just before the `return mem_start;` line.

For kernels from 1.1.33 onwards you would need to add the line:

```
tdd_init();
```

to the end of the `chr_dev_init()` function just before the `return 0;` line.

One of the main jobs performed by the driver `init()` function is to register the device driver with the kernel. This involves telling the kernel which major device number the driver will use and also giving the kernel a pointer to the driver's `file_operations` structure so that the kernel can enter this pointer in the appropriate character driver table entry. The registration is performed by calling the kernel's `register_chrdev()` function as follows:

```
register_chrdev(major, name, file_op)
```

where *major* is the major device number to be used by this driver (or zero to get the kernel to allocate a free major number), *name* is a string that gives the name of the driver, and *file_op* is a pointer to the driver's `file_operations` structure.

The return value from `register_chrdev()` is negative if the registration is unsuccessful. If *major* is given as zero and the registration is successful then the function returns the kernel allocated major device number. If *major* is specified and the registration is successful then the value zero is returned.

As you will see in the next section, for kernels up to 1.1.32, the `mem_start` parameter value passed into the driver's `init()` function can be used to allocate some working memory for the driver to use during its execution.

25.2 Working Storage

Very often a device driver will need some internal working storage space to keep temporary values during its execution. This can range from a few bytes just to store some internal variables, to large numbers of data buffers where a lot of data needs to be stored in transit, perhaps for several device special files which may be open at the same time.

Linux makes several different data buffering techniques available to the device driver writer, each of which has its own advantages and disadvantages.

25.2.1 Private Buffers

The simplest way to allocate memory to a device driver is just to declare a variable in the driver source code which is the required number of bytes in size. So, for instance, if you need an 800-byte buffer for some reason, to be used for working storage, this could just be declared in the code as a global array:

```
static char buffer[800];
```

The use of the keyword `static` outside any of the functions means that the buffer will only be visible to the code contained in the same file as the declaration (i.e. just to this device driver).

The use of private buffers like this has several disadvantages:

- The memory allocated in this way cannot be used anywhere except within this driver.
- The amount of memory cannot be increased if it should happen that your estimate of the amount required proves to be insufficient.
- The block of memory is allocated for your use even if it will not be used – perhaps the hardware device isn't even connected.

25.2.2 mem_start

The last of these problems can be overcome by using another memory allocation mechanism – `mem_start`. This is a Linux specific memory allocation mechanism used at system boot time, when a device driver's `init()` function is called, though, for kernels from 1.1.33 onwards, this technique is no longer available.

The value `mem_start` is a pointer to the start of available memory. This value is passed as a parameter into your device driver's `init()` function. When the `init()` function terminates, it is expected to return the same thing – a pointer to the start of available memory. This gives `init()` the opportunity to grab some system memory for use by the driver, just by adding the required memory size to the `mem_start` value received as a parameter and then returning this new value back to the kernel instead.

So, the sequence now is that when the `init()` function has successfully registered the device driver and its major device number, and tested that the hardware is present, it should then add to the `mem_start` value the size, in bytes, of any memory buffers the driver will need.

The new value of `mem_start` is then returned by the `init()` function and the block of memory of the required size starting at the old `mem_start` address is then reserved for the sole use of the driver.

The obvious advantages of this over straight private buffers are that the memory block need not be allocated if the hardware is not present or if the driver could not be registered, and that these decisions are left until system boot time so that each time the system is booted the outcome may be different.

Using this technique still has the disadvantage that memory allocation is a 'one-off' operation, meaning that no extra memory can be allocated after the initial block is taken and also that the block of memory cannot be released even if the driver has no further use for it.

25.2.3 kmalloc Function

To overcome these problems what is required is a kernel version of the dynamic memory allocation scheme provided to user processes by the library functions malloc() and free.

This functionality is provided in the kernel by the kmalloc() and kfree() functions. The prototype for kmalloc() is:

```
void *kmalloc(size_t size, int priority);
```

where *size* is the number of bytes of memory you want to have allocated, and the return value is a pointer to the start of the allocated memory or a zero pointer on error.

The *priority* parameter requires a little explanation. Basically, it is possible when you make a request for a particular block of memory that the kmalloc() function will be unable to comply immediately. However, if you are prepared for your driver routines to sleep while the memory is made available, usually by rearranging some memory pages via swap space, then kmalloc() can usually satisfy your request eventually.

If you are prepared to wait when necessary then the *priority* value GFP_KERNEL should be used. In situations where an indeterminate-length wait would be unacceptable (and there are some) then the *priority* value GFP_ATOMIC should be used instead. In this case, if kmalloc() is unable to satisfy your request immediately then it will return with the value zero.

An important case where you need to have the GFP_ATOMIC *priority* available is where you need to call kmalloc() from within an interrupt service routine. This is because, as a general rule, you must not allow your interrupt service routines to sleep.

Another option is that you might want to make sure that it is possible to do DMA transfers into the memory block returned by kmalloc(). On many machines this isn't a problem but on some PCs DMA transfers can only occur in the first 16 Mbytes of memory. To make sure it isn't a problem you just need to OR the value GFP_DMA into the *priority* value and kmalloc() will return a memory block guaranteed to be usable for DMA transfers.

Using kmalloc(), blocks of up to 128 KB of memory can be allocated (actually, a few bytes less than this because of administrative overhead).

Memory allocated with `kmalloc()` can be released back to the system with `kfree_s()`, whose prototype is:

```
void kfree_s(void *ptr, int size);
```

where *ptr* is a pointer value, previously returned by `kmalloc()` and *size* is the size of the memory block being freed, in bytes. The *size* value should be the same as the size parameter passed to `kmalloc()` when the memory was allocated. If the size of the memory block is unknown for some reason, then `kfree_s()` can be called with a *size* parameter of zero, in which case it will use an internal search to find the size.

Rather than call `kfree_s()` with a zero *size* parameter, there is a Linux macro, defined in `<linux/malloc.h>` called `kfree()`:

```
#define kfree(n) kfree_s((n), 0)
```

25.2.4 vmalloc

Blocks of memory allocated by `kmalloc()` are physically contiguous, as required in some hardware applications. Where this constraint can be relaxed, a relatively new memory allocation function can be used instead:

```
void *vmalloc(unsigned long size);
```

where *size* is the required memory block size, in bytes. The function returns a pointer to the allocated memory block or zero on error.

The memory supplied by `vmalloc()` cannot be used for DMA transfers, nor can `vmalloc()` be called from within an interrupt service routine.

Any memory blocks allocated with `vmalloc()` can be released back to the system with `vfree()`:

```
void vfree(void *ptr);
```

where *ptr* is a pointer value returned by a previous `vmalloc()` call.

As you can see, these last two memory allocation techniques overcome all the disadvantages of the private buffer and `mem_start` methods and they should be used in preference in any serious device driver you write.

25.3 Basic Entry Points

Having now seen how to register your character device drivers with the kernel, and how to allocate memory for use within a driver, we now turn our attention to the main entry points into the driver, whose addresses will appear in the driver's `file_operations` structure.

The main system calls for use with a character device or file are: `open()`, `close()`, `read()`, `write()` and `ioctl()`. Each of these system calls, when it has been established that they are intended for your driver, can result in the appropriate driver function being executed.

25.3.1 open Function

The driver's `open()` function is called when a user process executes an `open()` system call on a device special file associated with this driver. The `open()` function has the prototype:

```
int open(struct inode *inode, struct file *file);
```

where the *inode* parameter is a pointer to the inode structure of the device special file which was accessed, and *file* is a pointer to the file structure for this device.

Typical actions for the `open()` function are:

- Determine that the associated hardware (if any) is available and on-line.
- Verify that the minor device number in `MINOR(inode->i_rdev)` is valid (i.e. in the expected range).
- If only one process should be able to open the device at a time then `open()` should test and set a driver flag to busy the device, or return -EBUSY if the flag is already set.
- Return a negative value if any kind of error occurs.
- Return the value zero on success.

25.3.2 release Function

The driver's `release()` function is only called when the last user process which has the device open `close()`s it:

```
void release(struct inode *inode, struct file *file);
```

where *inode* is a pointer to the inode structure of the device special file, and *file* is a pointer to the file structure for this device.

The `release()` function may be required to:

- Perform cleanup actions if there is any unfinished I/O in progress.
- Release hardware resources if necessary.
- Reset any exclusive access flags set by `open()`.

25.3.3 read Function

The driver's `read()` function is called whenever a `read()` system call is executed on a device special file associated with this character device driver:

```
void read(struct inode *inode, struct file *file,
          char *buf, int count);
```

where *inode* is a pointer to the inode structure of the device special file, *file* is a pointer to the file structure for this device, *buf* is a pointer to a buffer in user space whose address was passed by the user process into the `read()` system call, and *count* is the number of bytes required by the user process (also passed into the `read()` system call).

The function of `read()` is to copy up to *count* bytes of data from the hardware device (if present) or allocated kernel memory, out to the buffer in user memory given by *buf*.

Care must be taken when performing the copy as the pointer in *buf* is an address located in user memory, not an address which can be used directly from within the kernel. In order to perform the copy correctly you should use one of several special copy functions provided specifically for this purpose. They are defined in `<asm/segment.h>`:

```
void put_user_byte(char data_byte, char *u_addr);
void put_user_word(short data_word, short *u_addr);
void put_user_long(long data_long, long *u_addr);
void memcpy_tofs(void *u_addr, void *k_addr, unsigned long cnt);
```

where, for the `put_user...()` functions, *data_byte*, *data_word* and *data_long* are the `char`, `short` and `long` values, respectively, to be copied into user space at address *u_addr* and, for `memcpy_tofs()`, *cnt* bytes will be copied from kernel space address *k_addr* to user space address *u_addr*.

For backward compatibility with older kernels (older is up to and including early 0.99), three other functions are provided:

```
void put_fs_byte(char data_byte, char *u_addr);
void put_fs_word(short data_word, short *u_addr);
void put_fs_long(long data_long, long *u_addr);
```

but these are exactly equivalent to the three previous `put_user_XXX` functions.

Additionally, if you are careful with your pointer types, all of these function calls can be replaced in newer kernels (newer is 1.3 and beyond) with a single call:

```
void put_user(type value, type *u_addr);
```

This call is implemented as a macro in `<asm/segment.h>`, whose expansion depends on the data `type` of the pointer parameter `u_addr`. The `type` of object that the u_addr pointer is pointing to is used to determine how many bytes of `value` to transfer to user memory space.

Before you use any of these functions to write into user memory, however, it is important for you to verify that the address in user space passed to you by the user process actually points to an area of memory to which the user has write access. This is done with the kernel's `verify_area()` function:

```
#include <linux/mm.h>

int verify_area(int access, void *u_addr, unsigned long size);
```

where *access* is one of `VERIFY_WRITE` or `VERIFY_READ` depending on whether you wish to write to or read from the user memory, *u_addr* is the start address in user space and *size* is the size in bytes of the memory block to be accessed.

The `verify_area()` function returns the value zero if the specified access is permitted or `-EFAULT` on error.

25.3.4 write Function

The `write()` function in the driver is called whenever a `write()` system call is performed on a device special file belonging to this driver:

```
void write(struct inode *inode, struct file *file,
           char *buf, int count);
```

where *inode* is a pointer to the special file's inode structure, *file* is a pointer to the file structure, *buf* is a pointer to a buffer in user space, passed into the `write()` system call, from which user characters will be written, and *count* is the number of bytes to transfer (also passed into the `write()` system call).

The purpose of the device driver's `write()` function is to copy up to *count* bytes of data from the buffer *buf* in user space out to the hardware (if applicable) or the internal buffer.

As with `read()`, the value in *buf* is an address in user space and so, again, one of the following special functions should be used to perform the copy operation:

```
unsigned char get_user_byte(char *u_addr);
unsigned short get_user_word(short *u_addr);
unsigned long get_user_long(long *u_addr);
void memcpy_fromfs(void *k_addr, void *u_addr, unsigned long cnt);
```

where the `get_user...()` functions return the `char`, `short` or `long` value contained at the user space address *u_addr* and for `memcpy_fromfs()`, *cnt* bytes will be copied to kernel space address *k_addr* from user space address *u_addr*.

Again, for backward compatibility with older kernels, three other functions are provided:

```
unsigned char get_fs_byte(char *u_addr);
unsigned short get_fs_word(short *u_addr);
unsigned long get_fs_long(long *u_addr);
```

that are equivalent to the three previous `get_user_XXX` functions.

Newer kernels also support the single call:

```
type get_user(type *u_addr);
```

which is implemented as a macro in `<asm/segment.h>` whose expansion depends on the data type of the pointer parameter `u_addr`. The `type` of object that the `u_addr` pointer is pointing to is used to determine how many bytes of data to transfer from user memory space and also the return `type` of the `get_user()` call itself.

Just as in the case of the device driver's `read()` function, you should arrange to call the `verify_area()` function before using any of the previous functions to read from user memory.

25.4 Special Control Functions

In addition to the basic open, close, read and write operations, you have also seen that sometimes it is desirable to send control information to the device driver or to take status information from it. For example, changing the baud rate on a serial port does not lend itself to being performed by the basic open, close, read, write paradigm. In this case (and many others like it) you have seen that the solution is to use the `ioctl()` system call. This system call is implemented by just calling an `ioctl()` function in the device driver to deal with it.

This is necessary because different device drivers will not all want to implement the same functions – there are many devices for which trying to change the baud rate would make no sense.

The device driver `ioctl()` function has the prototype:

```
int ioctl(struct inode *inode, struct file *file,
    unsigned int cmd, unsigned long arg);
```

where *inode* and *file* are the same as before, *cmd* is a device driver specific code for the command to be performed and *arg* is any kind of 4-byte thing (typically an `int` or a `struct *`) which provides a parameter for the particular *cmd* value. The *cmd* and *arg* parameters are obtained from the second and third parameters to the `ioctl()` system call.

Don't forget that if the *arg* parameter is a pointer to a block of memory in user space then you must use the special copy functions we looked at earlier to put and get values to and from this memory block.

In general, you are free to use any numbers you wish for *cmd* values, except that Linux uses four special values which it interprets before your `ioctl()` routine gets called:

FIONBIO	0x5421	set/reset O_NONBLOCK from *arg*;
FIONCLEX	0x5450	clear close-on-exec flag;
FIOCLEX	0x5451	set close-on-exec flag;
FIOASYNC	0x5452	set/reset O_SYNC from *arg*.

If you use any of these four *cmd* values for your own `ioctl()` commands then your routines will never be called because the kernel gets to them first.

25.5 Interrupts

In addition to the functions accessed via the `file_operations` structure, a device driver can also supply an `interrupt()` service routine. This will only be required where there is underlying hardware involved, capable of generating an interrupt signal.

In much the same way as you need to register your device driver with the kernel so that access to device special files with your major device number will call your driver's routines, you also need to request that the kernel associates a particular interrupt request line (IRQ) with your interrupt service routine, so that when the interrupt occurs, your routine will get called. This is done with the `request_irq()` function:

```
#include <linux/signal.h>

int request_irq(unsigned int irq, void (*handler)(int),
                unsigned long type, char *name);
```

where *irq* is the interrupt (IRQ) number you are trying to register, *handler* is a pointer to the interrupt service routine, *type* is a flag which specifies whether this should be a normal or fast interrupt, and *name* is the name of your device driver.

The difference between a normal and fast interrupt is that, on return from executing a normal interrupt routine, the kernel can take the opportunity to run the scheduler (via a call to the kernel `schedule()` function) to see if there is a more appropriate process to execute than the current one. If there is, then the current process will be preempted and the new process will run instead. In the case of a fast interrupt this scheduling is not performed so that the interrupted process will be resumed when the interrupt service routine returns.

The values for *type* are zero for normal interrupts and the symbolic constant `SA_INTERRUPT` for fast interrupts.

Interrupt handlers can also be un-registered by use of the `free_irq()` function:

```
void free_irq(unsigned int irq);
```

where *irq* is the IRQ number to free.

25.6 Device Driver Installation

Once you have your device driver written, the next task is to have it compiled and installed into a bootable kernel. This is actually quite a straightforward task, performed in a few simple steps as follows:

- The first job is to copy your *driver.c* file and any associated *driver.h* file into the directory which contains the source code for character device drivers. This is in `drivers/char` under the top level Linux source directory.
- Next, you should add a call to your driver's `init()` routine to the end of the function `chr_dev_init()` in the file `drivers/char/mem.c`.
- Now edit the `Makefile` in the `drivers/char` directory and add your *driver.o* name to the end of the definition for `OBJS` and your *driver.c* name to the end of the definition for `SRCS`.
- Now change directory to the top level Linux source directory and just build and install your new kernel using the steps described back in Section 7.4.

If you use `lilo` to boot your system, it is a good idea to treat your new kernel as experimental and generate an extra Linux boot section in the `lilo.conf` file so that you can still boot from your old kernel if the new one fails to boot or fails to perform correctly for some reason.

As a general precaution when modifying kernel code, it is always advisable to make a backup of anything on your machine that you do not feel prepared to lose. The chances are that, for most problems, either the new code will just not work or it will cause the kernel to panic. In general, neither of these events will cause any lasting damage to your system, especially if you can reboot your machine from the old kernel. However, in theory, it is possible for bugged kernel code to do absolutely anything, including scrapping data on your hard disk. So, it is always better to be safe than sorry.

Chapter 26

Tiny Device Driver – Case Study

In order to make some of the material we have now covered on device drivers a little more concrete we'll work through a simple example character device driver. The specification for the device driver we are going to develop may seem a bit artificial but it does allow you to see several interesting ideas put into practice.

The specification is as follows – Implement a character device driver which uses two device special files to allow a pair of processes to send short variable-length text messages to each other. The driver should make sure that multiple readers and multiple writers are not permitted and also that `read()`s will not block even when there are no messages to read and that `write()`s will not block however many messages are written before the next `read()` occurs.

I should point out straight away that this last requirement, about unlimited write capacity, is dangerous as it is possible for some kind of error to stop the consumer process from reading any data. This leaves the producer process writing messages unchecked until, eventually, the system runs out of space to store them. In fact, for long lived processes there doesn't even need to be any kind of error for this problem to occur eventually. All that is required is that, on average, the producer is generating messages faster than the consumer can use them up. With this in mind, it might be sensible to set some arbitrary, but large, limit on the number of messages that can be stored simultaneously within the device driver. I leave this safety check as a coding exercise for you to add later.

In effect, this device driver is just going to control some system memory as its 'hardware device' and effectively provide an extra IPC mechanism in addition to those already available. The IPC semantics provided by this new driver, however, are quite different from those available with the existing IPC mechanisms.

26.1 Header Information

In order to implement the requirements of the specification, the first task is to decide what the device driver's internal data structures will look like. What is required is that the device driver should be capable of storing a number of short text messages which are in transit between two processes. The number of messages the driver is required to hold is supposed to be infinite (infinite on a computer usually means 'until you run out') but in practice it would probably only hold a few messages until they could be read. This means that you really want to use a variable number of dynamically allocated buffers which can be built up into a FIFO queue which is best implemented as a linked list. This will require a kernel mechanism for the dynamic allocation and release of blocks of memory.

Note that the standard library `malloc()` and `free()` functions cannot be used because the standard library is not available from within the kernel. As you will see, however, there is a kernel equivalent to `malloc()` which can be used instead.

The structure from which the linked list of messages will be built has the following layout:

```
struct tdd_buf
{
    int buf_size;
    char buffer[MAX_BUF];
    struct tdd_buf *link;
};
```

where `buffer[]` is the array that holds one of the short messages, `buf_size` says how many characters in the `buffer[]` array are in use, and `link` is the linked list pointer to the next `tdd_buf`. The symbolic constant `MAX_BUF` can be set to whatever matches your idea of the maximum length of a 'short' message. My default is 120 characters.

Notice that the prefix used in the tiny device driver to make its identifiers unique will be `tdd_`, though many of the identifiers are declared to be `static` so that they will not be visible outside the source file for the driver anyway.

Bearing this in mind, the tiny device driver header information is as follows:

```
/* 1 */
#define KERNEL

#include <linux/kernel.h>
#include <linux/sched.h>
#include <linux/tty.h>
#include <linux/signal.h>
#include <linux/errno.h>
#include <linux/malloc.h>

#include <asm/io.h>
```

```c
#include <asm/segment.h>
#include <asm/system.h>
#include <asm/irq.h>

#include "tdd.h"

/* 2 */
static int tdd_trace;
static int write_busy;
static int read_busy;
static struct tdd_buf *qhead;
static struct tdd_buf *qtail;

/* 3 */
static int tdd_read(struct inode *, struct file *, char *, int);
static int tdd_write(struct inode *, struct file *, char *, int);
static int tdd_ioctl(struct inode *, struct file *, unsigned int,
unsigned long);
static int tdd_open(struct inode *, struct file *);
static void tdd_release(struct inode *, struct file *);
extern void console_print(char *);

struct file_operations tdd_fops =
{
    NULL,
    tdd_read,
    tdd_write,
    NULL,
    NULL,
    tdd_ioctl,
    NULL,
    tdd_open,
    tdd_release,
    NULL,
    NULL,
    NULL,
    NULL
};
```

The following list refers to the numbered comments in the header information:

1. The first section includes all the relevant header files. Notice the definition of the KERNEL symbol; this is used in some header files (tdd.h included) conditionally to include extra items and definitions when the header file is being used within kernel code. Ordinary user code does not define this symbol and, therefore, does not include these extras.

2. These are the static variables used within the driver. The variable `tdd_trace` is used as a flag to turn on and off the debug trace output, `write_busy` and `read_busy` are flags used to prevent multiple writers or readers, and `qhead` and `qtail` are the head and tail pointers to the linked list of messages.
3. This section sets up the `file_operations` structure to point to the other device driver routines. A pointer to this structure will be passed into the kernel at boot time by the initialization routine. Function prototypes for otherwise undeclared kernel functions are also declared here.

Over and above this header code, there is also a header file called `tdd.h` which contains the `#defines` and structure declaration required by the device driver and also by user code wishing to use this driver:

```
#ifdef KERNEL                           /* If we're in kernel code */

#define TRACE_TXT(text) \
    { \
        if (tdd_trace) \
        { \
            console_print(text); \
            console_print("\n"); \
        } \
    }

#define TRACE_CHR(chr) \
    { \
        if (tdd_trace) \
            console_print(chr); \
    }

#define TDD_WRITE 0             /* /dev/tddw minor device number */
#define TDD_READ 1              /* /dev/tddr minor device number */

#endif

#define FALSE 0
#define TRUE 1
#define MAX_BUF 120             /* Size of struct tdd_buf buffer */
#define TDD_TRON  (('M'<<8)|0x01)   /* Trace on cmd for ioctl() */
#define TDD_TROFF (('M'<<8)|0x02)   /* Trace off cmd for ioctl() */

struct tdd_buf
{
    int buf_size;
    char buffer[MAX_BUF];
    struct tdd_buf *link;
};
```

The only things here which require some explanation are the macro definitions for TRACE_TXT() and TRACE_CHR(). These are provided to give a very simple trace facility for debugging purposes. At various strategic locations throughout the device driver code, calls to these macros are inserted so that 'got here' type messages can be displayed on the machine's console terminal. Trace messages are displayed on the console screen using the kernel's internal function: console_print(). The display of trace messages is controlled by the state of a flag variable whose value can be set or reset via an appropriate ioctl() call. The two commands to ioctl() dealt with by the driver are TDD_TRON to turn tracing on and TDD_TROFF to turn it off again. Neither of these ioctl() commands takes any other parameters.

26.2 init Function

Moving on into the driver code proper, the first thing to look at is the initialization function, tdd_init():

```
void tdd_init(void)
{
    tdd_trace = TRUE;

    if (register_chrdev(30, "tdd", &tdd_fops))
        TRACE_TXT("Cannot register tdd driver as major device 30")
    else
        TRACE_TXT("Tiny device driver registered successfully")

    qhead = 0;
    write_busy = FALSE;
    read_busy = FALSE;
    tdd_trace = FALSE;
    return;
}
```

This routine is executed at system boot time. Remember that a call to the routine needs to be added to the chr_dev_init() function in the file:

/usr/src/linux/drivers/char/mem.c

assuming your kernel source is stored in /usr/src/linux.

When tdd_init() is executed it calls the kernel function register_chrdev() to add its file_operations structure to the character device routine address table. A message is displayed on the machine console, using the debug trace facility, to report the success or failure of this operation. The routine then initializes the driver's static variables and finally returns.

26.3 open Function

The device driver's open function (`tdd_open()`) is called whenever an `open()` system call is performed on one of the two device special files associated with this driver:

```
static int tdd_open(struct inode *inode, struct file *file)
{
    TRACE_TXT("tdd_open")

    /* 1 */
    switch (MINOR(inode->i_rdev))
    {
    /* 2 */
    case TDD_WRITE:
        if (write_busy)
            return -EBUSY;
        else
            write_busy = TRUE;
            return 0;

    /* 3 */
    case TDD_READ:
        if (read_busy)
            return -EBUSY;
        else
            read_busy = TRUE;
            return 0;

    default:
        return -ENXIO;
    }
}
```

If there were any hardware involved with the device driver then this routine would arrange to bring it into service. As it is, our routine just manages the semantic requirement that the associated device special files may only be opened once each, as follows:

1. The first task is to pick out the minor device number for the device special file associated with this `open()` call. This can be extracted by the `MINOR()` macro from the `i_rdev` field in the structure pointed to by the `inode` parameter.
2. If the device special file is `TDD_WRITE` (i.e. `/dev/tddw`) then the `write_busy` flag is checked to see if this device is already open. If it is then an `EBUSY` error is returned; otherwise the flag is set to TRUE to busy the device against further `open()` calls and a zero value is returned, indicating no errors.

3. Similarly, if this is an open() request for /dev/tddr (using TDD_READ) then the read_busy flag is checked and, if necessary, set to ensure exclusive access to the device special file.

26.4 release Function

The release function, tdd_release(), is called when the last process that is holding open each of the device special files associated with this device driver closes it with a close() call. In fact, since only one process at a time can open each of the device special files for this driver, then a close() from this process will also call the driver release routine (tdd_release()):

```
static void tdd_release(struct inode *inode, struct file *file)
{
    TRACE_TXT("tdd_release")

    switch (MINOR(inode->i_rdev))
    {
    case TDD_WRITE:
            write_busy = FALSE;
            return;

    case TDD_READ:
            read_busy = FALSE;
            return;
    }
}
```

All that tdd_release() does is to reset the appropriate read or write busy flag, ready for the next open() operation to take place on the device special file.

26.5 write Function

The write function, tdd_write(), is called every time a process uses the write() system call on an open file descriptor associated with one of the device special files belonging to this device driver:

```
static int tdd_write(struct inode *inode, struct file *file,
char *buffer, int count)
{
    int i, len;
    struct tdd_buf *ptr;
```

```
    TRACE_TXT("tdd_write")

    /* 1 */
    if (MINOR(inode->i_rdev)!=TDD_WRITE)
        return -EINVAL;

    /* 2 */
    if ((ptr = kmalloc(sizeof(struct tdd_buf), GFP_KERNEL))==0)
        return -ENOMEM;

    /* 3 */
    len = count<MAX_BUF?count:MAX_BUF;

    if (verify_area(VERIFY_READ, buffer, len))
        return -EFAULT;

    for (i = 0; i<count && i<MAX_BUF; ++i)
    {
        ptr->buffer[i] = get_user_byte(buffer+i);
        TRACE_CHR("w")
    }

    /* 4 */
    ptr->link = 0;

    if (qhead==0)
        qhead = ptr;
    else
        qtail->link = ptr;

    qtail = ptr;
    TRACE_CHR("\n")

    /* 5 */
    ptr->buf_size = i;
    return i;
}
```

The third and fourth parameters to tdd_write() are the buffer and character count passed by the user process into the write() system call. The contents of this buffer need to be copied into the device driver's internal linked list of messages. Remember, though, that you cannot access the user space memory directly via the *buffer* parameter to tdd_write(); you have to use one of the special data transfer functions for that job. The numbered comments in the listing are as follows:

1. Check and ensure that only the process with /dev/tddw open writes messages.

2. Allocate a block of kernel memory large enough for a single message. Check to make sure there are no problems and return an error if necessary.
3. Verify that the kernel can read from the specified memory block, then copy count or BUF_MAX characters, whichever is the smaller, from user space into the kernel allocated message space.
4. Link the new message structure on to the end of the linked list in the device driver.
5. Set up the actual message length in the message structure and also return this value from tdd_write(). This value will also become the return value to the calling process from the write() system call.

26.6 read Function

The tdd_read function is called when a user process calls the read() system call to read from a device special file controlled by this device driver:

```
static int tdd_read(struct inode *inode, struct file *file,
char *buffer, int count)
{
    int i, len;
    struct tdd_buf *ptr;

    TRACE_TXT("tdd_read")

    /* 1 */
    if (MINOR(inode->i_rdev)!=TDD_READ)
        return -EINVAL;

    /* 2 */
    if (qhead==0)
        return -ENODATA;

    /* 3 */
    ptr = qhead;
    qhead = qhead->link;

    /* 4 */
    len = count<ptr->buf_size?count:ptr->buf_size;

    if (verify_area(VERIFY_WRITE, buffer, len))
        return -EFAULT;

    for (i = 0; i<count && i<ptr->buf_size; ++i)
    {
        put_user_byte(ptr->buffer[i], buffer+i);
```

```
        TRACE_CHR("r")
    }

    TRACE_CHR("\n")

    /* 5 */
    kfree_s(ptr, sizeof(struct tdd_buf));
    return i;
}
```

Once again, the *buffer* and *count* parameters into `tdd_read()` are a pointer to a buffer in user space and a character count which were passed as parameters into the associated `read()` system call, the obvious difference between this and the `tdd_write()` function being that this time the buffer is to receive characters from a message structure in the device driver. The numbered comments are:

1. Only `read()`s from `/dev/tddr` are permitted.
2. If there are no messages in the queue then the `read()` call will not block, but will return the value -1 with the variable `errno` set to the value `ENODATA`.
3. Unlink the head message from the queue and set the variable `ptr` to point to it.
4. Verify that the kernel can write to the specified memory block then copy either the number of characters asked for (`count`) or the actual number of characters in the message buffer (`ptr->buf_size`) whichever is the smaller, into the user space provided (`buffer`). It is the user's responsibility to ensure that the specified buffer is large enough to hold the requested number of characters – the kernel cannot do exhaustive checks.
5. Finally, free the old message structure back to the kernel and return the actual number of characters transferred.

26.7 `ioctl` Function

The `ioctl()` function for this driver is very simple but it does serve to illustrate the idea. Two new `ioctl()` calls are provided by this driver to switch the trace facilities on and off. This is done using the `TDD_TRON` and `TDD_TROFF` commands to `ioctl()` respectively:

```
static int tdd_ioctl(struct inode *inode, struct file *file,
unsigned int cmd, unsigned long arg)
{
    TRACE_TXT("tdd_ioctl")

    switch(cmd)
    {
```

```
        case TDD_TRON:
            tdd_trace = TRUE;
            return 0;

        case TDD_TROFF:
            tdd_trace = FALSE;
            return 0;

        default:
            return -EINVAL;
    }
}
```

The *cmd* and *arg* parameters to `tdd_ioctl()` are the same values as were passed in the user process to the `ioctl()` system call. In this case, the value of `arg` is not significant. Only the two values TDD_TRON and TDD_TROFF have any special significance to this driver and that is when they are used as *cmd* values. The only action performed by these `ioctl()` commands is to set and reset the `tdd_trace` flag.

Chapter 27

Block Device Drivers

Many of the ideas you have seen regarding character device drivers are also directly applicable to block device drivers. In this chapter, therefore, I will try to concentrate on the differences between the two.

Let me say to start with that creating block device drivers under Linux seems to be a much more fiddly affair altogether, with quite a large degree of reliance placed upon macro definitions which try to hide some of the underlying complexity but which, in doing so, make your code look like it contains many 'magic incantations' whose purpose is not immediately apparent.

27.1 Block Driver Concepts

Just as with character device drivers, a block device driver is a collection of routines that get called as various operations are performed on the devices controlled by the driver.

This list of functions includes any or all of: `open()`, `release()`, `ioctl()`, `interrupt()`, `init()` and `request()`. The first four of these have the same format and function as their character device driver counterparts.

The first thing to do when you come to write a block device driver is to choose a block major device number for your driver and add it to the file:

   `/usr/include/linux/major.h`

Contained in this file is a list of all the major device numbers used in the standard kernel and a symbolic name for each one. You should add a definition for a symbolic name and a major device number to the list. For example:

   `#define MY_MAJOR 30`

Once this is done you can begin to write your device driver code, which should start with lines like the following:

```
#include <linux/blkdev.h>

#define MAJOR_NR MY_MAJOR

#include "blk.h"
```

Notice the definition of `MAJOR_NR` to specify the major device number that this device driver will use. This definition needs to appear before the `#include "blk.h"` line, because the symbol will be used in the `blk.h` file, as you will see later. The definition of `MY_MAJOR` will automatically be included because `<linux/blkdev.h>` itself includes the file `<linux/major.h>`, which you just modified.

27.1.1 Buffer Cache

You have already seen that physical I/O to block devices is an expensive operation in terms of time, and one which is automatically avoided wherever possible. This is accomplished by using a portion of the system's memory as a buffering mechanism between process reads and writes and the device driver itself. This mechanism is the *buffer cache*.

What this means is that your block device driver should not contain a `read()` or a `write()` function, as a user process which calls either of the `read()` or `write()` system calls on a device special file controlled by your device driver will automatically have its request dealt with by the buffer cache mechanism instead.

Only when it is absolutely essential, will the buffer cache need to call your device driver to perform physical I/O. It does this by adding its I/O request to a queue of such requests for your device and then arranging for the `request()` function in your device driver to be called to deal with the queue of requests.

27.1.2 The request Routine

The `request()` routine, when called, has the task of reading each of the pending I/O requests in turn from the request queue and arranging to perform the physical read or write operations specified. Each I/O request in the queue is stored in a structure called `struct request`, which is defined in the file:

`/usr/include/linux/blkdev.h`

The general layout of a `request()` function in a device driver without an interrupt service routine is quite straightforward, as shown here:

```
static void do_my_request(void)
{
loop:
```

```
    INIT_REQUEST;

    if (MINOR(CURRENT->dev)>MY_MINOR_MAX)
    {
        end_request(0);
        goto loop;
    }

    if (CURRENT->cmd==READ)
    {
        end_request(my_read());
        goto loop;
    }

    if (CURRENT->cmd==WRITE)
    {
        end_request(my_write());
        goto loop;
    }

    end_request(0);
    goto loop:
}
```

The first thing to note here is that CURRENT is a pointer to the struct request at the head of the request queue. CURRENT is defined in the header file "blk.h".

The request() function begins with the INIT_REQUEST macro (also defined in "blk.h"), which checks to make sure that there is at least one request waiting in the queue. If there are no more requests (i.e. CURRENT==0) the INIT_REQUEST macro causes your request() function to return, with its task complete.

Assuming that there is at least one request in the queue, your request() function should now deal with the request at the head of the queue. When the request has been dealt with, your request() function should then call end_request().

If the I/O operation was completed successfully, the end_request() function should be called with a parameter value of 1. If the I/O was unsuccessful, a parameter value of zero should be used instead.

The end_request() function logs an error message if necessary, removes the processed request from the queue, arranges to restart any processes that were waiting for this I/O request to complete, and then sets CURRENT to point to the next request if there is one.

After the end_request() call, the request() function loops back to the start to repeat the process with the next request.

In our simple example, the processing of the requests themselves is handled in a very easy manner. Most of the work is based around the contents of the CURRENT request. The `request` structure layout is as follows:

```
struct request
{
    int dev;
    int cmd;
    int errors;
    unsigned long sector;
    unsigned long nr_sectors;
    unsigned long current_nr_sectors;
    char *buffer;
    struct semaphore *sem;
    struct buffer_head *bh;
    struct buffer_head *bhtail;
    struct request *next;
};
```

The main fields in this structure and the tasks that they perform are:

dev	specifies the physical device for this request;
cmd	command to perform (READ or WRITE);
sector	sector number to start the read or write;
nr_sectors	number of sectors to read or write;
buffer	kernel memory buffer for data read or written.

In processing a request, first, some kind of simple sanity check is performed to make sure that the CURRENT request specifies a valid physical device. If an error is detected at this point then the `end_request()` function is called with a zero parameter value.

If the device is valid, the value of CURRENT->cmd is used to call either the `my_read()` or `my_write()` function as appropriate. The return values from these two functions must be either 0 (if an error occurs) or 1 (if everything is okay), and these values are then passed straight into `end_request()` to terminate the CURRENT request with the correct value.

The `my_read()` and `my_write()` functions will use the `sector`, `nr_sectors` and `buffer` fields of the CURRENT structure to transfer the data as requested.

27.2 Registering Block Devices

Registering a block device driver is rather more complicated than the character device driver equivalent operation, as it requires some effort at kernel boot time, like characters drivers, but it also requires some kernel compile time additions.

27.2.1 Boot Time Registration

The boot time registration is performed by the driver's `init()` function which, for kernels from 1.1.33 on, has the prototype:

```
void my_init(void);
```

In order for the kernel to call your `init()` function at boot time, a line of code needs to be added to the kernel's `blk_dev_init()` function. This function is contained at the end of the file:

```
/usr/src/linux/drivers/block/ll_rw_blk.c
```

Your extra line of code should be inserted just before the `return 0;` line at the end of the `blk_dev_init()` function, and it should have the general format:

```
my_init();
```

When the kernel executes your `init()` function at boot time, it has to check that any required hardware exists and can be initialized and it also has to register the major device number that the driver will use, and at the same time, to pass to the kernel a pointer to the driver's `file_operations` structure.

The `file_operations` structure used for block device drivers is the same as the one for character devices, but some of the fields have fixed addresses inserted so that standard kernel routines get called, instead of calling your device driver functions. Typically, the structure might be filled in as follows:

```
struct file_operations my_fops =
{
    0,
    block_read,         /* kernel function */
    block_write,        /* kernel function */
    0,
    0,
    my_ioctl,    /* device driver function */
    0,
    my_open,     /* device driver function */
    my_release,  /* device driver function */
    block_fsync,        /* kernel function */
    0,
    0,
    0
};
```

The `block_read()`, `block_write()` and `block_fsync()` kernel functions should generally be called from all block device drivers. This means that you need not (and, indeed, should not) include these functions in your driver code. The example also shows that `ioctl()`, `open()` and `release()` functions can be called and need to be included in your driver.

Once you have decided which major device number your driver will use and set up its `file_operations` structure, the device driver can be registered with `register_blkdev()` function:

```
if (register_blkdev(MY_MAJOR, "my_bdev", &my_fops))
{
    printk("MY_BDEV: Unable to register device\n");
    return; /* return mem_start; for pre 1.1.33 kernels */
}
```

The first parameter to `register_blkdev()` is the major device number to be used for this driver, the second parameter is a name string for the device and the third parameter is a pointer to the `file_operations` structure. When used in this form, the function returns zero if all is well, or a negative value on error. If you specify a zero value for the major device number then `register_blkdev()` will search for a free device number and supply this as its return value instead.

You have already seen that when the kernel needs to perform physical I/O it will call your driver's `request()` function. However, the address of this function is not contained in the `file_operations` structure. So, another task of your driver's `init()` function is to inform the kernel of the address of the `request()` function. This is done by including the standard line of code:

```
blk_dev[MY_MAJOR].request_fn = DEVICE_REQUEST;
```

This assumes that you are using the major device number `MY_MAJOR`. The symbollic name `DEVICE_REQUEST` is defined to be the name (and hence address) of the driver's `request()` function (we'll look at where the definition for it is given, in a moment).

The final thing that the `init()` function needs to set up is information to tell the buffer cache the size of a data block (in bytes) on the devices controlled by your new driver:

```
my_block_size = 512;
blksize_size[MY_MAJOR] = &my_block_size;
```

Again, this stores the value in an array which is indexed on the major device number.

27.2.2 Compile Time Registration

Up to now, you still have not told the kernel where to find your `request()` function, except in terms of the symbol `DEVICE_REQUEST`. In order to complete the registration procedure you need to add this macro along with several others to the file "blk.h" in the block driver's source directory:

    /usr/src/linux/drivers/block

To do this, you need to find a line in that file which appears like:

    #endif /* MAJOR_NR == whatever */

and then, immediately before this line, you need to add the following set of macro definitions:

    #elif (MAJOR_NR==MY_MAJOR)

    static void do_my_request(void);

    #define DEVICE_NAME "My Block Driver"
    #define DEVICE_REQUEST do_my_request
    #define DEVICE_NR(device) (MINOR(device))
    #define DEVICE_ON(device)
    #define DEVICE_OFF(device)

It should be obvious by inspection that you are entering your block of code into the correct place in the file because it will end up immediately after similar blocks of macro definitions for other drivers.

The various macros are defined as follows:

DEVICE_NAME	short driver description string;
DEVICE_REQUEST	pointer to driver's request() function;
DEVICE_NR(d)	calculates physical device number from minor number;
DEVICE_ON(d)	used for devices that need to be turned on;
DEVICE_OFF(d)	used for devices that need to be turned off (floppy).

27.3 Interrupts

Associating an interrupt service routine with a particular interrupt request line is done in the same way for block device drivers as you have already seen for character device drivers – using the request_irq() function.

The general sequence of events for device drivers containing an interrupt service routine is as follows:

- A user process performs some kind of I/O request (say a read() system call) which eventually, perhaps via the buffer cache, requires some physical device I/O to take place.
- The device driver read() function, or perhaps the request() function, will then be called to send instructions to the hardware to perform the I/O operation. The device driver now needs to wait for the operation to take place.
- After some time, the hardware becomes ready to perform the specified operation and generates an interrupt to flag the fact.

- The interrupt causes your driver's interrupt service routine to be called, which then has the task of copying the requested data from the hardware into a device driver memory buffer, and informing the waiting `read()` (or `request()`) function that the data is now available.
- With the data available, the `read()` or `request()` function can now complete its task in making the data available to the user process.

This picture is a bit simplistic and needs to be tightened up in several places, but it does give a reasonable starting point. The main problems occur in three areas:

- What happens if an interrupt routine needs to change some data which other parts of the kernel might also want to change?
- What do the `read()`, `write()` and `request()` driver functions do while a hardware I/O request is taking place?
- Why don't interrupt routines just copy data directly to and from user space?

27.3.1 Critical Sections

When two sections of kernel code both need to access and modify particular kernel data structures, their efforts must be carefully coordinated if disastrous consequences are to be avoided. Nowhere is this more true than when an interrupt service routine is involved as one of the sections of kernel code which can make the changes.

Consider the following scenario:

> Some part of the kernel is making modifications to the structure of a linked list. A new node is being added to the list by breaking a link at the appropriate place in the list and adding the new element. At some point in this process the data structure could well be in an unstable state, where only part of the job has been completed and one or more pointers could be pointing to incorrect places. Normally, this doesn't matter because two or three statements later, when the addition is complete, everything has been restored to a stable state and it is safe for other code to use the list again. If, however, an interrupt were to occur while the list was unstable, and if the interrupt service routine then needed to access or modify the same list, then I'm sure you can see the potential for problems.

Problems of this nature come under the general heading of *critical sections*. In this context, critical section refers not to the data structure, but to the sections of code that make critical access to it. Obviously, the idea here is to guarantee the accuracy and integrity of the data.

Any code in the kernel that contains a critical section with respect to some kernel data structure, must have a mechanism available to allow it to protect itself from interruption at the times when its critical sections are executing.

When a critical section of code is identified, the standard technique for dealing with the problem is to disable interrupts for the duration of the critical section. Obviously, critical sections should be kept a short as possible so that interrupts are not delayed any longer than necessary. Interrupt requests can be enabled and disabled whenever necessary from within kernel code by the use of two special instructions:

```
#include <asm/system.h>

sti();
cli();
```

Both `sti()` and `cli()` are macros defined in `<asm/system.h>`. The `sti()` call is used to enable interrupt requests, while `cli()` disables requests.

27.3.2 sleep and wakeup

When an I/O request is made by a device driver function on a piece of hardware that can generate interrupts, the function must wait until the hardware completes its function, generates an interrupt, and the interrupt service routine has copied the data into memory. Only then can the original device driver function continue. It would be quite possible for the function just to enter a `while` loop of some kind looking for the interrupt service routine to complete its task. This, however, would be ridiculously inefficient in terms of processor use, especially since any amount of time might elapse before the requested data was finally made available.

The real problem here is that once a piece of code within the kernel gets control of the CPU, it stays in control until it gives up the processor voluntarily.

Don't forget that functions within a device driver get called as a result of a user process issuing a system call, so that these functions are actually executing in the kernel but on behalf of the user process. This means that nothing further will happen with the user process until its I/O request has been satisfied, and, therefore, that the process does not need to hang on to its control of the CPU. If the process was running in user code then control of the CPU would be taken from it automatically. As the process is running in kernel code it must give up control itself, to allow other processes to continue while it waits for its I/O to complete.

In order to release the CPU, the device driver function will call the `sleep_on()` function:

```
#include <linux/sched.h>

void sleep_on(struct wait_queue **ptr);
void interruptible_sleep_on(struct wait_queue **ptr);
```

As far as the function which calls it is concerned, a call to `sleep_on()` is just like a call to any other function, except that this call will not return until the event for which the function is waiting has occurred.

It is possible that more than one process may wish to wait for the same event to occur. This is handled in Linux by putting all the processes waiting for a particular event onto a single *wait queue*. A wait queue is actually a circular linked list of `struct wait_queue` nodes which is automatically built up by the `sleep_on()` function when it is called.

In order to start a new wait queue you need to declare a pointer to a wait queue node and initialize it to zero. The address of this pointer can then be passed to `sleep_on()`, which will add the current process to the wait queue, flag the process as sleeping so that the Linux scheduler will not choose this process to run, and then call the scheduler to pick the next process to run:

```
#include <linux/sched.h>

static struct wait_queue *p = 0;

sleep_on(&p);
```

If you use the `sleep_on()` call then only a `wake_up()` call on the same wait queue will wake it up. The `interruptible_sleep_on()` function is the same as the `sleep_on()` function except that sending signals or timeouts to the sleeping processes can also be used to wake them up.

When an event occurs (such as I/O ready) for which one or more processes are waiting, then a call to the `wake_up()` function with a particular wait queue as a parameter, will cause all the processes on that queue to be flagged as runnable again, so that the scheduler will consider them as eligible to run when next it is called:

```
#include <linux/sched.h>

void wake_up(struct wait_queue **ptr);
void wake_up_interruptible(struct wait_queue **ptr);
```

In the case of a device driver, the `wake_up()` call is usually issued by the interrupt service routine, after it has copied the required data into kernel memory.

Remember that a `wake_up()` call will resume *all* process sleeping on the specified wait queue. This can have some consequences if, for example, the event for which the processes are waiting is for some piece of hardware to become free so that they can write to it. In this case, the first one of the newly woken processes that gets to run will take the hardware device out of service again. This means that, even though the device was free when they were woken, by the time the other processes get to run again the device has become busy again. When this type of scenario is a possibility, it shows the need to re-test the device before it is used, and go back to sleep if it is busy – even if the process has only just been woken from a previous sleep.

The `wake_up_interruptible()` function is the same as the `wake_up()` function, except that it will only wake up the interruptible processes on the specified wait queue, whereas the `wake_up()` function will wake them all.

27.3.3 Memory Access

As you have seen, a process is made to sleep (the device driver calls `sleep_on()`) while it waits for physical I/O to take place, thus allowing other processes to use the CPU at this time. It follows, then, that when the interrupt occurs and the interrupt service routine runs, the service routine will not be running in the context of the process for which the data is eventually intended. Indeed, that process is sleeping, waiting to be woken at the end of the interrupt service routine.

Because the currently running process is definitely not the one for which the data is intended, under NO circumstances should the interrupt service routine copy the data from the hardware straight into user space. What the service routine should do is copy the data into a kernel memory buffer associated with the device driver and then wake up the sleeping process. This will cause the original `sleep_on()` call to return the next time that process runs. As this code is running in the correct context, it is then safe to copy the data to user space, but not before.

27.4 Timers

Usually, `sleep_on()` and `wake_up()` are used in the `read()`/`write()`/`request()` and interrupt functions respectively. However, some drivers do not have an interrupt routine but still need to sleep and be woken after some time delay.

There is an easy way to write a function to support this requirement in just a few lines of code:

```
#include <linux/sched.h>

extern unsigned long jiffies;

void my_delay(unsigned long jiffs)
{
    current->state = TASK_INTERRUPTIBLE;
    current->timeout = jiffies+jiffs;
    schedule();
}
```

The `jiffies` variable is globally declared and is a timer whose value is initialized at machine boot time and which is incremented 100 times per second (i.e. every 10 ms). The `jiffs` parameter to `my_delay()` should also be specified in 10 ms chunks.

It is also possible that, due to a hardware failure or similar cause, an expected interrupt never arrives. This could mean that a sleeping process may never get woken up. A solution in this case is to use a kernel timer via a pair of functions called add_timer() and del_timer() and a structure called struct timer_list:

```
struct timer_list
{
    struct timer_list *next, *prev;
    unsigned long expires, data;
    void (*function)(unsigned long);
};


void add_timer(struct timer_list *timer);
void del_timer(struct timer_list *timer);
```

The add_timer() call sets up a specified *function* to be executed at a given time (given in jiffies). The chosen function will be executed at the specified time unless the timer is canceled. If the event for which the process is waiting occurs normally, then the interrupt service routine can cancel the timer (with del_timer()). If the interrupt fails to occur for any reason, then the timer will expire and call the specified *function*. This will usually flag that the error has taken place and wake_up() the sleeping process to deal with it.

Part V
INTERNALS

Chapter 28

Process Scheduling

In a multi-tasking operating system, one of the most fundamental operations is process scheduling. In any system where you would like to be able to run multiple processes concurrently on a machine with a single processor, some form of process scheduling must take place. This is obvious when you consider that, at any particular instant, the CPU can only be executing a single instruction, and that on behalf of a single process. For several processes to be making progress on the machine together, the CPU time must be shared between the processes that are ready to run. The task of the scheduler, then, is to choose which of the processes that are ready to run should be allocated the CPU next.

28.1 Background

In trying to perform its task, the scheduler has various objectives that it must try to achieve. And, as we shall see, several of these objectives will make demands on the scheduler that will pull in opposite directions. Among the more important objectives are:

- Give each process a fair share of the CPU.
- Minimize the CPU idle time (i.e. keep the CPU busy).
- Maximize throughput. This means maximizing the number of processes completed in a given time.
- Minimize the time the system takes to respond to user requests.

An obvious way in which these objectives conflict is with regard to user requests. Here, it seems as though user requests should be favored in some way, though this obviously conflicts with the idea of giving all processes a fair share of the CPU.

One problem that the scheduler faces immediately is that, in general, very little is known about a process when it starts up. In particular, such things as how long the process will use the CPU on average before it has to stop to wait for some I/O to take place, and how long on average the process must wait for an I/O event to take place once it is requested, are unknown.

Another question is what to do with a process which uses a very large amount of CPU time before it does any I/O; can it be allowed just to go on hogging the processor? Well, obviously it can't, otherwise such a process could virtually stop all the other processes from making any progress.

This implies that there needs to be some mechanism for switching the CPU to another process when the current process has had long enough. But where is the decision to do this taken and how?

In general, there are two possibilities here, the first is to allow the processes themselves to release control of the CPU voluntarily when they have had a reasonable time on the CPU, and the second is to find some mechanism to force a process to release its CPU control. The first of these is called non-preemptive scheduling and the second is called preemptive scheduling.

As we shall see when we look at threads, it is perfectly feasible to run a system of co-operating pieces of code that use non-preemptive scheduling to switch between them. However, for process scheduling in a multi-user environment, it is usually safer to assume that the processes may be, at best, unaware of each other's existence or, at worst, positively antagonistic towards each other in terms of their CPU use.

Consequently, in a multi-user environment, preemptive scheduling is used almost without exception – and Linux is no exception.

The way that this is achieved is that each process it given a maximum length of time it will be allowed to have on the CPU without a break. In addition, the system will generate fairly rapid and periodic clock timer interrupts, which will be counted and used to determine when the process has had its allocated time slice.

When the time slice of the current process has elapsed, the scheduler will be forced to run to determine if there is another process ready to run and more eligible to run than the process whose time slice on the CPU has just expired. If there is, then it will be run in place of the current process. If there is not, then the current process can be allowed to continue.

Obviously, from the previous discussion, there are several states in which a process may find itself and several transitions between states that can occur in response to various events. Figure 28.1 shows a greatly simplified state transition diagram for processes under the control of the CPU scheduler and labels six transitions between the states which occur in the following circumstances:

1. When a process is first started (by `fork()` in Linux) it is not given control of the CPU straight away. Instead, it joins a list of other processes that are in the position that they can proceed immediately, as soon as they have time on the CPU. This, then, is the starting transition which puts the process into the runnable state.
2. Eventually, a process that is runnable will be selected by the scheduler to execute for a time on the CPU. Transition 2 takes the process from the runnable list and starts it running.

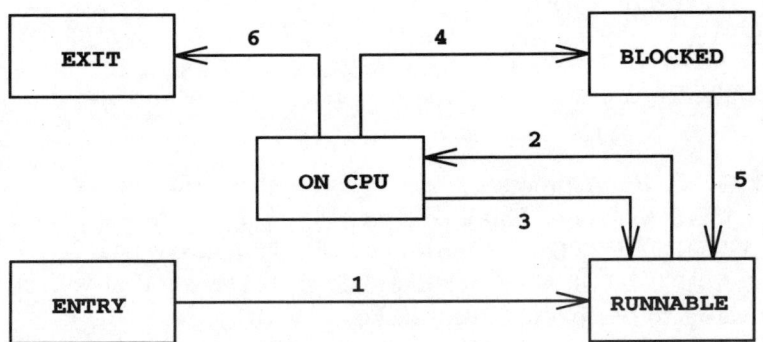

Figure 28.1 Simplified state transition diagram for CPU scheduler.

3. There are several ways for a process to move from the 'on CPU' state. Transition 3 is the one which takes the currently running process and places it back on the runnable list. This happens when the process has used up its allocated time slice on the processor and must be pre-empted to give other processes a chance to run.

4. The other main way for a process to lose control of the processor occurs when it requests some I/O operation which will involve a time delay while the machine hardware responds to the request. During this I/O wait, the process is not in a position to run even if the processor becomes totally free. Consequently, when a process blocks waiting for I/O in this way, it cannot be returned to the runnable list, because it simply isn't runnable. It is therefore transferred via transition 4 into a blocked state awaiting the completion of its I/O request.

5. When the I/O event for which a blocked process has been waiting occurs, the process becomes eligible to run once again. However, the process is not immediately given CPU time to deal with its I/O but is only returned to the runnable list to await selection once more by the scheduler. This is transition 5.

6. The final way to lose control of the processor, shown on this simplified diagram, occurs when a running process terminates. Transition 6 shows the event leading to process termination.

Surprisingly perhaps, this state transition diagram is generally applicable regardless of the actual algorithm used by the CPU scheduler to determine which process should run next.

There are many possible algorithms which can be used for CPU scheduling, including lots of theory about which is best in various sets of circumstances. However, rather than engage in a general discussion of scheduling algorithms here, we shall just concentrate on the details of the Linux scheduling algorithm itself.

28.2 Detail

During its lifetime, a Linux process may be in one of several states, the main ones being:

TASK_RUNNING A process is only considered for running by the scheduler when it is in this state. This is equivalent to the 'runnable' state in Figure 28.1.

TASK_INTERRUPTIBLE A process in this state is sleeping, but will be set to TASK_RUNNING if it receives a signal, so that it can deal with it. This is equivalent to the 'blocked' state in Figure 28.1.

TASK_UNINTERRUPTIBLE This is similar to the previous state except that signals have no effect on the process state. The usual way to restart a sleeping process is with wake_up(). Using wake_up() is the usual way for a process to take transition 5 from Figure 28.1.

Each process in Linux is represented internally by a `struct task_struct`, which contains the details of much of the environment in which the process executes. This structure is declared in the file:

`/usr/src/linux/include/linux/sched.h`

and the structure is dynamically allocated to the process in the `do_fork()` kernel function when the process is first created. The `do_fork()` function is contained in the file:

`/usr/src/linux/kernel/fork.c`

One of the members of the `task_struct` is called `counter`, and we shall see that it plays an important role in the scheduling of the process. The higher the value of `counter` in a TASK_RUNNING process, the more likely it is to be chosen to run the next time the scheduler is executed. Values of `counter` usually lie in the range 0 to 70, though in some circumstances, values outside this range are possible.

A process executing on the CPU will be required to give it up, so other processes may take a turn, in four main situations:

1. When the process requests that some I/O operation should take place on its behalf (such as a disk access operation) and the operation will take some time to complete. In this situation, even a time delay of only a few milliseconds is sufficient to warrant a reschedule.
2. Various signal related activities can give rise to a reschedule, such as calling the `pause()` or `sigsuspend()` system calls, or receiving a signal with `ptrace()` on.
3. When an interrupt occurs on some hardware event and wakes up a process which was sleeping on the event. If the woken process has a `counter` value that is significantly higher than the `counter` value of the current process, then a reschedule will be requested.

4. If a process is not stopped in any other way, then eventually it will use up its CPU time allocation and this will cause a reschedule to take place. The `counter` value in the `task_struct` is a count of the number of `jiffies` (10 ms timer interrupts) left in the CPU time allocation of the process.

Conceptually, the Linux scheduler has remained virtually unchanged since its early days, though the 1.3 kernel versions have seen the code tidied up on several occasions, and have seen support added for multi-processor systems. For a single processor, the operation of the scheduler is quite straightforward, and we shall examine it in some detail.

The scheduling task itself is performed by a single function within the kernel called `schedule()`. This function is contained in the file:

```
/usr/src/linux/kernel/sched.c
```

The following pseudo code program details the steps taken by a single-processor version of the `schedule()` kernel function:

```
Execute any functions on the scheduler task queue

FOR each process
    IF the process has a real time interval timer running
        IF the interval timer has expired
            Send a SIGALRM to the process
            Restart the interval timer if required
        END_IF
    END_IF

    IF the process state is TASK_INTERRUPTIBLE
        IF process has had a signal or has an expired timeout
            Set process state to TASK_RUNNING
        END_IF
    END_IF
END_FOR

FOR each process
    IF process state is TASK_RUNNING
        Remember the process with the highest counter value
    END_IF
END_FOR

IF all runnable processes have a counter value of zero
    FOR each process
        Recalculate process counter value from its priority
    END_FOR
```

```
    END_IF

    Switch context to the remembered 'highest counter' process
```

As you can see, this is a very simple scheduling algorithm that depends largely on the `counter` value to determine how likely a process is to run and, when it does run, the size of its time slice.

In kernels which can support multiple processors there is a simple modification to the way in which the `counter` value is used to select the next process to run. Instead of just using the `counter` on its own, there are extra terms added to give some advantage to processes on the same processor and also to give a small advantage to the current process.

With these notes and a copy of your Linux kernel scheduler source code to hand, it should be fairly easy for you to run through the code and sort out how it works.

Chapter 29

Tiny Threads – Case Study

You have seen that in Linux the main unit of concurrency is the process. In order to switch between executing one process and the next quite a lot of work is involved. This context switch overhead is necessary because, in general, Linux needs to make sure that any pair of processes are protected from interfering with each other, especially when you consider that the processes may not even belong to the same user.

Very often, however, you will want to write programs that are aware of the existence of each other and which can co-operate with each other towards some common goal. The standard solution to this problem is interprocess communication mechanisms.

It doesn't matter which of the IPC mechanisms you choose to use; there is still the context switch overhead to contend with whenever normal processes need to work together.

The way to overcome this is to use the concept of *threads*. Each Linux process has its own text, data and system memory areas and data structures, and its own time slices on the processor so that each process can proceed independently at its own pace. The idea behind threads is that each process can have its processor time slices shared between several concurrent threads, each of which also shares the memory and data structures of the process to which it belongs.

The amount of effort involved in context switching between two co-operating threads within a single process is much smaller than the effort of switching between two processes. This is mainly because the threads within a process are all sharing the same text, data and system memory areas and data structures so that no effort is expended in rearranging these things.

Since the threads are specifically designed to be co-operative and not antagonistic, nothing needs to be done by the kernel to protect the threads within a single process from each other.

Threads may, therefore, be considered as lightweight processes; light in the amount of effort required to context switch between them when compared to the effort involved with context switching standard (heavyweight) processes.

Threads can generally be implemented in one of two different ways:

- within the kernel, as a kernel task;
- within the process itself, as a user space task.

When threads are implemented within the kernel, the scheduling of the threads can be preemptive, in a similar way to the scheduling of processes themselves. This means that, whatever a thread is doing, when its time is up the kernel will interrupt it and pass control to the next thread to run.

In the case of threads provided in user space, the implementation is very much simpler, though now the thread scheduling becomes non-preemptive. This means that a context switch between threads can only take place when the current thread voluntarily releases control of the processor itself.

Non-preemptive scheduling is usually avoided in multi-user environments because it allows one user to hog the processor by refusing to give up control to allow other users to take a turn.

In the case of threads, however, non-preemptive scheduling does not present this problem as the threads are supposed to be co-operating on some task, not fighting over the processor.

The only real problem that does occur with user level threads, which can be avoided by kernel level threads, is with blocking I/O. With a non-preemptive scheduler, if one of the threads was to block on I/O (waiting for keyboard input, for instance), then that thread would be unable to release its control of the processor to allow another thread to run. This would effectively bring all the threads within that particular process to a halt until the blocked I/O was complete and control could be transferred. This just means that care must be taken when using user level threads to ensure that blocking a thread on I/O does not take place.

There are one or two packages available for Linux which implement threads in various ways. In general, they seem to be rather complex for our purposes so I will present a new, and very simple, user level threads library that you can easily incorporate into your own programs to experiment with the ideas behind threads.

29.1 Library Calls

The tiny threads library really is very simple, especially in terms of the user interface. Threads are created dynamically at run time, as they are required. This is done with a call to the `new_thread()` function:

```
int new_thread(int (*start_addr)(void), int stack_size)
```

where `start_addr` is a pointer to a function which will act, for the newly created thread, like the `main()` function acts for a process. The `stack_size` parameter specifies how much space, in bytes, should be set aside for this thread to use as its stack.

Whenever `new_thread()` is called, a new thread structure is created and initialized and added to a circular doubly linked list of thread structures. This list is used by the thread context switcher (scheduler) to determine which is the next thread to execute when the current thread gives up its control of the processor.

The first time `new_thread()` is called, usually from within the `main()` function of a process, the execution of `main()` itself is suspended and the thread scheduler started up. Only when all the threads created within a particular process have terminated is control finally returned to the `main()` function, to the point just after the initial `new_thread()` call.

On all calls to `new_thread()`, other than the first, a return is made immediately so that the calling thread can continue its execution. The return value from `new_thread()` is 0 on error (`malloc()` failure) or 1 on success.

The only other function needed to use the tiny threads library is the call which allows a thread to give up its control of the processor back to the thread scheduler:

```
int release(void);
```

Calling this function will cause the thread scheduler to pass execution control to the next thread in the circular list of thread structures created by `new_thread()`. Though not covered here, it is a straightforward task to create a simple preprocessor which will automatically add `release()` statements to your threads code in all the necessary places. To be on the safe side, you should add a `release()` to your code anywhere where it might loop, so that even an infinite loop will not stop the other threads from being scheduled. Using this criterion, the places that need `release()` statements are: inside the body of each `while`, `for` and `do` loop, after each program label so that a `goto` can't cause a loop without a `release()`, and also at the start of each function so that a recursive function isn't a problem either.

In the situation where two or more threads need to communicate with each other, this can be achieved by the use of variables which are global to the whole process (and therefore to each of its threads). Remember that all the threads within a process share the same program and data memory – their only private data storage area is their stack, which is not used to store global variables.

Communication via global variables is common with threads, but suffers somewhat from being asynchronous. This means that without setting up some kind of special arrangement, a data producing thread which writes to a global variable has no way to know that the data has been read by a data consuming thread when it needs to replace the current contents of the variable with the next data value.

In order to make it easier to write threads whose communication is synchronized, the tiny threads library provides a simple communication mechanism between threads, based on the rendezvous concept. The basic idea behind a rendezvous is that it doesn't matter which of the two communicating partners (producer or consumer) arrives at the rendezvous point in its code first; its execution will be suspended until the other partner arrives at the same point. At this time, the data is passed between the two threads, the suspended thread's execution is resumed, and both threads then continue their execution with the communication guaranteed to have taken place.

The tiny threads library provides three function calls related to the rendezvous mechanism: `get_channel()`, `send()` and `receive()`.

The `get_channel()` call has the prototype:

```
int get_channel(int number);
```

Where *number* is the communication channel number you wish to use, and the return value is a channel descriptor whose value will be passed forward into the other rendezvous related calls (or zero on error). This is rather similar in concept to opening a file except that you use a channel number instead of a file name, and get a channel descriptor returned instead of a file descriptor.

The first `get_channel()` call on a particular channel number will dynamically create the channel and return its channel descriptor. Subsequent `get_channel()` requests on the same channel number will just return the channel descriptor of the existing channel, and not create a new one.

The way that channels are implemented allows multiple producers and consumers all to share access to the same channel. In this case, the library will ensure that the producer's messages are properly queued and that each message can only be read by one consumer and will then be removed from the channel, in FIFO order.

Having obtained a channel descriptor, messages can be communicated over the channel with `send()` and `receive()`:

```
int send(int cd, char *buf, int size);
int receive(int cd, char *buf, int size);
```

where *cd* is a channel descriptor returned from a `get_channel()` call, *buf* is a pointer to a buffer from which data will be sent or to which data will be received, and *size* is the size of the data to be transferred, in bytes.

If matching `send()` and `receive()` calls specify different data sizes then the smaller of the two will be used. The return values from both the `send()` and `receive()` calls will be the actual number of bytes transferred.

29.2 Calling C Functions

In order to understand the operation of the tiny threads library, it is first necessary to look at how C programs implement function calls, and at how they deal with passing parameter values.

Every C program starts by executing the function `main()`. In fact, when you compile a C program and link it for execution, a system specific piece of code is bolted onto the front of your program which deals with any command line parameters and performs a call to the program's `main()` function.

Functions are called in the same way as subroutines are called in machine code, that is, a return address is pushed onto the machine stack and then control is transferred to the start of the called function. When this function terminates, the return address on the top of the stack is used to get back to the calling function at the instruction following the subroutine call.

In fact, not only is the stack used to store function return addresses, but it is also used for passing function parameter values and for holding the values of automatic local variables declared within functions. This means that some care must be taken not to confuse any values stored on the stack, as any form of stack corruption can lead to some pretty tricky bugs.

When you call a function, any parameter expressions, whose values you will pass into the function, are first evaluated and their values pushed onto the stack. Next, a machine code call is made to the function which also results in a return address being stacked. At the top of the called function, the names of any parameter variables specified, are used to label the appropriate positions on the stack where the parameter values have already been pushed. In this way, any parameter values are automatically assigned to their respective parameter variables.

Once inside the function proper, the value of one of the processor registers (`ebp` in fact, which is the extended base pointer register) is also pushed onto the stack because that register is going to be used as a place holder to be able to find the return address on the stack when the function terminates. The value of `ebp` on entering the function, is pushed right next to the return address and then the current stack pointer value (pointing to the `ebp` value just pushed) is copied into the `ebp` register, overwriting its previous value, which is now safely stored on the stack.

After `ebp` is dealt with, the stack pointer is decremented to allow space on the stack for any automatic local variables declared within the function body. Decrementing the stack pointer is the correct operation to perform to make space on the stack because the stack grows from high memory addresses downwards. That is, the stack pointer is decremented when pushing values onto the stack and incremented when popping them off again.

When a function terminates, all the values on the stack related to the operation of that function need to be discarded in order to get the stack back to the state it was in before the function call occurred. This is done in four stages:

- First, the current value of `ebp` is copied into the stack pointer. This automatically discards any local variables for which stack space was previously set aside, and leaves the stack pointer pointing to the saved `ebp` value.
- Second, the top stack entry is popped into the `ebp` register. This restores the saved value of `ebp` and leaves the stack pointer pointing at the return address to get back to the calling function.
- Third, a return instruction is executed which transfers control of execution back to the calling function and leaves the stack pointer pointing to any

422 *Tiny Threads – Case Study*

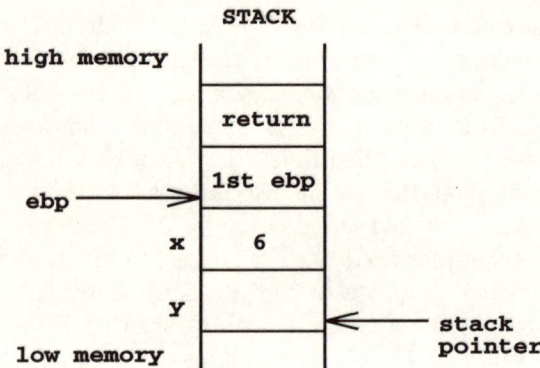

Figure 29.1 Stack layout in `main()` just before calling `twice()`.

parameter values that were passed into the called function.
- Fourth, back in the calling function the stack pointer is incremented by the correct amount to step it over any pushed parameter values. This has the effect of discarding these values and restoring the stack to its prefunction-call state.

To illustrate the operation of the stack during the execution of a program, we will look at two snap-shots of the stack taken during the operation of the following very simple piece of code:

```
main()
{
    int x, y;

    x = 6;
    /* snap-shot one here */
    y = twice(x);
}

twice(int n)
{
    int r;

    r = 2*n;
    /* snap-shot two here */
    return r;
}
```

The first snap-shot (see Figure 29.1) is taken inside the `main()` function just before the call to the `twice()` function. It shows the return address that was pushed onto the stack when the `main()` function was called, the original value of `ebp` pushed

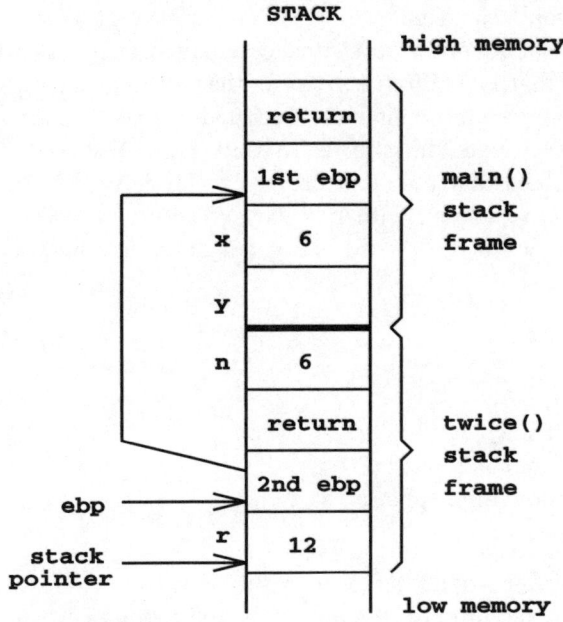

Figure 29.2 Stack layout in `twice()` just before `return`.

next on the stack, with the ebp register set to point to this stack location, the stack locations set aside for the local variables x and y, the current position of the stack pointer, and the value of 6, assigned to the variable x on the stack.

The second snap-shot (see Figure 29.2) is taken at the end of the `twice()` function, just before the execution of the `return` statement. It shows that, after the stack frame for the `main()` function, the value 6 was pushed onto the stack (as the value of the parameter passed into the `twice()` function), which was later labeled with the name n. After this, the machine code call to the function `twice()` caused another return address to be pushed onto the stack. This was followed by stacking the value in ebp and updating the ebp register to point to the saved value. By this mechanism, the ebp register has effectively been set up as the head pointer to a linked list of function stack frames, all stored on the stack. Finally, the variable r is allocated space on the stack to which the calculation subsequently assigns the value 12.

29.3 Thread Scheduling

Remember that all the threads within a single process share the program and all the global environment of the process. The only private parts of a thread are the contents of any significant processor registers and the stack, which it uses during its execution, as you have seen.

This suggests that in order to switch contexts between two threads within a single process, all that is required is to swap the values in a few processor registers – specifically, the program counter (or instruction register), ebp and the current stack pointer. In fact, you will soon see that all that really needs to be saved is the current ebp value, and that the other values can be derived from this.

Each thread has associated with it a data structure, which is used to save the per thread context when the thread is not currently running. The data structure has the following layout:

```
struct context
{
    int ebp;
    char *stack;
    struct context *next;
    struct context *prev;
};
```

The next and prev fields of the structure are used to form the forward and backward links that tie this structure into the doubly linked, circular list of structures which form the scheduling loop. The stack field is a pointer to an array of bytes which is used as the private stack space for this thread, and the ebp field is used as a temporary store for the contents of the processor ebp register when the CPU is processing some other thread.

29.4 Context Switching

The first piece of threads library code to look at is the release() function, which is called by a thread when it wants to pass its control of the CPU on to the next thread in the scheduling loop. When you examine this code, keep in mind that the variable current is a pointer to the struct context associated with the currently running thread:

```
release(void)
{
    /* 1 */
    if (thread_count<=1)
        return 0;

    /* 2 */
    current = current->next;
    switch_context(current->prev, current);
    return 1;
}
```

```
static switch_context(struct context *from, struct context *to)
{
    /* 3 */
    __asm__
    (
        "movl 8(%ebp),%eax\n\t"
        "movl %ebp,(%eax)\n\t"
        "movl 12(%ebp),%eax\n\t"
        "movl (%eax),%ebp\n\t"
    );
}
```

Notice that the `release()` function calls another function (`switch_context()`) which is declared to be `static` so that it cannot be called by any code outside the threads library file. Notice also that the `switch_context()` function consists of a few lines of embedded assembly code, which are used to allow direct access to specific processor registers – a level of control not directly available in standard C. This does mean that the library will not be portable to other processor architectures as it uses specific knowledge about the internal layout of the CPU. The numbered comments are:

1. If there is only one thread in the scheduling loop then there is no point in doing a context switch at all. In this case, the `release()` function just returns straight away and hence the current thread resumes execution until the next `release()` call is encountered.
2. Move `current` to point to the next thread in the scheduling loop. Then call `switch_context()`, passing the old value of `current` and its new value as parameters.
3. Inside the `switch_context()` function there are four instructions in 386 assembly code. All these instructions do is to take the CPU `ebp` register contents and store them in the `ebp` field of the `from` structure, and then load the CPU `ebp` register from the `ebp` field of the `to` structure instead. The `switch_context()` function then returns.

So, how does a thread context switch take place just by changing the `ebp` register around? To answer this question we will need to take a look at stack use again.

Imagine that a thread which has been running for a while calls the `release()` function. What happens is that this function call and the subsequent call to `switch_context()` both take place using the stack of this thread. Figure 29.3 shows part of the stack layout for this thread just before it starts executing the assembly code section of the `switch_context()` function.

The assembly code section saves the current value of the CPU `ebp` register into the `ebp` field of this thread's `struct context`, then loads the CPU `ebp` register

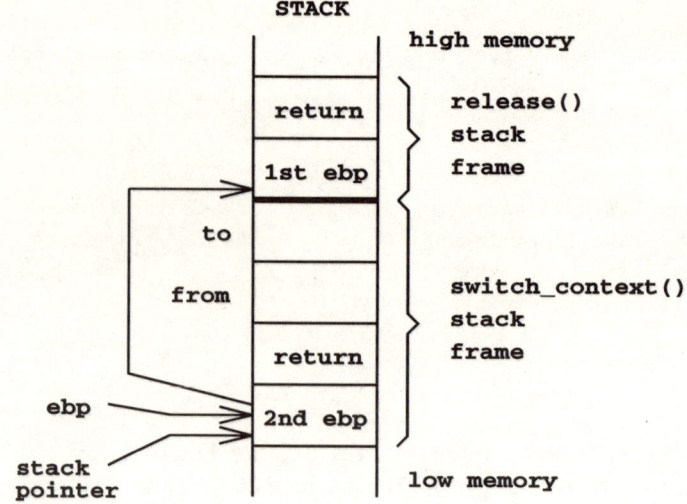

Figure 29.3 Thread stack layout just before context switch.

from the `ebp` field of the `struct context` belonging to the next thread to run, and then the `switch_context()` function returns.

Eventually, the CPU will have executed every thread in the scheduling loop up to its next `release()` call, so that the thread we are following gets its next turn to run. When this happens, the thread before ours in the scheduling loop will execute a `release()` call, and, by the time the assembly code section of `switch_context()` has run, the CPU `ebp` register will have been reloaded with our thread's saved `ebp` register value. Notice, however, that the stack pointer will still be pointing to the previous thread's stack and that the program counter will be pointing to the instructions at the end of the `switch_context()` function, and will be about to execute them.

What happens at the end of every function is that the stack pointer is set equal to the value in `ebp`, to discard any local variables. In this case, the `switch_context()` function has no local variables but the assignment is done anyway. This has the beneficial side effect of moving the stack pointer so that it points back to the correct place in our thread's stack. The other actions which take place at the end of a function are popping the `ebp` register from the current stack (our thread's stack) and then using the return address on the stack to get back to the calling function.

This means that our thread's code resumes execution by an ordinary return from the `release()` function. In fact, as far as any of the threads is concerned, they just call `release()` at intervals, which then returns, allowing them to continue. The threads themselves are unaware of anything unusual happening during the `release()` call.

29.5 Starting New Threads

Starting a new thread just means creating a `struct context` for the thread and allocating a block of memory for its stack. These data structures can then be initialized and added to the scheduling loop to get the opportunity to run. It all sounds straightforward when you say it fast but in fact it is a little bit tricky and requires some attention to detail. The tricky bit is initializing the thread's stack, as several values need to be hand crafted into the empty stack before it can be used:

```
new_thread(int (*start_addr)(void), int stack_size)
{
    struct context *ptr;
    int esp;

    /* 1 */
    if (!(ptr = (struct context *)malloc(sizeof(struct context))))
        return 0;

    /* 2 */
    if (!(ptr->stack = (char *)malloc(stack_size)))
        return 0;

    /* 3 */
    esp = (int)(ptr->stack+(stack_size-4));
    *(int *)esp = (int)exit_thread;
    *(int *)(esp-4) = (int)start_addr;
    *(int *)(esp-8) = esp-4;
    ptr->ebp = esp-8;

    /* 4 */
    if (thread_count++)
    {
        /* 5 */
        ptr->next = current->next;
        ptr->prev = current;
        current->next->prev = ptr;
        current->next = ptr;
    }
    else
    {
        /* 6 */
        current = ptr->next = ptr->prev = ptr;
        switch_context(&main_thread, current);
    }

    return 1;
}
```

The new_thread() function takes two parameters, the first is the address of the function where execution of this thread will begin and the second is the size of the memory block (in bytes) to allocate for stack space to the new thread. The numbered comments in the code are as follows:

1. Use malloc() to create a struct context for this thread. Check that the memory allocation was successful and return a zero value on error.
2. Use malloc() again to allocate a block of memory of the specified size for the thread's stack. The stack pointer in the new struct context is set to point to the stack memory. Again, a memory allocation error will cause a zero to be returned by new_thread().
3. Initialize the stack to the state shown in Figure 29.4. Remember that the pointer to the stack memory in the struct context points to the lowest numbered address of the block, whereas the action on the stack is taking place at the high address end of the block.
4. The next part depends on whether or not this is the first new thread within the current process. If it is, execution of the main program is suspended and a context switch to the new thread is performed; otherwise the new thread is just added to the scheduling loop to await its turn to run.
5. Adding a new thread to an existing scheduler loop is made a little more complex by the fact that the loop is doubly linked so that a forward and backward set of pointers need to be set up. A new thread is inserted into the scheduling loop in such a way that it will automatically be the next thread to run when the current thread performs a release().
6. Here, no threads are currently running so the scheduling loop needs to be created and started by a first call to switch_context(). In order to make sure that the main program is suspended, the switch_context() call stores its ebp register contents in a static struct context called main_thread. This structure is not part of the scheduling loop and so the main program will not be executed again, except by special arrangement, when there are no more threads left to run.

Figure 29.4 shows that the ebp element of the struct context associated with the new thread is set to point into the thread's stack. When a context switch is made to the new thread, this value is loaded into the CPU ebp register. The return from the switch_context() function then causes the stack pointer to point to the same stack location. Performing a stack pop into ebp loads this register appropriately and also makes the stack pointer point to the thread start function. Finally, performing a return from subroutine will pop the start address into the program counter, thus performing a jump to the beginning of the thread start function.

An extra twist is required when a thread's start function terminates in order to remove the thread from the scheduling loop and free its malloc()ed memory back to the system. These actions are performed by the exit_thread() function. So that you don't need to remember to call this function at the end of each thread's

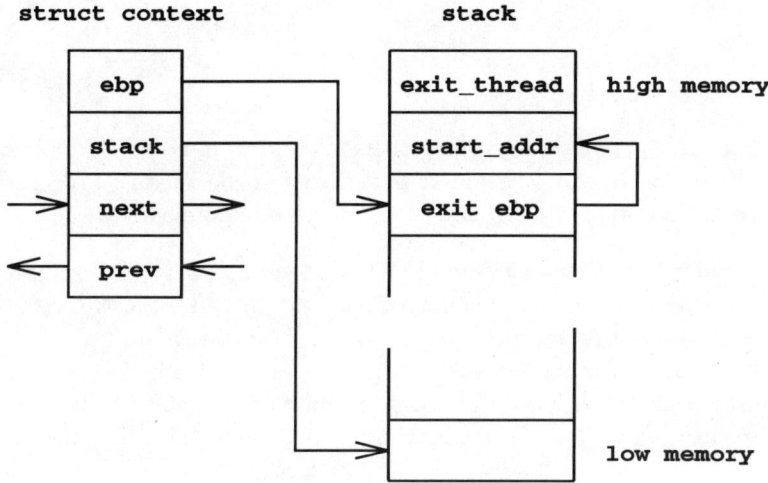

Figure 29.4 Data structures set up in new_thread.

start function, a jump to the function is automatically crafted into the thread's stack. This means that the function is automatically executed when the thread's start function terminates, using a similar trick to the one which executed the start function in the first place.

The code for the exit_thread() function appears as follows:

```
static exit_thread(void)
{
    struct context dump, *ptr;

    /* 1 */
    if (--thread_count)
    {
        /* 2 */
        ptr = current;
        current->prev->next = current->next;
        current->next->prev = current->prev;
        current = current->next;
        free(ptr->stack);
        free(ptr);
        switch_context(&dump, current);
    }
    else
    {
        /* 3 */
        free(current->stack);
        free(current);
        switch_context(&dump, &main_thread);
```

        }
}

The exit_thread() function terminates the thread pointed to by current. The fact that the exit_thread() function is declared to be static prevents it from being called from outside the library. The numbered comments are:

1. If current is not the last thread in the scheduling loop, then unlink it from the scheduler and switch context to the next thread; otherwise, as there are no more threads to execute, resume execution of the main thread.
2. Take a copy of the pointer to the current thread. Unlink the current thread from the scheduling loop, then reassign current to point to the next thread to execute. Now free() the malloc()ed memory associated with the terminating thread and finally switch_context() from this thread to the new current thread.
3. Here, it is only necessary to free() the malloc()ed memory associated with the final thread in the scheduling loop and then switch_context() back to the main program, to resume its execution.

29.6 Rendezvous

Two new data structures are used in the implementation of the rendezvous mechanism. The first (struct channel) is provided on a *per message channel* basis. The second (struct message) is used on a *per blocked message* basis. These two structures, along with the declaration of struct context and some global variables, etc., are all supplied in a separate header file, called def.h, which should be #included at the top of the program. The full contents of def.h are as follows:

```
#include <string.h>

struct context                          /* One structure for each thread */
{
    int ebp;              /* Base pointer (stack frame pointer) store */
    char *stack;          /* Pointer to memory block for thread stack */
    struct context *next;     /* Round robin circular list pointer */
    struct context *prev;     /* Round robin circular list pointer */
};

struct channel     /* One structure for each communication channel */
{
    int number;                                     /* Channel number */
    int sr_flag;      /* 0=no queue, 1=send queued, 2=receive queued */
    struct channel *link;         /* Link to next channel in list */
    struct message *message_list;        /* Head of message queue */
```

```
        struct message *message_tail;         /* Tail of message queue */
};

struct message          /* One structure for each pending send/receive */
{
    int size;                           /* Size of message in bytes */
    char *addr;                         /* Pointer to start of message */
    struct message *link;        /* Link to next message in queue */
    struct context *thread;    /* Which thread blocks on this struct */
};

static struct context main_thread;       /* Storage for main() details */
static struct context *current;          /* Currently executing thread */
static int thread_count = 0;         /* Number of threads to schedule */
static struct channel *channel_list = 0;    /* List of all channels */

static int switch_context(struct context *, struct context *);
static int exit_thread(void);
static int rendezvous(struct channel *, char *, int, int);
```

As each channel is created, a `struct channel` is allocated and added to a linked list of all the channels within the current process. Whenever an unmatched `send()` or `receive()` is performed on a channel, a `struct message` is allocated and entered on to the end of a message queue, hanging off the channel structure. Whenever a thread is blocked in a rendezvous awaiting a communication partner, the thread structure is unlinked from the scheduling loop and linked instead to its message structure. Figure 29.5 illustrates how the various structures are interconnected when `send()` and `receive()` operations are pending.

The diagram shows the existence of three communication channels in this example, whose data structures are linked together, with `channel_list` as the pointer to the head of the list. A `send()` operation has been performed on channel 1 and a message structure has been attached to the channel structure. The context structure for the thread wich performed the `send()` has been removed from the scheduling loop and attached to the message structure. This ensures that the thread cannot be run again until a matching `receive()` operation is performed on the same channel, at which time the context structure will be easy to locate and re-connect to the scheduling loop.

The diagram also shows that a second `send()` operation has also been performed by another thread on the same channel and that it, too, is queued on the channel awaiting the second `receive()` operation. Communication channel 2 has been created but there are no pending messages queued. Channel 3 shows that a `receive()` has been performed and that a `send()` on the channel is awaited.

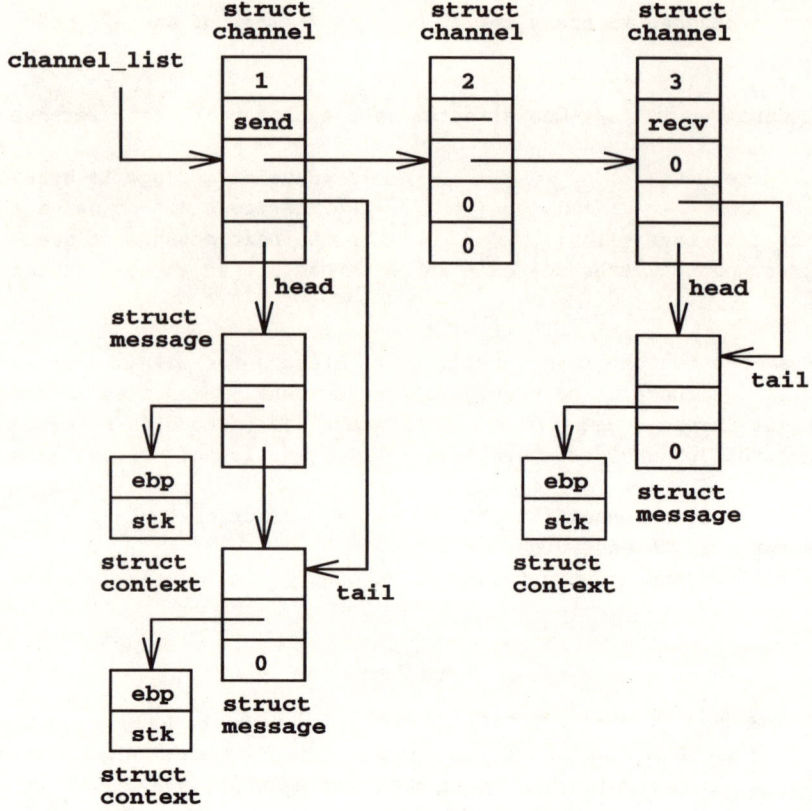

Figure 29.5 Structure links created during rendezvous.

29.7 Creating Channels

New communication channels are created with the get_channel() function as follows:

```
get_channel(int number)
{
    struct channel *ptr;

    /* 1 */
    for (ptr = channel_list; ptr; ptr = ptr->link)
        if (ptr->number==number)
            return((int)ptr);

    /* 2 */
    if (!(ptr = (struct channel *)malloc(sizeof(struct channel))))
        return 0;
```

```
        /* 3 */
        ptr->number = number;
        ptr->message_list = 0;
        ptr->message_tail = 0;
        ptr->sr_flag = 0;
        ptr->link = channel_list;
        channel_list = ptr;
        return((int)ptr);
}
```

Remember that the `get_channel()` function returns a channel descriptor given a channel number as a parameter. If the channel does not already exist, then it will be created. The numbered comment are:

1. Starting at `channel_list`, search down the linked list of existing channels looking to see if the specified channel number already exists. If the specified number is found in the list then the address of the associated `struct channel` is cast to an `int` value and returned as the channel descriptor.
2. If the channel number does not already exist, then a new `struct channel` is allocated, or a zero is returned on error.
3. After the new `struct channel` has been successfully created its fields are initialized and the structure is added to the head of the channel list. Finally, the address of the new structure is cast to `int` and returned as the channel descriptor.

29.8   send and receive

Once a channel descriptor has been obtained all that remains is to use `send()` and `receive()` to pass messages between threads. In fact, as the following code shows, `send()` and `receive()` are fully symmetrical operations so that they both make an internal call to the function `rendezvous()` with just an extra flag parameter to specify in which direction the data transfer should be made:

```
send(int chan, char *addr, int size)
{
    /* 1 */
    return(rendezvous((struct channel *)chan, addr, size, 1));
}


receive(int chan, char *addr, int size)
{
    /* 2 */
```

```c
        return(rendezvous((struct channel *)chan, addr, size, 2));
}


static int rendezvous(struct channel *chan, char *addr,
int size, int sr_flag)
{
    struct message *ptr;
    int nbytes;

    /* 3 */
    if (sr_flag==3-chan->sr_flag)
    {
        /* 4 */
        ptr = chan->message_list;
        chan->message_list = ptr->link;
        ptr->thread->next = current->next;
        ptr->thread->prev = current;
        current->next->prev = ptr->thread;
        current->next = ptr->thread;
        ++thread_count;
        /* 5 */
        nbytes = (size<ptr->size)?size:ptr->size;
        ptr->size = nbytes;

        /* 6 */
        if (sr_flag==1)
            memcpy(ptr->addr, addr, nbytes);
        else
            memcpy(addr, ptr->addr, nbytes);

        /* 7 */
        if (!chan->message_list)
            chan->sr_flag = 0;

        return(nbytes);
    }
    else
    {
        /* 8 */
        ptr = (struct message *)malloc(sizeof(struct message));

        if (!chan->message_list)
            chan->message_list = ptr;
        else
            chan->message_tail->link = ptr;
```

```
            chan->message_tail = ptr;
            ptr->link = 0;
            ptr->size = size;
            ptr->addr = addr;
            chan->sr_flag = sr_flag;
            ptr->thread = current;
            current->prev->next = current->next;
            current->next->prev = current->prev;

            /* 9 */
            if (--thread_count)
            {
                current = current->next;
                switch_context(ptr->thread, current);
            }
            else
                switch_context(ptr->thread, &main_thread);

            /* 10 */
            nbytes = ptr->size;
            free(ptr);
            return(nbytes);
        }
    }
```

The send() and receive() functions both take three parameters. The first is a channel descriptor, the second is a memory buffer from which, or to which, the data transfer will take place, and the third parameter specifies the size of the data transfer, in bytes. The return value from both functions is the number of bytes actually transferred. This will be the smaller of the two sizes specified as the third parameters to the two functions. The numbered comments are:

1. The send() parameter values are passed directly to rendezvous() with an added fourth parameter value to specify the data transfer direction.
2. The receive() parameter values are passed directly to rendezvous() with with an added fourth parameter value to specify the data transfer direction.
3. Inside rendezvous(), the first test checks to see if there is a communication partner of the correct type already queued. If there is, then the partner's struct context needs restoring to the scheduling loop and the data needs to be copied between threads before the threads can continue their execution. If no partner is queued, then the current thread is removed from the scheduling loop and the communication request added to the queue of requests associated with this channel.

436   *Tiny Threads – Case Study*

4. This code section re-links the thread's `struct context` to the scheduling loop and increments the count of the number of threads ready to run.
5. The calculation is performed to determine the number of bytes that will be transferred. This value is also saved where the communication partner can get at it on its next turn to run.
6. The data transfer now takes place, making sure to copy the data in the right direction.
7. If this was the last message queued in the channel, then the message type flag is reset and the number of bytes transferred is returned to the caller.
8. In this section of code a new message is to be queued as no matching partners are ready yet. A new `struct message` is allocated and added to the channel message list. The thread needs to block while waiting for a communication partner so this code section also removes the thread's `struct context` from the scheduling loop and stores it under the message structure.
9. The number of runnable threads is decremented and a context switch is performed to the next thread in the loop. As the newly blocked thread needs to find a communication partner before it can resume execution, there should always be other threads to which control can be passed. If for any reason this proves not to be the case then the context switch arranges to resume execution of the main thread.
10. The next time this thread gets scheduled will be after the rendezvous has taken place, when the number of bytes transferred can be recovered and, after `free()`ing the used `struct message`, can be returned.

29.9 Unbounded Buffers

As a simple example of the use of the tiny threads library, the following code presents a fairly elegant solution to the unbounded buffer problem:

```
int buffer(void);
int start(void);

int ch_desc1, ch_desc2;

main(void)
{
    ch_desc1 = get_channel(1);
    ch_desc2 = get_channel(2);
    new_thread(start, 1024);
}

start(void)
{
    int i, n;
```

```
    new_thread(buffer, 1024);

    for (i = 0; i<10, ++i)
    {
        send(ch_desc1, &i, sizeof(int));
        release();
    }

    for (i = 0; i<10, ++i)
    {
        receive(ch_desc2, &n, sizeof(int));
        printf("i=%d n=%d\n", i, n);
        release();
    }
}

buffer(void)
{
    int i;

    receive(ch_desc1, &i, sizeof(int));
    new_thread(buffer, 1024);
    send(ch_desc2, &i, sizeof(int));
}
```

I'll leave you to sort out how this works. However, I will just say that you will find two channels in use here with multiple senders and receivers. Also, you will find that the program uses one instance of the **start()** function, but several simultaneously running instances of the **buffer()** function.

Notice also how this solution dynamically creates more buffer space as it is required and how it dynamically tidies up after itself when the buffer elements are finished with.

Chapter 30

Memory

The memory management in Linux is one of the more complex areas of the kernel. In the main this is because it uses many of the facilities provided by the CPU itself, and they in turn are quite involved. Consequently, we'll begin this exploration of the memory management in Linux with a look at the CPU and the part it has to play in these events.

30.1 Protected Mode Addressing

Many of the instructions executed by the CPU need to perform a memory access. This would seem to be a straightforward thing, where the machine code instruction specifies the address whose contents are to be fetched or modified. If only it were that simple!

In the situation where you want to have many processes in memory and running at the same time, it is much easier if they can all run as though they each have the machine to themselves. The way that this is achieved is that various forms of address translation are performed within the CPU between an instruction specifying an address to access (called a logical or effective address) and the actual hardware making the access in physical memory.

To start with, a process is split into several segments for instructions, data and stack, and each segment has associated with it a segment descriptor. Each segment descriptor is an 8-byte block which contains the base address for the start of the segment, the size of the segment and the access rights granted on it. Sets of segment descriptors are collected into a descriptor table and a CPU internal register is used to access the base address of the table.

In addition to this, the CPU contains a set of segment registers. These registers each point to one of the segment descriptor entries in a descriptor table. Now, when any kind of memory access takes place, one of the CPU's segment registers is selected (either implicitly by the memory access type, or explicitly by the instruction

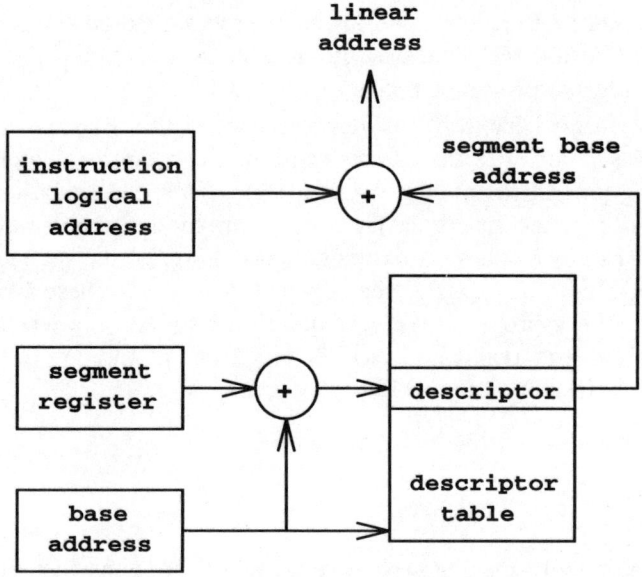

Figure 30.1 Calculation of a linear address.

making the access) to be involved in the memory address calculation. The result of this calculation is called a linear address. Figure 30.1 illustrates the calculation of a linear address given a logical address and a segment register.

What is shown here is that for each memory access, the CPU uses the contents of an internal register to find the base address of a descriptor table. To that base address is added the contents of one of the segment registers (with the low 3 bits of the register value set to zeros). The result of that operation is a pointer to one of the 8 byte entries in the descriptor table. Remember, the segment descriptor entries contain the base address of the segment in memory, the size of the segment and the access rights to the segment.

The instruction which is accessing memory will also have provided an address itself. This address is a logical (or effective) address within the memory segment whose segment descriptor has already been obtained. The logical address from the instruction is now added onto the base address of the segment to provide a new address called the linear address. This linear address has to be checked to ensure that it lies inside the segment (i.e. not outside the segment's specified size) and that the type of access requested (read, write or execute) is permitted within this segment. If these checks are passed, the CPU now has an address which can be used to access the machine's memory.

The main table of segment descriptors we have been looking at is called the global descriptor table or GDT, and the CPU register which points to the start of the table is called GDTR. In a multi-tasking environment you may wish each process to have access to its own memory segments. To cope with this requirement the CPU can also supply another descriptor table for each process, called the local descriptor table or LDT. If used, the local descriptor table is accessed via an entry in the GDT and the internal processor register called LDTR.

If it were performed for every memory access, all this looking up of values in descriptor tables (which are themselves contained in memory) would form a very time consuming part of the task of the processor. To speed things up enormously there are several registers inside the CPU which are hidden and not directly accessible to the programmer. These registers are used to cache the segment descriptors currently associated with each of the segment registers. These hidden registers are loaded with the appropriate segment descriptor values only when the values in the associated segment register change, or when one of the descriptor table base addresses change in GDTR or LDTR.

30.2 Paging

A perfectly viable multi-tasking system could be set up using just the facilities we have seen so far to organize its memory accesses. This is provided that each process knew, when it started running, how much memory it was going to require so that suitably placed and sized memory segments could be allocated to the process from the start, which wouldn't then need to be changed for the life of the process.

Linux, however, is rather more sophisticated than this simple model would suggest. For example, it can allow a process to grow in its memory requirements without considering other processes that may be physically next to it in memory. It is also possible for Linux to be running more processes at the same time than a simple sum of their memory requirements would suggest could fit into the available memory.

The mechanism used by Linux to allow these things to happen is the paging facility offered by the processor. Whether or not paging is used in the CPU is controlled by a single bit in a processor control register. If paging is switched on then a 32-bit linear address is treated as though it were split into two separate pieces. The high order 20 bits are treated as a page number and the low order 12 bits are treated as an offset address within the page. This means that a linear address can access a million 4 K-byte pages. One of the main things that paging does is to change the 20-bit page number supplied in the linear address into another 20-bit number which is the corresponding 4 K page in the physical memory of the machine. The practical upshot of this is that any 4 K page in physical memory can be made to appear on any of the million 4 K page boundaries in the linear address space of the processor.

This address translation is performed by using lookup tables in memory, where the high 20 bits of the linear address effectively specify the index into a big array of 32-bit elements. The 32-bit value thus accessed provides the required 20-bit translation plus a number of other bits which specify things like:

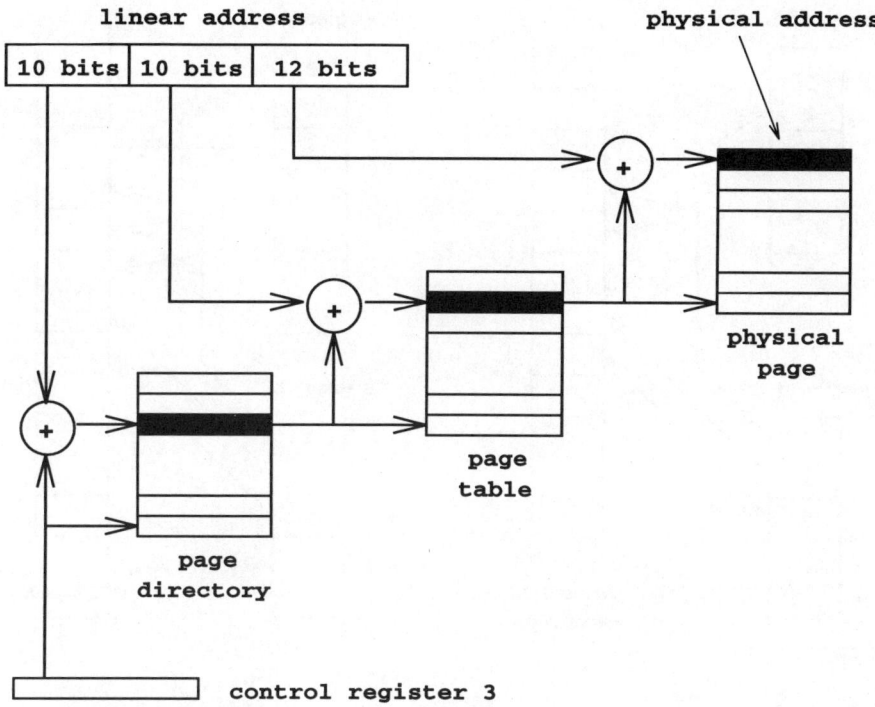

Figure 30.2 How paging translates linear to physical addresses.

- Is the accessed page read-write or read-only?
- Do user level processes have access to this page, or is it accessible only by processes in supervisor mode?
- Has any address in the page been accessed for read or write?
- Has any address in the page been written to?
- Is the page present in physical memory or is it stored on disk?

Rather than have a single huge page table a two-level hierarchy is used which avoids unnecessarily having to reserve a very large contiguous range of linear addresses to hold the table. The way that the two-level hierarchy is arranged is that the high 20 bits of the linear address are actually further subdivided into two separate 10-bit values. Control register 3 within the CPU contains the address of a 4 K page in memory which will be used as the top level page directory table. A 4 K page split into 32-bit entries is 1024 entries long. The high 10 bits of a 20-bit page number are exactly the right size to select one of the 1024 entries in the page directory. The top 20 bits of the selected entry in the page directory are used to point to another 4 K page called a page table. Again, this page holds 1024 entries, each 32 bits long, and this time the low 10 bits of the page number given in the original linear address will select exactly one of the entries in the page table. The 32-bit value

442 *Memory*

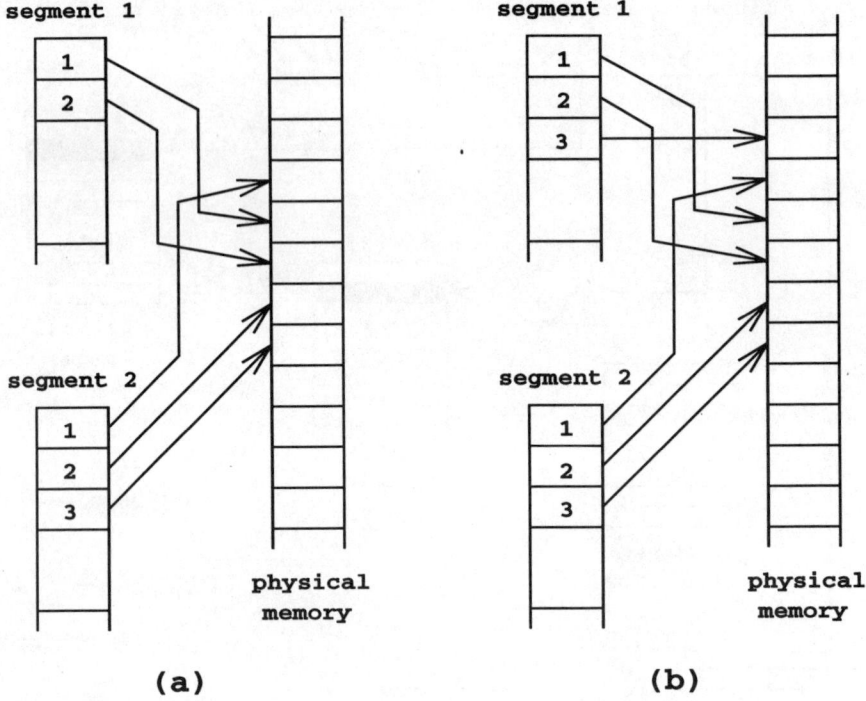

Figure 30.3 Paging allows easy memory segment growth.

thus selected contains the required 20-bit physical page number plus the other bits discussed previously.

Figure 30.2 illustrates this address translation arrangement from linear to physical addresses. Once again, if this translation were to be performed fully for each linear address access it would require an extra two memory reads to access the page directory and page table – a very expensive operation in terms of time. The solution used, as before, is to have some extra registers inside the CPU which are used to store the most recent address translations, making the lookup very much faster. These extra registers form the translation lookaside buffer (TLB).

30.2.1 Segment Growth

Paging is very useful in the situation where you wish to increase the size of a memory segment which is boxed-in in physical memory. Figure 30.3 illustrates the point.

Part (a) shows two memory segments composed of several pages which are mapped into the physical memory pages on the right of the diagram. Notice how, in physical memory, the pages for segment 1 are enclosed by the pages used for segment 2. Without paging, it would not be possible to increase the size of segment 1 without moving the entire segment to a new area of contiguous physical memory that was large enough to contain the enlarged segment.

Part (b) shows that, with paging, enlarging the size of segment 1 is a simple task as contiguous pages in the linear address space of segment 1 do not need to be physically contiguous, so that the new page (linear page 3) can just be allocated any free physical page, which just gets mapped to make it appear in the right place in segment 1.

30.2.2 Swapping

The other main use for paging is called swapping (it is called this for historical reasons – old versions of UNIX). The idea behind swapping is that it is possible to have more processes running on the system than could possibly fit into memory at the same time. This involves setting aside an area of swap space (usually on disk) to act like a memory overflow area. When you wanted to start up a new process and there was not enough room in memory to do so, the swapper would be called, which would chose one or more of the processes currently in memory to be written to the swap space in order to make room for the new process to be loaded and run. As processes progress some will block waiting for I/O and others will terminate. This gives the opportunity to bring swapped out processes back into memory (maybe at the expense of other processes being swapped out) so that they can continue their execution.

Using paging to perform the swapping function means that you do not need to swap out entire processes to disk, but only enough pages to make room for the new process to run. In fact, in Linux it is even better than that because it uses a technique called demand paging. In order for demand paging to work, the entries in the page tables need to contain information to say whether or not the contents of the pages to which the entries point are actually loaded into memory or not. With this information available, whenever the CPU tries to access a physical memory page which is not present in memory, an exception can be raised (called a page fault). This exception forces a call to an exception handler which will load the page into physical memory. The instruction which caused the page fault can then be restarted, and this time it should succeed.

This is such a good idea that new processes can be loaded into memory using the technique (and Linux does). What happens is that whenever the running process tries to execute an instruction at an address which is not yet loaded, a page fault occurs and is dealt with, after which the process can continue.

Studies on executing code soon reveal that for reasonable-sized programs a large proportion of the code does not get executed on any particular run. With demand paging, the implication of this is that, after a while, the process will have loaded the pages it requires and it will settle down to running with few new page faults and also with many of its pages not loaded into memory at all. Even if a particular program run does require access to all the program pages, then at any one time and for a significant length of time the process is typically only using a small subset of the pages, so that paging still reaps huge benefits.

30.3 Linux Specifics

The only way to start a new process under Linux is to use the `fork()` system call. This starts off by allocating two pages of memory, one for the task structure associated with the new process and one for use as stack space in the kernel when the kernel is running on behalf of the new process.

Next, the child task structure is copied from the parent, and some changes are made to set up the necessary differences such as process ID and session leadership. Finally, all the process information, including the memory map, is copied across to the new child. The child process has its own local descriptor table (LDT) and, therefore, its own text data and stack segments and it also has its own page tables which initially are just a copy of the parent's tables. The `fork()` call conceptually makes the child a copy of the parent's text, data and stack segments. However, this would be an expensive operation in terms of time, especially when in all probability the child is going to execute an `exec()` system call almost immediately and replace the contents of these segments with those belonging to a new program. To overcome this waste, Linux only copies the page tables from parent to child and not the pages to which they give access.

In the case of the text segment, this technique is fine as the text segment is flagged as read only anyway and the two processes cannot tell, just by reading, that they are sharing the code. However, the data and stack segment is read-write so sharing here will cause problems as soon as one of the processes wants to write some data. The Linux solution to this problem is called *copy on write*. What happens is that whenever one of the processes wants to write to a data or stack page that is currently shared, that page is copied and the page tables are updated so that each process now has its own copy of that page and can write to it without interfering with the other process.

When the `exec()` system call is used to start off a new program, then demand paging is used to load the pages needed for the process to run.

There are many occasions when new memory pages need to be allocated to a process. Eventually, the free page list will become exhausted. At this point Linux will try to steal a page from somewhere else, writing it to swap space if necessary, in order to satisfy the request. The possibilities for obtaining a page include reducing the number of pages used for disk buffer cache, as the boundary between buffer cache memory and ordinary process memory is dynamic in Linux. If it is necessary to steal a page of process memory to satisfy the memory request, then choosing to steal a page from the text segment of some process means that it doesn't need to be written out to swap space before it is freed as it is read-only (so it can't have changed) and it can be demand paged back in again from the original executable file.

Chapter 31

Filestore

In order to access the contents of a filesystem under Linux it is necessary to mount that file system into the directory hierarchy. You have already seen that this is done with the `mount` command. What we have not seen, however, is that there are many filesystem types, any or all of which can be mounted in any combination, almost without limit.

31.1 VFS

It is the job of the Virtual Filesystem Switch (VFS) to make it possible for Linux to be able to mount and access all of the various filesystem types. The main task of the VFS is effectively to add a layer of indirection into the Linux filestore to switch filesystem calls to the appropriate routines in the code for the correct filesystem type.

There are many filesystem types currently supported by Linux via the VFS, these include:

minix This is the earliest filesystem type supported by Linux; indeed, originally, it was the only supported filesystem type. Its two main disadvantages are that it only supports disk partitions up to 64Mb and it only allows file names up to 14 characters long.

ext The extended filesystem was soon added to Linux and it overcame the problems with the minix filesystem by offering disk partitions up to 2Gb and file names up to 255 characters in length. However, it had its own problems in terms of facilities and performance and was soon superseded.

xiafs This was one of two main attempts to replace the Ext filesystem and was based largely on the minix filesystem but with extensions to overcome its problems. However, Xiafs soon lost its popularity in favor of another filesystem type with greatly improved performance and facilities.

ext2 The second extended filesystem is now (as I write this) almost the universally accepted standard filesystem for Linux and it is also being ported to other systems. The system will allow disk partitions up to a staggering 4 Tb in size with file names up to 255 characters.

System V The System V filesystem is the filesystem type supported by early UNIX systems and it is now also available under Linux. This is only for compatibility with existing System V systems and would not normally be used seriously unless the compatibility point was paramount. It suffers the same kinds of limitations as the minix filesystem.

NFS The Network File System (NFS) originally developed by SUN, allows filesystems on one machine to be mounted over a directory on another machine, with the connection being made over a network. Apart from a small speed penalty, the network link is transparent and allows disk partitions and files to be shared all over a network.

ISO 9660 This is the filesystem associated with CD-ROM disks and has also been implemented for Linux. A CD can hold up to about 650 Mb of data, and many very useful Linux related CDs are available at this time. The standard ISO filesystem has a file name format like DOS though there are extensions to the standard which allow the more normal (for UNIX systems) long file names.

/proc This is a special filesystem type built into the Linux kernel to allow access to the various parts of the system and its processes.

msdos Standard DOS disks and partitions can be mounted and accessed under Linux. The system tries to make these filesystems appear as UNIX like as possible, though they are still subject to DOS limitations for things like file name length and format.

UMSDOS This a filesystem type used mainly to allow you to try out Linux on your DOS box without having to repartition your hard disks. Effectively, it allows you to put ordinary Linux files into a DOS partition and use them as. though they were in an ordinary Linux filesystem. This is achieved by using index files to provide a transparent lookup arrangement between the standard Linux file names and the more limited DOS file names.

In order to understand some of the problems and choices associated with filesystem design, we will look briefly at a small selection of the filesystem types supported by Linux to see some of the evolution that has taken place in this area.

31.2 System V

The layout of a disk partition configured as a standard UNIX System V file-system is very simple and is illustrated in Figure 31.1.

As you can see, each disk partition is split into just four parts:

boot block Contains the code to boot the machine if this is the boot partition; otherwise this block is not used (though it is still allocated).

448 *Filestore*

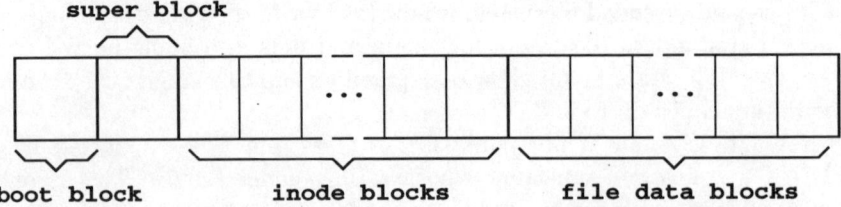

Figure 31.1 System V disk partition layout.

super block This block holds administrative information about the filesystem contained on this partition. We will look at this in more detail later.

inode blocks A set of disk blocks allocated to hold all the inodes for this filesystem. Once the filesystem has been created on the partition the number of disk blocks allocated to inodes (and hence the number of inodes available on this filesystem) is fixed and cannot be changed.

file data blocks The rest of the blocks on the partition are used to hold the actual data stored in the files on this filesystem. The blocks are allocated to files dynamically as they are required.

In the case of inodes and data blocks, some method is required to show when they are free to be allocated, or when they are already allocated and in use. For the System V filesystem a list of free inodes and data blocks is kept in the super block to make allocation faster when they are required, though the way in which they are held is different for the two things.

31.2.1 File Data Block Free List

It is generally not possible, by a simple inspection of a data block's contents, to determine whether or not the block is in use. This is because all of a data block's bytes are used to hold file contents, and a file's contents can be any sequence of bytes at all. This means that it is not possible to store a particular sequence of bytes in a data block to indicate that the block is free for allocation. The necessary solution to this problem is to have some data structure which lists those data blocks that are free.

This is actually implemented as a form of linked list, the first part of which is stored in the filesystem's super block. Data blocks on the disk partition are numbered sequentially and are thus each given a unique block number. When the filesystem is first created, all of the data blocks are obviously free and should, therefore, all appear on the free list. However, the space in the super block for this list is limited and only a small part of the list will fit. The next part of the list is stored in one of the free data blocks, the number of which is arranged to be the last block number in the super block list. This idea is repeated, using free blocks to store lists of free block numbers, and making sure that the last free block number

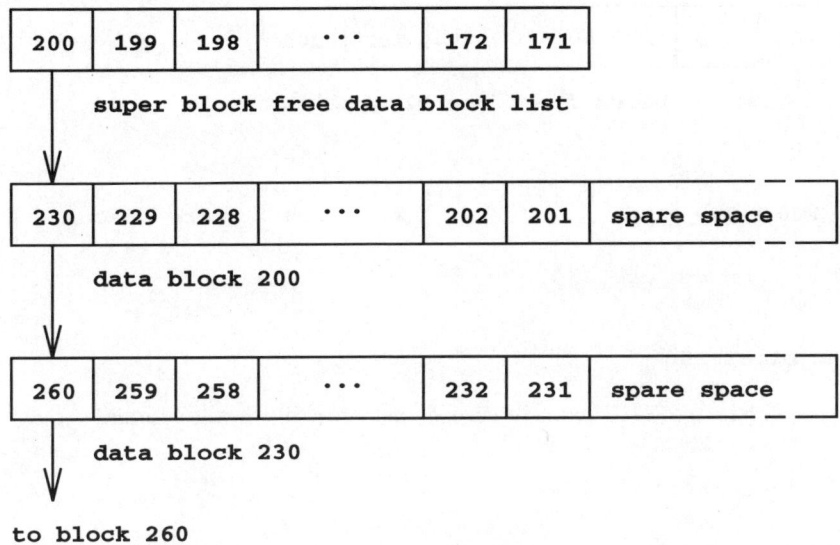

Figure 31.2 The initial data block free list.

in each list is a pointer to the next list of free block numbers. This idea is shown in Figure 31.2.

Using this arrangement, when a request is made for a new data block, the next free one on the super block list will be allocated (blocks will be allocated right to left in the diagram). As more data blocks are requested, this will be repeated until the super block list has only one entry left in it. Don't forget that this last block in the super block list contains the block numbers of the next part of the free block list. Therefore, these block numbers need to be copied into the super block list before the block which contained them is allocated, which it can be once the copy has taken place.

Figure 31.3 shows the situation after all the initial list of free block numbers in the super block have been allocated and the contents of block number 200 have been copied into the super block, just before block 200 was allocated as free.

When files are deleted and data blocks become free, their block numbers are just added to the free list in the super block. When this list becomes full and another data block becomes free (say, 188), then there is no space left to store the number. In this situation what happens is that the portion of the data block free list which is in the super block is copied into the newly freed block (188) and then the super block list is emptied and the newly freed block (188) is made the leftmost (and only) entry in the super block list.

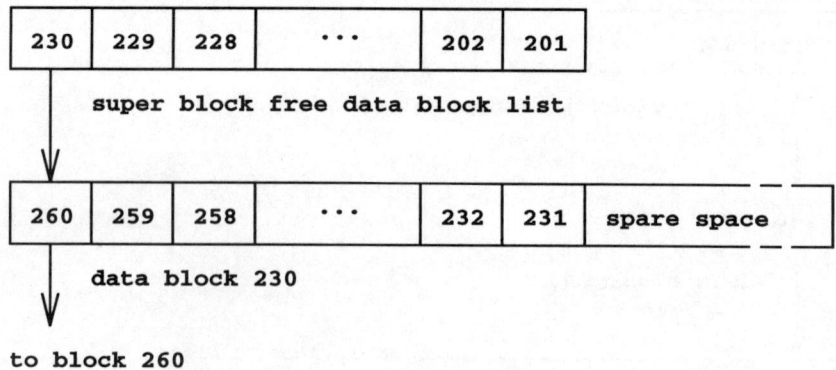

Figure 31.3 Data block free list after block allocations.

31.2.2 Inode Free List

The case of inode allocation is different to the allocation of disk data blocks for several reasons and, consequently, the free inode information is stored in a different format to that of free data blocks. The main reasons for the difference are:

- An inode is not very large and the structure contains no sensible place to store a large list of free inode numbers, unlike free data blocks, where the whole block could be used if necessary.
- With a data block, there is no way to determine from just a simple inspection of its contents whether or not it is free. This means that all the free data block numbers need to be stored; otherwise they are lost. In the case of an inode, when it is free it is flagged internally as such, which means that free inodes can always be found just by a simple linear search through the inode array.
- In general, there are many data blocks in a file so that data blocks tend to be allocated at a much greater rate than inodes. This means that occasional inefficiencies in finding inodes are more tolerable than inefficiencies in finding data blocks.

Taking these points into account, the kernel could just do a linear search through the inode array to find a free inode every time a request for a new inode was made. While this strategy could be made to work, it is made much more efficient by having a set of free inode numbers available in the super block. Unlike the case of free data blocks, however, the free inode list in the super block is just a stand alone list, so that there can be many inodes that are free and yet do not appear in the list. The use of the super block inode free list is illustrated in Figure 31.4, parts (A) to (F) as follows:

(A) This is meant to show the initial state of the super block inode free list. The `index` shows the inode number that will be used when the next allocation

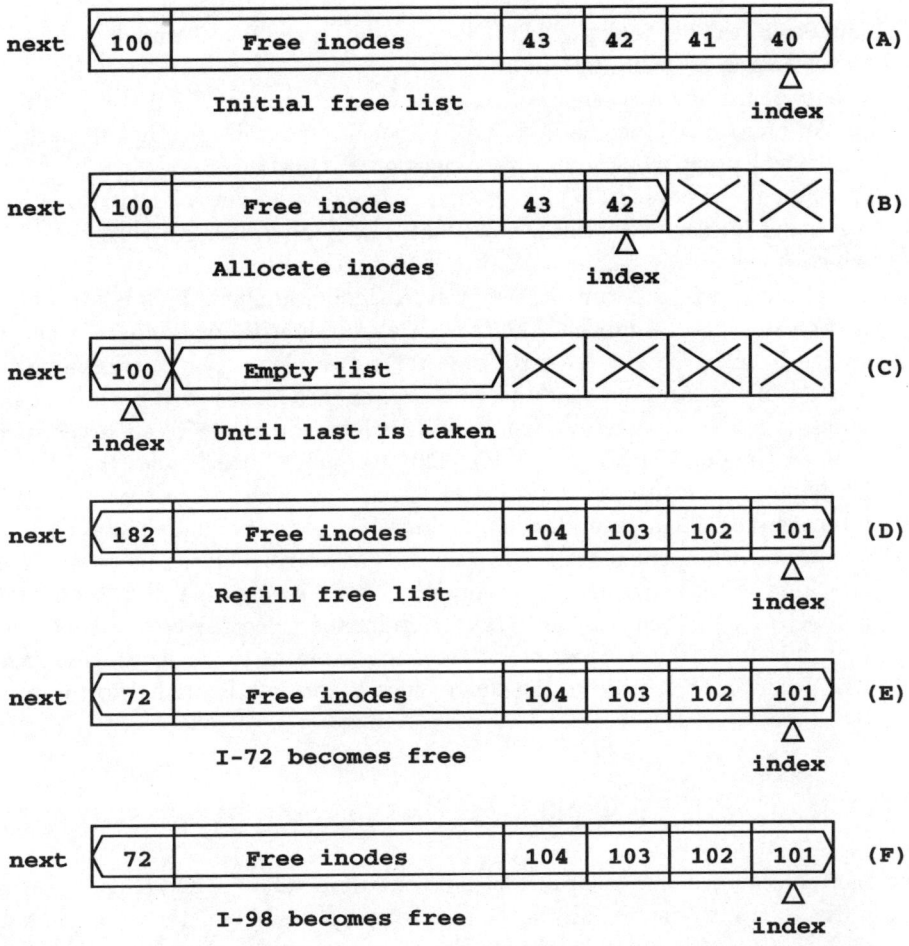

Figure 31.4 Allocation and release of free inodes.

request is made. The inode numbers which appear in the list were discovered on a linear search of the inode array. During the search, the super block list is filled from right to left (in the diagram) so that the leftmost inode number in the list is the largest free inode so far discovered.

(B) Here two inodes have been allocated (I-40 and I-41) and the index has been moved accordingly.

(C) After several more inode numbers have been allocated, the super block free list eventually gets to its last entry. When this inode is allocated, a new search is made through the inode array to find more free inode numbers with which to refill the super block list. However, there is no point in searching the inode array from the beginning because we already know that all the inodes up to 100 (in our example) are already in use. This suggests that the leftmost inode number in the original free inode list should be used as the `next` start point in the search for more free inodes.

(D) The inode free list has been refilled again from right to left, so that the leftmost inode number will be the last one to allocate and will once again mark the `next` start point when more free inodes are required.

(E) This scheme works just fine for as long as inodes are being allocated and none are being released. Suppose, now, that inode 72 is released when the file to which it belongs is deleted. With the free inode list in the super block full, there is nowhere to store the newly freed inode number. This is a problem, as we can't just let inode 72 go free. If we do, it will not be found when we search from inode 182 the next time the super block list needs refilling. In order to make sure that we don't lose freed inodes in this way, the `next` inode number in the super block list is replaced by the newly freed lower inode number (inode 72 in the example). This technique ensures that the leftmost inode number in the super block free list is always the correct place to start the next inode array search when looking for more free inode numbers.

(F) No special arrangements need to be made to remember the numbers of inodes that become free when the super block list is already full, if their inode numbers are greater than the `next` inode number, because they will be automatically found by a linear search starting at `next`. If an inode is released when there is free space in the super block it can just be added to the super block list.

31.2.3 Inode Data Block Pointers

Now that a mechanism exists for allocating a new inode to a file and for finding disk data blocks to add to the file, all that is now required is some method for accessing the data blocks in a file given its inode. The most obvious mechanism for this is to have the data block numbers listed in the inode. Sadly, for any reasonably large file, this solution is impracticable due to the amount of space it would require within the inode.

Looking at the average sizes of files created by typical users shows that the majority are 1024 bytes or less in size and that, as the size of files increases beyond this, the number of files of each size gets less. This suggests that an arrangement which makes accesses to small files quick and efficient, even at the expense of some speed for larger files, would be an acceptable compromise. It is this type of arrangement which System V implements.

Inside a System V inode there is an array of 13 elements, each of which can hold the number of a disk data block (see Figure 31.5). The first ten elements of the array are used to hold the data block numbers of the first ten data blocks assigned to storing the file's contents.

Assuming, for the purposes of illustration, that each disk data block is 1024 bytes in size, then these ten data block pointers will allow files to be created that are up

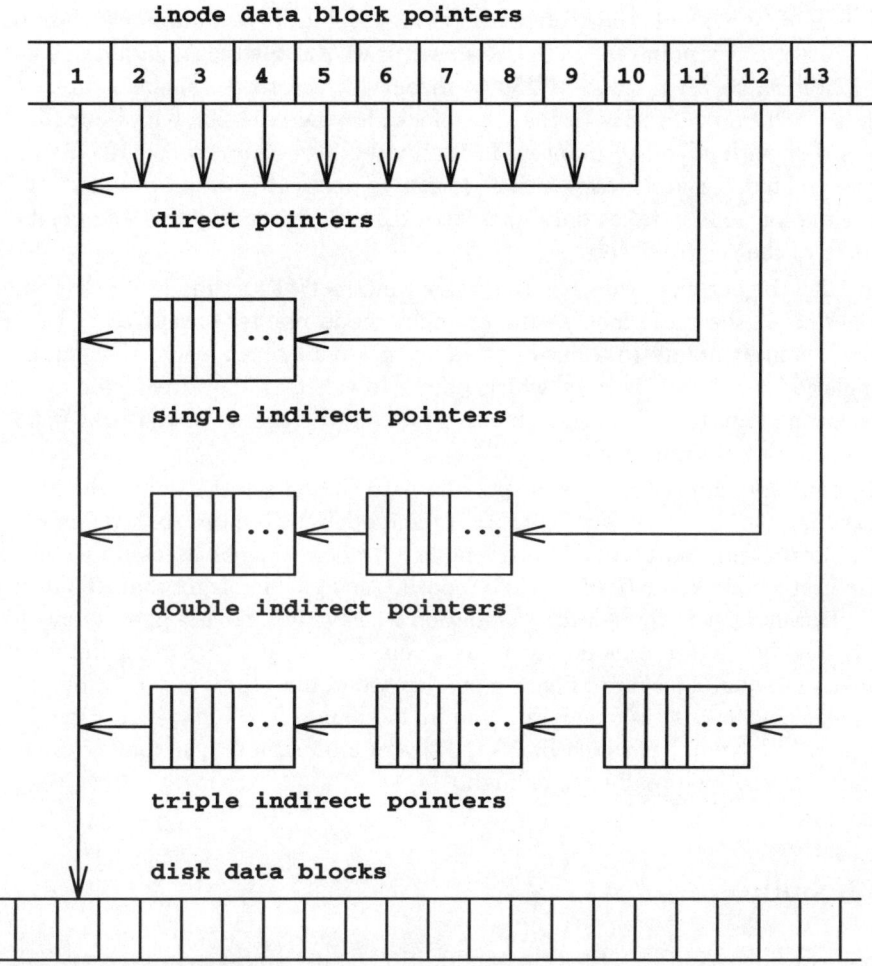

Figure 31.5 Data block pointers in an inode.

to 10 Kb in size. As you can see, for the large majority of files it should be possible to access the data with nothing more than a direct lookup required to find the data block that contains any particular data byte.

With this scheme, once a file has grown to 10 Kb, there are only three block pointers in the inode left to use, whatever the eventual size of the file. Obviously, some new arrangement must be found so that the three remaining block pointers will suffice for any realistic file size, while at the same time not degrading the data access time too much.

This goal is achieved by using the idea of indirect block pointers. Specifically, when an 11th data block needs to be allocated to the file, the 11th inode block pointer is used, but instead of pointing to the block which will contain the data, the

11th pointer is a single indirect pointer which points to a data block filled with a list of direct block pointers. In our example, if we assume that a data block number is a 32-bit value, then a list of 256 of them will fit into the single indirect block. This list will point directly to the data blocks for the next 256 Kb of our file. This means that with 11 block pointers in the inode, files of up to 266 Kb (10 + 256) can be created. True, it takes a little longer to access the data beyond the first 10 Kb in the file, but it takes only one extra disk block read to find the position on the disk of the required data.

For files bigger than 266 Kb the double indirect (12th) inode block pointer is used. This is the same idea as the previous inode pointer except that the double indirect pointer points to a list of pointers in a data block, each of which is itself a single indirect block pointer which points to a list of 256 direct block pointers. This means that the 12th inode block pointer gives access to the next 65536 Kb (256×256) of data in our file.

By now, you should be able to spot the pattern and see that when the file grows bigger than 64 Mb (actually 65802 Kb), the inode's 13th data block pointer will be used, but this time as a triple indirect pointer, which will give access to a staggering 16 Gb (256×256×256 Kb) of extra file space. A single file bigger than 16 Gb sounds huge. However, even though the calculation we have just done suggests that this file size is possible with the inode layout as given, in fact there are other factors which limit the maximum size of a file to a smaller value than this. For example, the size of a file, in bytes, is stored separately in its inode in a field of type `unsigned long`. This is a 32-bit number which limits the size of a file to 4 Gb, so that 13 data block pointers in an inode really are enough.

31.3 minix

The minix filesystem was the first (and initially, only) filesystem type available for Linux as, in its earliest incarnations, Linux sources needed a minix system so you could compile and run them.

From the user's point of view, the design of the minix filesystem is just the same as the System V filesystem from the previous section. However, as you will see, there are several differences between the two, which become apparent when you look at the internals.

To start with, minix uses a very similar arrangement to System V inside its inodes, to allocate data blocks to a file. The only real differences are that it uses only seven direct data block pointers and it does not support the triple indirect block pointer, making nine pointers in the inode in all. By default, minix uses 1 Kb disk data blocks and 16-bit data block pointers. This means that an indirect disk block can hold 512 pointers, which gives a maximum filesystem size of just over 256 Mb (seven direct data blocks plus 512 data blocks via the single indirect block pointer plus 512×512 data blocks via the double indirect block pointer). At

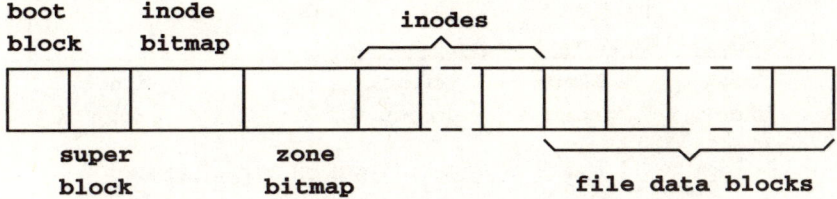

Figure 31.6 minix filesystem layout on a disk partition.

least, this would be the case were it not for the fact that with 16-bit block pointers you can only point at a maximum of 65536 data blocks (i.e. 64 Mb).

The layout of a minix filesystem on a disk partition is a little more complex than the System V equivalent, and is shown in Figure 31.6. Part of the reason for the extra complexity is that the minix filesystem uses the concept of zones as groups of data blocks, though, by default, zones and data blocks are the same thing and are both 1 Kb in size.

The rest of the extra complexity is because of the addition of the inode and zone bitmaps. Essentially, these replace the System V free inode and free data block lists in the super block. The advantage of bitmaps is that they take up relatively little space, as only a single bit is required for each inode and zone to specify whether it is in use or free. The practical consequence of this is that whole bitmaps can be stored in memory for as long as the filesystem is mounted. Searching a bitmap in memory is a far faster operation than sequentially searching through the inode array on disk, or reading a disk block's contents from the disk in order to fill the super block inode and data block free lists when this is required.

The reason for the zone bitmap rather than a data block bitmap is that disk space is allocated in zones. A zone is a power-of-two-sized set of data blocks grouped together and treated as a single entity when it comes to allocating the space to a file. This means that a zone can be 1, 2, 4, 8, etc., data blocks in size (1 data block in size by default). With this arrangement it is possible to have minix filesystems that are larger than 64 Mb because all the pointers accessed via the inode are really pointing to zones which can be larger than the 1 Kb default.

31.4 ext2

The second extended filesystem is virtually the standard filesystem type used on all Linux distributions and installations. It is very powerful and flexible and has been extensively optimized for performance. To see that this is so we shall look at some of the differences between it and the other two systems you have seen to observe the improvements.

To start with, the inodes in the `ext2` filesystem contain 15 block pointers, each 32 bits in size. These are arranged as 12 direct data block pointers and then one

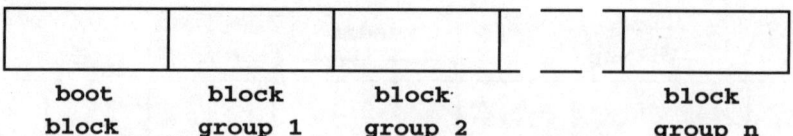

Figure 31.7 ext2 filesystem layout on a disk partition.

single, one double and one triple indirect block pointer.

Next, file names in ext2 are not limited to a fixed-sized record with a maximum of 14 characters as they are in the standard System V and minix filesystems. In ext2, directory entries are of variable length so as not to waste space and have a maximum length of 255 characters – more than enough for any application.

The layout of the filesystem on a disk partition has also been updated to make it faster and more efficient for data reads and writes. Figure 31.7 shows the top level structure of a partition.

The diagram shows that the partition consists of a boot block followed by a set of repetitions of a structure called a block group. The idea behind block groups is that they should improve the reliability of the filesystem and also improve its speed compared to the other filesystems we have examined.

The reliability is improved by using block groups because each block group contains a duplicate copy of system critical information, specifically the super block and the filesystem descriptors. This means that if one copy of this data should become corrupted, then it is always possible to obtain access to a backup copy.

The rest of the information in the filesystem, which consists of the block and inode bitmaps, the inode array and the file data blocks, is then distributed between the block groups so that each block group has a piece of each structure. This is shown in Figure 31.8, which gives the layout for a single block group.

In order to increase data access speed with this scheme, the ext2 filesystem uses a combination of several optimizations including:

- Whenever data blocks are allocated to a file, ext2 will always attempt to allocate the blocks in the same block group as the file's inode. This ensures that the inode and the data blocks are all physically close to each other on the disk to reduce the amount of disk head movement required to access a file and its data.
- When you write to a file and need to allocate new data blocks to the file, ext2 will try to preallocate up to eight contiguous data blocks into which the file can grow. Using a block bitmap this is an easy operation because eight contiguous data blocks will be represented by eight consecutive bits (i.e. a single byte) in the bitmap.
- When sequential read operations are taking place on a file and a physical read of the disk is required, ext2 can take advantage of the way that the data was written. Because of the preallocation of contiguous data blocks on write, it is likely that the data being read is contained in contiguous blocks. This makes

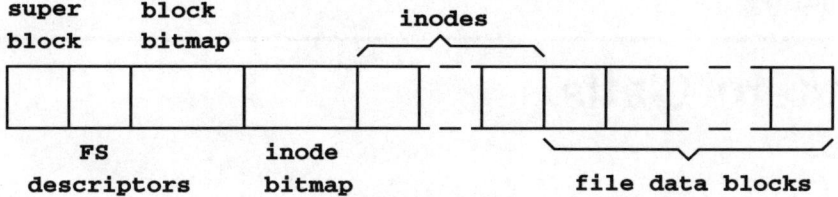

Figure 31.8 Layout of an ext2 block group.

it worth doing a read ahead of several blocks at the same time into the buffer cache, while the disk heads are in the right place, so that the data will already be in the cache when it is required.

There are many other facilities provided by the ext2 filesystem which make it the best current choice as a general purpose Linux filesystem. It also has the flexibility for much future expansion, and development is continuously in progress.

Chapter 32
System Calls

Back in Part 3 we took quite a detailed look at the more important system calls provided by Linux. The list we looked at does not represent the complete list of available system calls, nor could it, as this list is not fixed in size but can be extended as the need arises. Having said this, the list of system calls does not get extended all that often, but it has happened from time to time.

This chapter takes a look at the basic mechanism used by Linux to execute its system calls and then goes on to explain how you could add system calls of your own to the Linux kernel.

32.1 Interrupts and Exceptions

Most modern microprocessors, including all the PC processors upon which Linux will run, can have their processing interrupted by an event which has a higher priority than the currently executing code.

These special events come in several 'flavors' but, collectively, they are known as *interrupts and exceptions*. In general, an interrupt is a hardware generated 'prod' to the processor, caused by some external event. These events include hard disk and floppy disk activity, as well as things like keyboard input and modem control activity. An exception, on the other hand, is generated in response to some types of system error and also in response to some special machine code instructions that can be executed in program code.

Whichever interrupt or exception is raised, the processor's response is quite similar. A special piece of code will be executed, called either the interrupt handler or the exception handler. Normally, there is a separate handler for each interrupt and exception type in use on a particular system.

The way this works is that each interrupt and exception type is given a unique number in the range 0 to 255. Whenever an interrupt or exception is raised, this number (called the *vector number*) is used as an index into an array of pointers (the interrupt and exception vector table). Each pointer in the table is the address of a routine which will be called in order to deal with its particular interrupt or exception type. Most interrupts and exceptions are treated like function calls, so that the interrupted code resumes from where it left off when the interrupt or exception handler finishes.

32.2 System Call Mechanism

So, why am I telling you all this? Well, under Linux, system calls are implemented as one of the exception types which can be generated by executing an appropriate machine code instruction. One of the important side effects of generating an interrupt or an exception is that the system automatically gets switched from user mode into kernel mode to deal with it. This means that executing the system call exception instruction will automatically switch the system into kernel mode and arrange to execute an exception handler which knows how to deal with the call.

The actual instruction used by Linux to perform the system call exception is:

```
int     $0x80
```

This uses interrupt/exception vector number 128 (80 hex) in order to pass control to the kernel.

In order that you do not need to do any machine code programming when you make a system call, the standard C library contains a short routine for each system call which does the machine code bit for you. In fact, the machine code bit is quite straightforward; all that happens is that any parameter values to be passed into the system call are loaded up into CPU registers and then the `int 0x80` instruction is executed. The system call will then be run and any return value from the call will be returned in one of the CPU registers. The standard library routine takes this return value and arranges for it to be passed back to your code.

In order to make easy the task of executing a system call manually, Linux provides a set of pre-processor macros which can be used from within your own code. These macros take parameters which, when the macro is expanded, will tailor the expansion so that it becomes a specific function for calling a particular system call.

These macros all have names of the form:

```
_syscallN(parameters)
```

where N is replaced by the number of parameters the system call will take, and parameters is replaced by a set of parameters which tailor the expansion for a particular system call. For example, in order to create a function to call the setuid() system call you would use the _syscall1() macro as follows:

```
_syscall1(int, setuid, uid_t, uid)
```

460 *System Calls*

The first and second parameters to any of the _syscallN() macros are the return type that the generated function will give (int here) and the name of the generated function itself (setuid here).

After that, for each parameter value that the system call takes, the associated _syscallN() macro has two extra parameters, which specify the type and the name of each system call parameter (uid_t and uid in the example).

One restriction on the data types that can be used as system call parameters is that they must not be more than 4 bytes in size because, when the int 0x80 instruction is executed to make the call, the values of the parameters are all stored in 32-bit CPU registers. Another limitation due to using CPU registers to pass the parameters is that there is a maximum number of parameters which can be passed into a system call. This limit is five, so that there are only six different _syscallN() macros defined (_syscall0() to _syscall5()).

Once the expansion of one of the _syscallN() macros has been performed with an appropriate set of parameters for a particular system call, the result is a function with the name of that system call which can be run from user programs to execute that call.

32.3 Adding New Calls

Once you understand the mechanism by which Linux programs execute system calls, it is a fairly straightforward task to add your own system calls to your kernel.

In order to make sure you understand this process better we will actually develop a very trivial new system call and add it to the kernel. The system call to be added will be:

```
int printcons(char *mess, int len);
```

The printcons() call takes two parameters, mess, which is a pointer to a message stored in an array of characters, and len, which is the number of characters in the array. All that the new call will do is just to display the message characters on the console terminal screen. If successful, printcons() will return the value zero, otherwise -1 will be returned and errno will be set appropriately.

32.3.1 Coding the Call

The first task is to write the code to be added to the kernel. This is just a function which you will add to one of the kernel files, and it is a very similar task to writing a device driver function, something which you have seen previously. The code for the printcons() system call appears as:

```
asmlinkage int sys_printcons(char *mess, int len)
{
```

```
    char *kmess;

    /* 1 */
    if (verify_area(VERIFY_READ, mess, len))
        return -EFAULT;

    /* 2 */
    if ((kmess = vmalloc(len+1))==0)
        return -ENOMEM;

    /* 3 */
    memcpy_fromfs(kmess, mess, len);
    kmess[len] = '\0';
    console_print(kmess);

    /* 4 */
    vfree(kmess);
    return 0;
}
```

For such a trivial task as printing text to the console screen, this code may seem like overkill, but it does illustrate several points. The simplest place to enter this code, assuming that your kernel sources are in the standard place (/usr/src/linux) is at the end of the file:

/usr/src/linux/kernel/sys.c

The first thing to notice about the code itself is that the name of the function is just the name of the new system call with sys_ added to the front. Parameters are then declared as if the system call was going to be used just like a function.

The text for each of the numbered comments in the code is:

1. This system call is going to display the contents of a string on the console screen using the console_print() kernel function. The pointer to the text message (mess) is an address in user memory and so the message needs to be copied into kernel memory before it can be printed. The first task, then, is to check that memory accesses to the given address are legal for the user on whose behalf they will be performed. This check is done by calling the verify_area() kernel function. Our system call will return an EFAULT error if the required access is not permitted.
2. In order to be able to cope with messages of any length, the next step is to use the kernel vmalloc() function dynamically to grab a block of memory into which a user text message can be copied. Notice that the size of the requested memory block is one byte larger than the number of characters to be copied from user space. This is to ensure that space is available into which a zero

byte may be written to terminate the message and make it into a C string for printing. The pointer returned by vmalloc() is assigned to the variable kmess. Any failure here results in the return of an ENOMEM error.

3. The next three lines of code get the user's message, copying it from mess to kmess with the memcpy_fromfs() function, add a zero byte to the end of the message to prepare it for printing and then use the kernel console_print() function to display the message on the screen.

4. Finally, the last two lines tidy up by using vfree() to release the vmalloc()ed memory back to the system and then the last line returns a zero to the calling process to show that the call was successful.

32.3.2 Linking the Call In

Having written the code for the new system call, the next task is to make the rest of the kernel aware of the existence of the code and then to build a new kernel which contains the system call code within it.

In order to add the links from the existing kernel code into your new function you will need to edit two files. Depending on which version of the kernel you are running, the first of these is either:

    /usr/src/linux/include/linux/unistd.h

for kernels up to and including version 1.2 or, for kernels at version 1.3 and higher, the file is:

    /usr/src/linux/include/asm-i386/unistd.h

The file contains a list of #defines used to allocate to each system call a unique number. Each line in the list has the format:

    #define __NR_name   NNN

where name is replaced with the system call name and NNN is that system call's corresponding number. You should add your call's name to the end of the list and allocate to it the next available system call number in sequence. The line for our example system call might be:

    #define __NR_printcons   149

The second file to change also depends on which version of the kernel you are modifying. For kernels up to and including 1.1 the file is:

    /usr/src/linux/include/linux/sys.h

and what you need to do is to add the name of your new kernel function to the end of the list which is initializing the `sys_call_table[]` array. By doing this, you are adding a pointer to your new kernel function on to the end of an array of pointers to functions which point to each of the system calls in the kernel. To stop the compiler complaining about your function name in the array you will also need to add an `extern` declaration of your function to the end of the list of similar declarations that occur before the definition of the `sys_call_table[]` array.

For kernels of version 1.2 and higher, the second file to modify is:

```
/usr/src/linux/arch/i386/kernel/entry.S
```

which contains the initialization of the same array of pointers as the previous version, but this time written in assembly code rather than in C. Don't worry about the file being in assembly code – you don't need to understand it to modify it successfully. All you do is look for a list of assembler directives with the format:

```
.long _sys_name
```

followed by another assembler directive with the format:

```
.space (NR_syscalls-NNN)*4
```

where `NNN` in the formula is the total number of system calls. All that you need to do is to add a new `.long` line with your own kernel function name plus an underscore (_) on the front and then increment the `NNN` value to include your new call. The result for our example could be:

```
.long _sys_printcons
.space (NR_syscalls-149)*4
```

At this point, all that remains is to rebuild and run the new kernel. In the previous explanation references to `i386` in the pathnames of certain files may be replaced with the appropriate names if your work needs to be carried out on other machine architectures to which Linux has been ported.

32.3.3 Using a New Call

All that remains now is to sort out how to use your new system call from within your programs. Don't forget that a code stub for your new system call does not exist in the standard C library, so you must create one for yourself.

This is really easy, using the `_syscallN()` macros. A short C program to use the new `printcons` system call could be:

```
#include <linux/unistd.h>

_syscall2(int, printcons, char *, mess, int, len)
```

```
main()
{
    char message[] = "Print straight to console\n";

    if (printcons(message, strlen(message))==-1)
        printf("Error occurred in printcons() call\n");
}
```

The _syscall2() macro is used here because our system call has two parameters. The macro itself will be expanded into a function in your program called printcons() which the subsequent call inside main() will execute. The preprocessor generated code inside the printcons() function in your program will contain all the necessary machine code instructions to load the appropriate CPU registers with your system call's parameter values and then execute the int 0x80 exception. When the exception returns, the return value from your kernel function will be examined and an appropriate value returned to your code in main().

Linux Permuted Index

There are many commands, system calls, library functions and other Linux facilities which are not directly covered in this book. One of the biggest difficulties with using these facilities is just discovering their existence in the first place. This index is an attempt to make it easier to find many of the facilities which would otherwise remain unknown.

To this end, I have gathered together the names of a large number of facilities for which manual pages exist, along with simple descriptions of these facilities and I have created an index from the names and the keywords in the descriptions.

All you need to do in order to use the index, is just think of one or more keywords that might be related to the topic in which you are interested and then lookup those keywords. What you will find is a list of the names, manual sections and descriptions for any facilities containing your keywords.

For example, suppose you didn't know how to delete a DOS file on a floppy disk. Obvious keywords here would be things like: `delete` or DOS. In fact, either one of these will lead you to the discovery of the `mdel` command in section (1) of the manual.

An index lookup on the keyword `delete` will give the following entries:

delete - `lprm` (1) - delete queued printer jobs
delete - `mdel` (1) - mtools delete a DOS file
delete - `rm` (1) - delete files
delete - `rmdir` (1) - delete empty directories
delete - `rmdir` (2) - delete a directory
delete_module - `delete_module` (2) - kernel loadable module support

As you can see, not only do you get a lead to `mdel` but also to other commands and functions concerned with the deletion of other things as well. You should remember that, on your system, the list of manual pages you have available will depend on which Linux distribution you have installed and which software packages from that distribution you have chosen to load.

.   -   .   (1) - bash built-in commands
:   -   :   (1) - bash built-in commands
1970 - kernel_mktime (9) - convert struct mktime into seconds since 1 January, 1970
8086 - vm86 (2) - enter virtual 8086 mode
abnormal - abort (3) - cause abnormal process termination
abort - abort (3) - cause abnormal process termination
abs - abs (3) - absolute value math function
absolute - abs (3) - absolute value math function
absolute - fabs (3) - absolute value of floating point number
absolute - labs (3) - absolute value of a long int
absolute - realpath (3) - make absolute pathname from relative pathname or symbolic link
accept - accept (2) - accept a connection on a socket
access - access (2) - check user's permissions on a file
accounting - acct (2) - switch process accounting on or off
accounting - pac (8) - display printer accounting information
acct - acct (2) - switch process accounting on or off
acos - acos (3) - arc cosine trig function
acosh - acosh (3) - inverse hyperbolic cosine trig function
across - gpm (1) - cut and paste across virtual consoles
addftinfo - addftinfo (1) - modify troff font files for use with groff
addmntent - addmntent (3) - access fstab and mtab file entries
address - elmalias (1) - expand and display elm address aliases
address - mailaddr (7) - mail address description
address - newalias (1) - install new elm mail address aliases
addresses - inet_addr, inet_network, inet_ntoa, inet_makeaddr, inet_lnaof, inet_netof (3) - manipulate Internet addresses
add_timer - add_timer (9) - kernel event timers
adjtimex - adjtimex (2) - tune kernel clock
adjust_clock - adjust_clock (9) - set kernel clock to GMT from time-zone value
administrative - intro (8) - introduction to administrative/privileged commands
Adobe - afm2tfm (1) - convert Adobe font metrics to TeX font metrics
afm2tfm - afm2tfm (1) - convert Adobe font metrics to TeX font metrics
afmtodit - afmtodit (1) - create font files for use with groff
afs_syscall - afs_syscall (2) - unimplemented system calls
agetty - agetty (8) - getty for login prompt
alarm - alarm (2) - set a clock for an alarm signal
alias - alias (1) - bash built-in commands
alias - checkalias (1) - test if an alias is defined
aliases - elmalias (1) - expand and display elm address aliases
aliases - listalias (1) - display elm aliases
aliases - newalias (1) - install new elm mail address aliases
alloca - alloca (3) - allocate memory
allocate - alloca (3) - allocate memory
allocation - calloc, malloc, free, realloc (3) - dynamic memory allocation functions
alphasort - alphasort (3) - search a directory for entries with particular attributes
alter - renice (8) - alter running process priorities
amount - sleep (1) - sleep for a specified amount of time
amount - sleep (3) - sleep for a specified amount of time
amslatex - amslatex (1) - text formatting and typesetting
amstex - amstex (1) - text formatting and typesetting
anagram - strfry (3) - generate an anagram of a string
analog - xclock (1) - analog and digital clock for X-windows
analysis - gnuan (6) - produce a chess game analysis
analyzer - flex (1) - fast lexical analyzer generator
anonymous - pipe (2) - create anonymous pipe
another - write (1) - send a message to another user
ANSI - ansi2knr (1) - convert ANSI C to Kernighan & Ritchie C
ansi2knr - ansi2knr (1) - convert ANSI C to Kernighan & Ritchie C
answer - answer (1) - elm phone message system
a.out - ld.so (8) - a.out linker
application's - appres (1) - list application's X resources
applications - xlsclients (1) - list client applications running on a display
appres - appres (1) - list application's X resources
apropos - apropos (1) - list manual entries relevant to a query
ar - ar (1) - create, modify, and extract from archives
arc - acos (3) - arc cosine trig function
arc - asin (3) - arc sine trig function
arc - atan (3) - arc tangent trig function
arc - atan2 (3) - arc tangent trig function of two variables
arch - arch (1) - display processor architecture
architecture - arch (1) - display processor architecture
archive - funzip (1) - extract files from a ZIP archive
archive - ranlib (1) - generate an index for an ar archive
archive - size (1) - list section sizes in archive and object files
archive - unzip (1) - extract compressed files from a zip archive
archive - zip, zipcloak, zipnote, zipsplit (1) - package and compress (archive) files
archive - zipinfo (1) - list detailed information about a zip archive
archives - ar (1) - create, modify, and extract from archives
archives - cpio (1) - copy files to and from archives
archives - fiz (1) - data recovery from damaged zoo archives
archives - shar (1) - create shell archives
archives - unzipsfx (1) - creat self-extracting zip archives
archives - zoo (1) - manipulate compressed file archives
archiving - tar (1) - tape archiving utility

argument - stdarg (3) - variable argument list macros
ARP - arp (8) - manipulate system ARP tables
arp - arp (8) - manipulate system ARP tables
array - bcmp, bcopy, bzero, memccpy, memchr, memcmp, memcpy, memfrob, memmem, memmove, memset (3) - byte array operations
array - bsearch (3) - binary search a sorted array
array - qsort (3) - quick sort an array
as - banner (6) - print text as a large banner
as - pstree (1) - display process hierarchy as a tree
as - znew (1) - recompress .Z files as .gz files
ascii - ascii (7) - ascii character set
ascii - asctime, ctime, difftime, gmtime, localtime, mktime (3) - convert date and time to ascii
ascii - hexdump (1) - display file contents in hexadecimal decimal ascii and octal
ascii - pfbtops (1) - translate a .pfb postscript font to ascii
ascii - uuencode (1) - ascii encode a binary file
asctime - asctime (3) - convert date and time to ascii
asin - asin (3) - arc sine trig function
asinh - asinh (3) - inverse hyperbolic sine trig function
assert - assert (3) - terminate process if assertion is false
assertion - assert (3) - terminate process if assertion is false
assign - putenv (3) - assign a value to an environment variable
at - at (1) - manipulate batch jobs for later execution
atan - atan (3) - arc tangent trig function
atan2 - atan2 (3) - arc tangent trig function of two variables
atanh - atanh (3) - inverse hyperbolic tangent trig function
atexit - atexit (3) - call function on program termination
atobm - atobm (1) - bitmap editor and utilities for X11
atof - atof (3) - convert a string to a double
atoi - atoi (3) - convert a string to an integer
atol - atol (3) - convert a string to a long integer
atoms - xlsatoms (1) - list interned atoms defined on server
atq - atq (1) - manipulate batch jobs for later execution
atrm - atrm (1) - manipulate batch jobs for later execution
atrun - atrun (8) - run batch jobs queued for later execution
attribute - mattrib (1) - change attribute bit flags for DOS files
attributes - chattr (1) - change file attributes in second extended filesystems
attributes - lsattr (1) - list file attributes on a second extended filesystem
attributes - rcs (1) - change revision control system file attributes
attributes - scandir, alphasort (3) - search a directory for entries with particular attributes
attributes - setterm (1) - set terminal attributes

attributes - termios, tcgetattr, tcsetattr, tcsendbreak, tcdrain, tcflush, tcflow, cfgetospeed, cfgetispeed, cfsetispeed, cfsetospeed (2) - get and set terminal attributes and controls
audio - workbone (1) - play audio compact discs on a CD-ROM reader
audio - workman (1) - play audio compact discs on a CD-ROM reader
authority - mcookie (1) - generate magic cookies for the X authority system
authority - xauth (1) - X11 authority file utility
authorization - iceauth (1) - display or set ICE authorization information
auto-key - kbdrate (8) - set keyboard auto-key repeat rate and initial repeat delay time
automatic - depmod, modprobe (1) - automatic handling of loadable modules
average - tload (1) - gives graphic display of system load average
awaiting - select (2) - sleep awaiting file descriptor events
backgrounds - bggen (1) - generate colored backgrounds for X11
bad - badblocks (8) - search for bad blocks on a disk partition
badblocks - badblocks (8) - search for bad blocks on a disk partition
badwidth - lbxproxy (1) - low network badwidth proxy server for X11
banner - banner (6) - print text as a large banner
basename - basename (1) - strip directory prefix from file pathname
bash - :, ., alias, bg, bind, break, builtin, bye, case, cd, command, continue, declare, dirs, echo, enable, eval, exec, exit, export, fc, fg, for, getopts, hash, help, history, if, jobs, kill, let, local, logout, popd, pushd, pwd, read, readonly, return, set, shift, source, suspend, test, times, trap, type, typeset, ulimit, umask, unalias, unset, until, wait, while (1) - bash built-in commands
bash - bash (1) - GNU Bourne-Again SHell
batch - at, batch, atq, atrm (1) - manipulate batch jobs for later execution
batch - atrun (8) - run batch jobs queued for later execution
batch - fastmail (1) - quick batch mail interface
bcmp - bcmp (3) - byte array operations
bcopy - bcopy (3) - byte array operations
BDF - fstobdf (1) - create BDF file from X11 font
bdflush - bdflush (2) - control disk buffer daemon
bdflush - bdflush (8) - daemon to flush buffers back to disk
bdftopcf - bdftopcf (1) - X11 font conversion program
beforelight - beforelight (1) - X11 screen saver
behaviour - reboot (2) - reboot Linux or modify Ctrl-Alt-Del behaviour
behaviour - siginterrupt (3) - change signal behaviour with system calls
Bessel - j0, j1, jn, y0, y1, yn (3) - Bessel math functions
bg - bg (1) - bash built-in commands

bggen - `bggen (1)` - generate colored backgrounds for X11
bibliographic - `gindxbib (1)` - create an inverted index for a bibliographic database
bibliographic - `glookbib (1)` - search bibliographic reference databases
bibliographic - `grefer (1)` - preprocessor for groff bibliographic references
bibliographic - `lkbib (1)` - find keys in bibliographic databases
bibliography - `bibtex (1)` - make bibliography for a LaTeX document
bibtex - `bibtex (1)` - make bibliography for a LaTeX document
binary - `bpe (1)` - binary file editor
binary - `bsearch (3)` - binary search a sorted array
binary - `dsplit (1)` - split binary files into pieces
binary - `uuencode (1)` - ascii encode a binary file
bind - `bind (1)` - bash built-in commands
bind - `bind (2)` - bind a name to a socket
bindings - `lesskey (1)` - manipulate key bindings for less
bit - `ffs (3)` - returns position of first bit set in a word
bit - `mattrib (1)` - change attribute bit flags for DOS files
bit - `null, zero (4)` - bit bucket special files
bitmap - `bitmap, bmtoa, atobm (1)` - bitmap editor and utilities for X11
BitmapBitOrder - `BitmapBitOrder (3)` - Xlib image formating functions and macros
BitmapPad - `BitmapPad (3)` - Xlib image formating functions and macros
BitmapUnit - `BitmapUnit (3)` - Xlib image formating functions and macros
bits - `chmod (1)` - change file access permission bits
bits - `chmod, fchmod (2)` - change file access permission bits
block - `dumpe2fs (8)` - display filesystem super block and block-group information
block - `pause (2)` - block a process and wait for a signal
block - `sum (1)` - generate checksum and block count for a file
block - `xtetris (6)` - X-window block dropping game
block-group - `dumpe2fs (8)` - display filesystem super block and block-group information
blocks - `badblocks (8)` - search for bad blocks on a disk partition
blocks - `readv, writev (3)` - transfer several data blocks using multiple buffers
bmtoa - `bmtoa (1)` - bitmap editor and utilities for X11
board - `xvier (6)` - X11 board game
boot - `bootparam (7)` - Linux kernel boot time parameters
bootparam - `bootparam (7)` - Linux kernel boot time parameters
bounding - `psbb (1)` - get bounding box size from a postscript document
Bourne-Again - `bash (1)` - GNU Bourne-Again SHell
box - `psbb (1)` - get bounding box size from a postscript document
boxes - `dialog (1)` - handle dialog boxes from shell scripts
bpe - `bpe (1)` - binary file editor
break - `break (1)` - bash built-in commands
break - `break (2)` - unimplemented system calls
breaks - `more (1)` - display file contents with page breaks
bridge - `xcutsel (1)` - cut and paste bridge program
brk - `brk (2)` - change process data segment size
bsearch - `bsearch (3)` - binary search a sorted array
bucket - `null, zero (4)` - bit bucket special files
buffer - `bdflush (2)` - control disk buffer daemon
buffer - `dmesg (8)` - display/control the kernel message buffer
buffer - `sync (2)` - flush filesystem buffer cache
buffer - `sync (8)` - flush filesystem buffer cache
buffering - `setbuf, setbuffer, setlinebuf, setvbuf (3)` - file output buffering operations
buffers - `bdflush (8)` - daemon to flush buffers back to disk
buffers - `readv, writev (3)` - transfer several data blocks using multiple buffers
build - `column (1)` - build columns from lists
buildhash - `buildhash (1)` - spell checker
built-in - `:, ., alias, bg, bind, break, builtin, bye, case, cd, command, continue, declare, dirs, echo, enable, eval, exec, exit, export, fc, fg, for, getopts, hash, help, history, if, jobs, kill, let, local, logout, popd, pushd, pwd, read, readonly, return, set, shift, source, suspend, test, times, trap, type, typeset, ulimit, umask, unalias, unset, until, wait, while (1)` - bash built-in commands
builtin - `builtin (1)` - bash built-in commands
bye - `bye (1)` - bash built-in commands
byte - `bcmp, bcopy, bzero, memccpy, memchr, memcmp, memcpy, memfrob, memmem, memmove, memset (3)` - byte array operations
byte - `htonl, htons, ntohl, ntohs (3)` - translate between host and network byte order
byte-order - `swab (3)` - swap word byte-order
bytes - `cksum (1)` - crc-check and count the bytes in a file
bytes - `read (2)` - read bytes from an open file description
bytes - `wc (1)` - print the number of bytes, words, and lines in files
bzero - `bzero (3)` - byte array operations
cache - `sync (2)` - flush filesystem buffer cache
cache - `sync (8)` - flush filesystem buffer cache
cal - `cal (1)` - display a calendar
calculate - `difftime (3)` - calculate seconds between two times
calculates - `div (3)` - calculates quotient and remainder on integer division
calculation - `hypot (3)` - Pythagoras distance calculation
calendar - `cal (1)` - display a calendar
call - `atexit (3)` - call function on program termination
call - `globfree (3)` - free memory from previous glob call
call - `idle (2)` - internal system call to make process-0 idle
call - `socketcall (2)` - socket system call entry point

calloc - calloc (3) - dynamic memory allocation functions
calls - afs_syscall, break, gtty, lock, mpx, prof, quotactl, stty (2) - unimplemented system calls
calls - intro (2) - introduction to system calls
calls - siginterrupt (3) - change signal behaviour with system calls
calls - strace (1) - run a command and trace system calls and signals
can - securetty (5) - list of ttys from which root can login
capability - printcap (5) - printer capability data base
capability - termcap (5) - terminal capability database
capability - terminfo (5) - terminal capability database
card - spider (1) - double deck card game
case - case (1) - bash built-in commands
case - strcasecmp, strncasecmp (3) - compare two strings and ignore case
case - toupper, tolower (3) - convert letters to upper or lower case
cat - cat (1) - concatenate files
catalog - catopen, catclose, catgets (3) - message catalog operations
catclose - catclose (3) - message catalog operations
catgets - catgets (3) - message catalog operations
catopen - catopen (3) - message catalog operations
cause - abort (3) - cause abnormal process termination
cause - exit (3) - cause program termination
cbrt - cbrt (3) - cube root math function
cccp - cccp (1) - C preprocessor
cd - cd (1) - bash built-in commands
CD-ROM - workbone (1) - play audio compact discs on a CD-ROM reader
CD-ROM - workman (1) - play audio compact discs on a CD-ROM reader
cdtin - cdtin (1) - network news readers
ceil - ceil (3) - smallest integer value not less than x
cfdisk - cfdisk (8) - curses based fdisk
cfgetispeed - cfgetispeed (2) - get and set terminal attributes and controls
cfgetospeed - cfgetospeed (2) - get and set terminal attributes and controls
cfsetispeed - cfsetispeed (2) - get and set terminal attributes and controls
cfsetospeed - cfsetospeed (2) - get and set terminal attributes and controls
character - ascii (7) - ascii character set
character - fgetc, fgets, getc, getchar, gets, ungetc (3) - string and character input functions
character - fputc, fputs, putc, putchar, puts (3) - string and character output functions
character - groff_char (7) - groff input character list
character - index, rindex (3) - find character in string
character - isalnum, isalpha, iscntrl, isdigit, isgraph, islower, isprint, ispunct, isspace, isupper, isxdigit (3) - character test functions and macros
character - iso_8859_1 (7) - map of character set

character - mblen (3) - get length of a multi-byte character
character - mbstowcs (3) - convert multi-byte to wide character strings
character - mbstowcs (3) - convert wide character to multi-byte strings
character - strchr, strrchr (3) - find character in string
character - wctomb (3) - convert a wide character to a multi-byte character
characteristics - reset (1) - reset terminal characteristics to sane values
characters - mbtowc (3) - convert multi-byte characters to wide characters
characters - strpbrk (3) - finds any of a set of characters in a string
characters - strspn, strcspn (3) - return length of string containing given characters
characters - tr (1) - translate characters
characters - xfd (1) - display the characters in a given X11 font
chat - ytalk (1) - a multi-user chat program
chattr - chattr (1) - change file attributes in second extended filesystems
chdir - chdir (2) - change current working directory
check - access (2) - check user's permissions on a file
check - clearerr, feof, ferror, fileno (3) - reset and check stream status
check - dosfsck (8) - check/repair DOS filesystems
check - e2fsck (8) - check second extended filesystem
check - fsck (8) - integrity check and fix a filesystem
check - fsck.minix (8) - integrity check and fix a minix filesystem
check - login (1) - password check program
check - md5sum (1) - generate or check MD5 message signatures
check - pathchk (1) - check for valid file names
check - xfsck (8) - xiafs filesystem consistency check and repair
checkalias - checkalias (1) - test if an alias is defined
checked - rcsfreeze (1) - freeze a set of sources checked in under RCS
checker - frag (8) - filesystem fragmentation checker
checker - ispell (4) - spell checker dictionary format
checker - ispell, buildhash, munchlist, findaffix, tryaffix, icombine, ijoin (1) - spell checker
check-in - ci (1) - revision control system check-in files
check-out - co (1) - revision control system check-out files
checksum - sum (1) - generate checksum and block count for a file
chess - cmail (6) - for e-mail chess games
chess - gnuan (6) - produce a chess game analysis
chess - gnuchess (6) - chess game
Chess - xboard (6) - X-windows user interface for GNU Chess
chfn - chfn (1) - change finger information
chgrp - chgrp (1) - change file group ownership
child - clone (2) - create a child process
child - fork, vfork (2) - create a child process

chmod - chmod (1) - change file access permission bits
chmod - chmod (2) - change file access permission bits
chown - chown (1) - change the user and group ownership of files
chown - chown (2) - change file ownership
chroot - chroot (2) - change root directory
chroot - chroot (8) - execute a program with a new root directory
chsh - chsh (1) - change your login shell in password file
chsh - shells (5) - file of pathnames to login shells for use with chsh
ci - ci (1) - revision control system check-in files
cksum - cksum (1) - crc-check and count the bytes in a file
clean - rcsclean (1) - clean up unmodified rcs working files
clear - clear (1) - clear terminal screen
clearerr - clearerr (3) - reset and check stream status
client - rstart (1) - rsh remote start client
client - xclipboard (1) - X-windows clipboard client
client - xlsclients (1) - list client applications running on a display
clients - xkill (1) - close connections to X11 clients
clipboard - xclipboard (1) - X-windows clipboard client
clock - adjtimex (2) - tune kernel clock
clock - adjust_clock (9) - set kernel clock to GMT from time-zone value
clock - alarm (2) - set a clock for an alarm signal
clock - clock (3) - return processor time used by process
clock - clock (8) - manipulate the CMOS clock
clock - oclock (1) - X11 clock
clock - xclock (1) - analog and digital clock for X-windows
clone - clone (2) - create a child process
close - close (2) - close a file descriptor
close - closedir (3) - close a directory
close - fclose (3) - close a file pointer
close - xkill (1) - close connections to X11 clients
closedir - closedir (3) - close a directory
closelog - closelog (3) - send text to the system message and error logger
cmail - cmail (6) - for e-mail chess games
CMOS - clock (8) - manipulate the CMOS clock
cmp - cmp (1) - compare two files
co - co (1) - revision control system check-out files
code - fig2dev (1) - translate Fig code to other graphics languages
code - rpcgen (1) - C code generator for RPC protocols
col - col (1) - remove reverse line feeds from input
colcrt - colcrt (1) - translate nroff output for screen viewing
color - dircolors (1) - set ls color parameters
color - xcmsdb (1) - X11 color management system
colored - bggen (1) - generate colored backgrounds for X11
colormap - xcmap (1) - display default X11 colormap
colormap - xstdcmap (1) - X-windows standard colormap utility

color-name - showrgb (1) - uncompile an rgb color-name database
colrm - colrm (1) - remove columns from a file
column - column (1) - build columns from lists
columns - colrm (1) - remove columns from a file
columns - column (1) - build columns from lists
combination - ctrlaltdel (8) - set the function of the Ctrl-Alt-Del combination
combines - merge (1) - combines multiple independent modifications to a file
comm - comm (1) - compare two sorted files
command - command (1) - bash built-in commands
command - getopt (1) - parse command line options
command - getopt (3) - parse command line options
command - gnroff (1) - emulate the nroff command using groff
command - grog (1) - generate a groff command with parameter options
command - killall (1) - send signal to processes by command name
command - magic (4) - magic numbers for file command
command - man.config (5) - configuration file for man command
command - nohup (1) - run a command set to ignore hangup signals
command - strace (1) - run a command and trace system calls and signals
command - system (3) - execute a Linux command
command - tee (1) - add a tee to a command pipeline to write to a file
command - whereis (1) - locate files related to a command
command - xargs (1) - execute command lines from stdin
command - xon (1) - run an X-windows command on a remote machine
commands - :, ., alias, bg, bind, break, builtin, bye, case, cd, command, continue, declare, dirs, echo, enable, eval, exec, exit, export, fc, fg, for, getopts, hash, help, history, if, jobs, kill, let, local, logout, popd, pushd, pwd, read, readonly, return, set, shift, source, suspend, test, times, trap, type, typeset, ulimit, umask, unalias, unset, until, wait, while (1) - bash built-in commands
commands - intro (1) - introduction to user commands
commands - intro (8) - introduction to administrative/privileged commands
commands - rcsintro (1) - introduction to revision control system commands
commands - resize (1) - generate shell commands to set TERMCAP and TERM to current xterm size
commands - which (1) - display path name of commands
common - join (1) - join two sorted files line by line on a common field
communication - ipc (5) - System-V interprocess communication mechanisms
communication - minicom (1) - serial communication program

communication - socket (2) - create a communication endpoint
communication - talk (1) - interactive user communication
communication - talkd (8) - talk communication daemon
communications - runscript (1) - script interpreter for minicom communications program
compact - workbone (1) - play audio compact discs on a CD-ROM reader
compact - workman (1) - play audio compact discs on a CD-ROM reader
compare - cmp (1) - compare two files
compare - comm (1) - compare two sorted files
compare - rcsdiff (1) - compare revision control system files
compare - strcasecmp, strncasecmp (3) - compare two strings and ignore case
compare - strcmp, strncmp, strcoll (3) - compare two strings
comparison - x11perfcomp (1) - X11 server comparison program
comparisons - test (1) - generate exit status for file type-checks and value comparisons
comparisons - zcmp, zdiff (1) - perform comparisons on compressed files
compatible - gtroff (1) - gnu troff compatible document format program
compile - gtbl (1) - compile table description for groff
compiled - term (5) - format of compiled term file
compiled - untic (1) - uncompile the contents of a compiled terminfo file
compiler - g++ (1) - GNU C++ compiler
compiler - gcc (1) - GNU C compiler
compiler - tic (1) - terminfo compiler
compiler - zic (8) - time zone compiler
complementary-error - erf, erfc (3) - error and complementary-error math functions
compress - compress, uncompress, zcat (1) - compress and expand file contents
compress - gzip, gunzip, zcat (1) - compress and uncompress files
compress - sq (1) - compress a sorted word list
compress - zip, zipcloak, zipnote, zipsplit (1) - package and compress (archive) files
compressed - gzexe (1) - create self extracting compressed executable file
compressed - unzip (1) - extract compressed files from a zip archive
compressed - zcmp, zdiff (1) - perform comparisons on compressed files
compressed - zgrep (1) - search compressed files for a regular expression
compressed - zmore (1) - display compressed text
compressed - zoo (1) - manipulate compressed file archives
concatenate - cat (1) - concatenate files
concatenate - strcat, strncat (3) - concatenate two strings
concatenate - tac (1) - concatenate and reverse file contents
configuration - fpathconf, pathconf (3) - get file configuration option values
configuration - inittab (5) - configuration file for init to process
configuration - man.config (5) - configuration file for man command
configuration - resolver (5) - configuration file for resolv
configuration - setserial (8) - get and set Linux serial port configuration
configuration - sysconf (3) - get runtime configuration information
configuration - syslog.conf (5) - syslogd configuration file
configuration-dependent - confstr (3) - get configuration-dependent string variable values
configure - ifconfig (8) - configure a network interface
configure - plipconfig (8) - configure PLIP device parameters
configured - filesystems (9) - details the table of configured filesystems
confstr - confstr (3) - get configuration-dependent string variable values
connect - connect (2) - make a socket connection
connected - getpeername (2) - get name of peer connected to a given socket
connected - socketpair (2) - create a pair of connected sockets
connection - accept (2) - accept a connection on a socket
connection - connect (2) - make a socket connection
connection - shutdown (2) - shutdown all or part of a full-duplex socket connection
connections - listen (2) - specify queue length for incoming socket connections
connections - netstat (8) - display status information on active network connections
connections - xkill (1) - close connections to X11 clients
consistency - xfsck (8) - xiafs filesystem consistency check and repair
console - console (4) - console terminal
console - setfont (8) - load EGA or VGA console screen font
console - xconsole (1) - monitor system console messages with X-windows
consoles - gpm (1) - cut and paste across virtual consoles
containing - strspn, strcspn (3) - return length of string containing given characters
contents - compress, uncompress, zcat (1) - compress and expand file contents
contents - hexdump (1) - display file contents in hexadecimal decimal ascii and octal
contents - ls, dir, vdir (1) - list directory contents
contents - more (1) - display file contents with page breaks
contents - mtype (1) - display contents of a DOS file
contents - od (1) - display file contents in octal or other formats
contents - tac (1) - concatenate and reverse file contents
contents - untic (1) - uncompile the contents of a compiled terminfo file
continue - continue (1) - bash built-in commands
control - bdflush (2) - control disk buffer daemon
control - ci (1) - revision control system check-in files

control - co (1) - revision control system check-out files
control - ctermid (3) - get control terminal name
control - dmesg (8) - display/control the kernel message buffer
control - init, telinit (8) - setup and control process initialization
control - ioctl (2) - input and output device control
control - lpc (8) - control line printer system
control - msgctl (2) - System-V IPC control message operations
control - mt (1) - control a magnetic tape drive
control - ptrace (2) - debug process trace control
control - rcs (1) - change revision control system file attributes
control - rcsdiff (1) - compare revision control system files
control - rcsfile (1) - format of revision control system file
control - rcsfile (5) - format of revision control system file
control - rcsintro (1) - introduction to revision control system commands
control - rcsmerge (1) - merge revision control system files
control - rmt (8) - control remote magnetic tape drives
control - semctl (2) - System-V IPC control semaphore operations
control - shmctl (2) - System-V IPC shared memory control
control - timedc (8) - timed control program
control - xhost (1) - server access control program for X-windows
controlling - tty (1) - print the special file name of the controlling terminal
controlling - tty (4) - controlling terminal special file
controls - termios, tcgetattr, tcsetattr, tcsendbreak, tcdrain, tcflush, tcflow, cfgetospeed, cfgetispeed, cfsetispeed, cfsetospeed (2) - get and set terminal attributes and controls
conversion - bdftopcf (1) - X11 font conversion program
conversion - ddate (6) - date conversion program
converts - xvpictoppm (1) - converts XV thumbnail files to standard PPM format
cookies - mcookie (1) - generate magic cookies for the X authority system
copy - copysign (3) - copy the sign of a double
copy - cp (1) - copy files
copy - cpio (1) - copy files to and from archives
copy - dd (1) - file and disk partition copy
copy - install (1) - copy files and setup owner and permission modes
copy - lndir (1) - make a copy of a directory tree with symbolic links
copy - mcopy (1) - mtools copy DOS files to or from Linux
copy - mread (1) - copy a DOS file to Linux
copy - mwrite (1) - copy a Linux file to DOS
copy - rcp (1) - remote file copy
copy - strcpy, strncpy (3) - copy a string
copysign - copysign (3) - copy the sign of a double

corresponding - psignal (3) - print message corresponding to signal
cos - cos (3) - cosine trig function
cosh - cosh (3) - hyperbolic cosine trig function
cosine - acos (3) - arc cosine trig function
cosine - acosh (3) - inverse hyperbolic cosine trig function
cosine - cos (3) - cosine trig function
cosine - cosh (3) - hyperbolic cosine trig function
count - cksum (1) - crc-check and count the bytes in a file
count - messages (1) - count of messages in mail folder
count - sum (1) - generate checksum and block count for a file
cp - cp (1) - copy files
cpio - cpio (1) - copy files to and from archives
cpp - cpp (1) - C preprocessor
CPU - top (1) - display processes with highest CPU usage
crash - elvprsv (1) - recover modified version of an elvis edited file after a crash
crash - elvrec (1) - recover an unsaved elvis editor file after a crash
crc-check - cksum (1) - crc-check and count the bytes in a file
creat - creat (2) - open or create a file or device
create_module - create_module (2) - kernel loadable module support
creates - transfig (1) - creates a makefile for portable LaTeX figures
creation - umask (2) - set file creation mask
cron - crond (8) - cron daemon
cron - crontab (5) - tables for driving cron
crond - crond (8) - cron daemon
crontab - crontab (1) - manipulate per-user crontabs
crontab - crontab (5) - tables for driving cron
crontabs - crontab (1) - manipulate per-user crontabs
crypt - crypt (3) - data encryption function
csplit - csplit (1) - split a file into sections
ctags - ctags (1) - generates tags and refs files
ctermid - ctermid (3) - get control terminal name
ctime - ctime (3) - convert date and time to ascii
ctrlaltdel - ctrlaltdel (8) - set the function of the Ctrl-Alt-Del combination
Ctrl-Alt-Del - ctrlaltdel (8) - set the function of the Ctrl-Alt-Del combination
Ctrl-Alt-Del - ctrl_alt_del (9) - handle keyboard Ctrl-Alt-Del sequence
ctrl_alt_del - ctrl_alt_del (9) - handle keyboard Ctrl-Alt-Del sequence
Ctrl-Alt-Del - reboot (2) - reboot Linux or modify Ctrl-Alt-Del behaviour
cube - cbrt (3) - cube root math function
current - chdir, fchdir (2) - change current working directory
current - domainname (1) - set/print domain of current host
current - execl, execlp, execle, exect, execv, execvp (3) - execute new program in current process
current - execve (2) - execute new program in current process
current - _exit (2) - terminate the current process

current - getcwd, get_current_dir_name, getwd (3) - get current working directory
current - gethostid, sethostid (2) - manipulate the current host identifier
current - localeconv (3) - get information for current locale
current - nice (2) - change current process priority
current - raise (3) - signal current process
current - resize (1) - generate shell commands to set TERMCAP and TERM to current xterm size
current - setlocale (3) - set the current locale
current - sysfs (2) - get current filesystem type information
current - telldir (3) - return current position in directory stream
current - uname (2) - return information about the current kernel
current - vhangup (2) - simulate a hangup on the current terminal
current - zdump (8) - display the current time in a given time zone
currently - users (1) - display the login names of users currently logged in
curses - cfdisk (8) - curses based fdisk
curses - curses (3) - terminal screen handling library
cut - cut (1) - select fields from each line of a file
cut - gpm (1) - cut and paste across virtual consoles
cut - xcutsel (1) - cut and paste bridge program
daemon - bdflush (2) - control disk buffer daemon
daemon - bdflush (8) - daemon to flush buffers back to disk
daemon - crond (8) - cron daemon
daemon - fingerd (8) - user information lookup daemon
daemon - ftpd (8) - Internet file transfer protocol daemon
daemon - inetd (8) - Internet super-server daemon
daemon - klogd (1) - kernel message log daemon
daemon - lpd (8) - line printer daemon
daemon - mountd (8) - NFS mount daemon
daemon - nfsd (8) - NFS server daemon
daemon - nntpd (8) - network news transfer protocol daemon
daemon - pop3d (1) - remote mail daemon
daemon - pppd (8) - point-to-point Internet protocol daemon
daemon - rexecd (8) - remote execution daemon
daemon - rlogind (8) - remote login daemon
daemon - routed (8) - network routing daemon
daemon - rpc.rusersd (8) - rusers logged in users daemon
daemon - rpc.rwalld (8) - rwall message daemon
daemon - rshd (8) - remote shell daemon
daemon - rstartd (1) - rsh remote start helper daemon
daemon - rwhod (8) - user and system status daemon
daemon - talkd (8) - talk communication daemon
daemon - telnetd (8) - telnet daemon
daemon - tftpd (8) - trivial file transfer protocol daemon
daemon - timed (8) - time server daemon
damaged - fiz (1) - data recovery from damaged zoo archives

DARPA - portmap (8) - RPC program number to DARPA port number mapper
data - brk, sbrk (2) - change process data segment size
data - crypt (3) - data encryption function
data - fiz (1) - data recovery from damaged zoo archives
data - printcap (5) - printer capability data base
data - proc (5) - pseudo-filesystem for access to kernel data structures
data - readv, writev (3) - transfer several data blocks using multiple buffers
database - gindxbib (1) - create an inverted index for a bibliographic database
database - locatedb (5) - file name database for locate
database - makemap (8) - generate database maps for sendmail
database - psupdate (8) - update the ps kernel database
database - showrgb (1) - uncompile an rgb color-name database
database - termcap (5) - terminal capability database
database - terminfo (5) - terminal capability database
database - updatedb (1) - update file name database
database - whatis (1) - search the whatis database
database - workmanrc, workmandb (5) - database and preference files for workman
database - xrdb (1) - X11 server resource database utility
databases - glookbib (1) - search bibliographic reference databases
databases - lkbib (1) - find keys in bibliographic databases
databases - locate (1) - display file names from databases which match a regular expression
date - asctime, ctime, difftime, gmtime, localtime, mktime (3) - convert date and time to ascii
date - date (1) - display/set the system date and time
date - ddate (6) - date conversion program
date - ftime (2) - manipulate date and time
date - ftime (3) - get date and time
date - gettimeofday, settimeofday (2) - manipulate date and time
date - netdate (8) - set date and time
date - stime (2) - set system time and date
date - strftime (3) - format date and time
day - motd (5) - message of the day file
dd - dd (1) - file and disk partition copy
ddate - ddate (6) - date conversion program
debug - ptrace (2) - debug process trace control
debugfs - debugfs (8) - ext2 filesystem debugger
debugger - debugfs (8) - ext2 filesystem debugger
debugger - gdb (1) - GNU symbolic debugger
decimal - hexdump (1) - display file contents in hexadecimal decimal ascii and octal
deck - spider (1) - double deck card game
declare - declare (1) - bash built-in commands
decode - uudecode (1) - decode a uuencoded file
default - xcmap (1) - display default X11 colormap
defined - checkalias (1) - test if an alias is defined

defined - `xlsatoms` (1) - list interned atoms defined on server
delay - `kbdrate` (8) - set keyboard auto-key repeat rate and initial repeat delay time
delete - `lprm` (1) - delete queued printer jobs
delete - `mdel` (1) - mtools delete a DOS file
delete - `rm` (1) - delete files
delete - `rmdir` (1) - delete empty directories
delete - `rmdir` (2) - delete a directory
delete_module - `delete_module` (2) - kernel loadable module support
deliver - `deliver` (8) - local mail transport
del_timer - `del_timer` (9) - kernel event timers
dependencies - `ldd` (1) - display program shared library dependencies
dependencies - `make` (1) - maintain program dependencies
depmod - `depmod` (1) - automatic handling of loadable modules
describing - `strerror` (3) - return string describing errno
describing - `strsignal` (3) - return string describing signal
descriptor - `close` (2) - close a file descriptor
descriptor - `dup, dup2` (2) - duplicate a file descriptor
descriptor - `getdtablesize` (2) - get file descriptor table size
descriptor - `isatty` (3) - test a file descriptor for a tty
descriptor - `modify_ldt` (2) - get/set process local descriptor table
descriptor - `select` (2) - sleep awaiting file descriptor events
design - `mf, inimf, virmf` (1) - font and logo design tools
detailed - `file_table` (9) - detailed description of the kernel file table
detailed - `zipinfo` (1) - list detailed information about a zip archive
details - `filesystems` (9) - details the table of configured filesystems
details - `hd` (4) - details MFM/RLL/IDE hard disk device special files
determine - `setmetamode` (1) - determine handling of the keyboard meta key
device - `fd` (4) - floppy disk device
device - `hd` (4) - details MFM/RLL/IDE hard disk device special files
device - `ioctl` (2) - input and output device control
device - `lp` (4) - line printer device special file
device - `MAKEDEV` (8) - create device special files
device - `mkswap` (8) - create a swap device
device - `open, creat` (2) - open or create a file or device
device - `plipconfig` (8) - configure PLIP device parameters
device - `ram` (4) - RAM disk device special file
device - `rdev` (8) - display or modify kernel root device, swap device, RAM disk size, and video mode
device - `ttyname` (3) - get the pathname of an open terminal device
device - `ttys` (4) - serial device special files
device - `ttytype` (5) - terminal name and device file

device - `tunelp` (8) - manipulate parameters for the lp printer device
devices - `mmap, munmap` (2) - manipulate mapping of files and devices into memory
devices - `setfdprm` (8) - load parameters into floppy disk devices
devices - `swapon, swapoff` (2) - enable/disable devices and files for paging
devices - `swapon, swapoff` (8) - enable/disable devices and files for paging
df - `df` (1) - summarize free disk partition space
dialog - `dialog` (1) - handle dialog boxes from shell scripts
dictionaries - `english` (4) - format for English spelling dictionaries
dictionary - `ispell` (4) - spell checker dictionary format
diff - `diff` (1) - find differences between two files
diff - `patch` (1) - update a file with a diff
diff3 - `diff3` (1) - find differences between three files
differences - `diff` (1) - find differences between two files
differences - `diff3` (1) - find differences between three files
difftime - `difftime` (3) - calculate seconds between two times
difftime - `difftime` (3) - convert date and time to ascii
dig - `dig` (1) - send domain-name queries to name servers
digital - `xclock` (1) - analog and digital clock for X-windows
dir - `dir` (1) - list directory contents
dircolors - `dircolors` (1) - set ls color parameters
directed - `tsort` (1) - sort nodes in a directed graph
directories - `rmdir` (1) - delete empty directories
directory - `basename` (1) - strip directory prefix from file pathname
directory - `chdir, fchdir` (2) - change current working directory
directory - `chroot` (2) - change root directory
directory - `chroot` (8) - execute a program with a new root directory
directory - `closedir` (3) - close a directory
directory - `dirname` (1) - extract directory prefix from file pathname
directory - `find` (1) - list file names in a directory hierarchy
directory - `ftw` (3) - execute a function on file names in a directory tree
directory - `getcwd, get_current_dir_name, getwd` (3) - get current working directory
directory - `getdirentries` (3) - read directory entries
directory - `link` (2) - make a new directory link to an existing file
directory - `lndir` (1) - make a copy of a directory tree with symbolic links
directory - `ls, dir, vdir` (1) - list directory contents
directory - `manpath` (1) - display directory paths searched for manual pages
directory - `mcd` (1) - mtools change DOS directory
directory - `mdir` (1) - mtools display a DOS directory
directory - `mkdir` (1) - create a directory

directory - mkdir (2) - create a directory
directory - mkdirhier (1) - create a directory
    hierarchy
directory - mklost+found (8) - create a lost+found
    directory on a filesystem
directory - mount, umount (2) - mount and
    unmount filesystems to the directory hierarchy
directory - mount, umount (8) - mount and
    unmount filesystems to the directory hierarchy
directory - mrd (1) - remove a DOS directory
directory - opendir (3) - open a directory
directory - pwd (1) - display name of present
    working directory
directory - readdir (2) - read a directory
directory - rename (2) - change the name or
    directory of a file
directory - rewinddir (3) - reset stream pointer to
    start of directory
directory - rmdir (2) - delete a directory
directory - scandir, alphasort (3) - search a
    directory for entries with particular attributes
directory - seekdir (3) - set the position of the next
    readdir in a directory
directory - telldir (3) - return current position in
    directory stream
directory - unlink (2) - remove a file from a
    directory
dirname - dirname (1) - extract directory prefix
    from file pathname
dirs - dirs (1) - bash built-in commands
disable - mesg (1) - enable or disable write access to
    your terminal
disable - swapon, swapoff (2) - enable/disable
    devices and files for paging
disable - swapon, swapoff (8) - enable/disable
    devices and files for paging
discs - workbone (1) - play audio compact discs on a
    CD-ROM reader
discs - workman (1) - play audio compact discs on a
    CD-ROM reader
disk - badblocks (8) - search for bad blocks on a
    disk partition
disk - bdflush (2) - control disk buffer daemon
disk - bdflush (8) - daemon to flush buffers back to
    disk
disk - dd (1) - file and disk partition copy
disk - df (1) - summarize free disk partition space
disk - du (1) - summarize disk usage
disk - fd (4) - floppy disk device
disk - fdformat (8) - low-level format a floppy disk
disk - fdisk (8) - manipulate disk partition tables
disk - fsync (2) - write a file's in-core memory state
    to disk
disk - hd (4) - details MFM/RLL/IDE hard disk
    device special files
disk - mformat (1) - mtools add a DOS filesystem to
    a low-level formatted floppy disk
disk - ram (4) - RAM disk device special file
disk - rdev (8) - display or modify kernel root device,
    swap device, RAM disk size, and video mode
disk - sd (4) - SCSI disk driver
disk - setfdprm (8) - load parameters into floppy
    disk devices
disk - setup (2) - initialize hard disk driver
display - arch (1) - display processor architecture
display - cal (1) - display a calendar

display - date (1) - display/set the system date and
    time
display - dmesg (8) - display/control the kernel
    message buffer
display - dumpe2fs (8) - display filesystem super
    block and block-group information
display - dumpkeys (1) - display keyboard
    translation tables
display - echo (1) - display text from the shell
display - elmalias (1) - expand and display elm
    address aliases
display - file (1) - display file types
display - free (1) - display memory and swap space
    statistics
display - fsinfo (1) - display X11 font server
    information
display - fuser (1) - display PIDs of processes using
    specified files
display - grep, egrep, fgrep (1) - display lines
    matching a regular expression
display - groups (1) - display a user's groups
display - gxditview (1) - display gtroff output on an
    X display
display - head (1) - display the first part of a file
display - hexdump (1) - display file contents in
    hexadecimal decimal ascii and octal
display - hostid (1) - display or set system host id
display - hostname (1) - display or set the system
    hostname
display - iceauth (1) - display or set ICE
    authorization information
display - id (1) - display real and effective user and
    group IDs
display - ksyms (1) - display exported kernel
    symbols
display - last (1) - display past user/terminal login
    records
display - ldd (1) - display program shared library
    dependencies
display - listalias (1) - display elm aliases
display - locate (1) - display file names from
    databases which match a regular expression
display - logname (1) - display user login name
display - look (1) - display lines with a given string
    prefix
display - lpq (1) - display status information for
    printer job queue
display - manpath (1) - display directory paths
    searched for manual pages
display - mdir (1) - mtools display a DOS directory
display - more (1) - display file contents with page
    breaks
display - mtype (1) - display contents of a DOS file
display - netstat (8) - display status information on
    active network connections
display - nm (1) - display object file symbol table
display - od (1) - display file contents in octal or
    other formats
display - pac (8) - display printer accounting
    information
display - printenv (1) - display environment
    variables
display - printf (1) - format and display parameter
    strings
display - ps (1) - display process status

display - pstree (1) - display process hierarchy as a tree
display - pwd (1) - display name of present working directory
display - rdev (8) - display or modify kernel root device, swap device, RAM disk size, and video mode
display - ref (1) - display C function headers
display - rlog (1) - display information about RCS files
display - route (8) - display and manipulate kernel IP routing tables
display - rpcinfo (8) - display RPC information
display - showkey (1) - display scancodes or keycodes from the keyboard
display - strings (1) - display printable strings in a file
display - stty (1) - change or display terminal line settings
display - tload (1) - gives graphic display of system load average
display - top (1) - display processes with highest CPU usage
display - traceroute (8) - display the route taken by network packets
display - uname (1) - display system information
display - uptime (1) - display how long the system has been running
display - users (1) - display the login names of users currently logged in
display - vmstat (8) - display virtual memory statistics
display - which (1) - display path name of commands
display - xcmap (1) - display default X11 colormap
display - xdm (1) - X-windows display manager
display - xdpyinfo (1) - display X-windows server information
display - xfd (1) - display the characters in a given X11 font
display - xlock (1) - locks the X-windows display until a password is entered
display - xlsclients (1) - list client applications running on a display
display - xv (1) - interactive image display for X-windows
display - xwud (1) - display dump file image in X11
display - zdump (8) - display the current time in a given time zone
display - zmore (1) - display compressed text
displayer - xlsfonts (1) - server font list displayer for X-windows
displayer - xprop (1) - property displayer for X-windows
DisplayHeight - DisplayHeight (3) - Xlib image formating functions and macros
DisplayHeightMM - DisplayHeightMM (3) - Xlib image formating functions and macros
DisplayWidth - DisplayWidth (3) - Xlib image formating functions and macros
DisplayWidthMM - DisplayWidthMM (3) - Xlib image formating functions and macros
distance - hypot (3) - Pythagoras distance calculation
div - div (3) - calculates quotient and remainder on integer division

division - div (3) - calculates quotient and remainder on integer division
division - ldiv (3) - perform long integer division
dmesg - dmesg (8) - display/control the kernel message buffer
dn_comp - dn_comp (3) - resolver library functions
dn_expand - dn_expand (3) - resolver library functions
dnsquery - dnsquery (1) - query domain-name servers using resolver
document - bibtex (1) - make bibliography for a LaTeX document
document - fig2ps2tex (1) - include a postscript file in a TeX document
document - groff (1) - text and document formatting system
document - gtroff (1) - gnu troff compatible document format program
document - psbb (1) - get bounding box size from a postscript document
documentation - flexdoc (1) - documentation for flex
documentation - info (1) - hypertext documentation system
documents - ghostview (1) - use ghostscript to view postscript documents
domain - domainname (1) - set/print domain of current host
domain - getdomainname, setdomainname (2) - get/set host domain name
domain - host (1) - look up hostnames or numbers using domain name server
domain - personality (2) - set execution domain for a process
domain-name - dig (1) - send domain-name queries to name servers
domain-name - dnsquery (1) - query domain-name servers using resolver
domainname - domainname (1) - set/print domain of current host
DOS - dosfsck (8) - check/repair DOS filesystems
DOS - mattrib (1) - change attribute bit flags for DOS files
DOS - mcd (1) - mtools change DOS directory
DOS - mcopy (1) - mtools copy DOS files to or from Linux
DOS - mdel (1) - mtools delete a DOS file
DOS - mdir (1) - mtools display a DOS directory
DOS - mformat (1) - mtools add a DOS filesystem to a low-level formatted floppy disk
DOS - mkdosfs (8) - create a DOS filesystem
DOS - mkmanifest (1) - help restore Unix file names modified by DOS name restrictions
DOS - mlabel (1) - label a DOS partition/volume
DOS - mmd (1) - create a DOS subdirectory
DOS - mrd (1) - remove a DOS directory
DOS - mread (1) - copy a DOS file to Linux
DOS - mren (1) - rename a DOS file
DOS - Mtools (1) - tools for manipulating DOS files
DOS - Mtools (5) - tools for manipulating DOS files
DOS - mtype (1) - display contents of a DOS file
DOS - mwrite (1) - copy a Linux file to DOS
dosfsck - dosfsck (8) - check/repair DOS filesystems
double - atof (3) - convert a string to a double
double - copysign (3) - copy the sign of a double
double - spider (1) - double deck card game

double - strtod (3) - convert numeric string to double
down - shutdown (8) - shut the system down
drand48 - drand48 (3) - random number generator
draw - gpm-root (1) - gpm handler to draw menus on the root window
draw - xfig (1) - X11 draw and paint program
drem - drem (3) - floating point remainder math function
drive - mt (1) - control a magnetic tape drive
driver - grops (1) - groff postscript driver
driver - grotty (1) - groff tty driver
driver - lpcntl (8) - manipulate line printer driver
driver - sd (4) - SCSI disk driver
driver - setup (2) - initialize hard disk driver
drives - rmt (8) - control remote magnetic tape drives
driving - crontab (5) - tables for driving cron
dropping - xtetris (6) - X-window block dropping game
dsplit - dsplit (1) - split binary files into pieces
du - du (1) - summarize disk usage
dump - xwd (1) - create a dump file image from an X-window
dump - xwud (1) - display dump file image in X11
dumpe2fs - dumpe2fs (8) - display filesystem super block and block-group information
dumpkeys - dumpkeys (1) - display keyboard translation tables
dup - dup (2) - duplicate a file descriptor
dup2 - dup2 (2) - duplicate a file descriptor
duplicate - dup, dup2 (2) - duplicate a file descriptor
duplicate - strdup (3) - duplicate a string
duplicate - uniq (1) - remove duplicate lines from a sorted file
dvi - dvilj4, dvilj4l, dvilj2p, dvilj (1) - convert dvi files for HP laser printers
dvi - dvips (1) - make postscript from a dvi file
dvi - dvitype (1) - make a dvi file human readable
DVI - gftodvi (1) - translate generic font files to DVI format
dvi - grodvi (1) - convert groff to dvi format
DVI - xdvi (1) - DVI previewer for X-windows
dvilj - dvilj (1) - convert dvi files for HP laser printers
dvilj2p - dvilj2p (1) - convert dvi files for HP laser printers
dvilj4 - dvilj4 (1) - convert dvi files for HP laser printers
dvilj4l - dvilj4l (1) - convert dvi files for HP laser printers
dvips - dvips (1) - make postscript from a dvi file
dvitype - dvitype (1) - make a dvi file human readable
dynamic - calloc, malloc, free, realloc (3) - dynamic memory allocation functions
e2fsck - e2fsck (8) - check second extended filesystem
echo - echo (1) - bash built-in commands
echo - echo (1) - display text from the shell
echo - ping (8) - echo packets from network hosts
ecvt - ecvt (3) - convert a floating point number to a string
ed - ed (1) - text editor
edit - vipw (8) - edit the password file
edited - elvprsv (1) - recover modified version of an elvis edited file after a crash
editor - bitmap, bmtoa, atobm (1) - bitmap editor and utilities for X11
editor - bpe (1) - binary file editor
editor - ed, red (1) - text editor
editor - editres (1) - resource editor for X
editor - elvis, ex, vi, view, input (1) - Unix standard editor
editor - elvrec (1) - recover an unsaved elvis editor file after a crash
editor - sed (1) - inline editor
editor - vim (1) - improved vi text editor
editres - editres (1) - resource editor for X
effective - getgid, getegid (2) - get real/effective group identity
effective - getuid, geteuid (2) - get real or effective user ID number
effective - id (1) - display real and effective user and group IDs
effective - setregid, setegid (2) - set real and effective group ID
effective - setreuid, seteuid (2) - set real and effective user ID
effective - whoami (1) - print effective userid
EGA - setfont (8) - load EGA or VGA console screen font
egrep - egrep (1) - display lines matching a regular expression
elm - answer (1) - elm phone message system
elm - elm (1) - interactive mail reader
elm - elmalias (1) - expand and display elm address aliases
elm - listalias (1) - display elm aliases
elm - newalias (1) - install new elm mail address aliases
elmalias - elmalias (1) - expand and display elm address aliases
elvis - elvis (1) - Unix standard editor
elvis - elvprsv (1) - recover modified version of an elvis edited file after a crash
elvis - elvrec (1) - recover an unsaved elvis editor file after a crash
elvprsv - elvprsv (1) - recover modified version of an elvis edited file after a crash
elvrec - elvrec (1) - recover an unsaved elvis editor file after a crash
e-mail - cmail (6) - for e-mail chess games
embedded - unshar (1) - unpack shar files embedded in mail messages
empty - rmdir (1) - delete empty directories
emulate - gnroff (1) - emulate the nroff command using groff
emulator - seyon (1) - X11 modem terminal emulator
emulator - xterm (1) - terminal emulator for X-windows
enable - enable (1) - bash built-in commands
enable - mesg (1) - enable or disable write access to your terminal
enable - swapon, swapoff (2) - enable/disable devices and files for paging
enable - swapon, swapoff (8) - enable/disable devices and files for paging
encode - uuencode (1) - ascii encode a binary file
encoded - uuencode (5) - format of an encoded file

encryption - crypt (3) - data encryption function
end - put_file_last (9) - move a file to the end of the kernel file table
end - tail (1) - output the tail end of a file
endgrent - endgrent (3) - manipulate group file entries
endhostent - endhostent (3) - manipulate network host entries
endmntent - endmntent (3) - access fstab and mtab file entries
endnetent - endnetent (3) - get networks file entries
endpoint - socket (2) - create a communication endpoint
endprotoent - endprotoent (3) - get protocols file entries
endpwent - endpwent (3) - get fields from password file entries
endservent - endservent (3) - get services file entries
endusershell - endusershell (3) - get shells file entries
endutent - endutent (3) - access entries in utmp login record file
English - english (4) - format for English spelling dictionaries
english - english (4) - format for English spelling dictionaries
enhanced - less (1) - enhanced version of more
enter - vm86 (2) - enter virtual 8086 mode
entered - xlock (1) - locks the X-windows display until a password is entered
entries - apropos (1) - list manual entries relevant to a query
entries - getdirentries (3) - read directory entries
entries - getgrent, setgrent, endgrent (3) - manipulate group file entries
entries - gethostbyname, gethostbyaddr, gethostent, sethostent, endhostent, herror (3) - manipulate network host entries
entries - getmntent, setmntent, addmntent, endmntent, hasmntopt (3) - access fstab and mtab file entries
entries - getnetent, getnetbyaddr, getnetbyname, setnetent, endnetent (3) - get networks file entries
entries - getprotoent, getprotobyname, getprotobynumber, setprotoent, endprotoent (3) - get protocols file entries
entries - getpwent, setpwent, endpwent, getpwnam, getpwuid (3) - get fields from password file entries
entries - getservent, getservbyname, getservbyport, setservent, endservent (3) - get services file entries
entries - getusershell, setusershell, endusershell (3) - get shells file entries
entries - getutent, getutid, getutline, pututline, setutent, endutent, utmpname (3) - access entries in utmp login record file
entries - grow_files (9) - add a page of entries to the file table
entries - scandir, alphasort (3) - search a directory for entries with particular attributes
entry - fgetgrent (3) - get entry from group file
entry - fgetpwent (3) - get entry from password file
entry - get_empty_filp (9) - find an unreferenced entry in the kernel file table
entry - getpw (3) - get password line entry for given user
entry - putpwent (3) - write password file entry
entry - remove_file_free (9) - remove a kernel file table entry
entry - socketcall (2) - socket system call entry point
env - env (1) - run a program in a modified environment
environ - environ (5) - user environment
environment - env (1) - run a program in a modified environment
environment - environ (5) - user environment
environment - getenv (3) - get environment variable value
environment - printenv (1) - display environment variables
environment - putenv (3) - assign a value to an environment variable
environment - setenv (3) - set or change an environment variable value
equation - geqn (1) - equation formatting for troff
erand48 - erand48 (3) - random number generator
erf - erf (3) - error and complementary-error math functions
erfc - erfc (3) - error and complementary-error math functions
errno - perror (3) - print error message from errno value
errno - strerror (3) - return string describing errno
error - closelog, openlog, syslog (3) - send text to the system message and error logger
error - erf, erfc (3) - error and complementary-error math functions
error - perror (3) - print error message from errno value
etex - etex (1) - extended TeX
eval - eval (1) - bash built-in commands
evaluate - expr (1) - evaluate expressions
event - add_timer, del_timer, init_timer (9) - kernel event timers
events - mev (1) - report mouse events
events - select (2) - sleep awaiting file descriptor events
ex - ex (1) - Unix standard editor
exec - exec (1) - bash built-in commands
execl - execl (3) - execute new program in current process
execle - execle (3) - execute new program in current process
execlp - execlp (3) - execute new program in current process
exect - exect (3) - execute new program in current process
executable - gzexe (1) - create self extracting compressed executable file
execute - chroot (8) - execute a program with a new root directory
execute - execl, execlp, execle, exect, execv, execvp (3) - execute new program in current process
execute - execve (2) - execute new program in current process

execute - ftw (3) - execute a function on file names in a directory tree
execute - system (3) - execute a Linux command
execute - xargs (1) - execute command lines from stdin
execution - at, batch, atq, atrm (1) - manipulate batch jobs for later execution
execution - atrun (8) - run batch jobs queued for later execution
execution - personality (2) - set execution domain for a process
execution - profil (2) - generate process execution profile
execution - rexecd (8) - remote execution daemon
execution - usleep (3) - suspend process execution for a time given in microseconds
execv - execv (3) - execute new program in current process
execve - execve (2) - execute new program in current process
execvp - execvp (3) - execute new program in current process
existing - link (2) - make a new directory link to an existing file
existing - ln (1) - make new links to existing files
exit - exit (1) - bash built-in commands
_exit - _exit (2) - terminate the current process
exit - exit (3) - cause program termination
exit - false (1) - return zero exit status
exit - on_exit (3) - register a user exit function
exit - test (1) - generate exit status for file type-checks and value comparisons
exit - true (1) - do nothing and return a true exit status
exp - exp (3) - exponential, logarithmic and power math functions
expand - compress, uncompress, zcat (1) - compress and expand file contents
expand - elmalias (1) - expand and display elm address aliases
expand - expand (1) - convert tabs to spaces
exponential - exp, log, log10, pow (3) - exponential, logarithmic and power math functions
export - export (1) - bash built-in commands
exported - exports (5) - exported NFS filesystems
exported - ksyms (1) - display exported kernel symbols
exports - exports (5) - exported NFS filesystems
expr - expr (1) - evaluate expressions
expression - fnmatch (3) - search a string for a regular expression
expression - grep, egrep, fgrep (1) - display lines matching a regular expression
expression - locate (1) - display file names from databases which match a regular expression
expression - zgrep (1) - search compressed files for a regular expression
expression - zipgrep (1) - search zip'ed files for a regular expression
expressions - expr (1) - evaluate expressions
ext2 - debugfs (8) - ext2 filesystem debugger
extended - chattr (1) - change file attributes in second extended filesystems
extended - e2fsck (8) - check second extended filesystem

extended - etex (1) - extended TeX
extended - lsattr (1) - list file attributes on a second extended filesystem
extended - mke2fs (8) - create a second extended filesystem
extended - tune2fs (8) - manipulate parameters in second extended filesystems
extension - zforce (1) - force a .gz file extension on all gzip'ed files
extract - ar (1) - create, modify, and extract from archives
extract - dirname (1) - extract directory prefix from file pathname
extract - funzip (1) - extract files from a ZIP archive
extract - modf (3) - extract the integral and fractional parts of a floating point number
extract - objdump (1) - extract low level information from object files
extract - strtok (3) - extract token from string
extract - unzip (1) - extract compressed files from a zip archive
extracting - gzexe (1) - create self extracting compressed executable file
fabs - fabs (3) - absolute value of floating point number
false - assert (3) - terminate process if assertion is false
false - false (1) - return zero exit status
fast - flex (1) - fast lexical analyzer generator
fastmail - fastmail (1) - quick batch mail interface
fc - fc (1) - bash built-in commands
fchdir - fchdir (2) - change current working directory
fchmod - fchmod (2) - change file access permission bits
fchown - fchown (2) - change file ownership
fclose - fclose (3) - close a file pointer
fcntl - fcntl (2) - manipulate open file descriptions
fcvt - fcvt (3) - convert a floating point number to a string
fd - fd (4) - floppy disk device
fdformat - fdformat (8) - low-level format a floppy disk
fdisk - cfdisk (8) - curses based fdisk
fdisk - fdisk (8) - manipulate disk partition tables
fdopen - fdopen (3) - file open functions
feeds - col (1) - remove reverse line feeds from input
feof - feof (3) - reset and check stream status
ferror - ferror (3) - reset and check stream status
fflush - fflush (3) - flush a file pointer
ffs - ffs (3) - returns position of first bit set in a word
fg - fg (1) - bash built-in commands
fgetc - fgetc (3) - string and character input functions
fgetgrent - fgetgrent (3) - get entry from group file
fgetpos - fgetpos (3) - manipulate a file pointer
fgetpwent - fgetpwent (3) - get entry from password file
fgets - fgets (3) - string and character input functions
fgrep - fgrep (1) - display lines matching a regular expression
field - join (1) - join two sorted files line by line on a common field

fields - cut (1) - select fields from each line of a file
fields - getpwent, setpwent, endpwent, getpwnam, getpwuid (3) - get fields from password file entries
Fig - fig2dev (1) - translate Fig code to other graphics languages
fig2dev - fig2dev (1) - translate Fig code to other graphics languages
fig2ps2tex - fig2ps2tex (1) - include a postscript file in a TeX document
figures - Psfig/TeX (7) - postscript figures in TeX
figures - transfig (1) - creates a makefile for portable LaTeX figures
fileno - fileno (3) - reset and check stream status
file's - fsync (2) - write a file's in-core memory state to disk
filesystem - debugfs (8) - ext2 filesystem debugger
filesystem - dumpe2fs (8) - display filesystem super block and block-group information
filesystem - e2fsck (8) - check second extended filesystem
filesystem - frag (8) - filesystem fragmentation checker
filesystem - fsck (8) - integrity check and fix a filesystem
filesystem - fsck.minix (8) - integrity check and fix a minix filesystem
filesystem - hier (7) - filesystem hierarchy description
filesystem - lsattr (1) - list file attributes on a second extended filesystem
filesystem - mformat (1) - mtools add a DOS filesystem to a low-level formatted floppy disk
filesystem - mkdosfs (8) - create a DOS filesystem
filesystem - mke2fs (8) - create a second extended filesystem
filesystem - mkfs (8) - create a minix filesystem
filesystem - mklost+found (8) - create a lost+found directory on a filesystem
filesystem - mknod (2) - create a filesystem node
filesystem - mkxfs (8) - create an xiafs filesystem
filesystem - statfs, fstatfs (2) - get filesystem statistics
filesystem - sync (2) - flush filesystem buffer cache
filesystem - sync (8) - flush filesystem buffer cache
filesystem - sysfs (2) - get current filesystem type information
filesystem - xfsck (8) - xiafs filesystem consistency check and repair
filesystems - chattr (1) - change file attributes in second extended filesystems
filesystems - dosfsck (8) - check/repair DOS filesystems
filesystems - exports (5) - exported NFS filesystems
filesystems - filesystems (9) - details the table of configured filesystems
filesystems - fstab (5) - mount information about filesystems
filesystems - mount, umount (2) - mount and unmount filesystems to the directory hierarchy
filesystems - mount, umount (8) - mount and unmount filesystems to the directory hierarchy
filesystems - tune2fs (8) - manipulate parameters in second extended filesystems

file_table - file_table (9) - detailed description of the kernel file table
file_table_init - file_table_init (9) - initialize the kernel file table
filter - filter (1) - process incoming mail messages before adding to mailbox
filter - ul (1) - filter to do underlining
filter - unexpand (1) - filter to convert spaces to tabs
find - diff (1) - find differences between two files
find - diff3 (1) - find differences between three files
find - find (1) - list file names in a directory hierarchy
find - get_empty_filp (9) - find an unreferenced entry in the kernel file table
find - glob (3) - find pathnames matching a pattern
find - ident (1) - find RCS keyword patterns in files
find - index, rindex (3) - find character in string
find - lkbib (1) - find keys in bibliographic databases
find - strchr, strrchr (3) - find character in string
find - strstr (3) - find substring
findaffix - findaffix (1) - spell checker
finds - strpbrk (3) - finds any of a set of characters in a string
finger - chfn (1) - change finger information
finger - finger (1) - lookup user information
fingerd - fingerd (8) - user information lookup daemon
finite - finite (3) - test for infinity
first - ffs (3) - returns position of first bit set in a word
first - head (1) - display the first part of a file
fix - fsck (8) - integrity check and fix a filesystem
fix - fsck.minix (8) - integrity check and fix a minix filesystem
fiz - fiz (1) - data recovery from damaged zoo archives
flags - mattrib (1) - change attribute bit flags for DOS files
flex - flex (1) - fast lexical analyzer generator
flex - flexdoc (1) - documentation for flex
flexdoc - flexdoc (1) - documentation for flex
floating - drem (3) - floating point remainder math function
floating - ecvt, fcvt (3) - convert a floating point number to a string
floating - fabs (3) - absolute value of floating point number
floating - fmod (3) - floating point remainder function
floating - frexp (3) - split floating point number to integer and fractional parts
floating - gcvt (3) - convert floating point number to string
floating - ldexp (3) - multiply floating point number by a power of 2
floating - modf (3) - extract the integral and fractional parts of a floating point number
flock - flock (2) - set or reset open file lock
floor - floor (3) - largest integer value not greater-than x
floppy - fd (4) - floppy disk device
floppy - fdformat (8) - low-level format a floppy disk
floppy - mformat (1) - mtools add a DOS filesystem to a low-level formatted floppy disk
floppy - setfdprm (8) - load parameters into floppy disk devices

flush - **bdflush** (8) - daemon to flush buffers back to disk
flush - **fflush, fpurge** (3) - flush a file pointer
flush - **sync** (2) - flush filesystem buffer cache
flush - **sync** (8) - flush filesystem buffer cache
fmod - **fmod** (3) - floating point remainder function
fmt - **fmt** (1) - simple text format program
.fmt - **initex** (1) - special version of TeX for making .fmt files
fnmatch - **fnmatch** (3) - search a string for a regular expression
fold - **fold** (1) - format text to specified width
folder - **messages** (1) - count of messages in mail folder
folder - **readmsg** (1) - get messages from a mail folder
font - **addftinfo** (1) - modify troff font files for use with groff
font - **afm2tfm** (1) - convert Adobe font metrics to TeX font metrics
font - **afmtodit** (1) - create font files for use with groff
font - **bdftopcf** (1) - X11 font conversion program
font - **fsinfo** (1) - display X11 font server information
font - **fslsfonts** (1) - list X11 fonts supplied by font server
font - **fstobdf** (1) - create BDF file from X11 font
font - **gftodvi** (1) - translate generic font files to DVI format
font - **gftopk** (1) - translate generic font files to packed font files
font - **gftype** (1) - translate generic font files to human readable format
font - **groff_font** (5) - groff font description file format
font - **gsftopk** (1) - convert a ghostscript font to TeX pk format
font - **mf, inimf, virmf** (1) - font and logo design tools
font - **mkfontdir, fonts.dir, fonts.scale, fonts.alias** (1) - create an index of X11 font files
font - **pfbtops** (1) - translate a .pfb postscript font to ascii
font - **pktype** (1) - make a packed font file human readable
font - **pltotf** (1) - convert properties files to TeX font metric format
font - **setfont** (8) - load EGA or VGA console screen font
font - **tfmtodit** (1) - create font files for use with groff
font - **tftopl** (1) - convert TeX font metric files to properties
font - **vptovf** (1) - convert virtual properties to virtual and TeX font metrics
font - **xfd** (1) - display the characters in a given X11 font
font - **xfs** (1) - X11 font server
font - **xlsfonts** (1) - server font list displayer for X-windows
fonts - **fslsfonts** (1) - list X11 fonts supplied by font server
fonts - **pktogf** (1) - translate packed fonts to generic fonts

fonts - **vftovp** (1) - convert virtual fonts to virtual properties
fonts.alias - **fonts.alias** (1) - create an index of X11 font files
fonts.dir - **fonts.dir** (1) - create an index of X11 font files
fonts.scale - **fonts.scale** (1) - create an index of X11 font files
fopen - **fopen** (3) - file open functions
for - **for** (1) - bash built-in commands
force - **zforce** (1) - force a .gz file extension on all gzip'ed files
fork - **fork** (2) - create a child process
formating - **ImageByteOrder, BitmapBitOrder, BitmapPad, BitmapUnit, DisplayHeight, DisplayHeightMM, DisplayWidth, DisplayWidthMM, XListPixmapFormats, XPixmapFormatValues** (3) - Xlib image formating functions and macros
formats - **intro** (5) - introduction to file formats
formats - **od** (1) - display file contents in octal or other formats
formats - **time2posix, posix2time** (3) - convert time formats
formatted - **mformat** (1) - mtools add a DOS filesystem to a low-level formatted floppy disk
formatted - **scanf, fscanf, sscanf, vscanf, vsscanf, vfscanf** (3) - formatted input functions
found - **mklost+found** (8) - create a lost+found directory on a filesystem
fpathconf - **fpathconf** (3) - get file configuration option values
fprintf - **fprintf** (3) - output format functions
fpurge - **fpurge** (3) - flush a file pointer
fputc - **fputc** (3) - string and character output functions
fputs - **fputs** (3) - string and character output functions
fractal - **xfractint** (1) - X11 fractal generator
fractional - **frexp** (3) - split floating point number to integer and fractional parts
fractional - **modf** (3) - extract the integral and fractional parts of a floating point number
frag - **frag** (8) - filesystem fragmentation checker
fragmentation - **frag** (8) - filesystem fragmentation checker
fread - **fread** (3) - file read and write functions
free - **df** (1) - summarize free disk partition space
free - **free** (1) - display memory and swap space statistics
free - **free** (3) - dynamic memory allocation functions
free - **globfree** (3) - free memory from previous glob call
freeze - **rcsfreeze** (1) - freeze a set of sources checked in under RCS
freopen - **freopen** (3) - file open functions
frexp - **frexp** (3) - split floating point number to integer and fractional parts
frm - **frm** (1) - list from and subject lines in mail messages
fscanf - **fscanf** (3) - formatted input functions
fsck - **fsck** (8) - integrity check and fix a filesystem
fsck.minix - **fsck.minix** (8) - integrity check and fix a minix filesystem

fseek - fseek (3) - manipulate a file pointer
fsetpos - fsetpos (3) - manipulate a file pointer
fsinfo - fsinfo (1) - display X11 font server information
fslsfonts - fslsfonts (1) - list X11 fonts supplied by font server
fstab - fstab (5) - mount information about filesystems
fstab - getmntent, setmntent, addmntent, endmntent, hasmntopt (3) - access fstab and mtab file entries
fstab - nfs (5) - NFS fstab file format
fstat - fstat (2) - get file statistics
fstatfs - fstatfs (2) - get filesystem statistics
fstobdf - fstobdf (1) - create BDF file from X11 font
fsync - fsync (2) - write a file's in-core memory state to disk
ftell - ftell (3) - manipulate a file pointer
ftime - ftime (2) - manipulate date and time
ftime - ftime (3) - get date and time
ftok - ftok (3) - generate a System-V IPC key
ftp - ftp (1) - file transfer program
FTP - xferlog (5) - FTP server logfile
ftpd - ftpd (8) - Internet file transfer protocol daemon
ftruncate - ftruncate (2) - shorten a file to a given length
ftw - ftw (3) - execute a function on file names in a directory tree
full-duplex - shutdown (2) - shutdown all or part of a full-duplex socket connection
funzip - funzip (1) - extract files from a ZIP archive
fuser - fuser (1) - display PIDs of processes using specified files
fvwm - fvwm (1) - X11 window manager
fwrite - fwrite (3) - file read and write functions
g - g (1) - GNU C++ compiler
game - gnuan (6) - produce a chess game analysis
game - gnuchess (6) - chess game
game - othello (6) - othello game
game - spider (1) - double deck card game
game - xlander (6) - X11 game
game - xmahjongg (6) - X11 game
game - xroach (6) - X11 game
game - xtetris (6) - X-window block dropping game
game - xvier (6) - X11 board game
games - cmail (6) - for e-mail chess games
games - intro (6) - introduction to games
gamma - lgamma (3) - log gamma math function
gawk - gawk (1) - language for string pattern manipulation
gcc - gcc (1) - GNU C compiler
gcvt - gcvt (3) - convert floating point number to string
gdb - gdb (1) - GNU symbolic debugger
gdb - xxgdb (1) - X11 interface to gdb
generator - drand48, erand48, lrand48, nrand48, mrand48, jrand48, srand48, seed48, lcong48 (3) - random number generator
generator - flex (1) - fast lexical analyzer generator
generator - rand, srand, random, srandom, initstate, setstate (3) - random number generator
generator - rpcgen (1) - C code generator for RPC protocols
generator - xfractint (1) - X11 fractal generator
generator - Yacc (1) - LALR-1 parser generator
generic - gftodvi (1) - translate generic font files to DVI format
generic - gftopk (1) - translate generic font files to packed font files
generic - gftype (1) - translate generic font files to human readable format
generic - pktogf (1) - translate packed fonts to generic fonts
genksyms - genksyms (8) - generate symbol version files
geometry - vgaset (1) - setup X11 screen geometry
geqn - geqn (1) - equation formatting for troff
getc - getc (3) - string and character input functions
getchar - getchar (3) - string and character input functions
get_current_dir_name - get_current_dir_name (3) - get current working directory
getcwd - getcwd (3) - get current working directory
getdirentries - getdirentries (3) - read directory entries
getdomainname - getdomainname (2) - get/set host domain name
getdtablesize - getdtablesize (2) - get file descriptor table size
getegid - getegid (2) - get real/effective group identity
get_empty_filp - get_empty_filp (9) - find an unreferenced entry in the kernel file table
getenv - getenv (3) - get environment variable value
geteuid - geteuid (2) - get real or effective user ID number
getgid - getgid (2) - get real/effective group identity
getgrent - getgrent (3) - manipulate group file entries
getgrgid - getgrgid (3) - get group file information
getgrnam - getgrnam (3) - get group file information
getgroups - getgroups (2) - manipulate group access list
gethostbyaddr - gethostbyaddr (3) - manipulate network host entries
gethostbyname - gethostbyname (3) - manipulate network host entries
gethostent - gethostent (3) - manipulate network host entries
gethostid - gethostid (2) - manipulate the current host identifier
gethostname - gethostname (2) - manipulate hostname
getitimer - getitimer (2) - manipulate interval timer value
get_kernel_syms - get_kernel_syms (2) - kernel loadable module support
getmntent - getmntent (3) - access fstab and mtab file entries
getnetbyaddr - getnetbyaddr (3) - get networks file entries
getnetbyname - getnetbyname (3) - get networks file entries
getnetent - getnetent (3) - get networks file entries
getopt - getopt (1) - parse command line options
getopt - getopt (3) - parse command line options
getopts - getopts (1) - bash built-in commands
getpagesize - getpagesize (2) - return kernel page size

getpass - getpass (3) - prompt for and read a password
getpeername - getpeername (2) - get name of peer connected to a given socket
getpgrp - getpgrp (2) - set or get process group ID
getpid - getpid (2) - get process ID numbers
getppid - getppid (2) - get process ID numbers
getpriority - getpriority (2) - manipulate process scheduling priority
getprotobyname - getprotobyname (3) - get protocols file entries
getprotobynumber - getprotobynumber (3) - get protocols file entries
getprotoent - getprotoent (3) - get protocols file entries
getpw - getpw (3) - get password line entry for given user
getpwent - getpwent (3) - get fields from password file entries
getpwnam - getpwnam (3) - get fields from password file entries
getpwuid - getpwuid (3) - get fields from password file entries
getrlimit - getrlimit (2) - manipulate process resource limits
getrusage - getrusage (2) - manipulate process resource limits
gets - gets (3) - string and character input functions
getservbyname - getservbyname (3) - get services file entries
getservbyport - getservbyport (3) - get services file entries
getservent - getservent (3) - get services file entries
getsockname - getsockname (2) - get socket name
getsockopt - getsockopt (2) - manipulate socket options
gettimeofday - gettimeofday (2) - manipulate date and time
getty - agetty (8) - getty for login prompt
getuid - getuid (2) - get real or effective user ID number
getusershell - getusershell (3) - get shells file entries
getutent - getutent (3) - access entries in utmp login record file
getutid - getutid (3) - access entries in utmp login record file
getutline - getutline (3) - access entries in utmp login record file
getwd - getwd (3) - get current working directory
gftodvi - gftodvi (1) - translate generic font files to DVI format
gftopk - gftopk (1) - translate generic font files to packed font files
gftype - gftype (1) - translate generic font files to human readable format
ghostscript - ghostview (1) - use ghostscript to view postscript documents
ghostscript - gs (1) - ghostscript language interpreter
ghostscript - gsftopk (1) - convert a ghostscript font to TeX pk format
ghostview - ghostview (1) - use ghostscript to view postscript documents

gindxbib - gindxbib (1) - create an inverted index for a bibliographic database
given - getpeername (2) - get name of peer connected to a given socket
given - getpw (3) - get password line entry for given user
given - look (1) - display lines with a given string prefix
given - strspn, strcspn (3) - return length of string containing given characters
given - truncate, ftruncate (2) - shorten a file to a given length
given - usleep (3) - suspend process execution for a time given in microseconds
given - xfd (1) - display the characters in a given X11 font
given - zdump (8) - display the current time in a given time zone
gives - tload (1) - gives graphic display of system load average
gld - gld (1) - GNU linker
glob - glob (3) - find pathnames matching a pattern
glob - globfree (3) - free memory from previous glob call
globfree - globfree (3) - free memory from previous glob call
glookbib - glookbib (1) - search bibliographic reference databases
GMT - adjust_clock (9) - set kernel clock to GMT from time-zone value
gmtime - gmtime (3) - convert date and time to ascii
gnroff - gnroff (1) - emulate the nroff command using groff
GNU - bash (1) - GNU Bourne-Again SHell
GNU - g++ (1) - GNU C++ compiler
GNU - gcc (1) - GNU C compiler
GNU - gdb (1) - GNU symbolic debugger
GNU - gld (1) - GNU linker
gnu - gpic (1) - gnu pic generates pictures for troff or TeX
gnu - gtroff (1) - gnu troff compatible document format program
GNU - xboard (6) - X-windows user interface for GNU Chess
gnuan - gnuan (6) - produce a chess game analysis
gnuchess - gnuchess (6) - chess game
gnuchess - postprint (6) - postscript output from gnuchess
gpic - gpic (1) - gnu pic generates pictures for troff or TeX
gpm - gpm (1) - cut and paste across virtual consoles
gpm - gpm-root (1) - gpm handler to draw menus on the root window
gpm-root - gpm-root (1) - gpm handler to draw menus on the root window
graph - tsort (1) - sort nodes in a directed graph
graphic - tload (1) - gives graphic display of system load average
graphics - fig2dev (1) - translate Fig code to other graphics languages
greater-than - floor (3) - largest integer value not greater-than x
grefer - grefer (1) - preprocessor for groff bibliographic references
grep - grep (1) - display lines matching a regular expression

grodvi - grodvi (1) - convert groff to dvi format
groff - addftinfo (1) - modify troff font files for use with groff
groff - afmtodit (1) - create font files for use with groff
groff - gnroff (1) - emulate the nroff command using groff
groff - grefer (1) - preprocessor for groff bibliographic references
groff - grodvi (1) - convert groff to dvi format
groff - groff (1) - text and document formatting system
groff - groff_char (7) - groff input character list
groff - groff_font (5) - groff font description file format
groff - groff_me, groff_mm, groff_ms (7) - groff macros
groff - groff_out (5) - format of groff intermediate output
groff - grog (1) - generate a groff command with parameter options
groff - grops (1) - groff postscript driver
groff - grotty (1) - groff tty driver
groff - gsoelim (1) - include .so files in groff input
groff - gtbl (1) - compile table description for groff
groff - man (7) - groff macros to format manual pages
groff - tfmtodit (1) - create font files for use with groff
groff_char - groff_char (7) - groff input character list
groff_font - groff_font (5) - groff font description file format
groff_me - groff_me (7) - groff macros
groff_mm - groff_mm (7) - groff macros
groff_ms - groff_ms (7) - groff macros
groff_out - groff_out (5) - format of groff intermediate output
grog - grog (1) - generate a groff command with parameter options
grops - grops (1) - groff postscript driver
grotty - grotty (1) - groff tty driver
group - chgrp (1) - change file group ownership
group - chown (1) - change the user and group ownership of files
group - fgetgrent (3) - get entry from group file
group - getgid, getegid (2) - get real/effective group identity
group - getgrent, setgrent, endgrent (3) - manipulate group file entries
group - getgrnam, getgrgid (3) - get group file information
group - getgroups, setgroups (2) - manipulate group access list
group - group (5) - user group list file
group - id (1) - display real and effective user and group IDs
group - in_group_p (9) - match group IDs
group - initgroups (3) - initialize group access list from group file
group - killpg (3) - send signal to process group
group - newgrp (1) - change to a new user group
group - setgid (2) - set group ID
group - setpgid, getpgrp, setpgrp (2) - set or get process group ID
group - setregid, setegid (2) - set real and effective group ID

group - setsid (2) - create new session and process group
groups - groups (1) - display a user's groups
grow_files - grow_files (9) - add a page of entries to the file table
gs - gs (1) - ghostscript language interpreter
gsftopk - gsftopk (1) - convert a ghostscript font to TeX pk format
gsoelim - gsoelim (1) - include .so files in groff input
gtbl - gtbl (1) - compile table description for groff
gtroff - gtroff (1) - gnu troff compatible document format program
gtroff - gxditview (1) - display gtroff output on an X display
gtty - gtty (2) - unimplemented system calls
gunzip - gunzip (1) - compress and uncompress files
gxditview - gxditview (1) - display gtroff output on an X display
.gz - zforce (1) - force a .gz file extension on all gzip'ed files
.gz - znew (1) - recompress .Z files as .gz files
gzexe - gzexe (1) - create self extracting compressed executable file
gzip - gzip (1) - compress and uncompress files
gzip'ed - zforce (1) - force a .gz file extension on all gzip'ed files
halt - halt (8) - shutdown the system
handle - ctrl_alt_del (9) - handle keyboard Ctrl-Alt-Del sequence
handle - dialog (1) - handle dialog boxes from shell scripts
handler - gpm-root (1) - gpm handler to draw menus on the root window
handling - curses (3) - terminal screen handling library
handling - depmod, modprobe (1) - automatic handling of loadable modules
handling - ncurses (3) - screen handling package
handling - setmetamode (1) - determine handling of the keyboard meta key
handling - signal, sigaction, sigvec, sigsuspend, sigreturn, sigpause, sigpending, sigblock, sigmask, siggetmask, sigsetmask, siginterrupt (2) - signal handling functions
hangup - nohup (1) - run a command set to ignore hangup signals
hangup - vhangup (2) - simulate a hangup on the current terminal
hard - hd (4) - details MFM/RLL/IDE hard disk device special files
hard - setup (2) - initialize hard disk driver
hardware - SuperProbe (1) - probe and identify video hardware
hash - hash (1) - bash built-in commands
hasmntopt - hasmntopt (3) - access fstab and mtab file entries
hd - hd (4) - details MFM/RLL/IDE hard disk device special files
head - head (1) - display the first part of a file
header - makedepend (1) - add header files to a makefile
headers - ref (1) - display C function headers
help - help (1) - bash built-in commands
help - mkmanifest (1) - help restore Unix file names modified by DOS name restrictions

helper   - rstartd (1) - rsh remote start helper daemon
herror   - herror (3) - manipulate network host entries
hexadecimal - hexdump (1) - display file contents in hexadecimal decimal ascii and octal
hexdump - hexdump (1) - display file contents in hexadecimal decimal ascii and octal
hier   - hier (7) - filesystem hierarchy description
hierarchy - find (1) - list file names in a directory hierarchy
hierarchy - hier (7) - filesystem hierarchy description
hierarchy - mkdirhier (1) - create a directory hierarchy
hierarchy - mount, umount (2) - mount and unmount filesystems to the directory hierarchy
hierarchy - mount, umount (8) - mount and unmount filesystems to the directory hierarchy
hierarchy - pstree (1) - display process hierarchy as a tree
highest - top (1) - display processes with highest CPU usage
history - history (1) - bash built-in commands
host   - domainname (1) - set/print domain of current host
host   - getdomainname, setdomainname (2) - get/set host domain name
host   - gethostbyname, gethostbyaddr, gethostent, sethostent, endhostent, herror (3) - manipulate network host entries
host   - gethostid, sethostid (2) - manipulate the current host identifier
host   - host (1) - look up hostnames or numbers using domain name server
host   - hostid (1) - display or set system host id
host   - htonl, htons, ntohl, ntohs (3) - translate between host and network byte order
host   - rwall (1) - send a message to users logged in on a specified host
hostid   - hostid (1) - display or set system host id
hostname - gethostname, sethostname (2) - manipulate hostname
hostname - hostname (1) - display or set the system hostname
hostname - hostname (7) - hostname format description
hostnames - host (1) - look up hostnames or numbers using domain name server
hosts   - ping (8) - echo packets from network hosts
HP   - dvilj4, dvilj4l, dvilj2p, dvilj (1) - convert dvi files for HP laser printers
htonl   - htonl (3) - translate between host and network byte order
htons   - htons (3) - translate between host and network byte order
hyperbolic - acosh (3) - inverse hyperbolic cosine trig function
hyperbolic - asinh (3) - inverse hyperbolic sine trig function
hyperbolic - atanh (3) - inverse hyperbolic tangent trig function
hyperbolic - cosh (3) - hyperbolic cosine trig function
hyperbolic - sinh (3) - hyperbolic sine trig function

hyperbolic - tanh (3) - hyperbolic tangent trig function
hypertext - info (1) - hypertext documentation system
hyphenation - patgen (1) - generate TeX hyphenation patterns
hypot   - hypot (3) - Pythagoras distance calculation
ICE   - iceauth (1) - display or set ICE authorization information
iceauth - iceauth (1) - display or set ICE authorization information
icombine - icombine (1) - spell checker
ID   - getpid, getppid (2) - get process ID numbers
ID   - getuid, geteuid (2) - get real or effective user ID number
id   - hostid (1) - display or set system host id
id   - id (1) - display real and effective user and group IDs
ID   - setgid (2) - set group ID
ID   - setpgid, getpgrp, setpgrp (2) - set or get process group ID
ID   - setregid, setegid (2) - set real and effective group ID
ID   - setreuid, seteuid (2) - set real and effective user ID
ID   - setuid (2) - set user ID
ID   - su (1) - run a shell with swapped user ID
IDE   - hd (4) - details MFM/RLL/IDE hard disk device special files
ident   - ident (1) - find RCS keyword patterns in files
identification - issue (4) - system identification message file
identification - issue (5) - system identification message file
identifier - gethostid, sethostid (2) - manipulate the current host identifier
identify - SuperProbe (1) - probe and identify video hardware
identity - getgid, getegid (2) - get real/effective group identity
idle   - idle (2) - internal system call to make process-0 idle
IDs   - id (1) - display real and effective user and group IDs
IDs   - in_group_p (9) - match group IDs
if   - if (1) - bash built-in commands
ifconfig - ifconfig (8) - configure a network interface
ignore   - nohup (1) - run a command set to ignore hangup signals
ignore   - strcasecmp, strncasecmp (3) - compare two strings and ignore case
ijoin   - ijoin (1) - spell checker
image   - ImageByteOrder, BitmapBitOrder, BitmapPad, BitmapUnit, DisplayHeight, DisplayHeightMM, DisplayWidth, DisplayWidthMM, XListPixmapFormats, XPixmapFormatValues (3) - Xlib image formating functions and macros
image   - xv (1) - interactive image display for X-windows
image   - xwd (1) - create a dump file image from an X-window
image   - xwud (1) - display dump file image in X11
ImageByteOrder - ImageByteOrder (3) - Xlib image formating functions and macros

imake - imake (1) - preprocessor to generate make files
Imakefile - xmkmf (1) - create a makefile from an Imakefile
improved - vim (1) - improved vi text editor
include - fig2ps2tex (1) - include a postscript file in a TeX document
include - gsoelim (1) - include .so files in groff input
incoming - filter (1) - process incoming mail messages before adding to mailbox
incoming - listen (2) - specify queue length for incoming socket connections
in-core - fsync (2) - write a file's in-core memory state to disk
indent - indent (1) - C program pretty printer
independent - merge (1) - combines multiple independent modifications to a file
index - gindxbib (1) - create an inverted index for a bibliographic database
index - index (3) - find character in string
index - index (3) - string functions
index - makeindex (1) - generate index files for LaTeX
index - mkfontdir, fonts.dir, fonts.scale, fonts.alias (1) - create an index of X11 font files
index - ranlib (1) - generate an index for an ar archive
indicator - setleds (1) - set the keyboard indicator lights
inet_addr - inet_addr (3) - manipulate Internet addresses
inetd - inetd (8) - Internet super-server daemon
inet_lnaof - inet_lnaof (3) - manipulate Internet addresses
inet_makeaddr - inet_makeaddr (3) - manipulate Internet addresses
inet_netof - inet_netof (3) - manipulate Internet addresses
inet_network - inet_network (3) - manipulate Internet addresses
inet_ntoa - inet_ntoa (3) - manipulate Internet addresses
infinity - isinf, isnan, finite (3) - test for infinity
info - info (1) - hypertext documentation system
in_group_p - in_group_p (9) - match group IDs
inimf - inimf (1) - font and logo design tools
init - init (8) - setup and control process initialization
init - inittab (5) - configuration file for init to process
init - simpleinit (8) - small version of init program
initex - initex (1) - special version of TeX for making .fmt files
initgroups - initgroups (3) - initialize group access list from group file
initial - kbdrate (8) - set keyboard auto-key repeat rate and initial repeat delay time
initialization - init, telinit (8) - setup and control process initialization
initialize - file_table_init (9) - initialize the kernel file table
initialize - initgroups (3) - initialize group access list from group file
initialize - setup (2) - initialize hard disk driver
initialize - startx (1) - initialize an X11 session
initialize - tzset (3) - initialize time zone information
initializer - xinit (1) - X11 system initializer
init_module - init_module (2) - kernel loadable module support
initstate - initstate (3) - random number generator
inittab - inittab (5) - configuration file for init to process
init_timer - init_timer (9) - kernel event timers
inline - sed (1) - inline editor
inode - utime, utimes (2) - change access or modification times in an inode
input - col (1) - remove reverse line feeds from input
input - fgetc, fgets, getc, getchar, gets, ungetc (3) - string and character input functions
input - groff_char (7) - groff input character list
input - gsoelim (1) - include .so files in groff input
input - input (1) - Unix standard editor
input - ioctl (2) - input and output device control
input - ioperm (2) - set input and output access permissions on a port
input - iopl (2) - change input and output privilege level
input - popen, pclose (3) - start a process with piped input or output
input - readline (3) - take interactive line of input
input - scanf, fscanf, sscanf, vscanf, vsscanf, vfscanf (3) - formatted input functions
input - stdio (3) - standard input/output library functions
insmod - insmod (1) - install loadable kernel modules
install - insmod (1) - install loadable kernel modules
install - install (1) - copy files and setup owner and permission modes
install - mapscrn (8) - install user specified screen output mapping table
install - newalias (1) - install new elm mail address aliases
integer - atoi (3) - convert a string to an integer
integer - atol (3) - convert a string to a long integer
integer - ceil (3) - smallest integer value not less than x
integer - div (3) - calculates quotient and remainder on integer division
integer - floor (3) - largest integer value not greater-than x
integer - frexp (3) - split floating point number to integer and fractional parts
integer - ldiv (3) - perform long integer division
integer - rint (3) - round to nearest integer
integral - modf (3) - extract the integral and fractional parts of a floating point number
integrity - fsck (8) - integrity check and fix a filesystem
integrity - fsck.minix (8) - integrity check and fix a minix filesystem
interactive - elm (1) - interactive mail reader
interactive - readline (3) - take interactive line of input
interactive - talk (1) - interactive user communication
interactive - xv (1) - interactive image display for X-windows

interactively - nslookup (8) - interactively query Internet name servers
interface - fastmail (1) - quick batch mail interface
interface - ifconfig (8) - configure a network interface
interface - sliplogin (8) - convert a serial line into a SLIP network interface
interface - telnet (1) - telnet protocol interface program
interface - xboard (6) - X-windows user interface for GNU Chess
interface - xmh (1) - send and read mail with an X11 interface
interface - xxgdb (1) - X11 interface to gdb
intermediate - groff_out (5) - format of groff intermediate output
internal - idle (2) - internal system call to make process-0 idle
interned - xlsatoms (1) - list interned atoms defined on server
Internet - ftpd (8) - Internet file transfer protocol daemon
Internet - inet_addr, inet_network, inet_ntoa, inet_makeaddr, inet_lnaof, inet_netof (3) - manipulate Internet addresses
Internet - inetd (8) - Internet super-server daemon
Internet - NcFTP (1) - Internet file transfer program
Internet - nslookup (8) - interactively query Internet name servers
Internet - pppd (8) - point-to-point Internet protocol daemon
Internet - sendmail (8) - Internet mail transport program
interpreter - gs (1) - ghostscript language interpreter
interpreter - runscript (1) - script interpreter for minicom communications program
interprocess - ipc (5) - System-V interprocess communication mechanisms
interval - getitimer, setitimer (2) - manipulate interval timer value
into - csplit (1) - split a file into sections
into - dsplit (1) - split binary files into pieces
into - kernel_mktime (9) - convert struct mktime into seconds since 1 January, 1970
into - mmap, munmap (2) - manipulate mapping of files and devices into memory
into - setfdprm (8) - load parameters into floppy disk devices
into - slattach (8) - put a serial line into network mode
into - sliplogin (8) - convert a serial line into a SLIP network interface
into - split (1) - split a file into pieces
into - strsep (3) - split string into tokens
intro - intro (1) - introduction to user commands
intro - intro (2) - introduction to system calls
intro - intro (3) - introduction to library functions
intro - intro (4) - introduction to special files
intro - intro (5) - introduction to file formats
intro - intro (6) - introduction to games
intro - intro (7) - introduction to miscellaneous
intro - intro (8) - introduction to administrative/privileged commands
inverse - acosh (3) - inverse hyperbolic cosine trig function
inverse - asinh (3) - inverse hyperbolic sine trig function
inverse - atanh (3) - inverse hyperbolic tangent trig function
inverted - gindxbib (1) - create an inverted index for a bibliographic database
ioctl - ioctl (2) - input and output device control
ioperm - ioperm (2) - set input and output access permissions on a port
iopl - iopl (2) - change input and output privilege level
IP - route (8) - display and manipulate kernel IP routing tables
IPC - ftok (3) - generate a System-V IPC key
ipc - ipc (5) - System-V interprocess communication mechanisms
ipc - ipcs (8) - provide ipc status information
IPC - msgctl (2) - System-V IPC control message operations
IPC - msgget (2) - System-V IPC create a message queue
IPC - msgop (2) - System-V IPC message operations
IPC - semctl (2) - System-V IPC control semaphore operations
IPC - semget (2) - System-V IPC create a semaphore set
IPC - semop (2) - System-V IPC semaphore operations
IPC - shmctl (2) - System-V IPC shared memory control
IPC - shmget (2) - System-V IPC create a shared memory segment
IPC - shmop (2) - System-V IPC shared memory operations
ipcs - ipcs (8) - provide ipc status information
isalnum - isalnum (3) - character test functions and macros
isalpha - isalpha (3) - character test functions and macros
isatty - isatty (3) - test a file descriptor for a tty
iscntrl - iscntrl (3) - character test functions and macros
IsCursorKey - IsCursorKey (3) - Xlib keysym test macros
isdigit - isdigit (3) - character test functions and macros
IsFunctionKey - IsFunctionKey (3) - Xlib keysym test macros
isgraph - isgraph (3) - character test functions and macros
isinf - isinf (3) - test for infinity
IsKeypadKey - IsKeypadKey (3) - Xlib keysym test macros
islower - islower (3) - character test functions and macros
IsMiscFunctionKey - IsMiscFunctionKey (3) - Xlib keysym test macros
IsModiferKey - IsModiferKey (3) - Xlib keysym test macros
isnan - isnan (3) - test for infinity
iso_8859_1 - iso_8859_1 (7) - map of character set
ispell - ispell (1) - spell checker
ispell - ispell (4) - spell checker dictionary format
IsPFKey - IsPFKey (3) - Xlib keysym test macros
isprint - isprint (3) - character test functions and macros

IsPrivateKeypadKey - IsPrivateKeypadKey (3) - Xlib keysym test macros
ispunct - ispunct (3) - character test functions and macros
isspace - isspace (3) - character test functions and macros
issue - issue (4) - system identification message file
issue - issue (5) - system identification message file
isupper - isupper (3) - character test functions and macros
isxdigit - isxdigit (3) - character test functions and macros
its - nice (1) - run a program and change its scheduling priority
j0 - j0 (3) - Bessel math functions
j1 - j1 (3) - Bessel math functions
jn - jn (3) - Bessel math functions
job - lpq (1) - display status information for printer job queue
jobs - at, batch, atq, atrm (1) - manipulate batch jobs for later execution
jobs - atrun (8) - run batch jobs queued for later execution
jobs - jobs (1) - bash built-in commands
jobs - lprm (1) - delete queued printer jobs
join - join (1) - join two sorted files line by line on a common field
jrand48 - jrand48 (3) - random number generator
kbd_mode - kbd_mode (1) - get/set the keyboard mode
kbdrate - kbdrate (8) - set keyboard auto-key repeat rate and initial repeat delay time
kernel - add_timer, del_timer, init_timer (9) - kernel event timers
kernel - adjtimex (2) - tune kernel clock
kernel - adjust_clock (9) - set kernel clock to GMT from time-zone value
kernel - bootparam (7) - Linux kernel boot time parameters
kernel - dmesg (8) - display/control the kernel message buffer
kernel - file_table (9) - detailed description of the kernel file table
kernel - file_table_init (9) - initialize the kernel file table
kernel - get_empty_filp (9) - find an unreferenced entry in the kernel file table
kernel - get_kernel_syms, create_module, init_module, delete_module (2) - kernel loadable module support
kernel - getpagesize (2) - return kernel page size
kernel - insmod (1) - install loadable kernel modules
kernel - klogd (1) - kernel message log daemon
kernel - kmem (4) - kernel memory
kernel - ksyms (1) - display exported kernel symbols
kernel - loadkeys (1) - load kernel keyboard translation tables
kernel - proc (5) - pseudo-filesystem for access to kernel data structures
kernel - proc_sel (9) - kernel function for process selection
kernel - psupdate (8) - update the ps kernel database
kernel - put_file_last (9) - move a file to the end of the kernel file table
kernel - rdev (8) - display or modify kernel root device, swap device, RAM disk size, and video mode
kernel - readprofile (1) - read kernel profiling information
kernel - remove_file_free (9) - remove a kernel file table entry
kernel - rmmod (1) - unload a loaded kernel module
kernel - route (8) - display and manipulate kernel IP routing tables
kernel - uname (2) - return information about the current kernel
kernel_mktime - kernel_mktime (9) - convert struct mktime into seconds since 1 January, 1970
Kernighan - ansi2knr (1) - convert ANSI C to Kernighan & Ritchie C
key - ftok (3) - generate a System-V IPC key
key - lesskey (1) - manipulate key bindings for less
key - setmetamode (1) - determine handling of the keyboard meta key
keyboard - ctrl_alt_del (9) - handle keyboard Ctrl-Alt-Del sequence
keyboard - dumpkeys (1) - display keyboard translation tables
keyboard - kbd_mode (1) - get/set the keyboard mode
keyboard - kbdrate (8) - set keyboard auto-key repeat rate and initial repeat delay time
keyboard - keytables (5) - keyboard description tables
keyboard - loadkeys (1) - load kernel keyboard translation tables
keyboard - setleds (1) - set the keyboard indicator lights
keyboard - setmetamode (1) - determine handling of the keyboard meta key
keyboard - showkey (1) - display scancodes or keycodes from the keyboard
keycodes - showkey (1) - display scancodes or keycodes from the keyboard
keymaps - xmodmap (1) - utility for modifying keymaps in X-windows
keys - lkbib (1) - find keys in bibliographic databases
keysym - IsCursorKey, IsFunctionKey, IsKeypadKey, IsMiscFunctionKey, IsModiferKey, IsPFKey, IsPrivateKeypadKey (3) - Xlib keysym test macros
keytables - keytables (5) - keyboard description tables
keyword - ident (1) - find RCS keyword patterns in files
kill - kill (1) - bash built-in commands
kill - kill (1) - send signal to process
kill - kill (2) - send signal to process
killall - killall (1) - send signal to processes by command name
killed - yes (1) - output a string repeatedly until killed
killpg - killpg (3) - send signal to process group
klogd - klogd (1) - kernel message log daemon
kmem - kmem (4) - kernel memory
ksyms - ksyms (1) - display exported kernel symbols
label - mlabel (1) - label a DOS partition/volume
labs - labs (3) - absolute value of a long int
LALR-1 - Yacc (1) - LALR-1 parser generator

lamstex - `lamstex` (1) - text formatting TeX macro package
language - `gawk` (1) - language for string pattern manipulation
language - `gs` (1) - ghostscript language interpreter
languages - `fig2dev` (1) - translate Fig code to other graphics languages
large - `banner` (6) - print text as a large banner
largest - `floor` (3) - largest integer value not greater-than x
laser - `dvilj4, dvilj4l, dvilj2p, dvilj` (1) - convert dvi files for HP laser printers
last - `last` (1) - display past user/terminal login records
later - `at, batch, atq, atrm` (1) - manipulate batch jobs for later execution
later - `atrun` (8) - run batch jobs queued for later execution
LaTeX - `bibtex` (1) - make bibliography for a LaTeX document
latex - `latex` (1) - text formatting and typesetting system
LaTeX - `makeindex` (1) - generate index files for LaTeX
LaTeX - `slitex` (1) - generate slides with LaTeX
LaTeX - `transfig` (1) - creates a makefile for portable LaTeX figures
lbxproxy - `lbxproxy` (1) - low network badwidth proxy server for X11
lcong48 - `lcong48` (3) - random number generator
ldd - `ldd` (1) - display program shared library dependencies
ldexp - `ldexp` (3) - multiply floating point number by a power of 2
ldiv - `ldiv` (3) - perform long integer division
ld.so - `ld.so` (8) - a.out linker
length - `listen` (2) - specify queue length for incoming socket connections
length - `mblen` (3) - get length of a multi-byte character
length - `strlen` (3) - return the length of a string
length - `strspn, strcspn` (3) - return length of string containing given characters
length - `truncate, ftruncate` (2) - shorten a file to a given length
less - `ceil` (3) - smallest integer value not less than x
less - `less` (1) - enhanced version of more
less - `lesskey` (1) - manipulate key bindings for less
lesskey - `lesskey` (1) - manipulate key bindings for less
let - `let` (1) - bash built-in commands
letters - `toupper, tolower` (3) - convert letters to upper or lower case
level - `iopl` (2) - change input and output privilege level
level - `objdump` (1) - extract low level information from object files
lexical - `flex` (1) - fast lexical analyzer generator
lgamma - `lgamma` (3) - log gamma math function
library - `curses` (3) - terminal screen handling library
library - `intro` (3) - introduction to library functions
library - `ldd` (1) - display program shared library dependencies

library - `resolv, res_query, res_search, res_mkquery, res_send, res_init, dn_comp, dn_expand` (3) - resolver library functions
library - `stdio` (3) - standard input/output library functions
library - `uselib` (2) - select a shared library
lights - `setleds` (1) - set the keyboard indicator lights
limits - `getrlimit, getrusage, setrlimit` (2) - manipulate process resource limits
lineprinter - `lptest` (1) - generate lineprinter test output
link - `link` (2) - make a new directory link to an existing file
link - `readlink` (2) - read a symbolic link
link - `realpath` (3) - make absolute pathname from relative pathname or symbolic link
link - `symlink` (2) - create a symbolic link to a file
linker - `gld` (1) - GNU linker
linker - `ld.so` (8) - a.out linker
links - `ln` (1) - make new links to existing files
links - `lndir` (1) - make a copy of a directory tree with symbolic links
listalias - `listalias` (1) - display elm aliases
listen - `listen` (2) - specify queue length for incoming socket connections
lists - `column` (1) - build columns from lists
lists - `lsmod` (1) - lists loaded modules
lkbib - `lkbib` (1) - find keys in bibliographic databases
ln - `ln` (1) - make new links to existing files
lndir - `lndir` (1) - make a copy of a directory tree with symbolic links
load - `loadkeys` (1) - load kernel keyboard translation tables
load - `setfdprm` (8) - load parameters into floppy disk devices
load - `setfont` (8) - load EGA or VGA console screen font
load - `tload` (1) - gives graphic display of system load average
loadable - `depmod, modprobe` (1) - automatic handling of loadable modules
loadable - `get_kernel_syms, create_module, init_module, delete_module` (2) - kernel loadable module support
loadable - `insmod` (1) - install loadable kernel modules
loaded - `lsmod` (1) - lists loaded modules
loaded - `rmmod` (1) - unload a loaded kernel module
loadkeys - `loadkeys` (1) - load kernel keyboard translation tables
local - `deliver` (8) - local mail transport
local - `local` (1) - bash built-in commands
local - `modify_ldt` (2) - get/set process local descriptor table
local - `ruptime` (1) - show status of local network machines
local - `rusers` (1) - list users logged in on local network machines
local - `rwho` (1) - list users logged in on local network machines
locale - `locale` (7) - multi-language support
locale - `localeconv` (3) - get information for current locale
locale - `setlocale` (3) - set the current locale

localeconv - localeconv (3) - get information for current locale
localtime - localtime (3) - convert date and time to ascii
locate - locate (1) - display file names from databases which match a regular expression
locate - locatedb (5) - file name database for locate
locate - whereis (1) - locate files related to a command
locatedb - locatedb (5) - file name database for locate
lock - flock (2) - set or reset open file lock
lock - lock (2) - unimplemented system calls
locks - xlock (1) - locks the X-windows display until a password is entered
log - klogd (1) - kernel message log daemon
log - lgamma (3) - log gamma math function
log - log (3) - exponential, logarithmic and power math functions
log - script (1) - make a log of a terminal session
log - syslogd (8) - log system messages
log10 - log10 (3) - exponential, logarithmic and power math functions
logarithmic - exp, log, log10, pow (3) - exponential, logarithmic and power math functions
logfile - xferlog (5) - FTP server logfile
logged - rpc.rusersd (8) - rusers logged in users daemon
logged - rusers (1) - list users logged in on local network machines
logged - rwall (1) - send a message to users logged in on a specified host
logged - rwho (1) - list users logged in on local network machines
logged - users (1) - display the login names of users currently logged in
logged - w (1) - show who is logged on and what they are doing
logged - who (1) - show who is logged on
logger - closelog, openlog, syslog (3) - send text to the system message and error logger
logger - logger (1) - write messages to the syslog
logging - sysklogd (1) - Linux logging system
login - agetty (8) - getty for login prompt
login - chsh (1) - change your login shell in password file
login - getutent, getutid, getutline, pututline, setutent, endutent, utmpname (3) - access entries in utmp login record file
login - last (1) - display past user/terminal login records
login - login (1) - password check program
login - logname (1) - display user login name
login - nologin (5) - allow only root to login to the system
login - rlogin (1) - remote login program
login - rlogind (8) - remote login daemon
login - securetty (5) - list of ttys from which root can login
login - shells (5) - file of pathnames to login shells for use with chsh
login - users (1) - display the login names of users currently logged in
login - utmp, wtmp (5) - format of login records
logname - logname (1) - display user login name

logo - mf, inimf, virmf (1) - font and logo design tools
logo - xlogo (1) - X-window system logo
logout - logout (1) - bash built-in commands
long - atol (3) - convert a string to a long integer
long - labs (3) - absolute value of a long int
long - ldiv (3) - perform long integer division
long - strtol (3) - convert string to long
long - strtoul (3) - convert string to unsigned long
long - uptime (1) - display how long the system has been running
look - look (1) - display lines with a given string prefix
lookup - finger (1) - lookup user information
lookup - fingerd (8) - user information lookup daemon
lost - mklost+found (8) - create a lost+found directory on a filesystem
low - lbxproxy (1) - low network badwidth proxy server for X11
low - objdump (1) - extract low level information from object files
lower - toupper, tolower (3) - convert letters to upper or lower case
low-level - fdformat (8) - low-level format a floppy disk
low-level - mformat (1) - mtools add a DOS filesystem to a low-level formatted floppy disk
lp - lp (4) - line printer device special file
lp - tunelp (8) - manipulate parameters for the lp printer device
lpc - lpc (8) - control line printer system
lpcntl - lpcntl (8) - manipulate line printer driver
lpd - lpd (8) - line printer daemon
lpq - lpq (1) - display status information for printer job queue
lpr - lpr (1) - spool files to line print
lprm - lprm (1) - delete queued printer jobs
lptest - lptest (1) - generate lineprinter test output
lrand48 - lrand48 (3) - random number generator
ls - dircolors (1) - set ls color parameters
ls - ls (1) - list directory contents
lsattr - lsattr (1) - list file attributes on a second extended filesystem
lseek - lseek (2) - position file offset in an open file description
lsmod - lsmod (1) - lists loaded modules
lstat - lstat (2) - get file statistics
machine - xon (1) - run an X-windows command on a remote machine
machines - ruptime (1) - show status of local network machines
machines - rusers (1) - list users logged in on local network machines
machines - rwho (1) - list users logged in on local network machines
macro - lamstex (1) - text formatting TeX macro package
macros - groff_me, groff_mm, groff_ms (7) - groff macros
macros - ImageByteOrder, BitmapBitOrder, BitmapPad, BitmapUnit, DisplayHeight, DisplayHeightMM, DisplayWidth, DisplayWidthMM, XListPixmapFormats, XPixmapFormatValues (3) - Xlib image formating functions and macros

macros - isalnum, isalpha, iscntrl, isdigit, isgraph, islower, isprint, ispunct, isspace, isupper, isxdigit (3) - character test functions and macros
macros - IsCursorKey, IsFunctionKey, IsKeypadKey, IsMiscFunctionKey, IsModiferKey, IsPFKey, IsPrivateKeypadKey (3) - Xlib keysym test macros
macros - man (7) - groff macros to format manual pages
macros - stdarg (3) - variable argument list macros
magic - magic (4) - magic numbers for file command
magic - mcookie (1) - generate magic cookies for the X authority system
magnetic - mt (1) - control a magnetic tape drive
magnetic - rmt (8) - control remote magnetic tape drives
magnify - xmag (1) - magnify parts of the screen
mail - deliver (8) - local mail transport
mail - elm (1) - interactive mail reader
mail - fastmail (1) - quick batch mail interface
mail - filter (1) - process incoming mail messages before adding to mailbox
mail - frm, nfrm (1) - list from and subject lines in mail messages
mail - mailaddr (7) - mail address description
mail - messages (1) - count of messages in mail folder
mail - newalias (1) - install new elm mail address aliases
mail - newmail, wnewmail (1) - notify users of new mail
mail - pop3d (1) - remote mail daemon
mail - popclient (1) - get mail using post office protocol
mail - printmail (1) - format mail messages for printing
mail - readmsg (1) - get messages from a mail folder
mail - sendmail (8) - Internet mail transport program
mail - unshar (1) - unpack shar files embedded in mail messages
mail - xmh (1) - send and read mail with an X11 interface
mailaddr - mailaddr (7) - mail address description
mailbox - filter (1) - process incoming mail messages before adding to mailbox
maintain - make (1) - maintain program dependencies
make - make (1) - maintain program dependencies
makedepend - makedepend (1) - add header files to a makefile
MAKEDEV - MAKEDEV (8) - create device special files
makefile - makedepend (1) - add header files to a makefile
makefile - transfig (1) - creates a makefile for portable LaTeX figures
makefile - xmkmf (1) - create a makefile from an Imakefile
makeindex - makeindex (1) - generate index files for LaTeX
makemap - makemap (8) - generate database maps for sendmail
making - initex (1) - special version of TeX for making .fmt files

malloc - malloc (3) - dynamic memory allocation functions
man - man (1) - on-line manual
man - man (7) - groff macros to format manual pages
man - man.config (5) - configuration file for man command
management - xcmsdb (1) - X11 color management system
manager - fvwm (1) - X11 window manager
manager - smproxy (1) - X11R6 session manager support
manager - twm (1) - window manager for X11
manager - xdm (1) - X-windows display manager
manager - xsm (1) - X-windows session manager
manager - xsmclient (1) - X-windows session manager tester
man.config - man.config (5) - configuration file for man command
manipulate - arp (8) - manipulate system ARP tables
manipulate - at, batch, atq, atrm (1) - manipulate batch jobs for later execution
manipulate - clock (8) - manipulate the CMOS clock
manipulate - crontab (1) - manipulate per-user crontabs
manipulate - fcntl (2) - manipulate open file descriptions
manipulate - fdisk (8) - manipulate disk partition tables
manipulate - fgetpos, fseek, fsetpos, ftell, rewind (3) - manipulate a file pointer
manipulate - ftime (2) - manipulate date and time
manipulate - getgrent, setgrent, endgrent (3) - manipulate group file entries
manipulate - getgroups, setgroups (2) - manipulate group access list
manipulate - gethostbyname, gethostbyaddr, gethostent, sethostent, endhostent, herror (3) - manipulate network host entries
manipulate - gethostid, sethostid (2) - manipulate the current host identifier
manipulate - gethostname, sethostname (2) - manipulate hostname
manipulate - getitimer, setitimer (2) - manipulate interval timer value
manipulate - getpriority, setpriority (2) - manipulate process scheduling priority
manipulate - getrlimit, getrusage, setrlimit (2) - manipulate process resource limits
manipulate - getsockopt, setsockopt (2) - manipulate socket options
manipulate - gettimeofday, settimeofday (2) - manipulate date and time
manipulate - inet_addr, inet_network, inet_ntoa, inet_makeaddr, inet_lnaof, inet_netof (3) - manipulate Internet addresses
manipulate - lesskey (1) - manipulate key bindings for less
manipulate - lpcntl (8) - manipulate line printer driver
manipulate - mmap, munmap (2) - manipulate mapping of files and devices into memory
manipulate - mprotect (2) - manipulate access permissions on memory regions

manipulate - `pr` (1) - manipulate text files for page printing
manipulate - `rarp` (8) - manipulate system RARP table
manipulate - `route` (8) - display and manipulate kernel IP routing tables
manipulate - `sxpm` (1) - manipulate XPM files
manipulate - `tune2fs` (8) - manipulate parameters in second extended filesystems
manipulate - `tunelp` (8) - manipulate parameters for the lp printer device
manipulate - `zoo` (1) - manipulate compressed file archives
manipulating - `Mtools` (1) - tools for manipulating DOS files
manipulating - `Mtools` (5) - tools for manipulating DOS files
manipulation - `gawk` (1) - language for string pattern manipulation
manpath - `manpath` (1) - display directory paths searched for manual pages
manual - `apropos` (1) - list manual entries relevant to a query
manual - `man` (1) - on-line manual
manual - `man` (7) - groff macros to format manual pages
manual - `manpath` (1) - display directory paths searched for manual pages
map - `iso_8859_1` (7) - map of character set
mapper - `portmap` (8) - RPC program number to DARPA port number mapper
mapping - `mapscrn` (8) - install user specified screen output mapping table
mapping - `mmap, munmap` (2) - manipulate mapping of files and devices into memory
maps - `makemap` (8) - generate database maps for sendmail
mapscrn - `mapscrn` (8) - install user specified screen output mapping table
mask - `umask` (2) - set file creation mask
match - `in_group_p` (9) - match group IDs
match - `locate` (1) - display file names from databases which match a regular expression
matching - `glob` (3) - find pathnames matching a pattern
matching - `grep, egrep, fgrep` (1) - display lines matching a regular expression
math - `abs` (3) - absolute value math function
math - `cbrt` (3) - cube root math function
math - `drem` (3) - floating point remainder math function
math - `erf, erfc` (3) - error and complementary-error math functions
math - `exp, log, log10, pow` (3) - exponential, logarithmic and power math functions
math - `j0, j1, jn, y0, y1, yn` (3) - Bessel math functions
math - `lgamma` (3) - log gamma math function
math - `sqrt` (3) - square root math function
mattrib - `mattrib` (1) - change attribute bit flags for DOS files
mblen - `mblen` (3) - get length of a multi-byte character
mbstowcs - `mbstowcs` (3) - convert multi-byte to wide character strings

mbstowcs - `mbstowcs` (3) - convert wide character to multi-byte strings
mbtowc - `mbtowc` (3) - convert multi-byte characters to wide characters
mcd - `mcd` (1) - mtools change DOS directory
mcookie - `mcookie` (1) - generate magic cookies for the X authority system
mcopy - `mcopy` (1) - mtools copy DOS files to or from Linux
MD5 - `md5sum` (1) - generate or check MD5 message signatures
md5sum - `md5sum` (1) - generate or check MD5 message signatures
mdel - `mdel` (1) - mtools delete a DOS file
mdir - `mdir` (1) - mtools display a DOS directory
mechanisms - `ipc` (5) - System-V interprocess communication mechanisms
mem - `mem` (4) - system memory
memccpy - `memccpy` (3) - byte array operations
memchr - `memchr` (3) - byte array operations
memcmp - `memcmp` (3) - byte array operations
memcpy - `memcpy` (3) - byte array operations
memfrob - `memfrob` (3) - byte array operations
memmem - `memmem` (3) - byte array operations
memmove - `memmove` (3) - byte array operations
memory - `alloca` (3) - allocate memory
memory - `calloc, malloc, free, realloc` (3) - dynamic memory allocation functions
memory - `free` (1) - display memory and swap space statistics
memory - `fsync` (2) - write a file's in-core memory state to disk
memory - `globfree` (3) - free memory from previous glob call
memory - `kmem` (4) - kernel memory
memory - `mem` (4) - system memory
memory - `mmap, munmap` (2) - manipulate mapping of files and devices into memory
memory - `mprotect` (2) - manipulate access permissions on memory regions
memory - `shmctl` (2) - System-V IPC shared memory control
memory - `shmget` (2) - System-V IPC create a shared memory segment
memory - `shmop` (2) - System-V IPC shared memory operations
memory - `vmstat` (8) - display virtual memory statistics
memset - `memset` (3) - byte array operations
menus - `gpm-root` (1) - gpm handler to draw menus on the root window
merge - `merge` (1) - combines multiple independent modifications to a file
merge - `paste` (1) - merge lines from multiple files
merge - `rcsmerge` (1) - merge revision control system files
mesg - `mesg` (1) - enable or disable write access to your terminal
message - `answer` (1) - elm phone message system
message - `catopen, catclose, catgets` (3) - message catalog operations
message - `closelog, openlog, syslog` (3) - send text to the system message and error logger
message - `dmesg` (8) - display/control the kernel message buffer

message - issue (4) - system identification message file
message - issue (5) - system identification message file
message - klogd (1) - kernel message log daemon
message - md5sum (1) - generate or check MD5 message signatures
message - motd (5) - message of the day file
message - msgctl (2) - System-V IPC control message operations
message - msgget (2) - System-V IPC create a message queue
message - msgop (2) - System-V IPC message operations
message - perror (3) - print error message from errno value
message - psignal (3) - print message corresponding to signal
message - recv, recvfrom, recvmsg (2) - get a message from a socket
message - rpc.rwalld (8) - rwall message daemon
message - rwall (1) - send a message to users logged in on a specified host
message - send, sendto, sendmsg (2) - send a message from a socket
message - wall (1) - write a message to all users
message - write (1) - send a message to another user
messages - filter (1) - process incoming mail messages before adding to mailbox
messages - frm, nfrm (1) - list from and subject lines in mail messages
messages - logger (1) - write messages to the syslog
messages - messages (1) - count of messages in mail folder
messages - printmail (1) - format mail messages for printing
messages - readmsg (1) - get messages from a mail folder
messages - syslogd (8) - log system messages
messages - unshar (1) - unpack shar files embedded in mail messages
messages - xconsole (1) - monitor system console messages with X-windows
meta - setmetamode (1) - determine handling of the keyboard meta key
metafont - mft (1) - translate metafont program to TeX file
metric - pltotf (1) - convert properties files to TeX font metric format
metric - tftopl (1) - convert TeX font metric files to properties
metrics - afm2tfm (1) - convert Adobe font metrics to TeX font metrics
metrics - vptovf (1) - convert virtual properties to virtual and TeX font metrics
mev - mev (1) - report mouse events
mf - mf (1) - font and logo design tools
MFM - hd (4) - details MFM/RLL/IDE hard disk device special files
mformat - mformat (1) - mtools add a DOS filesystem to a low-level formatted floppy disk
mft - mft (1) - translate metafont program to TeX file
microseconds - usleep (3) - suspend process execution for a time given in microseconds

minicom - minicom (1) - serial communication program
minicom - runscript (1) - script interpreter for minicom communications program
minix - fsck.minix (8) - integrity check and fix a minix filesystem
minix - mkfs (8) - create a minix filesystem
miscellaneous - intro (7) - introduction to miscellaneous
mkdir - mkdir (1) - create a directory
mkdir - mkdir (2) - create a directory
mkdirhier - mkdirhier (1) - create a directory hierarchy
mkdosfs - mkdosfs (8) - create a DOS filesystem
mke2fs - mke2fs (8) - create a second extended filesystem
mkfifo - mkfifo (1) - create a named pipe
mkfontdir - mkfontdir (1) - create an index of X11 font files
mkfs - mkfs (8) - create a minix filesystem
mklost - mklost (8) - create a lost+found directory on a filesystem
mkmanifest - mkmanifest (1) - help restore Unix file names modified by DOS name restrictions
mknod - mknod (1) - create special files
mknod - mknod (2) - create a filesystem node
mkstemp - mkstemp (3) - create a unique temporary file from a name template
mkswap - mkswap (8) - create a swap device
mktemp - mktemp (3) - create a unique temporary file name
mktime - kernel_mktime (9) - convert struct mktime into seconds since 1 January, 1970
mktime - mktime (3) - convert date and time to ascii
mkxfs - mkxfs (8) - create an xiafs filesystem
mlabel - mlabel (1) - label a DOS partition/volume
mmap - mmap (2) - manipulate mapping of files and devices into memory
mmd - mmd (1) - create a DOS subdirectory
mode - kbd_mode (1) - get/set the keyboard mode
mode - rdev (8) - display or modify kernel root device, swap device, RAM disk size, and video mode
mode - slattach (8) - put a serial line into network mode
mode - vm86 (2) - enter virtual 8086 mode
modem - seyon (1) - X11 modem terminal emulator
modes - install (1) - copy files and setup owner and permission modes
modf - modf (3) - extract the integral and fractional parts of a floating point number
modification - utime, utimes (2) - change access or modification times in an inode
modifications - merge (1) - combines multiple independent modifications to a file
modified - elvprsv (1) - recover modified version of an elvis edited file after a crash
modified - env (1) - run a program in a modified environment
modified - mkmanifest (1) - help restore Unix file names modified by DOS name restrictions
modify - addftinfo (1) - modify troff font files for use with groff
modify - ar (1) - create, modify, and extract from archives

modify - `rdev` (8) - display or modify kernel root device, swap device, RAM disk size, and video mode
modify - `reboot` (2) - reboot Linux or modify Ctrl-Alt-Del behaviour
modifying - `xmodmap` (1) - utility for modifying keymaps in X-windows
modify_ldt - `modify_ldt` (2) - get/set process local descriptor table
modprobe - `modprobe` (1) - automatic handling of loadable modules
module - `get_kernel_syms, create_module, init_module, delete_module` (2) - kernel loadable module support
module - `rmmod` (1) - unload a loaded kernel module
modules - `depmod, modprobe` (1) - automatic handling of loadable modules
modules - `insmod` (1) - install loadable kernel modules
modules - `lsmod` (1) - lists loaded modules
monitor - `xconsole` (1) - monitor system console messages with X-windows
more - `less` (1) - enhanced version of more
more - `more` (1) - display file contents with page breaks
motd - `motd` (5) - message of the day file
mount - `fstab` (5) - mount information about filesystems
mount - `mount, umount` (2) - mount and unmount filesystems to the directory hierarchy
mount - `mount, umount` (8) - mount and unmount filesystems to the directory hierarchy
mount - `mountd` (8) - NFS mount daemon
mount - `showmount` (8) - show NFS mount information
mountd - `mountd` (8) - NFS mount daemon
mouse - `mev` (1) - report mouse events
move - `mv` (1) - move/rename a file
move - `put_file_last` (9) - move a file to the end of the kernel file table
mprotect - `mprotect` (2) - manipulate access permissions on memory regions
mpx - `mpx` (2) - unimplemented system calls
mrand48 - `mrand48` (3) - random number generator
mrd - `mrd` (1) - remove a DOS directory
mread - `mread` (1) - copy a DOS file to Linux
mren - `mren` (1) - rename a DOS file
msgctl - `msgctl` (2) - System-V IPC control message operations
msgget - `msgget` (2) - System-V IPC create a message queue
msgop - `msgop` (2) - System-V IPC message operations
mt - `mt` (1) - control a magnetic tape drive
mtab - `getmntent, setmntent, addmntent, endmntent, hasmntopt` (3) - access fstab and mtab file entries
mtools - `mcd` (1) - mtools change DOS directory
mtools - `mcopy` (1) - mtools copy DOS files to or from Linux
mtools - `mdel` (1) - mtools delete a DOS file
mtools - `mdir` (1) - mtools display a DOS directory
mtools - `mformat` (1) - mtools add a DOS filesystem to a low-level formatted floppy disk
Mtools - `Mtools` (1) - tools for manipulating DOS files

Mtools - `Mtools` (5) - tools for manipulating DOS files
mtype - `mtype` (1) - display contents of a DOS file
multi-byte - `mblen` (3) - get length of a multi-byte character
multi-byte - `mbstowcs` (3) - convert multi-byte to wide character strings
multi-byte - `mbstowcs` (3) - convert wide character to multi-byte strings
multi-byte - `mbtowc` (3) - convert multi-byte characters to wide characters
multi-byte - `wctomb` (3) - convert a wide character to a multi-byte character
multi-language - `locale` (7) - multi-language support
multiple - `merge` (1) - combines multiple independent modifications to a file
multiple - `paste` (1) - merge lines from multiple files
multiple - `readv, writev` (3) - transfer several data blocks using multiple buffers
multiply - `ldexp` (3) - multiply floating point number by a power of 2
multi-user - `ytalk` (1) - a multi-user chat program
munchlist - `munchlist` (1) - spell checker
munmap - `munmap` (2) - manipulate mapping of files and devices into memory
mv - `mv` (1) - move/rename a file
mwrite - `mwrite` (1) - copy a Linux file to DOS
named - `mkfifo` (1) - create a named pipe
names - `find` (1) - list file names in a directory hierarchy
names - `ftw` (3) - execute a function on file names in a directory tree
names - `locate` (1) - display file names from databases which match a regular expression
names - `mkmanifest` (1) - help restore Unix file names modified by DOS name restrictions
names - `pathchk` (1) - check for valid file names
names - `users` (1) - display the login names of users currently logged in
NcFTP - `NcFTP` (1) - Internet file transfer program
ncurses - `ncurses` (3) - screen handling package
nearest - `rint` (3) - round to nearest integer
netdate - `netdate` (8) - set date and time
netstat - `netstat` (8) - display status information on active network connections
network - `gethostbyname, gethostbyaddr, gethostent, sethostent, endhostent, herror` (3) - manipulate network host entries
network - `htonl, htons, ntohl, ntohs` (3) - translate between host and network byte order
network - `ifconfig` (8) - configure a network interface
network - `lbxproxy` (1) - low network badwidth proxy server for X11
network - `netstat` (8) - display status information on active network connections
network - `nntpd` (8) - network news transfer protocol daemon
network - `ping` (8) - echo packets from network hosts
network - `routed` (8) - network routing daemon
network - `ruptime` (1) - show status of local network machines
network - `rusers` (1) - list users logged in on local network machines

network - rwho (1) - list users logged in on local network machines
network - slattach (8) - put a serial line into network mode
network - sliplogin (8) - convert a serial line into a SLIP network interface
network - tin, rtin, cdtin, tind (1) - network news readers
network - traceroute (8) - display the route taken by network packets
networks - getnetent, getnetbyaddr, getnetbyname, setnetent, endnetent (3) - get networks file entries
network-transparent - X (1) - portable network-transparent window system
new - chroot (8) - execute a program with a new root directory
new - execl, execlp, execle, exect, execv, execvp (3) - execute new program in current process
new - execve (2) - execute new program in current process
new - link (2) - make a new directory link to an existing file
new - ln (1) - make new links to existing files
new - newalias (1) - install new elm mail address aliases
new - newgrp (1) - change to a new user group
new - newmail, wnewmail (1) - notify users of new mail
new - reconfig (1) - convert old Xconfig files to new XF86Config format
new - setsid (2) - create a new process session
new - setsid (2) - create new session and process group
new - setsid (8) - run a program in a new session
newalias - newalias (1) - install new elm mail address aliases
newgrp - newgrp (1) - change to a new user group
newmail - newmail (1) - notify users of new mail
news - nntpd (8) - network news transfer protocol daemon
news - tin, rtin, cdtin, tind (1) - network news readers
next - seekdir (3) - set the position of the next readdir in a directory
nfrm - nfrm (1) - list from and subject lines in mail messages
NFS - exports (5) - exported NFS filesystems
NFS - mountd (8) - NFS mount daemon
NFS - nfs (5) - NFS fstab file format
nfs - nfs (5) - NFS fstab file format
NFS - nfsd (8) - NFS server daemon
NFS - showmount (8) - show NFS mount information
nfsd - nfsd (8) - NFS server daemon
nice - nice (1) - run a program and change its scheduling priority
nice - nice (2) - change current process priority
nl - nl (1) - number lines in text files
nm - nm (1) - display object file symbol table
nntpd - nntpd (8) - network news transfer protocol daemon
node - mknod (2) - create a filesystem node
nodes - tsort (1) - sort nodes in a directed graph
nohup - nohup (1) - run a command set to ignore hangup signals

nologin - nologin (5) - allow only root to login to the system
nothing - true (1) - do nothing and return a true exit status
notify - newmail, wnewmail (1) - notify users of new mail
nrand48 - nrand48 (3) - random number generator
nroff - colcrt (1) - translate nroff output for screen viewing
nroff - gnroff (1) - emulate the nroff command using groff
nslookup - nslookup (8) - interactively query Internet name servers
ntohl - ntohl (3) - translate between host and network byte order
ntohs - ntohs (3) - translate between host and network byte order
null - null (4) - bit bucket special files
number - drand48, erand48, lrand48, nrand48, mrand48, jrand48, srand48, seed48, lcong48 (3) - random number generator
number - ecvt, fcvt (3) - convert a floating point number to a string
number - fabs (3) - absolute value of floating point number
number - frexp (3) - split floating point number to integer and fractional parts
number - gcvt (3) - convert floating point number to string
number - getuid, geteuid (2) - get real or effective user ID number
number - ldexp (3) - multiply floating point number by a power of 2
number - modf (3) - extract the integral and fractional parts of a floating point number
number - nl (1) - number lines in text files
number - portmap (8) - RPC program number to DARPA port number mapper
number - rand, srand, random, srandom, initstate, setstate (3) - random number generator
number - wc (1) - print the number of bytes, words, and lines in files
numbers - getpid, getppid (2) - get process ID numbers
numbers - host (1) - look up hostnames or numbers using domain name server
numbers - magic (4) - magic numbers for file command
numeric - strtod (3) - convert numeric string to double
objdump - objdump (1) - extract low level information from object files
object - nm (1) - display object file symbol table
object - objdump (1) - extract low level information from object files
object - size (1) - list section sizes in archive and object files
object - strip (1) - remove symbol table from object files
oclock - oclock (1) - X11 clock
octal - hexdump (1) - display file contents in hexadecimal decimal ascii and octal
octal - od (1) - display file contents in octal or other formats

od   - od (1) - display file contents in octal or other
           formats
office   - popclient (1) - get mail using post office
           protocol
offset   - lseek (2) - position file offset in an open file
           description
old   - reconfig (1) - convert old Xconfig files to new
           XF86Config format
on_exit - on_exit (3) - register a user exit function
on-line - man (1) - on-line manual
only   - nologin (5) - allow only root to login to the
           system
open   - fcntl (2) - manipulate open file descriptions
open   - flock (2) - set or reset open file lock
open   - fopen, fdopen, freopen (3) - file open
           functions
open   - lseek (2) - position file offset in an open file
           description
open   - open, creat (2) - open or create a file or
           device
open   - opendir (3) - open a directory
open   - read (2) - read bytes from an open file
           description
open   - ttyname (3) - get the pathname of an open
           terminal device
open   - write (2) - write to an open file description
opendir - opendir (3) - open a directory
openlog - openlog (3) - send text to the system
           message and error logger
operations - bcmp, bcopy, bzero, memccpy,
             memchr, memcmp, memcpy, memfrob, memmem,
             memmove, memset (3) - byte array operations
operations - catopen, catclose, catgets (3) -
             message catalog operations
operations - msgctl (2) - System-V IPC control
             message operations
operations - msgop (2) - System-V IPC message
             operations
operations - semctl (2) - System-V IPC control
             semaphore operations
operations - semop (2) - System-V IPC semaphore
             operations
operations - setbuf, setbuffer, setlinebuf,
             setvbuf (3) - file output buffering operations
operations - shmop (2) - System-V IPC shared
             memory operations
option   - fpathconf, pathconf (3) - get file
           configuration option values
options - getopt (1) - parse command line options
options - getopt (3) - parse command line options
options - getsockopt, setsockopt (2) - manipulate
           socket options
options - grog (1) - generate a groff command with
           parameter options
order   - htonl, htons, ntohl, ntohs (3) - translate
           between host and network byte order
othello - othello (6) - othello game
other   - fig2dev (1) - translate Fig code to other
           graphics languages
other   - od (1) - display file contents in octal or other
           formats
output   - colcrt (1) - translate nroff output for
           screen viewing
output   - fputc, fputs, putc, putchar, puts (3) -
           string and character output functions

output   - groff_out (5) - format of groff intermediate
           output
output   - gxditview (1) - display gtroff output on an
           X display
output   - ioctl (2) - input and output device control
output   - ioperm (2) - set input and output access
           permissions on a port
output   - iopl (2) - change input and output
           privilege level
output   - lptest (1) - generate lineprinter test output
output   - mapscrn (8) - install user specified screen
           output mapping table
output   - popen, pclose (3) - start a process with
           piped input or output
output   - postprint (6) - postscript output from
           gnuchess
output   - printf, fprintf, sprintf, vprintf,
           vfprintf, vsprintf (3) - output format
           functions
output   - setbuf, setbuffer, setlinebuf, setvbuf
           (3) - file output buffering operations
output   - stdio (3) - standard input/output library
           functions
output   - tail (1) - output the tail end of a file
output   - yes (1) - output a string repeatedly until
           killed
owner   - install (1) - copy files and setup owner and
           permission modes
ownership - chgrp (1) - change file group ownership
ownership - chown (1) - change the user and group
            ownership of files
ownership - chown, fchown (2) - change file
            ownership
pac   - pac (8) - display printer accounting information
package - lamstex (1) - text formatting TeX macro
           package
package - ncurses (3) - screen handling package
package - zip, zipcloak, zipnote, zipsplit (1) -
           package and compress (archive) files
packed   - gftopk (1) - translate generic font files to
           packed font files
packed   - pktogf (1) - translate packed fonts to
           generic fonts
packed   - pktype (1) - make a packed font file human
           readable
packets - ping (8) - echo packets from network hosts
packets - traceroute (8) - display the route taken
           by network packets
page   - getpagesize (2) - return kernel page size
page   - grow_files (9) - add a page of entries to the
           file table
page   - more (1) - display file contents with page
           breaks
page   - pr (1) - manipulate text files for page printing
pages   - man (7) - groff macros to format manual
           pages
pages   - manpath (1) - display directory paths
           searched for manual pages
paging   - swapon, swapoff (2) - enable/disable
           devices and files for paging
paging   - swapon, swapoff (8) - enable/disable
           devices and files for paging
paint   - xfig (1) - X11 draw and paint program
pair   - socketpair (2) - create a pair of connected
           sockets

parameter - grog (1) - generate a groff command with parameter options
parameter - printf (1) - format and display parameter strings
parameter - xsetroot (1) - root window parameter setting utility for X11
parameters - bootparam (7) - Linux kernel boot time parameters
parameters - dircolors (1) - set ls color parameters
parameters - plipconfig (8) - configure PLIP device parameters
parameters - setfdprm (8) - load parameters into floppy disk devices
parameters - tune2fs (8) - manipulate parameters in second extended filesystems
parameters - tunelp (8) - manipulate parameters for the lp printer device
parse - getopt (1) - parse command line options
parse - getopt (3) - parse command line options
parser - Yacc (1) - LALR-1 parser generator
part - head (1) - display the first part of a file
part - shutdown (2) - shutdown all or part of a full-duplex socket connection
particular - scandir, alphasort (3) - search a directory for entries with particular attributes
partition - badblocks (8) - search for bad blocks on a disk partition
partition - dd (1) - file and disk partition copy
partition - df (1) - summarize free disk partition space
partition - fdisk (8) - manipulate disk partition tables
partition - mlabel (1) - label a DOS partition/volume
parts - frexp (3) - split floating point number to integer and fractional parts
parts - modf (3) - extract the integral and fractional parts of a floating point number
parts - xmag (1) - magnify parts of the screen
Pascal - tangle (1) - convert WEB source to a Pascal program
passwd - passwd (1) - change user password
passwd - passwd (5) - system password file
password - chsh (1) - change your login shell in password file
password - fgetpwent (3) - get entry from password file
password - getpass (3) - prompt for and read a password
password - getpw (3) - get password line entry for given user
password - getpwent, setpwent, endpwent, getpwnam, getpwuid (3) - get fields from password file entries
password - login (1) - password check program
password - passwd (1) - change user password
password - passwd (5) - system password file
password - putpwent (3) - write password file entry
password - vipw (8) - edit the password file
password - xlock (1) - locks the X-windows display until a password is entered
past - last (1) - display past user/terminal login records
paste - gpm (1) - cut and paste across virtual consoles
paste - paste (1) - merge lines from multiple files
paste - xcutsel (1) - cut and paste bridge program

patch - patch (1) - update a file with a diff
patgen - patgen (1) - generate TeX hyphenation patterns
path - which (1) - display path name of commands
pathchk - pathchk (1) - check for valid file names
pathconf - pathconf (3) - get file configuration option values
pathname - basename (1) - strip directory prefix from file pathname
pathname - dirname (1) - extract directory prefix from file pathname
pathname - realpath (3) - make absolute pathname from relative pathname or symbolic link
pathname - ttyname (3) - get the pathname of an open terminal device
pathnames - glob (3) - find pathnames matching a pattern
pathnames - shells (5) - file of pathnames to login shells for use with chsh
paths - manpath (1) - display directory paths searched for manual pages
pattern - gawk (1) - language for string pattern manipulation
pattern - glob (3) - find pathnames matching a pattern
patterns - ident (1) - find RCS keyword patterns in files
patterns - patgen (1) - generate TeX hyphenation patterns
pause - pause (2) - block a process and wait for a signal
pclose - pclose (3) - start a process with piped input or output
peer - getpeername (2) - get name of peer connected to a given socket
perform - ldiv (3) - perform long integer division
perform - tex, virtex (1) - perform text formatting and typesetting
perform - zcmp, zdiff (1) - perform comparisons on compressed files
performance - x11perf (1) - X11 server performance test
permission - chmod (1) - change file access permission bits
permission - chmod, fchmod (2) - change file access permission bits
permission - install (1) - copy files and setup owner and permission modes
permissions - access (2) - check user's permissions on a file
permissions - ioperm (2) - set input and output access permissions on a port
permissions - mprotect (2) - manipulate access permissions on memory regions
perror - perror (3) - print error message from errno value
personality - personality (2) - set execution domain for a process
per-user - crontab (1) - manipulate per-user crontabs
.pfb - pfbtops (1) - translate a .pfb postscript font to ascii
pfbtops - pfbtops (1) - translate a .pfb postscript font to ascii
phone - answer (1) - elm phone message system

pic - gpic (1) - gnu pic generates pictures for troff or TeX
pic - pic2tpic (1) - convert pic files to tpic format
pic2tpic - pic2tpic (1) - convert pic files to tpic format
pictures - gpic (1) - gnu pic generates pictures for troff or TeX
PIDs - fuser (1) - display PIDs of processes using specified files
pieces - dsplit (1) - split binary files into pieces
pieces - split (1) - split a file into pieces
ping - ping (8) - echo packets from network hosts
pipe - mkfifo (1) - create a named pipe
pipe - pipe (2) - create anonymous pipe
piped - popen, pclose (3) - start a process with piped input or output
pipeline - tee (1) - add a tee to a command pipeline to write to a file
pk - gsftopk (1) - convert a ghostscript font to TeX pk format
pktogf - pktogf (1) - translate packed fonts to generic fonts
pktype - pktype (1) - make a packed font file human readable
play - workbone (1) - play audio compact discs on a CD-ROM reader
play - workman (1) - play audio compact discs on a CD-ROM reader
PLIP - plipconfig (8) - configure PLIP device parameters
plipconfig - plipconfig (8) - configure PLIP device parameters
pltotf - pltotf (1) - convert properties files to TeX font metric format
pointer - fclose (3) - close a file pointer
pointer - fflush, fpurge (3) - flush a file pointer
pointer - fgetpos, fseek, fsetpos, ftell, rewind (3) - manipulate a file pointer
pointer - rewinddir (3) - reset stream pointer to start of directory
point-to-point - pppd (8) - point-to-point Internet protocol daemon
pool - pooltype (1) - convert a WEB pool file to a text file
pooltype - pooltype (1) - convert a WEB pool file to a text file
pop3d - pop3d (1) - remote mail daemon
popclient - popclient (1) - get mail using post office protocol
popd - popd (1) - bash built-in commands
popen - popen (3) - start a process with piped input or output
port - ioperm (2) - set input and output access permissions on a port
port - port (4) - system ports
port - portmap (8) - RPC program number to DARPA port number mapper
port - setserial (8) - get and set Linux serial port configuration
portable - transfig (1) - creates a makefile for portable LaTeX figures
portable - X (1) - portable network-transparent window system
portmap - portmap (8) - RPC program number to DARPA port number mapper
ports - port (4) - system ports

position - ffs (3) - returns position of first bit set in a word
position - lseek (2) - position file offset in an open file description
position - seekdir (3) - set the position of the next readdir in a directory
position - telldir (3) - return current position in directory stream
posix2time - posix2time (3) - convert time formats
post - popclient (1) - get mail using post office protocol
postprint - postprint (6) - postscript output from gnuchess
postscript - dvips (1) - make postscript from a dvi file
postscript - fig2ps2tex (1) - include a postscript file in a TeX document
postscript - ghostview (1) - use ghostscript to view postscript documents
postscript - grops (1) - groff postscript driver
postscript - pfbtops (1) - translate a .pfb postscript font to ascii
postscript - postprint (6) - postscript output from gnuchess
postscript - psbb (1) - get bounding box size from a postscript document
postscript - Psfig/TeX (7) - postscript figures in TeX
pow - pow (3) - exponential, logarithmic and power math functions
power - exp, log, log10, pow (3) - exponential, logarithmic and power math functions
power - ldexp (3) - multiply floating point number by a power of 2
PPM - xvpictoppm (1) - converts XV thumbnail files to standard PPM format
pppd - pppd (8) - point-to-point Internet protocol daemon
pr - pr (1) - manipulate text files for page printing
preference - workmanrc, workmandb (5) - database and preference files for workman
preference - xset (1) - user preference utility for X-windows
prefix - basename (1) - strip directory prefix from file pathname
prefix - dirname (1) - extract directory prefix from file pathname
prefix - look (1) - display lines with a given string prefix
preprocessor - cccp, cpp (1) - C preprocessor
preprocessor - grefer (1) - preprocessor for groff bibliographic references
preprocessor - imake (1) - preprocessor to generate make files
present - pwd (1) - display name of present working directory
pretty - indent (1) - C program pretty printer
previewer - xdvi (1) - DVI previewer for X-windows
previous - globfree (3) - free memory from previous glob call
print - banner (6) - print text as a large banner
print - domainname (1) - set/print domain of current host
print - lpr (1) - spool files to line print
print - perror (3) - print error message from errno value

print - psignal (3) - print message corresponding to signal
print - tty (1) - print the special file name of the controlling terminal
print - wc (1) - print the number of bytes, words, and lines in files
print - whoami (1) - print effective userid
printable - strings (1) - display printable strings in a file
printcap - printcap (5) - printer capability data base
printenv - printenv (1) - display environment variables
printer - indent (1) - C program pretty printer
printer - lp (4) - line printer device special file
printer - lpc (8) - control line printer system
printer - lpcntl (8) - manipulate line printer driver
printer - lpd (8) - line printer daemon
printer - lpq (1) - display status information for printer job queue
printer - lprm (1) - delete queued printer jobs
printer - pac (8) - display printer accounting information
printer - printcap (5) - printer capability data base
printer - tunelp (8) - manipulate parameters for the lp printer device
printers - dvilj4, dvilj4l, dvilj2p, dvilj (1) - convert dvi files for HP laser printers
printf - printf (1) - format and display parameter strings
printf - printf (3) - output format functions
printing - pr (1) - manipulate text files for page printing
printing - printmail (1) - format mail messages for printing
printmail - printmail (1) - format mail messages for printing
priorities - renice (8) - alter running process priorities
priority - getpriority, setpriority (2) - manipulate process scheduling priority
priority - nice (1) - run a program and change its scheduling priority
priority - nice (2) - change current process priority
privilege - iopl (2) - change input and output privilege level
privileged - intro (8) - introduction to administrative/privileged commands
probe - SuperProbe (1) - probe and identify video hardware
proc - proc (5) - pseudo-filesystem for access to kernel data structures
process - abort (3) - cause abnormal process termination
process - acct (2) - switch process accounting on or off
process - assert (3) - terminate process if assertion is false
process - brk, sbrk (2) - change process data segment size
process - clock (3) - return processor time used by process
process - clone (2) - create a child process
process - execl, execlp, execle, exect, execv, execvp (3) - execute new program in current process
process - execve (2) - execute new program in current process
process - _exit (2) - terminate the current process
process - filter (1) - process incoming mail messages before adding to mailbox
process - fork, vfork (2) - create a child process
process - getpid, getppid (2) - get process ID numbers
process - getpriority, setpriority (2) - manipulate process scheduling priority
process - getrlimit, getrusage, setrlimit (2) - manipulate process resource limits
process - init, telinit (8) - setup and control process initialization
process - inittab (5) - configuration file for init to process
process - kill (1) - send signal to process
process - kill (2) - send signal to process
process - killpg (3) - send signal to process group
process - modify_ldt (2) - get/set process local descriptor table
process - nice (2) - change current process priority
process - pause (2) - block a process and wait for a signal
process - personality (2) - set execution domain for a process
process - popen, pclose (3) - start a process with piped input or output
process - proc_sel (9) - kernel function for process selection
process - profil (2) - generate process execution profile
process - ps (1) - display process status
process - pstree (1) - display process hierarchy as a tree
process - ptrace (2) - debug process trace control
process - raise (3) - signal current process
process - renice (8) - alter running process priorities
process - setpgid, getpgrp, setpgrp (2) - set or get process group ID
process - setsid (2) - create a new process session
process - setsid (2) - create new session and process group
process - times (2) - get process times
process - usleep (3) - suspend process execution for a time given in microseconds
process - wait, waitpid, wait3, wait4 (2) - wait for process termination
process-0 - idle (2) - internal system call to make process-0 idle
processes - fuser (1) - display PIDs of processes using specified files
processes - killall (1) - send signal to processes by command name
processes - top (1) - display processes with highest CPU usage
processor - arch (1) - display processor architecture
processor - clock (3) - return processor time used by process
proc_sel - proc_sel (9) - kernel function for process selection
produce - gnuan (6) - produce a chess game analysis
production - virtex (1) - TeX version for production typesetting
prof - prof (2) - unimplemented system calls

profil - profil (2) - generate process execution profile
profile - profil (2) - generate process execution profile
profiling - readprofile (1) - read kernel profiling information
prompt - agetty (8) - getty for login prompt
prompt - getpass (3) - prompt for and read a password
properties - pltotf (1) - convert properties files to TeX font metric format
properties - tftopl (1) - convert TeX font metric files to properties
properties - vftovp (1) - convert virtual fonts to virtual properties
properties - vptovf (1) - convert virtual properties to virtual and TeX font metrics
property - xprop (1) - property displayer for X-windows
protocol - ftpd (8) - Internet file transfer protocol daemon
protocol - nntpd (8) - network news transfer protocol daemon
protocol - popclient (1) - get mail using post office protocol
protocol - pppd (8) - point-to-point Internet protocol daemon
protocol - telnet (1) - telnet protocol interface program
protocol - tftpd (8) - trivial file transfer protocol daemon
protocols - getprotoent, getprotobyname, getprotobynumber, setprotoent, endprotoent (3) - get protocols file entries
protocols - rpcgen (1) - C code generator for RPC protocols
provide - ipcs (8) - provide ipc status information
proxy - lbxproxy (1) - low network badwidth proxy server for X11
ps - ps (1) - display process status
ps - psupdate (8) - update the ps kernel database
psbb - psbb (1) - get bounding box size from a postscript document
pseudo-filesystem - proc (5) - pseudo-filesystem for access to kernel data structures
Psfig - Psfig (7) - postscript figures in TeX
psignal - psignal (3) - print message corresponding to signal
pstree - pstree (1) - display process hierarchy as a tree
psupdate - psupdate (8) - update the ps kernel database
ptrace - ptrace (2) - debug process trace control
pushd - pushd (1) - bash built-in commands
put - slattach (8) - put a serial line into network mode
putc - putc (3) - string and character output functions
putchar - putchar (3) - string and character output functions
putenv - putenv (3) - assign a value to an environment variable
put_file_last - put_file_last (9) - move a file to the end of the kernel file table
putpwent - putpwent (3) - write password file entry

puts - puts (3) - string and character output functions
pututline - pututline (3) - access entries in utmp login record file
pwd - pwd (1) - bash built-in commands
pwd - pwd (1) - display name of present working directory
Pythagoras - hypot (3) - Pythagoras distance calculation
qsort - qsort (3) - quick sort an array
queries - dig (1) - send domain-name queries to name servers
query - apropos (1) - list manual entries relevant to a query
query - dnsquery (1) - query domain-name servers using resolver
query - nslookup (8) - interactively query Internet name servers
queue - listen (2) - specify queue length for incoming socket connections
queue - lpq (1) - display status information for printer job queue
queue - msgget (2) - System-V IPC create a message queue
queued - atrun (8) - run batch jobs queued for later execution
queued - lprm (1) - delete queued printer jobs
quotactl - quotactl (2) - unimplemented system calls
quotient - div (3) - calculates quotient and remainder on integer division
raise - raise (3) - signal current process
RAM - ram (4) - RAM disk device special file
ram - ram (4) - RAM disk device special file
RAM - rdev (8) - display or modify kernel root device, swap device, RAM disk size, and video mode
rand - rand (3) - random number generator
random - drand48, erand48, lrand48, nrand48, mrand48, jrand48, srand48, seed48, lcong48 (3) - random number generator
random - rand, srand, random, srandom, initstate, setstate (3) - random number generator
ranlib - ranlib (1) - generate an index for an ar archive
RARP - rarp (8) - manipulate system RARP table
rarp - rarp (8) - manipulate system RARP table
rate - kbdrate (8) - set keyboard auto-key repeat rate and initial repeat delay time
rb - rb (1) - receive xmodem, ymodem and zmodem files
rcp - rcp (1) - remote file copy
RCS - ident (1) - find RCS keyword patterns in files
rcs - rcs (1) - change revision control system file attributes
rcs - rcsclean (1) - clean up unmodified rcs working files
RCS - rcsfreeze (1) - freeze a set of sources checked in under RCS
RCS - rlog (1) - display information about RCS files
rcsclean - rcsclean (1) - clean up unmodified rcs working files
rcsdiff - rcsdiff (i) - compare revision control system files

rcsfile - rcsfile (1) - format of revision control system file
rcsfile - rcsfile (5) - format of revision control system file
rcsfreeze - rcsfreeze (1) - freeze a set of sources checked in under RCS
rcsintro - rcsintro (1) - introduction to revision control system commands
rcsmerge - rcsmerge (1) - merge revision control system files
rdev - rdev (8) - display or modify kernel root device, swap device, RAM disk size, and video mode
read - fread, fwrite (3) - file read and write functions
read - getdirentries (3) - read directory entries
read - getpass (3) - prompt for and read a password
read - read (1) - bash built-in commands
read - read (2) - read bytes from an open file description
read - readdir (2) - read a directory
read - readlink (2) - read a symbolic link
read - readprofile (1) - read kernel profiling information
read - xmh (1) - send and read mail with an X11 interface
readable - dvitype (1) - make a dvi file human readable
readable - gftype (1) - translate generic font files to human readable format
readable - pktype (1) - make a packed font file human readable
readdir - readdir (2) - read a directory
readdir - seekdir (3) - set the position of the next readdir in a directory
reader - elm (1) - interactive mail reader
reader - workbone (1) - play audio compact discs on a CD-ROM reader
reader - workman (1) - play audio compact discs on a CD-ROM reader
readers - tin, rtin, cdtin, tind (1) - network news readers
readline - readline (3) - take interactive line of input
readlink - readlink (2) - read a symbolic link
readmsg - readmsg (1) - get messages from a mail folder
readonly - readonly (1) - bash built-in commands
readprofile - readprofile (1) - read kernel profiling information
readv - readv (3) - transfer several data blocks using multiple buffers
real - getgid, getegid (2) - get real/effective group identity
real - getuid, geteuid (2) - get real or effective user ID number
real - id (1) - display real and effective user and group IDs
real - setregid, setegid (2) - set real and effective group ID
real - setreuid, seteuid (2) - set real and effective user ID
realloc - realloc (3) - dynamic memory allocation functions
realpath - realpath (3) - make absolute pathname from relative pathname or symbolic link

reboot - reboot (2) - reboot Linux or modify Ctrl-Alt-Del behaviour
reboot - reboot (8) - shutdown the system
receive - rx, rb, rz (1) - receive xmodem, ymodem and zmodem files
recompress - znew (1) - recompress .Z files as .gz files
reconfig - reconfig (1) - convert old Xconfig files to new XF86Config format
record - getutent, getutid, getutline, pututline, setutent, endutent, utmpname (3) - access entries in utmp login record file
records - last (1) - display past user/terminal login records
records - sort (1) - sort records in text files
records - utmp, wtmp (5) - format of login records
recover - elvprsv (1) - recover modified version of an elvis edited file after a crash
recover - elvrec (1) - recover an unsaved elvis editor file after a crash
recovery - fiz (1) - data recovery from damaged zoo archives
recv - recv (2) - get a message from a socket
recvfrom - recvfrom (2) - get a message from a socket
recvmsg - recvmsg (2) - get a message from a socket
red - red (1) - text editor
ref - ref (1) - display C function headers
reference - glookbib (1) - search bibliographic reference databases
references - grefer (1) - preprocessor for groff bibliographic references
refresh - xrefresh (1) - refresh an X11 screen
refs - ctags (1) - generates tags and refs files
regions - mprotect (2) - manipulate access permissions on memory regions
register - on_exit (3) - register a user exit function
regular - fnmatch (3) - search a string for a regular expression
regular - grep, egrep, fgrep (1) - display lines matching a regular expression
regular - locate (1) - display file names from databases which match a regular expression
regular - zgrep (1) - search compressed files for a regular expression
regular - zipgrep (1) - search zip'ed files for a regular expression
related - whereis (1) - locate files related to a command
relative - realpath (3) - make absolute pathname from relative pathname or symbolic link
relevant - apropos (1) - list manual entries relevant to a query
remainder - div (3) - calculates quotient and remainder on integer division
remainder - drem (3) - floating point remainder math function
remainder - fmod (3) - floating point remainder function
remote - pop3d (1) - remote mail daemon
remote - rcp (1) - remote file copy
remote - rexecd (8) - remote execution daemon
remote - rlogin (1) - remote login program
remote - rlogind (8) - remote login daemon
remote - rmt (8) - control remote magnetic tape drives

remote - rsh (1) - remote shell
remote - rshd (8) - remote shell daemon
remote - rstart (1) - rsh remote start client
remote - rstartd (1) - rsh remote start helper daemon
remote - xon (1) - run an X-windows command on a remote machine
remove - col (1) - remove reverse line feeds from input
remove - colrm (1) - remove columns from a file
remove - mrd (1) - remove a DOS directory
remove - remove_file_free (9) - remove a kernel file table entry
remove - strip (1) - remove symbol table from object files
remove - uniq (1) - remove duplicate lines from a sorted file
remove - unlink (2) - remove a file from a directory
remove_file_free - remove_file_free (9) - remove a kernel file table entry
rename - mren (1) - rename a DOS file
rename - mv (1) - move/rename a file
rename - rename (2) - change the name or directory of a file
renice - renice (8) - alter running process priorities
repair - dosfsck (8) - check/repair DOS filesystems
repair - xfsck (8) - xiafs filesystem consistency check and repair
repeat - kbdrate (8) - set keyboard auto-key repeat rate and initial repeat delay time
repeatedly - yes (1) - output a string repeatedly until killed
report - mev (1) - report mouse events
reset - clearerr, feof, ferror, fileno (3) - reset and check stream status
reset - flock (2) - set or reset open file lock
reset - reset (1) - reset terminal characteristics to sane values
reset - rewinddir (3) - reset stream pointer to start of directory
res_init - res_init (3) - resolver library functions
resize - resize (1) - generate shell commands to set TERMCAP and TERM to current xterm size
res_mkquery - res_mkquery (3) - resolver library functions
resolv - resolv (3) - resolver library functions
resolv - resolver (5) - configuration file for resolv
resolver - dnsquery (1) - query domain-name servers using resolver
resolver - resolv, res_query, res_search, res_mkquery, res_send, res_init, dn_comp, dn_expand (3) - resolver library functions
resolver - resolver (5) - configuration file for resolv
resource - editres (1) - resource editor for X
resource - getrlimit, getrusage, setrlimit (2) - manipulate process resource limits
resource - xrdb (1) - X11 server resource database utility
resources - appres (1) - list application's X resources
res_query - res_query (3) - resolver library functions
res_search - res_search (3) - resolver library functions
res_send - res_send (3) - resolver library functions

restore - mkmanifest (1) - help restore Unix file names modified by DOS name restrictions
restrictions - mkmanifest (1) - help restore Unix file names modified by DOS name restrictions
return - clock (3) - return processor time used by process
return - false (1) - return zero exit status
return - getpagesize (2) - return kernel page size
return - return (1) - bash built-in commands
return - strerror (3) - return string describing errno
return - strlen (3) - return the length of a string
return - strsignal (3) - return string describing signal
return - strspn, strcspn (3) - return length of string containing given characters
return - telldir (3) - return current position in directory stream
return - true (1) - do nothing and return a true exit status
return - uname (2) - return information about the current kernel
returns - ffs (3) - returns position of first bit set in a word
returns - sysinfo (2) - returns system statistics
rev - rev (1) - reverse each of the lines in a file
reverse - col (1) - remove reverse line feeds from input
reverse - rev (1) - reverse each of the lines in a file
reverse - tac (1) - concatenate and reverse file contents
revision - ci (1) - revision control system check-in files
revision - co (1) - revision control system check-out files
revision - rcs (1) - change revision control system file attributes
revision - rcsdiff (1) - compare revision control system files
revision - rcsfile (1) - format of revision control system file
revision - rcsfile (5) - format of revision control system file
revision - rcsintro (1) - introduction to revision control system commands
revision - rcsmerge (1) - merge revision control system files
rewind - rewind (3) - manipulate a file pointer
rewinddir - rewinddir (3) - reset stream pointer to start of directory
rexecd - rexecd (8) - remote execution daemon
rgb - showrgb (1) - uncompile an rgb color-name database
rindex - rindex (3) - find character in string
rindex - rindex (3) - string functions
rint - rint (3) - round to nearest integer
Ritchie - ansi2knr (1) - convert ANSI C to Kernighan & Ritchie C
RLL - hd (4) - details MFM/RLL/IDE hard disk device special files
rlog - rlog (1) - display information about RCS files
rlogin - rlogin (1) - remote login program
rlogind - rlogind (8) - remote login daemon
rm - rm (1) - delete files
rmdir - rmdir (1) - delete empty directories
rmdir - rmdir (2) - delete a directory

rmmod - rmmod (1) - unload a loaded kernel module
rmt - rmt (8) - control remote magnetic tape drives
root - cbrt (3) - cube root math function
root - chroot (2) - change root directory
root - chroot (8) - execute a program with a new root directory
root - gpm-root (1) - gpm handler to draw menus on the root window
root - nologin (5) - allow only root to login to the system
root - rdev (8) - display or modify kernel root device, swap device, RAM disk size, and video mode
root - securetty (5) - list of ttys from which root can login
root - sqrt (3) - square root math function
root - xsetroot (1) - root window parameter setting utility for X11
round - rint (3) - round to nearest integer
route - route (8) - display and manipulate kernel IP routing tables
route - traceroute (8) - display the route taken by network packets
routed - routed (8) - network routing daemon
routing - route (8) - display and manipulate kernel IP routing tables
routing - routed (8) - network routing daemon
RPC - portmap (8) - RPC program number to DARPA port number mapper
RPC - rpcgen (1) - C code generator for RPC protocols
RPC - rpcinfo (8) - display RPC information
rpcgen - rpcgen (1) - C code generator for RPC protocols
rpcinfo - rpcinfo (8) - display RPC information
rpc.rusersd - rpc.rusersd (8) - rusers logged in users daemon
rpc.rwalld - rpc.rwalld (8) - rwall message daemon
rsh - rsh (1) - remote shell
rsh - rstart (1) - rsh remote start client
rsh - rstartd (1) - rsh remote start helper daemon
rshd - rshd (8) - remote shell daemon
rstart - rstart (1) - rsh remote start client
rstartd - rstartd (1) - rsh remote start helper daemon
rtin - rtin (1) - network news readers
run - atrun (8) - run batch jobs queued for later execution
run - env (1) - run a program in a modified environment
run - nice (1) - run a program and change its scheduling priority
run - nohup (1) - run a command set to ignore hangup signals
run - setsid (8) - run a program in a new session
run - splitvt (1) - run two shells on a split screen
run - strace (1) - run a command and trace system calls and signals
run - su (1) - run a shell with swapped user ID
run - xon (1) - run an X-windows command on a remote machine
running - renice (8) - alter running process priorities
running - uptime (1) - display how long the system has been running

running - xlsclients (1) - list client applications running on a display
runscript - runscript (1) - script interpreter for minicom communications program
runtime - sysconf (3) - get runtime configuration information
ruptime - ruptime (1) - show status of local network machines
rusers - rpc.rusersd (8) - rusers logged in users daemon
rusers - rusers (1) - list users logged in on local network machines
rwall - rpc.rwalld (8) - rwall message daemon
rwall - rwall (1) - send a message to users logged in on a specified host
rwho - rwho (1) - list users logged in on local network machines
rwhod - rwhod (8) - user and system status daemon
rx - rx (1) - receive xmodem, ymodem and zmodem files
rxvt - rxvt (1) - VT100 terminal for X11
rz - rz (1) - receive xmodem, ymodem and zmodem files
sane - reset (1) - reset terminal characteristics to sane values
saver - beforelight (1) - X11 screen saver
sb - sb (1) - send xmodem, ymodem and zmodem files
sbrk - sbrk (2) - change process data segment size
scancodes - showkey (1) - display scancodes or keycodes from the keyboard
scandir - scandir (3) - search a directory for entries with particular attributes
scanf - scanf (3) - formatted input functions
scheduling - getpriority, setpriority (2) - manipulate process scheduling priority
scheduling - nice (1) - run a program and change its scheduling priority
screen - beforelight (1) - X11 screen saver
screen - clear (1) - clear terminal screen
screen - colcrt (1) - translate nroff output for screen viewing
screen - curses (3) - terminal screen handling library
screen - mapscrn (8) - install user specified screen output mapping table
screen - ncurses (3) - screen handling package
screen - setfont (8) - load EGA or VGA console screen font
screen - splitvt (1) - run two shells on a split screen
screen - vgaset (1) - setup X11 screen geometry
screen - xmag (1) - magnify parts of the screen
screen - xrefresh (1) - refresh an X11 screen
script - runscript (1) - script interpreter for minicom communications program
script - script (1) - make a log of a terminal session
scripts - dialog (1) - handle dialog boxes from shell scripts
SCSI - sd (4) - SCSI disk driver
sd - sd (4) - SCSI disk driver
search - badblocks (8) - search for bad blocks on a disk partition
search - bsearch (3) - binary search a sorted array
search - fnmatch (3) - search a string for a regular expression

search - glookbib (1) - search bibliographic reference databases
search - scandir, alphasort (3) - search a directory for entries with particular attributes
search - whatis (1) - search the whatis database
search - zgrep (1) - search compressed files for a regular expression
search - zipgrep (1) - search zip'ed files for a regular expression
searched - manpath (1) - display directory paths searched for manual pages
second - chattr (1) - change file attributes in second extended filesystems
second - e2fsck (8) - check second extended filesystem
second - lsattr (1) - list file attributes on a second extended filesystem
second - mke2fs (8) - create a second extended filesystem
second - tune2fs (8) - manipulate parameters in second extended filesystems
seconds - difftime (3) - calculate seconds between two times
seconds - kernel_mktime (9) - convert struct mktime into seconds since 1 January, 1970
seconds - time (2) - get time in seconds
section - size (1) - list section sizes in archive and object files
sections - csplit (1) - split a file into sections
securetty - securetty (5) - list of ttys from which root can login
sed - sed (1) - inline editor
seed48 - seed48 (3) - random number generator
seekdir - seekdir (3) - set the position of the next readdir in a directory
segment - brk, sbrk (2) - change process data segment size
segment - shmget (2) - System-V IPC create a shared memory segment
select - cut (1) - select fields from each line of a file
select - select (2) - sleep awaiting file descriptor events
select - uselib (2) - select a shared library
selection - proc_sel (9) - kernel function for process selection
self - gzexe (1) - create self extracting compressed executable file
self-extracting - unzipsfx (1) - creat self-extracting zip archives
semaphore - semctl (2) - System-V IPC control semaphore operations
semaphore - semget (2) - System-V IPC create a semaphore set
semaphore - semop (2) - System-V IPC semaphore operations
semctl - semctl (2) - System-V IPC control semaphore operations
semget - semget (2) - System-V IPC create a semaphore set
semop - semop (2) - System-V IPC semaphore operations
send - closelog, openlog, syslog (3) - send text to the system message and error logger
send - dig (1) - send domain-name queries to name servers
send - kill (1) - send signal to process

send - kill (2) - send signal to process
send - killall (1) - send signal to processes by command name
send - killpg (3) - send signal to process group
send - rwall (1) - send a message to users logged in on a specified host
send - send, sendto, sendmsg (2) - send a message from a socket
send - sx, sb, sz (1) - send xmodem, ymodem and zmodem files
send - write (1) - send a message to another user
send - xmh (1) - send and read mail with an X11 interface
sendmail - makemap (8) - generate database maps for sendmail
sendmail - sendmail (8) - Internet mail transport program
sendmsg - sendmsg (2) - send a message from a socket
sendto - sendto (2) - send a message from a socket
sequence - ctrl_alt_del (9) - handle keyboard Ctrl-Alt-Del sequence
serial - minicom (1) - serial communication program
serial - setserial (8) - get and set Linux serial port configuration
serial - slattach (8) - put a serial line into network mode
serial - sliplogin (8) - convert a serial line into a SLIP network interface
serial - ttys (4) - serial device special files
server - fsinfo (1) - display X11 font server information
server - fslsfonts (1) - list X11 fonts supplied by font server
server - host (1) - look up hostnames or numbers using domain name server
server - lbxproxy (1) - low network badwidth proxy server for X11
server - nfsd (8) - NFS server daemon
server - timed (8) - time server daemon
server - x11perf (1) - X11 server performance test
server - x11perfcomp (1) - X11 server comparison program
server - xdpyinfo (1) - display X-windows server information
server - xferlog (5) - FTP server logfile
server - xfs (1) - X11 font server
server - xhost (1) - server access control program for X-windows
server - xlsatoms (1) - list interned atoms defined on server
server - xlsfonts (1) - server font list displayer for X-windows
server - xrdb (1) - X11 server resource database utility
servers - dig (1) - send domain-name queries to name servers
servers - dnsquery (1) - query domain-name servers using resolver
servers - nslookup (8) - interactively query Internet name servers
services - getservent, getservbyname, getservbyport, setservent, endservent (3) - get services file entries
session - script (1) - make a log of a terminal session

session - setsid (2) - create a new process session
session - setsid - create new session and process group
session - setsid (8) - run a program in a new session
session - smproxy (1) - X11R6 session manager support
session - startx (1) - initialize an X11 session
session - xsm (1) - X-windows session manager
session - xsmclient (1) - X-windows session manager tester
set - set (1) - bash built-in commands
setbuf - setbuf (3) - file output buffering operations
setbuffer - setbuffer (3) - file output buffering operations
setdomainname - setdomainname (2) - get/set host domain name
setegid - setegid (2) - set real and effective group ID
setenv - setenv (3) - set or change an environment variable value
seteuid - seteuid (2) - set real and effective user ID
setfdprm - setfdprm (8) - load parameters into floppy disk devices
setfont - setfont (8) - load EGA or VGA console screen font
setgid - setgid (2) - set group ID
setgrent - setgrent (3) - manipulate group file entries
setgroups - setgroups (2) - manipulate group access list
sethostent - sethostent (3) - manipulate network host entries
sethostid - sethostid (2) - manipulate the current host identifier
sethostname - sethostname (2) - manipulate hostname
setitimer - setitimer (2) - manipulate interval timer value
setleds - setleds (1) - set the keyboard indicator lights
setlinebuf - setlinebuf (3) - file output buffering operations
setlocale - setlocale (3) - set the current locale
setmetamode - setmetamode (1) - determine handling of the keyboard meta key
setmntent - setmntent (3) - access fstab and mtab file entries
setnetent - setnetent (3) - get networks file entries
setpgid - setpgid (2) - set or get process group ID
setpgrp - setpgrp (2) - set or get process group ID
setpriority - setpriority (2) - manipulate process scheduling priority
setprotoent - setprotoent (3) - get protocols file entries
setpwent - setpwent (3) - get fields from password file entries
setregid - setregid (2) - set real and effective group ID
setreuid - setreuid (2) - set real and effective user ID
setrlimit - setrlimit (2) - manipulate process resource limits
setserial - setserial (8) - get and set Linux serial port configuration
setservent - setservent (3) - get services file entries

setsid - setsid (2) - create a new process session
setsid - setsid (2) - create new session and process group
setsid - setsid (8) - run a program in a new session
setsockopt - setsockopt (2) - manipulate socket options
setstate - setstate (3) - random number generator
setterm - setterm (1) - set terminal attributes
settimeofday - settimeofday (2) - manipulate date and time
setting - xsetroot (1) - root window parameter setting utility for X11
settings - stty (1) - change or display terminal line settings
setuid - setuid (2) - set user ID
setup - init, telinit (8) - setup and control process initialization
setup - install (1) - copy files and setup owner and permission modes
setup - setup (2) - initialize hard disk driver
setup - vgaset (1) - setup X11 screen geometry
setusershell - setusershell (3) - get shells file entries
setutent - setutent (3) - access entries in utmp login record file
setvbuf - setvbuf (3) - file output buffering operations
several - readv, writev (3) - transfer several data blocks using multiple buffers
seyon - seyon (1) - X11 modem terminal emulator
shar - shar (1) - create shell archives
shar - unshar (1) - unpack shar files embedded in mail messages
shared - ldd (1) - display program shared library dependencies
shared - shmctl (2) - System-V IPC shared memory control
shared - shmget (2) - System-V IPC create a shared memory segment
shared - shmop (2) - System-V IPC shared memory operations
shared - uselib (2) - select a shared library
SHell - bash (1) - GNU Bourne-Again SHell
shell - chsh (1) - change your login shell in password file
shell - dialog (1) - handle dialog boxes from shell scripts
shell - echo (1) - display text from the shell
shell - resize (1) - generate shell commands to set TERMCAP and TERM to current xterm size
shell - rsh (1) - remote shell
shell - rshd (8) - remote shell daemon
shell - shar (1) - create shell archives
shell - su (1) - run a shell with swapped user ID
shells - getusershell, setusershell, endusershell (3) - get shells file entries
shells - shells (5) - file of pathnames to login shells for use with chsh
shells - splitvt (1) - run two shells on a split screen
shift - shift (1) - bash built-in commands
shmctl - shmctl (2) - System-V IPC shared memory control
shmget - shmget (2) - System-V IPC create a shared memory segment
shmop - shmop (2) - System-V IPC shared memory operations

shorten - truncate, ftruncate (2) - shorten a file to a given length
show - ruptime (1) - show status of local network machines
show - showmount (8) - show NFS mount information
show - w (1) - show who is logged on and what they are doing
show - who (1) - show who is logged on
showkey - showkey (1) - display scancodes or keycodes from the keyboard
showmount - showmount (8) - show NFS mount information
showrgb - showrgb (1) - uncompile an rgb color-name database
shut - shutdown (8) - shut the system down
shutdown - halt, reboot (8) - shutdown the system
shutdown - shutdown (2) - shutdown all or part of a full-duplex socket connection
shutdown - shutdown (8) - shut the system down
sigaction - sigaction (2) - signal handling functions
sigblock - sigblock (2) - signal handling functions
siggetmask - siggetmask (2) - signal handling functions
siginterrupt - siginterrupt (2) - signal handling functions
siginterrupt - siginterrupt (3) - change signal behaviour with system calls
sigmask - sigmask (2) - signal handling functions
sign - copysign (3) - copy the sign of a double
signal - alarm (2) - set a clock for an alarm signal
signal - kill (1) - send signal to process
signal - kill (2) - send signal to process
signal - killall (1) - send signal to processes by command name
signal - killpg (3) - send signal to process group
signal - pause (2) - block a process and wait for a signal
signal - psignal (3) - print message corresponding to signal
signal - raise (3) - signal current process
signal - siginterrupt (3) - change signal behaviour with system calls
signal - signal (7) - list of supported signals
signal - signal, sigaction, sigvec, sigsuspend, sigreturn, sigpause, sigpending, sigblock, sigmask, siggetmask, sigsetmask, siginterrupt (2) - signal handling functions
signal - strsignal (3) - return string describing signal
signals - nohup (1) - run a command set to ignore hangup signals
signals - signal (7) - list of supported signals
signals - strace (1) - run a command and trace system calls and signals
signatures - md5sum (1) - generate or check MD5 message signatures
sigpause - sigpause (2) - signal handling functions
sigpending - sigpending (2) - signal handling functions
sigreturn - sigreturn (2) - signal handling functions
sigsetmask - sigsetmask (2) - signal handling functions
sigsuspend - sigsuspend (2) - signal handling functions
sigvec - sigvec (2) - signal handling functions

simple - fmt (1) - simple text format program
simpleinit - simpleinit (8) - small version of init program
simulate - vhangup (2) - simulate a hangup on the current terminal
sin - sin (3) - sine trig function
since - kernel_mktime (9) - convert struct mktime into seconds since 1 January, 1970
sine - asin (3) - arc sine trig function
sine - asinh (3) - inverse hyperbolic sine trig function
sine - sin (3) - sine trig function
sine - sinh (3) - hyperbolic sine trig function
sinh - sinh (3) - hyperbolic sine trig function
size - brk, sbrk (2) - change process data segment size
size - getdtablesize (2) - get file descriptor table size
size - getpagesize (2) - return kernel page size
size - psbb (1) - get bounding box size from a postscript document
size - rdev (8) - display or modify kernel root device, swap device, RAM disk size, and video mode
size - resize (1) - generate shell commands to set TERMCAP and TERM to current xterm size
size - size (1) - list section sizes in archive and object files
sizes - size (1) - list section sizes in archive and object files
slattach - slattach (8) - put a serial line into network mode
sleep - select (2) - sleep awaiting file descriptor events
sleep - sleep (1) - sleep for a specified amount of time
sleep - sleep (3) - sleep for a specified amount of time
slides - slitex (1) - generate slides with LaTeX
SLIP - sliplogin (8) - convert a serial line into a SLIP network interface
sliplogin - sliplogin (8) - convert a serial line into a SLIP network interface
slitex - slitex (1) - generate slides with LaTeX
small - simpleinit (8) - small version of init program
smallest - ceil (3) - smallest integer value not less than x
smproxy - smproxy (1) - X11R6 session manager support
snoop - ttysnoop (8) - snoop on a user's terminal
.so - gsoelim (1) - include .so files in groff input
socket - accept (2) - accept a connection on a socket
socket - bind (2) - bind a name to a socket
socket - connect (2) - make a socket connection
socket - getpeername (2) - get name of peer connected to a given socket
socket - getsockname (2) - get socket name
socket - getsockopt, setsockopt (2) - manipulate socket options
socket - listen (2) - specify queue length for incoming socket connections
socket - recv, recvfrom, recvmsg (2) - get a message from a socket
socket - send, sendto, sendmsg (2) - send a message from a socket

socket - shutdown (2) - shutdown all or part of a full-duplex socket connection
socket - socket (2) - create a communication endpoint
socket - socketcall (2) - socket system call entry point
socketcall - socketcall (2) - socket system call entry point
socketpair - socketpair (2) - create a pair of connected sockets
sockets - socketpair (2) - create a pair of connected sockets
sort - qsort (3) - quick sort an array
sort - sort (1) - sort records in text files
sort - tsort (1) - sort nodes in a directed graph
sorted - bsearch (3) - binary search a sorted array
sorted - comm (1) - compare two sorted files
sorted - join (1) - join two sorted files line by line on a common field
sorted - sq (1) - compress a sorted word list
sorted - uniq (1) - remove duplicate lines from a sorted file
sorted - unsq (1) - uncompress a sorted word list
source - source (1) - bash built-in commands
source - tangle (1) - convert WEB source to a Pascal program
sources - rcsfreeze (1) - freeze a set of sources checked in under RCS
space - df (1) - summarize free disk partition space
space - free (1) - display memory and swap space statistics
spaces - expand (1) - convert tabs to spaces
spaces - unexpand (1) - filter to convert spaces to tabs
special - hd (4) - details MFM/RLL/IDE hard disk device special files
special - initex (1) - special version of TeX for making .fmt files
special - intro (4) - introduction to special files
special - lp (4) - line printer device special file
special - MAKEDEV (8) - create device special files
special - mknod (1) - create special files
special - null, zero (4) - bit bucket special files
special - ram (4) - RAM disk device special file
special - tty (1) - print the special file name of the controlling terminal
special - tty (4) - controlling terminal special file
special - ttys (4) - serial device special files
specified - fold (1) - format text to specified width
specified - fuser (1) - display PIDs of processes using specified files
specified - mapscrn (8) - install user specified screen output mapping table
specified - rwall (1) - send a message to users logged in on a specified host
specified - sleep (1) - sleep for a specified amount of time
specified - sleep (3) - sleep for a specified amount of time
specify - listen (2) - specify queue length for incoming socket connections
spell - ispell (4) - spell checker dictionary format
spell - ispell, buildhash, munchlist, findaffix, tryaffix, icombine, ijoin (1) - spell checker

spelling - english (4) - format for English spelling dictionaries
spider - spider (1) - double deck card game
split - csplit (1) - split a file into sections
split - dsplit (1) - split binary files into pieces
split - frexp (3) - split floating point number to integer and fractional parts
split - split (1) - split a file into pieces
split - splitvt (1) - run two shells on a split screen
split - strsep (3) - split string into tokens
splitvt - splitvt (1) - run two shells on a split screen
spool - lpr (1) - spool files to line print
sprintf - sprintf (3) - output format functions
sq - sq (1) - compress a sorted word list
sqrt - sqrt (3) - square root math function
square - sqrt (3) - square root math function
srand - srand (3) - random number generator
srand48 - srand48 (3) - random number generator
srandom - srandom (3) - random number generator
sscanf - sscanf (3) - formatted input functions
standard - elvis, ex, vi, view, input (1) - Unix standard editor
standard - stdio (3) - standard input/output library functions
standard - suffixes (7) - list of standard file name suffixes
standard - xstdcmap (1) - X-windows standard colormap utility
standard - xvpictoppm (1) - converts XV thumbnail files to standard PPM format
start - popen, pclose (3) - start a process with piped input or output
start - rewinddir (3) - reset stream pointer to start of directory
start - rstart (1) - rsh remote start client
start - rstartd (1) - rsh remote start helper daemon
startx - startx (1) - initialize an X11 session
stat - stat (2) - get file statistics
state - fsync (2) - write a file's in-core memory state to disk
state - update_state (8) - update system state
statfs - statfs (2) - get filesystem statistics
statistics - free (1) - display memory and swap space statistics
statistics - stat, fstat, lstat (2) - get file statistics
statistics - statfs, fstatfs (2) - get filesystem statistics
statistics - sysinfo (2) - returns system statistics
statistics - vmstat (8) - display virtual memory statistics
status - clearerr, feof, ferror, fileno (3) - reset and check stream status
status - false (1) - return zero exit status
status - ipcs (8) - provide ipc status information
status - lpq (1) - display status information for printer job queue
status - netstat (8) - display status information on active network connections
status - ps (1) - display process status
status - ruptime (1) - show status of local network machines
status - rwhod (8) - user and system status daemon
status - test (1) - generate exit status for file type-checks and value comparisons

status - true (1) - do nothing and return a true exit status
stdarg - stdarg (3) - variable argument list macros
stdin   - xargs (1) - execute command lines from stdin
stdio   - stdio (3) - standard input/output library functions
stime   - stime (2) - set system time and date
strace - strace (1) - run a command and trace system calls and signals
strcasecmp - strcasecmp (3) - compare two strings and ignore case
strcasecmp - strcasecmp (3) - string functions
strcat - strcat (3) - concatenate two strings
strcat - strcat (3) - string functions
strchr - strchr (3) - find character in string
strchr - strchr (3) - string functions
strcmp - strcmp (3) - compare two strings
strcmp - strcmp (3) - string functions
strcoll - strcoll (3) - compare two strings
strcoll - strcoll (3) - string functions
strcpy - strcpy (3) - copy a string
strcpy - strcpy (3) - string functions
strcspn - strcspn (3) - return length of string containing given characters
strcspn - strcspn (3) - string functions
strdup - strdup (3) - duplicate a string
strdup - strdup (3) - string functions
stream - clearerr, feof, ferror, fileno (3) - reset and check stream status
stream - rewinddir (3) - reset stream pointer to start of directory
stream - telldir (3) - return current position in directory stream
strerror - strerror (3) - return string describing errno
strfry - strfry (3) - generate an anagram of a string
strfry - strfry (3) - string functions
strftime - strftime (3) - format date and time
string - atof (3) - convert a string to a double
string - atoi (3) - convert a string to an integer
string - atol (3) - convert a string to a long integer
string - confstr (3) - get configuration-dependent string variable values
string - ecvt, fcvt (3) - convert a floating point number to a string
string - fgetc, fgets, getc, getchar, gets, ungetc (3) - string and character input functions
string - fnmatch (3) - search a string for a regular expression
string - fputc, fputs, putc, putchar, puts (3) - string and character output functions
string - gawk (1) - language for string pattern manipulation
string - gcvt (3) - convert floating point number to string
string - index, rindex (3) - find character in string
string - look (1) - display lines with a given string prefix
string - strcasecmp, strcat, strchr, strcmp, strcoll, strcpy, strcspn, strdup, strfry, strlen, strncat, strncmp, strncpy, strncasecmp, strpbrk, strrchr, strsep, strspn, strstr, strtok, strxfrm, index, rindex (3) - string functions
string - strchr, strrchr (3) - find character in string
string - strcpy, strncpy (3) - copy a string
string - strdup (3) - duplicate a string
string - strerror (3) - return string describing errno
string - strfry (3) - generate an anagram of a string
string - strlen (3) - return the length of a string
string - strpbrk (3) - finds any of a set of characters in a string
string - strsep (3) - split string into tokens
string - strsignal (3) - return string describing signal
string - strspn, strcspn (3) - return length of string containing given characters
string - strtod (3) - convert numeric string to double
string - strtok (3) - extract token from string
string - strtol (3) - convert string to long
string - strtoul (3) - convert string to unsigned long
string - strxfrm (3) - string transformation
string - yes (1) - output a string repeatedly until killed
strings - mbstowcs (3) - convert multi-byte to wide character strings
strings - mbstowcs (3) - convert wide character to multi-byte strings
strings - printf (1) - format and display parameter strings
strings - strcasecmp, strncasecmp (3) - compare two strings and ignore case
strings - strcat, strncat (3) - concatenate two strings
strings - strcmp, strncmp, strcoll (3) - compare two strings
strings - strings (1) - display printable strings in a file
strip   - basename (1) - strip directory prefix from file pathname
strip   - strip (1) - remove symbol table from object files
strlen - strlen (3) - return the length of a string
strlen - strlen (3) - string functions
strncasecmp - strncasecmp (3) - compare two strings and ignore case
strncasecmp - strncasecmp (3) - string functions
strncat - strncat (3) - concatenate two strings
strncat - strncat (3) - string functions
strncmp - strncmp (3) - compare two strings
strncmp - strncmp (3) - string functions
strncpy - strncpy (3) - copy a string
strncpy - strncpy (3) - string functions
strpbrk - strpbrk (3) - finds any of a set of characters in a string
strpbrk - strpbrk (3) - string functions
strrchr - strrchr (3) - find character in string
strrchr - strrchr (3) - string functions
strsep - strsep (3) - split string into tokens
strsep - strsep (3) - string functions
strsignal - strsignal (3) - return string describing signal
strspn - strspn (3) - return length of string containing given characters
strspn - strspn (3) - string functions
strstr - strstr (3) - find substring
strstr - strstr (3) - string functions

strtod - strtod (3) - convert numeric string to double
strtok - strtok (3) - extract token from string
strtok - strtok (3) - string functions
strtol - strtol (3) - convert string to long
strtoul - strtoul (3) - convert string to unsigned long
struct - kernel_mktime (9) - convert struct mktime into seconds since 1 January, 1970
structures - proc (5) - pseudo-filesystem for access to kernel data structures
strxfrm - strxfrm (3) - string functions
strxfrm - strxfrm (3) - string transformation
stty - stty (1) - change or display terminal line settings
stty - stty (2) - unimplemented system calls
su - su (1) - run a shell with swapped user ID
subdirectory - mmd (1) - create a DOS subdirectory
subject - frm, nfrm (1) - list from and subject lines in mail messages
substring - strstr (3) - find substring
suffixes - suffixes (7) - list of standard file name suffixes
summarize - df (1) - summarize free disk partition space
summarize - du (1) - summarize disk usage
super - dumpe2fs (8) - display filesystem super block and block-group information
SuperProbe - SuperProbe (1) - probe and identify video hardware
super-server - inetd (8) - Internet super-server daemon
supplied - fslsfonts (1) - list X11 fonts supplied by font server
supported - signal (7) - list of supported signals
suspend - suspend (1) - bash built-in commands
suspend - usleep (3) - suspend process execution for a time given in microseconds
swab - swab (3) - swap word byte-order
swap - free (1) - display memory and swap space statistics
swap - mkswap (8) - create a swap device
swap - rdev (8) - display or modify kernel root device, swap device, RAM disk size, and video mode
swap - swab (3) - swap word byte-order
swapoff - swapoff (2) - enable/disable devices and files for paging
swapoff - swapoff (8) - enable/disable devices and files for paging
swapon - swapon (2) - enable/disable devices and files for paging
swapon - swapon (8) - enable/disable devices and files for paging
swapped - su (1) - run a shell with swapped user ID
switch - acct (2) - switch process accounting on or off
sx - sx (1) - send xmodem, ymodem and zmodem files
sxpm - sxpm (1) - manipulate XPM files
symbol - genksyms (8) - generate symbol version files
symbol - nm (1) - display object file symbol table
symbol - strip (1) - remove symbol table from object files
symbolic - gdb (1) - GNU symbolic debugger

symbolic - lndir (1) - make a copy of a directory tree with symbolic links
symbolic - readlink (2) - read a symbolic link
symbolic - realpath (3) - make absolute pathname from relative pathname or symbolic link
symbolic - symlink (2) - create a symbolic link to a file
symbols - ksyms (1) - display exported kernel symbols
symlink - symlink (2) - create a symbolic link to a file
sync - sync (2) - flush filesystem buffer cache
sync - sync (8) - flush filesystem buffer cache
sysconf - sysconf (3) - get runtime configuration information
sysfs - sysfs (2) - get current filesystem type information
sysinfo - sysinfo (2) - returns system statistics
sysklogd - sysklogd (1) - Linux logging system
syslog - logger (1) - write messages to the syslog
syslog - syslog (3) - send text to the system message and error logger
syslog.conf - syslog.conf (5) - syslogd configuration file
syslogd - syslog.conf (5) - syslogd configuration file
syslogd - syslogd (8) - log system messages
system - system (3) - execute a Linux command
System-V - ftok (3) - generate a System-V IPC key
System-V - ipc (5) - System-V interprocess communication mechanisms
System-V - msgctl (2) - System-V IPC control message operations
System-V - msgget (2) - System-V IPC create a message queue
System-V - msgop (2) - System-V IPC message operations
System-V - semctl (2) - System-V IPC control semaphore operations
System-V - semget (2) - System-V IPC create a semaphore set
System-V - semop (2) - System-V IPC semaphore operations
System-V - shmctl (2) - System-V IPC shared memory control
System-V - shmget (2) - System-V IPC create a shared memory segment
System-V - shmop (2) - System-V IPC shared memory operations
sz - sz (1) - send xmodem, ymodem and zmodem files
table - filesystems (9) - details the table of configured filesystems
table - file_table (9) - detailed description of the kernel file table
table - file_table_init (9) - initialize the kernel file table
table - getdtablesize (2) - get file descriptor table size
table - get_empty_filp (9) - find an unreferenced entry in the kernel file table
table - grow_files (9) - add a page of entries to the file table
table - gtbl (1) - compile table description for groff
table - mapscrn (8) - install user specified screen output mapping table

table - modify_ldt (2) - get/set process local
    descriptor table
table - nm (1) - display object file symbol table
table - put_file_last (9) - move a file to the end of
    the kernel file table
table - rarp (8) - manipulate system RARP table
table - remove_file_free (9) - remove a kernel file
    table entry
table - strip (1) - remove symbol table from object
    files
tables - arp (8) - manipulate system ARP tables
tables - crontab (5) - tables for driving cron
tables - dumpkeys (1) - display keyboard translation
    tables
tables - fdisk (8) - manipulate disk partition tables
tables - keytables (5) - keyboard description tables
tables - loadkeys (1) - load kernel keyboard
    translation tables
tables - route (8) - display and manipulate kernel IP
    routing tables
tabs - expand (1) - convert tabs to spaces
tabs - unexpand (1) - filter to convert spaces to tabs
tac - tac (1) - concatenate and reverse file contents
tags - ctags (1) - generates tags and refs files
tail - tail (1) - output the tail end of a file
take - readline (3) - take interactive line of input
taken - traceroute (8) - display the route taken by
    network packets
talk - talk (1) - interactive user communication
talk - talkd (8) - talk communication daemon
talkd - talkd (8) - talk communication daemon
tan - tan (3) - tangent trig function
tangent - atan (3) - arc tangent trig function
tangent - atan2 (3) - arc tangent trig function of
    two variables
tangent - atanh (3) - inverse hyperbolic tangent trig
    function
tangent - tan (3) - tangent trig function
tangent - tanh (3) - hyperbolic tangent trig function
tangle - tangle (1) - convert WEB source to a
    Pascal program
tanh - tanh (3) - hyperbolic tangent trig function
tape - mt (1) - control a magnetic tape drive
tape - rmt (8) - control remote magnetic tape drives
tape - tar (1) - tape archiving utility
tar - tar (1) - tape archiving utility
tcdrain - tcdrain (2) - get and set terminal
    attributes and controls
tcflow - tcflow (2) - get and set terminal attributes
    and controls
tcflush - tcflush (2) - get and set terminal
    attributes and controls
tcgetattr - tcgetattr (2) - get and set terminal
    attributes and controls
tcsendbreak - tcsendbreak (2) - get and set
    terminal attributes and controls
tcsetattr - tcsetattr (2) - get and set terminal
    attributes and controls
tee - tee (1) - add a tee to a command pipeline to
    write to a file
telinit - telinit (8) - setup and control process
    initialization
telldir - telldir (3) - return current position in
    directory stream
telnet - telnet (1) - telnet protocol interface
    program

telnet - telnetd (8) - telnet daemon
telnetd - telnetd (8) - telnet daemon
template - mkstemp (3) - create a unique temporary
    file from a name template
tempnam - tempnam (3) - create a unique temporary
    file name
temporary - mkstemp (3) - create a unique
    temporary file from a name template
temporary - mktemp (3) - create a unique temporary
    file name
temporary - tempnam (3) - create a unique
    temporary file name
temporary - tmpfile (3) - create a temporary file
temporary - tmpnam (3) - create a name for a
    temporary file
TERM - resize (1) - generate shell commands to
    set TERMCAP and TERM to current xterm
    size
term - term (5) - format of compiled term file
TERMCAP - resize (1) - generate shell commands
    to set TERMCAP and TERM to current
    xterm size
termcap - termcap (5) - terminal capability database
terminal - clear (1) - clear terminal screen
terminal - console (4) - console terminal
terminal - ctermid (3) - get control terminal name
terminal - curses (3) - terminal screen handling
    library
terminal - last (1) - display past user/terminal
    login records
terminal - mesg (1) - enable or disable write access
    to your terminal
terminal - reset (1) - reset terminal characteristics
    to sane values
terminal - rxvt (1) - VT100 terminal for X11
terminal - script (1) - make a log of a terminal
    session
terminal - setterm (1) - set terminal attributes
terminal - seyon (1) - X11 modem terminal
    emulator
terminal - stty (1) - change or display terminal line
    settings
terminal - termcap (5) - terminal capability
    database
terminal - terminfo (5) - terminal capability
    database
terminal - termios, tcgetattr, tcsetattr,
    tcsendbreak, tcdrain, tcflush, tcflow,
    cfgetospeed, cfgetispeed, cfsetispeed,
    cfsetospeed (2) - get and set terminal
    attributes and controls
terminal - tty (1) - print the special file name of the
    controlling terminal
terminal - tty (4) - controlling terminal special file
terminal - ttyname (3) - get the pathname of an
    open terminal device
terminal - ttysnoop (8) - snoop on a user's terminal
terminal - ttytype (5) - terminal name and device
    file
terminal - vhangup (2) - simulate a hangup on the
    current terminal
terminal - xterm (1) - terminal emulator for
    X-windows
terminate - assert (3) - terminate process if
    assertion is false
terminate - _exit (2) - terminate the current process

termination - abort (3) - cause abnormal process termination
termination - atexit (3) - call function on program termination
termination - exit (3) - cause program termination
termination - wait, waitpid, wait3, wait4 (2) - wait for process termination
terminfo - terminfo (5) - terminal capability database
terminfo - tic (1) - terminfo compiler
terminfo - untic (1) - uncompile the contents of a compiled terminfo file
termios - termios (2) - get and set terminal attributes and controls
test - checkalias (1) - test if an alias is defined
test - isalnum, isalpha, iscntrl, isdigit, isgraph, islower, isprint, ispunct, isspace, isupper, isxdigit (3) - character test functions and macros
test - isatty (3) - test a file descriptor for a tty
test - IsCursorKey, IsFunctionKey, IsKeypadKey, IsMiscFunctionKey, IsModiferKey, IsPFKey, IsPrivateKeypadKey (3) - Xlib keysym test macros
test - isinf, isnan, finite (3) - test for infinity
test - lptest (1) - generate lineprinter test output
test - test (1) - bash built-in commands
test - test (1) - generate exit status for file type-checks and value comparisons
test - x11perf (1) - X11 server performance test
tester - xsmclient (1) - X-windows session manager tester
TeX - afm2tfm (1) - convert Adobe font metrics to TeX font metrics
TeX - etex (1) - extended TeX
TeX - fig2ps2tex (1) - include a postscript file in a TeX document
TeX - gpic (1) - gnu pic generates pictures for troff or TeX
TeX - gsftopk (1) - convert a ghostscript font to TeX pk format
TeX - initex (1) - special version of TeX for making .fmt files
TeX - lamstex (1) - text formatting TeX macro package
TeX - mft (1) - translate metafont program to TeX file
TeX - patgen (1) - generate TeX hyphenation patterns
TeX - pltotf (1) - convert properties files to TeX font metric format
TeX - Psfig/TeX (7) - postscript figures in TeX
tex - tex (1) - perform text formatting and typesetting
TeX - tftopl (1) - convert TeX font metric files to properties
TeX - virtex (1) - TeX version for production typesetting
TeX - vptovf (1) - convert virtual properties to virtual and TeX font metrics
TeX - weave (1) - create a TeX file to view a WEB program
text - amslatex (1) - text formatting and typesetting
text - amstex (1) - text formatting and typesetting
text - banner (6) - print text as a large banner

text - closelog, openlog, syslog (3) - send text to the system message and error logger
text - echo (1) - display text from the shell
text - ed, red (1) - text editor
text - fmt (1) - simple text format program
text - fold (1) - format text to specified width
text - groff (1) - text and document formatting system
text - lamstex (1) - text formatting TeX macro package
text - latex (1) - text formatting and typesetting system
text - nl (1) - number lines in text files
text - pooltype (1) - convert a WEB pool file to a text file
text - pr (1) - manipulate text files for page printing
text - sort (1) - sort records in text files
text - tex, virtex (1) - perform text formatting and typesetting
text - vim (1) - improved vi text editor
text - zmore (1) - display compressed text
tfmtodit - tfmtodit (1) - create font files for use with groff
tftopl - tftopl (1) - convert TeX font metric files to properties
tftp - tftp (1) - trivial file transfer program
tftpd - tftpd (8) - trivial file transfer protocol daemon
thumbnail - xvpictoppm (1) - converts XV thumbnail files to standard PPM format
tic - tic (1) - terminfo compiler
time - asctime, ctime, difftime, gmtime, localtime, mktime (3) - convert date and time to ascii
time - bootparam (7) - Linux kernel boot time parameters
time - clock (3) - return processor time used by process
time - date (1) - display/set the system date and time
time - ftime (2) - manipulate date and time
time - ftime (3) - get date and time
time - gettimeofday, settimeofday (2) - manipulate date and time
time - kbdrate (8) - set keyboard auto-key repeat rate and initial repeat delay time
time - netdate (8) - set date and time
time - sleep (1) - sleep for a specified amount of time
time - sleep (3) - sleep for a specified amount of time
time - stime (2) - set system time and date
time - strftime (3) - format date and time
time - time (2) - get time in seconds
time - time2posix, posix2time (3) - convert time formats
time - timed (8) - time server daemon
time - tzfile (5) - time zone information
time - tzset (3) - initialize time zone information
time - usleep (3) - suspend process execution for a time given in microseconds
time - zdump (8) - display the current time in a given time zone
time - zic (8) - time zone compiler
time2posix - time2posix (3) - convert time formats
timed - timed (8) - time server daemon

timed - timedc (8) - timed control program
timedc - timedc (8) - timed control program
timer - getitimer, setitimer (2) - manipulate interval timer value
timers - add_timer, del_timer, init_timer (9) - kernel event timers
times - difftime (3) - calculate seconds between two times
times - times (1) - bash built-in commands
times - times (2) - get process times
times - utime, utimes (2) - change access or modification times in an inode
timestamps - touch (1) - update file timestamps
time-zone - adjust_clock (9) - set kernel clock to GMT from time-zone value
tin - tin (1) - network news readers
tind - tind (1) - network news readers
tload - tload (1) - gives graphic display of system load average
tmpfile - tmpfile (3) - create a temporary file
tmpnam - tmpnam (3) - create a name for a temporary file
token - strtok (3) - extract token from string
tokens - strsep (3) - split string into tokens
tolower - tolower (3) - convert letters to upper or lower case
tools - mf, inimf, virmf (1) - font and logo design tools
tools - Mtools (1) - tools for manipulating DOS files
tools - Mtools (5) - tools for manipulating DOS files
top - top (1) - display processes with highest CPU usage
touch - touch (1) - update file timestamps
toupper - toupper (3) - convert letters to upper or lower case
tpic - pic2tpic (1) - convert pic files to tpic format
tr - tr (1) - translate characters
trace - ptrace (2) - debug process trace control
trace - strace (1) - run a command and trace system calls and signals
traceroute - traceroute (8) - display the route taken by network packets
transfer - ftp (1) - file transfer program
transfer - ftpd (8) - Internet file transfer protocol daemon
transfer - NcFTP (1) - Internet file transfer program
transfer - nntpd (8) - network news transfer protocol daemon
transfer - readv, writev (3) - transfer several data blocks using multiple buffers
transfer - tftp (1) - trivial file transfer program
transfer - tftpd (8) - trivial file transfer protocol daemon
transfig - transfig (1) - creates a makefile for portable LaTeX figures
transformation - strxfrm (3) - string transformation
translate - colcrt (1) - translate nroff output for screen viewing
translate - fig2dev (1) - translate Fig code to other graphics languages
translate - gftodvi (1) - translate generic font files to DVI format
translate - gftopk (1) - translate generic font files to packed font files

translate - gftype (1) - translate generic font files to human readable format
translate - htonl, htons, ntohl, ntohs (3) - translate between host and network byte order
translate - mft (1) - translate metafont program to TeX file
translate - pfbtops (1) - translate a .pfb postscript font to ascii
translate - pktogf (1) - translate packed fonts to generic fonts
translate - tr (1) - translate characters
translation - dumpkeys (1) - display keyboard translation tables
translation - loadkeys (1) - load kernel keyboard translation tables
transport - deliver (8) - local mail transport
transport - sendmail (8) - Internet mail transport program
trap - trap (1) - bash built-in commands
tree - ftw (3) - execute a function on file names in a directory tree
tree - lndir (1) - make a copy of a directory tree with symbolic links
tree - pstree (1) - display process hierarchy as a tree
trig - acos (3) - arc cosine trig function
trig - acosh (3) - inverse hyperbolic cosine trig function
trig - asin (3) - arc sine trig function
trig - asinh (3) - inverse hyperbolic sine trig function
trig - atan (3) - arc tangent trig function
trig - atan2 (3) - arc tangent trig function of two variables
trig - atanh (3) - inverse hyperbolic tangent trig function
trig - cos (3) - cosine trig function
trig - cosh (3) - hyperbolic cosine trig function
trig - sin (3) - sine trig function
trig - sinh (3) - hyperbolic sine trig function
trig - tan (3) - tangent trig function
trig - tanh (3) - hyperbolic tangent trig function
trivial - tftp (1) - trivial file transfer program
trivial - tftpd (8) - trivial file transfer protocol daemon
troff - addftinfo (1) - modify troff font files for use with groff
troff - geqn (1) - equation formatting for troff
troff - gpic (1) - gnu pic generates pictures for troff or TeX
troff - gtroff (1) - gnu troff compatible document format program
true - true (1) - do nothing and return a true exit status
truncate - truncate (2) - shorten a file to a given length
tryaffix - tryaffix (1) - spell checker
tsort - tsort (1) - sort nodes in a directed graph
tty - grotty (1) - groff tty driver
tty - isatty (3) - test a file descriptor for a tty
tty - tty (1) - print the special file name of the controlling terminal
tty - tty (4) - controlling terminal special file
ttyname - ttyname (3) - get the pathname of an open terminal device
ttys - securetty (5) - list of ttys from which root can login
ttys - ttys (4) - serial device special files

ttysnoop - ttysnoop (8) - snoop on a user's terminal
ttytype - ttytype (5) - terminal name and device file
tune - adjtimex (2) - tune kernel clock
tune2fs - tune2fs (8) - manipulate parameters in second extended filesystems
tunelp - tunelp (8) - manipulate parameters for the lp printer device
twm - twm (1) - window manager for X11
type - sysfs (2) - get current filesystem type information
type - type (1) - bash built-in commands
type-checks - test (1) - generate exit status for file type-checks and value comparisons
types - file (1) - display file types
typeset - typeset (1) - bash built-in commands
typesetting - amslatex (1) - text formatting and typesetting
typesetting - amstex (1) - text formatting and typesetting
typesetting - latex (1) - text formatting and typesetting system
typesetting - tex, virtex (1) - perform text formatting and typesetting
typesetting - virtex (1) - TeX version for production typesetting
tzfile - tzfile (5) - time zone information
tzset - tzset (3) - initialize time zone information
ul - ul (1) - filter to do underlining
ulimit - ulimit (1) - bash built-in commands
umask - umask (1) - bash built-in commands
umask - umask (2) - set file creation mask
umount - umount (2) - mount and unmount filesystems to the directory hierarchy
umount - umount (8) - mount and unmount filesystems to the directory hierarchy
unalias - unalias (1) - bash built-in commands
uname - uname (1) - display system information
uname - uname (2) - return information about the current kernel
uncompile - showrgb (1) - uncompile an rgb color-name database
uncompile - untic (1) - uncompile the contents of a compiled terminfo file
uncompress - gzip, gunzip, zcat (1) - compress and uncompress files
uncompress - uncompress (1) - compress and expand file contents
uncompress - unsq (1) - uncompress a sorted word list
underlining - ul (1) - filter to do underlining
unexpand - unexpand (1) - filter to convert spaces to tabs
ungetc - ungetc (3) - string and character input functions
unimplemented - afs_syscall, break, gtty, lock, mpx, prof, quotactl, stty (2) - unimplemented system calls
uniq - uniq (1) - remove duplicate lines from a sorted file
unique - mkstemp (3) - create a unique temporary file from a name template
unique - mktemp (3) - create a unique temporary file name
unique - tempnam (3) - create a unique temporary file name

Unix - elvis, ex, vi, view, input (1) - Unix standard editor
Unix - mkmanifest (1) - help restore Unix file names modified by DOS name restrictions
unlink - unlink (2) - remove a file from a directory
unload - rmmod (1) - unload a loaded kernel module
unmodified - rcsclean (1) - clean up unmodified rcs working files
unmount - mount, umount (2) - mount and unmount filesystems to the directory hierarchy
unmount - mount, umount (8) - mount and unmount filesystems to the directory hierarchy
unpack - unshar (1) - unpack shar files embedded in mail messages
unreferenced - get_empty_filp (9) - find an unreferenced entry in the kernel file table
unsaved - elvrec (1) - recover an unsaved elvis editor file after a crash
unset - unset (1) - bash built-in commands
unshar - unshar (1) - unpack shar files embedded in mail messages
unsigned - strtoul (3) - convert string to unsigned long
unsq - unsq (1) - uncompress a sorted word list
untic - untic (1) - uncompile the contents of a compiled terminfo file
until - until (1) - bash built-in commands
unzip - unzip (1) - extract compressed files from a zip archive
unzipsfx - unzipsfx (1) - creat self-extracting zip archives
update - patch (1) - update a file with a diff
update - psupdate (8) - update the ps kernel database
update - touch (1) - update file timestamps
update - updatedb (1) - update file name database
update - update_state (8) - update system state
updatedb - updatedb (1) - update file name database
update_state - update_state (8) - update system state
upper - toupper, tolower (3) - convert letters to upper or lower case
uptime - uptime (1) - display how long the system has been running
usage - du (1) - summarize disk usage
usage - top (1) - display processes with highest CPU usage
uselib - uselib (2) - select a shared library
userid - whoami (1) - print effective userid
users - newmail, wnewmail (1) - notify users of new mail
users - rpc.rusersd (8) - rusers logged in users daemon
users - rusers (1) - list users logged in on local network machines
users - rwall (1) - send a message to users logged in on a specified host
users - rwho (1) - list users logged in on local network machines
users - users (1) - display the login names of users currently logged in
users - wall (1) - write a message to all users
usleep - usleep (3) - suspend process execution for a time given in microseconds

utilities - bitmap, bmtoa, atobm (1) - bitmap editor and utilities for X11
utility - tar (1) - tape archiving utility
utility - xauth (1) - X11 authority file utility
utility - xmodmap (1) - utility for modifying keymaps in X-windows
utility - xrdb (1) - X11 server resource database utility
utility - xset (1) - user preference utility for X-windows
utility - xsetroot (1) - root window parameter setting utility for X11
utility - xstdcmap (1) - X-windows standard colormap utility
utility - xwininfo (1) - window information utility for X11
utime - utime (2) - change access or modification times in an inode
utimes - utimes (2) - change access or modification times in an inode
utmp - getutent, getutid, getutline, pututline, setutent, endutent, utmpname (3) - access entries in utmp login record file
utmp - utmp (5) - format of login records
utmpname - utmpname (3) - access entries in utmp login record file
uudecode - uudecode (1) - decode a uuencoded file
uuencode - uuencode (1) - ascii encode a binary file
uuencode - uuencode (5) - format of an encoded file
uuencoded - uudecode (1) - decode a uuencoded file
valid - pathchk (1) - check for valid file names
variable - confstr (3) - get configuration-dependent string variable values
variable - getenv (3) - get environment variable value
variable - putenv (3) - assign a value to an environment variable
variable - setenv (3) - set or change an environment variable value
variable - stdarg (3) - variable argument list macros
variables - atan2 (3) - arc tangent trig function of two variables
variables - printenv (1) - display environment variables
vdir - vdir (1) - list directory contents
vfork - vfork (2) - create a child process
vfprintf - vfprintf (3) - output format functions
vfscanf - vfscanf (3) - formatted input functions
vftovp - vftovp (1) - convert virtual fonts to virtual properties
VGA - setfont (8) - load EGA or VGA console screen font
vgaset - vgaset (1) - setup X11 screen geometry
vhangup - vhangup (2) - simulate a hangup on the current terminal
vi - vi (1) - Unix standard editor
vi - vim (1) - improved vi text editor
video - rdev (8) - display or modify kernel root device, swap device, RAM disk size, and video mode
video - SuperProbe (1) - probe and identify video hardware
view - ghostview (1) - use ghostscript to view postscript documents
view - view (1) - Unix standard editor
view - weave (1) - create a TeX file to view a WEB program
viewing - colcrt (1) - translate nroff output for screen viewing
vim - vim (1) - improved vi text editor
vipw - vipw (8) - edit the password file
virmf - virmf (1) - font and logo design tools
virtex - virtex (1) - perform text formatting and typesetting
virtex - virtex (1) - TeX version for production typesetting
virtual - gpm (1) - cut and paste across virtual consoles
virtual - vftovp (1) - convert virtual fonts to virtual properties
virtual - vm86 (2) - enter virtual 8086 mode
virtual - vmstat (8) - display virtual memory statistics
virtual - vptovf (1) - convert virtual properties to virtual and TeX font metrics
vm86 - vm86 (2) - enter virtual 8086 mode
vmstat - vmstat (8) - display virtual memory statistics
volume - mlabel (1) - label a DOS partition/volume
vprintf - vprintf (3) - output format functions
vptovf - vptovf (1) - convert virtual properties to virtual and TeX font metrics
vscanf - vscanf (3) - formatted input functions
vsprintf - vsprintf (3) - output format functions
vsscanf - vsscanf (3) - formatted input functions
VT100 - rxvt (1) - VT100 terminal for X11
wait - pause (2) - block a process and wait for a signal
wait - wait (1) - bash built-in commands
wait - wait, waitpid, wait3, wait4 (2) - wait for process termination
wait3 - wait3 (2) - wait for process termination
wait4 - wait4 (2) - wait for process termination
waitpid - waitpid (2) - wait for process termination
wall - wall (1) - write a message to all users
wc - wc (1) - print the number of bytes, words, and lines in files
wctomb - wctomb (3) - convert a wide character to a multi-byte character
weave - weave (1) - create a TeX file to view a WEB program
WEB - pooltype (1) - convert a WEB pool file to a text file
WEB - tangle (1) - convert WEB source to a Pascal program
WEB - weave (1) - create a TeX file to view a WEB program
what - w (1) - show who is logged on and what they are doing
whatis - whatis (1) - search the whatis database
whereis - whereis (1) - locate files related to a command
which - locate (1) - display file names from databases which match a regular expression
which - securetty (5) - list of ttys from which root can login
which - which (1) - display path name of commands
while - while (1) - bash built-in commands
who - w (1) - show who is logged on and what they are doing
who - who (1) - show who is logged on

whoami - whoami (1) - print effective userid
wide - mbstowcs (3) - convert multi-byte to wide character strings
wide - mbstowcs (3) - convert wide character to multi-byte strings
wide - mbtowc (3) - convert multi-byte characters to wide characters
wide - wctomb (3) - convert a wide character to a multi-byte character
width - fold (1) - format text to specified width
window - fvwm (1) - X11 window manager
window - gpm-root (1) - gpm handler to draw menus on the root window
window - twm (1) - window manager for X11
window - X (1) - portable network-transparent window system
window - xsetroot (1) - root window parameter setting utility for X11
window - xwininfo (1) - window information utility for X11
wnewmail - wnewmail (1) - notify users of new mail
word - ffs (3) - returns position of first bit set in a word
word - sq (1) - compress a sorted word list
word - swab (3) - swap word byte-order
word - unsq (1) - uncompress a sorted word list
words - wc (1) - print the number of bytes, words, and lines in files
workbone - workbone (1) - play audio compact discs on a CD-ROM reader
working - chdir, fchdir (2) - change current working directory
working - getcwd, get_current_dir_name, getwd (3) - get current working directory
working - pwd (1) - display name of present working directory
working - rcsclean (1) - clean up unmodified rcs working files
workman - workman (1) - play audio compact discs on a CD-ROM reader
workman - workmanrc, workmandb (5) - database and preference files for workman
workmandb - workmandb (5) - database and preference files for workman
workmanrc - workmanrc (5) - database and preference files for workman
write - fread, fwrite (3) - file read and write functions
write - fsync (2) - write a file's in-core memory state to disk
write - logger (1) - write messages to the syslog
write - mesg (1) - enable or disable write access to your terminal
write - putpwent (3) - write password file entry
write - tee (1) - add a tee to a command pipeline to write to a file
write - wall (1) - write a message to all users
write - write (1) - send a message to another user
write - write (2) - write to an open file description
writev - writev (3) - transfer several data blocks using multiple buffers
wtmp - wtmp (5) - format of login records
X - appres (1) - list application's X resources
x - ceil (3) - smallest integer value not less than x
X - editres (1) - resource editor for X

x - floor (3) - largest integer value not greater-than x
X - gxditview (1) - display gtroff output on an X display
X - mcookie (1) - generate magic cookies for the X authority system
X - X (1) - portable network-transparent window system
X11 - bdftopcf (1) - X11 font conversion program
X11 - beforelight (1) - X11 screen saver
X11 - bggen (1) - generate colored backgrounds for X11
X11 - bitmap, bmtoa, atobm (1) - bitmap editor and utilities for X11
X11 - fsinfo (1) - display X11 font server information
X11 - fslsfonts (1) - list X11 fonts supplied by font server
X11 - fstobdf (1) - create BDF file from X11 font
X11 - fvwm (1) - X11 window manager
X11 - lbxproxy (1) - low network badwidth proxy server for X11
X11 - mkfontdir, fonts.dir, fonts.scale, fonts.alias (1) - create an index of X11 font files
X11 - oclock (1) - X11 clock
X11 - rxvt (1) - VT100 terminal for X11
X11 - seyon (1) - X11 modem terminal emulator
X11 - startx (1) - initialize an X11 session
X11 - twm (1) - window manager for X11
X11 - vgaset (1) - setup X11 screen geometry
X11 - x11perf (1) - X11 server performance test
X11 - x11perfcomp (1) - X11 server comparison program
X11 - xauth (1) - X11 authority file utility
X11 - xcmap (1) - display default X11 colormap
X11 - xcmsdb (1) - X11 color management system
X11 - xfd (1) - display the characters in a given X11 font
X11 - xfig (1) - X11 draw and paint program
X11 - xfractint (1) - X11 fractal generator
X11 - xfs (1) - X11 font server
X11 - xinit (1) - X11 system initializer
X11 - xkill (1) - close connections to X11 clients
X11 - xlander (6) - X11 game
X11 - xmahjongg (6) - X11 game
X11 - xmh (1) - send and read mail with an X11 interface
X11 - xrdb (1) - X11 server resource database utility
X11 - xrefresh (1) - refresh an X11 screen
X11 - xroach (6) - X11 game
X11 - xsetroot (1) - root window parameter setting utility for X11
X11 - xvier (6) - X11 board game
X11 - xwininfo (1) - window information utility for X11
X11 - xwud (1) - display dump file image in X11
X11 - xxgdb (1) - X11 interface to gdb
x11perf - x11perf (1) - X11 server performance test
x11perfcomp - x11perfcomp (1) - X11 server comparison program
X11R6 - smproxy (1) - X11R6 session manager support
xargs - xargs (1) - execute command lines from stdin
xauth - xauth (1) - X11 authority file utility

xboard - `xboard (6)` - X-windows user interface for GNU Chess
xclipboard - `xclipboard (1)` - X-windows clipboard client
xclock - `xclock (1)` - analog and digital clock for X-windows
xcmap - `xcmap (1)` - display default X11 colormap
xcmsdb - `xcmsdb (1)` - X11 color management system
Xconfig - `reconfig (1)` - convert old Xconfig files to new XF86Config format
xconsole - `xconsole (1)` - monitor system console messages with X-windows
xcutsel - `xcutsel (1)` - cut and paste bridge program
xdm - `xdm (1)` - X-windows display manager
xdpyinfo - `xdpyinfo (1)` - display X-windows server information
xdvi - `xdvi (1)` - DVI previewer for X-windows
XF86Config - `reconfig (1)` - convert old Xconfig files to new XF86Config format
XF86Config - `xf86config (1)` - generate an XF86Config file
xf86config - `xf86config (1)` - generate an XF86Config file
xfd - `xfd (1)` - display the characters in a given X11 font
xferlog - `xferlog (5)` - FTP server logfile
xfig - `xfig (1)` - X11 draw and paint program
xfractint - `xfractint (1)` - X11 fractal generator
xfs - `xfs (1)` - X11 font server
xfsck - `xfsck (8)` - xiafs filesystem consistency check and repair
xhost - `xhost (1)` - server access control program for X-windows
xiafs - `mkxfs (8)` - create an xiafs filesystem
xiafs - `xfsck (8)` - xiafs filesystem consistency check and repair
xinit - `xinit (1)` - X11 system initializer
xkill - `xkill (1)` - close connections to X11 clients
xlander - `xlander (6)` - X11 game
Xlib - `ImageByteOrder, BitmapBitOrder, BitmapPad, BitmapUnit, DisplayHeight, DisplayHeightMM, DisplayWidth, DisplayWidthMM, XListPixmapFormats, XPixmapFormatValues (3)` - Xlib image formating functions and macros
Xlib - `IsCursorKey, IsFunctionKey, IsKeypadKey, IsMiscFunctionKey, IsModiferKey, IsPFKey, IsPrivateKeypadKey (3)` - Xlib keysym test macros
XListPixmapFormats - `XListPixmapFormats (3)` - Xlib image formating functions and macros
xlock - `xlock (1)` - locks the X-windows display until a password is entered
xlogo - `xlogo (1)` - X-window system logo
xlsatoms - `xlsatoms (1)` - list interned atoms defined on server
xlsclients - `xlsclients (1)` - list client applications running on a display
xlsfonts - `xlsfonts (1)` - server font list displayer for X-windows
xmag - `xmag (1)` - magnify parts of the screen
xmahjongg - `xmahjongg (6)` - X11 game
xmh - `xmh (1)` - send and read mail with an X11 interface
xmkmf - `xmkmf (1)` - create a makefile from an Imakefile
xmodem - `rx, rb, rz (1)` - receive xmodem, ymodem and zmodem files
xmodem - `sx, sb, sz (1)` - send xmodem, ymodem and zmodem files
xmodmap - `xmodmap (1)` - utility for modifying keymaps in X-windows
xon - `xon (1)` - run an X-windows command on a remote machine
XPixmapFormatValues - `XPixmapFormatValues (3)` - Xlib image formating functions and macros
XPM - `sxpm (1)` - manipulate XPM files
xprop - `xprop (1)` - property displayer for X-windows
xrdb - `xrdb (1)` - X11 server resource database utility
xrefresh - `xrefresh (1)` - refresh an X11 screen
xroach - `xroach (6)` - X11 game
xset - `xset (1)` - user preference utility for X-windows
xsetroot - `xsetroot (1)` - root window parameter setting utility for X11
xsm - `xsm (1)` - X-windows session manager
xsmclient - `xsmclient (1)` - X-windows session manager tester
xstdcmap - `xstdcmap (1)` - X-windows standard colormap utility
xterm - `resize (1)` - generate shell commands to set TERMCAP and TERM to current xterm size
xterm - `xterm (1)` - terminal emulator for X-windows
xtetris - `xtetris (6)` - X-window block dropping game
xv - `xv (1)` - interactive image display for X-windows
XV - `xvpictoppm (1)` - converts XV thumbnail files to standard PPM format
xvier - `xvier (6)` - X11 board game
xvpictoppm - `xvpictoppm (1)` - converts XV thumbnail files to standard PPM format
xwd - `xwd (1)` - create a dump file image from an X-window
X-window - `xlogo (1)` - X-window system logo
X-window - `xtetris (6)` - X-window block dropping game
X-window - `xwd (1)` - create a dump file image from an X-window
X-windows - `xboard (6)` - X-windows user interface for GNU Chess
X-windows - `xclipboard (1)` - X-windows clipboard client
X-windows - `xclock (1)` - analog and digital clock for X-windows
X-windows - `xconsole (1)` - monitor system console messages with X-windows
X-windows - `xdm (1)` - X-windows display manager
X-windows - `xdpyinfo (1)` - display X-windows server information
X-windows - `xdvi (1)` - DVI previewer for X-windows
X-windows - `xhost (1)` - server access control program for X-windows
X-windows - `xlock (1)` - locks the X-windows display until a password is entered
X-windows - `xlsfonts (1)` - server font list displayer for X-windows
X-windows - `xmodmap (1)` - utility for modifying keymaps in X-windows

X-windows - xon (1) - run an X-windows command on a remote machine
X-windows - xprop (1) - property displayer for X-windows
X-windows - xset (1) - user preference utility for X-windows
X-windows - xsm (1) - X-windows session manager
X-windows - xsmclient (1) - X-windows session manager tester
X-windows - xstdcmap (1) - X-windows standard colormap utility
X-windows - xterm (1) - terminal emulator for X-windows
X-windows - xv (1) - interactive image display for X-windows
xwininfo - xwininfo (1) - window information utility for X11
xwud - xwud (1) - display dump file image in X11
xxgdb - xxgdb (1) - X11 interface to gdb
y0 - y0 (3) - Bessel math functions
y1 - y1 (3) - Bessel math functions
Yacc - Yacc (1) - LALR-1 parser generator
yes - yes (1) - output a string repeatedly until killed
ymodem - rx, rb, rz (1) - receive xmodem, ymodem and zmodem files
ymodem - sx, sb, sz (1) - send xmodem, ymodem and zmodem files
yn - yn (3) - Bessel math functions
ytalk - ytalk (1) - a multi-user chat program
.Z - znew (1) - recompress .Z files as .gz files
zcat - zcat (1) - compress and expand file contents
zcat - zcat (1) - compress and uncompress files
zcmp - zcmp (1) - perform comparisons on compressed files
zdiff - zdiff (1) - perform comparisons on compressed files
zdump - zdump (8) - display the current time in a given time zone
zero - false (1) - return zero exit status
zero - zero (4) - bit bucket special files
zforce - zforce (1) - force a .gz file extension on all gzip'ed files
zgrep - zgrep (1) - search compressed files for a regular expression
zic - zic (8) - time zone compiler
ZIP - funzip (1) - extract files from a ZIP archive
zip - unzip (1) - extract compressed files from a zip archive
zip - unzipsfx (1) - creat self-extracting zip archives
zip - zip (1) - package and compress (archive) files
zip - zipinfo (1) - list detailed information about a zip archive
zipcloak - zipcloak (1) - package and compress (archive) files
zip'ed - zipgrep (1) - search zip'ed files for a regular expression
zipgrep - zipgrep (1) - search zip'ed files for a regular expression
zipinfo - zipinfo (1) - list detailed information about a zip archive
zipnote - zipnote (1) - package and compress (archive) files
zipsplit - zipsplit (1) - package and compress (archive) files
zmodem - rx, rb, rz (1) - receive xmodem, ymodem and zmodem files
zmodem - sx, sb, sz (1) - send xmodem, ymodem and zmodem files
zmore - zmore (1) - display compressed text
znew - znew (1) - recompress .Z files as .gz files
zone - tzfile (5) - time zone information
zone - tzset (3) - initialize time zone information
zone - zdump (8) - display the current time in a given time zone
zone - zic (8) - time zone compiler
zoo - fiz (1) - data recovery from damaged zoo archives
zoo - zoo (1) - manipulate compressed file archives

GNU General Public Licence (GPL)

The following text is a verbatim copy of the Free Software Foundation's GNU General Public Licence (GPL) under which the Linux operating system and the vast majority of the software associated with it are written and distributed.

As you will see, if you intend to modify, update or improve any GPLed software then, for distribution purposes, your modified version must also be covered by the provisions of the GNU General Public Licence.

```
                    GNU GENERAL PUBLIC LICENSE
                       Version 2, June 1991

 Copyright (C) 1989, 1991 Free Software Foundation, Inc.
                    675 Mass Ave, Cambridge, MA 02139, USA
 Everyone is permitted to copy and distribute verbatim copies
 of this license document, but changing it is not allowed.

                            Preamble

  The licenses for most software are designed to take away your
freedom to share and change it.  By contrast, the GNU General Public
License is intended to guarantee your freedom to share and change free
software--to make sure the software is free for all its users.  This
General Public License applies to most of the Free Software
Foundation's software and to any other program whose authors commit to
using it.  (Some other Free Software Foundation software is covered by
the GNU Library General Public License instead.)  You can apply it to
your programs, too.

  When we speak of free software, we are referring to freedom, not
price.  Our General Public Licenses are designed to make sure that you
have the freedom to distribute copies of free software (and charge for
this service if you wish), that you receive source code or can get it
if you want it, that you can change the software or use pieces of it
in new free programs; and that you know you can do these things.
```

To protect your rights, we need to make restrictions that forbid anyone to deny you these rights or to ask you to surrender the rights. These restrictions translate to certain responsibilities for you if you distribute copies of the software, or if you modify it.

For example, if you distribute copies of such a program, whether gratis or for a fee, you must give the recipients all the rights that you have. You must make sure that they, too, receive or can get the source code. And you must show them these terms so they know their rights.

We protect your rights with two steps: (1) copyright the software, and (2) offer you this license which gives you legal permission to copy, distribute and/or modify the software.

Also, for each author's protection and ours, we want to make certain that everyone understands that there is no warranty for this free software. If the software is modified by someone else and passed on, we want its recipients to know that what they have is not the original, so that any problems introduced by others will not reflect on the original authors' reputations.

Finally, any free program is threatened constantly by software patents. We wish to avoid the danger that redistributors of a free program will individually obtain patent licenses, in effect making the program proprietary. To prevent this, we have made it clear that any patent must be licensed for everyone's free use or not licensed at all.

The precise terms and conditions for copying, distribution and modification follow.

GNU GENERAL PUBLIC LICENSE
TERMS AND CONDITIONS FOR COPYING, DISTRIBUTION AND MODIFICATION

0. This License applies to any program or other work which contains a notice placed by the copyright holder saying it may be distributed under the terms of this General Public License. The "Program", below, refers to any such program or work, and a "work based on the Program" means either the Program or any derivative work under copyright law: that is to say, a work containing the Program or a portion of it, either verbatim or with modifications and/or translated into another language. (Hereinafter, translation is included without limitation in the term "modification".) Each licensee is addressed as "you".

Activities other than copying, distribution and modification are not covered by this License; they are outside its scope. The act of running the Program is not restricted, and the output from the Program is covered only if its contents constitute a work based on the Program (independent of having been made by running the Program). Whether that is true depends on what the Program does.

1. You may copy and distribute verbatim copies of the Program's

source code as you receive it, in any medium, provided that you
conspicuously and appropriately publish on each copy an appropriate
copyright notice and disclaimer of warranty; keep intact all the
notices that refer to this License and to the absence of any warranty;
and give any other recipients of the Program a copy of this License
along with the Program.

You may charge a fee for the physical act of transferring a copy, and
you may at your option offer warranty protection in exchange for a fee.

  2. You may modify your copy or copies of the Program or any portion
of it, thus forming a work based on the Program, and copy and
distribute such modifications or work under the terms of Section 1
above, provided that you also meet all of these conditions:

   a) You must cause the modified files to carry prominent notices
   stating that you changed the files and the date of any change.

   b) You must cause any work that you distribute or publish, that in
   whole or in part contains or is derived from the Program or any
   part thereof, to be licensed as a whole at no charge to all third
   parties under the terms of this License.

   c) If the modified program normally reads commands interactively
   when run, you must cause it, when started running for such
   interactive use in the most ordinary way, to print or display an
   announcement including an appropriate copyright notice and a
   notice that there is no warranty (or else, saying that you provide
   a warranty) and that users may redistribute the program under
   these conditions, and telling the user how to view a copy of this
   License. (Exception: if the Program itself is interactive but
   does not normally print such an announcement, your work based on
   the Program is not required to print an announcement.)

These requirements apply to the modified work as a whole. If
identifiable sections of that work are not derived from the Program,
and can be reasonably considered independent and separate works in
themselves, then this License, and its terms, do not apply to those
sections when you distribute them as separate works. But when you
distribute the same sections as part of a whole which is a work based
on the Program, the distribution of the whole must be on the terms of
this License, whose permissions for other licensees extend to the
entire whole, and thus to each and every part regardless of who wrote it.

Thus, it is not the intent of this section to claim rights or contest
your rights to work written entirely by you; rather, the intent is to
exercise the right to control the distribution of derivative or
collective works based on the Program.

In addition, mere aggregation of another work not based on the Program
with the Program (or with a work based on the Program) on a volume of
a storage or distribution medium does not bring the other work under

the scope of this License.

3. You may copy and distribute the Program (or a work based on it, under Section 2) in object code or executable form under the terms of Sections 1 and 2 above provided that you also do one of the following:

    a) Accompany it with the complete corresponding machine-readable source code, which must be distributed under the terms of Sections 1 and 2 above on a medium customarily used for software interchange; or,

    b) Accompany it with a written offer, valid for at least three years, to give any third party, for a charge no more than your cost of physically performing source distribution, a complete machine-readable copy of the corresponding source code, to be distributed under the terms of Sections 1 and 2 above on a medium customarily used for software interchange; or,

    c) Accompany it with the information you received as to the offer to distribute corresponding source code. (This alternative is allowed only for noncommercial distribution and only if you received the program in object code or executable form with such an offer, in accord with Subsection b above.)

The source code for a work means the preferred form of the work for making modifications to it. For an executable work, complete source code means all the source code for all modules it contains, plus any associated interface definition files, plus the scripts used to control compilation and installation of the executable. However, as a special exception, the source code distributed need not include anything that is normally distributed (in either source or binary form) with the major components (compiler, kernel, and so on) of the operating system on which the executable runs, unless that component itself accompanies the executable.

If distribution of executable or object code is made by offering access to copy from a designated place, then offering equivalent access to copy the source code from the same place counts as distribution of the source code, even though third parties are not compelled to copy the source along with the object code.

4. You may not copy, modify, sublicense, or distribute the Program except as expressly provided under this License. Any attempt otherwise to copy, modify, sublicense or distribute the Program is void, and will automatically terminate your rights under this License. However, parties who have received copies, or rights, from you under this License will not have their licenses terminated so long as such parties remain in full compliance.

5. You are not required to accept this License, since you have not signed it. However, nothing else grants you permission to modify or distribute the Program or its derivative works. These actions are prohibited by law if you do not accept this License. Therefore, by

modifying or distributing the Program (or any work based on the
Program), you indicate your acceptance of this License to do so, and
all its terms and conditions for copying, distributing or modifying
the Program or works based on it.

6. Each time you redistribute the Program (or any work based on the
Program), the recipient automatically receives a license from the
original licensor to copy, distribute or modify the Program subject to
these terms and conditions. You may not impose any further
restrictions on the recipients' exercise of the rights granted herein.
You are not responsible for enforcing compliance by third parties to
this License.

7. If, as a consequence of a court judgment or allegation of patent
infringement or for any other reason (not limited to patent issues),
conditions are imposed on you (whether by court order, agreement or
otherwise) that contradict the conditions of this License, they do not
excuse you from the conditions of this License. If you cannot
distribute so as to satisfy simultaneously your obligations under this
License and any other pertinent obligations, then as a consequence you
may not distribute the Program at all. For example, if a patent
license would not permit royalty-free redistribution of the Program by
all those who receive copies directly or indirectly through you, then
the only way you could satisfy both it and this License would be to
refrain entirely from distribution of the Program.

If any portion of this section is held invalid or unenforceable under
any particular circumstance, the balance of the section is intended to
apply and the section as a whole is intended to apply in other
circumstances.

It is not the purpose of this section to induce you to infringe any
patents or other property right claims or to contest validity of any
such claims; this section has the sole purpose of protecting the
integrity of the free software distribution system, which is
implemented by public license practices. Many people have made
generous contributions to the wide range of software distributed
through that system in reliance on consistent application of that
system; it is up to the author/donor to decide if he or she is willing
to distribute software through any other system and a licensee cannot
impose that choice.

This section is intended to make thoroughly clear what is believed to
be a consequence of the rest of this License.

8. If the distribution and/or use of the Program is restricted in
certain countries either by patents or by copyrighted interfaces, the
original copyright holder who places the Program under this License
may add an explicit geographical distribution limitation excluding
those countries, so that distribution is permitted only in or among
countries not thus excluded. In such case, this License incorporates
the limitation as if written in the body of this License.

9. The Free Software Foundation may publish revised and/or new versions of the General Public License from time to time. Such new versions will be similar in spirit to the present version, but may differ in detail to address new problems or concerns.

Each version is given a distinguishing version number. If the Program specifies a version number of this License which applies to it and "any later version", you have the option of following the terms and conditions either of that version or of any later version published by the Free Software Foundation. If the Program does not specify a version number of this License, you may choose any version ever published by the Free Software Foundation.

10. If you wish to incorporate parts of the Program into other free programs whose distribution conditions are different, write to the author to ask for permission. For software which is copyrighted by the Free Software Foundation, write to the Free Software Foundation; we sometimes make exceptions for this. Our decision will be guided by the two goals of preserving the free status of all derivatives of our free software and of promoting the sharing and reuse of software generally.

                                NO WARRANTY

11. BECAUSE THE PROGRAM IS LICENSED FREE OF CHARGE, THERE IS NO WARRANTY FOR THE PROGRAM, TO THE EXTENT PERMITTED BY APPLICABLE LAW. EXCEPT WHEN OTHERWISE STATED IN WRITING THE COPYRIGHT HOLDERS AND/OR OTHER PARTIES PROVIDE THE PROGRAM "AS IS" WITHOUT WARRANTY OF ANY KIND, EITHER EXPRESSED OR IMPLIED, INCLUDING, BUT NOT LIMITED TO, THE IMPLIED WARRANTIES OF MERCHANTABILITY AND FITNESS FOR A PARTICULAR PURPOSE. THE ENTIRE RISK AS TO THE QUALITY AND PERFORMANCE OF THE PROGRAM IS WITH YOU. SHOULD THE PROGRAM PROVE DEFECTIVE, YOU ASSUME THE COST OF ALL NECESSARY SERVICING, REPAIR OR CORRECTION.

12. IN NO EVENT UNLESS REQUIRED BY APPLICABLE LAW OR AGREED TO IN WRITING WILL ANY COPYRIGHT HOLDER, OR ANY OTHER PARTY WHO MAY MODIFY AND/OR REDISTRIBUTE THE PROGRAM AS PERMITTED ABOVE, BE LIABLE TO YOU FOR DAMAGES, INCLUDING ANY GENERAL, SPECIAL, INCIDENTAL OR CONSEQUENTIAL DAMAGES ARISING OUT OF THE USE OR INABILITY TO USE THE PROGRAM (INCLUDING BUT NOT LIMITED TO LOSS OF DATA OR DATA BEING RENDERED INACCURATE OR LOSSES SUSTAINED BY YOU OR THIRD PARTIES OR A FAILURE OF THE PROGRAM TO OPERATE WITH ANY OTHER PROGRAMS), EVEN IF SUCH HOLDER OR OTHER PARTY HAS BEEN ADVISED OF THE POSSIBILITY OF SUCH DAMAGES.

                        END OF TERMS AND CONDITIONS

                How to Apply These Terms to Your New Programs

  If you develop a new program, and you want it to be of the greatest possible use to the public, the best way to achieve this is to make it free software which everyone can redistribute and change under these terms.

To do so, attach the following notices to the program. It is safest
to attach them to the start of each source file to most effectively
convey the exclusion of warranty; and each file should have at least
the "copyright" line and a pointer to where the full notice is found.

    <one line to give the program's name and a brief idea of what it does.>
    Copyright (C) 19yy <name of author>

    This program is free software; you can redistribute it and/or modify
    it under the terms of the GNU General Public License as published by
    the Free Software Foundation; either version 2 of the License, or
    (at your option) any later version.

    This program is distributed in the hope that it will be useful,
    but WITHOUT ANY WARRANTY; without even the implied warranty of
    MERCHANTABILITY or FITNESS FOR A PARTICULAR PURPOSE. See the
    GNU General Public License for more details.

    You should have received a copy of the GNU General Public License
    along with this program; if not, write to the Free Software
    Foundation, Inc., 675 Mass Ave, Cambridge, MA 02139, USA.

Also add information on how to contact you by electronic and paper mail.

If the program is interactive, make it output a short notice like this
when it starts in an interactive mode:

    Gnomovision version 69, Copyright (C) 19yy name of author
    Gnomovision comes with ABSOLUTELY NO WARRANTY; for details type `show w'.
    This is free software, and you are welcome to redistribute it
    under certain conditions; type `show c' for details.

The hypothetical commands `show w' and `show c' should show the appropriate
parts of the General Public License. Of course, the commands you use may
be called something other than `show w' and `show c'; they could even be
mouse-clicks or menu items--whatever suits your program.

You should also get your employer (if you work as a programmer) or your
school, if any, to sign a "copyright disclaimer" for the program, if
necessary. Here is a sample; alter the names:

    Yoyodyne, Inc., hereby disclaims all copyright interest in the program
    `Gnomovision' (which makes passes at compilers) written by James Hacker.

    <signature of Ty Coon>, 1 April 1989
    Ty Coon, President of Vice

This General Public License does not permit incorporating your program into
proprietary programs. If your program is a subroutine library, you may
consider it more useful to permit linking proprietary applications with the
library. If this is what you want to do, use the GNU Library General
Public License instead of this License.

Index

., 7
.., 7
.xinitrc configuration file, 181
/dev/null, 71
/dev/tty, 354
/proc directory, 221
: command, 107

absolute pathname, 5
accept system call, 291
access system call, 230
add_timer kernel function, 408
adduser command, 147
AF_INET, 289
AF_UNIX, 289
alarm system call, 321
apsfilter print filter, 174
archie service, 208
archive creation, 156
arp command, 194
at command, 154
atq command, 155
atrm command, 155
atrun command, 154

background process group, 246
backup creation, 156
bash, 49
    ~ notation, 97
    arithmetic operations, 105

back quotes, 100
background commands, 55
bg command, 58
command completion, 61
command substitution, 100
comments, 104
expression evaluation, 105
fg command, 58
functions, 62
here document, 54
history command, 59
history list, 59
I/O redirection, 51
IFS, 100
interactive input, 99
job control, 57
kill command, 58
output redirection, 52
pathname expansion, 49
pipeline, 55
positional parameters, 96
quoting mechanisms, 51
read command, 99
regular expressions, 49
script parameters, 96
tilde expansion, 97
batch command, 155
bdflush command, 345
bind system call, 290
blk_dev_init kernel function, 401

block device special files, 370
broadcast address, IP, 187
buffer cache, 233, 398

case command, 110
cat command, 9, 19
cd command, 7
Centronics printer interface, 171
change directory, 7
character device special files, 370
chat command, 195
chdir system call, 355
chgrp command, 149
child process, 26
chmod command, 25, 151
chmod system call, 252
chown command, 149
chown system call, 253
chr_dev_init kernel function, 375
cli, disable interrupts, 405
client, network, 288
close on exec flag, 267
close system call, 234, 242
closedir system call, 256
cmp command, 84
colon command, 107
comm command, 84
command line switches, 14
connect system call, 290
connectionless service, 287
control terminals, 246
copy on write, 444
cp command, 15
creat system call, 231
critical sections in device drivers, 404
crond command, 153
crontab command, 154
Ctrl-c, 4
Ctrl-d, 4, 98
current working directory, 6

daemon, 352
datagram, 287
date command, 83

demand paging, 443
device driver
    open function, 380
    read function, 381
    release function, 380
    write function, 382
device driver interrupts, 384
device driver ioctl function, 383
df command, 29
diff command, 86
dip command, 196
directory link, 17
disable interrupt call, 405
disk partitions, 16, 126
do_fork kernel function, 414
DOSEMU package, 215
dot directory, 7
dot-dot directory, 7
du command, 30
dumpkeys command, 162
dup system call, 277
dup2 system call, 280

EACCES, 230
EAGAIN, 242
EBADF, 234
ECHO, 245
echo
    -n switch, 99
    command, 93
EEXIST, 230
effective address, 438
electronic mail, 202
enable interrupt call, 405
end_request kernel function, 399
ENOENT, 230
EOF, keyboard, 4, 98
exceptions, 458
exec system call, 265
exit command, 101
exit status, 101
exit system call, 268
extended disk partitions, 127

false command, 109

fchmod system call, 252
fchown system call, 253
fcntl system call, 254, 268, 280
fdformat command, 136
fdisk command, 128
FIFOs, 281
file access permissions, 24
file command, 88
file descriptor, 227
file_operations structure, 376
filesystem, 16
filesystem creation, 133
filter commands, 65
find command, 68
for command, 109
foreground process group, 246
fork system call, 262
free command, 31
free_irq kernel function, 384
ftp command, 205
ftruncate system call, 254

gateway address, IP, 187
GDTR CPU register, 439
get_user kernel macro, 383
get_user_byte kernel function, 382
get_user_long kernel function, 382
get_user_word kernel function, 382
gethostbyaddr function, 293
gethostbyname function, 293
gethostname system call, 293
getservbyname function, 293
getty program, 168
gid, 10
global descriptor table (GDT), 439
gopher service, 211
gopherspace, 212
gpm command, 171
grep command, 65
gunzip command, 157
gzip command, 157

hardware requirements, 122
home directory, 7

host.conf configuration file, 191
hostent structure, 293
hostname command, 188
HOSTNAME configuration file, 188
hosts configuration file, 191
html, 213
htonl function, 294
htons function, 294
hypertext link, 212

ICANON, 245
if command, 102
ifconfig command, 188
inetd daemon, 190
init command, 168
init process, 26, 188
inode, 16, 248
Internet, 201
Internet Protocol, IP, 187, 286
interrupts, 373, 403, 458
ioctl system call, 242
IP address, 187, 287
IPC_CREAT, 283
IPC_EXCL, 283
IPC_PRIVATE, 283
ipcrm command, 285
ipcs command, 283
isatty system call, 245
ISIG, 245

kermit command, 198
kfree kernel function, 378
kfree_s kernel function, 378
kill command, 28, 112
kill system call, 320
kmalloc kernel function, 378

less command, 19
lilo boot loader, 136
lilo command, 138
limits.h, 227
linear address, 439
link in directory, 17
link system call, 256
Linux Distributions, 123

528   *Index*

linux/limits.h, 227
linux/socket.h, 292
listen system call, 290
ln, 17
ln -s, 18
loadkeys command, 161
loadlin command, 144
local descriptor table (LDT), 440
logical address, 438
logical disk partitions, 127
login prompt, 3
logout command, 4
lpc command, 172
lpd daemon, 172
lpq command, 172
lpr command, 172
lprm command, 172
ls, 8
ls -i, 17
ls -l, 23

major device number, 371
man command, 21
manual, 21
mapscrn command, 162
memcpy_fromfs kernel function, 382
memcpy_tofs kernel function, 381
memory management, 438
memory paging, 440
memory segments, 438
message passing IPC, 282
minor device number, 371
mkdir command, 14
mkdir system call, 255
mke2fs command, 133
mknod command, 281, 371
mknod system call, 281
mkswap command, 133
modem peripheral, 165
more command, 19
motd file, 15
mount command, 144, 344
mount system call, 344
mouse peripheral, 169

move command, 18
msgctl system call, 286
msgget system call, 286
msgrcv system call, 286
msgsnd system call, 286
mtools, 88
mv command, 18

name server address, IP, 187
named pipes, 281
netconfig command, 186
netdb.h, 293
netmask, IP, 187
netscape web browser, 213
network address, IP, 187
networking startup files, 189
networks configuration file, 191
newgrp command, 150, 223
non-preemptive scheduling, 412
ntohl function, 294
ntohs function, 294
null command, 107

O_APPEND, 229
O_CREAT, 229
O_EXCL, 229
O_NDELAY, 241
O_NOCTTY, 247
O_RDONLY, 228
O_RDWR, 228
O_SYNC, 233
O_TRUNC, 229
O_WRONLY, 228
od command, 87
open file description, 228
open system call, 228
OPEN_MAX, 227
opendir system call, 256
OPOST, 245

page fault, 443
parallel line IP (PLIP), 197
parent process, 26
partitioning hard disks, 126
passwd command, 10, 147

password file, 8
pathname, 5
pause system call, 321
PID, 26, 260
pipe, 55
pipes, 275
PPP
    authentication, 194
    networking, 192
pr command, 87
preemptive scheduling, 412
present working directory, 7
printcap configuration file, 173
process, 4, 26
process group, 246
process group leader, 246
process ID, 260
process identity number, 26
program, 26
protected mode addressing, 438
ps command, 26
put_user kernel macro, 381
put_user_byte kernel function, 381
put_user_long kernel function, 381
put_user_word kernel function, 381
pwd, 7

RAM, 30
random access memory, 30
rc.inet1 startup file, 189
rc.inet2 startup file, 189
rdev command, 136
read system call, 231, 241
readdir system call, 256
readonly command, 95
recv system call, 292
recvfrom system call, 292
register_blkdev kernel function, 402
register_chrdev kernel function, 376
regular expressions
    bash, 49
    grep, 66
    vi, 44
relative pathname, 6

rename command, 19
request_irq kernel function, 384
resolve.conf configuration file, 192
rm command, 15
rmdir, 15
rmdir system call, 255
route command, 188

S_IRGRP, 229
S_IROTH, 229
S_IRUSR, 229
S_IRWXG, 229
S_IRWXO, 229
S_IRWXU, 229
S_ISGID, 229
S_ISUID, 229
S_IWGRP, 229
S_IWOTH, 229
S_IWUSR, 229
S_IXGRP, 229
S_IXOTH, 229
S_IXUSR, 229
schedule kernel function, 415
sclient(), 298
sclose(), 298
sed command, 76
segment descriptor, 438
segment descriptor table, 438
select system call, 348
semaphore IPC, 282
semctl system call, 286
semget system call, 286
semop system call, 286
send system call, 292
sendmail command, 203
sendto system call, 292
serial line IP (SLIP), 196
servent structure, 293
server, network, 288
session, 246
session leader, 246
setfont command, 163
setgid permission bit, 151
sethostname(), 293

setserial command, 167
setsid system call, 247, 354
setuid permission bit, 151
setup command, 134
seyon command, 198
shared memory IPC, 282
shell, 4
shell scripts, 92
SHM_RDONLY, 284
shmat system call, 284
shmctl system call, 285
shmdt system call, 284
shmget system call, 282
showkey command, 161
shutdown command, 137
sigaction system call, 318
sigaddset function, 319
sigdelset function, 319
sigemptyset function, 319
sigfillset function, 319
sigismember function, 319
signal mask, 318
signal masks, 319
signal system call, 316
signals, 315
sigpending system call, 320
sigprocmask system call, 319
sleep command, 107
sleep_on kernel function, 405
smail command, 203
SOCK_DGRAM, 289
SOCK_STREAM, 289
socket, 286
socket creation, 289
socket descriptor, 288
socket system call, 289
sopen(), 298
sort command, 73
sserver(), 298
standard error output device, 228
standard input device, 228
standard output device, 228
startx command, 181
sti, enable interrupts, 405

stty command, 245
su command, 224
swap space, 30, 122
swapon command, 133
swapping, 443
symbolic link, 18
sync command, 345
sync system call, 345
syslogd daemon, 190
system calls, 21
System V IPC mechanisms, 282

tail command, 20
tar command, 158
TCGETA, 244
TCSADRAIN, 244
TCSAFLUSH, 244
TCSANOW, 244
TCSETA, 244
telnet command, 204
terminal control functions, 242
terminal I/O, 241
test command, 104
time system call, 346
times system call, 347
tiny shell interpreter, 325
top command, 32
touch command, 108
tr command, 80
translation lookaside buffer (TLB), 442
Transmission control protocol, TCP, 287
trap command, 112
true command, 109
truncate system call, 254
tty command, 28

uid, 10
umask command, 152, 220, 343
umask system call, 253, 343, 356
umount command, 145, 345
umount system call, 345
uniform resource locator, 213
uniq command, 86

unlink system call, 256
until command, 108
unzip command, 145
update command, 345
URL, 213
usenet news, 209
user data buffering, 234
User Datagram protocol, UDP, 287
useradd command, 147

verify_area kernel function, 382
vfree kernel function, 379
vi, 36
   command mode, 42
     deleting text, 46
     editor options, 46
     file manipulation, 43
     line numbers, 43
     quit commands, 42
     regular expressions, 44
     shell escape, 47
     string searching, 44
     text substitution, 45
   edit mode, 37
     cursor positioning, 38
     cut and paste text, 40
     replace and delete text, 39
     string searching, 39
     undo and repeat commands, 40
   insert mode, 40
     text substitution, 41
   ZZ command, 37
virtual filesystem switch (VFS), 446
virtual terminal, 27
vmalloc kernel function, 379
VMIN, 245
VTIME, 245

wait system call, 268, 319
wake_up kernel function, 405
wc command, 20
web pages, 212
which command, 12
while command, 106

who command, 147
world wide web (WWW), 212
write command, 222
write system call, 232, 242

X command, 180
xinit command, 181
xterm command, 184

zcat command, 157
zombie processes, 271, 319